T H E

Desktop
Multimedia
Bible

THE

JEFF BURGER

Desktop
Multimedia
Bible

Addison-Wesley Publishing Company

Reading, Massachusetts • Menlo Park, California • New York
Don Mills, Ontario • Wokingham, England • Amsterdam
Bonn • Sydney • Singapore • Tokyo • Madrid • San Juan
Paris • Seoul • Milan • Mexico City • Taipei

Library of Congress Cataloging-in-Publication Data
Burger, Jeff.
    The desktop multimedia bible / Jeff Burger.
       p. cm.
    Includes bibliographical references and index.
    ISBN 0-201-58112-4
    1. Data transmission systems   2. Hypermedia systems.   I. Title.
TK5105.B87   1993
621.389'7--dc20   91-42982
                                           CIP

Sponsoring Editor: Julie Stillman
Project Management: Elizabeth Rogalin and Claire Horne
Production Coordinator: Gail McDonald
Cover design: Jean Seal
Cover Photographs: Eric Fordham
Text design: David F. Kelly
Set in 10 point Cheltenham by CIP

Computer screen image on front cover from the MS-DOS version of ABC News InterActive, Inc. "Health: AIDS" from the "Understanding Ourselves" series.

ABC News InterActive, Inc.	Media Design, Inc.
7 West 66th Street	1445 Wampancag Trail
New York, NY 10023	E. Providence, RI 02915
(212) 456-4060	(401) 433-4255

1 2 3 4 5 6 7 8 9 -MU- 9695949392
First printing, December 1992

To Vickie Rinehart, without whose love, dedication, perseverance, talents, and immeasurable efforts this book would not have been possible.

In loving memory of my father, Paul Burger

Acknowledgments

I wish to extend profound thanks to the following people who have helped to make this monumental project come to life—directly and indirectly.

To Vickie Rinehart and Kent Jones who accepted the challenge of creating the volume of wonderful illustrations. To Rick Eberly, Magni Systems, ARC, and Commodore Business Machines for permission to use their illustrations and photos. To Image Club, 3G Graphics, T/Maker, TechPool Studios, Multi-Ad Services, and Online Arts for clip art that was used in creating some of the illustrations. To Aldus and Adobe for supplying Aldus Freehand and Adobe Photoshop that were used almost exclusively to create the illustrations.

To Bob Hoover for embracing and fulfilling a mammoth technical editing job. To Brent Hurtig, Chris Meyer, Brian Lanser, George Petersen, Lance Ong, and Craig Anderton for helping to bring additional technical clarity to many issues.

To Elizabeth Rogalin, Claire Horne, Gail McDonald, Keith Wollman, and Julie Stillman at Addison-Wesley for incredible patience, faith, and extensions on extensions. To my agent, Claudette Moore, for associating me with such publishing professionals. To Rob Mauhar at CIP for a great job in compositing all 600-plus pages.

To David Bunnell, Nancy Cutler, Eric Brown, Becky Waring, and all at *NewMedia* magazine for a regular home for my thoughts, words, and art. To Ken McGorry at *Post*, Bob O'Donnell at *Electronic Musician*, Jim Strothman at *Computer Pictures*, Dominic Milano at *Keyboard*, Daniel Todd at *Publish*, and all of the other magazines for whom I've written over the years for their support of my writing.

To Phil Hood for friendship, deep thoughts, cowboy songs, and rasta pasta (Connie, too!). To Dave Harding for friendship, reality checks, and long-distance perspective (Andromeda is still calling). To Joy Weigel for friendship, trust, and fuel for the Dream Machine (Hooversonics, too!). To Amy Miller for friendship, racquetball, Indian food, and an endless ear (Picard/Riker '96!). And to all my other close friends who haven't seen or heard much from me in the last year and a half because of some lame excuse about writing a book (here's the evidence!).

And to my mother, Luella Mattern, and the rest of my family for believing in me. (Dad, if you're watching, this one's for you!)

The following manufacturers gratiously contributed products for use in this project:

3-D Visions Corporation, 3G Graphics, Inc., Abacus Concepts, Abbate Video Consultants, Abbott Systems, AddStar, Inc., Adobe Systems, Inc., Advanced Software, Inc., AimTech Corporation, Aladdin Systems, Inc., Alde Publishing Inc., Aldus Corp., Alias Research Style! Division, Altsys Corporation, American Small Business Computers, Inc., Andromeda Software, Application Techniques, Argosy Software, Inc., ArtBeats, ASD Software, Ashton-Tate Corp., Attain Corporation, BeachWare, Berkana International, Bourbaki Inc., Bright Star Technology, Inc., Broderbund Software, C-Cube Microsystems, Caere Corporation, California Clip Art, Calliscope, Casady & Greene, Inc., Caseys' Page Mill, CE Software, Central Point Software, Ceres Software, Inc., Chartersoft Corp., Chena Software, Chinon America, Inc., Claris Corporation, Computer Friends, Inc., Computer Support Corp., Connectix Corporation, Corel Systems Corp., CoSa, CV Designs, Dantz Development Corporation, DataEase International, Inc., Davidson and Associates, Dayna Communications, Decathlon Corporation, Delta Tao Software, Inc., Deltapoint, Inc., Deneba Software, DesignCAD, Inc., Diaquest, Digi-Fonts, Inc., Digital Graphics Library Inc., DiVA Corp., Dream Maker Software, Educational Multimedia Concepts, LTD., Elan Design, Electronic Arts, Envisions Solutions Technology, Inc., Essential Software, Experience In Software, First Byte, Fisher Idea Systems, FontBank, Inc., Foundation Publishing, Inc., Fractal Design Corporation, Free Spirit Software, Inc., GeoQuery Corp., Gizmo Technologies, Gold Disk, Inc., Golden Software, Inc., Grafx Associates, Great Wave Software, Halcyon Software, HavenTree Software Limited, HSC Software, Husom & Rose Photographics, ICOM Simulations, Inc., Ideaform Inc., Illusion Art, Image Club Graphics, Image North Technologies, Imagine That, Inc., INBIT, Ingrimayne Software, Innovative Data Design, Inc., Insignia Solutions, ISLO TECH, Inc., ISM, Inc., Iterated Systems, Inc., Kaetron Software Corp., Kara Computer Graphics, Kiwi Software, Inc., Koala Acquisitions, Inc., LetterPerfect, LetterSpace, Light Source, Inc., LinksWare Corp., MacroMedia, Madrigal Residentail Designs, Mainstay, MasterSoft, Inc., Mathematica Incorporated, Maxa, Meta Software Corporation, Meyer Software, MichTron, Micro Logic, Microcom, Inc., MicroFrontier, Inc., MicroLogic Software, MicroMat Computer Systems, Microseeds Publishing, Inc., Migraph Inc., MindLink Inc., Multi-Ad Services, Inc., Multisoft Corporation, New England Software Inc., New Horizons Software, Nordic Software, Inc., Now Software, Inc., NTERGAID, Nu-Mega Technologies Inc., nView, Online Arts, Opcode Systems, OWL International, Pacific Rim Connections, Pantechnicon, Paragon Concepts, Inc., Passport Designs, Paul Mace Software, Performance Resources, PIXAR, Pixel Perfect, Poor Person Software, Postcraft International Inc., Power Up Software Corp., POWERSolutions for Business, Psybron Systems, Inc., Qualitas Trading Co., Quarterdeck Office Systems, RasterOps, Ray Dream, Inc., Rix SoftWorks, Inc., Rosesoft Inc., RT Graphics, Sabastian Software, Salient Solutions, Inc., Savitar Communications, ShirtPocket Software, Inc., Silicon Beach Software, Slide City, Softshell International, Ltd., Softstream International, Inc., Software Ventures, Inc., Software Workshop, Inc., Solutions, Inc., Sony Corporation, Spinnaker Software Corp., Starware Publishing Corp., STRATA INC., SunShine Graphics, SwivelArt, Symantec Corp., Symmetry, Synergy, T/Maker Company, Teach Yourself By Computer Software, Inc., TechPool Studios, Teknosys, TeleRobotics International, Terrace Software, Texture City, The Publishing Factory, Thunderware, TSP Software, Tulip Software, Userland Software, Inc., VideoLake, Ltd., VidTech, Virtual Reality Landscapes, Inc., Virtus Corporation, Vision Software, Visionary Software, Visual Business Systems, Vividus Corp, The Voyager Company, V_Graph Inc., Wacom, Inc., Wayzata Technology, Weber & Sons, Inc., Wildflower Software, Window Painters, Ltd., WINGS for Learning, Wolfram Research, Inc., ZSoft Corporation.

Preface

The twentieth century has fostered two of the most powerful communication tools in the history of the human race—television and the computer. Television and—by extension—video, have empowered people to see and hear events that expand our experience of the world and help us visualize information and concepts in ways that mere words cannot. The advent of the computer has given us the power to access vast amounts of data on demand, and this most versatile of machines has become a universal tool for the mind. The combination of the computer's interactive power with the communication capabilities of video is perhaps the simplest and most common vision of multimedia.

Desktop multimedia, however, is many things to many people. In fact, one of the problems that initially plagued the industry was a lack of definition. Perhaps the best technological description is "the integration of two or more different media with the personal computer." The candidates for the component media include text, graphics, animation, speech, music, and video.

But merely defining multimedia in the context of technology alone does no more justice to the concept than describing books as pages of paper with text printed on them. The uses for multimedia are even more diverse than the permutations of media combinations. The mainstream multimedia application at this writing is the corporate presentation that replaces the traditional slide or AV show, but multimedia is rapidly gaining ground in interactive training, personalized education, public information kiosks, retail kiosks, trade show demonstrations, consumer entertainment, and more.

On a conceptual level, the potential of multimedia represents a fundamental change in the way we communicate. Communication in the '90s must accomplish two fundamental tasks: satiating the demanding aesthetic tastes and expectations of today's sophisticated viewing audiences, and navigating the vast amount of knowledge, facts, and statistics that comprise the "Information Age." Multimedia allows us to use the best combination of media to present compelling information suited to specific situations. And it allows user-control over how and when that information is accessed.

This technology empowers anyone with a message to communicate their ideas effectively to others. It has been said that the power of the press belongs to those who own one. By extension, the power to communicate in the '90s belongs to media publishers and others with the tools and skills to use them effectively. Desktop publishing brought the power of the press to offices and individuals alike. Desktop multimedia adds the power of the recording studio, video studio, graphic design studio, animation house, computer lab, and more to potentially all of those same people.

THE EVOLUTION OF MULTIMEDIA

The term "multimedia" has roots preceding the computer. The word has been used for decades to describe productions incorporating multiple slide projectors, video monitors, audio tape decks, synthesizers, and/or other stand-alone media devices. Upon the arrival of the microprocessor, the hardware tools used in various media disciplines became programmable. This meant that various combinations of settings could be stored and recalled on demand, adding an order of magnitude to the ease of the associated production process. The same technology made it possible for devices to control each other with greater intimacy, and to synchronize their respective parts of the multimedia production more accurately. The combination of these factors led to far more ambitious productions and a maturing market for multimedia.

As the personal computer began taking its place in the world, it was quickly put to use controlling various media devices. Standards and protocols for device control evolved quickly, and suddenly the computer was controlling entire video editing suites, recording studios, and more.

Simultaneously, the more powerful computers and workstations were being used for computer graphics, animation, and digital audio. As the price/performance ratio of computing technology improved, personal computers assumed those abilities at moderate levels of quality. And as the lines between the capabilities of mainframe and desktop computers continued to blur, affordable computers themselves became the medium rather than merely controlling other media.

During this same period, the computer became a pervasive business tool, evolving from an often-feared curiosity to an indispensable friend and a permanent part of life. The desktop publishing revolution verified the personal computer as a professional publishing and communication tool, and impelled many individuals to create and produce communication material themselves, or at least, "in house."

The evolution from desktop publishing to other desktop media production was a natural technological and social process. Significant advances in the combined areas of storage media, memory, and processor speed have made it possible not only to create usable media on the computer, but to input, store, manipulate, and output real-world information in real time.

Multimedia's evolutionary course has not been without hurdles, however. The challenge—which drives all other considerations—is the sheer amount of digital data required to represent compelling media in general, and dynamic data in particular. One minute of stereo CD-quality audio requires 10MB of storage; full-fidelity digital video requires approximately 30MB per second! These are tall orders for even the best of today's desktop computers.

Since so many problems stem from too much data, one of the hottest areas in multimedia computing lies in compression technology aimed at reducing the amount of throughput and storage required. (While software compression exists, the quantum leap in quality comes with hardware implementations.) CD-ROM technology has simultaneously provided an inexpensive vehicle for storing and mass-producing large volumes of multimedia content. Unfortunately, both of these solutions take the form of non-standard hardware. (Even standard formats such as CD-ROMs are not yet standard hardware on everyone's computer.)

Speaking of standards, the acceptance and success of multimedia has been plagued by too few of them (or too many, depending upon how you look at it). The consumer video market is an excellent example of the acceptance pattern of new electronic media. Video didn't really take off until the war between Betamax and VHS was won by the latter: only then did we see a VCR in every living room and a video shop on every corner. Multimedia faces a similar challenge in that there are many entrenched platforms. Unlike the VCR world, however, the capabilities across different models and configurations of a given computer platform vary as well. You can create dazzling material on a PC clone, but there's no guarantee that it will play back faithfully (or at all!) on another PC—let alone a Macintosh. That's like needing the right model and configuration of VHS machine to be able to watch your favorite rented movie or home video of the grandkids!

Prematurity of product and manufacturers' myopia plagued the early days of multimedia. Shortly after the term desktop multimedia was coined, manufacturers raced to stake their claim on this new market. The aforementioned technological and standards problems resulted in a lot of smoke and lights, but little practical application. The early multimedia adopters and industry experts quickly realized that the technology was only half-baked. Moreover, in their efforts to sell products, manufacturers often overlooked the fact that multimedia is about communication, not technology.

Soon another reality set in: the industry hype implied that anyone could use this new technology to dazzle friends, clients, and co-workers. Just consider the desktop publishing nightmare of a million ugly newsletters created by untrained eyes. In multimedia, the combination of several unrelated components—on as grand a scale as audio and video—magnifies the potential for ineffective use by unskilled users. Today's on-the-go, media-saturated viewing audience is immersed in Hollywood glitz, MTV music videos, and fast-paced Madison Avenue commercials. Nobody cares whether the computer is sweating bullets at 40,000 megagoobers just to get this stuff on the screen and out the speakers. For better or for worse, the minute you put multimedia content on the screen, you are judged against television.

The combination of all of these factors has led to a lot of multimedia-bashing and skepticism. Multimedia has been called a technology in search of a market, a solution in search of a problem, a zero billion dollar industry. The good news is that despite all of its early problems, multimedia is alive and kicking. Microprocessors keep getting faster. Storage media keep getting larger. Software keeps getting cooler and easier to use. Manufacturers have also begun to make some serious in-roads standardizing hardware and software for multimedia. (The MPC hardware standard for PCs, Apple's QuickTime compression/synchronization standard for operating systems, and the Apple/IBM Kaleida collaboration are good examples.) And finally, users who want to produce multimedia content are becoming more savvy.

In only a few short years, multimedia has become powerful and accepted enough to begin taking its rightful place in changing the way we communicate. Thanks to the laptop computer, computer-based presentations are proliferating in corporate boardrooms and salespeople's briefcases. Retail kiosks are selling us merchandise in malls. CRTs and videowalls hawk new products at trade shows. Interactive training is being used to indoctrinate employees efficiently. Interactive multimedia is bringing personalization to education. And optical disc technology takes us to virtual museums in the comfort of our living rooms.

Where do we go from here? All computers will incorporate the requisite hardware and software to create and play multimedia productions in a few short years. Multimedia will melt away as a separate concept and blend into computing. Similarly, the lines between computer and television will continue to blur until we have, simply, media appliances. The seemingly disparate ingredients of videoconferencing, networks, and virtual reality will be stirred into this same cauldron. As the delivery platforms become more standardized and entrenched, multimedia programming will proliferate; you will buy it at the corner store and interact with it via the cable and phone lines coming into your home.

In many ways, the crystal ball remains cloudy in a stimulating and beckoning sort of way. Marshall McLuhan said "the medium is the message," meaning, in part, that new media actually change the nature and aesthetics of the content and can impact society in ways unforseen by its pioneers. Indeed, this is one of the most exciting aspects of multimedia's future.

This book is about harnessing the technology of the present and building toward that future. We now stand at an incredible time in the history of information and human communication. Those of you embracing multimedia today—as producers and users—pioneer a new way in which we interact with each other and the vast information of history and society. It is for them this book was written.

THE DESKTOP MULTIMEDIA BIBLE—THE CONCEPT

We know multimedia brings the promise of incredible communication powers to virtually anyone interested in presenting a message. The challenges lie in fulfilling that promise.

The first challenge is in understanding what the technology can do and keeping pace with the almost daily advances. The second is in learning enough to chose the right tools for the job. The third challenge is perhaps the most important—using the technology and tools for effective communication. Negotiating this trident of hurdles can be difficult in any given media. Desktop multimedia ups the ante by spreading each of these factors across many different media, then requiring their effective integration.

Those challenges to the user translate to challenges on the part of the author in distilling and communicating the most useful information. This concern led to several premises which guided the book's design. The first is that people are coming to multimedia from disparate media backgrounds. (A video professional may know little about computers, just as a talented graphic artist may know little about audio.) Moreover, people also come from different job descriptions and professional backgrounds—some technical in nature, some artistic, some from a business background.

The second premise is that technology and product development are changing so rapidly that detailed descriptions become outdated almost as soon as they are printed. (Simply put, this book would have already been obsolete before it went to press if it dwelled on the gory details of specific products.) In addition, desktop incarnations of products are more easily understood if we comprehend their traditional counterparts and forebearers—many of which still have their place in multimedia production.

The third premise is that even the ultimate desktop multimedia tools do not guarantee effective production, any more than owning a piano or a box of paints makes one a musician or an artist. Indeed, the ultimate vision of the desktop multimedia producer is that of Renaissance person—artist, animator, composer, musician, videographer, editor, writer, spokesperson, producer, director, designer, programmer, and more. Each of these is potentially a lifetime career.

This book addresses all of those challenges and premises in a carefully designed and orchestrated structure. The vast subject matter is first organized into logical sections or parts focusing on the individual media—computers, graphics, audio, video, and interactive media. Each of these parts is symmetrical in that it contains three chapters. The first chapter covers the underlying technology, framed in knowledge rather than facts. This background provides the reader with an understanding of how things currently work and the means of interpreting and understanding the seemingly daily new twists.

The second chapter in each part reviews the tools associated with a given technology and discipline, again presented categorically rather than specifically. This gives the reader a solid grounding in the tools of today and a framework in which to assimilate new products as they evolve.

The third chapter in each part encourages creative and efficient use of the associated media. People embracing the challenge of multimedia production on the desktop can benefit greatly from the tried-and-true experiences of traditional artists, photographers, composers, videographers, programmers and other creative professionals. They can also borrow invaluable perspectives from producers of traditional media when it comes to project management, media integration, legal issues, and more.

In finalizing my concept for this book, I was struck by how much the seemingly disparate media actually had in common. Moreover, I realized that everything comes back to square one—nature. Technology is simply the harnessing and manipulation of nature. And our ability to perceive the aural and visual results of multimedia is nature personified. I kick things off in Part I, therefore, with a perspective on the common natural threads and the universal concepts underlying all media technology.

The subject of multimedia is incredibly vast—far more than any one book can communicate. I wrap things up with appendices with recommendations for additional reading in specific areas, professional organizations that are involved in multimedia, and a listing of software and hardware products that are available at this writing.

You don't have to read this book from cover to cover in order to benefit from it—although doing so will broaden your perspectives significantly. Its modular design is intended to help you hit the ground running regardless of your background, experience, application, or platform. It is my hope that *The Desktop Multimedia Bible* helps you realize your dream and vision of multimedia. In doing so, you will have fulfilled mine.

— Jeff Burger
Redwood City, CA

Table of Contents

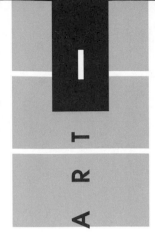

Fundamental Principles of Electronic Media

One of the most striking things about working with a combination of media is their similarity. Electronic tools—such as audio, video, and computer equipment—all operate on the same basic principles, as do their media. The way electronic media function parallels the way natural media and communication occur. Moreover, the operation of both natural and electronic media parallel the way the entire universe seems to work.

This part reviews some basic principles of media, science, and nature that lurk just out of sight when you are using electronic media. The concepts presented here will help you understand the subjects covered throughout the rest of the book. More importantly, they will help you utilize new multimedia technologies and tools to the fullest as they evolve.

Chapter 1 provides a synopsis of the natural phenomena that make sight, sound, and communication possible. Chapter 2 focuses on common concepts governing electronic media. Chapter 3 describes some of the basics that pertain to the electrical signals that enable and unite multimedia tools.

Indeed, Part I resembles a crash course in high school physics. Those of you who weren't distracted by other things in the tenth grade can skip right to Part II. For those who were daydreaming and otherwise occupied, as I was, this synopsis contains no intimidating formulas, few words of more than five syllables, only enough history to make it interesting, and—best of all—no test at the end. ❖

The Technology of Nature

Since multimedia is defined as the combination of two or more media, a definition of media is a good place to start. In the classic sense, a *medium* is something through which information travels. Air, water, space, and even solid objects are forms of media that carry information in nature.

Information that is carried through all natural media takes the form of *waves*—repeating patterns that oscillate back and forth. Light is a series of waves. Sound is a series of waves. Electricity is a series of waves. Radio and television transmissions are series of waves. Media are said to *propagate* or reproduce these waves.

ELEMENTS OF COMMUNICATION

The word medium also implies something intermediate or in the middle. This is an important concept, because it correctly infers that media mean nothing without two important adjuncts—stimulus and reception.

❖ Stimulus, Medium, and Reception

A medium must be stimulated into action for there to be any information to communicate. A train track can be a medium for sound if you put your ear next to it. However, you won't hear anything unless a train is coming to stimulate that medium into vibration. Likewise, your eyes can be wide open on a pitch black night, but you won't see much of anything unless the medium of air is stimulated by light.

Information must be received in order for the stimulus and communication media to have any purpose or meaning. This reflects on the old question, "If a tree falls in the forest and no one is around to hear it, does it really make a sound?" Current scientific thinking indicates that there is no event unless one is perceived.

In summary, all communication requires stimulus, a medium, and reception/perception. (See Figure 1.1.) Visual communication requires the stimulus of a light source, a medium such as space, air, water, or glass to transmit the image, and eyes to receive it. Sound requires a source of vibration in a given range, a transmitting medium such as air, water, wood, and ears to hear the message.

Figure 1.1

All communication is based on stimulus, a medium, and reception/perception.

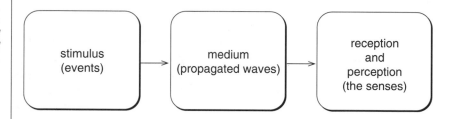

Response

While stimulus, media, and reception are integral to any form of communication, they all work synergistically. Say that two paddles are lying in the water on opposite sides of a small pond. If you move one paddle up and down or back and forth, the other will move in a similar fashion. The first paddle provides the stimulus, the pond acts as the medium, and the second paddle acts as a receptor. In essence, the medium acts as a direct link causing the receptor to move as one with the stimulus.

The key to this synergy is that both the medium and receptor are able to respond to the stimulus. If the pond were filled with mud instead of water, moving the first paddle would have less effect on the second. Similarly, sound does not exist in the vacuum of space because there's no medium to carry the physical vibrations regardless of the stimulus. On the other hand, space is an excellent medium for light and radio waves because these waves do not require physical matter in order to propagate.

Analogously, receptors must be capable of responding to the waves being transmitted through the medium in order for information to be perceived. A boat on a pond is significantly less responsive to waves created by a paddle than is another paddle. Likewise, the human ear can only perceive fluctuations in sound within certain ranges, and the naked eye can only perceive certain ranges of light. Moreover, the receptors have to match the overall type of waves being carried. The ear cannot respond to light waves any more than the eye can respond to sound.

Senses respond in scientific ways to waves that have quantifiable properties, such as frequency, amplitude, and waveform. The ultimate receptor—the brain—ascribes subjective attributes such as brightness, color, pitch, and volume to this input. The difference between reception and perception will be examined in greater detail later.

The weakest link principle

A fundamental rule of all communication is that the final result is only as good as the weakest link in the chain. Stimuli, media, and receptors share equal responsibility for the final quality of information. Applying quality media and quality reception to a poor stimulus only means that the poor stimulus will be represented accurately. (The best recording of a kazoo played through the best sound system will still sound like a kazoo.) Quality stimulus and quality reception mean nothing if the medium is poor. (Playing an audio CD into a telephone does not result in CD-quality audio on the other end.) Poor receptors can destroy the best source signal transmitted through the best medium. (A state-of-the-art broadcast can come across badly on a poor radio or television.) The *weakest link principle* recurs throughout all aspects of multimedia.

❖ **Making Waves**

The universe is in constant motion. Electrons move in a probabilistic pattern around the nuclei of atoms. On a much larger scale, the entire galaxy rotates within itself and in relation to other celestial bodies. Everything in between seems to be in motion as well, from a field of wheat oscillating in the wind to the daily tides. All of this motion shares a common bond—the motion manifests as waves.

A wave is the cyclic exchange of energy that occurs during transformation from a passive state into an active state and back again. The classic tool for visualizing wave action is the pendulum. If you pull a pendulum in one direction and hold it in place, gravity pulls against the mass of the pendulum but no energy is released. You've created a state exhibiting the greatest *potential energy* and the least *dynamic energy*. When you release the pendulum, it gathers momentum due to gravity. At the point closest to the ground the swinging pendulum exhibits the greatest dynamic energy and least potential energy.

A fundamental law of nature is that energy expended in one form must manifest itself in another form such as heat, light, or motion. In the case of the pendulum, the release of energy translates into further motion, and the momentum allows the mass to continue in an upward arc. When all of the momentum is overcome by gravity, the arc peaks, and the mass once again exhibits the greatest potential and the least dynamic energy. The continued influence of gravity starts the process over, and the pendulum swings back in the other direction. Without any outside influence such as friction, the pendulum will return to its starting point, and the cycle will repeat endlessly. This process is known as *self-propagation*.

Cycles and wavelength

The waves generated by the pendulum are best visualized by showing their action over time. The following example is hypothetical, but illustrative. Say you place a piece of paper under the pendulum and scroll it steadily at a right angle to the swinging action. If the pendulum weight contains a mechanism that sprays a thin stream of ink at the paper, the result will be a symmetric, repetitive, serpentine wave drawn on the paper. (See Figure 1.2.)

Figure 1.2

The pendulum is an example of a device that creates a natural wave.

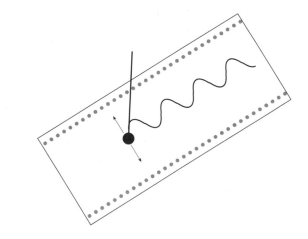

Each complete change—from potential energy to dynamic energy and back—is referred to as a *cycle*. A cycle can be referenced either by its *wavelength*—the distance between analogous points from one cycle to the next—or by its *period*—the time it takes to complete one cycle. (See Figure 1.3.) Waves exhibiting similar periods from cycle to cycle are referred to as *periodic* waves. The sound of a pitched musical instrument is periodic, for example.

Figure 1.3

A cycle describes one complete repetition of a wave.

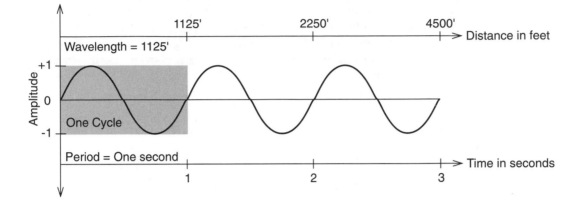

Sound waves exhibiting no discernible pitch—such as those result-ing from a cymbal crash—are *aperiodic waves*, waves whose peri-ods and wavelengths change erratically over the course of an event.

NATURAL MEDIA AND WAVES

Regardless of whether information is created and/or communi-cated electronically in a multimedia presentation, the ultimate ex-perience is conveyed to the eyes and ears of the audience in the form of light and sound. Both are examples of self-propagating waves.

❖ Sound Waves

Sound waves propagate in matter such as air, wood, and metal. You can use a tuning fork to illustrate how sound waves are cre-ated and transmitted. When the tuning fork is struck, the arm of the fork moves in the direction of the striking force. The air mol-ecules in that area become pressurized and exhibit high potential energy. Nature's propensity for a state of equilibrium forces the molecules to decompress outward. The dynamic energy expended during decompression causes neighboring groups of molecules to compress to a state of high potential energy. This process repeats in a sort of domino effect, pushing compressed air in all directions from the source.

So far the arm of the tuning fork has moved in only one direction. As with the pendulum, nature's propensity for equilibrium brings the arm not only back to its original position but past it. This action "pulls" on the volume of air previously occupied by the arm, producing an area of deficient compression or rarified air. A similar chain-reaction is set off, drawing the molecules previously pressured away from the source back toward it. As the tuning fork continues to vibrate, the pressure oscillations self-propagate through the surrounding air. (See Figure 1.4.)

Figure 1.4

Sound waves are waves of alternating air pressure.

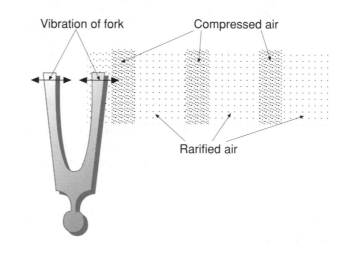

The waves created by the tuning fork resemble those created by the pendulum. If you were to attach a pen to the tuning fork and scroll a piece of paper under it at a constant rate, a depiction of the same basic waves would result.

Our ears are, of course, the main receptors for sound. The eardrum forms a membrane that is connected to a body of liquid and is sensitive to pressure changes within certain wavelengths. The pressure changes result in a hydraulic action that is converted into the electrical signals ultimately interpreted by the brain as sound. The properties of sound and its perception are covered in much greater depth in Part IV.

❖ Electromagnetic Waves

Electromagnetic waves include light, radio, x-rays, ultraviolet, infrared, and gamma waves. The only difference between these subclassifications is their wavelength. Electromagnetic waves behave similarly to sound waves, except that they are oscillations of electric and magnetic forces. To understand how these forces operate together, a bit of background on each is helpful.

Electrostatics and magnetism

Atoms normally have a neutral charge because they have an equal number of positively charged *protons* in their nuclei and negatively charged *electrons* in their various orbits. Positive and negative charges attract each other in a common bond. (Another quantum force maintains some distance between them.) All atoms seek an equal number of protons and electrons within their own atomic structure, thereby maintaining a neutral charge.

Envision two atoms in close proximity, each with an internally-balanced number of protons and electrons. Imagine that an outside force causes one atom to lose an electron to the other. The deficient atom is now positively-charged and the one with the extra electron is now negatively-charged. These opposing charges attract each other, resulting in electrical force attempting to resolve the imbalance of positive and negative charges. This attraction is manifested as a series of radiant lines of electrical force—an *electrostatic field*. (See Figure 1.5.)

Figure 1.5

Two electrons in close proximity that exhibit opposing charges create an electrostatic field.

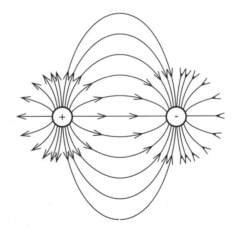

Electrostatic fields share many similarities with magnetic fields. Magnetism is thought to result from the patterns in which electrons orbit their nuclei. Every schoolchild has had the experience of placing iron filings on a piece of paper over a magnet. The magnet causes the filings to form curved lines connecting the poles to show the *magnetic field*. These visible lines correspond to invisible magnetic lines of force or *flux*—patterns that resemble the lines of electrical force in an electrostatic field. (See Figure 1.6.)

The magnetic field of a bar magnet, illustrating polarity and the law of inverse squares.

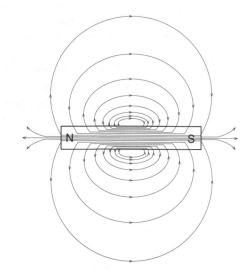

Other parallels exist between electrostatic and magnetic fields. First, electrostatic charges and magnetic fields can be imposed upon or *inducted* in neighboring objects through proximity. Second, the omni-directional dissipation of energy causes both types of fields to exhibit the *law of inverse squares*: The strength of the fields varies inversely as the square of the distance from the source. (For example, twice the distance from the source yields one-quarter the field strength.) Third, both have the capacity for opposite charges—positive and negative charges in electrostatic fields, and north and south polarity in magnetic fields.

The electromagnetic spectrum

The similarities between electrostatic and magnetic fields were not lost on nineteenth century scientists. Their experiments showed that these fields share a symbiotic relationship: An electrostatic field induces a magnetic field and a magnetic field induces an electrostatic field. This observation led to the conclusion that the two types of fields are properties of a single type of wave—the electromagnetic wave.

An electromagnetic wave is comprised of two types of fields perpetuating each other along a common axis extending away from the source. (See Figure 1.7.) The transformation of a dynamic electrostatic field into a dynamic magnetic field leads to the transformation of the dynamic magnetic field back into a dynamic electrostatic field—resulting in self-propagation. Unlike sound waves, electromagnetic waves require no physical medium in which to propagate since they consist of moving fields rather than moving particles.

Figure 1.7

Electromagnetic waves perpetuate each other along an axis perpendicular to their source.

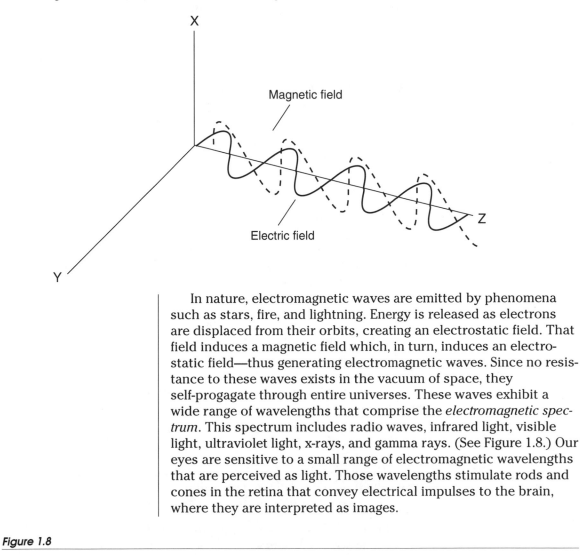

In nature, electromagnetic waves are emitted by phenomena such as stars, fire, and lightning. Energy is released as electrons are displaced from their orbits, creating an electrostatic field. That field induces a magnetic field which, in turn, induces an electrostatic field—thus generating electromagnetic waves. Since no resistance to these waves exists in the vacuum of space, they self-progagate through entire universes. These waves exhibit a wide range of wavelengths that comprise the *electromagnetic spectrum*. This spectrum includes radio waves, infrared light, visible light, ultraviolet light, x-rays, and gamma rays. (See Figure 1.8.) Our eyes are sensitive to a small range of electromagnetic wavelengths that are perceived as light. Those wavelengths stimulate rods and cones in the retina that convey electrical impulses to the brain, where they are interpreted as images.

Figure 1.8

The electromagnetic spectrum includes a wide range of wavelengths.

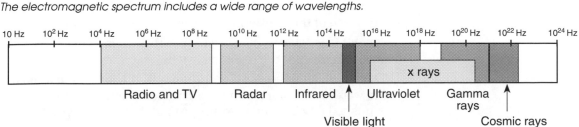

Electromagnetic principles as applied to electronic media are discussed in the next chapter. The properties of light and its perception are explored in greater depth in Part III.

MORE ABOUT WAVES

While sound, light, and other natural communication manifest in waves, waves also course through the electronic veins of computers, monitors, video recorders, tape decks, and other multimedia tools. Since all waves behave in a similar and predictable manner, a review of the nature of waves is in order.

❖ Newton Revisited

While quantum theory would later alter and expand our understanding of a universe in motion, Sir Isaac Newton had a pretty good understanding of overtly observable movement when he published his three laws of motion in the seventeenth century. For simplicity, they can be paraphrased as follows:

> First Law of Motion: A body at rest will stay at rest until acted on by a force. A body moving in a straight line at a constant speed will continue to do so unless acted on by an outside force.

> Second Law of Motion: When force is applied to a body, the resulting acceleration of that body is directly proportional to the amount of force applied and inversely proportional to the mass of the body.

> Third Law of Motion: For every action, there is an equal and opposite reaction.

The waves created by dropping a stone into a pond provide an excellent model for the understanding of all waves. Newton's work applies to this medium in the following manner:

> First Law: The surface of the pond is calm until the force of the stone striking it sets waves of water in motion. Once in motion, the waves would continue forever outward if not for the resistive force of the surrounding water or bordering land.

> Second Law: The harder the stone is thrown or the greater its mass, the deeper the resulting waves.

> Third Law: As the stone hits the surface, it loses momentum as the water gains momentum in a transfer of energy. As the water is pushed down a trough forms around it and some energy is

dissipated outward. The displaced water slides back into the trough with enough momentum to overshoot the surface level and cause a spike of water—an equal and opposite reaction. The spike of water then succumbs to gravity with enough momentum to cause another trough in another opposite reaction. This produces a series of similarly opposing events—self-propagating waves—until the energy is dissipated.

The troughs and peaks are equal distances—though in opposite directions—from the original surface level of the water. (See Figure 1.9.) The energy expended by the wave in its attempt to return to a state of equilibrium propagates the waves outward in an expanding radius from the point of impact.

Figure 1.9

A pebble striking a pond creates concentric waves that exhibit troughs and crests equidistant from the surface level.

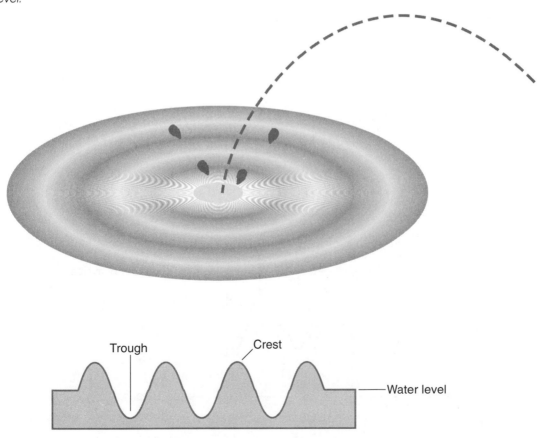

Trough Crest Water level

❖ **Frequency**

Waves are most commonly described by *frequency* rather than the wavelength of individual cycles. Frequency is a measurement of the number of waves that pass a fixed point in a specified period of time. The common way to refer to frequency is in *cycles per second (cps)*. If dropping the stone into the pond resulted in 30 waves passing a fixed point every second, the waves would have a frequency of 30 cps.

The more frequently-used nomenclature for one cycle per second is the *hertz* (abbreviated *Hz*), named after the German physicist Heinrich Hertz. One thousand hertz, or cycles per second, is referred to as 1 *kilohertz* (KHz); the shorthand for one million hertz is 1 *megahertz* (MHz).

The smaller the wavelength, the greater the frequency and vice versa. (See Figure 1.10.) Since waves of a given type (such as sound

---

Figure 1.10

The shorter the length of a wave, the greater its frequency. Note that amplitude does not depend on frequency.

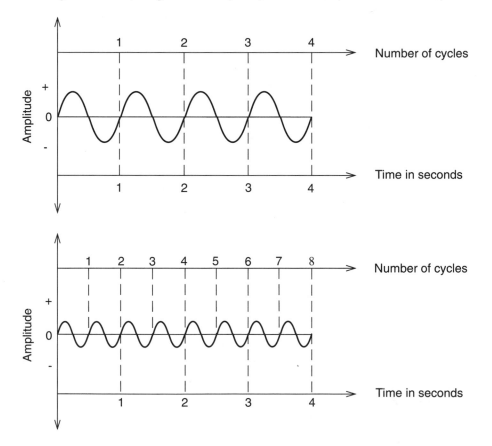

or light) travel through a given medium (such as air or water) at a fixed velocity, frequency is inversely proportional to wavelength:

velocity = frequency × wavelength

Frequency determines the pitches we perceive in sound, as well as the colors we see. In a broader sense, frequency influences the nature of the electricity that powers all our multimedia tools and represents the fundamental difference between light waves and various types of radio waves.

❖ Amplitude

As described earlier, the amount of force applied—in this case, the mass of the stone and the strength with which it is thrown—determines the height and depth of the wave's peaks and troughs, also referred to as the wave's intensity, or *amplitude*. Different portions of a wave can have positive amplitude or negative amplitude. (See Figure 1.11.) The point where amplitude has a value of zero is sometimes called the *zero-crossing point*.

Amplitude is measured on different scales depending upon the medium. It represents the loudness of sound, the brilliance of light, and the strength of the signals transmitted through wires and airwaves.

❖ Resistance

When traveling through a medium such as air or water, the amplitude of a wave lessens as it moves further in distance and/or time from the originating force. (See Figure 1.12.) This effect, known as

Figure 1.11

Two waves, one with twice the amplitude of the other. Note that frequency does not depend on amplitude.

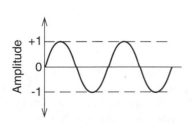
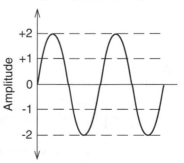

Figure 1.12

The damping of a sine wave due to resistance.

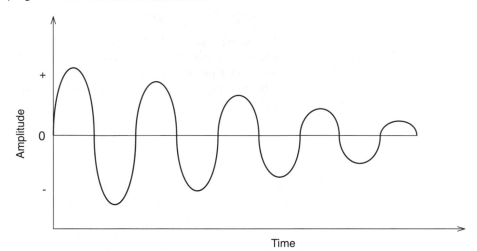

damping, is a result of two factors. First, the original energy of the event dissipates against increasingly greater mass as the waves radiate further from the source. Second, the medium itself applies *resistance* to the waves trying to set it in motion.

Resistance is a fixed property that can be attributed to a given medium. Molasses, for instance, is more dense than water, and therefore offers more resistance. Throwing the same stone into a pond of molasses with the same force would yield waves that dampen faster compared to those in pond water. Sand provides so much resistance that a stone has no perceptible wave effect on it. Note, however, that damping within a medium affects only amplitude as it propagates, not the frequency.

Resistance affects how the amplitude of sound and light diminish with distance and as they travel through different media. Resistance is also a major factor in how electric signals behave in the media of wires and circuits.

❖ Waveform Addition

The shape of a wave is referred to as its *waveform*. The waves created by dropping a stone in a pond represent the simplest of all waveforms—the *sine wave*. The smooth, symmetrical curve of the sine wave corresponds to the basic back-and-forth motion of most natural vibrations. The motion of the pendulum and tuning fork also describes sine waves.

Complex waves result from more than one thing vibrating at a time. If you drop a second stone into the pond right after the first, each stone will create a sine wave. However, the combined waves result in a waveform with a more complex shape than a simple sine wave. The more stones you throw, the further from a sine wave the resulting waves will be. Waves are *additive* in nature when they encounter each other. The amplitudes are added together at any given slice in time. (See Figure 1.13.)

The interaction of sine waves was studied by a French mathematician, Jean-Baptiste-Joseph Fourier, who postulated that all waveforms, regardless of their complexity, could be described by their component sine waves. Conversely, all complex waveforms are made up of simple sine waves—a theory that works well with the classical physics distillation of the universe into simple motions. In periodic waves, the component sine waves are integer multiples or *harmonics* of the fundamental frequency.

Differences in waveforms allow our ears to distinguish various sounds, such as instruments and voices, and enable our eyes to perceive differences between various hues of color. The electrical waveforms in audio and video gear determine the character of the sounds that emanate from our speakers and the images that appear on our monitors. Waveforms are also the building blocks of synthesis in electronic musical instruments.

❖ Phase

Imagine that after throwing the first stone, you were able to throw a second stone of exactly the same size into the pond with exactly the same force at exactly the same physical point as the first. While the impact of each stone would create identical sine waves whose amplitudes would be added together, it is likely that their cycles will not coincide with regard to time. In such a case, the waveforms are said to be out of phase. The term *phase* refers to the portion of a periodic wave's cycle that has elapsed from a predetermined point. (The phase of the moon is the point in its monthly cycle in relation to the full moon.)

Phase relationships are described in degrees, with the full cycle of a waveform being 360°. (See Figure 1.14.) The zero-crossing point before the positive portion of a wave is 0°. Since phase is a relative term, any given waveform is always in phase with itself. You can envision the relationship of multiple waves by mentally superimposing them. The phase relationship of two waves is the number of degrees difference between the 0° starting points of the two waves' cycles.

Figure 1.13

Sine waves are added together to create more complex waveforms. Adding the amplitudes of waves A and B results in wave C. Adding waves C and D results in wave E.

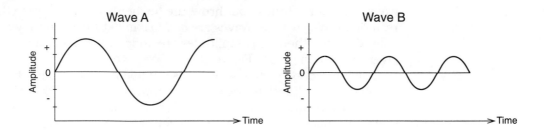

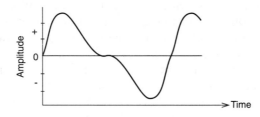

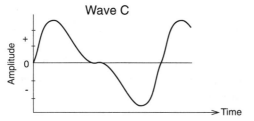

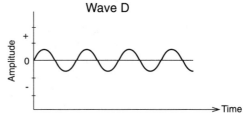

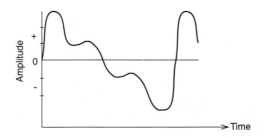

Figure 1.14

Each cycle of a waveform can be described as a phase shift over 360°.

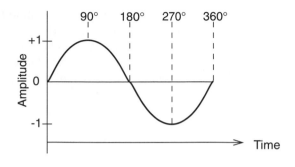

Since waves are additive, the waveform resulting from the combined waves will depend upon their phase relationship as well as their amplitude and frequency. Returning to the image of the pond, if you could somehow throw the second stone (still with identical size, force, and position) so that the wave it created was exactly in phase with that of the first, the result would be a sine wave with twice the amplitude, or height. (See Figure 1.15.) Throwing the second stone at any other time would result in the constructive/destructive interference of the two waveforms. The amplitude of the resulting waves would increase at certain phase relationships and diminish at others. (See Figure 1.16.)

Figure 1.15

The result of adding two waveforms in phase with each other.

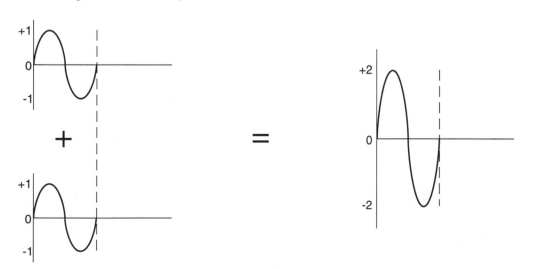

If two waves with the same frequency and amplitude were set into motion 180° out of phase in relation to each other, the wave actions would cancel each other out completely in a phenomenon aptly called *phase cancellation*. (See Figure 1.17.) Translation: no amplitude, no wave, no perceived stimulus.

Figure 1.16

The result of adding two waveforms 90° out of phase with each other.

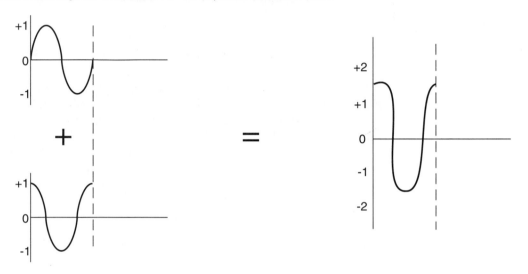

Figure 1.17

The result of adding two waveforms 180° out of phase with each other.

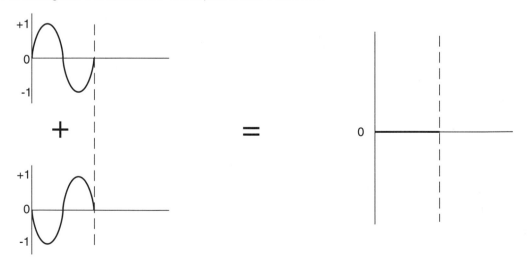

The concept of phase is important from an acoustic standpoint when placing multiple microphones and from an electrical standpoint when connecting stereo speakers and other devices. Phase cancellation effects influence timbre in music synthesis and is used to represent color encoding in video signals.

❖ Resonance and Sympathetic Vibration

Many objects or systems from atoms to planets have a frequency at which they naturally and easily vibrate when energy is applied. This is the object's *resonant frequency*. Transferring or coupling energy into a system at the system's resonant frequency and in phase with it will amplify its natural motion. If enough energy is added, the system becomes non-linear and will break. Force applied at any other frequency or phase will interfere with the natural motion in a constructive/destructive pattern.

A schoolchild might learn a little about resonance when pushing a friend on a swing. Once set into motion, the swing will naturally move at a resonant frequency. Pushing at the right time adds momentum; too much energy causes the swing to reach a point at the top of the curve where the chain goes slack and the natural motion is lost. Pushing at the wrong time detracts from the original motion and converts some of it to the influencing motion. The amount of coupling determines how long it takes the system to go from its original motion to the new motion.

An object will also vibrate at its resonant frequency with very little effort if influenced by energy at that resonant frequency. If you've ever heard an object in a room start buzzing of its own accord while you were listening to the stereo, you witnessed this phenomenon of *sympathetic vibration*: A frequency in the music matching the object's resonant frequency had enough energy to encourage vibration in the object.

Resonance determines which harmonics are naturally encouraged and discouraged in the waveforms around us. In audio, resonance determines the sonic signature of an instrument or other sound source, influences the aural character of speaker cabinets and listening environments, and is the source of unwanted feedback. In vision, resonance determines which colors are absorbed and reflected by surfaces on their way to the eye. Electronic circuits such as radio transmitters and receivers exhibit resonant frequencies that encourage or discourage the flow of electrons at certain frequencies.

❖ Encounters with Other Objects

The patterns in our imaginary pond also demonstrate how waves are affected when they encounter other objects. If they still have any strength when they hit the impasse of the solid ground at the edge of the pond, the waves are *reflected* back. The reflected waves mingle with any waves continuing to issue from the source, altering them in the process. The *angle of reflection* is always the same as the angle of incidence except on the opposite side of the *normal*—an imaginary line perpendicular to the reflective surface. (This can also be illustrated by a billiard ball bouncing off a rail or a rubber ball bouncing off a sidewalk.)

The amplitude of the reflected waves is reduced if some of the wave energy is absorbed when the waves strike the surface. The composition of the surface largely determines how much absorption occurs. A concrete wall offers no absorption, for example. Let's say the pond is instead ringed with a wall of sponges at the water line. As a wave hits the wall, the sponges absorb all the wave energy at that moment and reflect the rest back. If the wall was made of thin cheesecloth instead, only a small amount of wave energy would be absorbed or reflected. The rest would pass through the material, although the path of the wave would be slightly bent or *refracted*. (See Figure 1.18.) Refraction occurs when the velocity of a wave is altered by passing from one medium to another, such as light passing from air to water, or sound passing from air to wood.

Figure 1.18

Waves are reflected opposite their angle of incidence with diminished amplitude. Waves that are refracted through a medium continue at an altered angle with significantly reduced amplitude due to absorption by the medium.

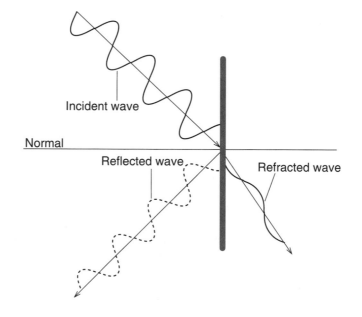

Incident wave

Normal

Reflected wave

Refracted wave

Finally, an obstacle in any medium (such as a rock protruding from the water's surface) will have one of two effects upon the waves striking it. A wave will be *diffracted*, or bent around, an object if the wavelength is greater than or equal to the size of the object; otherwise it will be reflected.

In multimedia, reflection, refraction, absorption, and diffraction properties influence the purity of what goes into presentations via microphones and cameras. They also influence the purity of information reaching the audience in the presentation environment. Understanding these properties also goes a long way in creating graphic and aural effects that accurately mimic the real world.

❖ ❖ ❖ ❖ ❖ ❖

While this chapter is far from being a comprehensive physics lesson, it provides an overview of nature's own technology. The next chapter offers a similar overview of multimedia technologies developed on the basis of these fundamental principles.

CHAPTER 2

The Nature of Technology

Increased understanding of the fundamental workings of nature has enabled the human race to harness these principles for its own purposes. The last century saw more scientific advances than all of previous human history. Exponential increases in scientific abilities have led directly to advances in the way people communicate. In particular, the evolution of electromagnetic and optical storage media, in conjunction with electronics, has provided the core technologies that make today's new media possible. The fundamental concepts that serve as a common thread in multimedia technology are the subject of this chapter.

ELECTRONIC MEDIA AND WAVES

Electronic media exhibit the same basic properties as natural media and carry waves with similar properties. However, electronic media have some capabilities and requirements that distinguish them from natural media, namely the abilities to record, duplicate, process, and synthesize information, as well as to convert it between radically different types of media.

❖ Transducers

When most people think of multimedia, they think of several electronic media—such as computer disks, audiotape, videotape, CD-ROMs, and laserdiscs—being used in parallel. The use of any of these communication tools implies the serial use of media. After all, we don't have jacks for audio, video, and digital data in our heads, nor do we have slots in which to insert physical media. Therefore, machines must not only employ some form of media, but also carry out stimulus and reception functions in communicating with other media.

Conversion between one medium and another requires a *transducer*—a device that converts one form of energy to another. Microphones are an example of transducers that convert sound waves into electrical waves. Similarly, video cameras convert light waves into electrical waves. Conversely, speakers convert electrical waves into sound waves, and monitors and projectors convert electrical waves into light waves.

Electronic media and their transducers, then, are only part of the chain leading to human perception in multimedia presentations. (See Figure 2.1.) As such, the weakest link principle applies to these stages of the communication process. Specific transducers are discussed in their appropriate sections throughout this book.

Figure 2.1

Electronic media form a link in a communication chain.

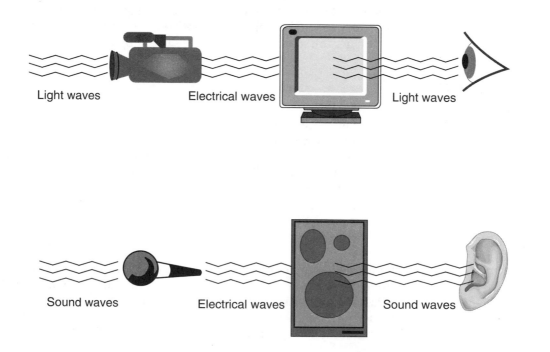

Light waves   Electrical waves   Light waves

Sound waves   Electrical waves   Sound waves

❖ Memory

For the most part, waves in nature must be perceived in real time or not at all. Air has no ability to remember a light wave, sound wave, or other stimulus. (Rock formations are examples of events recorded millions of years ago, but they are not exactly a good human communication medium.) Magnetic and optical media, such as tape and discs, can record or store waves for later retrieval. Indeed, one of the compelling aspects of multimedia is the ability to access stored information selectively.

Recall that waves move through natural media from stimulus to receptor. By contrast, information is stored in most electronic devices by moving the media past a stimulus in order to freeze the wave in the media. On playback, the media is moved past a receptor in order to reanimate the wave.

Natural communication media such as air and space can be thought of as linear—what goes in comes right back out. The storage process, on the other hand, is attributed to a medium's nonlinearity—what goes in does not come right back out. By extension, media that are good for storage are not good for real-time communication and vice versa.

The storage process typically involves the alteration of one or more properties of a medium. You can store a thought temporarily by drawing in the mud with your finger, for example. While this particular storage process doesn't take much effort, it doesn't take much effort to distort or destroy the message either. The drawing is much less susceptible to meaningful change after the mud dries, however. After that, the message can only be altered intelligibly after first returning it to its wet, malleable state.

The first important artificial communication medium with storage capability was the printed word. The pages of this book are a storage medium for keystrokes that were transduced from thought waves. The message is ultimately stored as systematic alterations in the coloration of the paper. You are retrieving that information by moving your visual receptors across the page; the brain transduces the image back into thought waves.

The venerable Victrola was one of the first mechanical recording devices. A stylus attached to a crude microphone was used to transduce sound waves into physical movements that were etched into a rotating wax cylinder. The sound was retrieved with an exact reverse of the process: a stylus translated the etched waves from the rotating cylinder back into sound waves that were amplified by a megaphone. Today's electromagnetic and optical recording media share this concept that recording and playback are inverse processes.

Replication and distribution

One other conceptual point that goes with storage is replication. More often than not, information that has been recorded into just about any medium can be duplicated. Paper can be photocopied. Tapes can be duplicated. Floppy disks can be copied.

Duplication leads to distribution in faithful form. Before paper, the distribution aspects of human communication were largely confined to word of mouth. Although we take replication and distribution for granted, these qualities represent an important difference between natural and electronic media.

Linear versus random access

Electronic media can be implemented in either linear or random-access fashion. Linear means that the information is retrieved in a start-to-finish fashion, like a story or movie. Audiotapes and videotapes are examples of linear media: You can move to another point, but not instantly or accurately. In contrast, information can be retrieved from any point in random-access media such as floppy disks, CDs, and laserdiscs.

❖ Processing

Sound waves and light waves in nature can certainly be manipulated or processed. You can draw the blinds or put on sunglasses to cut down light levels. You can stuff cotton in your ears to mute sound waves. Lenses and megaphones serve as amplifiers. The pitch of musical instruments is a direct result of manipulating wavelengths of strings and air passages.

Electronic media provide for much higher levels of manipulation and processing. Once in electronic form, information can be altered in a myriad of ways. Information can be selectively filtered, time-shifted, reversed, combined with other information, sorted, increased or diminished in intensity, distorted, and/or output in various formats.

The controls for volume, treble, and bass on your stereo govern rudimentary forms of processing, as do the brightness and contrast controls on your TV. Audio mixing consoles, video switchers, and special effects devices are examples of more sophisticated signal processors. Digital information can be processed in multimedia tools such as image processors, music sequencers, and direct-to-disk audio recorders.

Amplification and attenuation

One of the most fundamental parameters of an electronic signal that can be altered is its amplitude (volume in audio, brightness in video). Using fairly rudimentary electronics, amplitude can be increased to much higher levels or attenuated to much lower levels. In practice, most circuits in multimedia equipment operate at low signal strengths up to the point at which they need to go to a speaker or monitor. Microphones, electric guitars, synthesizers, video cameras, and recordings on any media all carry low-level signals. Audio power amplifiers and the predisplay circuitry inside video monitors and projectors are examples of devices that dramatically increase the amplitude of program material.

Electronic signals are eventually overcome by resistance and impedence when sent over long lengths of wire or split along many paths. These circumstances require amplification. A video distribution amplifier, for example, is used to boost the strength of a video signal when it is transmitted over long lengths of cable or driving multiple monitors.

Filters

While many other attributes of a program signal can be altered in an almost endless variety of ways, the *filter* is a processor that applies to many media. A filter does just what it implies: it screens out specified information—in the case of multimedia, selected frequencies.

Cut-off filters have a *cut-off point* at which attenuation occurs. A *low-pass filter* attenuates the frequencies above the cut-off point. These are used in sound synthesis and digital audio sampling. A *high-pass filter* is the opposite of a low-pass filter, attenuating frequencies below the cut-off point. High-pass is useful in removing extraneous sounds such as hum and microphone boom as well as enhancing the contrast in images. A *band-pass filter* rejects all frequencies except those in a certain frequency band—useful in isolating a voice or instrument. A *notch filter* is the opposite of a band-pass, attenuating only the frequencies in a certain band. This is useful for eliminating feedback in a live audio presentation.

Frequency-based filters have a *slope* characteristic whereby the cuts and boosts aren't linear—the effect on surrounding frequencies tapers off gradually. The sharper the slope, the more expensive the filter. Digital filters are more accurate than their analog counterparts. The application of filters is discussed in relation to various technology throughout the book.

FUNDAMENTAL PRINCIPLES OF ELECTRONIC MEDIA

❖ Synthesis

While microphones and cameras can serve as the eyes and ears of electronic media, many multimedia elements can be synthesized electronically. Synthesis bypasses input or stimulus from nature altogether. Although computer imagery can benefit from digitized artwork or photographs, extremely communicative visuals can be created solely within graphics applications. Similarly, even the least expensive music synthesizers can create a wider range of sounds than any single mechanical instrument or natural sound source.

Real-time generation of elements also eliminates the necessity for storage. Telling a graphics routine to draw an object or a synthesizer to play a note on demand consumes an infinitesimal amount of storage compared to the file sizes associated with actual images or sound passages. Synthesis, then, is an integral part of multimedia technology.

Artificial waveforms

The simplest electrical waveforms are sine waves, which are used to represent, manipulate, and generate natural waves such as sound. Several other types of electronic waveforms are created by equipment such as computers, video gear, and music synthesizers. (See Figure 2.2.) Electronic waveforms are typically created by a component called an *oscillator*—so named for the oscillating waves it generates.

Figure 2.2

Several examples of waveforms used in electronics.

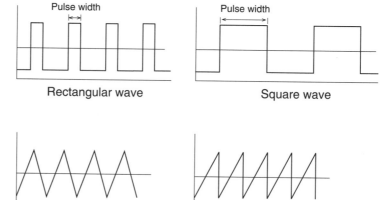

Rectangular wave

Square wave

Triangle wave

Sawtooth wave

The *triangle wave* resembles a sine wave in that it rises and falls smoothly from minimum to maximum amplitude. Unlike the sine wave, this action is linear rather than weighted. Triangle waves are used primarily in sound synthesis.

The *sawtooth wave* gets its name from its shape. Each cycle gradually builds up to its maximum voltage/amplitude, then immediately drops to its minimum value. This ramp-like quality has given the sawtooth wave the pseudonym of *ramp wave*. Sawtooth waves are employed in sound synthesis and in the control of electron guns in CRT displays, among other things.

The *rectangular wave* jumps abruptly from its minimum voltage/amplitude to its maximum. This yields a series of pulses that can be used either as timing signals for synchronization or as representations of on/off states. Rectangular waves are also called *pulse waves*. The duration of the on state is known as the *pulse width* or *duty cycle*. The *square wave* is a special type of rectangular wave that exhibits a 50 percent duty cycle yielding equal on and off times.

Modulation

More complex waveforms can be created using a technique known as *modulation*. The details aren't as important as the simple concept of one signal influencing or controlling a given parameter of another wave—such as frequency, amplitude, or pulse width. Music synthesizers, for example, rely heavily on modulation in the process of generating sound, as shown in Part IV.

Modulation is also used extensively in broadcast technology such as AM and FM radio and television transmissions. Frequency modulation is also used in another common area of technology—modem and fax transmission. The only difference is that the carrier frequencies being modulated by the analog representations of the actual data are in the audible range for purposes of telephone transmission.

ANALOG VERSUS DIGITAL

Waves and electromagnetic fields are *analog*, meaning that they are continuous signals capable of smooth fluctuations. Waves of water, sound, light, electromagnetism, and virtually everything else we deal with in nature are analog. Electric current is also analog, as were early electronics. Most modern electronic components are *digital*, meaning that the values are represented by numbers. As such, digital electronics represent value differences in discrete steps rather that the smooth transitions of analog waveforms.

Digital electronics have several major advantages over analog. The first is exacting representation of data and control over processes. Second, an amazing amount of manipulation can be performed on digital information. Third, digital components are more readily reduced in size compared to their analog counterparts. Finally, digital information is unaffected by the properties of a medium. Recordings on digital audiotape, for example, exhibit none of the tape noise associated with analog cassettes and reels. Similarly, digital signals signals are not subject to degradation or *generation loss* when copied.

Analog and digital components are both at work in most multimedia equipment. This section takes a closer look at the difference between these two ways of representing information and how they work together in electronic communications.

❖ Analog

Analog is characterized by a relationship of pressure and flowing current. Sound pressure results in a flowing current of air, just as water pressure results in a flowing current of water. Both of these examples are predicated on having a path that enables the flow. Air currents can't flow into an enclosed space once that space has been completely pressurized, any more than water can flow through a capped pipe once the pipe has filled completely.

The water pipe example also illustrates the statement that analog signals are capable of smooth fluctuations. Gradual changes in the valve position result in proportionately smooth changes in the water flow.

To use another meaning of analog, many of the electrical patterns flowing through audio and video devices are analogous to the sound and light waves they represent. Electricity is a flowing current of electrons resulting from the electrical pressure of charged atoms. Therefore electricity consists of waves of electric charges.

To visualize how wave crests are created, go back to the water pipe image. Varying the pressure by opening and closing the valve at regular intervals causes the water to surge up and down in response. The water pipe analogy, however, only illustrates *direct current* (DC)—current that flows in one direction. *Alternating current* (AC) oscillates by reversing its polarity and, therefore, its direction of flow at regular intervals. This back-and-forth movement of electrons exhibits the same oscillations found in sound waves and electromagnetic waves.

❖ Digital

Digital electronics is based on the concept that the simplest way to represent a piece of information is that it be either on or off. This correlates to the *binary* numbering system, literally meaning "two numbers." The number 0 corresponds to off or no, and the number 1 corresponds to on or yes. The piece of information exhibiting one of these states is a *bit* (short for "binary digit"). A combination of bits is usually required to convey a command or any meaningful data. This combination employs binary, or Base 2, arithmetic.

Humans employ *decimal*, or Base 10, arithmetic—not without coincidence to the fact that we have ten fingers. (Rest assured that if the human race evolved with eight fingers, we'd be counting in Base 8!) All numbering systems work in the same way: Each place value represents the next higher number above the maximum value that can be represented by all of the lower place values to the right combined. (It might help to think of the computer as having only two fingers!)

Batches of bits are gathered and manipulated like the digits of all numbering systems. A *byte* is a group of eight consecutive bits, in which each bit represents a different value position. The rightmost bit represents a 1, the next denotes a 2, the third a 4, and so forth. (See Figure 2.3.) Each bit is either on or off—a 1 or a 0—indicating the presence or lack of the number corresponding to that place value. By combining the status of the eight bits in a byte, any decimal number from 0 (00000000) to 255 (11111111) can be described. For example, the binary number 10001010 is the equivalent of 138 in decimal. (See Figure 2.4.) Note that in cases where decimal and binary numbers might be confused, the percent sign (%) precedes the binary numbers, as in %10001010.

Figure 2.3

The bits of a byte can represent a decimal value from 0 to 255.

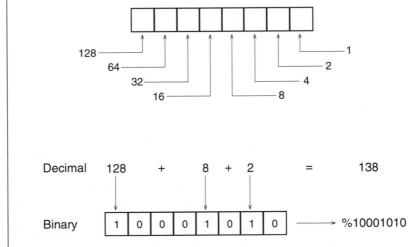

Figure 2.4

Any number can be represented in binary or decimal.

Representing numbers larger than 255 requires additional bits. The term *word* is used for groupings of bits of any size. For example, a 16-bit word refers to a grouping of 16 bits of data capable of representing 65,536 values.

A word can also represent positive and negative numbers with a trade-off of reduced range. This is accomplished by designating the bit in the highest position of a word as a sign bit that is to be applied to the value of the remaining bits. A 0 indicates positive; 1 indicates negative. This allows an 8-bit byte to represent the values of 127 to –128 and a 16-bit word to cover a range of 37,767 to –37,768. Non-integer or *floating point numbers* can be designated by assigning a certain number of bits to represent values and others to represent the position of the decimal point. Whether a word represents a full range of positive integers, a restricted range of positive and negative numbers, or floating point values is determined by the software that is translating the values.

At this point, it may become clearer why certain numbers keep reoccurring in high technology. Computers commonly offer palettes of 2, 4, 8, 16, 256, or 4,096 colors. Programmable equipment often has 8, 16, 32, 64, or 128 memory locations. High-resolution monitors often have a display of 1024 × 1024 pixels. The MIDI spec provides for 16 channels, 128 notes, 128 velocity levels, and 4,096 values for pitch bend. In every case, these values can be represented economically and exactly by small groupings of bits.

A large group of bytes is typically required to hold data of any significance. A group of 1024 bytes is referred to as a *kilobyte* or 1K. (In the binary numbering system 1024 is 2^{10}.) A *megabyte* (MB) is approximately one million bytes ($1024 \times 1024 = 2^{20} = 1,048,576$). A *gigabyte* (GB) is approximately one billion bytes ($1024 \times 1024 \times 1024 = 2^{30} = 1,073,741,824$).

❖ Conversion Between Analog and Digital

Since the waves in sight, sound, and electricity are analog and those in computers and many other modern electronic products are digital, some method of conversion between the two technologies is required. *Analog-to-digital converters* (also referred to as *A-to-D converters* or *ADCs*) accept an analog voltage and convert it into a series of discrete numbers in a process known as *digitizing* or *sampling*. *Digital-to-analog converters* (*D-to-A converters* or *DACs*) transform a group of discrete numbers into a continuous analog voltage. These circuits are used separately or together in various multimedia components such as graphic display cards, digital audio recorders,

Figure 2.5

ADCs and DACs convert information between analog and digital.

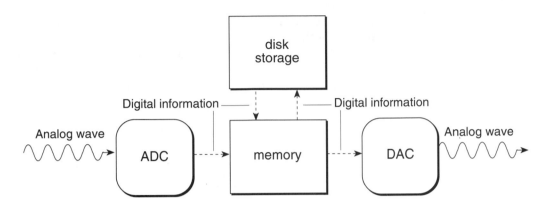

digital video recorders, CD-audio players, digital sampling keyboards, and video digitizers. (See Figure 2.5.)

Resolution

The larger the range of numbers used to describe a signal level, the more subtle are the gradations that can be represented. The number of bits reserved to represent the amplitude at each point of a wave is referred to as *resolution*. The greater the bit resolution, the larger the number of discrete amplitude values that can be represented. For example, audio CDs are standardized with 16-bit resolution: Amplitude values for each point in the audio waveform are represented by any of 65,536 numbers. By contrast, 8-bit audio only has 256 possible amplitude levels.

Quantization occurs when a source value falls between the values available at a given resolution. In the case of ADCs, the analog value is rounded, or quantized, to the closest available digital value. Quantization therefore produces a sort of "stair step" effect that causes the resulting output to be perceived as having an unnatural effect when the signal is output through a DAC. In audio, this effect manifests as a grainy sound. With visuals quantization results in bands of luminance. The unwanted effects caused by quantization become less obvious as resolution increases.

Sampling rate

The ADC essentially takes a snapshot or *sample* of an analog signal level—such as that from an audio or video source—at a given moment in time. Representing moving currents requires that snapshots be taken at regular intervals, similar to the way a movie comprises multiple still pictures. The *sampling rate* determines how often the analog signal is digitized.

Together, resolution and sampling rate—along with the component quality of the ADC and DAC—dictate how faithful the representation of a moving image or sound will be as compared to the original. (See Figure 2.6.) The DAC turns the numbers back into voltages at the same rate to render a representation of the original.

Figure 2.6

Resolution and sampling rate determine the similarity of a digital representation of a waveform to its analog counterpart.

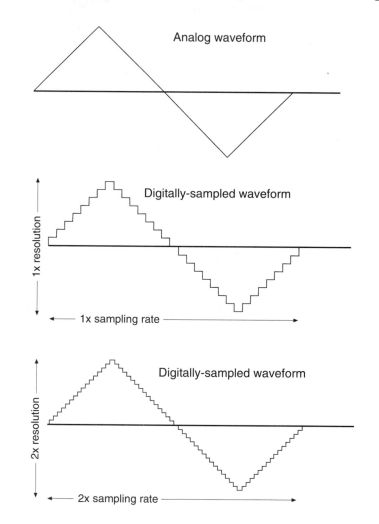

The *Nyquist theorem* essentially states that the sampling rate must be twice that of the highest frequency to be represented. This makes sense because each cycle of the waveform requires two values—one each for positive and negative amplitude levels. CD-quality audio, for example, exhibits a sampling rate of 44.1KHz, so the highest frequency that can be represented is 22.05KHz.

A phenomenon known as *aliasing* occurs when the sampling rate interferes with the frequency of the program material. This occurs when a frequency exceeding half the sampling rate is introduced to any sampling system. Aliasing is manifested as artifact frequencies called *sidebands*—sum and difference frequencies that contribute falsely to the amplitudes of low-frequency components.

In audio, aliasing introduces an unpleasant metallic distortion. In images, they appear as visible interference patterns. An image such as a herringbone jacket causes all sorts of bizarre artifacts on television because the high frequencies in the pattern interfere with the television scan rate. (In images, high frequencies represent sharp edges or changes, such as those found in the herringbone pattern.)

Two basic approaches are used to eliminate the unwanted effects of aliasing. The first is to apply a filter during sampling that allows all of the valid frequencies through, but blocks those that are too high for the sampling rate. In the example of 44.1KHz audio, the filter frequency would theoretically be about 22.05KHz. In practice, however, the sampling rate needs to be higher to compensate for the slope of the filter.

The second and more popular method of eliminating sideband artifacts is *oversampling*—sampling at a rate many times higher than twice the highest frequency. Once the information is in digital form, precise digital filters are used to remove frequencies that would cause problems at lower sample rates. The sample rate is then converted down to the normal rate for storage and manipulation. On playback, the signal is sometimes converted to a higher rate using *interpolation* to reconstruct the missing samples. The resulting signal lacks any high frequencies that could be undesirable. Otherwise, a more common analog filter is applied to the output of the DAC in order to smooth the "stair steps" of the quantized digital signal. It is cheaper and more accurate to build digital filters and faster DACs than it is to build sharp analog filters.

The GIGO principle

The subjects of resolution, quantizing, and sampling rate as they apply to different media are covered in greater detail in later sections on those media. One other thing to keep in mind about these conversion processes in general is component quality. Electronic components with the same basic specs come in a wide variety of quality levels and, as with most things, you get what you pay for.

The final output quality is only as good as the weakest link in the chain. A great DAC won't give you any better quality than the signal acquired by the ADC. This subset of the weakest link concept is the *GIGO principle* (Garbage In, Garbage Out). Similarly, a signal digitized using a great ADC will lose fidelity if output through a DAC of lesser quality.

COMMON MEDIA TERMS AND CONCEPTS

The fact that different media and waves share many common attributes means that they also share some of the same methods of qualitative evaluation. The following global terms and concepts are associated with a variety of audiovisual media and components. Application of these terms to specific media is discussed in greater depth later.

These concepts apply not only to media but the individual components that serve as both stimuli and receptors. This brings us back to the principle that any communication is only as good as the weakest link in the chain.

❖ Decibel

Perceivable levels of sound and light cover such a vast range that a logarithmic scale is used to measure them. A *decibel* is one tenth of a *bel*— a bel being a power ratio of 10:1. Decibels are covered in greater depth in Chapter 10.

❖ Frequency Response

Frequency response refers to the lowest and highest frequencies that can be transmitted or received by a component or medium within specified tolerances. An audio component with a frequency response specification of 30Hz to 20KHz ±3 dB, for example, indicates that the device can pass all frequencies between 30Hz and 20KHz with no more than a 3 dB variation in amplitude. Frequency response is said to be *flat* within a defined range if there is no perceptible amplitude deviation at any frequency within that range.

❖ Dynamic Range

Dynamic range describes the difference between the weakest signal and the strongest signal that can be faithfully represented by a given medium or component. Dynamic range is typically described in decibels.

❖ Noise

Noise can be loosely categorized as any unwanted element accompanying program material. Noise is aperiodic, exhibiting little or no patterned content. The extreme case is pure noise, containing an equal mixture of all frequencies. The audio and visual signals coming from a television receiving no broadcast are examples of pure noise.

❖ Signal-to-Noise Ratio

All circuitry and media contribute an inherent amount of background noise called the *noise floor*. You can hear noise when playing a blank tape, for example, or from most stereos even if there's no music playing. One of the most common specifications attributed to such products is *signal-to-noise ratio*. Signal-to-noise is typically expressed as the difference in decibels between the optimum program level and noise floor. The greater the difference, the better.

Signal-to-noise ratio has a simple real-world analogy. In a crowded room, the combined conversation and other noise in the room is the noise floor. To carry on a conversation, your voice has to be sufficiently higher in level in order to be distinguished. The lower the noise level in the room, the lower your voice has to be. Regardless of the background noise level, the louder your voice in comparison, the more effective the communication will be.

❖ Distortion

Distortion is any type of change in a signal from its original form. Many different types of distortion can adversely affect an electronic signal, including non-linear, frequency, and phase distortion.

Non-linear distortion is a result of output that does not rise and fall in direct proportion to the input. There are several sub-classes of non-linear distortion. *Amplitude distortion* describes differences in scale or ratio between input and output as amplitude changes. *Harmonic distortion* results from information at harmonic frequencies being added by a circuit or transducer, usually in amounts directly proportionate to input amplitude. *Intermodulation distortion* adds frequencies that are not necessarily harmonics of the component frequencies. *Flutter distortion* results from time-base deviations in physical mechanisms, such as tape transports, or electronic components, such as oscillators.

Frequency distortion is a phenomenon in which the output exhibits frequency content not present at the input. *Phase distortion* refers to phase relationships that differ between input and output.

❖ **Fidelity**

Fidelity means "faithful" in any context. Applied to audio, video, and photorealistic images, fidelity usually refers to how faithful the output image is to the original input. Frequency response, signal-to-noise ratio, and distortion are all part of the evaluation of fidelity.

❖ **Saturation**

Any medium or circuit reaches *saturation* when additional input cannot affect additional output. *Headroom* is the difference between the average signal level and the saturation level. Magnetic recording tape, electronic circuits, and colors and luminance in video are some of the elements in multimedia that are subject to saturation.

❖ **Bandwidth and Throughput**

Bandwidth is the difference between the extremes of a device's frequency response. A device capable of producing frequencies ranging from 20KHz to 100KHz, for example, would be said to have an 80KHz bandwidth. Since frequency determines how fast information can be transmitted in many aspects of multimedia, bandwidth determines data *throughput*—how much information can be communicated in a given interval of time.

Bandwidth and throughput are major issues in multimedia. For example, a medium with a bandwidth of 20MHz is capable of passing 20 million fluctuations per second. If each fluctuation represents one bit of digital data, that's 20 million bits per second. If you're trying to pump 30 frames of animation per second through this medium and each frame consists of 1 million bits of data, those needs exceed the medium's throughput capabilities by a factor of 50 percent. Bandwidth and throughput will be examined in greater detail throughout this book because they affect the ability of vehicles such as modems, networks, storage devices, and computer buses to communicate data describing audio and visual data.

ELECTROMAGNETIC MEDIA AND TRANSDUCERS

Audio tape, video tape, floppy disks, and hard disks are all forms of electromagnetic storage media. Broadcasts including radio, television, cellular phones, and broadband networks employ artificially-generated electromagnetic waves for communication.

❖ Harnessing Electromagnetism

The discussion of electromagnetic waves earlier in this chapter introduced the concept that electricity and magnetism are inextricably bound to one another. By extension, the passage of electrical current through a wire inducts a magnetic field around the wire.

Winding the wire into a coil increases that magnetic field; the strength of the field is determined by the number of turns in the coil, as well as its diameter and length. Coiling the wire around a ferrous material, such as iron, focuses the field when current is applied. When the current is lost, so is the magnetic field, hence the term *electromagnet*. Electromagnetism in various forms is the basic principle behind the electric motor, solenoid, volt-ohm meter, transformer, and many other sub-components common to audiovisual equipment.

The direction of current flow dictates the polarity of the electromagnetic field. The fluctuations in a magnetic field resulting from an AC current directly correspond to the fluctuations in that current. (See Figure 2.7.) Since current can represent audio and visual information, magnetic fields can represent them also.

Electromagnetism applies the other way around as well. Moving a magnet along a wire produces a current in that direction. Further, moving a magnet back and forth along a coiled wire (or moving a coiled wire past fixed magnets) will produce an alternating current in the wire. This principle of *electromagnetic induction* is the technology behind the generation of electricity from turbines, as well as some types of microphones.

❖ Electromagnetic Transducers

Let's put these two ways of looking at electromagnetism together in a simple system comprised of a microphone, a wire, and a speaker. The simple dynamic microphone consists of a diaphragm attached to a coil of wire suspended within a magnetic field. As sound waves pull the diaphragm in and out, the wire moves with it.

Figure 2.7

The electromagnetic field associated with an alternating current is a direct corollary to the waveform of that current.

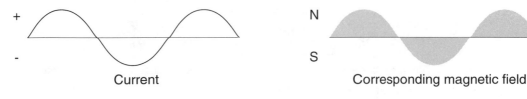

Current

Corresponding magnetic field

This causes fluctuations in the magnetic field which, in turn, induce an alternating current in the coil. This current is a direct corollary to the original sound waves.

Electric current travels through the wire to a speaker, which is similar in design to a microphone. A wire coil is suspended in a magnetic field and attached to a diaphragm. The alternating current causes fluctuation in the magnetic field which, in turn, causes the diaphragm to move in and out. This generates sound waves that are essentially the same as those that entered the microphone in the first place. In essence, the same information has been transmitted by various types of current—air pressure to magnetic field to electric current to magnetic field to air pressure. (See Figure 2.8.) Microphones and speakers are covered in greater depth in Part IV.

❖ Broadcasts

In Chapter 1, the universe was shown to be filled with electromagnetic radiation at a wide range of frequencies. Over the course of the twentieth century, people have learned how to receive, create, and control waves in an increasing number of these ranges.

The basic concept enabling the transmission and reception of radio, television, and satellite information is simple to understand given a knowledge of electromagnetic induction. The classic transmitter operates by running a strong alternating current into a long wire that serves as an *antenna*. The action of electrons running up and down the length of the antenna causes an alternating electric and magnetic field that causes an electromagnetic wave to radiate in all directions. The wavelength—and, therefore, the frequency—is determined by the rate of this alternation.

A receiving antenna is a passive length of wire attached to a circuit. When an electromagnetic wave strikes this wire, an alternating current is induced that mirrors the original source signal. By altering the circuitry of the receiver, it is tuned or made resonant with a given wavelength.

Figure 2.8

Sound waves are converted to an alternating electric current and back via electromagnetic induction.

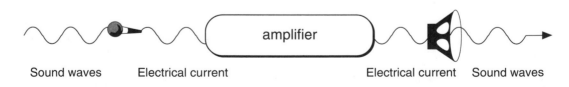

Sound waves   Electrical current   Electrical current   Sound waves

Modulation in broadcasts

The program signals representing audio and video information don't fall into the frequency ranges in which their signals are broadcast. While audio programming ranges from approximately 20Hz to 20KHz, for example, FM radio broadcasts transmit their signal at somewhere between 88MHz and 108MHz.

The transmission frequencies assigned by the Federal Communications Commission (FCC) are known as *carrier frequencies*. Carriers alone contain no actual program information. The carrier is modulated by the program signal to create a waveform that simultaneously adheres to the FCC frequency restrictions and contains meaningful information.

AM radio employs *amplitude modulation*, where frequency variations in the program are turned into variations in the carrier's amplitude. FM, or *frequency modulation*, converts frequency variations in the program signal into variations in the carrier signal's frequency. (See Figure 2.9.)

Figure 2.9

Amplitude modulation transforms changes in program frequency to amplitude changes in the carrier. Frequency modulation transforms changes in program frequency to frequency changes in the carrier.

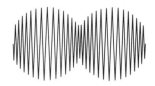

Amplitude modulation

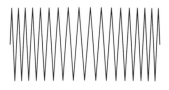

Frequency modulation

❖ Magnetic Recording

Until the recent innovations in optical media, *magnetic media* such as audiotape, videotape, and floppy disks have been the storage vehicles of the audio, video, and computer industries. Magnetic media all operate on the principles of electromagnetic induction.

All magnetic media employ a non-ferrous base substance as a backing material. A surface coating of ferrous particles, such as ferric oxide or chromium dioxide, is applied to this backing. The molecules of the oxide form areas called *domains*—the smallest particles known to be magnetizable. The polarity or magnetic alignment of these domains is initially random, although they can be easily influenced by outside magnetic forces.

The medium moves past a *record head* consisting primarily of an electromagnetic coil wrapped around a ferrous core. The core of the head has a gap cut in it at the point closest to the medium.

When current is applied to the head coil, it induces a field of magnetic flux—the magnetic equivalent of current—that flows through the medium. The flux, in turn, arranges the polarities of the ferrous domains on the medium into magnetic fields that are direct corollaries to the electric current. (See Figure 2.10.) Since an electrical current can represent audio, video, and computer data, all of these signals can be stored using magnetic media. In the case of analog, the magnetic field provides a direct corollary of the electrical signal. In the case of digital information, on/off bit values are represented by the discrete north/south polarization of domains.

Given the right attributes, the medium retains these magnetic patterns when the influence of the record head is removed. Information recorded in this manner can be retrieved by reversing the process. The media is moved past a *playback head*, similar to the record head except that it is unpowered. The magnetic flux on the medium induces a current into the head as the medium moves. All things being equal, these fluctuations are mirror images of the ones that caused the medium to magnetize in the first place.

❖ Attributes of Magnetic Media

As you might suspect, all things are not equal in magnetic recording. Most issues surround how the *formulation* or composition of the magnetic particles on the medium respond to the natural side effects of the recording process.

Figure 2.10

Fluctuations in the current of the electromagnetic head imprint magnetic fluctuations in the recording medium. On playback, the magnetic fluctuations in the medium induce a corresponding current in the electromagnetic head.

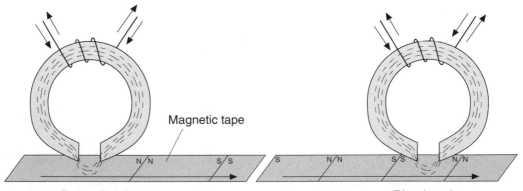

Magnetic tape

Recording head   Play head

Formulation and bias

The unaligned particles in any medium represent a noise floor that must be overcome with an appropriate signal-to-noise ratio. *Retentivity* and *remanence* are both terms (on different scales) that describe a medium's ability to retain a magnetic field after current is removed from the record head(s). As retentivity and remanence increase, so does the signal-to-noise ratio.

Sensitivity is the overall output level before saturation as compared to a standard reference. Higher sensitivity or output is desirable as long as the signal-to-noise ratio is preserved or improved.

The transfer of an electrical signal to magnetic media and back again is not a linear process. To simplify a rather complex subject, the magnetic domains on the medium exhibit a certain level of *coercivity*—resistance to being magnetized and demagnetized. This makes the recording process non-linear by nature, resulting in a distorted recording. The solution is *bias*—an ultra-high frequency signal that is added to the signal being recorded to improve headroom and significantly reduce distortion. (The bias signal itself is not perceived since it is well above the frequency range of the program material.) Bias essentially pre-excites the magnetic particles to a state in which they are receptive to undistorted magnetization by the program material.

The amount of bias required for optimum performance varies with the formulation of the medium. Ferric oxide, chromium dioxide, and metal particles offer progressively higher signal-to-noise ratios, in that order. Each requires a different bias setting for optimum performance. Issues of bias are fairly transparent to the user in the case of digital media such as floppy disks. The bias of analog audio tape recorders must be adjusted for the formulation of a specific tape, either via a switch or internal adjustments. Most video decks sense tape formulation automatically unless they require a specific type. Specific coverage of formulation and bias issues for audio and video are deferred to Parts V and VI.

Density

Particle density dictates the amount of information that can be recorded in a given time and space. This is quite evident in the case of floppy disks, where high-density disks are capable of storing almost twice the information in the same physical space as their standard counterparts. In the case of analog audio and video, higher density translates to improved dynamic range and frequency response.

In addition to formulation, the other solution to density is to move more particles by the head(s) in a given period of time. Wider tape formats in audio and video are capable of greater fidelity because there's simply more space available to store information. Similarly, the faster the tape speed, the more particles go by the head(s) in a given period—again resulting in higher fidelity.

Safe distance

One simple rule applies to all magnetic media including computer disks, audiotapes, and videotapes: Keep all magnetic media away from magnetic fields! What one magnetic field giveth, another taketh away. While this rule sounds simple, electromagnetic fields are everywhere. Speakers, televisions, monitors, and the electric motors found in vacuum cleaners and power tools are all examples of electromagnetic sources that can alter or erase valuable information stored in any magnetic form.

How far is safe for magnetic media? Since magnetic fields dissipate according to the law of inverse squares, a foot away from the average speaker or monitor is probably safe for disks and videotapes. Audiotapes are more susceptible and warrant an extra foot or so. If you have any doubts about proximity when installing equipment that generates magnetic fields, conduct some tests using some media that doesn't contain irreplaceable data.

Degeneration

Think of the aligned magnetic domains in a recorded magnetic media as being "stressed" in comparison to those in blank media, which are "unstressed." Over time, the magnetic domains tend to

Care of Magnetic Media

- Always keep magnetic media at a safe distance from sources of magnetic fields such as speakers, cables, and monitors.
- Dirt and dust are enemies of magnetic media. Always keep magnetic media in their protective cases or sleeves.
- Avoid storing magnetic media in environments exhibiting humidity and/or temperature extremes. Allow tapes and disks to acclimate after radical changes in temperature or humidity.
- Never touch the actual media, as oil from the skin can adversely affect both the media and the equipment that later accesses it.

tire of holding their pattern and start to become unaligned. Self-erasure can also result from heat and neighboring layers of tape. This degradation process certainly takes a long time, but it is quite common to find that an audiotape or videotape recorded ten years ago has degraded past the point of usability. Floppy disks are also susceptible to degradation, but seemingly less so. (Data formats are usually obsolete by the time this becomes a problem!)

A special form of degradation called *dropout* occurs when oxide flakes off the medium or dirt particles come between the head and the medium. Dropout translates to a corresponding dropout in program material on playback.

❖ Optical Media

The current trend in storage media is moving away from electromagnetic media and toward optical media. Audio CDs, CD-ROMs, laserdiscs, and fiber optics are examples of the optical media that are revolutionizing the communications and multimedia industries.

Optical media have several advantages over electromagnetic media. First, they hold vast amounts of data in a small surface area since they don't depend on domain sizes. (The average CD-ROM, for example, can hold about 600MB of digital data, as compared to about 1.2MB on a floppy disk of similar size.) Second, the media has an almost infinite lifetime and is virtually indestructable by comparison. Third, it is almost impossible to erase accidentally. Finally, optical media offers no degradation in signal integrity.

Lasers

Today's optical media owe their existence to the artificially-generated waves of the *laser*—an acronym for *light amplification by stimulated emission of radiation*. The normal light we perceive contains the wide, or *incoherent*, range of frequencies—all in various phase relationships. A laser heats gases in such a way that the light is *coherent*—confined to one predictable frequency and in uniform phase. This coherency allows the output to be focused. (The area of the light beam used to write and read optical media like CDs is 1.7 millionths of an inch!) Lasers can be turned on and off millions of times per second to correspond to the on/off values of digital bits, making lasers ideal for communicating large quantities of digital information.

Fiber optics

Fiber optics are slowly replacing wires as transmission lines for audio, video, and data communication. Fiber optic cables are essentially bundles of long glass strands called *optical fibers* which act as "light pipes" to carry the pulses of information created by lasers. The casing around the fibers is constructed to act as mirrors that reinforce the signal's amplitude. (One limitation is that fiber optics cannot be bent too much, since sharp angles can destroy the required angles of reflection.)

Since the material exhibits a high degree of optical purity, it offers a low degree of resistance to light. This provides data integrity across long transmission lines that require only periodic amplification. The actual couplings to the amplifiers represent a weak link in the chain. Fortunately, the technology of the couplings and fibers continues to improve as prices drop.

Due to lack of inductive properties, data can be transferred via fiber optics much faster than through inexpensive wires. A single fiber optic cable can carry vast amounts of data compared with a single-conductor wire of the same size.

Optical storage

At this writing, the creation of most affordable optical media such as CDs and laserdiscs starts with a mastering process. The digital information from master data is used to turn a laser on and off corresponding to the on/off states of the data. (In video laserdiscs, the width of the states is used to represent analog signals.) The laser is used to expose spots in the photographic film coating of a rotating glass master disk. After the film is developed, acid is used to etch the glass underneath. The film is then removed, leaving a glass *mother*. A metal master, made from the mother, is used to stamp or imprint the patterns of holes into heated plastic discs. A thin backing of reflective aluminum is applied (for the same effect as silvering a mirror), then sealed with a plastic coat to protect the disk from scratching.

On playback, the media rotates past a low-power laser. The aluminum reflects light into a photodiode according to the patterns in the plastic. These, in turn, are converted to electrical impulses that are routed to the appropriate processing system.

Technology is becoming available with price/performance ratio allowing the everyday user to record or write optical media on the desktop. The various implementations of optical media are discussed in Part VI.

❖　❖　❖　❖　❖　❖

This chapter has presented foundations that are common to all electronic media. The remaining chapter in this section deals with the concepts of powering and interconnecting electronic media tools.

CHAPTER 3

Power and Connections

The most fundamental artificial medium in multimedia is the wiring that powers and interconnects the electronic components. Electric current comprises the fundamental waves running through that medium. This chapter examines the basic concepts of powering and connecting multimedia equipment.

THE ELECTRIC PERSONALITY

Electricity is the lifeblood of computers, audio gear, and video equipment. It represents, manipulates, and conveys the wave-like properties of sound and light. A review of the basic principles of electricity will help you get the most from your multimedia endeavors. Taking a few minutes to review the basics of powering all the electronic tools of the trade will also help ensure both safety and equipment longevity.

❖ The Journey of the Electron

Most of the electricity we use involves the process of free electrons moving through a wire to form electrical current. This flow of electrons requires a complete loop—a *closed circuit*. Envision a closed circuit as a chain of atoms and an electromotive force, such as a battery, as an electron pump containing energy capable of pushing extra electrons. If the battery is inserted into a closed circuit, the negative terminal repels electrons into the wire. This sets off a chain reaction in which each normally neutral atom along the wire has electrons pushed onto it from its neighbor, causing it in turn to repel more electrons to its neighbor on the other side. This chain reaction continues through the rest of the wire to the other end, where the positive terminal of the power source is attracting electrons. (See Figure 3.1.)

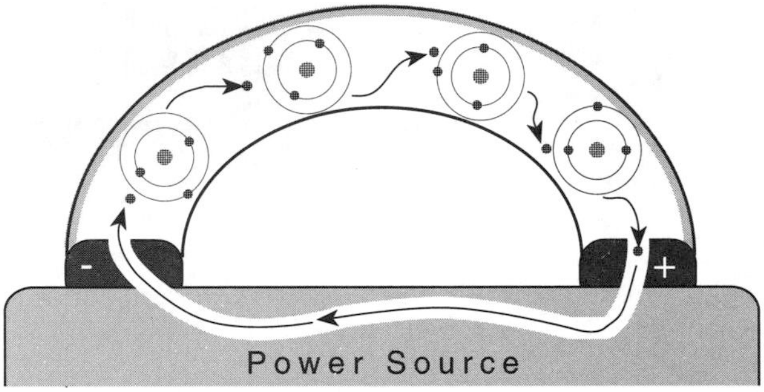

Figure 3.1

An electromotive force compels electrons to move through a closed circuit.

Power Source

The aforementioned example illustrates direct current (DC) in which electrons flow in a single direction. Recall the statement in Chapter 2 that alternating current (AC) reverses its polarity and, therefore, its direction of flow at regular intervals. The rate at which the electron flow alternates is referred to as frequency. While electronic components can internally vary the frequency of alternating current over a vast range, the electrical current coming from wall outlets in North America operates within a tolerance of 50 to 60Hz.

❖ Electrical Conductivity

Chapter 1 discussed how substances such as air, water, molasses, and sand offer varying resistance to the movement of an object like a dropping stone. Different materials also offer more or less unique levels of resistance to electrical current, because some types of atoms are more, or less, willing to part with their electrons. This variance allows poor conductors—like plastic, porcelain, and rubber—to act as *insulators* to confine the flow of electricity to good *conductors*—like copper and silver wiring.

Electricity cannot escape easily through an *open circuit*—one containing a broken wire or switch that is turned off. This is because air is not a good conductor of electricity. On the other hand, electricity can flow from a broken wire if it contacts a material that offers reasonable conductivity. Water is a good conductor, hence all those childhood warnings about keeping electrical appliances away from the bathtub. Earth is also a reasonable conductor, which is why electricians wear shoes made from an insulating material such as rubber. A *short circuit* results when a conductive path is made between two parts of a circuit in such a way as to bypass a portion of the circuit—a potentially dangerous situation unless it is part of the circuit's design.

❖ Amperage— Electrical Flow

As discussed earlier, the flow of electrons is known as current. The rate at which current flows past a given point in the wire or circuit is measured in *amperes* or *amps* (A). One ampere is equal to 6.8×10^{18} electrons per second flowing through a circuit. Devices requiring electrical power are said to draw current from a circuit. Table 3.1 shows how much current is drawn by some ordinary electrical devices.

Table 3.1. Examples of current drawn by typical household appliances.

ITEM	APPROXIMATE AMPERAGE
Flashlight	.25A
100-watt light	.8A
¼-h.p. electric motor	4.5A
Average heating appliance	10A
12-volt car battery	100-200A

❖ Voltage and Resistance

Voltage is the electrical pressure caused by electrons repelling other electrons and is measured in *volts* (v). The pressure of voltage causes current to flow. Voltage is said to be not only an electrical pressure, but an *electromotive force*. As discussed in Chapter 1, if the stone is tossed into a pond, the force with which that stone was thrown translates to amplitude. Therefore, voltage is a measurement of the amplitude of potential force in an electrical signal. The voltage of wall current in North America is 120 volts; in many other parts of the world it is 220 volts. Voltage levels running through most multimedia circuitry are usually significantly less than that—on the order of less than one to about 10 volts.

The amperage, or speed at which electrons can flow given a certain voltage, depends on the resistance of the circuit. Resistance is measured in *ohms* (Ω). These three parameters of electricity—voltage, amperage, and resistance—have a direct relationship as set forth in Ohm's Law:

current = voltage / resistance

   or

amps = volts / ohms

From this relationship, it's easy to see that current and voltage are directly proportional—more voltage creates more current and less voltage creates less current. The relationship between voltage and resistance appears inversely proportional—half the resistance creates twice the voltage, twice the resistance creates half the voltage, and so forth.

Resistance is determined by the size of a wire or electrical path, as well as the conductivity of the material. To put this in better perspective, let's return to the analogy of electricity flowing through a wire and water flowing through a pipe. The water pressure is not the amount of water coming into the pipe. The size of the pipe determines how much resistance the water encounters. The resistance, in turn, affects how much water flows at a given pressure. Increasing the size of the pipe lowers the resistance and increases the current. Decreasing the size of the pipe offers more resistance and decreases the current. Figure 3.2 illustrates the relationship of current, resistance, and voltage.

Since current, voltage, and resistance are inextricably related, varying a circuit's resistance can affect its voltage and current—and, therefore, amplitude. Most of the knobs on audio and video gear that govern amplitude-related functions, such as brightness and volume, are variable resistors. Resistance also has important implications in the following discussion of wiring.

Figure 3.2

Current is determined by the direct relationship of voltage and resistance.

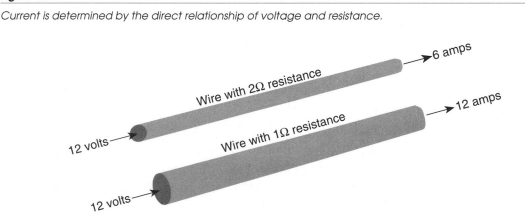

❖ **Capacitance**

Capacitance is the ability to store electric charges resulting from oppositely charged poles separated by a *dielectric*—a material that permits the lines of electrical flux to pass through it without actually being a conductor. This is the principle behind the capacitors commonly used in electronic circuits. The effects of capacitance vary with frequency and vice versa. Variable capacitors are associated with many of the frequency-dependent controls on audiovisual equipment, such as tone and contrast controls.

Capacitance comes into play in two areas of concern to those using electronic gear. First, be cautious when opening a piece of equipment, since capacitors can store an electrical charge even after the power is disconnected. (In particular, the picture tube inside a CRT or video monitor can store a dangerous level of voltage for long periods of time.) Second, capacitance affects the performance of the signal cables used to connect multimedia equipment. Cables are discussed later in this chapter.

❖ **Wattage— the Measurement of Electrical Power**

A fundamental law of nature is that energy expended in one form must manifest itself in some other form such as heat, light, or motion. Another way to look at this is to think of the difference between energy such as electricity and the actual work done by it. The part of an electrical circuit that utilizes electric energy is called the *load*. (Light bulbs and electric motors are examples of loads.) Ultimately, electrical energy is expended as power, measured in *watts*—more wattage, more output power, more electrical power consumption. For example, the output of power amplifiers and the power-handling capabilities of speakers are rated in watts. The power of radio transmitters is measured in *kilowatts* or thousands of watts.

Wattage is interrelated with amperage, voltage, and resistance. For those who are technically inclined, the formulas that apply follow. (For those not technically-oriented, don't sweat this one!)

$$power = voltage \times current$$
and
$$wattage = current^2 \times resistance$$
and
$$wattage = voltage^2 / resistance$$

A tangible example of the relationship between these electrical attributes is the load of the common light bulb on household current.

A 60-watt bulb puts out less light and heat than a 100-watt bulb, although they both receive the same 120 volts of electrical current. This owes to the differing resistance of the filaments used within the bulbs. Elements offering higher resistance to the flow of electricity provide lower current which translates to less wattage, heat, and light; those with lower resistance provide increased current which translates to greater wattage, heat, and light. (It's easy to remember this by relating it to dealing with people: the more resistance you encounter, the less work gets done.)

CONNECTIONS

Multimedia equipment deals with two basic classes of electrical signals. The first is the pure AC current or *line voltage* that powers everything. The other is actual audiovisual program material. Both have their own issues with regard to cables, signal efficiency, and safety.

❖ Electrical Safety

The more electronic equipment you use in a multimedia production and presentation environment, the greater the issue of proper power becomes. Professional audio, video, and computer facilities don't even consider installing equipment until the electrical foundation in the building is rock solid. How do you know if you're taxing your wiring? Here are some symptoms:

- Circuit breakers pop or fuses blow when a lot of equipment is on at once.
- Lights dim or the image on your video/computer monitor shrinks when other equipment is turned on or when the motor of an appliance kicks in.
- Equipment containing motors starts reluctantly and/or runs slowly.
- Power cords seem unusually hot.
- You smell smoke!

If any of these symptoms occurs, turn the equipment off immediately to avoid risking fire and/or damage to the equipment! These problems typically stem from too much current being drawn from a circuit at one time. Every electrical product you have plugged into a circuit draws some amperage away from it. Power in a home or building is distributed across multiple circuits, each rated to handle a given amount of amperage. When more amperage is being drawn than the circuit is rated for, a circuit breaker or fuse blows. In better buildings, circuits are rated at 20 amps; older buildings and those of poorer construction have circuits rated at 15 amps or less.

A wire has fixed resistance. In keeping with Ohm's Law, voltage decreases as more amperage is drawn from the circuit by additional equipment. If voltage decreases too much, individual pieces of gear don't receive enough voltage to run properly. (In the case of a VCR, tape deck, or other motorized product, low voltage can burn the motor out in addition to causing other damage.) Resistance is essentially an electrical form of friction. As it increases, so does heat. That's why a flimsy extension cord becomes hot if you have too many things plugged into it.

Since resistance is also a function of wire size, proper wiring is important. The *gauge* of a wire indicates its diameter, with lower gauge numbers indicating greater diameters. Outlets in modern buildings are powered by 12-gauge wire. A circuit is only as good as the weakest link in the chain, however. Household extension cords, for instance, are often problematic because they are made of 14-gauge wire or smaller, offering much greater inherent resistance than 12-gauge wire.

Power irregularities and protection

Even the best wiring can't compensate for irregularities in the power line coming into your building—blackouts, brownouts, and surges. A *blackout*, or complete power failure, doesn't have to last long to warrant bringing out the candles. An interruption of a fraction of a second is enough to cause equipment to lock up or restart. Data loss is the first problem in equipment with volatile memory. If a blackout occurs while a computer or similar product is writing information to storage media, the file may be damaged as well. A series of failures in rapid succession can cause damage in other areas such as the power supply.

Brownouts are temporary reductions in power levels. They can be as detrimental to electronic gear as overloading a circuit. Brownouts can be identified by dimming lights, the slowing of motorized equipment, and shrinking images on video monitors. *Power surges*—also known as *transients*, *glitches*, or *spikes*—are temporary jolts of high voltage usually undetected by lights and appliances, but potentially deadly to electronic gear. All electronic equipment worth its salt is protected from surges by internal fuses, but nothing's foolproof.

Fortunately, protection is available from these electrical anomalies. The least expensive option is plugging your equipment into a *surge protector* that guards against power transients. These can be purchased in stand-alone form, built into power strips, or incorporated into wall outlets. Be sure that you do not plug more equipment into a single surge protector than it is rated to handle.

The next level of protection is a battery-powered *standby power supply*. The device constantly monitors the line for brownouts and failures, and switches to its battery pack if it senses either. As a general rule, the faster the switching process, the better. Fifty milliseconds is about the maximum for multimedia gear.

The ultimate in power protection is an *uninterruptible power supply* (UPS). The output is powered by batteries that are constantly charged by the incoming line voltage. This method eliminates damage from power failures by buffering the equipment from the power source. Of course, standby and uninterruptible power supplies can only run so long on batteries, so work should be saved immediately and equipment powered down in the event of a lengthy failure. A self-contained generator is often employed as a backup power source in areas with a track record of blackouts, or by facilities where continued power is crucial.

Just because the flow of electric current is stabilized doesn't mean it is free from other anomalies. Line voltage can be contaminated or made "dirty" by electromagnetic interference and radio frequency interference—interference that can adversely affect the performance of audio, video, and computer equipment. Many devices that protect against power irregularities also have filters that remove interference.

Start-up precautions

Equipment draws the greatest amount of current when first switched on because more current is needed to start electrons and motors moving than to perpetuate that motion. As a result, the start-up process places the greatest stress on electronic equipment. Most audio and video studios, as well as computer professionals, leave their sophisticated equipment on all or most of the time for this reason. The cost of the power this practice incurs is less than the cost of constantly turning things on and off—not to mention the cost of service calls should equipment need repair.

Hard drives throw a bit of a wrench into the works. One common specification of hard drives is *mean time between failures* (MTBF), referring to how many hours they can run before they go to that Big Storage Device in the Sky. While these ratings are usually in the tens of thousands of hours, the system may be idle for long periods of time overnight. A healthy compromise is to leave the equipment on throughout the work day and turn it off overnight if it's not serving a function.

When turning on equipment, do not power up more than a few devices on the same circuit at the same time since doing so can cause a surge. Turning on a lot of equipment with a single switch is the primary thing to avoid. If you must link power strips, for example, switch each one on and off in sequence rather than using the one closest to the wall outlet as a master switch.

Grounding and polarity

All electrical power cables have at least two pins on the plug to constitute a closed circuit. For most modern electronic gear, it is important that proper polarity between positive and negative be maintained. In equipment using 2-wire cables, the two pins on the plug are physically polarized: One is slightly larger than the other and will only plug into the corresponding slot in an outlet. Equipment using 3-wire AC can also only be plugged in one way thanks to the *ground pin*. While these conventions ensure proper connections on the part of the user, they do not guarantee that the outlets themselves have polar continuity. Outlet wiring should be checked in the event of persistent power or ground problems. (Inexpensive circuit testers are available at local electronics stores.)

The ground pin also serves to connect the *electrical ground* for the equipment to the ground for the building, preventing the risk of electric shock when touching the gear. (Electronic devices with 2-pin power plugs aren't normally a safety hazard unless there is an internal short circuit.) Common grounding issues for multimedia studios are discussed in greater depth at the end of this chapter.

Old buildings, old wiring

Some older buildings with original wiring pose many potential problems. Poor amperage rating in circuits is one. Old insulation is much more susceptible to heat and fire than that of today. Further, electrical outlets have no grounds and no physical polarization dictating positive from negative. The best solution by far is to update the entire wiring system. In lieu of that, run a heavy insulated cable from the main ground pin of your power strip to a copper or steel water pipe going into the ground or to a 10-foot ground rod. Then get ahold of a test meter—and somebody to run it who knows what they're doing—to establish positive from negative on each of the outlets you intend to use for multimedia equipment. If things are this far gone, you would be well advised to obtain a professional rewiring opinion from an electrician if you plan to do much A/V work.

Electrical Dos and Don'ts

- If your equipment is overloading a circuit breaker or fuse, try plugging some of the equipment into a different circuit to spread the load. Always plug multimedia equipment into circuits that do not power heavily-motorized appliances like refrigerators.

- Use power strips rated for at least 15A, preferably ones with self-contained circuit breakers. Avoid "octopus" plugs. Where possible, make sure all wall outlets, power strips, and extension cords use 12-gauge wiring.

- Don't force a 3-pin power cord into 2-pin extension cord. Use a proper ground-lift adapter if you must use this type of connection. Never force a polarized plug into a non-polarized outlet.

- If you ever need to remove the cover of a piece of electronic gear, always disconnect the power first. Be aware that some components such as capacitors and CRTs can store an electrical charge long after the power has been removed.

- Wait at least five seconds between toggling an electronic device off and on. Leave sensitive equipment, like computers and recording devices, turned on for the duration of your work sessions to minimize start-up surges.

- Use a surge protector when powering sensitive equipment such as computers; look into a standby or uninterruptible power supply in areas with unreliable power.

❖ Inputs and Outputs

All signal connections on audiovisual gear are either inputs or outputs. While those terms are self-explanatory, the terms plug and jack are often confused. A *jack* is the connector on the panel of the equipment, while a *plug* is what's on the end of a cable.

Impedance

Connections between two or more audiovisual components are affected by *impedance*—the overall force that opposes signal flow in the circuit. Resistance and reactance are factors contributing to impedance.

The term *reactance* is derived from a cable's reaction to the signal being applied to it, especially with regard to frequency. Recall that the flow of electricity induces magnetism; in an AC circuit, this process results in *inductive reactance*—a magnetic field that opposes the current you are trying to create. This effect varies with frequency of the signal. Also recall that a capacitor is comprised of two opposing signals separated by a dielectric—exactly the description of a cable containing two leads of opposite polarity separated by an insulator. *Capacitive reactance* is the effect the capacitance in the cable has on the program signal. In particular, high capacitance results in high-frequency loss.

Impedance, then, is the combination of inductive reactance, capacitive reactance, and the inherent resistance in the circuit. Like resistance, impedance is measured in ohms, although the symbol Z is often used instead of Ω. Impedance ratings are generally divided into the categories of *low impedance* and *high impedance*. The long and short of impedance is that matched low impedances are optimal, and low-impedance outputs to high-impedance inputs work fine. Conversely, high-impedance into low-impedance does not work. Therefore, equipment outputs usually exhibit low source impedance (approximately 2 Ω to 600 Ω), while equipment inputs usually exhibit high load impedance (2 kΩ to 50 kΩ).

❖ Anatomy of a Cable

The cables that carry program signals between audiovisual devices have different, but equally important, aspects that bear closer inspection. These signals are typically low enough in level that shocks are not an issue. However, the quality of the information they carry requires more delicate handling in other ways to ensure fidelity. Many people spend thousands of dollars on multimedia equipment, then skimp on cables. Cables are very much a part of the weakest link principle. So remember that buying a cable that has the right physical connections on each end doesn't mean that it's the best cable for the job!

Shielding and balancing

Cables are natural antennae, inviting unwanted extraneous signals into electronic equipment. There are many types of interference, most of which have to do with electromagnetic induction.

Capacitive interference is induced by an AC circuit in close proximity. This even applies to an open circuit, such as an appliance or light that is not turned on, since the voltage or electrical potential is still present. *Inductive interference* comes from magnetic fields such as those generated by electric motors and current in AC cables. *Electromagnetic interference* (EMI) results when wires are subjected to a sea of electromagnetic waves ranging from fluorescent light ballasts to power tools and dimmers. And everyone has heard *radio frequency interference* (RFI) at some point—the effect of CB and AM radios bleeding into radios, TVs, and other electronic media.

The solution for most types of interference is *shielding*. Shielded cable places an electrical sheath around the cable that short-circuits electrical potential induced into the cable to ground before it can affect the signals in the wire. The more continuous the sheath, the better the shielding. The concentric nature of the conductors explains the term *coaxial cable*.

The lower the signal strength running through a cable, the more susceptible it is to interference. Hence, cables used to convey low-level signals—such as those from microphones, tape decks, and VCRs—employ shielding. High-level signals found in speaker cables and power cords are not shielded.

There are two classes of shielded cable—unbalanced and balanced. In an *unbalanced line*, the shield usually doubles as a conductor for the A/V signal ground. No shield is perfect, however, especially over long distances. In that light, professional studios and stage presentations employ *balanced lines* for low-level audio. Balanced lines employ two conductors—one positive, one negative—plus a signal ground, all sheathed in a shield. (Sometimes the shield serves as a ground.) The idea is that any interference penetrating the shield will enter both the positive and negative conductors and will therefore be eliminated through phase cancellation. Balanced lines can be run much further than unbalanced lines, but the input and output circuitry of the equipment on both ends of the cable must be balanced to reap the benefits of a balanced circuit. (See Figure 3.3.)

In general, balanced lines are used for low-impedance, low-level signals such as microphones. They are also employed in necessarily long cable runs such as from instruments on stage to a mixing

Figure 3.3

Unbalanced cables use the outer conductor as a shield, combatting interference in shorter cable runs. Balanced cables surround two conductors with a grounded shield, adding another layer of interference protection in longer cable runs.

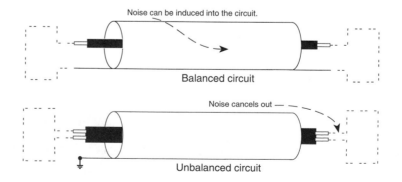

Noise can be induced into the circuit.

Balanced circuit

Noise cancels out —

Unbalanced circuit

console in the house. (High-impedance signals can be fed into low-impedance using an *impedance matching transformer*.) Unbalanced cables are used for moderate-level, high-impedance signals such as those from electronic musical instruments or composite video sources. While the maximum length for unbalanced high-impedance cables is approximately 25 feet, lengths should always be kept as short as possible to maximize frequency response and minimize the possibility of interference.

Cable construction

The next thing to consider is the substance from which the conductor is made. The best material will offer a combination of low electrical resistance and high physical flexibility. High resistance reduces the strength of the overall signal—higher frequencies in particular—in a system with unmatched impedance. Flexibility is important because cables are often moved, coiled, plugged, unplugged, and generally subjected to physical torture.

The purity of the material is also important. Tinned copper is used in run-of-the-mill cables. *Oxygen-free copper* (OFC) is used in the best cabling because it lacks impurities.

The choice of materials for the connectors on each end of the cable is not restricted by the issue of malleability. Their exposure makes oxidation a major issue, however. While gold connectors increase the cost a bit, they are the best because they are resistant to oxidation.

Just as the ideal wire has no resistance, it has no capacitance either. Neither is a real-world situation. Low-capacitance cable is the best there is. Capacitance is usually rated in capacitance per length of cable—the lower the better when comparing brands. Capacitance in cables is related to the insulating material. The material with the lowest (most desirable) dielectric constant is Teflon, although it is also the most expensive. Less costly polyvinyl chloride (PVC) is more commonly used, although it can have a much higher dielectric constant than Teflon.

While the specs on cable construction can tell you something, there is a much simpler rule in selecting the best cable. Simply put, better cable costs more to build and buy. Get the best you can afford!

❖ Avoiding Hum and Interference

Now that we've examined the two basic kinds of cables that carry power and information, let's see how they interact. For starters, power cables can be bundled together, and cables that carry program information can be bundled together. Indeed, this practice is often desirable for the sake of appearance and safety. The two different types of cables should not be bundled together, however, since the AC can induce audible side effects into the weaker program signals.

One particularly noticeable side-effect is *AC hum* or *60-cycle hum*. Current from wall outlets alternates at 60Hz; 60Hz is an audible frequency taking the form of a low-pitched hum. If line voltage frequencies bleed into an audio signal, even the most pristine audio will be tainted with a constant low-frequency or higher harmonics thereof. (A similar scenario applies to 50Hz AC lines outside of North America.)

The general rule of thumb is to keep power cables and audiovisual cables away from each other. This is often more idyllic than practical. If the two types of cable must cross, they should do so at right angles to provide a minimal opportunity for induction.

More about grounds

Two different kinds of grounds are used in multimedia equipment—signal ground and electrical ground. *Signal ground* is the ground for low-level audio or video information. Signal grounds are usually attached to chassis grounds, so that they go to the ultimate electrical drain—the earth.

The main idea behind an *electrical ground* is safety with regard to the AC line current used to power the equipment. If a wire inside an electrical device should come loose and touch the chassis or case, the potential for shock exists when someone touches the chassis. The same thing can happen when a drink is accidentally spilled inside a piece of equipment and the liquid shorts the circuit to the chassis. Either way, the path through unsuspecting flesh might be the most direct route the electrical charge can find to reach ground.

The 3-pin AC plug reduces the concern. A wire attaches the third pin directly to the chassis, reducing the risk of shock by providing a direct path to ground. This safety mechanism is obviated in a 2-pin AC plug. Fortunately, 2-pin plugs are used primarily on equipment with predominantly low risk of shock. There's also a good reason why the ground pin is missing on audiovisual equipment—it has to do with that pesky 60-cycle hum. Stay tuned.

In addition to interference, 60-cycle hum often occurs as a result of a *ground loop*. A ground loop exists where there is a difference in potential between points in an AC circuit. Let's say two power strips are plugged into two separate wall outlets. If the quality of the ground differs between the two outlets (which it typically does), then the voltage potential between the two power strips will be different. This potential, sometimes as small as millivolts, creates an alternating current in the ground path—the ground loop. So, simply plugging equipment with 3-pin grounds into different outlets or power strips can cause a ground loop. And plugging interconnected devices into outlets on different circuits is really asking for hum.

Solutions to hum induced via ground loops range from simple to very technical. The first rule of thumb is to ensure that all devices that are part of the audio chain be powered from a common power strip at best, and the same wall outlet at worst. You may have heard that using a ground lift adapter to lift or disconnect the ground pin on the AC plugs is a solution. While this has been known to work in a pinch, it should be considered extremely dangerous and is not advised. Removing the ground pin makes it possible for your body to become the path of least resistance for electricity to reach ground—not a fun thing!

An additional solution that works more times than not is to place a simple isolation transformer on the audio connections of one or more devices. (Radio Shack is one source.) Beyond these suggestions, the help of a qualified technician is highly recommended in sorting out your hum and ground loop problems safely.

Interference defenses

Ordinary light dimmers can cause electromagnetic interference. Professional studios use a special type of dimmer called a Variac that eliminates this problem.

If the tactics described so far don't eliminate your interference problems, there's more you can do. First, run all of your wires that carry program information through a conduit made from material like aluminum, then ground the conduit. This adds one more level of shielding around all of the cables.

Proximity to radio-frequency transmitter can pose special difficulties especially in metropolitan areas. In cases of extreme interference, a *Faraday cage* can be implemented around a facility. This is essentially a grid of wire mesh (much like window screening) running through every inch of the peripheral walls, floors, and ceiling—all connected to a common ground. The effect is that of one big shield around the facility. (Forget windows!) Professional advice is recommended if you are encountering interference problems of this magnitude.

❖ ❖ ❖ ❖ ❖ ❖

While the subject of electricity can be explored in significantly greater depth, these basic concepts should give you enough background to operate and connect equipment safely and fruitfully. The next part examines the tool at the center of today's multimedia technology—the computer.

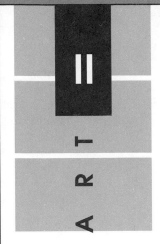

PART II

Computers

The computer has become not only an integral part of today's multimedia presentations, but also a catalyst in bringing production capabilities to the masses. Nonetheless, the inner workings of computers in general often remain a mystery or terror—even to people who use them every day. This is perfectly understandable. Computers have gone from being rows of mammoth monoliths requiring teams of technicians to personal productivity tools as common as any other appliance. Along the way the "high priesthood" of computing has attempted to cloak its secrets from the masses. Hollywood has even portrayed computers as doomsday machines with malevolent personalities. Ironically, multimedia technology is now an integral part of the entertainment industry.

Society seems to be evolving into roughly two classes of people—those who embrace computers and those who don't. Presumably readers of this book are in the former category. Chapter 4 dispels some common myths about computers and explains their inner workings in plain English. Chapter 5 contrasts the popular computer platforms in the context of multimedia. Chapter 6 sheds some light on making life with computers easier and utilizing them to their fullest potential. ❖

Computer Technology

Many people who use computers are hard-pressed to define what they are. The role of the computer is not defined in the same way as that of other machines. A sewing machine sews clothes and a lathe lathes wood—period. They are dedicated machines. A food processor or a toaster-oven is more general-purpose, but still has limitations. (They do several things, but you can't iron or vacuum with them, for instance.)

The computer is truly a multipurpose machine. It's not designed to do any one thing in particular, but is capable of being programmed to perform many different tasks. You still can't sew or lathe with one, but the computer can be made to control a sewing machine or a lathe. Multimedia is taking computers one step further. Computers can not only control video and audio devices, but extensions to the technology actually allow these silicon tools to become video and audio devices.

ANATOMY OF THE THINKING MACHINE

Computers are constantly being compared to the human brain; early incarnations were even called "thinking machines." This analogy to the brain helps to establish the first important distinction in computer technology—hardware versus software. *Hardware* is everything that has corporeal existence just as biological brains do—computers, disk drives, keyboards, printers, monitors, and the like. *Software*, on the other hand, is conceptual or intellectual property akin to our thoughts—programs, operating systems, and data.

Now, just because you're breathing and circulating blood doesn't mean you're actively thinking about it, any more than you have to think about how to think! This implies some intrinsic underlying functions associated with the task of simply being a human. In a computer, *firmware*, or *read-only memory* (ROM), contains permanent instructions associated with everyday low-level abilities. When the computer is first turned on, for example, the firmware knows to look for a "higher level of consciousness" from a disk. (Technically, you could say that firmware is software that is permanently embodied in hardware.)

Even though people are born with a sort of firmware, we have to learn how to walk, talk, eat, read, ride a bike, react instantly to danger, and other things that later become second nature. In doing so we develop an extension of the autonomic functions, the sum total of which allows us to deal with everyday life and to function as a normal member of society. In the computer, the *operating system* (OS) knows how to deal with standard procedures like accepting system commands or menu choices, and allocating and managing space in memory and on storage media.

As we learn more about life, we develop certain mental routines for performing specialized tasks like playing the piano, sailing a boat, or baking a cake. We invoke the associated thought processes only when we need to use a particular skill, ignoring them the rest of the time. The silicon analogy to these skills are *programs* or *applications*. They too are dedicated to performing specialized tasks above and beyond the basic system operation—tasks such as word processing, page layout, or electronic painting. They are invoked when their particular skill is needed and go unused the rest of the time.

The brain is constantly receiving *data*, or information, from the outside world via senses such as eyes and ears, just as it delivers information via speech, gestures, and writing. This data is also the content and substance of what we manipulate with our specialized skills. (We use data in the form of sheet music, wind direction, and recipes when employing the aforementioned skills of playing the piano, sailing, or baking.) The computer receives stimulus in the form of data from *input devices* such as keyboards, microphones, scanners, cameras, and mice. In turn, it sends data to *output devices* such as monitors, speakers, and printers. Data is the information that programs manipulate and operate upon.

The human brain makes endless decisions and calculations based on input, experience, and procedures, then stores the results in a seemingly infinite amount of memory. The computer uses a *microprocessor to* perform calculations based on input, memory, and procedures, and stores the results in *random-access memory* (RAM). Memory is therefore the immediate medium of both.

RAM is *volatile*, meaning that it only retains information until the computer is turned off. Compared to the brain, computers have limited amounts of memory. For these reasons, programs and data must be recorded permanently on *storage media* such as a magnetic or optical disk for later retrieval. In the human analogy, the storage process could be likened to writing down a thought or making entries in a log or ledger so you don't forget it—thus freeing up "brain space" to think about other things.

The nervous system in the human body serves to interconnect areas of the brain, as well as communicate with the senses and muscles. The electronic counterparts in the computer are various buses or electronic conduits that connect the microprocessor with memory, storage devices, and input/output hardware. The most obvious one is the *system bus* that extends the electronic pathways of the microprocessor to slots capable of holding add-on boards fulfilling specific needs such as audio and video input, output, and processing.

All of these hardware and software elements work synergistically to form the greatest productivity tool mankind has known to date—the computer. (See Figures 4.1 and 4.2.)

Figure 4.1

All hardware components of the basic computer model communicate with the microprocessor.

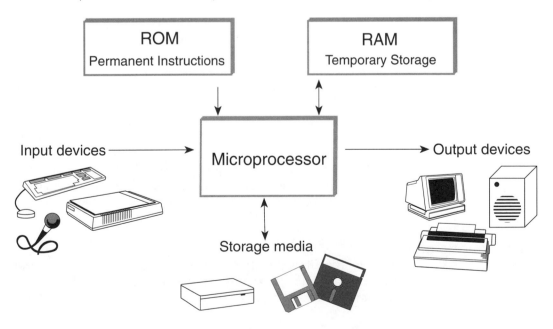

Figure 4.2

All software components of the computer communicate with the operating system.

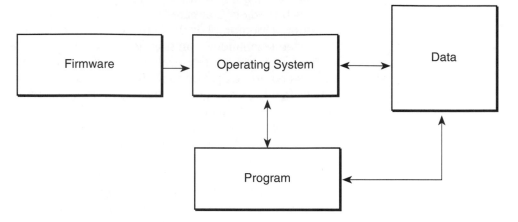

THE MICROPROCESSOR

One of the most significant inventions in the history of the human race has been the microprocessor. Microprocessors make "intelligent" machines possible. They make your microwave easier to use. They give your VCR programmability. And, of course, they are the brains of personal computers. Behind the scenes, microprocessors are a collection of several hundred thousand simple microscopic transistors and switches.

The microprocessor is the central clearinghouse through which most active data must pass. The microprocessor and support circuits that handle control and timing are collectively called the *central processing unit* (CPU). The term CPU is also often used to describe the entire main box that houses all internal components of a computer.

Microprocessors are often called "number crunchers" and for good reason: It's not only what they do best, but really the only thing they do! The information the numbers represent is what has meaning to people—text, graphics, sound, and the like. In its simplest form, then, the microprocessor takes a number from one place, manipulates it, and places the result somewhere else.

❖ The Language of the Microprocessor

The numbers flowing into the microprocessor are the ones and zeros of binary bits. These bits are grouped together into bytes and words to represent more complex information. These numbers would be meaningless without some guidelines as to what they symbolize. Each microprocessor has an intrinsic *instruction set*, or *machine language*, that correlates byte or word values to specific instructions. The way that a stream of bits is converted into a meaningful instruction can be compared to Morse code in which groupings of seemingly nondescript dots and dashes actually represent alphanumeric characters that have meaning for us. (See Figure 4.3.)

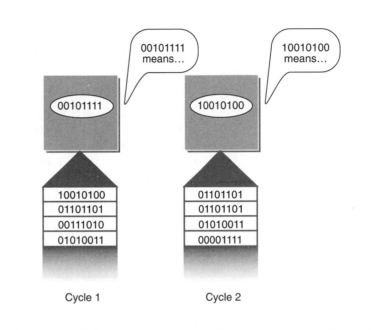

While many different programming languages are used to write applications, sooner or later they are all translated to machine instructions so that the microprocessor can execute them. While a discussion of computer programming is beyond the scope of this book, the following general categories of instructions might help in understanding the logic of the machine:

- Input: receive a piece of data from memory, disk, or a peripheral.
- Output: Send a piece of data to memory, disk, or a peripheral.
- Variable assignment: Assign the result of input or calculation to a variable that can later be referenced without regard for content.
- Calculation: Basic mathematic calculations.
- Loops: Repeat a specified set of instructions until a given condition is satisfied.

- Conditional statements: Evaluate a condition to be true/false or compare the mathematical relationship of two values, then act in a specified way based on the result.
- Branching: Direct the flow of program execution to another routine or portion of a program, usually in response to a conditional statement.

Taken separately, none of these instructions accomplish much. Used in combination, they form a powerful set of tools with which sophisticated tasks can be accomplished. As you will see in Part VI, these same programming concepts are used to create interactive productions using authoring systems.

❖ **Speed**

Microprocessors are driven by a *crystal clock* typically running anywhere from 7MHz to 50MHz. Each clock cycle triggers the acceptance and evaluation of the next group of bits and the processing of the embodied instruction. The faster the clock, the quicker the processing rate and the greater the throughput of data is. This might be likened to a bank teller servicing a single-file line of customers: The faster the teller works, the sonner the next person in line can be serviced.

All other things being equal, a CPU running at 14MHz will process twice the amount of data in a given time period as the same processor running at 7MHz. Even the fastest microprocessor can only process data as quickly as it can retrieve it from or return it to memory or disk, however. Each clock cycle that goes unfulfilled while waiting for RAM is called a *wait state*. Thus, a system exhibiting zero wait states is running optimally. On some systems, the bus itself can be slower than the processor and the RAM. Some accelerator cards work around this by putting the RAM onboard with a direct connection to the processor.

Today's CPUs are complex enough that clock rate alone does not accurately describe the number of instructions that can be computed in a given amount of time. *MIPS* (millions of instructions per second) describes how many integers, such as actual program instructions, the system can crunch through. *Mflops* (millions of floating point operations per second) describes the number of non-integer numbers the system can process. Floating point values are used extensively in 3-D rendering, for example.

❖ Architecture

The CPU's architecture refers to its ability to manipulate data and share it with the rest of the system. The increasing sophistication of microprocessor architecture is one of the main forces contributing to price/performance advances in today's computers over those of only a few years ago.

Internal architecture

The areas of the microprocessor that receive, hold, manipulate, and send pieces of data are called *registers*. All microprocessors have several registers. The more registers a microprocessor has, the more data it can quickly access.

Internal architecture refers to the size of a data word that the microprocessor can hold in one of its registers. The larger the register size, the fewer the number of instructions that have to be processed to perform mathematical operations on large values. For example, the only way to perform calculations on a 16-bit number using an 8-bit processor would be to break the number in half and operate on the high and low portions separately. Conversely, a 16-bit processor could process two pieces of 8-bit data in parallel assuming that the software is written properly. Table 4.1 shows the number of clock cycles that microprocessors of varying internal architecture would require in order to process digital audio and graphics in various formats. Note that anything but a one-to-one relationship of data word size to register size might be impractical in actual application.

Data bus

The second architecture consideration is the *data bus*, which sends and receives data between the microprocessor and memory locations. The "width" of the data bus dictates the maximum word size or value that can be transferred at any given moment. So, no matter how large a word the microprocessor can crunch internally,

Table 4.1. *The amount of data that a processor has immediate access to depends upon the size of the internal registers of the microprocessor.*

FORMAT	8-BIT PROCESSOR	16-BIT PROCESSOR	32-BIT PROCESSOR
8-bit mono audio	1 cycle	2 per cycle*	4 per cycle*
8-bit stereo audio	2 cycles	1 cycle	2 per cycle*
16-bit mono audio	2 cycles	1 cycle	2 per cycle*
16-bit stereo audio	4 cycles	2 cycles	1 cycle
8-bit graphics	1 cycle	2 per cycle*	4 per cycle*
16-bit graphics	2 cycles	1 cycle	2 per cycle*
32-bit graphics	4 cycles	2 cycles	1 cycle

*Some combinations are theoretical and not actually practical to implement.

the portion that can be communicated to and from the rest of the system in one clock cycle is limited by the capacity of the data bus. For example, while a system with a 32-bit processor and a 16-bit data bus can process an entire 32-bit word of graphic data in one clock cycle, it will still take two clock cycles to move each 16-bit half of the word in and out of memory via the data line. Table 4.1 therefore applies to data bus size as well.

Address bus

The final factor in evaluating microprocessor architecture is the size of the *address bus*. The address bus determines which memory location is being addressed, so its size dictates how much memory can be accessed directly. For example, the largest number that can be described by 24-bits is approximately 16 million, so 16MB is the maximum amount of memory that can be addressed directly by a 24-bit address bus. Note that some systems allow the utilization of more memory than provided for by the address bus. These techniques include paging and virtual memory, both of which are discussed later in this chapter.

Control line

The *control line* is responsible for specifying the functions associated with the data and address lines that allow the processor to read and write data in conjunction with specific locations of memory and peripherals. Think of the control line as a sort of traffic cop for data.

Figure 4.4 illustrates the function of the address, data, and control lines. Table 4.2 shows an architecture overview of the most popular microprocessor chips currently being used in personal computers.

Table 4.2. The architecture of popular microprocessors.

PROCESSOR	INTERNAL	DATA BUS	ADDRESS BUS	MAXIMUM RAM
Intel 8088	16-bit	8-bit	20-bit	1MB
Intel 8086	16-bit	16-bit	20-bit	1MB
Intel 80286	16-bit	16-bit	24-bit	16MB
Intel 80386SX	32-bit	16-bit	32-bit	4GB
Intel 80386/80386DX	32-bit	32-bit	32-bit	4GB
Intel 80486	32-bit	32-bit	32-bit	4GB
Motorola 68000	32-bit	16-bit	24-bit	16MB
Motorola 68020	32-bit	32-bit	32-bit	4GB
Motorola 68030	32-bit	32-bit	32-bit	4GB
Motorola 68040	32-bit	32-bit	32-bit	4GB

Figure 4.4

The main arteries of microprocessors are the address bus and data bus.

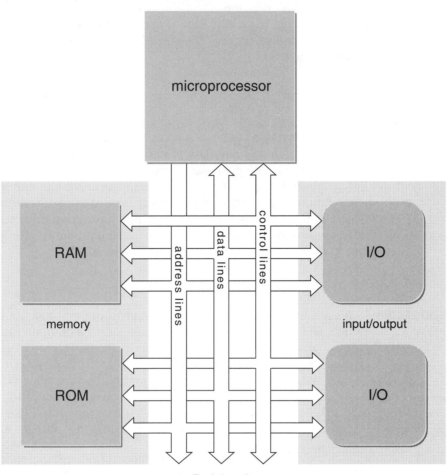

Peripherals

❖ **Caches** | Computers often perform repetitive tasks in a loop requiring data to be read from memory or disk over and over again. A *cache* (pronounced "cash") is an area of fast RAM retaining a history of recently accessed data that can be fed to the processor if it is needed again.

Some processors have a small amount of very fast memory attached directly to the processor that can be used to store the most recent instructions and/or data. These are known as *instruction caches* and *data caches*, respectively. Instruction and data caches are usually on or off, period.

A *disk cache* is based on the same idea, however data recently read from disk is placed in a reserved area of standard memory. If the same information is to be accessed again, the disk caching software looks in the cache first, since memory access is significantly faster than disk access. The size of these caches can typically be set by the user.

❖ The Stack

All microprocessors have a *stack*, which serves as a more intelligent version of a cache. It is a stack of data that exhibits the same first-in, first-out quality as a stack of plates does. The microprocessor can push a piece of data onto the top of the stack for safe keeping. When that data is required again, the processor can pull it off the top of the stack. This process is faster than addressing a location in RAM. Occasionally you will find a program that requires you to change the size of the stack. The actual procedure for altering the stack size varies from system to system.

❖ Coprocessors

It's not hard to envision how the microprocessor can get bogged down if virtually everything going on inside the computer has to go through it. The microprocessor can be likened to an overburdened manager who doesn't know how to delegate authority. *Coprocessors* take on the role of subordinates that handle specialized tasks, freeing up the main processor to oversee the entire operation.

The most common type is the *floating-point unit* (FPU) or *math coprocessor*, specifically designed to crunch non-integer and exponential values. Math coprocessors for the Motorola-based systems include the 68881 and the faster 68882 (about 1.5 to 2 times faster). The analogous chips in the Intel world are the 8087, 80287, and 80387. As a rule of thumb, the speed of the FPU should match that of the processor to prevent a processing bottleneck. In the multimedia world, math coprocessors are used for computation-intensive tasks such as 3-D rendering.

Several other types of coprocessors are found in various personal computers. The Macintosh II, for example, has a socket for a 68851 *paged memory management unit* (PMMU) that will allow a hard drive to be used as virtual memory. (The 68030 and 80386 have this feature built in; the 68040 and 80486 have the PMMU and the FPU onboard.) The Amiga and NeXT computers have several coprocessors for tasks including display management, audio playback, and high-speed transfer of graphic elements.

❖ **New Trends in Processing**

Coprocessing represents an important step in reducing the burden placed on the microprocessor. In the quest for greater speed, designers are making even more radical departures from the architecture that has distinguished personal computing—RISC, parallel processing, and DSP chips.

RISC

The instruction sets for the classic Motorola and Intel microprocessors incorporate instructions that are powerful in scope but bulky to execute. A new type of microprocessor has emerged in recent years known as *RISC* (reduced instruction set computing). RISC works on the principle that a small number of simpler, faster instructions can expedite many tasks more efficiently than a bulk of sophisticated instructions.

RISC is in use in some of the newer laser printers. RISC technology is also at the heart of new machines by Silicon Graphics, Hewlett-Packard, Sun, DEC, and the joint venture between Apple and IBM.

Parallel processing

In coprocessing, the main processor delegates specialized tasks to dedicated ancillary processors. *Parallel processing* or *multiprocessing* takes things one step further by employing many microprocessors operating in tandem to fulfill one or more tasks. This is viewed as a major step toward faster processing and closer emulation of the human brain. While parallel processing has largely been reserved for supercomputers, this technology is still being perfected for the desktop.

DSP chips

The real-time demands placed on the microprocessor by high quality audio, complex graphics, and real-time video are formidable. Digital signals representing these types of information require complex and specialized mathematical procedures, or *algorithms*, to be applied on the fly. Special *DSP* (digital signal processor) chips such as the Motorola 56001 are dedicated to efficiently accelerating these specialized processes while removing the burden from the microprocessor. While the price of these chips contributes to the increased cost of real-time media acceleration products, the improvement in speed often makes a critical difference in the performance.

SYSTEM BUS

The *system bus* is a series of signal paths that are tied directly to the microprocessor, extending the data, address, control, and other lines to add-in *boards* or *cards* via *slots* on the computer's motherboard. These slots are used to add video cards, sound cards, communications ports, internal modems, RAM, coprocessors, and a variety of other added-function cards. Examples of system buses include ISA and EISA on PC-compatibles, the Apple NuBus, IBM Micro Channel, Amiga Zorro, and NeXTBus.

The bus itself has a clock speed that can act as a bottleneck if it is slower than the processor clock speed. In such an event, it is advisable to find some way around the bus if possible. Some graphics accelerators, for example, go right on a graphics display card or bypass the bus via a card-to-card bridge. Advanced direct-to-disk audio recording systems connect hard drives right to their specialized boards in order to avoid the bus.

The system bus can prove a bottleneck in data width as well as speed. For example, adding an accelerator with 32-bit data and address lines will have limited effectiveness when plugged into a 16-bit system bus.

❖ Interrupts

The microprocessor basically has its own agenda in the form of the main program it's running. Pandemonium would break loose if all the other system components started flooding the processor with data anytime they chose. Most of today's computers uses a system of *interrupts*. When another component wants some processor time, it signals the processor via an interrupt request—akin to politely slipping a note under the processor's door that says "I've got something for you whenever you're ready." The processor can then find a convenient stopping point and store what it's doing in order to return to it later. To avoid conflict, each I/O device is given a unique interrupt number that identifies it for the processor. The numbers also tell the processor what priority the interrupt has (although the numbering systems vary between platforms).

On some systems interrupts are transparent to the user. On others—notably PC-compatibles—interrupts are configured via jumpers or DIP switches on the boards being added to the system bus. In this case, the user must manually set each card for a different interrupt number to assign priorities and avoid conflicts.

❖ **DMA**

DMA (direct memory access) allows data to be transferred directly between memory and I/O ports without going through the microprocessor, thus speeding up throughput. The I/O device sends a request to the processor, which then releases the address and data buses to the I/O device. Different devices are assigned to *DMA channels* to avoid conflicts in transfer and control. Bus control is returned to the processor after a previously-specified number of cycles. The microprocessor can perform internal operations during DMA transfers, although program operations that require bus access are suspended.

Handling and Installing Add-on Cards

- Never add or remove a computer component with the power on. Avoid even opening the cover with the power on.
- Static electricity can damage electronic components. Always touch a grounded metal object before handling a circuit board. Never lay a loose circuit board on a carpeted floor.
- Never touch the gold-plated contacts of the circuit board. The oil from your fingers can adversely affect the contacts.
- Never force a circuit board into a slot. Work it straight in gently with both hands.
- The gold contacts of PC-style add-in cards can become dirty through normal use. If you are having problems with a card, try removing it (with the power off) and cleaning the contacts with a clean pencil eraser, then isopropyl alcohol.
- Keep circuit boards in their protective anti-static sleeves or packing when not being used.

MEMORY

As previously introduced, there are two basic types of computer memory—RAM and ROM. These types of memory represent the real-time media of the computer.

❖ **Random-Access Memory**

RAM (random-access memory) is the electronic scratchpad and "thinking space" where your programs and data reside while you are working with them. This memory is volatile: When you turn the computer off, the information it contains is lost. The term random-access refers to the concept that each memory location is uniquely addressable and capable of being accessed as quickly as any other location. Indeed, you can think of each memory location as a mailbox that holds one byte or word of data.

RAM implementation differs between platforms. The most important memory issues for multimedia are how much, how fast, how accessed, and how used.

Capacity

As a general rule of thumb, the more memory you have, the better off you'll be. For openers, massive amounts of memory are required to represent and process individual files containing high quality sound, graphics, and video in digital form. During production many tasks benefit from multiple files being open in order to cut-and-paste data between files, merge files, or use one as a scratchpad. The more sophisticated an application is, the more memory the software itself requires. Having multiple applications in memory simultaneously during the production process prevents your having to quit one program to get to another.

Memory also comes in handy during presentation delivery. Since information is accessed faster from RAM than from storage media, delays can be avoided by preloading files and keeping them in memory. The more sophisticated the production, the greater the size of individual files and the greater the number of data types (such as audio and video) that you'll need to access simultaneously.

The amount of memory you can put in a computer is limited by two factors. The first is the maximum addressable memory provided for by the address bus. The second is the physical space available for RAM chips and the capacity or density of the chips installed. Today's RAM chips have capacities ranging from 256K to 16MB, and multiple chips are combined to create the total available memory.

Speed

RAM is also classified by how fast the chips can read and write data. Today's memory chips are predominantly in the 70 to 120 ns (nanosecond) range. As with microprocessors, you pay an additional premium for speed. Adding memory that is faster than your system can handle is no problem. Adding memory that is slower than what is recommended for your system, however, results in significant delays in the form of wait states. Therefore, significantly upgrading a microprocessor sometimes requires upgrades to faster RAM as well.

Physical installation

Memory configurations vary from machine to machine. Some systems provide sockets for RAM on the *motherboard*—the CPU's main circuit board. Others accept groups of chips preconfigured on a miniature circuit board called a *SIMM* (single in-line memory module). Yet another method entails memory cards that plug into the system bus. These memory cards often come *populated* with a certain number of memory chips, with the option of adding more chips in the future to expand memory further. A word of caution here: Some system buses are restricted to speeds or data widths that are less than that of the processor. In this case, adding RAM via expansion slots can cause a throughput bottleneck.

Intended usage

Another way to classify RAM is by its intended usage. *Dynamic RAM* (DRAM) is the standard memory used in most computers today. *Static RAM* (SRAM) is a fast, low-power version primarily used in laptops and RAM caches. *Video RAM* (VRAM) is dedicated to manipulating the video data that translates directly to the display screen.

❖ Read-Only Memory

ROM (read-only memory) is also addressable, however as the name implies, you can read information from it but not write to it. ROM is primarily used by manufacturers for storing firmware in the form of native programs, instructions, and routines. ROMs are often used for this purpose in microprocessor-based devices other than computers, such as video and audio accessories.

ROMs are also used to hold standard system routines that programmers use for everyday tasks. Tasks like accepting input from the keyboard and mouse are handled automatically, freeing programmers to worry about what to do with the input instead. PROMs, EPROMs, and EEPROMs are all forms of ROM, although ROM usage and distinctions in general are transparent to the user.

MAGNETIC STORAGE DEVICES

Since RAM is volatile, more permanent media are required to store data for later retrieval. In the early days of computing, data was stored on big reels of tape. The storage systems operated on the same basic principles as magnetic tape recording. Their drawbacks were twofold: They were clumsy and—more importantly—data was inherently stored in linear rather than random-access fashion. In desktop computing, tape is used in backup devices and for transporting and archiving large volumes of data. While housed in more manageable cartridges, they are still linear media. It was the advent of random-access floppy disks and hard drives that helped pave the way for the desktop computing revolution.

All disk drives have a circular *platter* that spins much as a record spins on a turntable (only much faster). Instead of having the spiral grooves found in an LP, however, the disk consists of concentric rings called *tracks*. The surface is further cross-sectioned into wedge-shaped *sectors*. The areas cross-referenced by the intersection of tracks and sectors are referred to as *blocks*. (See Figure 4.5.)

Figure 4.5

Disks are magnetically cross-sectioned by concentric tracks and wedge-shaped sectors to form blocks.

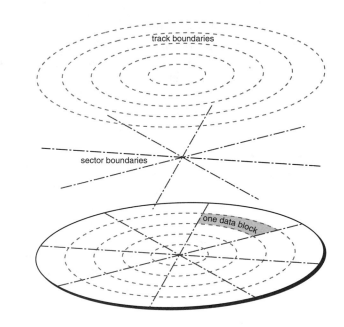

The disk surface is coated with ferrous particles that are susceptible to magnetic fields. An electromagnetic head attached to an *actuator* arm flies just above the surface of the spinning disk. A *disk controller* circuit turns digital information about track and sector positioning into a voltage that moves the actuator so that the head is positioned over the appropriate track. Strict synchronization then allows the electromagnetic head to be activated over the proper block within the track.

At the high level, disk operations include things like format, save, load, copy, delete, move, verify, and directory listing. At the lowest level, these operations are combinations of two basic head operations: write and read.

Each data bit is *written*, or recorded, to a unique microscopic portion of the disk as a series of adjacent magnetic fields. (See Figure 4.6.) The sequence of magnetic fields represents a sequence of digital data. The drive controller affects the polarity by simply changing the direction of the current flow through the head. When the data is *read*, the magnetic fields on the disk induce an electric current in the head, the direction of which corresponds to the polarity. The sequence and timing of the induced currents are evaluated as bit values.

Figure 4.6

The value of data bits is signified on disks by the relative polarity and timing of magnetic fields.

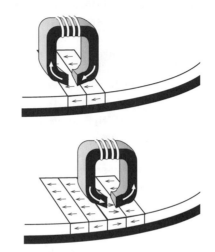

❖ **Floppy Disks**

The *floppy disk* gets its name from the fact that a flexible magnetic disk about the thickness and rigidity of photographic film is encased within a protective jacket. When you insert the disk in the drive, a spindle in the drive mechanism inserts and locks into the center hole of the disk. When the computer needs to access the disk, the spindle makes the disk spin at about 360 rpm. An opening in the jacket of the floppy disk provides a way for the electromagnetic read/write head(s) of the drive to touch the surface in order to read and write data.

The 5.25-inch disks became popular in the late '70s and early '80s. Recent years have seen the introduction and popularization of 3.5-inch disks. Though smaller, they hold more data, come encased in a hard plastic jacket for increased durability, and have a protective metal slide that covers the opening that the drive's read/write head uses to access the magnetic surface. The disks currently used in the Macintosh, Amiga, Atari, IBM PS-series, and most newer PC compatibles are all 3.5-inch.

Sides

The first disk drives had a single head, which meant that only one side of the disk could be used without turning it over. The floppy drives in multimedia-capable machines include two heads—one for each side of the disk—effectively doubling the storage capacity. In actuality, all floppy disks are manufactured with magnetic media on both sides. *Double-sided* disks are merely tested and certified by the manufacturer on both sides. More often than not, the other side of a disk rated as *single-sided* is perfectly usable—the manufacturer simply hasn't certified it. Since single-sided disks often cost less, many people get away with using them as double-sided. This unreliable practice is not recommended.

Density

The higher the density of the magnetic particles on the disk, the greater the number of tracks that can be formatted and the more data that can be held on the disk. *Single-density* disks are not normally used in conjunction with multimedia-capable machines. Double-sided, *double-density* 5.25-inch drives for the PC yield 720K Similar 3.5-inch disks with the same spec hold about 800K.

High-density (HD) disks have gained increasing popularity, although special drives are required in order to use them. Some PC drives can store 1.2MB on a 5.25-inch high-density floppy, whereas 3.5-inch high-density drives for the PC and Mac hold about 1.44MB of data—a welcome format given the size of multimedia files. High-density disks are distinguished by an additional rectangular hole opposite the write-protect tab, and usually bear the HD symbol on the shell. The actual density is dependent not only on the media, but on the sophistication of the drive mechanism as well as the formatting used by the operating system.

Write protection

All floppy disks can be physically *write-protected* so that data cannot be erased by accident. A mechanical sensor inside the drive mechanism is aligned with a hole in the disk's shell. On a 5.25-inch floppy an open hole indicates that writing is enabled; application of an adhesive tab prohibits altering the disk. (You might think of this as being opposite from the punch-out record tab on an audio cassette.) On 3.5-inch disks a simple slide "switch" determines this status; an open hole signifies write-protection.

Care and Handling of Floppy Disks and Drives

- Observe all precautions associated with magnetic media in general.
- Never bend a diskette. Always put a 5.25-inch floppy in something stiff when transporting or mailing it.
- Never write directly on a 5.25-inch diskette or affixed label with a sharp implement such as a pencil or ball-point pen. The resulting impression may damage the media. Always try to write a label before affixing it, otherwise use a soft felt-tip pen.
- Avoid using an eraser on the label, as the flakes can contaminate the media.
- Always lock the write-protect tab on a diskette containing valuable data in order to prevent accidental erasure.
- When computers are shipped, a disk-shaped cardboard or plastic insert is placed inside the drive mechanism to prevent the head from flying around. When moving a system with floppy drives, these inserts should be placed back in the drives for protection. (An old diskette containing no valuable information will work also.)

❖ Hard Disks

Hard disks or *fixed disks* get their name from the fact that their magnetic media is rigid and permanently mounted. Hard drives are much faster than floppy disks and offer significantly greater storage capacity. A 30MB drive, for example, holds the equivalent of almost forty 800K diskettes. Fortunately the price/performance of hard disks has improved at the same time that storage requirements have increased. It's hard to find a hard drive today smaller than 40MB, and drives with the capacity of hundreds of megabytes are commonplace.

Increased capacity is not only useful for storing vast amounts of data and programs; most operating systems are software-based and must be accessible at all times from one form of disk or another. Having the OS on a hard drive prevents the pesky business of swapping disks just to perform everyday file operations. Hard drives are a requisite for multimedia computing.

Physical differences between hard drives and floppy disks

Hard drives are permanently encased and sealed to isolate the precision mechanisms and prevent damage. Since the disk itself is rigid and permanently affixed to the spindle, the drive mechanism can position the read/write head with much greater accuracy than on a temporarily-inserted floppy disk. As a result, many more tracks are possible on a hard disk of similar size, translating to greater storage capacity. Hard disks also respond significantly faster because they are always spinning and don't have to get up to speed. They also rotate at about 3,600 rpm—ten times faster than a floppy.

The other major difference is that hard drives have multiple platters of magnetic media rotating on a common spindle. Each platter is formatted into tracks and sectors and has its own magnetic read/write head. (See Figure 4.7.) Unlike floppy disk mechanisms, the heads do not touch the media, but fly just above the surface. As a matter of fact, damage can occur to the heads and/or the magnetic surface should they come in contact. Drives should therefore be handled with care to avoid this type of *head crash*. (Dust caught between the heads and the media can cause a head crash as well.) Any hard drive worth its salt will have a method of *parking* the drive heads in a reserved area so that they cannot move around when being shipped.

Figure 4.7

Hard drives use multiple heads to access multiple platters.

Speed

When manufacturers rate the speed of a hard disk, they're talking about how fast data moves between the drive and the computer rather than how fast the platter spins. Hard drives with large capacities are typically faster than smaller ones for several reasons. First, the read/write heads are positioned using *voice-coil actuators* rather than the *stepper motors* employed by smaller-capacity drives. Stepper motors are rather brute force. As a result, tracks are fairly wide (limiting the capacity). Voice-coil actuators derive their name from the more subtle technology of the audio speaker and yield faster response, improved accuracy, and greater track density. Because the data is more dense, the head often has to move a shorter distance between desired tracks.

The second reason is that since the physical surface of the media is spread across multiple platters of small to moderate diameter, the heads have shorter distances to travel than in a drive employing fewer platters of larger diameter. The third factor that speeds higher-capacity drives is the dedication of the bottom-most platter as a *servo-platter* containing information used exclusively for positioning the heads over the other data platters. Smaller-capacity drives employ the *embedded servo method* in which positioning information is intermixed with user data on all platters.

Several factors determine the speed with which data can be written and read on a hard drive. The logical request must be correlated to a track/sector location and translated into the proper actuator voltage. *Seek time* is required to move the head stack to the proper cylinder and activate the appropriate head. Finally, *rotational latency* causes a delay while the platter rotates until the desired sector is under the read/write head.

The combination of translation time, seek time, and rotational latency determines the *average access time*—the typical amount of time between the request for information and the read operation. While this is the most common measurement of drive performance, it can only be an average since the location of track/sector locations to be accessed is variable. Current access times range from 80 *milliseconds* (ms) to less than 18 ms. (The smaller the number, the better.) The fastest access times are always desirable since multimedia work entails shuffling around large amounts of audio and visual data. The significant break point is 28 ms—the approximate minimum access time required to record and playback 16-bit CD-quality audio via a hard disk in real time.

Once the information has been accessed, the other measurement that comes into play is *transfer* rate—the time required for the data to go from the drive to the CPU. While this rating is important, it is typically less so than access time performance. As a purely electronic operation, it is usually limited by the electromechanical nature of the accessing process.

Control

Hard drives must have a controller in order to interface with the computer. The controller handles all the mundane tasks of positioning the heads and performing the read/write operations. In addition, it manages the flow of data between the drive and the computer. Depending upon the system, the controller can be built into the computer motherboard, or the drive, or can be a slot-bound card. (Floppy drives require controllers as well.)

Original *MFM* controllers such as the ST506 and ST412 found on PC XTs and ATs had all the intelligence and the drive had none. Since a "dumb" drive doesn't know whether it's going to read or write or where the heads are positioned, the controller is very active when a disk operation is performed. On a multitasking system this slows down the computer since the controller cards must be managed by the processor.

The move to intelligent drives is exemplified by the *ESDI* (Enhanced Small Device Interface) standard. More of the controller and data translation functions are embedded in the drive and therefore intimately know its architecture.

SCSI is a bus combined with a communications protocol that extends the system bus out to other SCSI-compatible devices. SCSI works with not only embedded controller drives, but also other types of devices such as scanners. While SCSI can be added to a PC-type computer via a host adapter, it is currently found as a standard connection on many computers including IRIS Indigo, all Macintosh and NeXT machines, and some Amigas. SCSI is discussed in greater detail later in this chapter.

Partitioning

All hard drives can be *partitioned* into smaller sub-sections given the proper software. Each partition appears as a separate logical storage device or *volume* to the computer. Partitioning is useful on larger drives when the number of files and directories becomes unwieldy and slows disk operations.

Partitioning is also useful in a networking environment. While most systems support simultaneous read operations from several users, writing is typically restricted to one user at a time per partition. Different partitions can be given separate password protection in a multi-user situation where data security is an issue. Some advanced partitioning software will allow partitions to have different operating systems.

Two partitioning methods are available. *Hard partitioning* creates sub-sections of fixed size, each with a separate directory. *Soft partitioning* maintains one common directory and partitions are dynamically sized. Each method has its pros and cons. Hard partitioning requires that the disk be reformatted in order to change the partition sizes, but each partition is an island of data. Soft partitioning is more flexible but permits damage to one partition to affect the directory for the entire drive.

Interleave

In some scenarios, a drive can read and write data faster than the card can transfer it or the CPU can process it. This bottleneck prevents data from being written to or read from contiguous portions of the disk in the same pass. Waiting for the drive to complete an entire revolution before writing more data is a waste of time. To work around this, some formatting software allows you to specify the *interleave* of the drive. Interleaving skips a certain number of sectors between reads or writes, giving the rest of the system a chance to keep pace with drive operations. A 1:1 interleave uses contiguous or adjacent sectors and is therefore optimal if the rest of the system can keep up. A 2:1 interleave reads and writes to every other sector, while a 3:1 interleave uses every third sector. (See Figure 4.8.) The sectors in between don't go unused, but are employed in interleave fashion to write on subsequent revolutions. Proper interleave settings are typically implemented or suggested by the manufacturer of the drive and/or system.

REMOVABLE MEDIA

As the need to store and transport data files of larger size and volume increases, *removable media* becomes valuable. This technology is a cross between a floppy disk and hard disk. A removable cartridge containing a rigid platter is inserted into a specially-designed drive mechanism. The cartridges have a sliding door that protects the magnetic surface when the cartridge is not in the drive.

Figure 4.8

Interleave is used to improve efficiency when accessing hard drives.

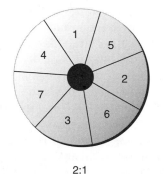

1:1   2:1   3:1

Care and Handling of Hard Drives

- Observe precautions associated with magnetic media in general.
- When choosing a new internal hard drive, make certain that your system's power supply is rated to handle the extra power requirements.
- Never remove the sealed inner case from a hard drive. Contact the manufacturer or authorized service center for problems at this level.
- Never move the drive while it is turned on, as this could cause a head crash.
- Always back up the data on a hard drive before transporting it.
- If you must transport a hard drive or a computer containing one, reduce vibrations by placing it on a cushion or car seat rather than on the floor or in the trunk. Buckle up!
- Allow a computer subjected to hot or cold extremes to adjust to room temperature before turning it on. (Hard drives operate safely within approximately the same freezing to 100° F range as floppies.)
- Never place more than one copy of an operating system in a given partition.
- If you must ship a computer with a hard drive, pack it very well—preferably in the original packing carton.

Removable technology offers the ability to extend your storage capacity by buying additional media without paying for duplicate mechanisms and power supplies. One cartridge might hold all your graphics applications, another your sound programs, another your scanned images, etc. Removable cartridges are also commonly used to transport large files associated with graphics, desktop publishing, and multimedia from one location to another. They also offer an alternative when backing up data and archiving projects. (While removable media is more expensive than the cassettes associated with tape backup technology, they have the advantage of being instantly accessible.)

Removable magnetic drive mechanisms are made by Syquest, Ricoh, and Bernoulli at this writing. These mechanisms are then packaged by a variety of companies who actually bring them to market. Current capacities are approximately 44MB and 90MB.

I/O—EXPANDING THE COMPUTER

The more computers are able to support communication forms that are meaningful to humans, the more useful and transparent they become. These communications can be broadly classified as input and/or output, hence the categoric reference *I/O*. All computers have a standard input device—the keyboard. The mouse is also an input device. All computers support standard output devices as well—the CRT display and some form of audio.

In addition to the system bus, the computer's I/O *ports*—connections for external hardware—enable a wide variety of devices to be appended to the system. These devices are often referred to as *peripherals*, broadly defined as anything that doesn't come as part of the main system. Input peripherals include cameras, scanners, microphones, and graphic tablets. Output peripherals include printers, film recorders, stereo systems, and monitors. Some peripherals such as MIDI instruments and modems act as both input and output devices.

Communication between various components of the computer can also be classified as synchronous or asynchronous. *Synchronous* communication refers to all devices operating at the same speed and synchronized with a timing source. *Asynchronous* refers to individual components operating without regard for the timing of other devices or the overall system.

Most of these devices can be connected to the computer via one of three common types of external I/O port—serial, parallel, and SCSI. The ports are built into the motherboard of some computers, but are added to others in the form of circuit boards that connect to the system bus. The concept of male and female connectors is used in many I/O connections. Note that the gender reference is to the pins, not the connector shell. **WARNING! Always turn the power off before connecting or disconnecting devices with any form of interface!**

❖ Serial Communications

Serial communication is used to connect computers with modems, some networks, and some printers. A serial interface refers to data being transferred between the computer and a peripheral device in a series or sequence, because only one data line is used in each direction. Since data is usually grouped within the computer in clusters of 8 or 16 bits, these groupings are broken down to a stream of bits on the transmitting end and paraded down the wire single file into a sort of electronic corral on the other end where they are reassembled into bytes or words again. Each reassembled piece of data is sent on for processing while the bit parade continues.

The common asynchronous serial protocol is *RS-232C*, a standard developed to define communications between computers and telecommunications devices. While definitions of 25 separate signal lines are specified for various functions, fewer are typically used in practice. The DB-25 connector is part of physical specification of the RS-232C standard. Various hardware manufacturers utilize other connectors for RS-232C signals, including an 8-pin DIN connector on the Mac and NeXT, and DB-9 connectors on some PCs. (See Figure 4.9.) Devices with dissimilar connectors can communicate given the right adapter, although the serial protocol makes no provisions for standardizing the content of the information being communicated.

Figure 4.9

The most common serial connectors are male DB-25 and DB-9, as well as Macintosh-style.

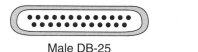

Male DB-25   Male DB-9   Macintosh

RS-422 is another common serial protocol. It is the data equivalent of the balanced lines in audio and can be run over longer distances and at higher speeds than RS-232C without interference.

❖ Parallel Communications

Parallel connections are primarily used for communicating with printers. Parallel, of course, refers to things happening simultaneously in a side-by-side fashion. A parallel interface uses eight data lines so that the eight bits of a byte can be transmitted and/or received simultaneously. All things being equal, parallel is about eight times faster than serial. Parallel cables can only be used for short runs, however, since they are more susceptible to interference. Parallel communications are most commonly implemented using a 25-pin female connector on the computer and a 36-pin female on the printer. (See Figure 4.10.)

Figure 4.10

The DB-25 and Centronics connectors are common to parallel communications.

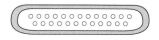 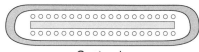

Female DB-25   Centronics

❖ **SCSI**

A more recent communications protocol for computers and peripherals is SCSI (pronounced "scuzzy"), an acronym for Small Computer System Interface. SCSI is hundreds of times faster than serial and parallel protocols. It is most commonly used to connect devices such as hard disks, CD-ROM drives, and scanners to computers. SCSI storage devices typically have embedded controllers, allowing other devices to simply make an access request and go on about their business. Many computers today have SCSI buses and connections built in; those that do not must add SCSI capabilities via a board that converts the system bus signals to SCSI and vice versa.

The SCSI spec calls for up to eight devices in a daisy-chain with a total cable length not to exceed 25 feet. Each device has an ID number from 0 to 7 that is set via software or hardware switches. (Most people find hardware switches easier to handle.) Each device in a SCSI chain must have a unique ID number so that it can be addressed individually. If two devices have the same address, the system will hang or lock up when switched on. Also, the ID numbers dictate priority when more than one device is sending SCSI data. Unfortunately, this numbering isn't standardized: Higher numbers have priority on the Mac, while lower numbers have priority on the PC, for example.

SCSI devices use either 25-pin or 50-pin connectors, and cables are available to convert between the two if necessary. (See Figure 4.11.) The 50-pin variety is preferable because it has a dedicated ground line for every data line; it is also rated for 10 times the number of insertions as its 25-pin counterpart.

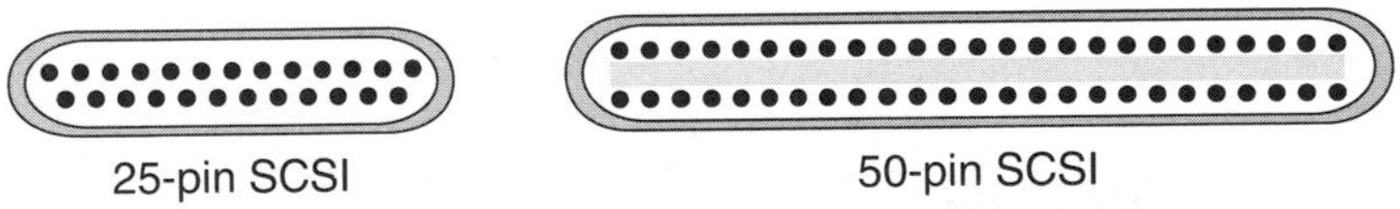

Figure 4.11

SCSI devices are connected via 25- and 50-pin SCSI connectors.

25-pin SCSI   50-pin SCSI

Since SCSI devices are chained together, any intermediate device in a SCSI chain must have two connectors to facilitate sending and receiving the signal in both directions. (Note that the physical position in the chain and the ID numbers have no relation.)

Each end of a SCSI chain should have a *terminator*—a resistor that keeps the voltage within the circuit at the appropriate level. Termination can be accomplished internally or externally. Internal termination is usually handled by a switch or jumper, while external terminators plug right into the SCSI port like a cable. (External terminators are easier to handle.) The SCSI ports on computers are already terminated. Devices in the middle of a SCSI chain should not be terminated as a rule. In short SCSI chains, however, you can sometimes get away with leaving an intermediate device terminated or the final device unterminated. All devices in a SCSI chain usually must be turned on to ensure proper system operation and prevent data loss.

At this writing SCSI II is being introduced. Announced features include connection of up to 14 devices and a speed increase of at least 200 percent.

POWER SUPPLIES

The most unexciting part of the computer is the power supply. Power supplies are rated in wattages that reflect their ability to handle different loads. Each internal electrical device you add to the system draws current. Circuit boards in slots draw current. Graphic cards draw current. And the motors of hard drives most definitely draw current.

A 65-watt power supply, for example, is typically not strong enough to handle a disk drive on a PC. A hard drive of moderate size combined with several full slots demands something on the order of a 145-watt supply; supplies in the 200-watt range are recommended for a large drive or several moderate-size drives and lots of filled slots. As another example, the 65-watt supply in the Mac IIsi powers the internal hard drive and video circuitry that ships with the unit, but won't support many third-party high-resolution graphics cards.

OPERATING SYSTEMS

If the microprocessor and memory form the computer's physical brain, the *operating system*, or OS, is the mind that inhabits and utilizes it. The OS acts as an overall system manager providing some or all of the following functions:

- Manages the access programs have to the various hardware components of the system, such as the processors, memory, system bus, mass storage devices, and external interfaces.
- Loads programs into memory and runs them.
- Keeps track of system memory and how it is being used by various software and system resources to prevent memory conflicts.
- Manages the organization of disks and the storage and retrieval of files.

- Provides a toolbox of standard routines that programs can use to perform common functions.
- Provides a way for various programs to share data.
- Manages how various programs share the microprocessor in a multitasking system.
- Handles memory paging in multitasking and virtual memory systems.

Common operating systems are MS-DOS and OS/2 on PC-compatibles and the IBM PS-series, the System on the Macintosh, AmigaDOS on the Amiga, and UNIX across a variety of platforms. (*DOS* is an acronym for *disk operating system* and is used fairly interchangeably with OS.)

❖ Bootstrapping

Virtually all computer operating systems today come in the form of software that resides on a disk. This provides manufacturers the flexibility of upgrading the operating system in the future by simply supplying a new version on disk instead of dealing with firmware upgrades. As described earlier in this chapter, ROMs contain routines that go looking for the operating system on disk when you start the computer. The operating system then loads itself into memory in a process known as *bootstrapping*. Ideally, this process happens automatically and *autoboots* from a hard drive. If the ROM can find no operating system, the computer will prompt the user to insert a disk containing one.

❖ Tasks

Earlier operating systems could only run one program at a time. Most of today's operating systems allow more than one program to reside in memory simultaneously. This is implemented in two basic forms: program switching and multitasking. *Program switching* is exemplified by Apple's MultiFinder. While two or more programs can reside in memory at once, only one program—the one in the foreground—can be active at a time. When you switch another program to the foreground, the previous one becomes inactive.

In a *multitasking* OS such as UNIX, NeXT's Mach, AmigaDOS, OS/2, and Microsoft Windows (in most modes), multiple programs not only can reside in memory simultaneously, but also can perform operations at the same time. Each activity is called a *task*, hence the term multitasking. In the strictest sense of the word, multitasking is the staggered processing of small chunks of each program. This inter-weaving of tasks happens so fast that it gives the illusion of simultaneous program operation. The OS assigns a *task priority* and sets up a proportionate time-sharing schedule in order to divide the processor's time. This might be likened to time-sharing of a resort condominium where the time allotted to different investors is proportionate to their importance.

❖ Memory Management

The OS is also responsible for *memory management*. On start-up the OS is loaded into a specific, predetermined area of memory. The OS then evaluates its own size and makes an entry in the *memory map* that certain RAM locations are no longer available for other use. It also knows that certain addresses are reserved for retrieving data from ROM as well.

When you tell the OS to run an application, it first looks at the memory map to determine where to place it, *allocates* enough RAM starting at that location, then copies the program into that memory. The memory map is updated to reflect the new status. When you open a file within the application, the request is handed to the OS. It again looks at the map to find and allocate some free space and copies the file into memory. (If creating a new file rather than loading an existing one, memory is allocated but there's obviously nothing to copy.) When you close a file or application, the memory it previously used is *deallocated* or made available again in the memory map. (See Figure 4.12.)

Ideally, the OS wants to keep a given file or application in contiguous memory locations. Things get interesting when more than one file is open simultaneously in an application. What happens when one file grows large enough to bump into the other's allocated space? What happens when having multiple programs in memory complicates this issue? Memory can be divided into equal-sized blocks called *pages*; more sophisticated microprocessors support the ability to swap one page with another. When a file in memory hits the wall, the processor can swap a page in the file's contiguous address space with one from an unused area of memory.

Virtual memory

While newer processors are capable of addressing gigabytes of memory, finding the space and money to actually implement that much RAM is another issue. *Virtual memory* techniques allow free space on a hard disk to be treated as memory. This is an extension of the paging concept previously described: Blocks of physical

Figure 4.12

The OS uses a memory map to keep applications and files from conflicting.

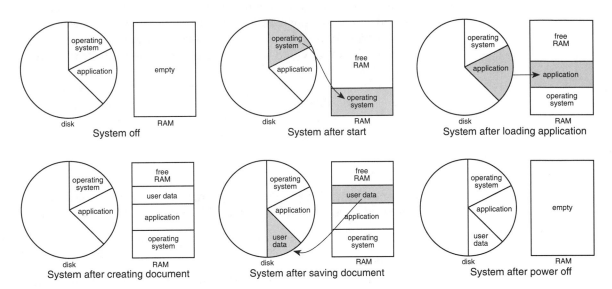

memory are exchanged for blocks of disk data. In effect, the hard disk becomes extra memory on an as-needed basis. Accessing a hard drive is much slower than accessing RAM, but 100MB of disk space is a lot more affordable than 100MB of RAM at this point.

Virtual memory is a concept of growing importance in multimedia work. Software for image processing and digital audio/visual editing, for example, can manipulate files that are significantly larger than the memory capacity of many of today's computers.

Startup files and device drivers

All modern desktop computers can perform special operations automatically when the computer is booted. The PC's *autoexec.bat* file and the Amiga's *s:startup-sequence* file, for example, are always invoked when those systems are powered up. These are text files that contain lines of commands that are automatically executed in sequence, as if you had typed them in yourself in real time. These commands cause the system to update the time and date, change directories, and execute programs automatically. A startup file can be used, for example, to automatically load and start a multimedia presentation when the system is turned on.

Another type of file is executed automatically when booting these systems. The *config.sys* file on the PC and the *devs:mount_list* file on the Amiga, for example, extend the system's capabilities by making the OS aware of the presence of other software or hardware devices, as well as how to communicate with them. Such software often takes the form of a *device driver*—a translator that tells the OS what type of peripheral you have—keyboard, printer, scanner, mouse, audio card, video board, or hard drive—and how to communicate with it.

Memory-resident programs are small programs that remain active or accessible in memory even while other programs are in use. INITs on the Mac and TSRs on the PC are examples of programs that are always active in the background.

❖ How the OS Organizes Data on a Disk

Data can't just be thrown into a disk drive. The drive must first be configured for use, and data must be organized in a way that it can be retrieved later.

Formatting

When you first insert a blank disk you must tell the OS to *format* it before using it. Imagine a disk as a valet parking lot, your data as a car, and the operating system as the lot manager. An unformatted disk is a parking lot without delineated, identifiable spaces, so the manager can't store your data/car in any organized way—let alone find it again. By formatting the disk, the available storage area is divided into clearly-defined, addressable spaces. As described earlier in this chapter, the disk surface is magnetically subdivided into concentric tracks cross-sectioned by sectors. Each of these subdivided areas can hold a block of data—usually 512 or 1024 bytes depending upon the machine. Each block typically contains a header that identifies its track/sector.

Directory maps

A real-world parking attendant keeps the keys to your car on a labeled hook so there's a way to find the cars. On a disk drive, the OS keeps track of what's parked where by creating and maintaining a *directory* or *file allocation table* (FAT) on each disk—a sort of map or index to where everything is. (See Figure 4.13.) The OS handles the details associated with summarizing, loading, saving, deleting, renaming, and otherwise manipulating disk files. So when you tell the computer to store your file, the OS just finds a place for it; when you want to retrieve the file, the location is automatically looked up and the file is retrieved. Directories usually record other data with each file, such as date and length.

Figure 4.13

Disks maintain directories that keep track of files and available space.

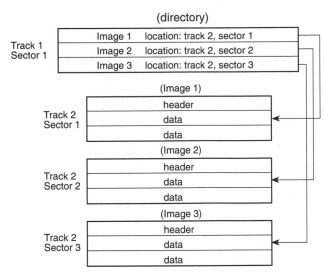

The formatting process usually *verifies* the integrity of every block on the disk. This is accomplished by first writing a magnetic pattern, then reading it and comparing it to what should have been written. If a bad sector is found, it is *locked out* by making an entry in the directory that permanently removes it from the list of available blocks.

Storing files

If your file is larger that a single block of disk space, the OS tries to park all the bytes in sequential locations on the disk. This is not always possible, so the OS has to stash various pieces of the file wherever it can and record additional directory information in order to keep track of where everything goes. Continuing the parking lot analogy, you hand over an entire caravan to the manager without regard for what space is available in the lot and say that you expect the caravan to come out in the same order in which it went in.

Files are typically stored with additional information at the beginning called the *header*. The header usually contains data such as file type and other attributes of specific interest to the programs that use the file.

Disks created on a computer running one OS can't be read by a computer running under a different OS since each OS organizes and stores data in a different way. Not only can the number of formatted tracks and sectors vary from system to system, but directories contain different information in a different order, and reside in different track/sector locations.

Hierarchical filing

Placing files on a disk randomly is akin to opening the door of an office and throwing documents all over the floor. While this is a way of life for some people, it is obviously not the most efficient filing system. In real life documents are placed in folders that are placed in drawers in filing cabinets. The same *hierarchical filing* concept applies to computers. The main or *root* directory should consist of a *tree* structure of other *subdirectories*, which in turn can contain files or even more subdirectories. On the graphically-oriented systems, subdirectories are depicted as folders or drawers.

What happens when you tell the OS to move a file from one subdirectory to another? The directory structure is rearranged, but the actual data stays where it was. In other words, the reference or index that points to it is moved, not the file. When a file is deleted, the corresponding entry in the directory is simply erased, making the disk locations previously used by the file available again.

❖ User Interface

People need a way to communicate their desires to the operating system—a *user interface*. If the microprocessor is likened to the brain, and the operating system to the mind, the user interface is the soul of the machine. Two types of user interface are currently in vogue—the command-line interface and graphic user interface.

Command-line interface

The *command-line interface* (CLI) gets its name from the fact that lines of *commands* are entered into the computer to give it instructions. The CLI is typified by a flashing cursor and screens full of text. MS-DOS, AmigaDOS, OS/2, and UNIX are examples of CLI. CLI gives users fairly intimate access to the system and a lot of power-user shortcuts. The downside is that users have to remember a sophisticated series of rather cryptic commands that must be typed correctly and in just the right order, or *syntax*.

Graphic user interface

The *graphic user interface* (GUI) is a more recent development that lets users interact with the computer in a more intuitive way than the method offered by CLIs. Examples of GUIs include the Macintosh Finder and MultiFinder, Amiga Workbench, Windows on the PC, UNIX X-Windows, NeXT Workspace Manager, and IBM's Presentation Manager. These are typified by pictographic *icons* that represent things like disk drives, command menus, and software tools.

The GUI is typically accompanied by a *mouse*—a device that the user rolls around the desk to control an on-screen pointer. Moving the mouse moves the pointer and clicking the mouse button performs an action associated with the object being pointed to. GUIs are often called *point-and-click* interfaces for this reason.

Pointing to the various items in the on-screen *menu* bar and holding down the mouse button reveals the associated commands in a *pull-down menu*. Releasing the mouse button while pointing to one of these menu commands invokes that command. Pointing to and clicking on the icon for a disk drive, for example, will visually highlight it and conceptually select it for subsequent operations. Double-clicking will usually open a *window* that displays icons depicting the contents or directory of the drive; files often have icons that pictographically identify their type, while sub directories are depicted as file folders or drawers. (See Figure 4.14.)

Figure 4.14

The Macintosh Finder is a good example of a graphic user interface.

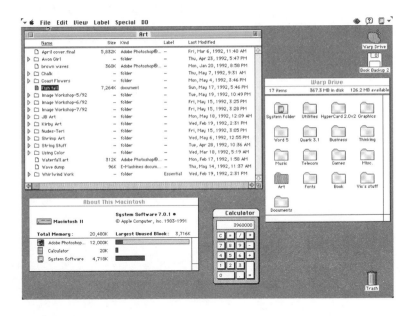

GUIs allow for many windows to be open simultaneously, although only one is usually active at any given moment. Since a directory might contain more entries than can be shown in a window, windows have *scroll bars* that scroll the contents within the window when clicked with the mouse. Windows also have mechanisms for sizing, moving, and closing.

GUIs are more intuitive than CLIs, but lack their power. Too many windows can overlap to the point of clutter on display screens of small to moderate size.

Hybrid interfaces

Some CLI-based systems offer a *shell*—a window that acts as a simplified and less-imposing environment for interacting with the system. While shells offer some of the shortcuts afforded by GUIs, they are primarily text-based.

Full-blown GUIs often reside on top of CLIs, acting as a sort of front panel. This symbiotic relationship is found between the Amiga Workbench and CLI, the NeXT user interface and the Mach operating system, Windows and MS-DOS, and Presentation Manager and OS/2. These hybrids are implemented with varying degrees of elegance and effectiveness. In fact, the Mac is the only personal computer lacking a CLI.

❖ ❖ ❖ ❖ ❖ ❖

While concepts that hold a special place in the multimedia world—graphics, sound, and interactive programming—have been deferred to dedicated sections later in this book, this chapter has explained how various components make computers tick. Chapter 5 uses this knowledge to contrast the capabilities of the popular personal computers used for multimedia productions.

Computers for Multimedia

While a conscious effort has been made to avoid detailing specific products in this book, a few words contrasting the viability of major desktop computers for multimedia are appropriate. Nonetheless, manufacturer's product lines change so rapidly that significant detail is in danger of becoming obsolete all too quickly. Dedicated books offer the best resources in harnessing the power of specific computers.

This discussion, then, offers an overview for those wishing to establish basic ways to evaluate classes of multimedia computers. It draws as much from past track records as from the silicon crystal ball. Many statements in this chapter are solely my personal views.

THE PLATFORMS

The major contenders for desktop multimedia at this writing include PC-compatibles, IBM PS/2, Apple Macintosh, Commodore Amiga, NeXTstation Color, and Silicon Graphics IRIS Indigo. These systems all have multimedia potential and can be purchased for less than $10,000—although anything more than a basic system may quickly exceed that price.

Several references are made to the graphic output capabilities of the various platforms. RGB is the common output supported by computer monitors, while NTSC is the broadcast video standard in North America. RGB is described fully in Chapter 6, as are the subjects of resolution and bit planes. NTSC and related topics are detailed in Chapter 13. Similarly, the differences between 8- and 16-bit audio are covered in Chapter 10.

❖ **Commodore
Amiga**

When the Amiga was released at the end of 1985, it represented the first true multimedia computer. Its design integrates dedicated chips that handle graphics, sound, I/O ports, and DMA. You can still buy a basic Amiga for less than any other multimedia-capable computer.

Graphics

Custom chips provide for coprocessed graphics, double-buffering for animation, and composite black-and-white video output. Graphics and animation are fast, smooth, and capable of being displayed on any NTSC monitor. While the video signal is not completely up to broadcast specs, the circuitry is so close that inexpensive devices, such as Mimetics' AmiGen, not only convert the output to color, but make it recordable, with the option of being superimposed over external video.

The Amiga's native graphics trade off physical resolution for color resolution. The video DACs have 12-bit resolution for a range of 4,096 colors. Standard modes include 320 x 200 non-interlaced with any 32 colors and 640 x 400 interlaced with any 16 colors. Most modes can be extended to accommodate NTSC video overscan through the addition of extra pixels.

The unique *HAM* (hold-and-modify) mode allows all 4,096 colors to be displayed on the screen simultaneously, but with some restrictions. Sixteen color registers are used as starting points, and the color of adjacent pixels is represented as a change in one of the RGB values. While this is a unique solution to resolution, HAM exhibits varying degrees of artifacting because only one RGB value can be changed per pixel unless the pixel is represented by another pure register value. Changing from all white to all black, for example, requires three pixels—one each for red, green, and blue values—unless black and white are both found in the 16 base registers. While some manufacturers use work-arounds, standard HAM mode is restricted to 320 horizontal resolution, not counting overscan.

The option of 24-bit color came late to the Amiga. The standard graphic modes are so deeply embedded in the hardware that the normal user interface is difficult to implement in 24-bit mode. While a number of 24-bit products are available, they span a wide range of non-standard, proprietary hardware/software work-arounds that are largely incompatible with each other and the native graphic modes. This is not to say that you can't get great looking 24-bit images out of the Amiga, just that the tools are not as synergistically related to each other and the overall system as on other platforms.

104

Sound

All Amigas include four DMA digital audio channels allowing sound to play without impeding other system activities. Although there are no internal speakers, the four voices are mapped to stereo RCA line-level jacks that can be connected to a sound system. Many products allow the audio circuitry to be used either for synthesizer voices or for digitized real-world audio. The hardware itself is 8-bit, with a top sampling rate of 15KHz—pretty low. A handful of external digital audio products with higher quality are beginning to emerge, and inexpensive MIDI interfaces proliferate.

Operating system and user interface

The Amiga's operating system is multitasking, adding to the potential of the system as a multimedia platform. The Amiga uses a combination of a CLI running AmigaDOS and a point-and-click GUI overlay called the Workbench. This combines the best of both worlds—power and simplicity.

While Amiga developers have not always designed user interfaces with uniformity, the machine's operating system implemented completely general multitasking from the beginning.

The Amiga's operating system is unique in that it is *reentrant*. This means that processes like disk accesses can be interrupted to give priority to something like redrawing the screen—a serious consideration in multimedia computing. The Amiga's multitasking capabilities are also tied to the system clock, allowing for real-time synchronization of dynamic data such as audio and animation. (Whether or not software developers implement this is a separate issue.)

The Amiga also supports Arexx, an interapplication communication protocol that signals another multimedia advantage. Commodore also ships AmigaVision, an easy-to-use authoring system, with most models.

Ports and drives

The Amiga comes standard with ports for serial, parallel, external floppy, mouse, RGB, and composite black-and-white video. SCSI is also built into the 3000 series. Floppies are 3.5-inch with 880K capacity. At this writing, Commodore has not released a high-density floppy format. Not all models are shipped with hard drives.

Special features and support

The Amiga utilizes a standard file type called *IFF* (Interchange File Format). This is an open format that allows multiple data types, such as sound, graphics, and animation, to be contained within the same file. Programs can access whichever data types are appropriate. As such, the IFF format is a logical vehicle for multimedia content.

The Amiga's custom graphics chips and inherent video-compatible output have always made it a natural for video tasks. More recently, NewTek's Video Toaster has transformed the Amiga into an integrated video switcher and 3-D animation station. (The Toaster is described in greater depth in Part V.) The Toaster pretty much takes over the Amiga, however, and does not lend itself to integration with other Amiga-resident production tools. As such, the Toaster-laden Amiga is more of a video production component than a delivery platform.

The Amiga is also the natural development platform for titles for CDTV—Commodore's consumer-oriented CD-ROM machine. In addition to a delivery option for the consumer market, the units make inexpensive delivery platforms for certain types of multimedia productions. (CDTV is described in Part VI.)

Market positioning

The Amiga 500 is available for less than $500 in a minimal configuration: black-and-white output, only 512K, 68000 processor, no monitor, and no hard drive. Serious production will require at least an Amiga 2000 or 3000 series—a minimum of $2,500 by the time you include a hard drive, color video, and enough RAM to do anything significant. Versions are available with full 32-bit buses, at higher costs.

Commodore is much stronger in Europe than in the U.S. Little domestic marketing effort is made in comparison to Apple and PC vendors. The Amiga has never been successfully positioned as a business computer in the U.S., making its entry into corporate multimedia a tough challenge.

Third-party support ranges from powerful to klunky to twinky; the behind-the-scenes distribution vehicle that most small developers rely on has crumbled several times, leaving little more than mail-order availability.

Conclusions

The Amiga was once "the little computer that could." Its architecture served as a landmark for multimedia computing. It is now seen in the U.S. multimedia market largely as "the little computer that could have been." In a world where 8-bit graphics is largely standard and 24-bit color is an integrated option, the Amiga's offbeat array of graphic modes and non-standard 24-bit graphics don't stand up well at this writing. Amiga's built-in interlace capabilities do lend themselves to video, however the resulting flicker can be annoying if you have to work in this mode all the time.

The Amiga does a great job at straightforward animations—such as titling and infographics—at a reasonable price, including video output with overscan. Its 3-D rendering to video frame buffers is reasonably powerful as well. Plenty of software is available to support all those tasks. Finally, many Amigas are purchased solely as an engine for the Video Toaster.

❖ Apple Macintosh

The Apple Macintosh was introduced in 1984 as the first commercially-available computer with an integrated point-and-click graphic interface. Apple introduced it as "the computer for the rest of us" in a direct assault on the high priesthood of the CLI world. This quickly led to WYSIWYG ("what you see is what you get") and the desktop publishing phenomenon.

Graphics

Graphics are integrated into the design of every Macintosh, although not necessarily video graphics. In color machines, 8-bit color is standard at 640 x 480 resolution and fewer bit planes can be used. You can easily integrate 32-bit display cards with 24-bit graphics and 8-bit alpha channels.

Apple's QuickDraw is essentially an integral part of the operating system that supports both bit-mapped and vector drawing routines. This has made it easy for developers to create programs that exhibit uniformity to the user. QuickDraw's vector drawing routines also provide the option of small files for images created using vectors.

Sound

The Mac has built-in 8-bit sound with a 22.05KHz sampling rate—not CD-quality, but adequate for everyday work. This is a hardware/software solution: Software is used to fill the sound buffer which the hardware then plays. This can use a substantial amount of CPU time. All models have a small built-in speaker and earphone jack; later models come with a small microphone for speech input. Several high-quality 16-bit stereo direct-to-disk systems are available, as are a plethora of sophisticated MIDI interfaces and professional music software. Internet 16-bit sound is also on the horizon at this writing.

Operating system and user interface

The Mac is one of the only computers that has no CLI anywhere. The entire user interface—the Finder—is point-and-click. Although Apple's MultiFinder can hold several programs in memory simultaneously and run some background operations such as print spooling, it is not truly multitasking.

Several interapplication communications protocols have emerged in recent years. One is System 7's "Publish and Subscribe" feature in which a master document, such as one created by a multimedia authoring system, references component documents. Changes made to a published external graphic, text, or sound file will appear the next time the subscribing master document is called up. Apple's MIDI Manager also acts as a communication bridge between MIDI software and device drivers.

One of the Mac's big attributes is the fact that Apple didn't stop at WYSIWYG. The company has delivered strong guidelines to developers regarding a standardized human interface. The result is that most Mac software is uniform in feel, style, and operation. With few exceptions, standard menu items are always found in the same place, key-equivalents and tool icons are standardized, and file formats have been tightly controlled. The Mac's Clipboard provides an easy way of cutting and pasting data between documents— even those of different applications. Fonts and printer drivers are installed globally and are accessible to any program.

Ports and drives

While Apple doesn't directly support parallel ports, all Macs come standard with two independent serial ports, a SCSI port, and an external floppy port. New machines support 1.44MB floppy drives that can read and write PC files given proper software. Multimedia level machines are usually delivered with hard drives as well. All Macs also come with LocalTalk on the motherboard, making basic networking simple and inexpensive via a serial port.

Special features and support

As this book is being published, Apple has announced but not released QuickTime—an extension to the operating system that claims to do for time-based media what QuickDraw does for graphics. QuickTime provides for new dynamic data types called *Movies*, which can contain multiple tracks of data including video and audio. While each track contains only one type of data, the system synchronizes the tracks.

QuickTime also provides compressors for photorealistic images, animation, and video. All compression is managed by QuickTime, so that the details of the compressors are transparent to applications. If a better compressor comes along, it is automatically used with complete transparency to the application and user. The same is true for devices: calls can be made to generic devices such as digitizers and video gear, and, given the appropriate driver(s), QuickTime will handle all the specific communications with the currently installed device(s).

Equally as important, QuickTime addresses one of the banes of multimedia delivery—the fact that software runs at different speeds on different processors. QuickTime prioritizes audio running at its intended rate, then drops animation or video frames, if needed, to keep everything in sync. QuickTime also has a standard Movie Toolbox for creating, editing, and playing back Movies, complete with a standardized human interface.

Apple also ships every Macintosh with *HyperCard*—a software package that provides relatively easy methods for developers and end-users alike to organize, interlink, present, and distribute information in standardized documents called stacks. While HyperCard is by no means the ultimate multimedia authoring system, its pervasiveness has helped to unite and further the Macintosh community.

Market positioning

A veritable silicon smorgasbord of software and hardware for graphics and sound is available for the Mac. Most are both professional and intuitive. Moreover, the Mac has become the preferred desktop computer for artists, publishers, and musicians.

The Mac's biggest drawback is price. A color machine capable of supporting multimedia is $3,000 at a bare minimum. Third-party hardware and software ranges from amazingly inexpensive to amazingly overpriced. The other problem is that the Mac has not been embraced by the business community to the degree the PC has, giving it an uphill battle in the corporate world.

Conclusions

The Mac has had a tremendous track record as a high-quality, intuitive computer preferred in its price range by the majority of creative types. QuickTime appears to make Apple's future equally bright in integrated media, although competitive pricing from other platforms is a concern.

While Apple's graphic standards are well-entrenched, NTSC video and double-buffering for animation are not native to the Mac.

Current multimedia demands are beginning to push a once-simple system to increasing complexity. Adhering to a venerable hardware heritage and backward-compatibility may be Apple's Achilles' Heel. Some industry analysts predict that Apple will exhibit little innovation in the next few years, claiming that the majority of its efforts will go toward the new Kaleida technology being developed in conjunction with IBM.

❖ PC-Compatibles

Ever heard the story about the one that got away? IBM probably holds the all-time record for losing a big one. Through lack of legal claim, the company that started the desktop computing revolution lost a large section of that market to "clone" manufacturers on both sides of the Pacific. As a result, there has been no such thing as a standard PC—with some recent exceptions fostered largely by multimedia.

Graphics

More PC graphics "standards" exist than you can shake a stick at. While the market is settling in with *VGA* and *Super VGA* (SVGA) display adapters, PCs can be configured into several different modes that trade physical resolution for color resolution. Moreover, the capabilities of many graphics cards hinge on how much memory is installed. VGA has a maximum resolution of 640 x 480 with any 16 colors out of 262,144, or 320 x 200 with any 256 colors out of 262,144.

Some VGAs can also accommodate double-buffering given enough memory. Many support both interlaced and non-interlaced modes, although actual NTSC video still requires special cards.

Many VGA cards also have *feature connectors* which allow other products to add graphic functionality. Cards built on the *8514* chip add 256 colors in resolutions ranging from 640 x 480 to 1024 x 768. The TIGA standard also adds higher physical and color resolutions to VGA, usually in conjunction with a dedicated VRAM frame buffer. TIGA cards have the advantage of a display list coprocessor that relieves the main processor of many graphics duties. Tasks such as scrolling become much faster in the process.

SVGA is a catch-all for formats that exceed the capabilities of VGA in physical and/or color resolution processed or coprocessed. Fortunately, most of these products adhere to *VESA*, an extension to the standard PC graphic calls that allows the plethora of graphics adapters to be be supported with one set of commands. The S3 chipset is a superset of SVGA that has become popular because of its built-in acceleration of Windows graphics commands.

16- and 24-bit boards such as the Targa have been available for years on the PC, but these products did not integrate with other PC graphics modes and required software that implemented their proprietary format. This is changing since 24-bit software and hardware are now supported under Windows.

Sound

The PC's built-in sound capabilities are virtually nonexistent. Add-on sound cards have been available for years, with the SoundBlaster leading the pack. Many of these products support both sampled digital audio and sound synthesis. While the average sound quality is rarely overwhelming, sound can be added to the PC for as little as $100. Several proprietary CD-quality, 16-bit, 44.1KHz direct-to-disk recording systems have been available for years, as well as a few 12-bit products. File formats across the board are fortunately becoming more standardized, and MIDI support has also become widespread.

Operating system and user interface

One of the reasons why PCs have been deemed unfriendly by many is MS-DOS. Until recently, this unforgiving command-line interface has been the main method of communicating with these machines until recently. Numerous GUIs and shells are now available, but everything has relied on keyboard entry until the last few years.

PCs have not endeared themselves to many users because user interfaces have historically been completely without standards. Simple tasks like loading and saving a file have been performed in completely different manners for each software program. To add insult to injury, PCs have traditionally required dedicated drivers to communicate with printers, and other software and hardware for each program.

Windows 3 from Microsoft is the most popular GUI that rides on top of DOS to offer a mouse-driven, point-and-click interface. Windows brings standard drivers, file formats, and user interfaces to a market segment that sorely needs them. Windows also supports color resolutions up to 24-bits, although the actual resolution still depends on the display card. It also provides a common clipboard for exchanging data between documents. Full suppot for sound has also been added in the Windows 3.1 update.

On the downside, Windows sits on top of DOS as an afterthought and acts as an intermediary, which can bog things down. The user still has to know something about DOS to configure and optimize the system for Windows!

The 80286, 80386, and 80486 microprocessors can run in several different modes, one of which is multitasking. Current PCs have grown out of an original design that only allowed for 640K of memory. Work-arounds have broken that memory barrier, but not without confusion and memory management issues. At this writing, manufacturers have made significant progress in resolving these memory management issues.

Ports and drives

Although standards exist for addressing ports, no standards exist for what hardware actually comes on the machines (short of the MPC standard discussed next). Even a mouse port is not necessarily built in. Most machines come with at least one serial and one parallel port. Both the newer 3.5-inch and the older 5.25-inch disks are still in use, and 1.44MB floppy drives are available. Hard drives are available on a mix-and-match basis, although most are not SCSI. (In general, SCSI costs extra on PCs.)

Special features and support

Multimedia Extensions for Windows (or Multimedia Windows) provides tools for developers to use in creating multimedia applications. Multimedia Windows focuses primarily on standard interfaces for devices such as scanners, videodisc players, sound digitizers, and MIDI interfaces. Compression is also supported, although currently only for 16- and 256-color files. CD audio can be controlled as well. Multimedia Windows also supports the *Microsoft Multimedia Movie* format that includes animation, sound, and some limited scripting. At this writing, Microsoft has not been very vocal about synchronization issues, however.

In a parallel move, Microsoft as announced the MPC (Multimedia Personal Computer) standard. Not actually a Microsoft product, it is a set of guidelines that dictates a minimum standard configuration to run multimedia applications. MPC-compatible machines from any manufacturer include:

- 80386 or better operating at 10MHz or greater
- 2MB of memory minimum
- 3.5-inch, 1.44MB floppy drive
- 30MB hard drive minimum
- CD-ROM drive with audio outputs
- 8-bit audio DAC with linear PCM playback at 22.05 and 11.025KHz rates

- 8-bit audio ADC with linear PCM sampling at 11.025KHz, mic-level input
- Music synthesizer and MIDI interface
- Analog audio mixing
- VGA display adapter
- 101-key keyboard and two-button mouse
- Ports for serial, parallel, and joystick

MPC signals a configuration that developers of multimedia titles can rely on for delivery. Considering the lack (or plethora, depending upon your view) of standards in the PC market, MPC is almost like a light from above. Unfortunately, although the list of hardware is fairly complete, the minimum requirements of each item are generally considered by the industry to be inadequate—in particular the processor, memory, and bit planes for graphics. Microsoft says these specs were provided to keep the prices affordable to consumers.

Market positioning

While PCs have never really endeared themselves to most artists and creative types, they dominate the business world. They have also overflowed into the consumer market as a result of clone prices and the desire to bring work home to a compatible machine. Since many multimedia presentations are business-oriented, the PC has an inevitable place in media production.

Price also has much to do with the PC's continued success. The cost seems to plummet as performance increases. Moreover, serious developers can build their own systems from parts.

Conclusions

Debating the viability of PCs for multimedia is a moot point. They are dirt-cheap and found everywhere. Their usefulness, sophistication, and standardization for multimedia delivery would be questionable without recent advances such as Windows 3, MPC, and color resolution. These developments ensure standards and capabilities that have begun to yield powerful software/hardware solutions for authoring, graphics, animation, and sound. The sheer volume of this market segment continues to ensure price/performance ratios that other platforms can only dream about.

Windows is still an afterthought, rather than being built in. Outside of MPC and Windows, support for the PC is still a free-for-all. The PC's evolution is a Frankenstein story—pieced together from parts, powerful, and clumsy. The PC has more raw computing power for the dollar than its direct multimedia competitor—the Mac—but lacks its entry-level simplicity.

❖ IBM PS/2

In 1987 IBM countered the PC-clone market with the PS/2 series. The biggest physical difference is the use of more proprietary hardware, making the machine hard to clone. In particular, the PS/2 models appropriate for multimedia—Model 50 and higher—employ a proprietary bus architecture called *Micro Channel Architecture* (MCA).

Graphics

The low end of the PS/2 employs the MCGA graphics standard, a precursor to VGA, with maximum resolutions of 320 x 200 with 256 colors or 640 x 480 with two colors. The machines one would choose for multimedia work come with VGA as standard, and 8514 video boards can be used with an adapter.

In 1990 IBM introduced XGA (Extended Graphics Array) exclusively for the PS/2. XGA uses coprocessed graphics for faster performance. This card offers 1024 x 768 interlaced output with 256 colors. XGA cards can display standard VGA with much better performance due to a 32-bit internal data path (as compared to the 8-bit data path of normal VGA). Displays of 640 x 480 with 65,536 colors are also available.

Sound

The PS/2 isn't delivered with any more audio capability than the PC-compatibles. MIDI, sound synthesis, and digital audio sound cards can be added.

Operating system and user interface

At this writing, IBM uses the 80286, 80386, and 80486 in various PS/2 machines. Most programs created for PC-compatibles will also run on the PS/2 unless they are dependent on incompatible bus hardware. That's because the PS/2 will operate under IBM's OS/2 operating system or under DOS and Windows. (OS/2 seems to have backfired on IBM. It was developed by Microsoft before Windows 3 and DOS 5 made their debut, and there have been allegations that Microsoft gave IBM a diluted version of its own later offerings.) Most applications for the PS/2 support the use of a mouse in a point-and-click environment.

Ports

The PS/2 comes with standard ports including serial, parallel, RGB, and mouse. Floppy drives are 3.5-inch high-density with 1.44MB capability.

Special features and support

The most distinguishing standard feature of the PS/2 is the MCA bus, although some models have an ISA bus. The MCA bus is physically and electrically incompatible with the buses found in clones. MCA is self-configuring, which shields the user from dealing with configuration switches, jumpers, and technical documents. It also provides for bus masters—cards containing their own processors that can operate independently from the main processor. MCA comes in both 16-bit and 32-bit versions.

IBM offers a plethora of hardware and software products, many of which are also available for PC-compatibles supporting multimedia:

- ActionMedia II: DVI option that records and plays back full-motion compressed digital video.
- M-Audio Capture Playback Adapter/A: 2-channel digital audio with microphone and line inputs.
- M-Motion Video Adapter/A: Displays NTSC video on PS/2 monitor, either full-screen or in a window.
- TouchSelect: Touch screen displays for user interface in delivery systems.
- PS/2 TV: Audio/video tuner.
- Video Capture Adapter/A: Captures and displays single frames of video.
- M-Control Program/2: Programming development tools that aid in controlling of multimedia and user interface devices.
- LinkWay: A simple, script-oriented program for development of hyper-documents.
- Learning System/1: Authoring and presentation system designed for developing courseware.
- Audio Visual Connection (AVC): Multimedia authoring and presentation software that uses IBM multimedia hardware options.
- Storyboard Live!: Presentation software that does not require special hardware.

Market positioning

Although the PS/2 offers some advantages over PC-compatibles, not everyone realizes or needs those features. PS/2 systems are more expensive than clones and more directly competitive with Apple—a problem in a market that has come to expect large discounts and little after-sale support. Incompatibility with existing PC-compatible bus hardware is also a stumbling block. Though IBM has lost significant market share to clones, the company's reputation as a quality supplier is very much intact. IBM is also well known for its service contracts.

Big Blue is putting its considerable weight behind multimedia—or "Ultimedia," as its marketing campaign suggests. Although similar multimedia hardware/software options are available from other vendors on other platforms, IBM offers a single-source solution for integrating media. The shear marketing clout of IBM, compared to its clone competitors, is a significant factor in the company's potential multimedia success.

Conclusions

There are a lot worse things one can do than bet on IBM. One bright spot is IBM's alliance with Intel in developing DVI technology, since this is a viable approach to uniting computers and television. (DVI is discussed in Part VI.) By offering complete turnkey multimedia development and delivery solutions, IBM has increased assurances to developers that multimedia is here, it works as reliably as anything else, and it is here to stay.

❖ NeXTstation Color

Steve Jobs, one of Apple's founders, has transformed his vision of what the Macintosh should be into the NeXT computer. Its low-end color model is called NeXTstation Color. The NeXTdimension is an add-on product that supercharges the machine's graphic and video power. While NeXT products are not mainstream choices for desktop multimedia at this writing, NeXT promises to be a stronger contender in the future.

Graphics

All NeXT computers use Display PostScript, which allows the screen to be driven in the same way as a PostScript printer. The 17-inch monitor displays 1120 x 832 at 92 dpi, and the 19-inch screen displays 1120 x 832 at 75 dpi. NeXTstation Color has 16-bit graphics (4,096 simultaneously displayable colors plus 4-bit alpha channel).

The NeXTdimension has full 32-bit graphics (16.7 million displayable colors plus 8-bit alpha channel). Graphics are handled by a dedicated RISC-based graphic processor for amazing speed. Video I/O hardware JPEG support is also built in.

Sound

NeXT models come with built-in 8-bit, 8KHz sampling and microphone for speech input, and CD-quality 16-bit, 44.1KHz dual-channel output. Higher quality digitizing options are available to bridge the disparity between input and output capabilities.

Operating system and user interface

NeXT systems use both a UNIX command-line interface and an intuitive GUI. UNIX is the most common standard for platform-independent communication, and its combination with a point-and-click interface is considered by many to be the best of both worlds.

NeXT machines at this writing are built around 68040 processors running at 25MHz, delivering a benchmark of 15 MIPS and 2 Mflops. NeXT systems offer true multitasking environments and networking is built in.

Ports and drives

Systems come standard with ports for SCSI-II, 10 Mbit/sec Ethernet, two serial devices, DSP, laser printer, and monitor. Standard floppy drives are 3.5-inch with 2.88MB capacity and can read 1.44MB and 760K DOS disks. A hard drive is standard.

Special features and support

Overall system architecture is based on eight DMA channels. All models come with Motorola DSP chips designed for optimized audio. RAM dedicated to DSP can be expanded to 576K.

The NeXTdimension board makes the machine a serious multimedia contender. It contains true NTSC video input and output along with C-Cube hardware compression that allows video to be recorded and played back from disk at up to 30 frames per second. The dedicated RISC processor is capable of 80 Mflops per second. Up to four NeXTdimension cards can be placed in a single NeXTstation, opening the door for sophisticated applications like video editing and multiple-monitor presentations.

Another interesting note: A group of NeXT computers can be used for parallel processing. This is a particularly interesting time-saver since a NeXT machine doing 3-D rendering and animation can go out over a LAN and delegate some of the work to idle NeXT machines.

Market positioning

NeXT's power is matched only by its lack of acceptance in the overall marketplace. This is due partially to the lack of wide software support from third parties and to the business world's unwillingness to spend so much money on an unproven standard with power they don't comprehend. These two factors form a vicious circle that causes developers to be wary. To date NeXT has not shown a strong marketing effort in the multimedia arena.

Conclusions

As businesses and multimedia presenters realize how much money goes into the additional hardware and software required to do multimedia and related tasks, they may realize that NeXT has most of those requirements built into a well-integrated environment. The sheer speed of the system in general is applicable to an increasing number of situations where productivity is important. If NeXT becomes more successful as a mainstream business computer, it will enjoy more attention as a multimedia system as well. Currently it offers interesting horizons only for multimedia producers who do installations, one-time shows, or video production—or those who use it as a cross-platform production tool rather than a mass delivery vehicle.

❖ Silicon Graphics IRIS Indigo

Silicon Graphics (SGI) has recently released its IRIS Indigo. Although this system was designed around a RISC processor, it is a compatible member of its high-end family of graphic workstations used in motion picture and television production.

Graphics

The Indigo is specifically designed to perform real-time 2-D and 3-D graphics and animation—up to 40 million pixels per second. This is made possible by displaying 8-bit dithered graphics from true 24-bit internal representations. The 24-bit data is saved for future rendering and frame-by-frame recording to video. The Indigo uses Display PostScript to display 1024 x 768 on a 16-inch monitor.

Sound

The Indigo records and plays true 16-bit stereo audio in real time with the aid of a Motorola 24-bit DSP chip. I/O includes stereo line-level ins and outs, mono microphone, internal speaker, headphone amp, and microphone pre-amp. The sampling rate is variable up to 48KHz to match the optional DAT deck. Somebody's thinking here: One DAT can be used for both digital audio and data backup/archiving. The serial ports accept MIDI interfaces designed for the Mac.

Operating system and user interface

Like the NeXT products, Silicon Graphics machines are UNIX-based with an intuitive GUI. Libraries of sophisticated routines for graphics, audio, and video derived from Silicon Graphics $60,000-plus workstations are integral to the Indigo. Speed is rated at a blinding 30 MIPS and 4.2 Mflops—the fastest device available in its price range at this writing. It can effectively process and display data as fast as it can come off a storage device. The system can be expanded to 96MB of RAM. A variety of popular networks are supported.

Ports and drives

Standard ports are provided for thick Ethernet, parallel, SCSI-II, and two serial devices. A bay is supplied that can hold a variety of storage devices, including SCSI hard drives, SCSI tape drive, 3.5-inch 1.44MB floppy, SCSI DAT drive, and CD-ROM.

Special features and support

Silicon Graphics has announced a video option card for the Indigo. Features include real-time composite video and S-Video input and output in NTSC and PAL standards, motion video in a window, single-frame video capture, genlock and keying of graphics and video in several combinations, and 24-bit RGB frame output for video sequencing—among other things.

Third-party developers appear to be clamoring to support the Indigo. Major players include Adobe, Time Arts, Alias, VPL Research, Wacom, and Xaos. Most offerings at this point are not cheap.

Market positioning

Indigo is unique in more ways than its graphics hardware and speed. It is the only desktop computer designed almost solely for graphics. Silicon Graphics' high-end products are the stuff that special effects in movies like *Terminator 2* and *The Abyss* are made of. Although Indigo has scientific applications as well as graphic applications, SGI does not appear to care if anybody ever runs a spreadsheet or word processor on its systems.

Conclusions

This machine is undeniably hot for graphics. The only question is whether SGI can successfully market the Indigo as a dedicated multimedia machine. It will not be a natural choice for businessmen, multisite kiosks, or home entertainment. It is, however, a viable candidate as a video and multimedia production tool, and as a dedicated delivery platform for one-time presentations.

Many variables determine the viability of platforms for multimedia, not the least of which is what you already have or what a client uses. Choices often depend upon the application and your definition of multimedia. Multimedia in one form or another can be produced on any of these systems. Potential throughput bottlenecks lurk at virtually every turn. Often specific needs with regard to graphics, animation, audio, video, and programming level will dictate a clear choice.

Price is also a serious consideration. A contract to install 500 kiosks across the country will most likely not bear the use of a NeXT or Silicon Graphics product. Creating state-of-the-art videos will most likely not happen on an MPC machine. Producing titles for the mass market may dictate MPC, on the other hand.

This leads to two conclusions. First, individual producers should choose the right tool for the job—if you have a lot of different jobs, a knowledge of all the available tools will be helpful. Second, cross-platform compatibility and development are improving. With some limitations, files can be transferred between different platforms if you know what you're doing. (If you do all your work on a Mac and you've got a client or co-worker with a PC, file conversion is a lot easier than starting over or changing horses.)

❖ ❖ ❖ ❖ ❖ ❖

This chapter has provided an overview of the main desktop computers being used for multimedia today. The subject of choosing the right tool for the job is explored furthur in Part VI. Regardless of which platform(s) you use, Chapter 6 offers suggestions for getting the most out of your hardware and software.

CHAPTER 6

Using Computers

Every field has various levels of expertise. In the computer world, people who approach using a computer from a standpoint of professionalism, safety, and efficiency have been dubbed power users. You don't have to take up rocket science, disavow any knowledge of good taste in clothes, or exhibit a lack of social graces. A good starting point is simply knowing what tools are available and why you might need them.

THE POWER USER'S TOOLBOX

You wouldn't set out on a long drive without a spare tire, jack, and jumper cables, right? Every computer power user has a set of software tools that can be used to prevent, diagnose, and repair problems. The power user's toolbox also contains software that optimizes system performance and makes productivity and storage media more efficient. The following is a brief list of highly recommended software tools.

❖ Hard Disk Utilities

If you have never had a disk error or unreadable file, notify the *Guinness Book of Records* and stake your claim. Many good disk utility packages are available, such as Norton Utilities and PC Tools, which offer a variety of invaluable functions.

121

Defragmenting

The more you use your hard drive or similar device, the more sluggish the read and write times may become. Since many files are too long to be stored in a single block on disk, they have to be stored across many blocks. On a newly-formatted disk, these blocks are contiguous—at least with respect to the interleave of the disk. If the file is deleted later, some of the space may be reused to write a smaller file. This process can leave gaps of unused data blocks. After a number of files have been written and deleted, the available blocks in which data can be stored become scattered throughout the disk. When new files are written that are longer than the largest contiguous chunk of disk space, they are broken up, or *fragmented*, so they can be stuffed into the available gaps between existing files. As fragmentation increases, the OS has to create a complex map to keep track of it all, and the read/write head has to move around a lot to read and write the data in a fragmented file. This process results in sluggish response and slower file access. As you might suspect, the problem is perpetuated as more files are added and deleted.

Fortunately, the solution is pretty straightforward. Several commercially available utilities can be used to *optimize* or *defragment* your hard drive. This procedure rewrites all the data on your disk in sequential order for faster access. (See Figure 6.1.)

Figure 6.1

Fragmentation occurs when the OS splits files into segments in order to fit them in available disk blocks, resulting in slower access times. Defragmentation rewrites the data contiguously.

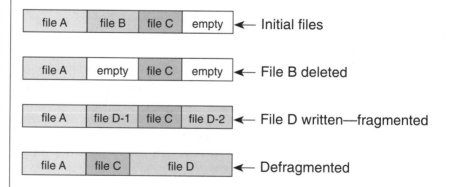

file A | file B | file C | empty ←— Initial files

file A | empty | file C | empty ←— File B deleted

file A | file D-1 | file C | file D-2 ←— File D written—fragmented

file A | file C | file D ←— Defragmented

Although the defragmentation process is designed to be as safe as possible, you should always have a safety copy of your data before running such a utility in case of power loss or a similar problem. (Some applications employ copy-protection schemes that install hidden files on the disk that can be destroyed by defragmenting procedures. Any such applications should be removed by the original installation program per the manufacturer's instruction before a defragmenting session.)

Disk analysis and repair

Sometimes you simply can't access a disk at all, or one or more files seem corrupted. Disk analysis and repair programs analyze the integrity of the directories and files, look for areas of the disk that have been assigned to more than one file, and seek out lost sectors that show as being in use but have no apparent file affiliation. If problems are found, these programs can attempt to make repairs. Most provide the ability to verify the integrity of each data block on the disk and lock out any bad blocks so that they cannot be written to subsequently.

Another function of this type of disk tool is recovering a file that has been deleted. Recall that files aren't actually erased when you delete them: the directory reference is simply changed to show that those blocks are available. If the actual data blocks haven't been written over by another file, a disk repair program can often reassemble a file and make a new directory entry for it. The same concept extends to entire disks that have been erased accidentally. Although the entire directory might be wiped out, most of the file data blocks can be found and referenced again.

Disk editors

Who knows what lurks in the hearts of disk drives? A disk editing utility enables you to examine every bit of data that resides on your disk. You can even edit and recover data from otherwise hopelessly corrupted disks. Disk editing is not for the weak of heart. If this level of surgery becomes necessary, research what you're doing, get help, and/or practice on backup copies.

❖ **Recovery Aids**

Some programs enable you to install a utility that keeps a log of all disk and file activities. Should you have to recover from a crash, the logs created by these utilities can act as an extra road map for the disk repair programs, increasing your chances of successful recovery.

❖ **Virus Protection and Disinfection**

Ten years ago, *computer viruses* would have made great science fiction. Today they are a serious threat to your productivity and to your data. They don't occur naturally—they are purposeful and malicious creations of unscrupulous hackers. Some viruses lurk behind the scenes and play little tricks. The most common ones embed themselves in the OS and cause system crashes. The most dangerous viruses can actually eat their way through files on your disk and corrupt them beyond recognition.

How does a computer get a virus? Viruses can often be contracted simply by inserting and/or accessing contaminated disks in a drive. They can also be aquired by modem if you receive a contaminated file and store it on your disk.

The answer lies in *disinfectants* and *virus protection* or *anti-virus* programs. The disinfectant will locate infected files on your disks and either free them of the virus or alert you that they are hopeless. Once your disks are clean, immediately install a virus protection program. These typically act as a sentry, checking each disk before you are allowed to access it. If a virus is found, you can do something about it before it contaminates your system.

Some protection programs allow you to choose various levels of automation in the testing process (always test, always prompt, test only when a key combination is held, and so forth). Always choose to test a disk whose integrity you are not absolutely certain of. If you lend it to somebody, test it the next time you use it unless you're certain their system also has adequate protection. Test any disks acquired from anybody whose virus protection is questionable.

Many programs are available to combat the growing number of computer viruses. New strains of viruses seem to make their way into the world every day, so I recommend that you look into a protection product made by a company with a continual upgrade and support policy.

❖ Screen Saver

CRTs can suffer from *burn-in* if you leave a static image on the screen too long. The persistence of the phosphors becomes altered so that you see a ghost of the burnt-in image for the rest of the monitor's life. (Burn-in time varies, but some manufacturers suggest adverse effects can occur if a static image remains on the screen for as little as one-half hour.) *Screen saver* utilities are startup or memory resident documents that time how long it's been since the screen last changed, and blank the screen automatically after a preset interval of time. Your work screen is returned when you touch the mouse or a key.

Screen savers present everything from psychedelic patterns to aquariums. The more flashy routines require more memory. Always remember to turn off or remove screen savers on delivery systems unless you want to be embarrassed during a presentation!

❖ **RAM Disk**

A RAM disk is almost the opposite of virtual memory in that it enables memory to act like a disk drive. After setting up a portion of memory as a logical volume, you can treat it like a disk. You could preload a series of images into the RAM disk, for example, then display them almost instantly using standard load commands within a presentation program. While some operating systems come with a RAM disk utility, most require a separate utility to configure a portion of memory in this way.

❖ **Emergency Disk**

I strongly advise that you compile a floppy disk with a minimal bootable OS and a complement of tools, such as the most useful hard disk utilities and virus disinfectant. That way you have a concise assortment of tools ready for action if your hard drive won't boot.

❖ **File Compression**

One of the major hurdles in multimedia is the size of the files associated with elements such as audio, graphics, animation, video, and interactive programs. As a result, various methods of compressing files for storage, distribution, telecommunication, and delivery are some of the hottest areas of technology right now.

The effectiveness of data compression is judged by the *compression ratio*. A 2:1 ratio would indicate that the compressed data is half the size of the original file; a 20:1 ratio would indicate that the compressed data is 1/20th size of the original file.

Compression falls into two basic categories: lossy and lossless. *Lossy* compression is used in conjunction with media such as digitized photographs, digital video, and digital audio where some pieces of data can be sacrificed as long as the overall impact of the content is not perceptibly altered. Lossy compression is implemented in methods that are unique to given media and is discussed in greater detail in those sections.

Lossless compression derives its name from the fact that the integrity of all data is preserved during compression. After all, compressing a textual document isn't effective if some of the characters are lost! Files compressed with a lossless technique must be decompressed before they can be read.

Most lossless data compression techniques operate by encoding redundant data. One of the simplest is *Huffman encoding*, which works well for text files and some data files. Huffman encoding works by replacing 8-bit ASCII bytes with tokens. The more frequently a character appears, the fewer the bits comprising the token. In this method, commonly reused characters—such as "e" and "a"—take only a few bits while infrequent characters like "q" and "z" take more.

Another common form of redundancy compression is *Lempel-Ziv-Welch* (LZW) compression. Where Huffman encoding creates tokens for each character, LZW creates tokens for common groupings of bytes. In the case of text, words such as "the," "is," and "of" are represented by tokens, while words with little redundancy remain in their natural form. Redundancy compression is quite useful for reducing text files by approximately 2:1.

Redundancy compression can also compact applications, though typically to a lesser degree. Images with large areas of continuous shades also work well with redundancy compression. As the image complexity increases, however, there is less redundancy to compress. (As you'll see in Part III, proprietary compression is intrinsic to some graphic file formats.)

Besides saving storage space and modem time, another popular use for lossless compression is in distribution. If you're trying to squeeze a presentation onto one or two disks to send out, compression programs are available that will compress the files complete with a self-decompressor that is transparent to the user.

BACKING UP YOUR WORK

Murphy's First Law of Computers states: "You will have a serious disk error when you are least able to recover from it." (Burger's Corollary to Murphy's First Law is: "If you have a safety copy of your data, you will never need it.")

One of the most dreaded terms in computerese is *crashed disk*—referring to a disk that has become unreadable. Encountering a crashed disk feels like being locked out of the house—all your valuables and tools are inside, but you can't get at them. A less disastrous event occurs when individual files become unreadable, or *corrupt*, due to a bad sector on a disk.

❖ Backups and Archiving

Backups imply separate storage media containing a duplicate copy of the data on which you're currently working. *Archiving* implies storing files or projects in a more permanent library after you're done with them, usually in a different location. (Companies whose data is their lifeblood often rent space in off-site fireproof, magnetically-shielded vaults to protect their archives.) Both processes enable you to restore the files to the form of their last safety copy.

Backups should be a way of life; the degree to which you take remote archiving seriously will depend upon your individual situation. The following section describes different backup methods, but the most important thing is to do it. The right time to do a backup is when you'd be out of luck if you couldn't recover your work! Make it part of your schedule, make it somebody's job—but do it religiously.

Restoring your work

Whenever you have to restore your work because of a corrupted file or disk, go back to square one with the media. For floppies, put the data on another disk and throw the problem disk away. For removables and hard drives, back up the files and reformat the disk with software sophisticated enough to identify and lock out bad sectors.

File organization

Regardless of what backup method you use, directory organization can help. Users tend to put files created by one application in the same directory as the application itself. This requires you to back up the entire drive or hunt through all your directories to find volatile data—unless you use an incremental backup described shortly. In contrast, all of your applications are inherently archived on the media on which they were originally delivered. The files you create with those applications can't be easily replaced. Putting all user-created documents in sub-directories within a common directory provides a backup method that consumes less time and backup media.

One fundamental way to organize files then becomes three directories at the root level: system, applications, and documents. You can have more subdirectories for various categories, but your day-to-day backup needs will always be in the documents directory. (Some applications require a specific directory structure that may make this organization method impractical.)

❖ **Backup Methods**

The simplest item to back up, of course, is a single file. This just requires saving a second copy on a separate disk at logical intervals. Next is copying a floppy disk. If a floppy contains original data, simply make a disk-to-disk copy.

The issue becomes more convoluted when backing up media with larger capacities. Overall backup methods fall into one of two categories—image backup or file-by-file backup. *Image backups* save the data from the original device on a byte-by-byte basis without regard for individual files. This often means that restoring a single file requires restoring the entire drive. *File-by-file backups* preserve the identity of individual files, making it easy to save and restore a single file or directory that has been corrupted or archived. Both methods usually have the option of *incremental backup*—identifying and storing only the files that have been altered since the last backup.

There are several other software considerations. One is speed, and many good computer magazines run frequent comparisons of backup software. Another is *automatically timed backups* that protect your data whether you're thinking about it or not. *Network backup and restore* capabilities allow a backup device attached to a file server to back up the hard drives in workstations attached to the network.

Several backup vehicles are available, each with its pluses and minuses. They include multiple floppies, removable media, disk mirroring, and tape streamers.

Multiple floppies

One way to make backups is to save each file to both a hard disk and floppy disk—either as you save the file(s) or at the end of the session. This can sometimes present a problem since some multimedia files are larger than the storage capacity of a single floppy disk. The file compression techniques described earlier can make the difference in whether files will fit on a floppy or not. Another solution is a backup utility that splits a large file into disk-sized pieces that can later be reassembled on the hard drive.

Many programs are commercially available that copy the entire contents of a hard drive to a series of floppy disks. These programs come in both image backup and file-by-file versions.

In the short term, multiple floppies might appear to be the cheapest way to ensure safety. This process requires a lot of time and patience, however. Backing up a 40MB drive to 800K floppies would require you to format and swap 50 disks without using compression. If you count time as money, this quickly becomes uneconomical. The only way this method is practical is with incremental backup or if documents are organized in a dedicated folder, as discussed in the previous section, and the multiple-floppy method is used on that directory alone—software permitting. Overall, the volume of today's multimedia makes floppies a poor total backup solution.

Removable media

The removable media described in Chapter 4 make interesting choices for backup devices because they double as regular storage media. Of course, a full 80MB hard drive will require two 44MB cartridges—anything above that is just a pain. A problem arises if you use removable cartridges as main storage media—what do you use to back them up? If you have a big enough hard drive with room to spare, the entire contents of a removable cartridge can be temporarily copied to the hard drive, then copied to a different cartridge.

Data mirroring and duplexing

Disk mirroring provides another backup alternative—writing data to two hard drives at the same time. This requires special software and a second drive with at least the same capacity as the main drive. The write time is somewhat longer because the disks share a single controller that only allows one write operation at any given moment. Read times are unaffected since only one drive is accessed. The advantage of disk mirroring is that you always have a current backup of everything as of the last save and you can be back on your feet after a crash by simply accessing the good drive. You still have to fix the crashed disk, but disk mirroring could be a lifesaver in a live presentation. A disadvantage is that you could lose the work on both drives simultaneously through disasters, mangled directories, viruses, and accidental erasures.

Data duplexing is similar to mirroring, except that an independent control channel is used for the second drive. This allows files to be written to both drives simultaneously. Duplexing usually incorporates a method where the data from both drives is compared for verification purposes after being written. Given the right software, duplexing also allows the drive pair to respond to requests for two simultaneous file reads.

Tape streamers

Tape streamers are the most common mechanism for backing up hard drives. Most of these come with software that supports image, incremental, and file-by-file backup options. Their disadvantage is that they are linear. Finding and restoring a given file can be time-consuming. Their advantage is that they can hold massive amounts of data on a single inexpensive tape cartridge.

Tape drives employ media and mechanisms borrowed from the audio and video recording industries. Like removable media, only a handful of companies make the mechanisms that are marketed in a variety of repackaged forms. Four categories are currently available—

cassettes (60MB to 525MB capacity), cartridges (similar in capacity to cassettes), DAT (up to 1.3GB capacity), and 8mm (up to 2.2GB capacity).

Beyond capacity, gross comparisons in speed can be made, but the software that comes with each drive and the volume of your data are the true determinations of speed. As a general guide, buy a drive with enough capacity to handle your current and medium-range expansion needs in one backup pass without having to swap tapes.

TROUBLESHOOTING

There comes a time in the life of every computer user when there seems to be a ghost in the machine. Exorcising these demons is easier with a few tips, but the best advice is to apply some preventive maintenance along the way.

❖ Preventive Maintenance

As in other walks of life, computer preventive maintenance is less painful in the long run than emergency fixes. Mixed with a little common sense, the following ideas should help keep your system up and running.

Conflicts

One of the joys of computers is that you can customize them to make them very much your own. Lots of software out there is very tempting. You know—the desk accessory that pops up offering a game of Global Nuclear Warfare when it senses your stress level is too high. Or the start-up file that downloads and plays the digital audio of this week's entire Billboard Top 10 whenever you boot your machine. Unfortunately, the ability to customize to your heart's content is also the ability to buy yourself lots of problems.

Different platforms have different names for files that extend the system's capabilities: INITs, Suitcases, device drivers, TSRs, start-up files and more. Whatever they're called, these little wonders can trip the OS or each other. The KISS principle most assuredly applies to computer systems. In general, anything you don't absolutely need as an active part of your system is a potential hazard—remove it! And never have two similar utilities, such as virus detectors, active at the same time.

If possible, avoid adding or changing more than one element in your system at a time. Don't install 15 new desk accessories, 5 device drivers, and 30 fonts at the same time that you load a new hard drive and a beta version of a new application. Make small changes or additions and test them. If everything works, make some more small changes and test them, and so forth. Problems are a lot easier to diagnose this way than after you have completely rearranged your silicon world.

Access

Determine who has access to your system and define rules for usage. In most cases, the computer should be regarded as a finely-tuned, high-performance automobile. You might allow others with a license to drive it, but nobody is allowed under the hood except a qualified mechanic!

❖ **Problem Solving**

The problems that can cause you and your computer grief, as well as the solutions to these problems, are difficult to document. The general approach is the systematic elimination of variables. The tips box offers some troubleshooting guidelines.

When Things Go Wrong

- Save your work (if possible) and reboot the system. The problem may be due to a power surge or other fluke.
- Check for compatibility and proper installation of all software, hardware, and drivers.
- Remove any unneeded hardware and active software, especially custom enhancements to the system.
- Replace the application(s) and drivers—and the OS if necessary—to ensure that they have not become corrupted.
- Recreate the configuration as a test on another machine. Also test a different document in the same environment.
- Make certain that there is enough memory provided for each element of the software environment.
- Isolate the problem through process of elimination, either by selectively removing elements or by starting from scratch and adding one element at a time. Problems often arise due to conflicts between drivers or extensions.

STREAMLINING YOUR SESSIONS

Automation is almost synonymous with computing. Batch files and macros enable users to put automation to work in customized ways.

❖ Batch Files

Most command-line oriented operating systems such as MS-DOS provide for *batch files*. Batch files allow you to define a series of instructions that are executed automatically with one command. The start-up files described in Chapter 4 are examples of batch files. In developing a multimedia presentation, you might want a batch file that automatically configures memory, installs device drivers for sound cards, video boards, and peripherals, assigns directories, and runs your favorite production tools. Batch files can also be used to automate the process of performing repetitive operations on successive files, such as rendering or the image-processing techniques described in Chapter 8.

When finalizing a presentation for delivery, the slick thing to do is set everything up in a batch file so that the presentation runs automatically when the computer is booted. Indeed, this must be done in the case of an installation that you will not be able to baby-sit all the time. The batch file might configure memory, set up a RAM disk, load graphic and sound files into the RAM disk, and execute the presentation—all as if you had done it yourself.

❖ Macros

A batch file is a form of *macro*—a function that performs a series of operations by invoking one simple command. In a CLI-based system, the batch file approach might be assigned to and subsequently invoked by one keystroke.

In systems that are based on GUIs, a macro can be created by recording a series of operations that you perform in real time using the mouse and keyboard. This works much like audio or video re-cording: everything you do is recorded, but you can edit out the undesirable parts. Each macro or series of operations created in this fashion can be assigned to individual keys on the keyboard. Pressing a key associated with a macro plays back all of the events recorded in that macro as if you had performed them yourself. These kinds of macros can be employed in the same way as their batch file counterparts.

Let's say that you are performing identical operations on a series of images in an image-processing program—say, selecting the entire image, scaling it by a certain factor, changing the color palette, remapping the colors, applying an effect such as anti-aliasing, and finally resaving the file. You could record this series of operations on the first image as a macro and then apply the same operation to a series of subsequent images by simply opening the next image and invoking the macro!

TELECOMMUNICATIONS: ON-LINE WITH THE WORLD

Computers have been reshaping our society in many ways. One of those catalysts has been the ability to transfer information electronically across standard phone lines. This *telecommunication* technology makes the automated teller, credit card verification, and the ubiquitous fax machine possible. It is also the vehicle that allows us to connect computers to the rest of the world without leaving our homes and offices.

In multimedia work, telecommunications can make the difference between exchanging desperately needed files or information with coworkers today instead of tomorrow. It can be used as a way to network with peers to solve common problems and establish business contacts. Telecommunications can be used to send a file between disparate computer platforms, and it can be used to update remote multimedia installations such as kiosks. While an in-depth discussion of telecommunications is beyond the scope of this book, we'll take a quick look at the most important concepts for multimedia.

❖ Basic Terminology

Going *on-line* refers to the overall telecommunication process. The act of initially accessing a remote computer is called *logging on* to that system; *logging off* signifies terminating that connection. *Downloading* is the process of receiving a file from a remote computer; *uploading* a file is the process of sending a file to a remote computer.

❖ Modems

Computers communicate across phone lines using a *modem* (short for *modulator/demodulator*) and *telecommunication software* on each end. The modem incorporates digital-to-frequency and frequency-to-digital conversion since the phone system is used to an analog signal on each end of a connection. Modems initially establish a connection via a *carrier* signal—a logical stage to the modem, a frequency to the telephone company, and a high-pitched tone to us. Each digital bit transmitted modulates the carrier frequency to a frequency representing either zero or one; the receiving modem turns those frequencies back into digital zeros and ones and passes them to the computer.

Communication speed

Modems are measured by their *baud rate*—how many times per second the signal can change states. While not exactly the same thing, baud is used synonymously with *bits per second* (bps). While modems became popular when standard bill of fare was 300 baud, today's models come standard with speeds of 1200 and 2400 baud. (9600-baud models are plummeting in price and even faster ones are available for professional use). Needless to say, you can transmit the same amount of information four times faster at 9600 baud than at 2400 baud.

Many newer modems have built-in compression schemes that apply redundancy compression on the fly. The *V.42bis* standard, for example, can effectively achieve an average throughput on a 2400-baud modem that approximates 9600 baud. It's also smart enough not to try to compress a file that has already been compressed by the user. Regardless of compression, modems on both ends of the connection need to operate at the same speed and protocol.

Speed is everything in a modem since time is money when you're on-line. If you intend to send a lot of large files, it makes economic sense to invest in the fastest modem you can find. Table 6.1 puts speed into perspective with some examples of approximate file transfer times given different baud rates and file sizes. Real-time compression is not taken into consideration.

❖ Telecommunications Protocols

Telecommunications or *terminal software* tells the modem how to handle incoming and outgoing data. Various parameters that make up this communications *protocol* must be set identically on both

Table 6.1. *Theoretical transfer times for various file sizes at different baud rates without compression.*

File Size	1200 baud	2400 baud	9600 baud	19,200 baud	38,400 baud
10K	1.4 seconds	44 seconds	22 seconds	11 seconds	5.5 seconds
100K	14 minutes	7 minutes	3.5 minutes	1.75 minutes	87.5 seconds
1MB	2.3 hours	1.16 minutes	35 minutes	17.5 minutes	8.75 minutes
10MB	23 hours	7 hours	3.5 hours	1.75 hours	.525 hours

ends: baud rate, duplex, data bits, stop bits, and parity. If a file is to be transferred, a *transfer protocol* also needs to be established.

Duplex

The arcane history of telecommunications has created several methods by which you see what you type while on-line. With *full-duplex*, what you type is echoed by the remote system. With *half-duplex*, your characters are echoed locally, thereby avoiding delays. *Local echo* allows you to force your keystrokes to echo locally if different settings on the other end are preventing you from seeing what you're typing. These settings are typically important only when communicating directly with another user. In this case, setting the same duplex on both ends is usually recommended.

Data bits and stop bits

The size of the data words must be standardized to seven or eight *data bits*. Since the ASCII code ranges from 0 to 127, ASCII files can be transferred using only seven data bits (the extra bit would go unused). Eight data bits can be used to double the number of codes that can be sent. However, non-ASCII codes from 128 to 255 will typically only have meaning to similar computers and/or software. Binary (non-ASCII) transfers are best accommodated by 8-bit data formats. Stop bits are simply extra framing bits that delineate data words. One or two data bits are the standard options.

Parity

Parity checking is primarily used to detect problems such as noise and bad connections that can occur over a telephone line. When parity is on, an extra bit is added to each word transmitted. Simple arithmetic is used to add the number of ones in each word sent. *Even parity* dictates that each word will contain an even number of ones; *odd parity* dictates that each word will have an odd number. (This is simple addition having nothing to do with the actual word values.) The transmitting computer evaluates the data bits of each outgoing word and sets the parity bit to a 1 or 0 to force the total to become even or odd as agreed upon by the users. The receiving computer evaluates each incoming word to verify that the total number of ones matches the even or odd parity spec. If a value does not match, the receiving computer is flagged. (Various protocols take different types of action at this point.)

❖ **File Transfer Protocols**

Various protocols allow computers to communicate—even those of different brands. All personal computers employ ASCII to identify basic text. Binary (non-text) files have a variety of options.

ASCII

The most fundamental communications standard is *ASCII* (American Standard Code for Information Interchange), which defines the characters associated with the first 128 values that can be described by a byte. Thanks to ASCII, every computer knows to send the character A as the number 65 (decimal); conversely they all know that receipt of the number 65 should be interpreted as the letter A. When two computers first connect, they communicate in the common tongue of ASCII, allowing the users to type back and forth to each other.

Word processors normally save files containing additional headers and formatting information that are beyond the ASCII code. These files cannot be transferred in ASCII format. Virtually all word processors have the ability to strip off this extra formatting information and save documents as straight ASCII *text files*. Text files can be read by any computer and brought into any word processing program or text editor. The formatting will be gone, but the text will be there.

ASCII files can be sent directly, in which case you can watch the characters flowing on the screen during transmission. They can also be sent using one of the binary standards listed below to facilitate enhanced error-checking.

Binary files

While a byte can have 256 values, codes beyond 127 are not defined by ASCII—they have different meanings to different computers. Moreover, files of any type can be transferred across phone lines without immediate regard for their meaning. This is often referred to as a *binary transfer*, since a series of bits are just being shuffled across the line and saved as a file. Whether the receiving computer can do anything with them later is another issue. Some software can save documents in formats that can be read by other software, sometimes on other platforms. For example, Microsoft Word is available on both the Macintosh and the PC; each can save in a format that can be read by the other. Also, CompuServe has a library of graphics saved as GIF files. Any computer with a GIF interpreter can turn these files into usable graphics.

Several types of transfer protocols have evolved for binary files, and the primary differences have to do with error-checking schemes. Most employ a *checksum*—a method of adding up the values of the bytes and comparing it on both ends. A few of the more popular transfer protocols are as follows:

- *XModem* sends packets of 128 bytes, comparing a checksum, and repeating. It is an older protocol and should only be used if YModem or ZModem are not available on both ends, or if the quality of the telephone line is in question.

- *YModem* evolved in tandem with better phone lines and larger files. It sends packets of 1K before invoking a checksum. Since there's less checking, less transfer time is required. YModem can also send and receive multiple files in a single transfer.

- *ZModem* was designed to record the progress of a transfer. If the connection is corrupted part way through a transmission, transmission can resume from that point in a subsequent call. This is quite handy when call-waiting or a bad connection interrupts a call 45 minutes into an hour-long transfer! ZModem-compatible software also senses the presence of an incoming ZModem transfer and automatically opens a file for it.

- *Kermit* transmits the exact number of bytes rather than padding bits to fill out a block. Kermit also communicates file names, handles multiple files, and has sophisticated error checking.

DIRECT FILE TRANSFER BETWEEN TWO COMPUTERS

Many times you have to transfer data between two machines, whether the platforms are the same or not. Even when developed on multiple machines that are compatible, multimedia files can quickly become too large to store on easily transported media. Networking isn't always practical, and using two modems side-by-side seems a bit silly, especially when files too large to transport will take forever to run through the average modem.

As multimedia continues to evolve on multiple platforms, files frequently need to be transferred between computers running different operating systems. In such a case, the receiving machine is referred to as *native*, and the sending machine is referred to as *foreign*. Three basic non-network solutions to direct file transfer are null-modem connection, direct linking, and foreign disk mounting. Implementing any of these solutions across platforms will likely require translation.

❖ Translators

As with modems, just because you can transfer files between two platforms doesn't mean you can do anything with them on the receiving end. If you can save a transferred file to the native system, you can see and manipulate it at the directory level, but often the content of the file won't be usable within a native program. There are exceptions to this scenario: ASCII files won't be a problem, and some applications on the originating end allow saving the file in a foreign format.

In most other cases, you'll need a *translator*—a program that allows you to specify to what type of format you want the internal data of the foreign file to be converted. Some programs will perform translation as part of the transfer process. Others translate formats subsequent to transfer and can even be used in converting between native graphic formats. You are at the mercy of what your software supports, but more formats are being implemented all the time.

❖ Null-modem Connections

A *null-modem* connection is a method of bypassing modems and connecting the serial ports of two computers. Telecommunications software is still used, but the restriction of modem speed is obviated. You can transfer at the fastest common speed supported by the terminal software on each end—usually 9600 or 19,200 baud. Any necessary translation must be implemented after transfer.

The only real trick to this process is the wiring. Modem cables switch pins 2 and 3—the actual data transmission and reception pins—so that the send pin on the modem goes to the receive pin on the computer, and the send pin on the computer to the receive pin on the modem. If you plugged two modem cables together, these connections would be switched twice to no avail. A null-modem cable directly connects the send pin on one end to the transmit pin on the other end and vice versa. Null-modem adapters are also available that connect two standard modem cables.

❖ Direct Links

Two computers can access each other's disk drives via a *direct link* package made up of software and specialized cable. These packages allow you to see and manipulate the directory of a second machine via remote control from the first. This can only be accomplished from within the dedicated software, so these packages do not fulfill the function of a network in which files can be accessed within any program. Packages such as LapLink on the PC provide for direct linkage between similar machines. Other programs, such as those from DataViz, perform the more formidable task of implementing this function across different platforms. MacLinkPlus/PC, for example, can send files in either direction between PCs and Macs. At the end of the process, the transferred file is saved in a format that can be read directly by the receiving machine. Translation can be part of the process: MacLinkPlus/PC, for example, comes with 150 different translators.

❖ Foreign Disk Mounting

Normally, if you insert a foreign disk in a computer, a message appears saying the disk is unreadable. With the right software—and sometimes hardware—you can actually access foreign disks. DosMounter, AccessPC, and Apple File Exchange are programs that allow DOS disks to be read by Mac FDHD SuperDrives. NeXT computers can also read DOS disks. Files can usually be transferred to the native format, sometimes with concurrent translation.

Don't confuse foreign disk mounting with platform *emulators*. These are typically hardware/software combinations that simulate the operating environment of a foreign platform. For example, Amaxx makes the Amiga emulate a Mac, and SoftPC lets the Mac emulate a PC. Interformat transfer capabilities are not necessarily part of the deal. Be forewarned: emulators must jump through a lot of software hoops to mimic other systems. Any purchases should be thoroughly tested since multimedia applications normally push their native systems to the limits.

LOCAL AREA NETWORKS

Computers can be linked together in a variety ways to form a *network*. The cheapest type of network is known as "sneaker net"— you grab a disk or other removable media and walk it to another computer! This same function can be fulfilled by connecting the computers with a cable and sending files between them without leaving your desk. This type of network is called a *local-area network* (LAN). In addition to sharing files, LANs send interoffice electronic mail and share hardware such as printers, mass storage, backup devices, and modems.

In short, networks make it possible to share intellectual and physical resources, thus increasing productivity and cutting the cost of redundant peripherals and data. The primary difference between network types and architectures is their efficiency in facilitating this sharing process.

In multimedia work networks come into play on several different levels. A production team can store, access, and back up elements, such as graphic and sound files, on one another's systems or on a common, centralized medium. They can also access common hardware devices that are too costly to duplicate and too much hassle to move around and connect.

A far more powerful future is looming for multimedia and networks—multimedia presentations via network. LAN-based electronic mail and telephone-based voice mail are both in widespread use today. Some companies are beginning to integrate voice mail into electronic mail. The next logical step will be video mail and one-to-many presentations within the corporate environment.

In general, implementing all but the simplest of networks is a complex task that requires research, specialists, or both. The following discussion provides perspective and concepts rather than step-by-step installation and design instructions.

❖ Network Architecture

A network is a combination of hardware and software. A cable connects devices such as computers and printers, and each connection is referred to as a *node*. When machines are connected in a network, individual computers are often referred to as *workstations*.

Most networks use serial communications to minimize the number of costly conductors in the cables. This serial nature necessitates having some way for the nodes to share the cables simultaneously—that's where the software comes in. All networks operate by sending groupings of data known as *packets* across the network. Each packet contains an ID header that specifies its originator, type, and intended destination. Other routines ensure that only one packet is zipping through the wires at a given moment. All the other nodes read and evaluate each packet to see if the header contains their ID. If the ID doesn't match, the packet is ignored; if it matches, the packet is interpreted and acted upon.

Peer-to-peer networks

The most rudimentary form of networking is sharing workstation hard drives without a file server. All users can *publish* their storage device(s) to the network; other users can log on to, or *mount*, published drives remotely as if the drives were part of their own system. This method of networking is quick, dirty, and cheap. On the downside, most implementations quickly clog the network. In addition, accessing the drive on a coworker's computer slows down whatever they are doing at the same time because the transferred data has to go through their microprocessor.

File server networks

Sophisticated networks use a central computer as a storage device that everybody on the network can access. This provides a central repository for shared files, electronic mail, and other common data. Applications themselves are usually run from local drives. The file server also usually acts as a *print server*, managing the traffic between all nodes and the printer(s). File serving has the added advantage of centralized backup: The responsibility for making safety copies of an organization's valuable data is given to one person on one device, rather than relying upon individual users to back up their respective files.

❖ Topology

Most networks can be set up in several different configurations, or *topologies*, depending upon the needs and the number of nodes and resources.

Daisy-chain topology

The simplest way to connect multiple nodes is in a daisy chain. Data is passed through each node in series. (See Figure 6.2.) The nodes at each end of the chain must be terminated with the proper resistors in order to maintain the correct impedance in the line. Daisy chains restrict the number of nodes that can be attached. Disconnecting a node in the middle of a daisy chain usually breaks the network into two smaller networks that cannot communicate with one another.

Figure 6.2

Daisy chains are the simplest networks.

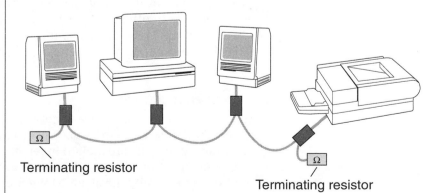

Terminating resistor

Terminating resistor

141

Backbone or trunk topology

Backbone, or *trunk*, *topology* is preferable to a daisy chain because jacks are provided along a trunk and various devices can be connected and disconnected without altering the rest of the network. (See Figure 6.3.) Clusters of daisy chains can also be branched off from the jacks. In some networks, lower gauge (greater diameter) wire can be used for the trunk line, thus lowering resistance and providing for greater distance. The ends of the trunk must be terminated.

Figure 6.3

Networks using trunk topology offer greater reliability and longer distances than daisy-chain networks.

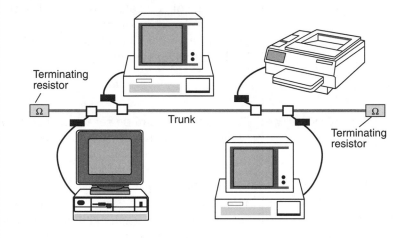

Star topology

Star topology gets its name from the concept of multiple branches connected to a central hub. (See Figure 6.4.) In office buildings, the hub is often the phone closet, because extra existing phone lines can be used for networks. In some star topologies, each branch can be used as a trunk or daisy chain, often serving groups of users clustered near one another. The flexibility of star topology is desirable when users are often relocated and/or existing phone-system wiring is used. As a general rule, the ends of the branches should be terminated.

Active versus passive

The daisy-chain, trunk, and star networks previously described are inherently *passive* since they have no electronics to boost the signal. All passive networks are limited in length because voltage levels cannot be maintained across long distances due to resistance. The solution is to amplify the signal along the way, making the network *active*. A *repeater* is a simple in-line amplifier between sections of

Figure 6.4

Trunk and daisy-chain topologies can be combined in a flexible star topology. An active controller is optionally used to increase the number and length of the branches connected by the hub.

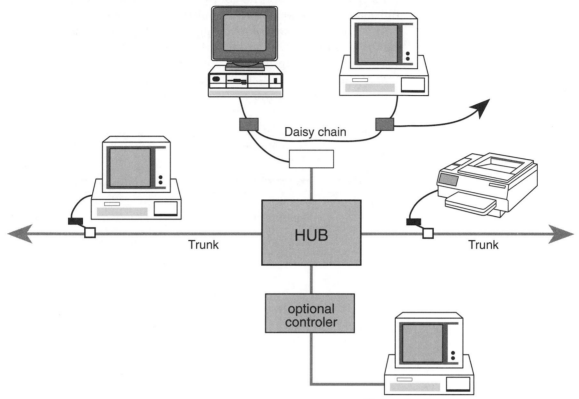

Daisy chain

HUB

Trunk

Trunk

optional controler

Optional network manager

long daisy-chains or trunks. A *router*, or *controller*, typically amplifies the signal and splits it off into several branches. The result is that overall wiring lengths can be many times longer than with passive topologies. Routers can also be used to isolate heavy users from network traffic routes so as not to impede other users.

❖ Common Network Types

The two most common network types used in desktop computing are Ethernet and Apple's LocalTalk. (IBM's Token Ring is also widely used.) Each of these is a hardware description that specifies the cabling, connections, and maximum bandwidth (speed) for the network. Software protocols determine how the packets are sent, trafficked, and interpreted. Their most significant difference is speed—230.4 kilobits/second for LocalTalk and 10 megabits/second for Ethernet.

Rather than explore the gory details of these networks, you can contrast their speed when transmitting files of various sizes. (See Table 6.2.) The amount of messaging significantly reduces the actual data bandwidth. In addition, the transfer times shown are based on the assumption that nothing else is trying to use the network at the same time—an unlikely event. (Actual times can be as much as ten times slower.)

Table 6.2. Time required to transfer representative file sizes via LocalTalk and Ethernet at optimal speeds. Transfer times do not take other network factors into account.

File Size	LocalTalk (230.4 kilobits/sec)	Ethernet (10 megabits/sec)
10K	.35 second	.01 second
100K	3.5 seconds	.1 second
1MB	30 seconds	1 second
10MB	5 minutes	8 seconds

As you can see, Ethernet is barely capable of handling real-time multimedia and LocalTalk is barely capable of handling non-real-time transfers of multimedia files. The crux of the matter is that current LANs are low-bandwidth systems designed to send packets of data in bursts, whereas audio and video are high-bandwidth media that are continuous and time-sensitive. The marriage of multimedia and LANs obviously has a lot of growing to do yet. Fiber optics and other technologies on the horizon are poised to transform their integration into pratical reality.

❖ ❖ ❖ ❖ ❖ ❖

This chapter has presented concepts that help you take control of your computing tools and put you well on the way to becoming a power user. This concludes our discussion of computers and sets the stage for the following section on computer graphics.

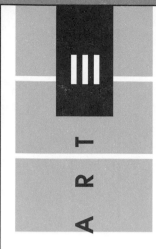

Computer Graphics

Computer graphics are a staple of today's media—from desktop publishing to on-screen presentations, slides, and broadcast video graphics. In the hands of artists, the computer is an ultimate power tool. The computer also empowers people who can't draw their way out of a paper bag to create effective—if not stunning—images as well. Artistic expression is primarily a function of the mind: Many artistically-talented people simply haven't developed the hand–eye coordination of the painter or sculptor. Sometimes all you need to create incredible computer graphics and animations is the right perspective combined with the right tools.

Chapter 7 covers the basic principles of light and color, as well as how computer technology represents and displays them. Chapter 8 provides an overview of the various types of computer graphics hardware and software used in creating presentation graphics and animations. Chapter 9 offers tips and techniques that can help you visualize and create aesthetically pleasing images. ❖

Graphics Technology

This chapter begins with a discussion of how light and color work in nature. While these concepts may seem a bit removed from multimedia, they apply to all light entering our eyes—including that from computer and video monitors. The discussion moves on to how computers manipulate and present images. Together, these concepts set the stage for a better understanding of computer graphic tools and the creation of more realistic and appealing images.

PROPERTIES OF LIGHT AND COLOR

In Chapter 1 visible light was identified as a rather narrow band of waves within the electromagnetic spectrum. As such, light also exhibits all of the classical wave attributes—frequency, amplitude, resonance, phase, reflection, refraction, absorption, and more.

❖ Amplitude

All light sources emit waves uniformly in all directions. The amplitude of the waves is perceived by the eye as brightness, or *luminance*. In space the light waves from stars travel unimpeded and their self-propagating quality perpetuates them infinitely. The earth's atmosphere contains particles and gases that absorb light waves, however. In all circumstances, the amplitude of light emitted from an electric bulb, candle, or other light source is distributed with distance according to the law of inverse squares. (Twice the distance yields one-quarter the luminance, three times the distance yields one-ninth the luminance, and so on.)

❖ Wavelength

The frequency of light is so high that traditional measurements in hertz become unwieldy. In common practice, wavelength is used as a reference. The wavelengths of visible light range from 380 to 760 *nanometers* (nm). The nanometer is also known as the *millimicron* (mμ). Another common unit of measurement is the *Angstrom* (Å)—one Å equals 10^{-8} cm. The wavelengths of visible light therefore range from 7600 to 3800 Å.

The exact wavelength of the light wave determines the color, ranging from red on the long end to violet on the short end—with a rainbow of colors in between. This range comprises the *color spectrum*. People rarely see any of these pure *spectral colors* in isolation except in a rainbow or through a prism. Most natural light sources are *polychromatic*, meaning they emit a combination of wavelengths. Some light sources, such as sodium lights or neon tubes, emit only waves in a narrow band of frequencies.

❖ Additive Color in Direct Light

The visual world is filled with millions of unique colors, each the result of a specific blend of wavelengths. Human visual perception is based on the *trichromatic theory of color*. Any colors can be realized by blending three basic, or *primary*, colors.

Direct light is light that is visible directly from the source—the sun, light bulbs, video/computer monitors, and projectors. The wavelengths of direct light are additive in nature, as are all waves. The three primary colors of direct light are red, green, and blue. Combinations of these three colors can result in most perceivable color variations.

Special circumstances apply to balanced mixtures of primaries. Equal mixtures of any two of the three primaries yields a *complementary color*: red and blue yield magenta, red and green yield yellow, and blue and green yield cyan. Identical amounts of all three primary colors result in various intensities of gray. A balanced mixture of primaries at full intensity produces white light; the absence of all primaries produces no color—black. (See Figure 7.1.)

❖ Subtractive Colors in Reflected Light

In the real world, people rarely look directly at actual light sources such as the sun or light bulbs. Most light that enters our eyes is a by-product of direct light encountering other objects. As such, most of what we see is influenced by the wave-like properties of reflection, absorption, refraction, and diffraction.

Figure 7.1

In direct light, the various colors we see result from additive mixtures of red, green, and blue wavelengths. In reflected light, the various colors we see result from subtractive mixtures of cyan, magenta, and yellow.

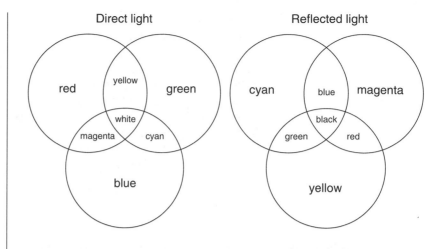

Objects themselves have no actual color properties. Various surfaces reflect certain wavelengths of light and absorb others. The colors that we attribute to a given object correspond to the wavelengths reflected by that object. When sunlight shines on the chlorophyll-filled leaves of a plant in bloom, the pigments in the surface reflect only the green wavelengths and absorb the others. (See Figure 7.2.) When the leaves die in the fall, the plant stops producing chlorophyll and the change in chemical balance allows the other colors to become more apparent.

Figure 7.2

The colors we attribute to objects are actually the colors reflected by their surfaces. All other colors are absorbed.

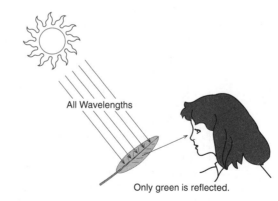

Reflected light operates on the principle of *subtractive color*. Consider the mixing of red and green paints. Red paint absorbs all but the red wavelengths including blue and green; green paint absorbs all but the green wavelengths including red and blue. In essence the red and green paints absorb everything, producing a very dark color approximating black.

Subtractive color theory must be taken into consideration when producing colors on reflective media such as paper. Reflective media require the use of the *subtractive primary colors* of magenta, cyan (light blue), and yellow. These are the complementary colors of the additive primaries. The reciprocal is true as well: Red, green, and blue are the complementary colors resulting from the equal combination of any two of the subtractive primaries. Color film is comprised of three separate emulsion layers, each sensitive to one of the subtractive primaries. Color printing employs separate plates that are used to apply ink for each of the subtractive primaries.

❖ Reflection

Reflective qualities are very important in creating images that seem realistic. In most two-dimensional graphics programs, the user is responsible for manually implementing reflection. In 3-D rendering, the user is responsible for specifying reflective attributes. Either way, the topic merits some attention.

As with other types of waves, light is reflected by an object at an angle that is complementary to the angle of incidence on the opposite side of the normal or perpendicular. The angles of incidence and reflection for any individual light wave striking any given point are all within a common plane. Although light waves fill the world, we only see those that reflect along planes that intersect with our eyes.

The concept of reflective planes can be visualized by thinking of bouncing a rubber ball (a light wave) off a sidewalk (a reflective surface) to a friend (the viewing eye). The ball stays in a plane between you and your friend—in this case a plane perpendicular to the ground. Your friend can catch only balls thrown along that plane or close to it The same concept applies to the perception of reflected light.

This example is too simple to account for all the light waves that enter our eyes. Let's extend the idea from a sidewalk to a racquetball court—a room with reflective surfaces on all four walls in addition to the floor and ceiling. For starters, the third dimension vastly increases the number of reflective planes. In addition, the ball can bouce off one surface to a second to a third, and so on, when propelled with enough energy. In this scenario, some balls will ultimately reach your friend's position and others will not, but the combination of reflective planes multiplies towards infinity.

The racquetball analogy validates the concept that everything we see that is not a direct light source is actually a myriad of reflections. (It also shows why most people find playing racquetball with a friend more intriguing than bouncing a rubber ball off a sidewalk!) But while we play racquetball with one ball at a time, an almost infinite number of light waves reflect simultaneously in our field of vision.

Light scattering

Our first encounter with reflected light is not an obvious one. Earth's atmosphere is filled with molecules of various gases. Since the size of these molecules is in the same range as the wavelengths of visible light, sunlight causes the atmospheric molecules to vibrate sympathetically. This produces additional sources of light, although they are reduced in amplitude. (Recall that a reflected wave has less amplitude that the original.) This light also reflects off neighboring molecules in a chain reaction. This effect of *light scattering* yields the *diffuse light*, or *ambient light*, that fills our visual world, even in shadows or in the absence of direct sunlight on a cloudy day.

Specular reflection

The reason some surfaces seem shinier and more reflective than others is a direct result of how smooth the surface is. Light waves travel from their source in nearly parallel paths. When they strike a smooth or highly polished surface—such as glass, plastic, crystal, liquid, or metal—they reflect along planes that are relatively parallel to one other.

The smoothest surfaces exhibit *specular reflection*, or mirror-like quality, because there are related angles of reflection for every point on the surface. If a specular surface is flat, the reflection will appear spatially undistorted (with the exception of the standard image reversal) because the relationship of all the angles of reflection is linear. Specular surfaces that are not flat will distort the reflection since the angles of incidence vary across the surface. A billiard ball will yield a non-linear fish-eye reflection because the angles of incidence are in the same relationship as the points on the sphere.

The images you see in a mirror are made up of light waves that have first struck other objects, then reflected into the mirror, and finally reflected into your eye. Similarly, if you place a billiard ball on a wooden table and illuminate the scene brightly from the proper angle, the wood grain of the table will appear as a reflection on the ball's surface. A combination of direct and ambient light strikes the ball and reflects into your eyes; it also hits the table's surface and reflects off the ball into our eyes. (See Figure 7.3.)

Figure 7.3

All visible objects are percieved via a complex series of reflections.

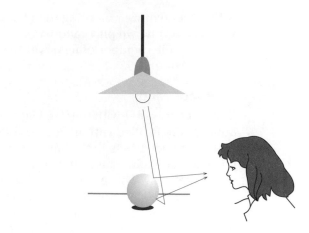

Highlights

Any place where direct reflections of light can be seen or focused causes a *hot spot*, or *highlight*. The closer the light is to the object, the larger the hot spot. The brighter the light source, the brighter the reflection. Smooth objects exhibiting specular reflection produce a small, well-defined highlight; the rougher an object is the more spread out and tapered the highlight appears.

The highlight will appear to move as you or the light source moves. This is because reflective planes align with your eye and vary with the relationship of your eye to the object and/or the light source. If you and a friend stand a few feet apart and view the reflective surface, you will each see a highlight at different physical points on the object. When you stand side-by-side looking into a mirror, you will both see similar yet different reflected images.

The earlier statement that objects reflect only certain wavelengths to yield the perception of color requires modification. Some surfaces, such as plastic, reflect all incoming wavelengths equally at the hot spot regardless of angle. The highlight on a billiard ball from a white light source will yield a white highlight, regardless of the ball's actual color. Metallic surfaces interact to different extents with light energy, depending upon the angle of reflection. In this phenomenon, shallow angles yield highlights bearing the color of the light source; sharper angles yield highlights tinted with the color of the surface.

Diffuse reflection

The opposite of specular reflection is *diffuse reflection*. Most surfaces are more porous than smooth—at least on the scale of the wavelength of light. At a microscopic level, each little bit of a surface such as concrete or wood is angled differently than its neighbors, causing incoming light waves to be diffused or reflected at different angles. The rougher the surface, the more these angles vary, and the further the object gets from exhibiting specular reflection. Returning to the bouncing ball analogy, the relative smoothness of a sidewalk compared to the size of the ball makes for predictable angles. If the surface is an old cobblestone walk or loose rocks, the angles become more random.

Diffuse reflectors such as cardboard are often called *matte* objects. The perfect diffuse surface reflects light equally in all directions at once. As such, it exhibits no highlights. However, nothing is a completely perfect specular or diffuse reflector. A piece of wood is a fairly diffuse reflector; adding a polished coat of varnish can add specular quality as well.

❖ Light Transmission

Not all objects simply reflect and/or absorb light: some *transmit* incoming light waves out the other side. The degree to which a material is opaque, translucent, or transparent is determined by the resistance of the medium to light waves. The nature of transmitted light has to do with the thickness of the object, the density of the material, and its color. Even objects that appear completely transparent offer some resistance or absorption. Although glass might appear transparent, glass that is several feet thick will transmit significantly less light than a normal windowpane. Increasing the opacity without increasing the thickness would have a similar effect. As for color, transmitted light is affected by the *body color* or internal color of the object. White light passing through a green gel on a spotlight yields green transmitted light.

Just as the surface of an object can exhibit specular and diffuse qualities, so can the internal materials. A window is an example of *specular transmission* where the angles of rays traveling in parallel are not disrupted. Slight imperfections in the glass—an air bubble, for example—can even result in a sort of internal highlight. *Diffuse transmission*, on the other hand, scatters light in equal directions and intensities, resulting in translucency. Ice block and typical stained-glass windows are examples of internal diffusion.

Refraction

As explained in Chapter 1, a wave traveling through one medium refracts when it encounters another medium. This is true of light waves as well. If you are standing knee deep in a clear pond, your legs will appear to protrude at an improbable angle rather than straight down. Light passing through a water glass or crystal will be refracted in the same manner. As you'll see in Chapter 8, many 3-D rendering products can automatically simulate light transmission through transparent and translucent materials.

❖ Shadows

A wave in any medium will be reflected by an object that is larger than the wavelength. This is most assuredly true of light waves, as evidenced by the phenomenon of shadows. The wavelengths of all visible light waves are smaller than any individual object you can see with the naked eye. Therefore, any opaque object large enough to be visible will cast a shadow opposite the light source because the light waves are reflected by the object.

The length of the shadow depends upon the positioning of the light source. The closer the light source is to being perpendicular to the object in relation to the background, the smaller the shadow will be. This can be seen easily in nature: at high noon shadows are much shorter than they are toward the beginning and end of the day. (See Figure 7.4.) The effective size of the light source with respect to the distances between the object, shadow, and source determines the diffusion in the shadow. In general, larger light sources create more diffuse or fuzzy shadows.

Figure 7.4

Shadows become longer and more diffuse as the angle of the light source moves further away from the normal.

Shadows are not necessarily solid black. Any available ambient light reflects off the shadowed surface, presenting a less brilliant version of the surface. Shadows appear darker as the object gets closer to the background surface, because more incidental light waves are occluded. Objects with reflective surfaces incur brighter shadows since the additional reflections illuminate the shadowed area. Also, the more reflective the background surface, the less noticeable the shadows.

Shadows are also affected by additional light sources. Positioning several light sources at different angles can create shadows in multiple directions. Where a second light source strikes part of a shadow, that area will become brighter. Whether the shadow is eliminated depends on the position, color, and intensity of the additional light source. The combination of lights to eliminate shadows is discussed further with regard to lighting for video in Part V.

COLOR PERCEPTION

Light and reflection are only part of the visual equation. The other part is how the human eye and brain perceive light. While the biological understanding of human vision still has a long way to go, many studies have been performed on perception and psychology. This section largely deals with perception; the psychology topic is deferred to Chapter 9.

❖ Subjective Color

Although humans see colors via the additive process in direct light and the subtractive process in reflected light, the way we think of color is more subjective. The three basic components to the way we perceive color are brightness, hue, and saturation.

Brightness

Brightness is simply a perception of how light or dark something is. It can be envisioned as a series of grays ranging from black to white. Black-and-white televisions or photographs can only represent differences in brightness, for example. Brightness is also referred to as *lightness*, although there is some discrepancy over subtle differences.

Hue

Hue refers to the spectral colors of red, orange, yellow, green, blue, and purple. A wide variety of subjective colors exists within each of these categories. Pink, brick red, and fire engine red, for example, all have a red hue. Hues are depicted as a circle in the order in which they appear in the spectrum. (See Figure 7.5.) This forms the basic of the standard *color wheel*.

Saturation

Saturation (sometimes called *chroma*) refers to the strength of a hue added to its pure brightness. Light with no saturation is *achromatic*,

Figure 7.5

Spectral colors are distin-guished by their hue.

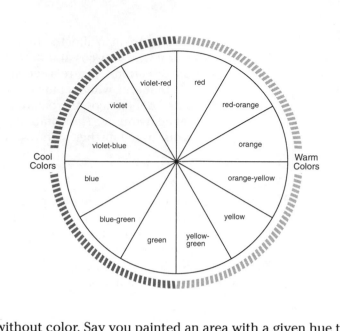

or without color. Say you painted an area with a given hue that in-creased from no saturation on one side to full saturation on the other. If you then took a black-and-white photo of it, the photo would appear solid gray because the brightness is constant. Pastels are examples of colors that exhibit only partial saturation.

Color space

The three properties of brightness, hue, and saturation can be en-visioned as a 3-dimensional *color space*. (See Figure 7.6.) The cen-tral column is the achromatic axis of brightness. Hues form circles around the brightness axis. The position along the axis perpen-dicular to the achromatic brightness axis describes the amount of saturation. Any color can be described by its position relative to all three axes.

Figure 7.6

Brightness, hue, and satura-tion form a 3-dimensional color space with which any color can be represented.

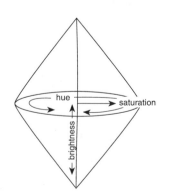

Color Temperature

You've probably heard colors referred to as having a temperature—cool blue or warm yellow, for example. The colors on one side of the color wheel are primarily warm (red, orange, and yellow); on the other side they are primarily cool (blue, violet, and green). Further, each hue has a relative warm and cool side. Red-violet, for example, is warmer than blue-violet. Finally, the colors opposite one another on the color wheel have opposite color temperatures.

❖ Theories of Color Perception

The iris of the eye determines how much light strikes the retina, which covers most of the back half of the eye. The retina contains about 120 million *rods* and *cones*. Cones are sensitive to bright light and are used in daylight. Rods are employed in night vision and are less sensitive to color—which explains why scenes appear to be less saturated at night (predominantly black-and-white).

Scientists have determined that rods contain a photopigment called *rhodopsin* that changes its chemical composition depending upon the balance of colors striking it. The chemical balances are converted to voltages that are sent to the brain for interpretation. While the color-discerning properties of cones have less scientific substantiation than rods, the current theory is that three different pigments must be involved—most likely embodied in three different types of cones.

The original *component theory*, or Young–Helmholtz theory, of color perception postulated that the three color receptors were red, green, and blue. While the trichromatic theory of color serves well in describing mixtures of color, the additive primaries are not necessarily the only component choices for how the eye actually works.

In the late 1870s, Ewald Hering developed the *opponent color theory*. Opponent colors are those opposite each other on the color wheel such as red/green or blue/yellow. One of the main factors behind this theory is the presence of *negative afterimages* in human vision. If you focus your vision on an area of a solid color for about 20 seconds or more and then look away, you will see a ghost of that image in the opponent color. (A red square will yield a green afterimage, for example.) Hering concluded that there must be three types of color discriminators—blue/yellow, red/green, and black/white. Each receptor would discriminate between its given opponent colors and toggle to present the brain with the necessary component information.

More recently, the *opponent-process theory* has blended the component and opponent color theories for an explanation that has gained a high degree of scientific acceptance. In essence, this theory states that cones responding to different thirds of the visible spectrum send signals to each of three opponent discriminators which, in turn, respond by altering the frequencies they send to the brain.

❖ Phenomena of Color Vision

Understanding the intricacies of the opponent-process theory is less important than the visual phenomena it explains. The first is negative afterimage. Another is *simultaneous color contrast*—a phenomenon wherein identical colors appear differently depending upon their background. A color with medium brightness and saturation will appear brighter against a background with lower brightness and saturation and darker against a background with higher brightness and saturation. Colors of equal brightness and saturation are only differentiated by hue and color temperature.

The opponent-process theory also explains why eyes become fatigued after lengthy exposure to intense colors that are high in contrast. The signals going through the nerves to the brain fluctuate greatly, causing a strain. Such contrasts are sometimes called vibrant colors. This phenomenon is more prominent as the value and saturation of two colors increase in similarity and as they become more opposite in hue and color temperature. In a related concept, using opponents for color differentiation can backfire in extended viewing situations, because negative afterimages tend to cancel out opposing color elements.

Proportion is also a contributing factor, as you can verify by the following experiment: Fill your monitor with a solid fully-saturated yellow background, then draw a solid fully-saturated 2-inch square on one side and a thin line in the same color of red on the other side. Notice that the red square seems more saturated than the red line due to the influence of the surrounding body of yellow on the eye. This owes to the fact that the eye has good luminance resolution, but poor chroma resolution.

❖ Abnormal Color Vision

Abnormal color vision (formerly called color blindness) affects a surprising portion of the world's population. Statistically about 8.5 percent of male Caucasians, 3 percent of black males, and 5 percent of Asian males have deficiencies in color perception in one form or another. By contrast, only about 0.5 percent of the entire female population of the world is so affected. Although you can't sacrifice artistic quality for small segments of the population, knowledge of abnormal color vision is important when creating information that is differentiated by color.

One reason the term color blindness is no longer preferred is that it is inaccurate on the whole. Only about 0.003 percent of Caucasian males exhibit *monochromatism*—the inability to differentiate various hues and saturations.

The most common form of abnormal color vision is confusion between red and green. This takes several forms including the inability to distinguish the difference between the two, and a bias toward one or the other in the perception of various shades of yellow. Fully 5 percent of Caucasian males, for example, require an extra amount of green in order to perceive a spectral yellow. One percent of Caucasian males require extra red balance in order to match any given yellow. Another 1 percent of Caucasian males confuse red and bluish-green and perceive red with less luminosity than normal. One percent also confuse red and pure green with near-normal perception of luminosity. Finally, only about 0.001 percent of the entire male population is affected by difficulties in distinguishing blue and yellow, accompanied with lower perception of blue luminosity.

People with normal vision appear to see differing amounts of yellow components in colors. Fatigue reduces overall ability to distinguish colors. The ultimate fatigue—old age—brings a yellow discoloration to the lenses of the eye, which boosts yellow and cuts blue.

MONITORS

A variety of software tools are available that can create computer-generated images. When all is said and done, everything you see on a computer monitor comes down to two components—the CRT and the display circuitry that drives it.

❖ Cathode-ray Tubes

The *CRT* (cathode-ray tube) is the picture tube used in televisions, oscilloscopes, radar, video monitors, and computer monitors. For the sake of simplicity, let's start by discussing a black-and-white CRT. At the highest conceptual level, the CRT consists of a screen coated with phosphorescent dots called *pixels* (short for *picture elements*). The phosphors glow when bombarded with electrons from an *electron gun* at the back of the tube. The glow lingers for a short time after bombardment has stopped due to a phenomenon known as *persistence*. The pattern and intensity of the bombardment determines the nature of the image we discern on the screen.

The CRT, like all vacuum tubes, is made of a glass envelope from which the air has been removed. The vacuum allows electrons to flow with much greater ease between two separated electrical poles without interference from air molecules. The electron gun itself consists primarily of a *cathode*—a pole connected to the negative voltage source in a circuit. *Filaments* at the back of the tube boil off electrons for the gun when excited with electricity. The *anode*, or positive pole, is attached to a conductive shield around the tube and is connected to the positive portion of the circuit. Given a high enough voltage in the circuit, electrons leap from the cathode toward the anode. Smaller anode collars in the gun serve to focus and accelerate the electron beam. (See Figure 7.7.)

Figure 7.7

The electron guns in a CRT project a stream of electrons that illuminate the phosphor dots on the screen.

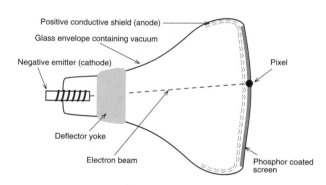

The relative strength of the voltage applied to the cathode/anode circuit determines the strength of the electron beam and, by extension, the brightness of the phosphor being bombarded. Monitors with phosphors of uniform tint and only a single electron gun are *monochrome*, or capable of displaying only various intensities of a single color. Black-and-white monitors employ white phosphors, for example.

Since a complete image is comprised of many phosphor dots, the electron beam must be systematically directed to illuminate all pixels, each with unique intensity. Movement of the electron beam is handled by applying control voltages to a *yoke*—a collar consisting of two electromagnetic coils wound at right angles to each other. The voltage applied to one coil determines the horizontal positioning, while the voltage applied to the other coil determines vertical positioning. Together they can direct the flow from the electron gun in a predictable pattern.

The basic element of that pattern is the *scanline*—one complete horizontal line of pixels. A sawtooth current applied to one of the coils directs the flow from the electron gun so that it scans horizontally across the screen from left to right, then shuts off while moving back to the other side. After this *horizontal retrace* or *horizontal blanking* interval, the next cycle of the sawtooth wave starts the process over again. The sawtooth wave that governs the timing of the horizontal scanlines and horizontal retrace is the *horizontal sync* signal.

Another slower sawtooth wave is simultaneously applied to the other coil in the yoke so that the overall flow is progressively directed down the screen. This allows the horizontal scans to create a raster—successive pattern of scanlines that fills the screen. When the last line is completed, the gun shuts off—*the vertical blanking interval*—and repositions to the upper-left corner again *vertical retrace*. The sawtooth wave that governs the timing of the vertical scanning and retrace is synchronized to the *vertical sync* signal. This *rasterizing* process repeats itself continually to refresh the screen as the phosphors fade from each previous pass. (See Figure 7.8.)

Figure 7.8

Varying electromagnetic fields are used to direct the electron beams in a series of horizontal scanlines that fill the screen from top to bottom.

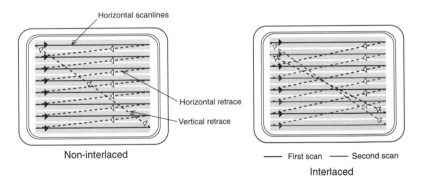

From there, things differ between monitors for computers or video. Most computer monitors draw every line in sequence from the top of the screen to the bottom at a rate of approximately 60 times per second. This is called a *non-interlaced signal*. Video, television, and some computer displays employ an *interlaced signal* that draws all the even lines, then all the odd lines. Each *field*, or complete set of odd or even scanlines, takes 1/60th of a second; each complete two-field screen is redrawn 30 times per second.

Color CRTs

Since CRTs are actually light sources, color versions work on the principle of the additive primary colors of red, green, and blue. While painters have experimented for centuries with various mixtures of color, French impressionists, such as Claude Monet and Georges Seurat, took the approach of placing isolated colors in close proximity rather than blending them. Even though Seurat's pointillistic *Sunday Afternoon in the Park* is composed of thousands of discrete color dots, viewing it from a distance gives the impression of a complete image rich in color. Color CRTs operate in much the same way.

Phosphors can be tinted so that they glow in unique colors when excited. In color CRTs, the phosphor dots inside the visible face of the screen are organized in tightly-grouped trios of red, green, and blue phosphors. Each multicolor phosphor trio comprises one *color pixel* that appears to the naked eye as a single color dot. The color signal coming into the CRT is separated into red, green, and blue components that are routed to three different electron guns. These guns are calibrated to hit each dot trio in unison as the beams play across the screen. (See Figure 7.9.) A *shadow mask* helps restrict the electron flow to the desired pixels. Applying various combinations of voltages to the three electron guns yields color pixels that appear as any one of a wide range of colors.

Figure 7.9

Three electron beams corresponding to the red, green, and blue components of the signal strike trios of red, green, and blue phosphors to create color pixels. A shadow mask between the electron guns and the screen ensures that the electron beams are restricted to their targeted dots.

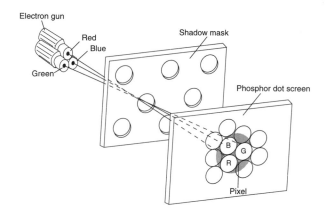

❖ Monitor Attributes

Various other attributes are frequently attached to manufacturer's monitor specs and publisher's monitor tests. *Tracking* measures the comparative intensity of the three electron guns in order to produce accurate color fidelity. Uneven tracking will yield displays that are biased toward the color of the more intense gun(s). *Focus* refers to the sharpness of the pixels, usually tested subjectively with fine text. *Distortion* usually manifests as bending and other anomalies in the image toward the screen edges.

Evaluating a monitor is largely a subjective exercise. Ask yourself the following questions while evaluating two different screens, one filled with repetition of a dense letter (such as a lower case *m*), the other with a variety of standard colors:

- Is there any fuzziness around the edges of the screen?
- Is the image crisp or smeared?
- Is the color true?
- Are the colors still true toward the edge of the screen?
- Do horizontal and vertical lines appear straight?

❖ Monitor Adjustments

Monitors come with a variety of controls that allow for adjustment by the user. *Convergence* refers to the accuracy with which the three guns hit their target phosphors. Misconvergence can happen as a result of jarring the monitor. Extreme misconvergence manifests as a tinted screen or in colored borders around objects, particularly geometrical shapes. Most monitors have a convergence control that can be used to bring the guns back into alignment while examining a test image. Be sure to let a monitor warm up for at least 20 minutes before adjusting convergence.

Contrast and brightness work just like they do on a TV set. Most monitors have detentes in the controls to indicate normal setting. In most cases, monitors should be set to normal before you start creating graphics so that your images will look similar on other systems down the line. Compare your monitor with others to establish a norm and make one-time adjustments if necessary. If adjustments are required, adjust the brightness until the darkest areas are black, then adjust the contrast so the whites are white.

H-size determines how much horizontal space a standard image will fill in the display area. *V-size* determines how much vertical space a standard image will fill in the display area. While most computer displays do not extend to the edges of the monitor, resist the urge to spread the image using the h-size and v-size controls. For one thing, monitors are less accurate at the edges. In addition, the relationship of display card dpi and monitor dot pitch have already been optimized by the manufacturer.

The Earth's natural magnetic field can build up a magnetic field within the monitor that negatively affects convergence and other performance. While turning the monitor off will eliminate this magnetic field, dedicated *degauss* buttons eradicate this contamination more elegantly.

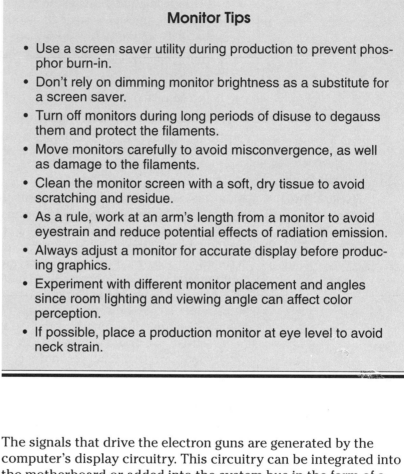

Monitor Tips

- Use a screen saver utility during production to prevent phosphor burn-in.
- Don't rely on dimming monitor brightness as a substitute for a screen saver.
- Turn off monitors during long periods of disuse to degauss them and protect the filaments.
- Move monitors carefully to avoid misconvergence, as well as damage to the filaments.
- Clean the monitor screen with a soft, dry tissue to avoid scratching and residue.
- As a rule, work at an arm's length from a monitor to avoid eyestrain and reduce potential effects of radiation emission.
- Always adjust a monitor for accurate display before producing graphics.
- Experiment with different monitor placement and angles since room lighting and viewing angle can affect color perception.
- If possible, place a production monitor at eye level to avoid neck strain.

DISPLAY TECHNOLOGY

The signals that drive the electron guns are generated by the computer's display circuitry. This circuitry can be integrated into the motherboard or added into the system bus in the form of a *display card, graphics adapter,* or *video card.* (This usage of the term "video" does not automatically imply compatibility with the television industry's definition of video.)

❖ Video Memory

The computer creates and stores graphic images in memory as a series of numbers, just like everything else it manipulates. A special memory area called *video memory* or *display memory* is used when an image or portion thereof needs to be displayed. This memory is sampled repeatedly at a rate compatible with the scan rate of the monitor. DACs in the associated circuitry convert the digital information in this display memory into the analog voltages required by the monitor's electron guns.

Standard memory and video memory differ both conceptually and physically. Video memory usually has faster access times than regular memory. While standard memory areas cannot be accessed by the video DACs, video memory can communicate with both the video DACs and standard RAM areas. (See Figure 7.10.) Standard memory is therefore used to calculate and/or conceptually represent an image in one of a variety of ways, while video memory is a direct digital representation of the electronic canvas that is displayed on the monitor. (On some systems like the Amiga, video memory can also be used as standard memory—but not the other way around.)

Figure 7.10

Although graphic calculations can be made in standard RAM, video RAM holds the final representation of a graphic image that is converted to analog for display.

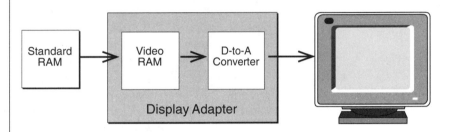

❖ Device Resolution versus Image Resolution

Device resolution is the measurement of the number of pixels that can be represented in a given space on an output device such as a monitor or printer. Device resolution is measured in *dots per inch* (dpi). The average laser printer, for example, has a resolution of 300 dpi. The average computer display has a resolution of 72 or 75 dpi. The *display resolution* is referenced by the number of pixels in a horizontal scanline times the number of scanlines. A display employing 640 pixels across each of 480 lines—a total of 307,200 pixels—would be commonly referred to as a *640 x 480 display.*

Image resolution can be completely independent from the device or display resolution. Let's use a scanned 4-inch square photograph as an example. The film has a resolution of thousands of dots per inch. Scanning the photograph into a computer at 100 percent with 300 dpi resolution will result in a digital representation with lower resolution than the original film. Printing the scanned image on a 300 dpi printer will result in a printout the same size as the original with same 300 dpi resolution as the digital representation. (See Figure 7.11.)

Figure 7.11

The image resolution determines the number of pixels per inch that represent the image.

| 36 dpi | 75 dpi | 150 dpi | 266 dpi |

Displaying such an image on-screen is a different matter, since monitors have far less resolution. (Lots of video memory would be required as well.) Images of higher resolution are stored and manipulated in standard RAM (or even virtual memory), and a representation of it is calculated and placed into video memory for display.

Say your monitor has a resolution of 75 dpi. If you ask for a 100 percent (dot-for-dot) representation on the screen, the image will be 16" x 16". Since this is larger than the average display, the video memory will only contain part of the picture. This effectively makes your display a scrollable window on a larger image because there are four times as many dots per inch in the image file than can be displayed on-screen. If you want to see the entire image on the monitor at its original size, the software will need to send every fourth pixel to the display buffer. (This process is transparent to the user.)

❖ Color Resolution

In a 1-bit display system, every pixel on the screen is represented by a bit in video memory. Since a bit is either on or off—a 1 or a 0—a pixel is either black or the monochrome color. Put another way, there are a total of 2^1 values per pixel. The memory used to represent one bit per pixel of an entire screen is called a *bit plane*.

Additional colors are added to the computer through the use of multiple bit planes, along with DACs and monitors that can accept their values. The number of bit planes used is referred to as the *color resolution* or pixel depth. Two bit planes yield four possible values per pixel (2^2), four bit planes yield 16 values (2^4), and eight bit planes yield 256 values (2^8). (The Amiga has some non-standard ways of using bit planes for color resolution.) The total of all the bit planes used to represent a graphic is referred to as a *bitmap*. The time required to process and display large numbers of bit planes will be discussed later in this chapter.

How these extra bit planes are viewed depends upon the monitor and the display card driving it. Having 8-bit color resolution means nothing if the monitor has only one electron gun and/or the DACs driving the display are of lower resolution. The next step up from 1-bit monochrome is the *gray-scale display*, mostly used in desktop publishing. Gray-scale monitors have a single electron gun and are usually capable of displaying 16 or 256 shades of gray, which correspond to four or eight bit planes, respectively. (See Figure 7.12.)

While 256 shades of gray are quite respectable in a non-color image, color is another ballgame altogether. With millions of natural colors bombarding our eyes from the world around us, 16 or even 256 colors barely scratch the surface when it comes to realism. Two solutions to overcome this barrier are currently in use—more bit planes for enhanced resolution and color mapping.

Enhanced color resolution

As discussed, any color can be created by combining different amounts of red, green, and blue. This statement assumes that you have a smooth range of values between zero intensity and full intensity for each of the three additive colors. The current paradigm

Figure 7.12

The number of bits per pixel determines the range of colors in an image.

| 1-bit (black and white) | 2-bit (4 shades) | 4-bit (16 shades) | 8-bit (256 shades) |

in color resolution is *24-bit color*—24 bit planes providing 8-bit values (256 levels) for each of the three color guns. (See Figure 7.13.) This yields a total of 256^3 or 2^{24} or 16.7 million possible colors—enough for the eye to perceive as being *photorealistic*, or of photographic quality. Any display system that stores implicit values for the RGB components is said to use *direct color*—regardless of color depth.

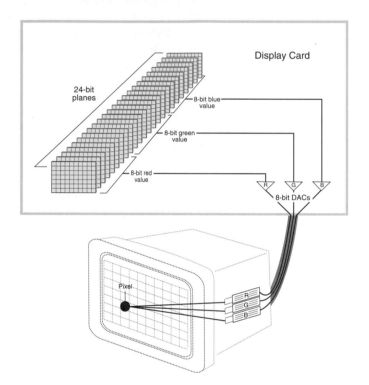

Figure 7.13

24-bit color systems employ 8-bit planes for each of the red, green, and blue component values.

If millions of colors seem extravagant, consider that a single leaf can have hundreds or thousands of subtle shades of green. An apple may have as many shades of red. Certainly the leaf or apple can be represented with fewer shades, but with less realism as well. If you have a leaf and an apple in the same image, the number of colors required increases. Place a bouquet of flowers in the image and you're looking at millions of colors.

Although some manufacturers boast 32-bit graphics, the extra eight bits comprise an *alpha channel* that is used for operations such as overlays and masks that don't have anything to do with color resolution. Some 16-bit systems are also in use. These employ four bits for each of the RGB colors plus a 4-bit alpha channel, or three 5-bit color values and a 1-bit alpha channel.

Unfortunately, 24-bit and 32-bit graphics require massive amounts of storage, not to mention a less than instantaneous display time. The bitmap of a 24-bit image the size of the average 640 x 480 display takes up about 921K of memory and storage before applying any compression techniques. These files sizes and associated load times are currently prohibitive for multimedia presentations that require a fast pace, quick visual response, and/or real-time animation.

Color mapping

The current compromise between speed, color resolution, and price is *color mapping*. Rather than having values fed directly to the DACs, each pixel on the screen has a value that corresponds to one of the locations in a color map, or *color look-up table* (CLUT), of limited size. Each location, or *color register*, in the CLUT is an index that references a larger value corresponding to a color with greater resolution. Systems employing CLUTS are often refered to as using *indexed color* for this reason. You can think of CLUTs as being similar to paint-by-number kits in which each area on the canvas contains a number indicating the proper paint pot to be used.

A CLUT with 256 color registers would limit each pixel value to an 8-bit number. Each of those 256 registers can reference a color of higher resolution—a 12-bit, 16-bit, or 24-bit value depending upon the system. (See Figure 7.14.) In this way the range of overall colors

Figure 7.14

The pixel value in the display memory points to the appropriate color register in the CLUT. The value contained in the register determines the values fed to the DACs for the red, green, and blue electron guns.

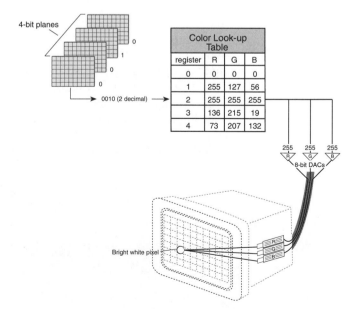

available to you is still vast, but the number of simultaneously displayable colors is limited. In the process, the same 640 x 480 bitmap has shrunk to 307K before compression.

An interesting side effect of color mapping is that by changing the referenced color within a register, you change all of the pixels on the screen that have already been painted from that register. This provides for some flexibilities and limitations that will be explained further in discussing graphics.

Gamma correction and 24-bit color mapping

Color maps are sometimes used in 24-bit systems as well. This has to nothing to do with color resolution, however, and everything to do with the *non-linear response* of human and electronic visual systems. (Linearity means that the output is directly proportional to input.) The change in brilliance of phosphors on the CRT is not linearly proportionate to the change in intensity of the electron beams striking it. To complicate matters, human perception of brilliance is not linearly proportionate to changes in phosphor brilliance.

Each monitor has a different response curve, the equation for which is called *gamma*. If a CLUT is created that compensates for gamma, all color values received from the computer can be translated through the CLUT to yield a linear response with regard to brilliance and color balance. This process of *gamma-correction*, or *linearizing*, is usually associated within an image-processing program.

Dithering

When two pixels of different colors are in close enough proximity, our brains average them together into one perceived median color. When using fewer than the optimum number of displayable colors, many programs will represent the unavailable colors by intermingling the dots of two available colors. This is called *dithering*. Several ratios of black and white dots are perceived as shades of gray. (See Figure 7.15.) Extending this theory to color, a 50 percent blend of red and yellow dots would approximate orange, a 50 percent blend of red and blue would approximate purple, and so forth.

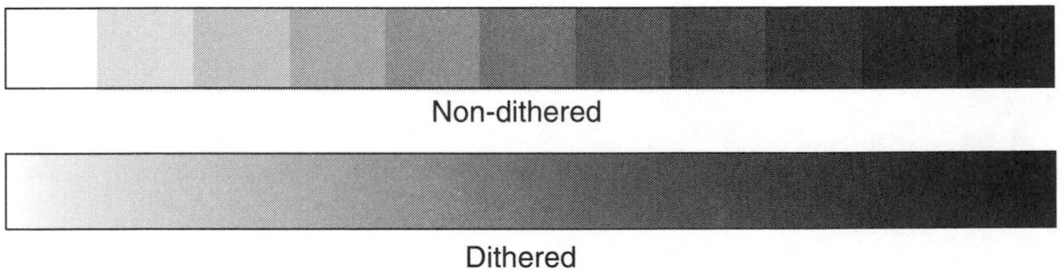

Figure 7.15

Dithering intermingles the dots where two different colors meet in order to create a smooth transition.

Non-dithered

Dithered

In multimedia graphics, dithering is used when filling an area with a gradation of colors so that the color transitions appear to be smooth. Dithering can also be used with reduced color palettes in order to fake colors that are not available.

Aliasing and anti-aliasing

In computer graphics, aliasing takes the form of jaggies, or the staircase effect exhibited by groups of pixels that are not confined to horizontal or vertical lines.

One way to soften the appearance of the edges is by adding transitional colors—a process appropriately known as *anti-aliasing*. (See Figure 7.16.) If you were placing a yellow triangle on a red background, anti-aliasing would smooth the appearance of the diagonal lines by changing the color of bordering pixels to orange. Anti-aliasing is specific to given graphics software; some implement it globally, while others localize its effect to certain painting tools. The quality of anti-aliasing depends heavily on having the necessary intermediate colors available in the palette.

Figure 7.16

Anti-aliasing smooths the appearance of jagged edges found in bitmapped images by changing the values of border pixels to intermediate colors.

aliased

anti-aliased

❖ Memory Trade-offs

Several factors are juxtaposed in a limited amount of display memory—image resolution, image size, color resolution, and the number of images. In many systems you can have either high physical resolution and low color resolution, or low physical resolution and high color resolution, for example. Some systems allow you to boost one or more of these factors by adding extra memory.

Display buffers

The memory required to hold the data for a single screen is often referred to as a *frame buffer*. Although this term is sometimes used to describe the display circuitry as a whole, some systems have enough video memory to hold more than one screen's worth of data.

One problem posed by multimedia is that animation redraws the screen very rapidly and not necessarily in sync with the rasterizing process of the monitor. Since the monitor is always looking at the display memory, the viewer often witnesses this single buffer being refilled with successive frames, yielding glitches in the animation. The solution is *double-buffering*—the use of two discrete buffers in one display card. With double-buffering, the next frame is always rendered in the buffer that the viewer is not watching; the buffers are simply swapped faster than the eye can see. This flip-flop process repeats so that redraws always occur in the invisible buffer where the viewer never sees them.

Double-buffering also helps in making transitions from one static screen to the next. With proper software support, a multimedia producer can display one image while loading the next into the invisible buffer. That image can then be popped right onto the screen or brought on with a fast transition that allows elements from both images to mingle.

Regardless of how it is used, double-buffering allows two images to reside in fast video memory simultaneously. This technology is made possible by a combination of hardware and software, not all of which support double-buffering. This can be a critical factor in determining the right tools for real-time animation and special effects.

❖ Enhancing Speed

The issue of throughput rears its ugly head when it comes to displaying graphics. Displaying graphics is very demanding for the microprocessor. The more information there is spatially and temporally, the more the CPU gets bogged down. Chapter 9 will explore design techniques that can enhance display speed. Several hardware solutions are available in the form of coprocessed video and graphics accelerators.

Coprocessed video

Graphics coprocessing technology dedicates circuitry to processing and displaying video without the help of the CPU. The CPU sends a management instruction, and the coprocessor does the rest, thereby freeing the CPU for other tasks.

Graphics accelerators

Screen refresh refers to the time it takes for the screen to redraw after you perform an operation that alters the screen. In various graphic applications, for example, screens sometime take a while to redraw after you move a menu or perform an operation that modifies the image. Due to the increase in the volume of data, 24-bit images take noticeably longer to refresh than 8-bit and lower resolutions.

Screen refresh can be greatly improved by installing a *graphic accelerator* board in a system bus slot. The distinction between graphic accelerators and processor accelerators is important. Processor acceleration affects the number crunching that determines what goes into the display buffer. For example, 3-D rendering time is enhanced by speeding up the computer's processing. Display accelerators simply enhance the speed with which graphic information in the display buffer fills the screen.

Although these are two independent processes and products, ideal system performance is enhanced by implementing both. At that point the system bus is often the slowest component, thus presenting a bottleneck. Some graphic accelerators and processor cards support direct connection, allowing the processor accelerator to send information directly to the display buffer associated with the graphic accelerator.

❖ Combining Monitors and Display Cards

The topics that follow relate to linking monitors and display circuitry. The issues involved primarily hinge on resolution, size, and scan formats.

Dot pitch

Monitors come with varying display resolution. This is the *dot pitch*—how fine the dots are. While dot pitch is roughly equivalent to its displayable dpi, it is independent of the dpi resolution coming from the computer. To clarify, the video buffer in the display card contains discrete digital information that the DACs turn into an analog signal. The electron guns in the monitor accept the analog signal and sweep it across the screen regardless of the dot pitch. If the dot pitch is fine enough to match the information conveying the original dpi, then you have a clear, crisp display; if the dot pitch is not as fine, the image will have less clarity and exhibit additional aliasing.

The distinction, then, is how much information is being sent by the display card compared to how much of it the monitor can let you see. Sending a monitor 800 x 600 pixels will yield more information than sending it 640 x 480. The only question is whether you'll be able to view that information clearly.

Size

Higher resolution and more pixels require larger memory. The price of RAM is the main reason 24-bit color costs more than 8-bit color. Not only do larger displays, like double-page color monitors, themselves cost more money, but the matching display cards require more RAM to accommodate the combined needs of more pixels and high color resolution.

Scan rates

You can't hook up any monitor to any display card: The scan rates of the two must match. More horizontal information requires a higher horizontal scan rate, and more vertical resolution requires a higher vertical scan rate. *Multisync*, or *multiscan*, monitors automatically adjust to sync rates within specified ranges. It is difficult, however, for manufacturers to build monitors that accept significant deviation in scan rates. This is partially because manufacturers determine the highest scan rate according to the dot pitch of the CRTs.

A 640 x 480 display has different display rate requirements than a 1000 x 800 display. While the larger horizontal display requires a higher horizontal scan rate, there are two choices for the vertical end: dedicate the display system to high range vertical scan rates for non-interlaced display, or restrict it to lower range scan rates and use interlace mode for higher resolutions. A display system employing the latter solution is typically a better choice for multimedia projects that must also accommodate interlaced video sources. (Refer to Part V for more information on the marriage of computer and video displays.)

BITMAPPED VERSUS STRUCTURED GRAPHICS

Video display memory contains bitmaps by nature. The actual graphics files may or may not be bitmaps. The other general file category is structured graphics. The differences are significant, and each has its own pluses and minuses.

❖ Bitmapped Graphics

Bitmapped graphics use one or more bit planes to represent the value of each pixel in an image file. Bitmapped graphics are often referred to as raster graphics, because the bitmap in the display buffer directly corresponds to the raster lines on the CRT. As such, they are the predominant type of graphic files used for multimedia presentations.

As discussed, bitmaps aren't necessarily the same resolution as the screen. The more resolution that is used to represent an image, the smoother the curves and other visual elements will appear when output to a device capable of rendering a matching resolution.

Fixed image resolution is fine when working with a device with the same resolution, but it has drawbacks when output or displayed on devices with varying resolution. Images whose actual resolution exceeds the screen resolution are inappropriate for final presentation on monitors. On the other hand, most film recorders benefit from higher resolution when making slides and transparencies.

While image processing programs can alter the resolution of an image, resolution-dependency is a major drawback in manipulating bitmaps. Their literal description of an image makes for imperfection in artistic tasks such as scaling and perspective. Such operations yield the greatest fidelity when performed with a conceptual knowledge of the image rather than a finite description.

Bitmapped images have fairly large file sizes. The greater the image resolution, image size, and color resolution, the more unwieldy the file becomes to store, manipulate, display, and animate. A 24-bit display with a size of 640 x 480 takes up about 921K before compression. The same size image at 300 dpi would require 3.8MB— and much larger image sizes and resolutions are common in the world of print production.

Some bitmapped file formats employ a form of automatic redundancy compression. Say you've drawn a horizontal black line 80 pixels long. Rather than storing 80 pieces of identical data, the software can store something like "color: black, occurrences: 80." In this manner, 80 pieces of data can be reduced to two or three. The Amiga IFF file formats are examples of built-in redundancy compression. (TIFF and TARGA offer redundancy compression as options.)

JPEG compression

One of the challenges in image file size is photorealism. Such images typically require 24-bit color, and the fact that colors vary subtly even between adjacent pixels renders redundancy compression fairly ineffective. The solution is to compress these images according to optical guidelines rather than statistical guidelines.

The *JPEG* (Joint Photographic Experts Group) compression standard is based on the way the human eye perceives color. Since people discern color areas and edges more readily than subtle shading, detail, and absolute brightness, JPEG works by compressing the variations in color and brightness. Put another way, the subtle color changes that defy redundancy compression are the most expendable form of information. JPEG compression is actually a series of steps:

- The RGB image is converted into a representation of luminance and chrominance that more closely parallels the eye's perception of light and color.

- The image is divided into tiles of 8 pixels by 8 pixels. The average luminance of each tile is evaluated with a process called *direct cosine transform* (DCT).
- Higher frequencies that are imperceptible to the eye are converted to zeros.
- Gradations of similar colors within tiles are quantized to more defined incremental levels. The amount of this quantization directly determines the amount of color compression.
- The restricted luminance values and quantized color values are subjected to standard redundancy compression techniques.

While images compressed via JPEG can be stored, copied, and sent over a modem, decompression must be applied in order for images to be viewed. This is accomplished by repeating the steps in reverse order. The decompressed files require considerably less memory than the original versions. Since the data that is discarded or quantized cannot be recouped, however, JPEG is a form of lossy compression. The compression ratio is dictated by the user. The amount of compression that is acceptable depends on the nature of each image. While compression approaching 200:1 is achievable, significant artifacting usually becomes apparent at between 20:1 and 25:1.

❖ **Structured Graphics**

The alternative to bitmaps is broadly termed *structured graphics*—also known as *object-oriented*, or *vector*, *graphics*. Rather than describing every dot in an image, these formats describe objects such as lines, circles, rectangles, and polygons. The descriptions typically include attributes like anchor points, size, angles, position, line weight, and hollow/fill characteristics. These commands are then rendered into a bitmap that matches the resolution of the output device (printer, monitor, film recorder). Structured graphics are said to be *device independent* or *resolution independent*—thereby obviating one of the problems of bitmapped graphics. (See Figure 7.17.)

Here's another way to look at structured graphics. A point represents a single conceptual position of infinitesimal size located on a plane. *Vector* refers to a conceptual line drawn between two points. You could draw that line as a series of individual dots with a pencil (high resolution), a felt-tip pen (medium resolution), or a magic marker (low resolution)—each yielding a physical representation with different resolution. The actual points and line are still conceptual: only their physical interpretation has changed.

Scaled bitmap   Scaled object

Structured graphics overcome the problem of bitmapped file sizes. If you draw a big solid green circle that covers most of the screen, the computer's internal representation of that might be something like "draw circle: center 4" in, 3" down; radius 2.5"; fill green." That set of instructions takes a handful of bytes; a bitmap of the same image could range from kilobytes to megabytes depending upon the physical and color resolution.

PostScript

PostScript is one of those seemingly simple ideas that everyone wishes they had thought of before somebody else got rich from it—in this case, Adobe. PostScript is a structured *page description language* (PDL) made up of object-oriented drawing commands that take the form of an ASCII text file. While this means that you can write your own PostScript program, popular implementations such as Adobe *Illustrator* and Aldus *Freehand* provide a graphic interface and standard drawing tools. The on-screen representations of lines, curves, and other geometric elements are internally represented as descriptions that ultimately become commands in the PostScript file that is saved.

PostScript graphics are only visible when interpreted by a PostScript-compatible output device and rendered at the resolution of that device. (PostScript drawing programs running on bitmapped displays provide on-screen representations that approximate the final output.) When output to a 300 dpi laser printer, the curves and gradients will be moderately smooth; when output to a 2540 dpi image setter, the curves and gradients will be pristine. This is one of the catalysts that has given rise to *service bureaus*. You can create and preview your documents on devices that are affordable enough for the average business, then send them to somebody else's high-priced, high-resolution output devices.

PostScript is universally accepted as a structured graphics and page definition language. Sophisticated programs are available across all major graphics platforms that can all output to any PostScript device. Files can even be interchanged across platforms. For example, not many service bureaus have Amigas, but you can use a modem to send an Amiga-generated PostScript file to a service bureau's Mac or PC from which the file can be printed.

PostScript has some disadvantages, however. For starters, PostScript interpreters are licensed by Adobe at a price that adds about $1,000 to the street price of the average printer. Also, PostScript has to calculate everything it displays, during both the creation and output processes. The more elements there are, the longer the calculations take.

In the last few years, *Display PostScript* has appeared, allowing PostScript files to be rendered directly to the screen. NeXT computers and Silicon Graphics IRIS Indigo have built-in Display PostScript and Digital F/X has licensed it for Macintosh computer/video applications. Display PostScript is expected to make stronger footholds over the next few years.

FONT TECHNOLOGY

In the computer world, *fonts*—or typefaces—are collections of graphic elements assigned to the keys on the keyboard. Their beauty and challenge is variety: There are hundreds of typefaces, each with many characters. There are also hundreds of useful sizes. Since the biggest usage of type is in printed materials, the various resolutions of hard-copy output devices are a consideration. The combination of all these options adds up to tremendous storage and memory requirements.

Not all fonts are always available: Each font you wish to use must be installed in the system. Beyond that, various manufacturers' solutions are a combination of bitmapped and structured graphics technologies.

❖ Bitmapped Fonts

Like all graphics, the fonts displayed on the screen are ultimately part of the bitmap in the display buffer. The variety of characters, sizes, and output resolutions associated with each font in a system make it impractical to keep a bitmap for each unique combination in memory, however. To cut down on all this font baggage, the most rudimentary solution is to support only the screen resolution. Next, only certain point sizes for each font are made available to the system as bitmapped characters, or *screen fonts*. The Amiga and stock

178

PC, for example, use only the specific point sizes installed when creating bitmapped images. If only 10-point and 12-point fonts are installed, you're out of luck if you want 11-point or 18-point. At this level, installed sizes will only be output to a printer at screen resolution.

The Macintosh operating system automatically interpolates a request for an uninstalled point size by scaling the closest installed size. While this is fast, the smoothness leaves much to be desired and the printed output is still 72 dpi.

Some PC systems employ printers that accept font cartridges containing the printer fonts for a given family. If a program encounters 12-point Helvetica, it displays the 12-point screen font and calls the higher-resolution version of 12-point Helvetica in the cartridge when printing. This approach leaves much to be desired in the world of graphic arts.

In a slightly more elegant solution, some printer manufacturers augment their screen fonts with bitmaps designed specifically for the resolution of their products. This higher-resolution version is sent to the printer when a print command is issued.

❖ Outline Fonts

A better solution is *outline font* technology—vector descriptions of fonts from which various sizes of bitmapped fonts can be interpolated. This scalable technology is implemented in both real-time and non-real-time forms.

Non-real time

SoftType on the PC, for example, creates bitmaps from outline fonts for various typefaces, but not in real time. Before using the fonts, the user tells the accompanying software to build screen fonts in specific sizes at screen resolution, along with matching bitmapped printer fonts at a specified resolution such as 300 dpi. The drawbacks are twofold: The user must predetermine each size that will be needed, and different printer fonts have to be built before outputting documents on printers of differing resolutions.

PostScript fonts

The most popular real-time outline font technology brings us back to PostScript. PostScript fonts are descriptions of the lines and curves that make up the characters. Bitmapped fonts are still used for screen display. When the document is output, however, the matching PostScript outline description is downloaded to the

PostScript output device where it is interpreted. As a result, the font is rendered in the desired size at the resolution of the output device.

PostScript fonts are said to be dumb fonts because the PostScript interpreter in the printer has to make all of the calculations. In an associated level, printer fonts must be downloaded for each weight and style within a common family. (PostScript printer fonts are referred to colloquially as *downloads* for this reason.)

Two versions of PostScript fonts are available—Type 1 and Type 3. The equations describing Type 1 fonts are encrypted in such a way that they print faster and render more faithfully at all sizes and resolutions than unencrypted versions. They also contain hints that help render point sizes smaller than about 12 points more accurately on output devices with 300 dpi or lower resolution. Type 1 fonts are not compatible with all PostScript clones and have no provision for stroked (unfilled) fonts, gray-scale fills, or composite characters. Type 3 fonts are unencrypted, so they print more slowly and less faithfully at all sizes and resolutions than do Type 1 fonts. They don't include hinting, but do provide for stroked characters, gray-scale fills, and composite characters.

These differences are summarized in Table 7.1. Until recently Type 1 was the exclusive domain of Adobe Systems, and all other PostScript fonts were Type 3. Adobe has since published the specs on Type 1 in light of competition.

Table 7.1. Differences between Adobe Type 1 and Type 3 formats.

Type 1	Type 3
Faster printing	Slower printing
Filled characters more true to outlines	Less-faithful filled characters
No composite characters	Can contain composites
No gray-scale fills	Can contain gray-scale fills
No stroked (unfilled) characters	Can contain stroked characters
Not compatible with all PostScript clones	Compatible with most clones
Can contain hints	Does not contain hints

Type 1 and Type 3 PostScript fonts can be accompanied by *Adobe Font Metrics* (AFM) files. These optional files contain special information about refinements, such as character widths and special kerned pairs, for a given typeface. Although PostScript fonts are available for both Mac and PC, they are not directly compatible—especially the metrics files.

Adobe Type Manager

A few years ago, *Adobe Type Manager* (ATM) became available for both the PC and Mac. ATM is a subset of PostScript that interprets and displays Type 1 fonts in real time. ATM interpolates requests for screen fonts in uninstalled sizes on the fly and renders them with moderate speed and optimum fidelity at display resolution. Further, ATM can send bitmaps of higher resolution to non-PostScript printers. For example, the HP DeskWriter and DeskJet printers are 300 dpi but not PostScript: ATM can render any PostScript font (and most object-oriented graphics) to one of these printers at 300 dpi. ATM requires that only one screen font size be installed along with the PostScript outline.

ATM must interpret each character, which is slower than displaying installed screen sizes. As a partial solution, ATM employs a temporary font cache that stores bitmaps for later use in a session after the first interpolation. Several utilities are available that can create permanent screen font sizes by interpolating an installed screen font size and the PostScript outline. Installation of screen fonts in the exact sizes required is recommended for multimedia applications, such as hypertext, that must display text on demand.

Adobe Multiple Masters

Adobe has recently announced *Multiple Masters*. This technology can render a Type 1 font in different weights based on two outlines containing light and heavy extremes. It can also render a range of widths based on two additional outline files containing condensed and expanded extremes.

COLOR MODELS IN COMPUTERS

Earlier in this chapter the additive properties of direct light, as well as the perception of brightness, hue, and saturation in a color space, were discussed. Computer graphics reference color in a variety of color spaces, or *color models*, such as RGB, HSB, and CMY—often within the same applications. Most color models have three basic parameters that can be visualized as three separate axes defining the color space. (See Figure 7.18.)

❖ RGB

RGB (red, green, blue) provides controls to directly manipulate the values of the numbers fed into each of the red, green, and blue DACs and, by extension, each electron gun in a CRT. This is the most direct and expedient mode for the computer to deal with. It is not always the most intuitive method for humans, however, since all colors are created and edited via extensive interaction of the three color controls. For example, all three controls must be set to

Figure 7.18

Various color models are optimized for specific tasks.

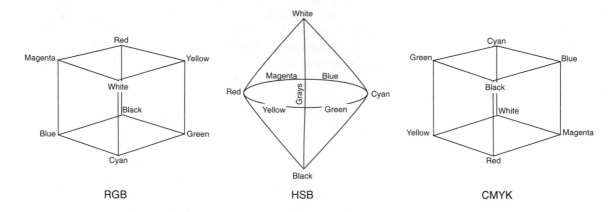

maximum to yield pure white or at minimum to yield pure black. Changing the overall brightness of a given color means altering each slider in equal increments.

❖ **HSB/HLS**

HSB (hue, saturation, brightness) is modeled after the human mind's perception of color described earlier in this chapter. This model is sometimes called *HLS* (hue, lightness, saturation). Brightness determines the overall amount of light intensity perceived by the eye. Technically, its value corresponds to the highest primary RGB value. Hue determines the spectral color added to that intensity, and saturation specifies the amount of that hue added to pure brightness. This system is much more intuitive for most applications since subtle variations in shading, color mixtures, and brightness are each easily adjusted with single controls. HSB is often offered as a parallel set of controls to RGB to provide the best of both worlds. HSB values are converted internally to RGB values for display.

❖ **HSV**

HSV (hue, saturation, value) is similar to HSB, except that parameters are specified in degrees and percentages. Hue is specified in the degrees of a color wheel, blue being 0° and 360°. Primary colors are 120° apart, complimentary colors are 60° apart, and direct compliments are 180° apart. This system is sometimes preferred by scientists and artists because commonly desired hue relationships can be specified precisely. Saturation and value are specified in percentage, with value being the same as brilliance in the HSB system.

❖ HSL

HSL (hue, saturation, luminance) is almost the same as HSB and HSV. Luminance differs from brightness in that its value is an average of the highest and lowest RGB primary values.

❖ CMY

CMY (cyan, magenta, yellow) is the subtractive color system used in print production. Why subtractive? RGB works by adding color intensities to a black screen, with full intensity of all colors yielding white. In printing, the paper is presumably white so colors have to be subtracted from it. Combining cyan, magenta, and yellow at full intensities yields black.

In practice, a black ink is also used independently of the CMY values in order to ensure the darkest blacks, enhance the range of densities, and help compensate for impurities in ink and paper. This is the standard CMYK, or *process color system*, used in four-color printing today. True CMYK separations can be viewed individually on a monitor, but not in combination since the color model is inverted. A more detailed discussion of CMYK and the color printing process is beyond the scope of on-screen multimedia.

❖ Pantone Color Matching System

Many image processing and color paint packages today support the *Pantone Color Matching System*. This is essentially a standard system that allows artists to reference thousands of specific colors by number—much like choosing paint at a store via a swatch booklet. As it is designed solely for ensuring exact color in the print process, a further discussion of Pantone is also beyond the scope of this book.

❖ ❖ ❖ ❖ ❖ ❖

This chapter has introduced the basic concepts of how light is transmitted in nature, perceived in human vision, and represented and displayed in computers. The next chapter takes a closer look at the tools used in creating computer graphics.

CHAPTER 8

Computer Graphics Tools

The technologies described in the previous chapter are the foundation of all computer graphics displays. This chapter focuses on the tools that enable creation of the visual content of multimedia presentations. Significant differences exist between displaying images on computer monitors and video monitors. Video technology and the issues of merging these two worlds are discussed in Part V.

The advantages of electronic art tools over traditional media are significant. The computer is extremely accurate and has measuring tools built in. Design elements can be moved, duplicated, and scaled instantly. Special effects that traditionally took hours to create now take seconds. And a simple command lets you back out of an unwanted modification.

At a fundamental level computers change the entire approach to creating graphics. Traditional artists often sketch out many drafts or test versions before putting paint to a canvas. Computer art tools breed experimentation. Since the image is always malleable, rough ideas can be transformed into a final image through a series of revisions, and existing art can be altered and manipulated easily without going back to the drawing board.

2-D AND 3-D COORDINATE SYSTEMS

Creating graphics is essentially the moving and placing of visual objects within a conceptual space. Our world and the objects in it exhibit the physical dimensions of height, width, and depth. Images on computer and video monitors are two-dimensional projections that lack depth. Further, display memory is a matrix that describe points according to their horizontal and vertical position on the screen. Projected images can only have perceived depth and perspective based on their relationship to other elements in the image.

In computer graphics, three dimensions are conceptualized along three axes: the *x-axis* is horizontal, the *y-axis* is vertical, and the *z-axis* runs from over your shoulder from an imaginary horizon within the screen. (See Figure 8.1.) Obviously, the computer can only physically place objects along the x- and y-axes. A significant difference between graphics applications is whether the computer is aware of the third dimension from the standpoint of the conceptual viewing space and/or objects within it.

If the computer is only aware of two axes for both the space and the object, you have classic *2-D graphics*. In these programs, the only way to create an impression of depth is through artistic means. Some programs are aware of a third dimension in the viewing space, but not with regard to objects. Objects in this *2-1/2-D* world are still flat, but the computer can intelligently scale and rotate them in a 3-D space. Graphics programs that are 3-D are actually aware of the third dimension in objects as well as the viewing space.

Figure 8.1

Three-dimensional systems reference all three physical dimensions to define a conceptual space.

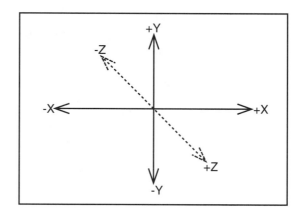

PAINT PROGRAMS

Paint programs loosely follow the metaphor of traditional paint and canvas in creating bitmapped graphics that are primarily 2-D. (Any perceived depth is the sole responsibility of the artist) The user has a palette of paint, painting tools, rulers, T-squares, protractors, compasses, and a canvas. There the similarity basically stops.

❖ Color Control

As in real painting, the colors placed on the canvas come from a palette. In electronic painting, the *color palette* varies depending upon the platform, display circuitry, application, and memory configuration. In general, images for multimedia work will be 8-bit or less in the interest of speed. The use of 24-bit color is largely reserved for image processing, frame-by-frame video output, and slide generation. (Outside the multimedia arena, 24-bit color is very important to print media.)

Color look-up tables in action

Color systems employing eight bits or less per pixel use a color look-up table (CLUT) as a palette. Each register in the CLUT acts as a paint pot. Most systems have a default palette that can be altered by the user. A color selector allows the user to specify the color value filling each register. This can be accomplished on a per-color basis via controls for RGB and/or HSB values. Some systems allow you to automatically create a smooth range of colors between two specified registers. Another option is the ability to load and save palettes for future use, including preset versions with shades such as earth tones, metallic, pastels, rainbow, and the like.

Any changes to the color value of a register will also change all pixels on the screen that were originally placed using paint from that location. If CLUT location 12 is navy blue and you paint a line on the screen using that color selection, changing the color of location 12 to light green will change the blue line you painted to light green as well.

Color cycling implements a sort of bucket-brigade in which the color in each CLUT register within a given range is poured into the successive register; the color in the register at the end of the range is transferred to the register at the beginning of the range. Continuing this end-over-end color swapping at a set speed provides an animation effect by moving the colors attributed to on-screen graphic elements rather than moving the actual pixels.

Foreground and background colors

Once a palette is established, you can begin painting with any of the colors on it. Most paint programs adhere to the concept of choosing current foreground and background colors. The *foreground color* specifies the paint to be used with the currently selected tool. The *background color* has several implications. First, it is the color to which the eraser tool erases and to which the screen changes when cleared. The background color usually also specifies the color that will be unaffected or transparent when cutting, pasting, and moving selections.

24-bit color

Systems with the ability to display 24-bit color rely on direct selection of color rather than a color look-up table. While the subtleties in shades and hues of 24-bit color can be breathtaking, finding a way to represent a palette with 16.7 million color choices can be a challenge—especially when an entire 640 x 480 display only has 307,200 pixels.

The solution is to choose one of the color models and divide color choices into ranges. The color selector and/or palette usually includes the ability to mix colors, just as you might with traditional paint and palette.

❖ Painting Tools and Modes

Most paint programs share a common core of painting tools such as pencil, paintbrush, spraycan/airbrush, lines, rectangles, squares, regular polygons, freeform polygons, circles, ellipses, arcs, and text. These tools often have associative attributes, such as line weight and anti-aliasing. These tools interact with other settings, such as color and ink modes, to determine exactly what winds up on the screen. Ink attributes can be roughly divided into two categories—painting effects that place new ink and those that rearrange existing colors.

Paint effects

Normal mode simply paints with the foreground color. *Cycle draw* draws while the foreground color steps through the color cycling range, making it possible to draw with a rainbow, for example. *Tint* has the effect of placing a colored gel over an area of the image. The basic tint color is taken from the hue and saturation of foreground color; the value or brightness is taken from the existing image to maintain the proper contrasts. *Blend* mixes the color of the foreground ink with that of the affected pixels. *Lighten* or *add* increases the brightness of all colors affected by the painting tool. *Darken* or *subtract* has the opposite effect, lowering all of the RGB values by uniform amounts.

Some programs have the ability to simulate different drawing media including charcoal, felt-tip, and crayon in addition to regular pencil and paint brush effects. (See Figure 8.2.) Programs are even beginning to emerge that automatically create strokes emulating the techniques of famous painters. All of these effects are very useful in creating images that don't look computer-generated.

A variety of preset patterns are usually available as an ink as well. Freehand painting with patterns can produce an effect akin to scraping off a layer of paint to reveal a wallpaper pattern underneath.

Figure 8.2

Various ink modes can be used in conjunction with painting tools.

Alteration effects

Smooth, or *blur*, is similar to a manual implementation of anti-aliasing. This nondirectional effect is sometimes implemented as a *waterdrop* tool due to its similarity to the effect of a waterdrop on a painted canvas. *Sharpen* is the opposite of anti-aliasing, adding distinction or harder edges to an area. *Smear, smudge,* or *blend* has the effect of dragging your finger from one area of wet paint through another with diminishing effect. *Diffusion* scrambles the pixels in the affected area to create a defocused look. *Mosaic* or *pixelate* creates a series of tiles of specified size out of the selected area. It has the visual effect of transforming the image to a lower resolution. (See Figure 8.3.)

Figure 8.3

Special ink modes can be used with paint tools to rearrange the existing pixels in an image.

Original

Sharpen

Blur

Smudge

189

❖ Fill Effects

Fill or *paint bucket* tools provide a way to fill any area of similarly colored pixels. The fill effect extends in all directions until it encounters pixels of dissimilar color. (Some applications also allow you to select an area with a lasso or similar selection tool, then fill the entire selection regardless of existing pixel colors.) The true power of these tools is in their ability to fill an area with something other than a solid color. A *gradient fill*, or *ramp fill*, covers the enclosed area with a range of color gradations according to a specified group of colors and a specified direction. (See Figure 8.4.)

Pattern fill is another popular option, filling an area with a pre-set pattern, such as a grid, brick wall, checkerboard, or other dot pattern. The selected pattern is repeated over and over as a tile to fill the desired area. Patterns are sometimes user-definable by direct editing or by selection tool. The latter allows you to copy any area of a painting and turn it into a fill tile.

Figure 8.4

Paint programs provide for a variety of area fill patterns including gradients, patterns, and tiles.

Gradient fill

Radial gradient fill

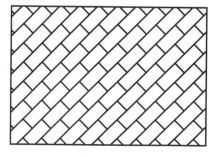

Pattern fill

Tile fill

❖ Area Selection and Transformation

One of the most powerful aspects of electronic painting is the ability to grab an isolated portion of the image and perform various operations on it. These operations range from simple movement to scaling, rotation, and dynamic transformations.

Selection

The area to be manipulated is usually selected via a *marquee*—a rectangular selection tool that derives its name from the dotted line that bounds the selected area. Other tools, such as the *lasso*, allow freehand selection of an exact area by tracing its perimeter. Any colors in the selection area that match the current background color will be transparent when the selection is pasted elsewhere.

Once the area is selected, it can be cut, copied, and pasted just as you might perform similar operations with text in a word processor. A simple cut can delete the element, cut-and-paste can be used to reposition the object, and multiple paste operations can duplicate the element as many times as needed. *Transparency* is a more advanced option that allows you to specify the opacity of a selection being pasted over another graphic element. Some systems allow you to turn a selection area into a tool that you can paint with. (See Figure 8.5.)

Figure 8.5

A selected area can be cut-and-pasted and often turned into a brush itself.

Transformation

After an area is selected, it can be transformed in a variety of ways. While implementation varies between programs, typical features include scaling, stretching, rotation, horizontal/vertical flipping, bending, skewing, and free-form distortion. (See Figure 8.6.) Another important transformation is perspective. While some programs are more intelligent about it, this attribute can add a sense of dimension to images.

Original

Perspective

Stretch

Flip

❖ Special Effects

Special effects provide some of the most striking differences between computer-generated art and art created by hand. As such, special effects capabilities are often the deciding factor between paint applications.

Mapping is essentially the process of selecting an area of a bitmap and making it conform to the shape of another area. *Symmetry* allows most painting actions to operate in many directions at once, much like drawing within a kaleidoscope. This effect might be used, for example, to yield an entire flower while drawing a single petal. A *trails* attribute can create effects such as concentric circles and radians from a single drawing action. *Trace* or outline functions allow you to make a simple outline from a complete element.

Much of the character of real-world images is a result of the relationship of objects to light sources. While most 2-D packages leave lighting attributes up to the user, a few more advanced paint packages allow positioning of an imaginary light in order to yield highlights and shadows automatically.

❖ Masks

Artists use *masks* to protect areas of a canvas from paint (hence the term masking tape). Masks in computer graphics serve the same functions as their real-world counterparts, but have much more power. For starters, anything that can be selected can usually be turned into a mask. Many programs provide for a mask layer that can be painted on using the entire compliment of painting tools. The entire layer can then be used as a mask. Masks can also often be specified by the colors which will be affected and unaffected by painting and selection operations.

Once created, masks can be used to protect certain drawing elements so that newly-drawn elements appear to be behind them. (See Figure 8.7.) They are also commonly used to give the effect of seeing through a cut-out into another scene in the background. Systems with alpha channels can use them for masks with 256 levels of transparency. The mask layer can be painted with 256 shades of gray that determine how much luminance of the image underneath will be allowed to shine through.

Figure 8.7

Masks can be used to protect portions of an image from painting effects.

Mask   Paint with mask protection

STRUCTURED DRAWING PROGRAMS

Structured drawing programs differ from painting programs in that they are entirely object-oriented. Images are created from descriptions of objects rather than from pixel-by-pixel representations. When you create a circle in a paint program, it merges into the overall bitmap. Enlarging the circle isn't much easier to do electronically than it would be with traditional paint and canvas. When you create a circle in a structured drawing program, it retains its identity as a circle. It can later be reselected, moved, resized, and given new attributes for weight, color, fill, and depth priority compared to other layers.

Structured drawing programs have several applications for multi-media graphics. First, some authoring packages support structured graphics. Structured files are significantly smaller than their bit-mapped counterparts. Second, some graphics applications allow the user to work within separate paint and drawing layers for the best of both worlds, although the tools available at each layer are typically less extensive than those found in software dedicated to one technique or the other.

❖ **Objects**

The drawing tools resemble some of those found in paint programs: squares, rectangles, lines, and curves. Unlike their bit-mapped counterparts, you can always click on these objects to make the anchor points, or *handles*, visible and manipulable. Objects composed of straight lines are sort of like a rubber band stretched around two or more nails: resizing and reshaping objects has the effect of moving the nails.

The more advanced structured drawing programs incorporate *Bezier curves*—sort of an electronic implementation of the mechanical French curve. The shape of Bezier curves can be altered either by moving the end point or by turning handles on the end points. (See Figure 8.8.)

Figure 8.8

Bezier curves have handles that can be used to alter the shape of a curve.

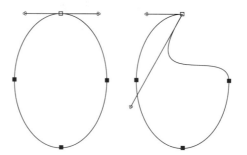

Object attributes that can be changed with a few mouse clicks include line weight, line type (solid, dashed, arrowheads), line color, fill color, and fill pattern. If an object is filled with diagonal lines and then scaled up, the pattern remains the same—there's just more of it. By contrast, a paint program would enlarge the pattern proportionally with the object. Text works like other objects in structured drawing. An invisible box is created to contain a group of characters you type. Selecting the text box thereafter provides a method of manipulating the text without re-entering it or affecting what's behind it in the image. All attributes including text content, position, font, size, style, and alignment can be changed at any point.

❖ Layers

Each object is drawn on its own conceptual *layer*. Each layer can be thought of as the electronic equivalent of acetate containing separate drawings. The order in which the layers overlap determines how the final image appears. (See Figure 8.9.) Filled objects occlude or mask underlying objects. Unfilled objects are transparent, allowing other layers to show through. Menu commands—such as "Send to front" and "Send backward"—are used to rearrange the order of the layers.

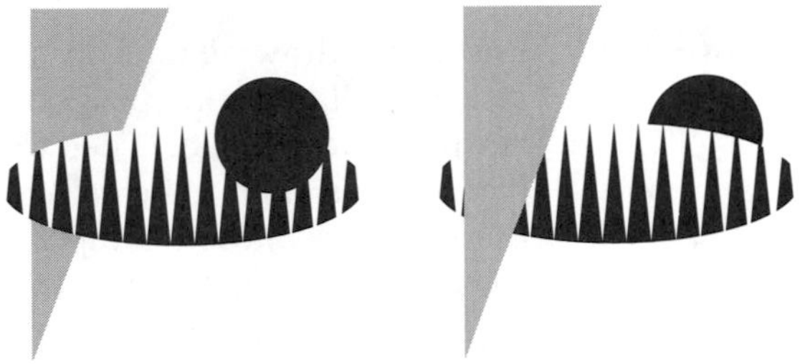

Figure 8.9

The priority of layers in a structured drawing program determines the visibility of different overlapping elements.

❖ Special Effects

Object-oriented programs contain some limited special effects depending upon the package. These can include stretching, shearing, perspective warp, and horizontal and vertical flips. Color palettes, dithering, and gradient fills are typically more limited than in bit-mapped programs.

❖ Resolution

Object-oriented programs can often print at a higher resolution than that of the screen. Although not directly related to on-screen multimedia work, supplements to a presentation can be laser-printed at higher resolutions. Some packages also offer PostScript output that can be sent to any PostScript device.

❖ The Best of Both Worlds

There are pros and cons to structured drawing programs and bit-mapped paint programs. Object-orientation makes structured drawing ideal for block diagrams, flow charts, and graphs where the information is both straightforward and subject to change. However, paint programs are significantly more powerful and intuitive as artistic tools.

Some packages offer two distinct layers for structured drawing and bit-mapped painting. Elements from one layer can usually be converted to the other format. This allows creation of block diagrams and similar graphics in the draw layer with artistic additions in the paint layer. The results can be saved for use in a multimedia presentation. File import and export options can be used in conjunction with other applications to make up for weak points in either layer.

ILLUSTRATION PROGRAMS

PostScript drawing packages are loosely referred to as *illustration programs*. Illustration programs are structured drawing programs in which every object is tied to a PostScript command. The resulting files are designed to be sent to PostScript output devices and are, therefore, resolution-independent. As such, they are primarily designed to create graphics that will be printed rather than displayed.

PostScript illustration programs have three basic functions in multimedia. First, some newer machines, like the NeXT and IRIS Indigo, utilize Display PostScript to render these types of files directly to the screen. Secondly, illustration software is capable of creating special effects that can be exported and translated for incorporation in bit-mapped images. Finally, they can be used to access and manipulate a wealth of PostScript clip art originally designed for desktop publishers.

❖ Paths

Illustration programs have almost all of the attributes of structured drawing programs. The biggest difference, other than PostScript output, is the concept of a *path*. A path is a series of anchor points that define segments to form a shape. In the case of straight line-segments, this is somewhat akin to the connect-the-dots drawings everyone has done.

Complex illustrations are much more than simple lines or curves—they are a series of subtly varying elements. Paths can be comprised of many points connected by lines with varying curvature. (See Figure 8.10.) Three types of point attributes determine what type of segment will be drawn between them. A point can be a corner joint between two straight line segments, a transition

Figure 8.10

Paths are collections of curves and lines that are grouped for common attributes and manipulation.

point between two Bezier curves, or a transition point between a line and a Bezier curve.

Points can be added to or deleted from a path as needed. They can also be changed to any of the point types as needed. Once the path is perfected, the segments can be grouped for common manipulation. An *open path* does not form a closed loop and might comprise a free-form sketch. A *closed path* connects with itself to form the outline of an object.

Various effects can be applied to paths. The line attributes of weight, color, and gradient can be adjusted on any path. Closed paths also have a wide variety of fill options, colors, and effects.

❖ Text Manipulation

One good reason to use an illustration package is to manipulate PostScript fonts. For starters, text can be stretched or compressed horizontally and/or vertically with less artifacting than with bitmap programs. Next, letters can be converted into paths. The path of each letter can be manipulated to achieve custom lettering. Text can also be bound to a path such as a curve for special effects. (See Figure 8.11.)

Figure 8.11

Illustration programs are great for manipulating PostScript fonts.

This is an example of text on a path

STRETCH

❖ Object Manipulation

Another common feature of illustration programs is automated duplication of an element. Changes in position, scale, rotation, and color can be specified so that they repeat a given number of times. This helps take the tedium and guesswork out of repetitive effects. Some illustration programs can specify a transition between two objects over a certain number of steps. This process is known as *morphing* (short for metamorphosis) and is found on only a handful of graphics products in any category. (See Figure 8.12.)

Figure 8.12

Morphing provides an automatic transition between two objects in given number of steps.

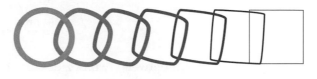

❖ Graphs

While plenty of spreadsheets and dedicated programs generate graphs, most are restricted in their customization abilities. Adobe *Illustrator* can automatically generate a wide variety of graphs and charts from numbers entered or imported into a matrix. The resulting objects can then be manipulated for a more artistic look. Even without automatic data importing, illustration programs can be quite useful in creating compelling charts and graphs because they combine artistic control with the malleability of structured objects.

❖ Using Bitmaps with Illustration Programs

Applications such as Corel DRAW! and Aldus *Freehand* allow color bitmap images such as scans to be imported and placed in the background for tracing purposes. Automatic tracing functions can produce a line art version of the image that can then be manipulated extensively. This automated feature works with varying degrees of effectiveness depending upon the software and complexity of the bit-mapped image. (Sometimes you get a billion little points and paths that are more of a hassle to clean up than they're worth.) The manual method of tracing over key elements of the bit-mapped image to create paths is often faster and more efficient. The bitmap itself cannot be edited and the layer is discarded after the trace.

Bitmaps can be imported and left in the background in the production of printed materials and slides. A high-resolution color bitmap merged with PostScript elements is being used more and more at the high end of these processes.

2-D ANIMATION

The basic theory of animation is simple: if a series of progressively varied static images are displayed fast enough, the viewer perceives motion. The average viewer perceives animation as more than a series of individual frames at around 16 *frames per second* (fps). The 24 fps frame rate used in film ensures smoothness.

Animation has come a long way since Walt Disney's Steamboat Willie made its silver screen debut more than 50 years ago. At worst, each frame was painstakingly drawn by hand. At best, each frame contained foreground character movements that were drawn by hand over a static or scrolling background. Anyway you cut it, that's a lot of work when 24 frames per second are flying by.

While standard animation techniques have certainly evolved, the computer has found a home as an animator's power tool—even at modern-day Disney Studios. The overall visual effect is still the same: enough individual frames are presented each second for smooth movement. Today's software packages, however, provide many different methods by which those frames can be generated.

❖ Types of 2-D Animation

In one sense 2-D animation has the additional dimension of time. One of the main distinctions between 2-D animation programs is the method in which images move through time and space. These include page flipping, cel animation, and object animation.

Page flipping

Since animation is a series of rapidly-projected frames, the simplest form of computer animation is *page flipping*. This term is derived from flip books that you bend and release to make the gradually changing images on successive pages seem to move. To create such animation on the computer, you can step through the frames and paint on each one electronically with the standard digital painting tools discussed earlier. You can also import images that have been created in other paint programs as backgrounds, objects, and/or entire frames. Frames can be inserted, deleted, rearranged, and copied, and individual elements can usually be cut-and-pasted between frames.

Cel animation

Characters like Fred Flintstone, Mickey Mouse, and Bugs Bunny are created in a process called *cel animation*. This term gets its name from the technique of layering multiple pieces of clear celluloid, or *cels*, that contain various elements of each frame. For starters, the background for a given scene need only be created once since all the action takes place in the foreground. A series of foreground cels depicting each unique character movement is then created.

Each final frame is created by overlaying one or more foreground cels over the background and filming it. (See Figure 8.13.) (The background is usually larger than the frame to allow the character to be positioned in his world.)

As Fred gets bowled over by an overeager Dino, only those two characters need be drawn for each frame since the background doesn't need to change. If Fred is standing frozen in his living room taking some obligatory admonishment from an off-screen Wilma, a single foreground cell can be rephotographed in position over the living room background for the duration of Wilma's tirade. If only Fred's mouth moves in response, a main cel might be created without the mouth, allowing the animator to overlay another series of cels containing various lip positions. Finally, if Fred walks through Bedrock, the animator first creates cels in which Fred simply walks in place. A separate background is created that is much longer than the width of a frame. For each final frame, a foreground cel is positioned on the background with a slight horizontal offset from the last and the camera is moved to compensate.

The movements of characters begin as sketches on onionskin. Only important *key frames* that mark significant action, events, and transitions are sketched initially. The frames in between are then sketched, or *tweened*, laying each new onionskin over the previous ones to gauge motion. This pencil test stage is primarily used for perfecting fluid motion, timing, and expression. Once the pencil test is approved, refined versions of the test frames are inked or traced onto clear celluloid. Finally, the areas enclosed by the inked outlines are painted.

Several animation programs provide the metaphor of cel animation (most notably Disney Animation Studio for the Amiga). The computer version of cel animation is used primarily for scenes that emulate traditional cartoons. In other words, while pristine logos might fly across the screen with smooth, predictable motion that is easily automated, characters like Fred and Wilma require each foreground cel to be drawn or altered by hand. Cel animation requires patience, practice, artistic skill, and a knowledge of organic motion in order to create anything close to Hollywood quality.

Object animation

Object animation loosely refers to moving unchanging objects over a series of frames. Where cel animation requires a different foreground element for each frame, a 2-D object such as a flying logo or spinning photo can be animated much more easily and automatically. The object's position and orientation at least along the x- and y-axis can change to provide a different orientation. The better packages support 2-1/2 D animation where 2-D objects can be moved and rotated in relation to a third axis as well. Some products also support objects that change in cyclic fashion, such as a walking figure or moving piston.

Most animation programs of this type provide for automation of object motion. The user typically specifies the number of frames, the start or end frame, the start or end object position, the distance the object is to be moved along each axis, and the amount of rotation around each axis. (See Figure 8.14.) This combination provides for slides, scrolls, zooms, spins, and flips in various combinations.

Figure 8.14

Object animation can be used to automate the movement of various elements along their own paths and axes.

Object movements can be automated forward or backward. If a start position and frame are defined, the specified moves are rendered over subsequent frames; if an end position and frame are defined, the specified moves are rendered up to that frame. Several different automated moves can be rendered to successive sets of frames in order for an object to change direction and/or rotation. Autodesk Animator allows the user to draw a path freehand that the object will follow over a series of frames.

Multiple objects can be animated in similar fashion, like a graphics version of the audio overdub. This allows very complex scenes to be created. Provision is made to prioritize the visibility of various objects. (Typically the objects rendered last have visual priority.) Another power feature is the ability to merge animations either sequentially or by controlled compositing.

Object animation lends itself to special effects. A handful of animation programs support the animated extension of morphing—*polymorphic tweening*. This feature automatically creates a gradual transition between two objects over a specified number of moves.

Some programs also provide for duplication of object movement. Several products, such as Deluxe Paint and Animator Pro, allow the user to capture object movements over a series of frames as a paint brush. You can then literally paint with the animated brush over one or more frames! This is quite handy for effects like quickly turning one flying bird into a flock.

❖ Speed and Memory Issues

The amount of data that must be processed and displayed for each frame of animation directly impacts on the speed with which a series of frames can be played. It also places practical limitations on the file sizes required for animation of any significant length or content. Chapter 9 offers some tips on cutting down this volume of data. Two technology solutions are available that also address this issue—motion compression and direct disk access.

Motion compression

Compression is a common solution to media storage and throughput problems. In the case of animation, *motion compression* stores the starting frame and then calculates and records only the differences between subsequent frames—a process called *frame differencing*. The resulting data stream is then typically compressed using *run-length encoding* (RLE). (This is a form of lossless compression.) On playback, the processor only has to deal with computing and displaying those differences rather than handling the volume of data required for a sequence of full frames.

Motion compression is most effective when there are small changes between frames, such as one or more small objects moving across a static background. The more change there is, the more information about those changes that must be stored and processed. Animations that contain radical changes in background or overall composition are therefore least enhanced by motion compression.

While the calculations required for the compression process don't usually happen in real time, software-only playback of those files is fast enough for some real-time animations. Due to throughput and storage limitations, motion compression is used in most animation programs. Several stand-alone packages are also available that will take a series of standard images or successive frames and apply motion compression. (Hardware compression is being developed that dramatically improves the performance of animations and video.)

Direct disk access

Some animation formats only support the ability to access successive frames from RAM, placing a severe limitation on animation length and content. More recent developments provide the ability to access the disk directly. While this doesn't speed up the process, it does pave the way for significantly longer animations.

3-D GRAPHICS

Three-dimensional graphic technology is behind the eye-popping fly-through logos of network television, the electronically-generated world of Disney's *Tron*, and special effects in movies like *The Abyss* and *Terminator 2*. The quantum visual leap that 3-D has taken over 2-D is due to a fundamental difference in the way the computer treats 3-D graphics. The user provides a three-dimensional description of each object's characteristics and their relationships to each other, the 3-D space, light sources, and the viewer's position. The software then computes this data and renders the scene based on the information supplied. To see the scene from another perspective, you simply change your viewpoint location and let the computer do the dirty work.

Since rendering a single frame can take hours on the average desktop computer, creating 3-D graphics is a study in patience. This process is also distinctly more like an exercise in mechanical drafting than like the traditional drawing and painting process. (Indeed, the CAD programs used by engineers are close relatives.) In return for patience, 3-D can provide spectacular results, stunning animation, and uncanny realism. The process is roughly divided into stages of modeling, scene description, rendering, and animation.

❖ 3-D Modeling

3-D *modeling* is the process of defining the shape and other characteristics of objects that will later be rendered and animated. There are several different types of modeling—solid, polygonal-surface, wire-frame, and parametric. Each has its own strengths and weaknesses, and the more advanced modeling packages include several modeling techniques.

Types of modelers

Solid modeling builds complex objects from simple 3-D solids or *primitives* such as cubes, cylinders, and cones. Most solid modelers allow the user to modify the object by reshaping it, cutting holes in it, and so forth—similar to sculpting. This method is usually used when cut-aways or inside views of objects are required.

Wire-frame modeling employs 2-D and 3-D skeletons of objects such as polygons, circles, and cubes. (See Figure 8.15.) Curves are usually supported in the form of *splines*. Although there are different types of splines, they are essentially curved lines with a mathematical relationship to two or more points. Modeling programs often implement splines with control levers similar to Bezier curves.

Figure 8.15

Wire-frame modeling is one of the most common methods of creating 3-D objects.

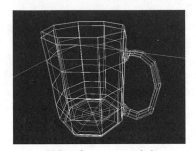 

Wire frame model   Rendered image

Various wire-frame elements can be joined at their vertices to form an object. Many packages allow the vertices to be moved individually in order to deform and reshape the object easily. The planes formed by the various wire-frame elements define surfaces that will later be rendered. Alternately, a series of linked objects can serve as a sort of skeleton over which the computer can drape a surface or skin—hence the term *skinning*. (The terms *lofting* and *loafing* are used interchangeably, the latter presumably named after the idea of reverse-engineering a loaf of bread from slices.) This technique can produce objects that are very difficult to produce by other methods.

Polygonal-surface modeling employs a series of 2-D polygons that are linked together and grouped to construct objects. The triangle is the most commonly-used polygon due to its flexibility. Polygons are useful for faceted surfaces; however, creating rounded or smooth surfaces can require a significant number of polygons. Polygons are often represented during the modeling process as a wire frame.

Polygons, circles, and other 2-D objects can be *extruded* to add a third-dimension. (See Figure 8.16.) An extruded circle becomes a cylinder, for example. Extrusion is popular for transforming existing 2-D artwork, such as a font or an architectural floor plan, into 3-D entities. Extruded objects can often be lathed around the axis of extrusion, similar to lathing a piece of wood. Lathing is handy for creating objects with polar symmetry, such as bottles and wine glasses.

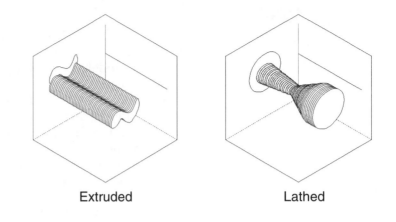

Extruded   Lathed

Surface properties

Once the shape of the model is created, the surface properties are specified. These properties include many of the object qualities described in Chapter 7—color, material, specular reflection, diffusion coefficient, opacity, index of refraction, and so forth. This prepares the objects for the rendering process.

Modeling environment

Modeling three-dimensional objects with a two-dimensional screen and mouse is challenging, to say the least. Two basic approaches are taken to the dilemma of user interface—world-view and tri-view. *World-view*, or single-view, environments give users one window on their virtual world: Navigation is accomplished by rotating and zooming with various key combinations and mouse moves. *Tri-view* provides a smaller window for each of the three axes, often with a fourth window showing a perspective that is not directly aligned with any axis. (See Figure 8.17.)

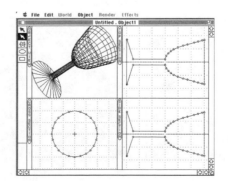

❖ 3-D Scene Description

After individual objects have been modeled, they must be arranged in a scene before rendering. Some packages incorporate scene description in the modeling software, others in the rendering software, and yet others in a dedicated motion-control module.

Scene description is fairly straightforward. The first step is defining the orientation, or *attitude*, of the modeled objects with respect to the virtual world. Attitude is defined by three factors: *roll* is rotation around the x-axis, *yaw* is rotation around the y-axis, and *pitch* is rotation around the z-axis. (See Figure 8.18.) Some packages also allow the option of importing and positioning a 2-D bit-mapped image in the scene. The next step is positioning virtual light sources in relation to the objects and specifying their intensity, color, and focus. Finally, the position of the viewer or camera is also specified.

❖ 3-D Rendering

After the objects and scene have been described to the computer, it's time for the final step of *3-D rendering*. This process turns descriptions of three-dimensional objects into standard two-dimensional graphic files that can be displayed on a monitor.

Chapter 7 explained that objects are visually perceived when the waves from light sources are reflected into the viewer's eyes. Some rendering packages employ *ray tracing* technology to simulate this effect. To be completely faithful to reality, the computer would have to calculate the paths of an almost infinite number of light waves, including those that never reach the eye. In actuality, ray tracing reverse-engineers this process so that only the calculations pertinent to visible screen pixels are performed. Even at its simplest,

Figure 8.18

Object rotation around the three axes are defined as roll, yaw, and pitch.

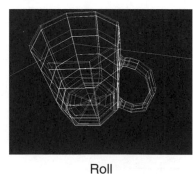
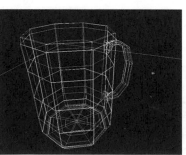
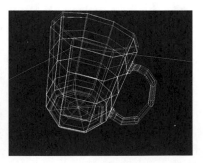

Roll   Yaw   Pitch

ray tracing must take into account what objects or portions thereof are visible to the camera and what is occluded by other objects. This is the function of the *hidden-surface algorithm*.

Shading models

Ray tracing must also take into account all object aspects specified in modeling, such as color, surface shapes/angles, and reflectivity. Even when limited to perceived pixels, ray tracing can take quite a long time to calculate and render a scene. The more complex the scene and the objects in it, the longer the rendering process. Using ordinary personal computers, rendering times take anywhere from half an hour to all night. Since that's a long time to wait to see whether you're even in the right ballpark, several non-ray tracing *shading models* are available that trade speed for realism. The faster, less realistic models are used for tests, while the slower, more realistic models or ray tracing are used to produce the final images.

Lambert shading, or *flat shading*, is the simplest and fastest shading model. The shading for each polygonal facet is determined based upon how light is reflected around the normal at any one point on the surface. Each point on a given facet is shaded the same using this method, yielding very fast rendering times. Lambert shading is noticeably lacking in subtle shading and highlights. Given Lambert shading, the only way to create smoother objects is to increase the number of polygons. Smooth-shading algorithms circumvent this problem by assuming that the existing polygons are actually smooth curves. Two popular smooth-shading models are Gouraud and Phong shading.

Gouraud shading (pronounced "guh-row") averages the normals of surrounding surfaces to establish a normal for the vertex, then calculates the shading for each vertex. Finally, the shading of the vertices that bound a polygon are averaged across the the polygonal surfaces, yielding diffuse shading. Gouraud shading is much more realistic than Lambert shading and is still relatively fast, but it is not without drawbacks. Delineations between facets are softened but not eliminated—an effect that becomes more noticeable as curvature increases. Highlights can only be calculated if they naturally fall on vertices. The shape of the facets also creates some artifacts that result from and betray the presence of underlying facets.

Phong shading is another type of smooth shading that resolves the aforementioned problems by calculating the appropriate shading values for each pixel. Phong shading is required for accurate shadows and yields better diffuse and specular reflection. As a result of the increased calculations, Phong shading takes significantly longer than Gouraud and Lambert shading.

Mapping

In rendering, mapping is the process of applying a two-dimensional image to a three-dimensional surface. While the use of maps increases the rendering time, the results can be well worth the wait. Several forms of mapping are popular in rendering packages.

Projection mapping is used to project a 2-D image like artwork or a photograph onto a 3-D surface. This is also called *texture mapping* when the image is a surface texture such as wood or marble. *Procedural shaders* create a surface texture map using algorithms that enable the user to control characteristics such as the burl and grain of the wood or the turbulence within the marble. *Reflection mapping* resembles projection mapping except that the algorithms employed create the illusion of the image being reflected in the surface. *Bump maps* translate the brightness levels of the map pixels into apparent height or depth in order to create the illusion of a surface that is not smooth. *Opacity mapping* allows the brightness values of the mapped image to determine surface opacity.

Most mapping schemes have several options regarding the relationship of the 2-D map to the 3-D objects. Coordinates usually can be specified to position the map as desired. Maps can simply be projected onto the surface, much like using a slide projector. They can also be wrapped around the object in all directions as in the case of a ball or wrapped around only one axis as in the case of mapping a logo on a soft drink can. Provisions are also made for maps that are smaller than the surface onto which they are being mapped: A single iteration can be applied like a decal or the image can be tiled in all directions out to the edges.

Other rendering options

Several other options offer trade-offs in rendering time versus image quality. Anti-aliasing can usually be turned on and off because this process consumes more time. In addition to choice of shading model, some packages also provide low-resolution previews with respect to pixel resolution, color resolution, or both. The better rendering packages support several output formats other than the resolution of standard computer monitors. Common options include film recorders with more than 1,000 lines of resolution and overscanned video.

❖ 3-D Animation

Like 2-D animation, 3-D animation is a series of frames that depict motion when viewed in rapid sequence. Each frame is rendered separately, and the illusion of motion is created by making changes to the object positions and scaling, lighting attributes, or viewer angle in the scene description.

Object motion allows objects to move independently from other elements. Scaling an object over time without changing other objects or the camera position makes the object appear to grow or shrink. Moving a focused light source over time can simulate a moving spotlight or searchlight. Dimming the light source over time will create a fade-out. Moving the camera allows the viewer to zoom in or out, walk or fly around the scene, and even pass through openings in objects. The TV network fly-through logos are examples of many of these effects used in combination.

Linking and hierarchy

Few objects stand alone in the real world; most are parts of other objects and have defined relative motion. The keys on a computer are attached to the keyboard, pistons in a car are connected to a crankshaft, and even the pages of this book are attached at the spine. In the 3-D world these items would be linked so that they could be manipulated in unison within the scene. The more advanced animation packages allow multiple objects to be linked hierarchically as they would be in reality. A finger is attached to a hand, which is attached to an arm, which is part of the body as a whole. In modeling such a construct, repositioning any element should affect the position of the elements lower in the hierarchy but not necessarily those above. (Moving the hand will move the finger, but not necessarily the arm or body.)

Hierarchy brings with it the parallel concept of restricted movement. Human joints are only capable of turning and bending in certain directions and at certain angles. Similarly, the movement of a piston is confined to its cylinder. Advanced modeling packages allow the user to restrict the possible motion of hierarchal objects. Hierarchy and restricted movement are very helpful in achieving realism when automating the 3-D animation process.

Linking can also be used for camera and light sources. Linking the camera to a moving object, for example, would force the viewer to follow the object. Linking a light source to a moving object yields the effect of a theatrical follow spot.

Automated motion

As with 2-D animation, key frames are used in 3-D animation as well. The software calculates the tweens over a specified number of frames and provides a wire-frame or bounding box rough of the animation before you commit to rendering. Options include ease-in and ease-out time curves. Advanced packages incorporate 3-D morphing for some very cool effects.

Viewing and recording 3-D animation

Once rendered, each image in a 3-D animation must be saved in one form or another. Saving them to disk is an option, but lots of disk space will be required even for short segments. The real problem, however, is viewing the animation. It usually takes a few seconds to retrieve and display 24-bit images. Accessing and displaying the number of frames per second required for animation is out of the question given current desktop technology.

One solution is to render images with either 8-bit resolution or smaller physical size. Alternately, 24-bit images can be cut down to 8-bit resolution with image processing packages. The files can then be placed into a 2-D animation program where the motion can be compressed.

Since the goal of most 3-D animation is to create stunning segments in 24-bit color, another solution is required—recording to video. After each frame is rendered, it is recorded sequentially to a frame on a video recorder, the next 3-D frame is rendered and recorded to the next video frame, and so forth. When played back in real time, the video will display the animation in all of its glory. This process requires a frame-accurate video recorder and is typically automated under software-control. This topic is discussed further in Part V.

IMAGE PROCESSING SOFTWARE

Image processors are increasingly important tools in the creation of effective electronic images. As software becomes more sophisticated, the fundamental differences between paint programs and image processors are becoming blurred. Both devices manipulate bitmaps. Their most fundamental difference correlates to the difference between the traditional disciplines of graphic art and film: The paintbrush is used to build an image in localized strokes, while film images are processed in a more global manner. The artist chooses brush, paint, and technique carefully for each motion. The photographer manipulates film, light, and chemicals in order to attain the overall light and color balance desired, or to create composite images.

The diverse capabilities of the image processor can be distilled to two basic functions for multimedia purposes—optimization of scanned images and special effects. Most image processing programs have the same basic tools found in paint programs—brushes, fills, cut-and-paste, rotate, flip, and so forth. The following discussion focuses on the areas that differentiate image processors from paint programs.

❖ Color Space

Image processors are available in both color and gray-scale versions—this discussion assumes a color system. The original and most widespread use of image processors is in preparing color separations of scanned photographs for printed output. As computer graphics and multimedia evolved, image processors became more adept at converting images between a variety of color spaces. Many color image processors can work in CMYK, RGB, HSB, and other color spaces. In most cases, each of the components in a given color space represents a *channel* that can be individually viewed, edited, and manipulated.

Basic controls

Basic controls affect common attributes of an image or selected area that result from poor photographs or poor scans. Brightness controls the overall luminance of all pixels. *Contrast* affects the balance between dark and light portions of the image. *Equalize* distributes the brightness values of pixels evenly across the brightness range, usually enhancing the contrast. Gamma affects the mid-range values, like details in shadows, without altering the extreme light and dark sections. These basic controls are often easier to use in conjunction with a *histogram*—a plot of how many pixels in an image or channel occur at various intensities. (See Figure 8.19.)

Figure 8.19

Histograms can aid in adjusting overall image attributes.

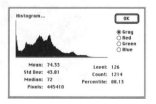

These types of controls can also be applied to individual channels or color space components. In RGB mode, for example, the entire image can be made to look more reddish by brightening the red component. In HSB mode, the entire image can be made more saturated in color by boosting the saturation control. A selected area can be altered in hue to a completely different set of colors: a green apple could be turned into a red apple using this technique, for example. These global controls offer far more powerful color manipulation than the localized per-color versions common to paint programs.

Palette creation

One critical function for multimedia is the ability to convert potentially thousands or millions of colors into a color look-up table with eight or fewer bits of resolution. Image processors are the consummate programs for this type of task. Suggestions for optimizing this process are discussed in the next chapter.

Sometimes extremely limited palettes are desired for artistic effect and/or reduced file size. *Threshold* determines the brightness value used as a breakpoint when converting an image with more than one bit plane to a single black-and-white bit plane. Everything above the threshold will be white, everything below will be black. (See Figure 8.20.) *Posterize* reduces the image to a user-determined number of colors. While threshold and posterize limit the number of colors in the image, they do not automatically reduce the number of bit planes.

Figure 8.20

Threshold is useful in turning color or gray-scale images into monochrome images.

Original   After Threshold

❖ Resampling

Scanned images are often the wrong size and/or resolution for a presentation. Another useful feature of image processors is the ability to *resample*, or alter, the resolution and size of an image. Given a fixed size, resampling to a lower resolution discards pixels, while resampling to a higher resolution adds pixels through interpolation. While the results of the latter are not as good as scanning or creating the image at a higher resolution in the first place, they are better than simply scaling up a bitmap in a paint program.

Resampling can affect image size as well as resolution. Say that you have an image that is 3" x 5" at 300 dpi and are using a monitor with 75 dpi. Image processors allow you to alter the viewing magnification so that you can see every pixel. Most multimedia programs, however, would display that image by preserving the size and displaying only every fourth pixel at screen resolution. (A few would correlate each 300 dpi image pixel to a 75 dpi display pixel, displaying only a portion of the image.)

If the image is to remain 3" x 5", the undisplayed pixels are extra baggage. Resampling to 75 dpi will produce the same display and a file one-sixteenth the size of the original. If the original image is doubled to 6" x 10" during the resampling process, every other pixel can be discarded in the process. The image fidelity will improve because more original pixels are displayed, but the file size will be only one-fourth of the original. Finally, one-to-one pixel conversion to 75 dpi would yield full fidelity in a virtual 12" x 20" image that could be cropped for a screen display.

❖ File Format Interchange

The power of image processors to perform operations on image size, image resolution, and color resolution works hand-in-hand with the ability to import and export a wide variety of graphic file formats. Image processors are often thought of and used secondarily as a sort of Grand Central Station for the interchange of graphic files.

❖ Advanced Selection

Selecting areas is more difficult with photorealistic images than with electronically-generated images. What the human eye perceives as an object, background, or pattern is just a series of pixels to the computer—usually pixels of differing colors. Many image processors offer the ability to select areas based on similarity of pixel colors or patterns. An associated strength adjustment determines how much deviation the program allows during the automatic selection process. This single-click solution is extremely powerful, since scanned photos can exhibit subtle differences in shading throughout a conceptual area. Many image processors also allow selection areas to be defined using object-oriented lines and paths. This permits the perimeter of the area to be extremely fine-tuned before an operation is performed on the selection.

Once defined, most global operations can be restricted to selected areas rather than the entire image. The selection can be

Figure 8.21

Selected areas can be cut-and-pasted with a variety of sophisticated attributes.

| 100% Opacity | 50% Opacity | 100% Opacity—
darken only | 100% Opacity—
lighten only |

inverted so that everything previously deselected is now selected and vice versa—a feature helpful in creating masks or isolating image elements. Selections can be cut and pasted with a variety of sophisticated options. (See Figure 8.21.) *Transparency* levels determine how much of the background image will show through the pasted object. *Feathering*, or *vignetting*, pastes an object with increasing transparency toward the edges for a smooth transition into the background.

❖ Channel and Multi-image Operations

Channels can be used for other purposes than color adjustment in more sophisticated software. Additional channels can be created and used as masks and overlays that can be manipulated separately, then combined with the original image in a variety of ways. For example, a channel might be created in which bit-mapped text is created and edited. When the the text is perfected, the channel can be merged with the main channels of an image so that the text is added to it.

Images can be combined in a wide variety of ways using image processors. Many systems allow the effects to work with individual channels or entire images. These effects operate by evaluating the corresponding pixels on two images or channels and performing some mathematical calculation. Common calculation options include adding, subtracting, multiplying, or differencing the pixel values, choosing either the lighter or darker values, or compositing the images with an optional mask. (See Figure 8.22.)

Figure 8.22

Image processors can perform powerful calculations to combine images in a variety of ways.

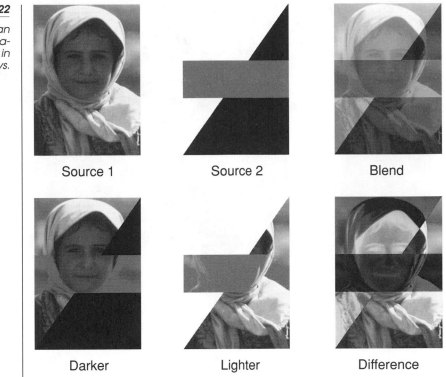

Source 1   Source 2   Blend

Darker   Lighter   Difference

❖ **Filters**

Filters can be applied to selection areas or entire images to subtly enhance the image or radically alter it. These effects are calculation-intensive and frequent usage can quickly lead to a desire to buy a processor accelerator. *Blur filters* soften the image by reducing the contrast between adjacent pixels. Variations on that theme include motion blur and radial blur. *Sharpen* filters increase the contrast between adjacent pixels to create a focusing effect. *Despeckle* filters can be used to remove the dot patterns that result from scanning an image that was originally created with the color printing process.

A wide variety of special effects available on more advanced packages can be used to add artistic style. (See Figure 8.23.) These include distorting the image via digital noise, waves, twirls, pinches, and altering the entire plane of the image via spherizing or polar coordinates. Diffusion jumbles the pixels for a more painted or frosted-glass appearance. *Emboss* creates the effect of stamping or raising an imprint of the image in a surface. *Trace* highlights the edges and discards the rest of the image. *Mosaic* averages the pixels within a certain tile size to one color per tile. *Facet* and *crystallize* create effects that emulate their namesakes. The list of filter effects

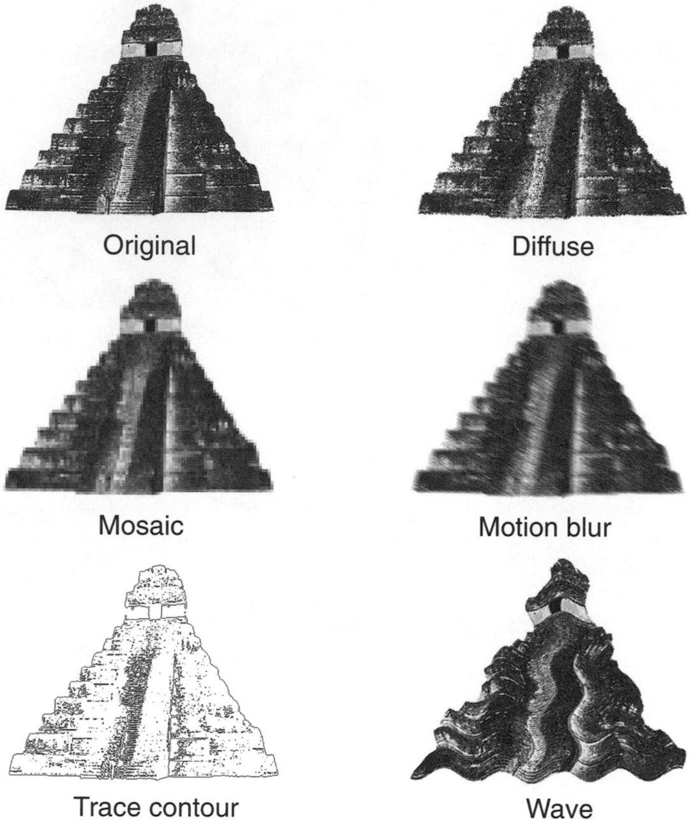

Figure 8.23

Filters can be applied that alter the entire image or selected area in various ways.

Original

Diffuse

Mosaic

Motion blur

Trace contour

Wave

goes on, and many filters have variable settings. Some programs like Adobe *Photoshop* have the option for plug-in filters that can be developed by third-party manufacturers.

DIGITIZING REAL-WORLD IMAGES

Although the electronic tools for creating images are extremely powerful, artistic images can still demand talent and/or hand-to-eye coordination not possessed by everyone needing to make presentations. *Scanners* or *digitizers* provide a way that any existing image can be digitized into the computer. Depending upon their quality, scanned images can be used for photorealism, line art, or templates over which electronic images can be painted.

There are several types of scanners, not all of which are appropriate for multimedia work. *Sheet-fed scanners* are primarily used for batch-feeding documents that are converted to text files via OCR software. Inexpensive *hand-held scanners* can be used to digitize small images or line art. However, they are spatially restricted and less accurate than other implementations. *Drum scanners* are used to digitize extremely high-resolution images for print production. All are omitted from this discussion. *Video digitizers* are used to capture images from a video camera, VCR, or other video device on the computer. Discussion of these devices is reserved for Part V.

❖ Flatbed Scanners

Flatbed scanners are the most popular scanners in use on the desktop today. They resemble small photocopy machines: The image to be scanned is placed face-down on a clear glass surface and scanned from underneath. A moving head containing a light source and mirror is moved along a track beneath the image. The light illuminates each line of the scanned image and the mirror reflects the image through a lens into a CCD array like those found in camcorders. The CCD converts the incoming light into voltages whose amplitude corresponds to the intensity of the light. Analog-to-digital converters transform these voltages into digital information. This process is repeated line-for-line until a complete digital representation of the image is available for storage and manipulation as a standard bitmap file.

Basic features

One-bit scanners only yield black and white according to a user-defined threshold level. Their best use is in scanning simple line art. Four-bit gray-scale scanners can distinguish 16 levels of gray including black and white—less than ideal for photos. Eight-bit gray-scale scanners up the ante to 256 levels—fine for black-and-white photos.

Multimedia work usually demands color scanners. Most provide 8-bit values for each of the RGB components to yield a 24-bit image. Three different sensors (or color filters in some designs) are required in order to distinguish these components. This was originally accomplished through the automation of three separate scanning passes, one for each color component. Not only do three passes take longer to complete, but subtle movement can jar the document being scanned enough to cause registration problems. Newer technology scans all three components in one pass for faster operation and fewer registration problems.

While color resolution affects the price of a scanner, so does *optical resolution*. The use of 300 dpi scanners is common, since they match the 300 dpi output of laser printers for desktop publishing.

Recently 400 dpi and 600 dpi scanners have started to proliferate. Some manufacturers use interpolation methods that increase the perceived resolution, often by a factor of two. Interpolation doesn't actually acquire more data, but averages existing information to add pixels in between the scanned ones.

Another price determinant is the scanning area—the size of the bed. While prices don't differ significantly between 8½" x 11" and 8½" x 14", going to 11" x 17" significantly increases the price. Most scanners use common interfaces such as SCSI, but interfaces can add to the cost if your computer isn't equipped with the proper interface.

The final monetary factor is whether the device can scan slides and transparencies. This process requires an additional attachment (about $500 worth) that illuminates the film from behind. These systems are often make-shift and do not offer the quality of dedicated film scanners.

Scanning software

Scanning software comes in two basic forms—dedicated programs and modules for image processors. In either case they provide for a *pre-scan*, which does a fast pass to provide a rough image on-screen. The user can drag a marquee around the desired area of the image in order to reduce scanning time and file size.

Scanning resolution and scale can also be specified. These two factors are independent of one another. Scale determines the physical size of the final image. Scaling a 4" x 5" original by 200 percent during scanning, for example, results in an image that will display and print as 8" x 10". Resolution determines how much detail is to be scanned. Scanning at 150 dpi on a 300 dpi scanner will scan every other dot, for example. The upper limit is the maximum optical resolution.

Other image processing controls are available such as brightness, contrast, and gamma. These controls can also discard data, so only adjust them at the scanning stage if you don't have the means to store and later manipulate all that information with an image processor. While scans can often be saved in a variety of formats, TIFF files are most common for this application.

Other considerations

Many scanner features are geared toward the use of scanned images in printed materials. If you intend to use a scanner for this purpose as well as multimedia, you may want to consider features like enhanced resolution. Multimedia alone, however, demands little resolution since monitors display less than 100 dpi. Although it's all right to scan at 300 dpi and lose some detail, paying for 600 dpi and then losing a lot of detail is carrying things a bit far.

When evaluating different scanners, inspect the sharpness in highlights and overall detail. In particular, look at how much detail shows up in darker areas and shadows. The other thing to evaluate is bias toward one or more of the component colors. While color bias can be compensated for in image processing, the results are not as accurate as those obtained with the optimal initial component balance. Finally, if you do a lot of scanning, the scanning time of individual models may be a deciding factor.

❖ Slide Scanners

Dedicated *slide scanners* do a better job of digitizing slides than add-on attachments for flatbeds. Scanned slides usually yield more luminance and saturation than scans of printed photos. Since this process employs transmitted light, exposure and gamma correction controls are usually available along with image size during the pre-scan process.

The resolution of slide scanners is measured in pixels rather than dpi. Typical ranges include 1024 x 1500 pixels on the low end, and up to 4096 x 6144 pixels on the high end.

OTHER GRAPHIC TOOLS

Although the tools described so far take the graphics spotlight, a complement of other hardware and software is often indispensable in boosting productivity. The remainder of this chapter highlights some products that you may find useful.

❖ Screen Capture Utilities

In some cases it is desirable to obtain an image containing the exact contents of a screen display. If you are doing on-line documentation for a program, for example, you'll want the ability to display a program workscreen complete with windows and pull-down menus. This can be accomplished with a *screen capture* utility. These programs run as memory-resident utilities that are invoked through menu commands or special keystroke combinations. The resulting bitmap can be brought into standard paint programs and/or authoring software for later use.

Screen capture programs have another use as well. Although most PostScript illustration programs do not export bitmaps directly, they do preview a bitmap representation on the screen so that you can see what you're drawing. Performing a screen capture on a preview screen provides you with a bitmap that can be manipulated in a paint program.

❖ Graphic File Conversion

Chapter 6 discussed programs that will translate files between formats and platforms. Some such programs support graphic files as well, but they constitute a special case. Dedicated programs are available that are designed to handle conversion between the myriad of graphic file types.

❖ Clip Art

Clip art has been a boon to people designing documents long before personal computers came along. The term derives from preproduced art that one purchases in paper form, clips out, and pastes into a layout. (The Yellow Pages are a study in clip art—good and bad.) Clip art went electronic when the desktop publishing industry saddled all sorts of non-artists with the task of creating newsletters and other publications that contained graphic content. A large body of clip art is available in PostScript format to fit the needs of desktop publishing. Image Club, 3G Graphics, and Art & Letters are excellent sources of PostScript clip art.

Although these files are both compact and resolution-independent, they are not directly compatible with bit-mapped screen displays. File conversion tools and screen capture utilities can convert clip art to bitmaps. Many of these images are unfilled line art that can easily be filled and otherwise manipulated in paint programs. The components of clip art images can usually be manipulated separately, simplifying the process of isolating the desired element from a complex drawing. PostScript objects can (and should) be resized to the desired size before conversion, yielding the least amount of artifacting associated with scaling.

With the increasing popularity of CD-ROM as a delivery vehicle, bit-mapped clip art and backgrounds are becoming more widely available. Most straddle the gap between desktop publishing and multimedia, providing the same image at a variety of bit-mapped resolutions. The backgrounds in particular are very useful in adding character and texture to multimedia images.

❖ **Stock Photography**

In a parallel vein to clip art, stock photography libraries have long been a resource of print designers. Tens of thousands of photos spanning all subjects are available through these agencies—excellent fodder for scanning. Fees are usually negotiated based on the usage. A few forward-thinking houses are beginning to offer selections on CD-ROM.

❖ **Library Software**

How do you know what you have when you have a CD-ROM with 7,000 pieces of clip art on it, or a hard drive full of graphic elements and sound effects you've built up over many projects? *Library software* provides a database for all this information and more. Features vary, but you can usually ascribe various descriptions to your files that can be searched as keywords when you need to find something. Well-organized CD-ROMs come with such a database. You can also see a thumbnail of an image or hear a snip of a sound without having to go to a dedicated program and load the whole file. Some library programs also perform file conversion.

❖ **Algorithmic Generators**

Although clip art is an invaluable resource for textured backgrounds, you can quickly run out of resources. *Algorithmic generators*—notably Pantechnicon's *TextureSynth*—produce patterns on the fly based on controls that determine patterns, grain, color, waveshapes, and so forth. You can tweek these controls as you watch the new patterns materialize on the screen, then save the ones you like both as control setting files and standard bitmaps.

❖ **Type Manipulation**

Programs like *LetraStudio*, *Arts & Letters*, and *TypeStyler* are designed to create special effects with type. With a few clicks, you can select a font then apply powerful effects such as stretch, compact, twist, and arch. Most of these functions can be applied to pathed text in an illustration program, but these type manipulation packages have a short learning curve and a smaller price tag.

❖ **Tablets**

Artists who have developed the hand-to-eye coordination associated with traditional painting often find the mouse hard to draw with. *Graphic tablets* provide a more intuitive pen-based input alternative. Most are pressure-sensitive, and the pressure values can be used to control intuitive things like stroke width, brush color, and airbrush density in the more sophisticated graphics and image processing packages. Tablets can also be used in the process of tracing photographs and existing art without the use of a scanner. The main considerations in choosing a tablet are surface area and resolution.

❖ ❖ ❖ ❖ ❖ ❖

The desktop tools available to today's electronic artists are nothing short of amazing! This technology was affordable only to institutions ten years ago and didn't exist at all a few decades ago. One wonders what some of the classic and impressionistic masters might have created with this technology. They would most likely be quick to point out that tools alone do not an artist make. In the next and final chapter on graphics, we examine the process of creating aesthetically pleasing and effective imagery.

CHAPTER 9

Using Graphics

Becoming a fine artist takes many years of dedication in developing both hand-eye coordination and unique style. Multimedia productions usually require more graphic design than fine art. The skill this discipline also requires is oriented toward effective communication. Some rules based on centuries of experience clearly define what works and what doesn't. This chapter sets out some of those basic design concepts and provides some ideas about how to get the most from computer-based graphic tools.

USING COLOR

The ability of computers to display millions of colors is a valuable and powerful resource, especially when photorealism is involved. In the artistic process, however, only a small subset of those millions of colors are typically used to communicate a given effect.

Colors play several roles in multimedia. They can communicate relationships between ideas and hierarchical levels. Colors can also be used to call attention to a desired piece of information or to direct the eye. Proper use of color enhances legibility and memorability. Perhaps most importantly, color speaks to the subconscience of the audience.

❖ Color Psychology

Each color in the spectrum conveys a silent statement to the viewer. This perception is a result of the manner in which our eyes work, our natural surroundings, and the subliminal effects of society and culture. Table 9.1 shows how various colors communicate via general impression and specific association.

Table 9.1. Colors can communicate general moods or associated items.

Color	Subliminal perception	Associated item examples
Red	Alert, danger, sexy, hot	Stop, fire engine, blood, roses, hell
Orange	Attention	Pumpkin, popsicle
Blue	Confident, royal, tranquil, comfort	Sky, water, public information signs
Yellow	Loyalty, fun	Sun, banana, lemon, yield sign, butter
Green	Nature, clean outdoors	Plants, forest, money, go
Brown	Earth	Dirt, national park signs, chocolate
White	Purity, cleanliness	Wedding dress, clouds, heaven
Black	Evil, elegant, mysterious	Night, tuxedo, death
Pastels	Soft, non-threatening, feminine	Female, Southwest, babies
Earth tones	Nature	Mother Earth
Saturated	Loud, bold, capable, happy, strong	Flags, corporate logos, crayons
Desaturated	Old, weathered, drab	Old photographs, expired products

Specific color combinations and categories can also carry implied meaning. This is especially so with regard to countries and flags. Red, white, and blue implies patriotism in the United States, while a combination of red, white, and green pulls at the heartstrings of Italians. Corporations also have color identities. A yellow box of film with red lettering trumpets Kodak, while white script on red background brings Coca-Cola to mind.

The point here is that various color combinations can work both for you and against you. Analyze your audience when choosing color schemes. White on saturated blue is a great choice if your audience is Greek. Yellow and red are a bad idea if you're making a presentation to Fuji. Pastels are fine for a kiosk in a store that caters to women. Day-glo and neon are bad choices for a presentation on retirement communities. You get the idea.

❖ Natural Color

In addition to certain colors being associated directly with nature, colors as a whole exhibit certain qualities in nature. Cool colors—purple, blue, and green—seem to recede into the distance and offer stability. This implies their effective use as background colors. The warm colors—red, yellow, and orange—appear to advance toward the viewer, implying foreground use. The colors that bound the two color temperatures—yellow-green and red-violet—are comfortable in the mid-range perspective.

Different brilliance levels send important messages as well. Brilliant colors can imply bright sunlight, a slight reduction in brilliance adds warmth, and dark colors imply lack of light. Colors also exhibit less saturation and brilliance in the distance than in the foreground. Objects that require dimension and depth can be simulated by applying gradients that follow those guidelines.

As an interesting parallel, dark items are psychologically attributed more weight than light items. This may be a result of our experience of a bright sky above a darker landscape. The implication is that darker objects are often best placed toward the bottom of the screen or that objects toward the bottom of the screen add appropriate weight if given darker colors.

If you intend to create visuals that convey realism, analyzing the world around you is a great place to start. For this reason, a review of the discussion in Chapter 7 regarding the properties of reflection, light transmission, and shadows is highly recommended.

❖ Color Harmony

Many novice artists choose colors individually and arbitrarily. Selecting colors according to *color harmony*—how they interact— yields more effective results. Many of the dos and don'ts of color mixture pertain to the discussion in Chapter 7 on visual phenomena such as negative afterimage, simultaneous color contrast, color vibration, area proportions, and color temperature. These properties should be taken into design consideration.

There's nothing wrong, for example, with using *direct complements* (those exactly opposite on the color wheel) in the same image. On the contrary, the result is vibrant! However, you don't want to subject your audience to a vibrant screen for very long before moving to another image. If you must use a saturated color over an extended period of time, contrast it with an unsaturated tone. If you must dwell on two potentially vibrant colors, see if you can reduce the saturation on one or both.

Direct complements could be said to be disharmonious. Harmonious colors have more in common. *Triadic complements*—those that are 120° apart on the color wheel—are less vibrant than direct complements, yet have somewhat of a disharmonious effect when highly saturated. *Split complements* are much more harmonious. The two split complements of a color are located 30° on either side of the direct complement.

❖ Color Contrast

Contrast in color primarily refers to differences in brightness between areas. Neighboring values of a given hue offer the least contrast. The silhouette—0 percent brightness against 100 percent brightness—is the most dramatic form of contrast. Although contrast need not be that blatant, smaller objects do require greater color contrast in relation to the background.

Contrast can also be a function of saturation. Many designers will choose a few saturated colors for foreground elements, then create backgrounds with less saturated colors to ensure that the important elements stand out.

When selecting colors as foreground and background, keep the effects of simultaneous contrast in mind. As you recall from Chapter 7, foreground colors appear differently depending on background color. Yellow, for example, appears warm on white yet harsh on black. Blue on white works fine, while blue on black is difficult to discern. Red on white is bright, red on black is warm. And yellow virtually ignites red.

In the print world where white pages are viewed in light environments, a dark element on a bright foreground will appear stronger than a bright element on a dark background. In multimedia, the same can hold true under normal lighting conditions. In a darkened viewing environment, white text on a dark background often has more strength.

Establishing contrasting colors becomes more difficult to rectify when a foreground color is to pass through many background colors. Labeling a pie chart or multi-colored graph is a prime example. Three solutions are apparent—vary the label colors, frame a standard-color label in a small box or outline, or place the labels outside of the colored background areas.

Gradients and photographs are often desirable in breaking the monotony of solid backgrounds. The problem of finding a contrasting foreground color is usually aggravated by these devices, however. One solution is to weight gradients so that severe changes in value do not fall where a foreground item such as text will be displayed. Another option is to outline the foreground element or place a single-color box between foreground and background. Finally, gradients can be restricted to ranges such as neighboring hues that do not themselves include serious contrasts.

❖ Color Continuity and Differentiation

Colors are extremely useful in establishing conceptual relationships. Concepts that share the same hierarchical level are often given the same colors: When the viewer sees the color again, the new information will automatically be associated with the desired level. This is of paramount importance when various levels of hierarchy are displayed on the same screen. The design and title color may remain the same on multiple screens while the background color scheme changes for variety. Conversely, different colors can also be used intentionally to differentiate ideas or objects that are conceptually unique.

❖ **Keep it Simple**

Working with color adds a new level of complexity to basic design. Most art courses start with black-and-white and move slowly into color, first adding one color, then two, and so forth. Restricting the number of colors in an image can make the design task easier, especially if you are new to art and design. Perhaps the best way to end our discussion of color usage is to revive the "KISS" principle. Properly chosen colors can make very powerful statements: adding unnecessary colors can dilute their effect.

USING LIGHT SOURCES

Shadows are very instrumental in adding depth and realism to any graphic image. 3-D graphics systems generate shadows automatically. Most 2-D graphics applications leave shadows up to the user. As a result, *drop shadows* have become the standard bill of fare in graphics today. This term refers primarily a simulated shadow "dropped" below and to the side of a graphic element. This position has become popular because most light in our lives comes from above, and the right-hand offset draws the eye in the same direction in which the eyes naturally move. Shadows can also be above the object as long as you wish to imply that the light comes from below. Shadows can even appear in front of the object if the light source is intended to be behind the object.

One of the cardinal sins of graphic novices is to have shadows going off in different directions. This implies—usually improperly—that the light source is in between those objects. Always create shadows, highlights, and gradients with a firm concept of where the light source is. Using the basic principles of light transmission put forth in Chapter 7, simulate ray tracing in your mind to ensure continuity.

One effect that lends refinement to an image is the use of translucence in creating soft shadows. This can be accomplished in a variety of ways, depending upon your paint program or image processor. Any sort of brush or filter that has a "darken" setting will help. More sophisticated effects can be obtained by using feathering in conjunction with pasting a darkened copy of the object behind the foreground object.

A review of our discussion of light yields some basic concepts that can be applied to create a proper spatial relationship between light sources, objects, and backgrounds.

USING PERSPECTIVE

Graphics have greater impact when dimension is applied. While shadows and highlights aid in creating this effect, the form of the object is also integral in communicating perspective, dimension, and distance.

The simplest way to create perspective is called *parallel projection*. In this process, a two-dimensional image is placed on a plane parallel to the viewing screen and extended along both axes without altering the size. (See Figure 9.1.) One way to accomplish this is to copy the original object, paste the duplicate in front of or behind the original, then create lines and fills to connect the planes. Another method is to turn the image into a brush and drag it or stamp it successively along the desired vector.

Figure 9.1

Parallel projection adds dimension via simple extrusion of a 2-D object along the x- and y-axes.

While parallel projection is fairly simple, true three-dimensional objects become smaller as they grow more distant and eventually recede into a *vanishing point*. The level of sophistication and associated difficulty in creating these objects increases depending upon how many axes are used as multiple vanishing points. Figures 9.2 and 9.3 show the use of one and two vanishing points, respectively.

(A third vanishing point can be added at the bottom, but the complex perspectives that result often distract the viewer.)

Grids make it easy to move objects forward–backward and right–left. They can be created as on-screen guidelines, then later erased. The vertical position of the viewer in relation to the horizon can be altered by vertically scaling the grid. Flipping the grid vertically will place the viewer underneath the objects being drawn.

Figure 9.2

Using a single vanishing point, the naturally parallel lines on the object face remain parallel, while the sides going into the distance follow the grid lines.

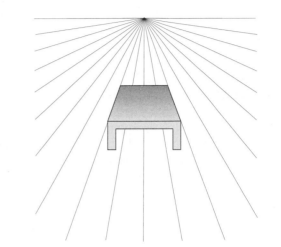

Figure 9.3

With two vanishing points only vertical lines that are naturally parallel remain parallel.

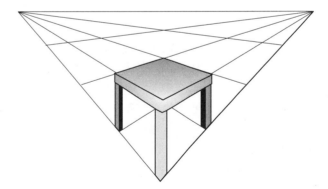

TYPOGRAPHY AND TITLING

Fonts make a big difference in how text messages and overall images are perceived. There are thousands of typefaces in the world, with more popping up every day. This section is designed to show you how to think about using typography for more effective presentations.

Much typographic terminology has developed since Guttenberg's printing press. In the classic definition, a *font* is a single collection of alphabetic and numeric characters in one size and style—18-point Helvetica Black, for example. A *series* is all of the sizes of an otherwise identical font. A *typeface* is technically a complete grouping of fonts that bear a family resemblance. (All Helveticas comprise a typeface.) With the advent of computer typography, the terminology has become a bit mixed up. In electronic publishing font is used to describe the classic series. Related series such as roman, italic, and bold are often referred to as *font families*.

❖ Anatomy of a Font

A whole slew of terms can be used to describe the various parts of a font's anatomy. (See Figure 9.4.) Perhaps the biggest overall distinguishing factor between fonts is the lack or presence of *serifs*, or feet. Serifs are designed to draw the eye easily from one character to the next across a line of type. Typefaces without serifs are called *sans serif*. (*Sans* is French for "without.")

Size and weight

In the United States, typographic elements are measured in *points*—a carryover from the days of hot-lead type. One point is equal to almost ¹⁄₇₂". Twelve points make up a *pica*, and there are 6 picas to an inch. The overall measurement of a font is its *point size*—the approximate distance between the bottom of the lowest descender and the top of the highest ascender. This measurement is not exact from font to font, however. Instead, the part that you can see or

---

Figure 9.4

Many terms are used to describe the anatomy of a font.

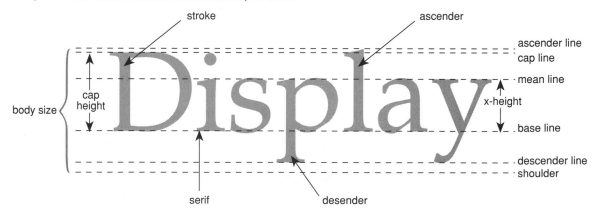

face sits in an invisible space called the *body*—and the body is the measurement of point size.

Set is the space taken by a character and the white space to its right. (See Figure 9.5.) The average set of different fonts in a given point size can affect the overall aesthetics of the text. Some families have members with extreme sets such as condensed and expanded. The *weight* of a font is the relative thickness or heaviness of the actual letter stems. (See Figure 9.6.)

Figure 9.5

The set of a font describes the relative amount of horizontal space required for the characters.

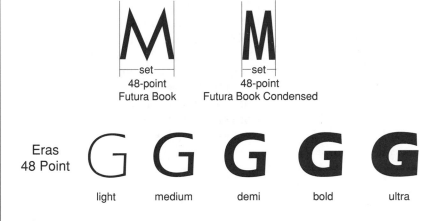

48-point
Futura Book

48-point
Futura Book Condensed

Figure 9.6

The weight of a font describes the relative thickness of the stroke.

Eras
48 Point

light   medium   demi   bold   ultra

Leading

The amount of space between lines of text is called *leading*. Leading is actually the distance from the baseline of one line of text to the baseline of the next. Designers commonly spec type as a point size in relation to leading: "10 on 12" means 10-point type with 12-point leading.

Spacing

The more elegant fonts today have *proportional spacing*, meaning that the amount of horizontal space allocated for each character changes according to each letter. The classic examples are the letters *i*, which requires much less space than other letters, and *m*, which requires much more. Monospaced type allots equal space for each letter regardless of letter width. Monospaced type tends to be harder to read, less aesthetically pleasing, and conveys the feel of a typewriter.

The standard distance between the letters of a font is the *letterspacing,* or *tracking*. Letterspacing is optimally set so that the individual letters are distinguishable, yet entire groupings of letters are

perceived as words. This can be augmented by the more conceptual aesthetic of *word spacing*—the space between words.

Special pairs of letters require special attention due to their
interaction. In the pair *Wo*, for example, the *o* looks orphaned if a
normal amount of letterspace occurs between the letters. *Kerning*,
or negative letterspace, can be used to tighten the letters up. Some
fonts and programs include tables containing automatically-kerned
pairs of letters; other times kerning must be done manually.

Alignment

Body copy can be aligned in several ways. Copy set flush left aligns
all type against the left margin leaving a ragged right edge. Flush
right text is aligned against the right margin, leaving a ragged left
edge. Justification spreads the word spacing out so that it is aligned
with both the left and right margins. This can leave unsightly gaps
of white space, often requiring that words be manually hyphenated
or kerned in order to bring more characters onto a line. Centering
positions each line of type in the center of a text area.

❖ Font Classifications

Fonts are usually designed with a particular function in mind. They
are logically best used in those contexts. Although there are thousands of fonts, they all fall into a handful of basic categories. (See
Figure 9.7.)

Figure 9.7

*Fonts are classed into basic
categories according to
their use.*

Times New Roman

serif

Futura Book

sans serif

Spring

script

Spumoni

display only

IRONWOOD

decorative

Serif fonts enhance the eye's flow from one character to another. Sans serif fonts have a clean, geometric, contemporary appearance and make for excellent headlines. Although the rule of thumb says that serif fonts are easier to read in long lines of text, tests indicate that sans serif fonts are quite legible given proper letterspacing and leading.

Both serif and sans serif fonts can be set in roman or italic. *Roman* type is straight type set perpendicular to the baseline. It is classically used for body copy and anything that requires detailed reading. *Italic* type is slanted to the right, usually at a 78-degree angle to the baseline. It is traditionally used for emphasis or an informal touch. Italic is often confused with *oblique* type. Italic is specifically crafted for a slanted appearance, while oblique is a simple skewing of the normal font. Neither italic nor oblique is appropriate for long streams of text or passages in which entire words are capitalized.

Script, or *cursive,* fonts mimic human handwriting. As such, they lack a sense of symmetry and generally convey a warm feeling. That said, different scripts can convey a wide range of personalities from feminine to informal to sophisticated. Scripts are inappropriate for long streams of text and passages set entirely in capital letters.

Decorative typefaces were first seen in the ornate scribing of monks before the advent of moveable type. They can be difficult to read and have few uses today, outside of initial caps, the church and, ironically, heavy metal!

Many contemporary fonts add subtle serifs to an otherwise geometric sans-serif look. Other contemporary fonts throw away the rules of symmetry and character-to-character continuity for a decidedly loud visual effect. While there is no formal name for this category, these are typically only appropriate for display purposes rather than body copy.

❖ Using Fonts

Fonts can be classified by the role they play in the overall design. In print design, the two major classifications are body copy and display type. *Body copy* is for the text of a story such as the words you are reading now. It is usually set in 10- or 12-point type. *Display type* is for everything else, including headlines and subtitles. In video applications, fonts smaller than about 18 points are impractical (a subject explored in greater depth in Part V). This restriction makes almost everything on a video screen display type. Computer monitors are capable of displaying fonts that are legible at 12 points and even smaller, providing for the possibility of body copy. Hypertext is an example where the rules of body copy should be applied in order to sustain interest and reduce eye fatigue.

General concepts

Fonts make statements and should always compliment the message and graphic elements with which they appear. Proper font usage invites the reader into the screen.

As a general rule, avoid using more than two font families on a screen, since it lends an effect of confusion to the image. If you have more than two levels of text, consider using a typeface that has enough family members for the weights and other variations to supply the required variety without clutter. Font combinations should be chosen with care so that they do not conflict or distract the eye with too much similarity or diversity. Designers often contrast one serif face with one sans-serif.

Continuity throughout a presentation is important. The titles for each chapter and heading in this book lend continuity and communicate conceptual levels; the same logic should be applied to on-screen presentations. Establish fonts and sizes that will be used to identify various elements and levels consistently throughout an entire presentation.

Remember that the proper sizes of screen fonts should be installed if you are not using a type presentation system such as TrueType or Adobe Type Manager. Even with those systems, noninstalled screen font sizes will usually take longer to render than installed versions.

Body copy

Body copy is aesthetically perceived on both the character and global levels. At the character level, the font subtly affects the viewer's psychological feelings about the subject and its presentation. The typeface categories are largely restricted to serif, sans serif, and contemporary. There's also a mechanical consideration: although serif fonts are traditionally used for body copy in printed materials, make certain that your choice of serifs render well at screen resolution.

The brain recognizes words more by their overall shape than their individual letters. For this reason, text set entirely in uppercase or "all caps" is less accessible than that set in a mixture of upper- and lowercase characters. The blocky form of all caps destroys the unique, identifying shape. Italic, bold, and underlined type have similar effects and should be used for emphasis only.

At the global level, the entire body of text should be graphically pleasing and inviting. Leading, line length, justification, and margins all play an important role at this level. Subject the overall body of text to the squint test: squint when looking at the screen so that your eye perceives overall form rather than detail.

In printed documents, body copy is often tweeked to perfection before it is published. Multimedia applications that employ hypertext may require that a small subset of a large volume of text be displayed on demand. Since this usually obviates any tweeking, basic body copy rules become more important.

Body copy is most often set flush left when an informal feel is desired or justified for a more formal effect. As a general rule, right-alignment and centering are reserved for purposeful artistic design. (The exception is that columns of figures are right-aligned.) In hypertext applications, left-alignment of body copy is recommended to avoid unsightly word gaps resulting from automatic formatting.

Paragraphs should not end with an *orphan*—a single word on the last line. While most presentations will not use more than one column of type, any that do should also avoid *widows*—single words on the first line of a new column. Letterspacing and kerning provide one way to control orphans, widows, and word gaps. Another method is to hyphenate words so that lines are better balanced. Some hypertext situations will provide automatic hyphenation dictionaries. In situations where you have control over hyphens, several rules apply. Avoid hyphenating words containing five characters or less, leaving a one- or two-character syllable on either line, or ending more than two successive lines with a hyphen. You will also find that words are best hyphenated according to the way they are pronounced rather than strictly by syllable breaks.

Fonts with larger x-heights and/or set in longer lines tend to need more leading to alleviate a feeling of confinement. Conversely, type restricted to minimal leading should flow in shorter lines or be set in a font that has minimal x-height.

Our eyes discern foreground and background colors differently. Studies show that black text set on white background can be read about 40 percent more efficiently than white text on black or gray backgrounds. Red and black combinations are extremely hard to read, and black on yellow is the easiest to read. While textures can add a lot to a background, they can conflict with perception of small type. The smaller the type, the simpler the immediate background should be.

Certainly the capabilities of hypertext-style applications are less sophisticated than page-layout applications. If more control is desired over body copy, it may be necessary to tweek the text in a dedicated program, then stamp the font down as a part of the bitmap. (A screen capture program provides one way of performing the latter function.) This also precludes the need to supply the actual font when configuring a presentation for delivery. This approach is practical only for short passages, however.

Display type

Display fonts should be chosen with great care since they make an immediate subconscious statement about the message and its presenter. (See Figure 9.8.) Like body copy, display fonts should match the overall style of the accompanying graphic elements. Valid font categories include roman, serif, sans serif, italic, script, and contemporary. Choose the weight of the font carefully. You will often find that the use of bold is not necessary in large titles.

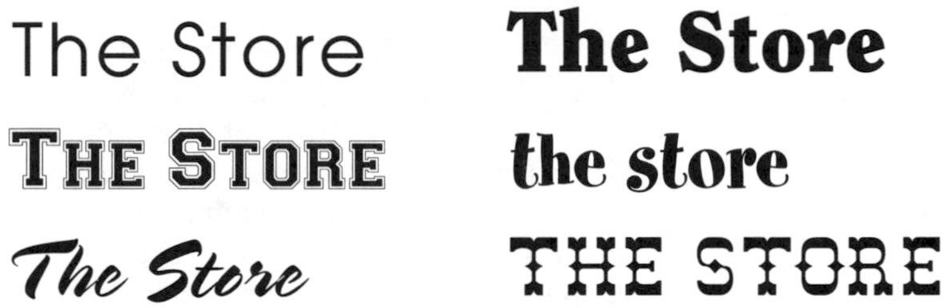

Figure 9.8

The choice of font can communicate a distinct subliminal impression to the viewer.

The Store   **The Store**

THE STORE   *the store*

The Store   THE STORE

Typeface choices for headlines and titles might be partially dictated by the background elements on which they are displayed. Geometric or blocky type will contrast best against softer or rounder background elements. Rounded fonts often stand out more effectively against geometric backgrounds.

The eye requires less letterspace and leading in text set in larger points sizes than in text set in smaller point sizes. Tighter tracking and leading is both more appealing and more conservative of space. The need for kerning in special pairs of letters also increases with type size. While many graphic programs offer little control over qualities like letterspace, kerning, and leading, there are two solutions. One is to hammer out the basic characters and then cut-and-paste their bitmaps to achieve better spacing. The other is to use a program with better typographic controls to tweek everything, then export them or use a screen capture program to import them into the graphic image.

Main titles are often centered. While you can use software tools to ensure perfect centering, manual centering is usually more visually pleasing. This applies both to the relationship of multiple lines of display type to one another, as well as to the positioning of the overall title in the image.

The overall shape of the display type is important. When using uneven lines, they should be top-heavy rather than bottom-heavy. This treatment is often referred to as the "inverted pyramid." (See Figure 9.9.) Another modern look employs justification in conjunction with expanded tracking and varying font sizes on individual lines.

Figure 9.9

Multiple-line titles can be made more effective by using an inverted pyramid shape.

This shape
is less accessible
than the next example

This is an example
of the inverted
pyramid

When using upper- and lowercase in combination, observe the same rules of capitalization in titles that magazines and newspapers use for headlines. Important words such as nouns, vowels, adjectives, and adverbs are capitalized; incidental words such as the, a, on, and at are not. More informal headlines can be rendered exclusively in lowercase with the exception of the first word and those which are capitalized regardless of circumstance. Don't break title lines with hyphens.

Another important tip about titles can be gleaned from the print publishing world: magazine logos and other titling elements on the cover almost invariably take on a color extracted from the photo or graphic on the cover. This effect lends harmony to the composite viewing experience and is quite appropriate for multimedia screens that contain both text and graphics.

Title colors should be selected so that they contrast the backgrounds on which they are displayed. If the background is dark, use light type and vice versa. In general, warm colors leap off of the screen more so than cool colors. Cases where the background varies behind the type call for additional effort. Following the guidelines for drop shadows described later in this chapter will help distinguish letters; however, they work best with bright letters and only provide a contrast in one direction.

The ultimate insurance that your font will stand out is the addition of an outline edge in a color that contrasts the body of the letters. The way this is accomplished varies depending upon the software. Some packages simply let you specify an outline—sometimes referred to as *stroke*—in addition to the fill characteristics. In a package offering only a choice between filled and outline font rendering, choose outline, fill the outline itself with the desired color, and then fill the body of the letter with a different color. Finally, some programs will let you select each letter as a brush, then outline the brush in a user-selected color. It is often effective to apply anti-aliasing to the entire area so that there is a perceived distinction between the font and background, yet a smooth edge.

Bullets or subheads should be in a smaller point size that the main title. The font should either be a member of the same family or one that is both significantly different and complimentary. Bullets can also be distinguished from other levels through use of color, but all text at the same level should be the same color. (An exception is when color is used to highlight each bullet in the sequence of a presentation.) Lowercase can often be used exclusively with bullets with the possible exception of the first letter of the first word. Avoid underlines. Use another graphic vehicle to distinguish bullet levels.

Although many presentation programs allow you to call up titles that are rendered on the fly, typically little control is available for tweeking kerning, letterspace, optical centers, and other previously discussed aesthetic concepts. Display type requiring these refinements should be stamped down into the bitmapped image after tweeking so that it becomes part of the graphic file.

Type as art

Main titles or logos require more than just choosing and placing fonts. Our daily visual experience includes so much type that some artistic flair makes the message stand out. Moreover, proper graphic treatment can simultaneously communicate the essence of the message.

The simplest effect is to alter the angle of the type. Rotating type at up to 45° can break the monotony of horizontal elements. Vertical orientation can also be effective, but only when used judiciously with large fonts and short words. (Rotate normally oriented text rather than stacking the letters.) Another technique that works well is reversing out a title element or placing it in a box. A popular approach—especially in main titles and logos—is the use of two elements with different size and aesthetic flavor. A common example would be a title consisting of one artistically scripted word and one in normal text. (See Figure 9.10.)

A more ambitious approach uses artistic elements as letters. In the word "Bowling," for example, you could use a bowling ball to represent the letter *o* and/or a bowling pin for the letter *l*. A globe could serve as the *o* in "World." A graphic element can also replace an entire word. The classic example of this treatment is the well-

known "I Love New York" where a heart replaces the word "Love."
This method is only effective when the meaning of the graphic element is implicit.

Just as art can serve as letters, letters can also serve as art. In the
normally precise world of computers, the most basic approach is to
draw letters freehand, possibly with some fill pattern applied afterward. A title having to do with kids, for example, might be rendered
effectively with the crude look of chalk or crayon. Image processing
and type manipulation programs can be used to alter standard fonts
in endless variations of stretches, distortions, and geometric contours. (See Figure 9.11.) Illustration programs can perform similar
functions, including binding type on a path such as a curve or arch.

Letters can also be filled with a wide variety of effects. Perhaps
the most popular is a filled gradation that ranges between two colors. This can be accomplished by applying a filled gradient to each
letter. A more challenging approach spreads the gradient range
across the entire title by masking the text over a gradient screen.
These masking techniques can be used to fill any title with a background image, as shown in Chapter 7.

DESIGN BASICS

In professional design, everything serves a purpose. Never decorate an image, always design it. Concentrate on communicating effectively rather than making an image look good. The challenge of presentation graphics is to make images so artistic that they subconsciously appeal to the viewer and reinforce the message, but not so eye-catching as to draw conscious attention to the graphics and away from the overall impact. Use of novelty, for example, can be very effective up to the point that it is distracting. In short, grow a style out of the needs of the message and the demographics of the audience, rather than forcing works of art on the audience.

❖ Establishing a Style

The first design step in establishing an overall style for presentation graphics is defining the audience. Certainly diverse scenarios such as museum displays, corporate training, educational programming for children, and trade show kiosks each have unique design needs. Once the audience and subject matter are identified, the next step is visualization. What imagery can be associated with the subject matter? What colors will work well for both the message and the audience? What font embodies the flavor of those messages?

While there are as many design styles as there are designers and applications, one simple rule prevails: Once you establish a style, stick with it! Continuity unifies your message and gives your audience a sense of comfort. Styles should only be mixed, well, as an intentional style!

The design grid

Many designers begin image development by establishing a grid, either electronically or with pencil and paper. The grid serves as a sort of visual outline and provides a method of working elements in together without being distracted by their details. The message and elements you have to work with will drive the formation of the grid; conversely, the grid will serve as an excellent indication that the design direction is too simple, too complex, or just right. Once a grid is established, it can be used in the design and production of the other screens in the presentation to ensure continuity. (See Figure 9.12.)

❖ Attracting the Viewer

One of the responsibilities of the graphic designer is to invite the viewer in and lead the eye through the image or subject matter. The use of a dominant object can be effective in getting the readers'

Figure 9.12

A design grid can help in both growing a style and creating a series of images with continuity.

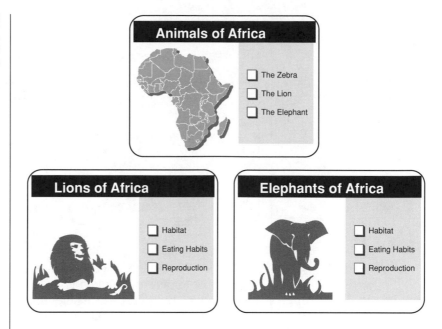

attention, after which they become more interested in exploring the rest of the screen. Without a dominant object, the viewer can become confused as to what's most important or where to start. Dominance can be established through several means. Shear size is the most obvious. Another is through use of colors and contrast. Finally, an image processor can make an element in a photograph more dominant by sharpening that element and blurring the rest.

Don't crowd elements into the screen. Space gives your text and graphics room to breathe and an area to dominate. Lack of space usually means there's too much information to absorb and subconsciously communicates a sense of claustrophobia and confusion that threatens viewers. Keeping things simple also avoids visual clutter and reduces the risk of elements competing for attention. If you have too much information to fit comfortably in one screen, use multiple screens or change portions of the screen through partial overlays.

❖ Leading the Eye

We normally read from left to right and top to bottom. Good design works with this tradition rather than fighting it. Images often benefit from having a visual anchor toward the bottom-center or bottom-right of the screen. This not only leads the eye down the screen, but provides a sense of weight. (See Figure 9.13.) Recalling our earlier discussion, the use of darker colors helps to accentuate that weight.

Figure 9.13

Place elements on the screen in such a way that they lead the eye in an expected path.

The eye is also led by elements in a picture or graphic that are pointing or appear to be moving in a given direction. Use these vehicles to lead the eye. Graphic elements placed on either side of the screen should reflect the eye back into the picture (unless your intention is to lead to the next screen). People, for example, should always face inward. Sometimes flipping a photo or image horizontally will yield the desired result for a given position. Those that cannot be flipped (such as an element containing text) should be moved to a more appropriate position.

❖ Keeping it Interesting

If realism is the goal, graphics should be created so that any elements they contain are in proper proportion to one another. Exaggerated scale can be effective when emphasizing or satirizing a point. Proper use of scale also applies to unrelated elements—such as text, boxed areas, photographs, graphic devices, and even blank space—that do not have implicit size relationships. Scaling these objects in relation to one another is largely a matter of feel, but the overall goal is to establish balance and priority.

In the real world, few things are the same shape. Regardless of whether the design is attempting realism or not, images are more appealing to the eye if they contain different shapes. Even the use of simple rectangles is more effective when they contain different proportions.

Centering everything is expected and boring. Images can be made much more appealing by staggering elements off-center. One extreme use of this technique is to bleed an image off of the edge of the screen.

Flat images are also boring. The most obvious way around this is the use of distinct foreground and background elements, often in conjunction with shadows. (See Figure 9.14.) Foreground elements can also be focused or highly-detailed, while background elements are made to be out-of-focus or less detailed. The use of perspective tools in paint and image processing software can also create the impression of dimension. Effective contrast of warm and cool colors or bright and dark lighting as described earlier in this chapter can also add depth.

Figure 9.14

Placing an element in the foreground is one way to establish depth.

Although full-fidelity photographs can be scanned, these images are sometimes too literal. Indeed, research indicates that audiences retain more information when images are less detailed. A line drawing is sometimes more effective than a photograph. The limitations of working with CLUTs can also cause problems in portraying photo-realism. Computer graphics tools—such as image processing filters, ink modes that emulate traditional painting styles, scans of traditional art, and textures—are all to be considered in making an image more accessible and artistically interesting.

Implied motion can also make a static image more compelling. Things usually come to rest in a horizontal orientation. Designers can capitalize on this by placing elements, such as titles or photographs, at an angle to add the perception of action or motion to an object. A sense of frozen motion can also be added to a static image. One method is to use an image processing effect such as a "motion blur" filter. Another option involves copying the object, then pasting it down several times at regular intervals, each with increasing opacity. (See Figure 9.15.) Note that images depicting motion are usually most effective when cropped more liberally or given larger frames.

Figure 9.15

The impression of motion can be created using angles and motion blur.

Working with frames

The effect of frames and boxes is one of confinement and isolation. These devices should be used sparingly. Too much confinement constricts the image and makes the information it contains seem less accessible. Too much isolation of elements fragments the message and threatens its synergy. This is not to say that frames have no place in design: they can prevent elements from floating meaninglessly. Alternatives to a simple box include the use of decorative borders and partial frames on only a few sides.

Scanned photos and filled areas form their own natural frames. Adding artificial framing usually detracts from these elements. In fact, it is often desirable to soften this effect by cropping them in irregular shapes such as circles, ovals, and silhouettes. (See Figure 9.16.) Feathering or vignetting the edges can be applied to any shape. Partial cut-outs can also be effective in emphasizing head shots of people and making objects characterizing frozen motion leap from the frame into their surroundings.

Figure 9.16

Unusual cropping can create interesting effects.

There's nothing that says you have to use a scanned photo on a 1:1 basis. Use scaling and/or cropping to emphasize a dominant element and discard distracting visual information. If you have enough disk space and memory, it is often handy to scan an entire element at the highest resolution in order to have access to as much detail as possible. A prime example is the use of extreme magnification of a photographic element. (See Figure 9.17.) Let the shape of the object dictate the shape of the frame. Overcropping can also be used as a special effect or in situations where the original photo makes normal cropping impossible.

Figure 9.17

Cropping and scaling can be used in conjunction to focus on a desired object.

When using two photos in the same image, put them in frames of the same size only if the scale shown in both pictures is the same. If this is not the case and cannot be rectified through scaling, use different sized frames in order to completely disassociate the scale of the images.

Basic Design Tips

- Keep the design simple. Focus on communication rather than art.
- Always design, never decorate.
- Establish master design using a grid, then use it as a template.
- Use space to give your elements room to breathe.
- Make one element dominant to give the viewer a starting point.
- Maintain a sense of proper balance and scale between the design elements.
- Employ contrasting shapes to keep things visually interesting.
- Use off-center positioning to break from the expected.
- Use foreground and background elements to establish a sense of depth.
- Lead the eye through the image using size, positioning, and color.
- Work with the natural flow of images. Flip or position objects so that they direct the eye into the page.
- Use a dark visual anchor toward the bottom of the page if needed.
- Lend a sense of motion to an image through use of angles or special effects.
- Use frames sparingly to preserve a sense of openness.
- Try partial framing devices such as graphic borders, drop shadows, and bleeds.
- Try non-rectangular frames to add interest.
- Crop and scale to highlight the dominant object.
- Use extreme magnification and extreme cropping for effect.
- Try full and partial silhouettes to make images stand out.
- Use frames of the same size in one image only if their contents exhibit the same scale.

COMPUTER GRAPHIC TECHNIQUES

There are as many artistic styles as there are artists. Regardless of your aesthetic tastes, it's important to work with technology rather than against it.

❖ Choosing the Right Resolution

For reasons of display speed and file size, most computer-based presentations rely on images created with the color look-up tables described in Chapter 7. Various tools and methods are available for converting and mapping palettes. The real challenge is choosing the right process and combination of colors for a given image or project.

Two basic concepts are involved in working with CLUTs—establishing the number of bit planes or the total number of displayable colors on a screen and choosing the exact colors in that palette. Although some paint programs can perform both functions to a limited degree, image processing packages are generally much better tools for both tasks.

One of the first questions to ask yourself is how many colors or bit planes an image requires. Fewer bit planes mean smaller files and faster load, display, and animation times. Images that use only four colors, for example, are inefficient if stored with more than 2-bit planes.

Ideally, scanned images should be acquired with 24-bit resolution, even though they will be converted down to 8-bit resolution or less. This provides the greatest amount of flexibility by relying on the many options of the image processor rather than the arbitrary conversion that occurs if you specify lesser color resolution during the scanning process.

Several mapping options are typically available when converting images from direct color to indexed color. Most systems have a *standard palette* chosen by the manufacturer. With the exception of a few authoring programs that support no customized palettes, this mapping option has limited use in dedicated productions. An *adaptive palette* offers the best selection of colors for a given image. A *custom palette* is defined elsewhere, such as in a reference image or as a stand-alone palette file. Many paint and authoring packages offer an assortment of preset custom palettes that are optimized for certain types of images. Metallic, earth tones, pastels, rainbow, flesh tones, and NTSC are common offerings.

Reducing the palette of an image can cause color artifacting in the form of halos or undesirable color banding. Various dithering options are available that mix pixels of two different values where they meet to create a smoother gradation. The most common and effective dithering scheme when reducing bit planes is *diffusion dither* because different colored pixels are diffused in a fairly organic pattern.

Conversion order for scanned images

The order in which the steps of a conversion process are performed affects the final image quality where high-resolution scans are involved. Let's say you have a 24-bit 300 dpi scan that needs to be reduced to an 8-bit 75 dpi image for use in a presentation. The physical resolution should be reduced first so that the color palette is derived only from pixels that will be in the final image. In other words, when restricting a palette to a limited number of colors, it should be derived from the smallest number of master colors. JPEG conversion should also be performed after any required resolution reductions.

On a similar note, if you plan to use only part of an image, crop out the unwanted part first so that the color reduction process doesn't have to consider colors that won't ultimately be used. Let's say you're using a scanned portion of a magazine cover depicting a lush green jungle. If you map the palette first, one or more color registers will be wasted on the magazine's logo. Cutting the logo and accompanying border away first will free those color registers for more shades of green.

Designing CLUTs at the project level

One of the biggest considerations in determining color palettes for images is how they need to work together in a project. Transitions in which portions of two images share the screen simultaneously are particularly problematic. Most authoring packages will retain the palette of the previous image while bringing on the next image, then switch the CLUT to that of the new image. If the color palettes of the two images don't match, the colors of the new image will initially appear wrong, then flash to their proper colors. Bad news.

One way around this problem is to use transitions that fade to black between screens. These fades are implemented by automatically reducing all of the color register values to 0, loading the new image, switching to the new palette, then fading all of the register values up to their actual values. Since the palette is switched while the entire screen is black, no color differences between images are noticeable. (Fade to white serves the same purpose.)

248

If you have a variety of digitized photographs in your presentation, you may find that the use of a common palette creates too much artifacting in the images. In this case, fading to black between images with unique adaptive palettes is probably the best solution.

For smooth transitions between two images, the images should have the same color palette. (A few authoring packages, such as Macromedia Director, offer an advanced palette transition feature that circumvents this somewhat.) The problem increases from choosing the optimal color palette for a single image to choosing the best common palette for all images. Perhaps the best method is to paste representative portions of each 24-bit image into a common document, then use an image processor to derive and save the optimal custom palette. Then use the image processor to reduce each individual image to that custom palette.

Forcing existing images of 8-bit resolution or less to conform to a common palette is more of a challenge. Under demanding circumstances, bring the 8-bit images into an image processor, bump them up to 24 bits, and implement the steps just described. In lieu of that, the remap function in many graphics programs and authoring systems can force images to conform to an existing CLUT. This is handy if one image is more demanding of accurate color or if you wish to overlap an object on a screen.

Remapping is most effective if the images or objects have similar colors but in a different order. The fidelity of remapping bears partially on the master colors: Mapping a 24-bit image down to an 8-bit palette will yield much better results than mapping one 8-bit palette to another.

Manual adjustment of colors after palette conversion sometimes aids in compromising color maps. If the image to be remapped has an orange, for example, and the closest color in the master CLUT is red, the orange will turn to red. Adjusting the red in the common CLUT to a red-orange might provide the best results. The order of the colors in the CLUT can also be manually rearranged so that adjacent colors are optimized for gradient fills or color cycling in images that will be created later. Remember to work with a master color map and remap any other images to that map.

Some programs allow you to lock certain color registers during remapping. This is handy when you have a subset of colors, such as those for a logo, that must remain absolutely true across images. Locked colors will not change while the rest of the palette is remapped. Another use for this feature is when a register (typically, 0) is used for video keying. Before mapping, set the register to a color that is not present in the image and lock it so that no valid colors are mapped to this ultimately invisible register.

❖ Different Programs, Different Fortes

Few artists can rely on a single graphics program to serve every design and production need. Even the best programs lack some features found in others. The more tools you become familiar with, the more flexibility you have in your graphic creations. Although image processing and paint applications are designed for two different purposes, they are beginning to share similar features. You might find that basic painting is best done with the tools in a paint program, while the final art might be improved via manipulation in the image processor. Similarly, charts and graphs are often easier to create and manipulate in an object-oriented environment, then converted to bitmaps for aesthetic touches.

Using multiple programs is made easier when the programs you are using support the same file formats. When this is not the case, file conversion software can often act as a go-between. The most incompatible images are usually bitmapped formats versus Post-Script files, due to their conceptual differences. Structured drawing and PostScript illustration programs are best suited for mechanical drawing and type manipulation. In addition, a large volume of clip art is available for the PostScript-based desktop publishing community. Bitmap packages are best suited for manipulating scanned images, creating complex color patterns, and emulating art created with traditional media. Bitmapped images are the most prominent image type supported by multimedia applications.

If your software does not support conversion of object-oriented files to bitmaps, all is not lost. Most illustration programs have a preview mode that lets you see an image in a variety of magnifications. Use the scale and magnification controls to display the image at the right size compared to the screen. Then use a screen capture accessory to take a digital snapshot of the screen. This creates a bitmap file that can be pasted into paint and image processing packages.

❖ Working with Bitmaps

Bitmapped images at screen resolution are "jaggy" by nature. It is important to ensure that the image doesn't degenerate below screen resolution. The primary rules for bitmap manipulation pertain to scaling and rotation.

Scaling

Ideally, bitmapped elements should be created at the size at which they will be displayed and never be scaled. The cardinal rule is to avoid enlarging the scale of a bitmap! Say you scale a bitmap element by 200 percent. The average paint program will replace each pixel with two pixels, yielding a severe case of aliasing. Now let's say you scale the same original by 50 percent. The computer has to lose pixels rather than manufacture them. While this has its own side effects, it is far preferable to having the computer manufacture pixels. (See Figure 9.18.)

Figure 9.18

Effects of scaling a bitmap.

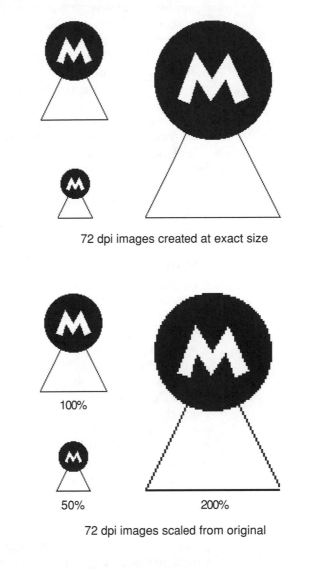

72 dpi images created at exact size

100%

50%   200%

72 dpi images scaled from original

A common scenario where this issue arises is a logo that is reused in different sizes throughout a presentation. Scan or create such a logo at the largest size in which it will be used, refine and save it at that size, then scale it down to the smaller size. This will yield more appealing results than starting small and enlarging. When performing the reduction, try a few variations on size since some will produce a more faithful transformation. Evenly divisible increments such as 50 percent or 25 percent usually work best. Scaling by 50 percent basically tells the computer to lose every other pixel—a fairly straight-forward task. If, on the other hand, you scale by an irregular factor such as 77 percent, you're asking the computer to loose fractions of pixels—an impossible task that produces artifacting problems.)

If you are forced to scale a bitmap up, all is not lost. The first option is to tweek the results by hand, adding and deleting pixels as needed to smooth out the appearance of the image. Many image processors support a more sophisticated interpolation method than paint programs do for generating additional pixels. A more roundabout method involves importing the bitmap into the background of an illustration program, tracing it in the drawing layer, scaling the object, then exporting or screen-capturing to yield a bitmap again. This method is most effective with simple elements and is particularly useful when several different sizes of the same element are required.

Angles

Most paint applications will let you draw lines and geometric elements at any angle, as well as rotate objects at any angle. The problem is that edges that look fine at horizontal and vertical orientations degrade at virtually all other angles. Working with pixels is much like working with graph paper: you can fill in a sequence of adjacent horizontal or vertical elements and have a smooth line, yet a diagonal will appear to have a stairstep effect. The key is to work with angles that produce the least artifacting. An angle of 45° is the best since the pixels are still more or less linear. The next best angles are 30°, 60°, 15°, and 75°. When drawing lines endpoint-to-endpoint or rotating elements freeform, the marquees will provide edges that you can use to judge how well the element will translate at various angles. (See Figure 9.19.)

Duplication

Copying and pasting elements can be a tremendous time saver, especially when used with other tools like flipping. The classic example would be cleaning up a poorly scanned logo. Most typefaces share a common geometry throughout their alphanumeric components. Elements such as serifs, stems, and ascenders are duplicated,

Figure 9.19

Certain angles yield less artifacting when rotating objects.

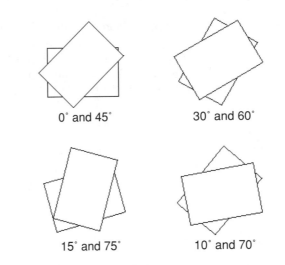

0° and 45°   30° and 60°

15° and 75°   10° and 70°

which means that you can use the duplication power of graphics programs to simplify the clean-up task.

Let's start with the serifed capital I as an example. The letter is completely symmetrical, so all we have to do is perfect one quarter of it, then copy, flip, and paste it several times to fine-tune the rest of the letter. Then the bottom of the I can be pasted over the bottoms of the letters F, H, K, N, T, P, R, and Y as well. Extending this concept, an R can be made from a perfected P, a Q from a perfected O, and so forth. Repetitive letters should just be duplicated from a single clean one.

Other effects can be used in conjunction with duplication. Simple drop shadows can be created easily by cutting out an element, changing the color to black or to a "darken" mode, stamping it down, then changing back to normal mode and pasting the element down offset over the shadow.

Progressive saves

It's difficult to extract elements once they are integrated into bitmaps. Save any individual elements or development stages of images so that they are easily accessible if you want to make changes or use them for another task. Similarly, take advantage of the layering capabilities of object-oriented graphics applications in order to isolate design elements.

Anti-aliasing

Bitmapped images can be polished as a finishing touch by running them through a program with global anti-aliasing or blur capabilities. This effect should be used with caution, however, as it tends to blur thin lines and small type. Some programs get around this problem by offering control over the level of anti-aliasing. Alternately, anti-aliasing can be used before those elements are added to the final image. Applying anti-aliasing to areas that were created using anti-aliased paint tools in the first place may create too much blur.

❖ Working with Animation

Animation taxes the throughput capabilities of your computer. Full-frame, full-speed, full-color, full-length is a tall order for today's processors. The motion compression and direct disk access technologies described in Chapter 8 can help. Fortunately, several production techniques can be used to maintain smooth and manageable animations.

Smaller files

The goal is to reduce the volume of information to improve throughput. The more bit planes the frames of an animation contain, the more number crunching is required. Reduce the CLUT to the minimum number required for the subject matter or aesthetic value. The same caveat goes for image size. Fewer changing pixels mean faster loads and faster rendering. Try reducing your animation so that it fits into a frame, window, or background screen that doesn't change.

Use of motion compression precludes storing and redrawing redundant information. As a general rule, the more complex an image is, the less effective motion compression will be. Avoid using dithers, patterns, anti-aliasing, and textures—at least in portions of an image that have moving objects. The eye will naturally be drawn to motion over detail, anyway. (A sustained final frame is a possible exception to this rule, since the viewer may dwell on it for a while.)

Animate during delivery

Many presentation packages allow objects to be manipulated during delivery. This allows the object(s) to be saved independently from the image. As a result, you only need storage, memory, and load times associated with a single frame and a single object, as opposed to that required for many frames. This is particularly conservative of resources when an element like a logo is used many times during a presentation. The actual speed of performance of real-time animation, as compared to motion-compressed animation, varies between products, so some experimentation might be in order to help decide which process to use for certain production requirements.

In a similar concept, some presentation packages directly support drawing commands. Although not effective for complex images, you can conserve resources by composing simple images in real-time during delivery using lines, circles, fills, and so forth. This can be combined with double-buffering so that the drawing process is hidden to the audience while viewing the previous screen.

Animation ideas

There are as many animation techniques as design techniques. Following are some animation examples to get (or keep) the wheels turning.

Line drawings and logos with a scripted or artistic element lend themselves to being drawn before the viewer's eyes. This process is simple if not tedious. Establish a range of frames in which the drawing will take place, then paste the complete element into the last frame. Now copy it to the previous frame, erase a little, copy that to the previous frame, erase a little more, and continue this process until you have "undrawn" the entire element backwards through the scene. Playing the segment back normally will give the appearance of the element being drawn in real-time. (See Figure 9.20.)

Figure 9.20

An image can be made to appear to draw itself by "undrawing" it backwards over a series of frames.

Frame 150

Frame 300

Frame 450

Frame 600

Another powerful animation effect is to have an image, such as a logo, assemble itself for the viewer. The first step is isolating the individual elements that make up the final image (a perfect case for saving different stages of your work). Animate the movement of each element by stamping it down in position on the final frame and having the animation path lead up to that frame and position. Work from background to foreground to add each object and path, and save after each added element is animated satisfactorily so that you're free to experiment in getting each subsequent pass right. Some fairly complex animations can be built up in this fashion. (See Figure 9.21.)

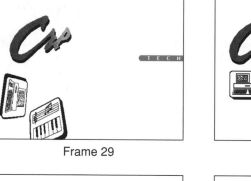

Frame 29

Frame 49

Frame 63

Frame 79

Frame 104

If you can't beat 'em, join 'em. If your image size and quality will yield less that smooth animation—less than, say, 16 frames per second—exaggerate the jerkiness and turn it into an artistic stop-animation effect. This can be particularly effective on a sequence of video frames that are digitized one per beat to an accompanying soundtrack, for example. The effect can be enhanced by adding a motion blur effect to each frame or painting right on the frame (the latter is a technique called *rotoscoping*).

Pop TV commercials often seem to have titles or backgrounds that are alive. This can be accomplished by hand-drawing a series of, say, four frames that vary slightly, then looping them. Playing the loop back at rapid speed will produce a psychedelic effect. This short series of frames can be replicated end-on-end into a longer set of frames. Additional animated elements can then be added in the foreground so that they play themselves out over the repeating background.

Color cycle animation

The effects of color cycling can create animated effects with only one frame. Changing the colors in the paint registers will also change the on-screen colors originally painted with those registers. Since color values can be shifted through the CLUT registers at a much faster rate than a series of complete frames can be displayed, these effects offer impressive speed alternatives. The key to cycle animation is careful planning of the palette and restricting the cycling effects to portions of the palette.

Cycling can be used to simulate TV commercials that rapidly flash text at the viewer. Set contrasting foreground and background colors and define them as the cycle range. Paint the text with one color and the background with other. Turn cycling on at high speed, and the image will flash by inverting the colors. (See Figure 9.22.) A variation on this theme will create a straight flash without inverting the background. Let's say you fill the background with register 0, and paint the text with register 1. If you set register 2 to the same value as the background (color 0) and set the cycle range to encompass only registers 1 and 2, cycling will force the text to flash on a static background.

These principles can be extended to animate the movement of colors through an image. Color cycling can create the effect of an animated marquee if each bulb is painted using successive colors in the cycle range. A highlight can also be made to run through an image by specifying matching ranges for gradients and cycling.

A similar technique can be applied to tasks like animating arrows to illustrate flow. This technique is only effective when you

Figure 9.22

Color cycling can be used to create a flashing image or element with little overhead.

have a plain background color under the objects whose color is being cycled. First, select a small cycle range, say three paint pots, and fill them with three distinct colors. Paint a stream of arrows with the three successive colors, either using cycle draw or by manually selecting the colors. Finally, set the color of two of the registers to match the background color, and the third for the desired arrow color. When cycling is turned on, only one of the three sets of arrows will be visible at any moment, since the others blend invisibly into the background.

❖ Working with Scanners and Image Processors

Working with scanners and image processors entails all of the considerations of working with bitmaps and more. Always align the source material as straight as possible before scanning. If the result of the scan does not look straight, adjust the positioning and rescan for better alignment. These steps can save lots of clean-up work later. Scanned text will often need some clean-up no matter how straight it is. Any time you can replace scanned text with fresh text using a real font, do it. If the scanned text is part of a background, consider placing the fresh text on a plaque or similar device to replace the entire localized area.

Printed materials containing photographs or shading (halftones, screens, and the like) are actually a series of dots. Scans of printed images often emphasize those dot patterns. Many image processors offer a despeckle filter to remove individual dots: This type of filter can greatly improve the appearance of scans of printed materials. (Note, this does not usually apply to actual photographs, only printed reproductions.)

For the sake of detail and flexibility, scan at the optical resolution of the scanner if you have the means to store and later manipulate the data. It's easier to throw detail away than to manufacture it! Memory requirements and processing time are formidable on large or high-resolution images, however. One approach is to make a low-res working copy of the image(s) for use during a comping process, then apply the perfected techniques to the original hi-res files. Many image processors store nonimage information such as selections and masks in their native files. Perfected images will take less disk space when saved in standard display formats.

Image Processing Tips

- Perform complex operations with as few applications and windows open as possible. This provides a greater chance for complex manipulations to occur in RAM rather than the slower virtual memory of a disk drive.
- Perform complex selections on a gray-scale version of a file for faster operation and easier contrasts. Save the selection as a mask, then import and apply it to the color version of the image.
- Store non-displayed information, such as masks and alpha channel gradations, in a separate file and remove them from the final graphic file. This makes for smaller image files.
- If scanning time and file size are an issue, always pre-scan images so you only scan the information needed.
- Clean the glass scanner bed and dust the physical photos or art before scanning.

❖ ❖ ❖ ❖ ❖ ❖

Although this chapter has presented a lot of rules and ideas for graphic design, they are merely starting points. True learning experience comes from experimentation given an awareness of the basics. Many graphic designers in the '90s may tell you that their first rule is to break all the rules!

Audio

Music, speech, and sound effects are as integral to the communication process as visual information. Today's sonic devices include digital audio tools for the computer in addition to the analog and digital resources of the traditional recording studio. The advent of MIDI, sequencers, and inexpensive digital synthesizers has brought the ability to compose and record original music to the masses. As with the visual arts, electronic technology enables creative individuals lacking hand–eye coordination to experiment with compositions ranging from simple melodies to sophisticated orchestrations.

Chapter 10 sets out the basic principles of sound in both acoustic and electronic forms. Chapter 11 explores the various audio tools available to musicians, engineers, and producers. Chapter 12 offers suggestions for using these tools effectively. ❖

Audio Technology

As with the preceding discussion of visual information, the best way to begin studying sound is with its occurrence in nature. No matter how much electronic equipment is involved, human perception relies on both the acoustic phenomenon of pressure waves in the air reaching the eardrums and the translation of those waves to neural information.

The discussion leads to the principles enabling both analog and digital technology to represent, convey, and manipulate sound. The chapter concludes with a look at the MIDI technology that has revolutionized the composition, recording, and performance processes.

PRINCIPLES OF SOUND

Sound can be described as oscillations of air pressure that stimulate the eardrum and, by extension, the auditory nerves and the brain. To create that stimulation, the oscillations must occur in a range of frequencies and amplitudes. Just as absolute measurements of frequency and amplitude in light are perceived as color and brightness, the same qualities in sound are perceived as pitch and loudness. This chapter assumes knowledge of the basics of waves and media covered in Part 1.

❖ Frequency and Pitch

The hearing range of the average person is approximately 20Hz to 17KHz. As we age—and/or listen to lots of loud music—the upper end of our hearing range decreases to 15KHz or lower. Sounds above our hearing range—*ultrasonic* sounds—simply go undetected by the human ear, although many animals can hear well above 20KHz.

The lower threshold of sound is much more distinguishable, however. Have you ever listened carefully to a lawn mower or chain saw as it starts up? At low throttle, the "putt, putt, putt..." sound can be heard about five times per second—the engine is firing at a frequency of 5Hz. As the throttle is increased and the speed of the engine increases, so does the frequency of the sound it emits. At around 20Hz, the repetitions of the engine can be perceived as an extremely low pitch. If the throttle is increased further, the pitch will rise accordingly.

Frequency and pitch are related, but differ in several important ways. First, frequency is a scientific measurement corresponding to one of the physical characteristics of a waveform, whereas pitch is the subjective quality our brains perceive from frequency. Second, the relationship of frequency to pitch is approximately exponential: The 200Hz difference between 100Hz and 300Hz is significantly perceptible, whereas the same 200Hz difference between 10KHz and 10.2KHz is not. Finally, frequency is an absolute measurement, whereas pitch is relative.

The effects of frequency and pitch are related to Newton's Second Law of Motion: Given two moving objects of similar material and shape but different size, the larger object produces a longer wavelength—and therefore lower frequency and pitch—than its smaller counterpart. This relationship is seen in the world of musical instruments: larger bells have a lower pitch than smaller ones, cellos are pitched lower than violins, tubas sound lower than trumpets, etc.

Taking the idea of wavelength and pitch one step further, let's examine a guitar string. As it is tightened, the mass between the endpoints is lessened and the restoring force is increased: the wavelength is shortened and the pitch is increased. (Lessening the tension, of course, has the opposite effect.) Pitch is further determined by pushing the string down with the finger so that it contacts the fingerboard. The mass is increased, and restoring force is decreased. As a result, the wavelength is shortened and the pitch is raised. (See Figure 10.1.)

This same relationship between wavelength and pitch occurs in every pitched instrument. The piano, for example, has a series of increasingly shorter strings that correspond to higher notes. The pipe organ applies this concept to moving columns of air, where shorter pipes produce air columns with shorter wavelengths and correspondingly higher pitches. Brass and wind instruments employ a similar principle, except the wavelength of the air column is

Figure 10.1

The pitch and fundamental frequency ranges for common instruments.

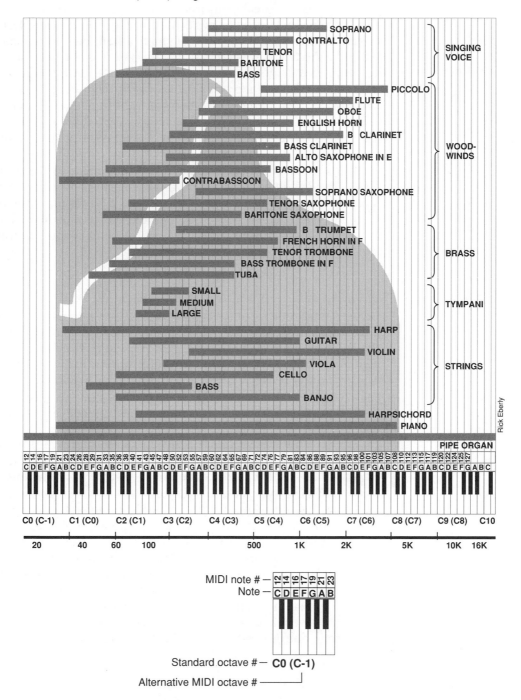

increased and decreased by opening and closing holes or valves—resulting in a pitch change.

The largest musical measurement of pitch is the *octave*. Taking any pitch one octave higher will exhibit twice the frequency of the original tone; one octave lower will have a frequency of one-half of the original pitch. In Western music the octave is subdivided into 12 *half-steps* that correspond to the notes available on pitched instruments such as the piano or guitar. (Some other cultures employ fewer or greater numbers of subdivisions of the octave.) Half-steps are further subdivided into 100 smaller increments knows as *cents*. The smallest change the average ear can perceive is approximately five cents.

Each instrument or other sound source has a range of frequencies and perceived pitches. (See Figure 10.1.) Since pitch is relative, some method of standardization is required. The internationally recognized standard is that the A above Middle C on the piano be tuned to 440Hz. This is known as *concert pitch* and that particular note is logically referred to as *A-440*.

❖ Amplitude and Loudness

Greater amplitude results when objects are set into motion with greater force. Just as we derive the relative perception of pitch from the absolute frequency of sound waves, we derive the relative perception of loudness from their absolute amplitude. The human ear is an extremely sensitive organ. At a frequency of 2KHz, for example, the ear can respond to sound pressure levels that are a trillion (10^{12}) times more powerful than the smallest perceivable sound—an incredibly wide range.

The ear perceives sound pressure in logarithmic ratios. Doubling the sound energy doesn't result in the perception of twice the volume. Two violins, for example, do not seem to be twice as loud as a single violin. Only when the intensity of a sound is increased approximately tenfold do we perceive it as having doubled in loudness.

The unit of measurement associated with a tenfold increase in power is the *bel*, named after Alexander Graham Bell. This measurement is divided by ten to yield the increment of the decibel (dB) as an everyday measurement of sound pressure level (SPL). Conveniently, a change of 1 dB represents the smallest difference in intensity that the trained ear can normally perceive at a frequency of 1000Hz. Given that, doubling the actual sound power—two violins rather than one, for instance—yields a 3 dB increase in sound pressure.

Figure 10.2

The sound pressure levels of a variety of common noises.

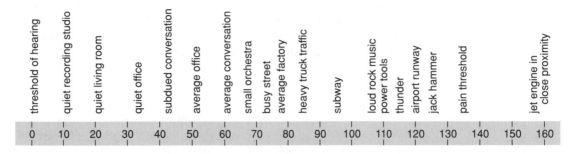

Since the decibel is a relative concept, a reference point is needed. Therefore, 0 dB has been established as the threshold of human hearing—the softest sound the average person can perceive. All other decibel statistics are referenced to this standard. (See Figure 10.2.)

Equal loudness contour

The human ear's perception of frequency and loudness has a non-linear relationship. The standard *Fletcher–Munson curves* show that the ear is less sensitive to lower and higher frequencies at reduced sound pressure levels. (See Figure 10.3.) This aspect of human hear-

Figure 10.3

The Fletcher–Munson curves show the ear's heightened sensitivity to frequencies between 1KHz and 6KHz at reduced sound levels.

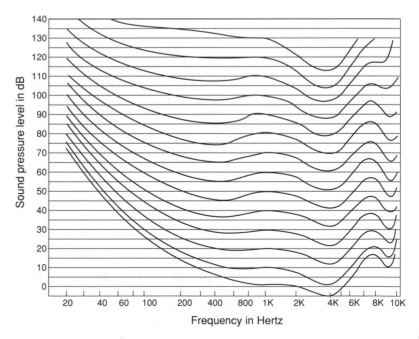

ing is known as *equal loudness contour*. The loudness button on many stereo receivers boosts the bass and treble ranges to compensate for the ear's frequency response at lower listening levels.

Volume and loudness are not the same. Volume refers to the amount of sonic power at which the ear perceives various degrees of loudness depending upon the frequency range.

❖ Sonic Signatures

The sine wave represents the simplest possible motion that could result in a sound. (The steady tone accompanying the test pattern displayed by television stations during nonbroadcast hours is a simple sine wave.)

If our aural world were made up of only simple sine waves, we wouldn't have any way to distinguish between different sound sources. Each instrument, person, and object in the world has its own sonic signature or waveform when emitting sound. The perception of the characteristic of an audio waveform is referred to as *timbre* or *tone color*.

Harmonics

Fourier's theory that any waveform is a blend of various sine waves applies to sound. The sine wave with a frequency corresponding to that of the actual note being played—such as A-440—is called the *fundamental frequency*. Almost all natural sounds also have a series of harmonics or higher-frequency sine waves that blend with the fundamental (technically the first harmonic) to create a more complex waveform and richer timbre. In pitched sounds, these harmonics are all integer multiples of the fundamental. (See Figure 10.4.) The frequency of the second harmonic is twice that of the fundamental, the frequency of the third harmonic is three times that of the fundamental, and so forth. (Harmonics are sometimes referred to as overtones, although the first overtone is technically equivalent to the second harmonic.)

Each sound has its own complex combination of harmonic overtones, and each harmonic has its own amplitude. (See Figure 10.5.) The drawbars on the original Hammond organs and the stops on pipe organs add harmonics in controlled amounts, for example. The primary difference between the rather static sound of an organ and the more animated qualities of other sounds is due to the fact that most sound waves exhibit harmonics that change amplitude independently of one another over time.

The exact interaction of harmonics, amplitudes, and durations that characterize a sound are largely determined by the molecular

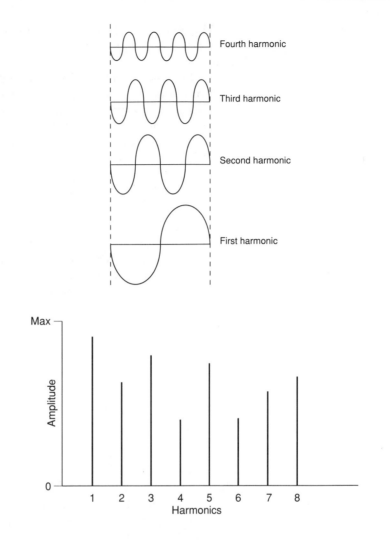

make-up of the associated materials, and the shape of the object. For example, the timbre of the violin owes to the combined properties of the string, bow, fingerboard, body, and even the human finger that controls the wavelength. The shape and materials of the instrument's body further contribute to the harmonic structure in addition to acting as a natural amplifier.

The stronger the higher harmonics are, the brighter the sound will be. More force is required in nature to set higher harmonics in motion than their lower counterparts. The combination of these factors results in brightness increasing with loudness. A piano sounds considerably brighter when the keys are struck harder, for example.

The collective harmonic attributes of the elements comprising a sound source dictate its resonant frequencies. This applies to sound sources as diverse as instruments, voices, and speaker cabinets. The construction of the violin dictates a resonant frequency of approximately 350Hz. Human voices are distinguished from one another partially by the vocal chords and partially by the resonant frequencies of the air cavities in the body and mouth. Speaker cabinets also form air cavities with their own resonant frequencies. The sensitivity of the ear to the frequencies between 1KHz and 6KHz is actually resonance owing to the shape of the ear canal itself.

Harmonics and sound reproduction

Harmonic content affects the frequency response required to reproduce sounds faithfully. Few instruments produce fundamental frequencies above 5KHz, but many exhibit overtones that extend higher than the range of human hearing. For example, while the fundamental frequency of the note two octaves above Middle C is 1024Hz, the presence of a 16th harmonic in the sound source would incur an overtone of 16,384Hz—a frequency whose reproduction can suffer at the hands of many media and sound systems.

Amplitude transformation over time

In addition to the interactions of individual harmonic amplitudes with time, global changes in amplitude of all harmonics over time determine the other primary factor that makes up the sonic signature. Four primary temporal elements exist with respect to sound. (See Figure 10.6.) *Attack* is the time required for the sound to reach peak amplitude after force is applied. *Sustain level* is the amplitude that is maintained while the initiating force is still applied. *Initial decay* is the time it takes the sound to fall from maximum amplitude

Figure 10.6

The way in which the overall amplitude of a sound changes over time is an important part of its sonic signature.

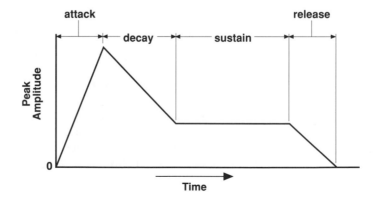

to the sustain level. *Release* is the time required for the amplitude to fall from the sustain level back to zero after the initiating force is removed.

A few examples will bring these parameters into perspective. Most wind instruments exhibit less than immediate attack and release because time is required for the air to start and stop moving through their cavities; sustain level is determined by the air pressure being applied. Percussion instruments are typically characterized by immediate attacks, no sustain level, and fairly short decay/release times. An electronic organ exhibits immediate attack, full sustain level with no decay as long as a key is depressed, and immediate release when a key is released. A piano offers percussive attack, no sustain level, and long decay; equally long releases are available when the sustain pedal is depressed.

All other factors the same, the size of the sound source will also influence the attack, decay, and release times. More time is required to fill and evacuate the larger pipes in the lower registers of the pipe organ than the smaller ones in the higher registers, for example. The same is true of all wind, brass, reed, and stringed instruments. (Tubas and cellos exhibit longer attack and decay times than trumpets and violins.) While percussive instruments exhibit instantaneous attack, the sound of larger drums, bells, and the like take longer to die out than smaller ones.

Highly percussive sounds exhibit a *transient attack*. This is typified as a sharp amplitude spike at the onset of the sound that falls off very quickly. Sounds with high transients provide an additional challenge to the recording and amplification process.

Unpitched sound

Unpitched sounds, such as cymbals and drums, contain overtones that are not integer multiples of the fundamental. (One cymbal can be perceived as being categorically higher or lower in pitch than another, but an actual note value cannot be identified.) The waveforms of unpitched sounds are aperiodic. The more frequencies an aperiodic sound has, the closer it comes to being pure *noise*—sound that exhibits all frequencies at once. (The sound you hear from a television when the antenna or cable is disconnected is an example of pure noise.)

Speech

Human speech is an extremely complex pattern of changing frequencies, harmonics, and amplitudes. Consonants and vowels are essentially variations in harmonic structure. (You can speak in a monotone voice and still be intelligible.) Inflection is the result of variations in fundamental frequency or perceived pitch over time. The amplitude characteristic determines emphasis and the levels ranging from a whisper to a shout.

COMBINING COMPLEX SOUNDS

When two or more sound sources are combined, all of the properties of waveform addition and phase relationships described in Chapter 1 apply. Several additional points deserve brief mention.

When two or more sounds are combined, one that is significantly louder can obscure a softer one in a phenomenon called *masking*. More commonly, masking occurs at specific frequencies when sounds contain similar harmonics. Masking becomes a major issue when ensuring the clarity of various instruments and voices in an audio mix. (Mixing tips are offered in Chapter 12.)

When two similar sound waves vary slightly in frequency, their combination produces a phenomenon known as *beating*. Beating is apparent when one instrument is slightly out of tune with a pitch reference such as another instrument.

While beating of any significance can be annoying and dissonant, subtle beating can add sonic richness. A single trumpet or violin sounds fairly sterile compared to two, three, or an entire section of similar instruments playing the same notes. The piano offers another example in that the middle register has two strings per note and the upper register has three. In both of these examples, the additional sound sources increase the volume; the slight differences in frequency produce a fuller, more animated sound as well. Beating comes into play when tuning instruments, synthesizing interesting sounds, and creating full-sounding musical productions.

❖ Acoustics

Sound waves can be reflected, absorbed, or refracted by an object, or simply bent around it. Consideration of these qualities with respect to all of the physical aspects of a listening environment is the study of *acoustics*. The resulting ambiance of a listening environment determines much about not only what we hear, but how we feel about the listening experience.

Reflection in sound

The most obvious form of sonic reflection is the *echo* that occurs when you shout into an area like a canyon. First you hear the actual sound leaving your mouth. Next you hear the first reflection as the sound bounces off the canyon wall and returns back to your ear. The amount of delay in the first reflection is dictated by your proximity to the wall.

Additional echoes usually follow the first. They might come from the original sound striking an additional surface. The echoes themselves may bounce off additional surfaces. Each reflection has its own delay time as a result of relative distances. As you can imagine, these reflections can add up to some fairly complex interactions hitting your ear. The natural sonic qualities of a listening environment are perceived as *ambiance*.

In a canyon echoes can be perceived individually. Confined spaces—such as concert halls, recording studios, and meeting rooms—exhibit similar reflective qualities, but the shorter distances between surfaces result in such small delays between reflections that human ears cannot perceive them individually. A concert hall might produce reflections that take 30 milliseconds (30/1000ths of a second) to reach the ear, rather than a second or more for canyon echoes. Moreover, confined space provides more reflective surfaces, hence more reflections and angles. The combination of sounds reflecting off all of the surfaces in close proximity is perceived as a sort of lingering rumble known as *reverberation*. (See Figure 10.7.)

Figure 10.7

Reverberation is the composite of all the sonic reflections in a listening environment.

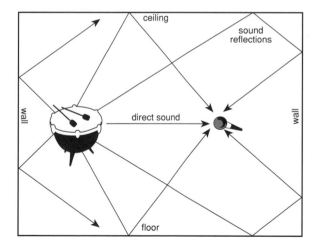

Factors that contribute to the reverberant quality of a listening environment include the number of walls and objects, their distances, composition, sizes, and angle in relation to the sound. Like all waves, sound is reflected at an equal and opposite angle to the one at which it strikes a surface. Many similar paths of sonic reflection crisscross one another. All of those whose angles intersect with the ear will be perceived as a composite reverberant quality. A generalization can be made that, given two different sized rooms with similar proportions, the larger room will exhibit longer reverberation times.

As another generalization, harder surfaces produce brighter sounding reflections than softer surfaces. This is due to the relationship between the particles in the materials and the higher audio frequencies. The reflective qualities associated with sound parallel those attributed to light in Chapter 7.

Amplification

As with light, sound amplitude decreases over distance according to the law of inverse squares—making amplification an important part of acoustics. Most acoustic amplification is caused by reflection. Acoustically-designed concert environments, like amphitheaters, employ a shell behind the performers. As the original sounds encounter this structure, they are reflected in the direction of the audience to increase projection. In a concert hall sound reflects off many walls many times, which adds reverberation as well as volume. Conversely, the outer ear focuses and reflects sounds into the ear as a means of amplification.

The same principles are at work in most acoustic instruments. The reeds, strings, mouthpieces, and membranes of most acoustic instruments create little air pressure alone. The cavities of the instruments provide for a chain reaction of reflections with such short delays that perceptible echoes and reverberations are replaced by significant amplification and complex phase interaction. (The shape and materials of the cavities also influence the resonant frequencies.) Similarly, speaker cabinets amplify and redirect the oscillations in air pressure produced behind the speaker cone.

Absorption

The harder (more dense) a surface, the more reflective it is. The less reflective it is, the more absorptive it is. If the sound passing through an object is not completely absorbed, the remaining waves will be refracted on the other side. This principle is demonstrated by muffled sounds heard through a closed door or solid wall. Shorter wavelengths are normally absorbed and/or reflected, while longer wavelengths are not.

The contents of a room also affect its acoustics. Furniture and human beings tend to absorb sound. You have probably noticed that rooms are more reverberant when they're empty. Similarly, a concert hall sounds completely different when it is filled with people than when it is empty.

Sound waves will bend around an object if their wavelengths are greater than or equal to the size of the object. An obstacle such as a partial room divider will obstruct selected frequency components, but will not block a sound entirely.

Room resonance and standing waves

Envision for a moment a sound wave reflecting from one parallel wall to another. When the wave is reflected again, it encounters similar waves still coming from the original source. At intervals that are integer multiples of the wavelength (such as 1/2 the room dimension), the waves will reinforce each other causing greater amplitude at that frequency. When the two waves are 180 degrees out of phase, they will cancel out and the listener will hear nothing at that frequency. In practice, these frequencies may seem louder or softer depending upon where you are in the room! These phenomena are known as *standing waves*.

Since rooms are relatively sealed cavities, standing waves can make a room resonate like an instrument. Each of the three dimensions of a room with parallel walls will cause the room to resonate at a frequency with a wavelength corresponding to twice the dimension. For example, if one of a room's dimensions is 10 feet, the room will resonate at the 55Hz frequency that corresponds to a wavelength of 20 feet. (Resonance can also occur at higher harmonics of the fundamental resonant frequency.) Each parallel dimension will create its own resonant frequency, the relative amplitudes of which will correspond to the materials of the surfaces.

The effect of such resonance is that the corresponding frequencies will have a greater sound pressure level, causing them to seem stronger in this environment. A recording whose sound is mixed in such a room will sound deficient at those same frequencies when played back in another room of different dimensions. Any resonant characteristics of the playback environment will affect the perceived frequency balance of even the most pristine recording mix.

Due to the influence of all these acoustic properties, ideal recording and listening environments are designed so that frequency response is balanced. Parallel walls (including the ceiling) are eliminated where possible and reflective and absorptive materials are used appropriately. Where physical design solutions are not practical, electronic equalization is used to flatten the frequency response of the room. Practical solutions to acoustic problems are discussed in greater detail in Chapter 12.

❖ Psychoacoustics

The number of reflections combined with their delay times determines an overall perception of the listening experience. Up to a point the bigger the sound is, the bigger the experience seems. A cavernous cathedral could be damped with absorptive materials for less reverberation, but the spacious sound quality reinforces the sensation of deity. On the other end of the scale, a conversation in an acoustically deadened, or *anechoic*, room becomes uncomfortable because it feels unnatural. And the pleasure derived from singing in the shower is due largely to the plethora of nice, short reverberations that the surrounding tile offers!

Issues of frequency are equally important. Too much low-frequency content in reverberation sounds boomy or muddy, while not enough low frequency makes a sound seem to lack warmth. Too much high-frequency content can cause annoyance and pain, while not enough causes an apparent lack of clarity.

Directionality

Our sense of direction is largely dependent on our ears. The method we use to locate a sound differs for frequencies above and below 100Hz. Below 100Hz the waves that reach one ear are out of phase with those reaching the other because the wavelength is greater than the distance between the ears. The brain can associate some directionality with this phenomenon, but attributing an exact location to the sound source is difficult. Since the wavelength of frequencies above 100Hz is shorter than the distance between the ears, the sound waves reaching both ears are in phase; their difference in amplitude provides the brain with a way to pinpoint the location of the sound source.

This explains why we are less able to identify the location of low-frequency instruments and sounds. Some stereo systems exploit this phenomenon by using a single large monophonic bass cabinet to supplement a pair of stereo speakers that handle the higher frequencies.

ANALOG AUDIO

Until the nineteenth century, sound could only be manipulated physically. Some of the earliest examples of acoustic manipulation are found in the designs of Greek amphitheaters and baroque concert halls. The evolution of the small chamber music ensemble to the orchestra owed largely to acoustic necessities rather than aesthetic sensibilities. As population centers grew, so did the size of the listening halls—and more instruments were added to increase the volume. The parallel evolution of the clavichord and harpsichord into the pianoforte—the modern-day piano—stemmed in part from similar desires to amplify the volume of the instrument.

In the late 1800s, many inventors were working on converting acoustic sound to electrical sound. One of their goals was to amplify the sound beyond what was possible by acoustic manipulation alone. Conquering this problem would also mean that sound could be transferred over previously impossible distances and would lead to concepts of storage and manipulation as well.

Part 1 of this book laid the basic foundation of electronic handling of sound. Sound waves emanating from voices, instruments, or other natural sources are transduced into electric current via a microphone. Once in electrical form, the sound can be manipulated, combined selectively with other sounds, and/or stored for later retrieval. Sounds can also be created entirely at the electronic stage. Finally, the electrical waves are transduced back in sound pressure waves via a speaker.

❖ Signal Levels

Several corollaries to the decibel are used to reference electronic audio levels—dBu, dBm, and dBV. The background required to understand the differences is formidable. However, most multimedia work requires no such knowledge. More important are the concepts of impedance presented in Chapter 3 and the fact that audio signals fall into several basic categories that are incompatible without amplification or attenuation.

Microphones emit extremely weak signals—in the range of 1 millivolt. These *mic level* signals are extremely susceptible to interference and noise. Therefore, balanced low-impedance cables and circuits are desirable for microphones in general and mandatory with cables of any length.

Line level is referenced to two different standards. Most equipment used for home recording, semi-pro recording/amplification, and multimedia production/presentation is standardized at .316 volts. Professional recording gear in the U.S. is standardized at 1.23 volts. The former is referenced as -10 dB, while the latter is referenced as +4 dB. (Technically this refers to -10 dBu and +4 dBV, respectively. The differences in scale are much less important than the idea that pro signals are significantly "hotter" in voltage than semi-pro.)

Instruments, such as electric guitars, that employ pickups (transducers) typically emit signals that fall somewhere between mike level and line level. Electronic musical instruments, like synthesizers and drum machines, are typically in the semi-pro line level range.

The amplified signals used to drive speakers are significantly higher than line levels. The output voltage of an amplifier varies with the volume set in the previous stages. For example, a speaker with 8 ohms of impedance receiving the full output of a 10-watt amplifier is getting approximately 9 volts.

Audio stages and level matching

The voltage levels in the audio chain span such a wide range as to be incompatible. Connecting a microphone to a power amplifier input yields little or no result. Conversely, connecting the output of an amplifier to a line level input likely would result not only in massive overload and distortion, but also in damage. Since it is impractical for manufacturers to build a single circuit to accommodate such disparate signal levels, the audio chain is divided into various stages.

Perhaps the most important delineation is that between *preamplifiers* (preamps) and *power amplifiers* (amps). Since it is most practical to work with lower voltage signal levels, audio information is attenuated, modified, switched, mixed, and so forth at the preamp stage. The results of the preamp stage are then sent to a power amplifier whose sole purpose is to increase the signal level. The average home stereo receiver integrates the preamp and amp in one package. These functions are separate components in advanced stereo systems. Recording and mixing consoles output preamp level signals that also must be amplified to drive speakers.

The extremely low level outputs of microphones require special mike preamps to bring the signals up to the other levels at the preamp stage. Mike preamps are built into the better mixing consoles.

Most devices that accept audio inputs have some means of limiting the strength of the incoming signals. *Attenuators* are basic variable resistors that allow continuous control over input level. *Pads* are buffers that reduce signal levels at the input stage by an arbitrary amount.

Proper levels at each stage of the audio chain are essential in maintaining optimal fidelity. Each analog stage adds a certain degree of noise. As the signal is boosted at a given stage, so is the noise level. Each stage has a range of signal levels within which it works with optimal efficiency. Exceeding that range can add noise and distortion that is further amplified later in the chain. Ensuring optimal performance at each stage in an audio chain is important in addressing the weakest link principle.

Input signals higher than a circuit is designed to handle result in distortion or *clipping*. Peaks exceeding the levels the circuit can handle without distortion are flattened out, or clipped. This results in a sort of amplitude plateau. The more clipping occurs, the more the waveform begins to resemble a square wave—a sound similar to that of a clarinet. (See Figure 10.8.) Clipping results when transients exceed the circuit's design specs, even if the average program level is not clipping. Tips on maximizing the fidelity throughout the audio chain are presented in Chapter 12.

Figure 10.8

One of the most common forms of audio distortion occurs when amplitudes exceeding the circuit's capacity are clipped.

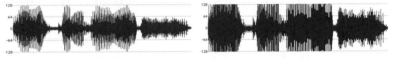

Audio waveform at optimum signal level   Same waveform clipped

Meters

Most audio systems that accept input from other devices have some form of meter that enables the user to monitor the signal levels within the device. Meters are calibrated in *VU* (volume units), with 0 VU corresponding to the optimum signal level the internal circuitry can handle without distortion.

The classic *VU meter* has a needle that swings back and forth in response to the music. These meters show only an average level because the response time is less than instantaneous. The ballistics of these meters are too sluggish to reflect the transients associated with snare drums and other highly percussive sounds. The better modern-day VU meters include a *peak light*, an LED that illuminates instantaneously whenever the signal begins clipping.

Most modern audio meters use an LED ladder—a series of LEDs that track the signal levels. These devices take less space and respond instantly to signal levels including peaks. Some incorporate a *peak hold* feature, where the peak level readings are sustained for a short period in a different color while the regular metering process continues. This feature is very helpful in visualizing transients.

❖ Audio Fidelity

Audio fidelity is dependent on and measured by many attributes. Although many of these were introduced categorically in Chapter 2, a brief recap in the context of audio is appropriate.

Frequency response describes the range of frequencies that a component or medium can reproduce accurately. Although optimal audio frequency response is 20Hz to 20KHz, few adults can hear frequencies or harmonics above approximately 17KHz. Uniform, or flat, response across the frequency range is also very important.

Given a constant input signal, many audio devices and media exhibit increases or decreases in amplitude in certain frequency ranges. (See Figure 10.9.) While graphs provide the greatest detail about frequency response, this data is more commonly stated numerically, such as 40Hz–16KHz ±3 dB. Although ±3 dB is a fairly common disclaimer, it represents 6 dB worth of deviation—a considerable amount. Smaller variances are better.

Figure 10.9

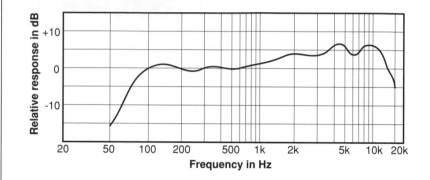

Dynamic range is the variation between the softest and loudest amplitude levels that a component or medium can reproduce. Given that the comfortable listening range of the human ear spans silence, or 0 dB, to somewhere around 90 dB, the 96 dB dynamic range of the audio CD is about perfect for audio reproduction. By contrast, the average audio cassette has a dynamic range of around 48 dB. Dynamic range is distinct from loudness. You could amplify a cassette of any music until your ears bleed, but that would not necessarily guarantee the ability to distinguish the subtleties between softer and louder passages or to experience the full impact of transients.

Signal-to-noise ratio is the ratio between the optimum amplitude of the audio program material (just before distortion) and the inherent noise of a circuit or medium. Headroom is the difference between the average amplitude of the program material and the clipping level. Chapter 12 explains that a major part of recording and mixing is positioning the amplitude of the program material so that it is high enough to mask the noise floor while maintaining enough headroom to avoid clipping of transients.

The weakest link principle applies to most of these attributes on the global level. A CD with full frequency content and dynamic range, for example, will be degraded if recorded, mixed, and/or amplified using components or media with lesser characteristics. The GIGO principle is equally applicable at every stage of the audio chain: If the dynamic range, frequency range, or signal-to-noise ratio is less than optimal or degraded at one stage, little can be done at subsequent stages to improve those qualities.

❖ Connections

Audio equipment employs both balanced and unbalanced lines as described in Chapter 3. The actual connectors vary depending upon the usage and manufacturer. (See Figure 10.10.) Adapters and cables are typically available to convert one type to another.

Figure 10.10

Various types of connectors used with audio equipment.

1/4"   XLR   RCA

Balanced lines typically employ XLR connectors. Unfortunately a discrepancy exists between American and European manufacturers as to whether the "hot" pin is 2 or 3. Check the specifications of both pieces of equipment being connected with XLR balanced lines to insure pinout compatibility. Alternately, stereo 1/4" connectors are sometimes used for balanced connections.

RCA phono connectors are used for interconnecting consumer electronic equipment; the exception is the use of stereo mini-phone plugs on portable equipment. For musical instruments and unbalanced semi-pro microphones 1/4" phone connections are used. Semi-pro recording gear uses some 1/4" phone and some RCA phono. Headphones use stereo 1/4" phone or mini-phone connectors. Most speakers either have terminals for bare wires or banana plugs.

DIGITAL AUDIO

Digital audio follows the principles of all digital media, as outlined in Chapter 2. Analog-to-digital converters are used to transform analog sound into numeric representations. Once in digital form, the information can be manipulated, stored, transmitted, and copied without degradation. Digital-to-analog converters transform the numbers back into analog signals that can be amplified and sent via speakers.

❖ Sampling Rates and Resolution

All digital audio is not created equal. The number of bits of resolution determines the dynamic range. Each bit contributes 6 dB of dynamic range. Therefore, 8-bit audio yields 48 dB of dynamic range—about that of a portable cassette deck. Similarly, 12-bit yields 72 dB—the dynamic range of an average open-reel recorder. 16-bit audio yields the 96 dB of dynamic range found in CDs—nearly the dynamic range of the human ear.

The quantization process used in digitizing audio sometimes yields artifacts known as *quantization noise*. This is one of the factors that cause some audiophiles to label digital audio as more harsh than analog. Some manufacturers employ a dithering technique to digital audio to smooth things out. Strange as it may seem, this is accomplished by adding white noise to the signal! Filters are also employed in the D-to-A conversion stage to smooth the "stair steps" resulting from the combination of sampling rate and quantization.

Sampling rate determines the frequency response of the recording according to the Nyquist theorem. Aliasing caused by attempting to record frequencies that exceed half the sampling rate manifests as anomalous noise in the recording that is decidedly unwanted. The cutoff slopes of the low-pass filters used to eliminate high frequencies that are potential causes of aliasing usually dictate that the effective frequency response is slightly less than half the sampling rate. Hence, the 44.1KHz sampling rate common to audio CDs yields about 20KHz frequency response.

Higher sampling rates and resolutions result in greater demand on throughput and storage. For example, 16-bit data contains twice as much information as 8-bit data. 44.1KHz sampling rate requires twice as much as 22.05KHz; stereo requires twice as much as mono. This results in storage and throughput requirements ranging from approximately 1.25MB per minute of mono 8-bit audio at 22.01KHz to 10MB per minute of stereo 16-bit audio at 44.1KHz.

Two other basic factors also determine the quality of digital audio. First, the quality of the circuit designs and components used in the ADCs and DACs is independent of the resolution and sampling rate specifications. Your ear can be as much a judge of audio quality as the specifications. Second, the weakest link and GIGO principles apply. Feeding garbage into the finest digital recording system will produce an immaculate recording of garbage. The most pristine recording will only sound as impressive as the remainder of the audio chain.

❖ **Digital Audio Protocols**

Sometimes digital audio information needs to be transferred in real time between devices. The communication protocols you are most likely to encounter in desktop multimedia production are AES/EBU, SDIF-2, and S/PDIF.

AES/EBU was developed jointly by the Audio Engineering Society and the European Broadcast Union and is common to most professional digital audio systems. It is a 2-channel RS-422 interface using balanced lines and either XLR or D-sub connectors. *SDIF-2* (Sony Digital Interface Format) is found on videotape-based PCM recording devices. It uses 75-ohm balanced lines with BNC connectors.

S/PDIF (Sony/Phillips Digital Interface Format) was developed jointly by Sony and Phillips. It is essentially an unbalanced version of the AES/EBU protocol and uses either RCA or fiber optic connections. S/PDIF is used with DAT recorders, CD players, and F1 encoders with digital interfaces.

THE MIDI REVOLUTION

Until 1983 most sophisticated electronic musical instruments could communicate only with products from the same manufacturer. While many proprietary system approaches were available, infinitely expandable synergistic electronic music systems were still a dream. The inclusion of a microprocessor in instruments paved the way for *MIDI* (Musical Instrument Digital Interface), a serial communications protocol designed specifically for electronic music devices. A joint group of electronic music manufacturers aptly named the MIDI Manufacturers Association (MMA) is responsible for the development and evolution of MIDI.

MIDI (pronounced "mid-ee") revolutionized the recording industry almost overnight by allowing many instruments to be centrally-controlled like one electronic orchestra. Few pop records are made without it. MIDI is now found in the vast majority of electronic musical instruments and has paved the way for a sort of global electronic music village. MIDI interfaces and software are available for virtually every personal computer as well.

❖ **MIDI Overview**

MIDI does not embody digital audio. Instead, it contains instructions controlling how and when devices like digital synthesizers produce sound. You can think of MIDI as a sort of PostScript for music. PostScript describes objects, rather than casting them into bitmapped form. MIDI describes the elements of the musical performance, rather than casting them into the bit streams of digital audio. Like PostScript, MIDI is device- and resolution-independent. A MIDI performance can be orchestrated on any MIDI-compatible equipment and the sound quality will be that of the output device(s).

In its simplest form, connecting the MIDI output from one instrument (the *master*) to the MIDI input of another (a *slave*) allows a performer to control the slave from the master. So if you play Middle C on the master, Middle C on the slave will sound. The immediate benefit is the layering of timbres from two or more instruments.

The power of MIDI stems from its ability to send and receive performance information on any of 16 discrete channels. The concept of channels correlates to television broadcasts and receivers. While the cable or antenna running into your home carries broadcasts on many different channels simultaneously, your TV receiver picks up only the information corresponding to the channel you set it to receive on. The same is true of MIDI. While many channels of performance data might be going through the MIDI pipeline simultaneously, a slave set to receive on channel 1 will only act on data with a matching channel ID.

Many of today's digital instruments can sound more than one timbre simultaneously, each responding to a different MIDI channel. This is similar to digital televisions that can display multiple channels in simultaneous windows.

The importance of MIDI becomes evident with the addition of a *sequencer*—hardware and/or software that records, edits, and plays back MIDI data in real time. Like multitrack tape recorders, sequencers have multiple tracks that can be used to record discrete performance elements. The ability to assign tracks to transmit on discrete MIDI channels and instrument timbres to receive on discrete MIDI channels paves the way for the sophisticated electronic composition and orchestration at the heart of many of today's hit recordings and movie soundtracks. This same technology is of growing importance to multimedia soundtracks.

The advantages of MIDI sequencing over magnetic recording are many. First, the performance and its orchestration is completely malleable while in MIDI form. Second, since only the performance information is recorded, the audio quality is that of the instruments and sound system and suffers no generation loss unless subsequently recorded. Finally, the amount of data (and therefore disk space and RAM) needed to represent a MIDI performance is virtually inconsequential compared to that of digital audio. (A typical four-minute song might only require around 50K of MIDI data.)

A discussion of MIDI encompasses products as diverse as synthesizers, digital samplers, drum machines, sequencers, mixing consoles, signal processors, and more—all of which are discussed in Chapter 11. The following section describes the MIDI protocol. Although references are made to keys and keyboard instruments for simplicity, the same concepts apply to MIDI wind controllers, percussion controllers, and similar non-keyboard devices.

❖ MIDI Connections

MIDI is a classic example of success through standardization. All MIDI devices employ 5-pin DIN connectors for communications between devices, and a MIDI cable is a MIDI cable in any corner of the electronic music world. (Although similar in appearance, European audio DIN cables should not be used as MIDI cables.) One restriction on MIDI cables is that they should not exceed 50 feet in length.

While they all share the same type of jack, three distinct types of MIDI connectors are used on electronic devices. *MIDI In* accepts MIDI signals from another device. *MIDI Out* sends signals generated inside the device to the MIDI In of other devices. *MIDI Thru* passes information arriving at a device's MIDI In connector to other devices without regard for internally generated MIDI data.

Connecting two MIDI devices is simple: the MIDI Out from the designated master is connected to the MIDI In of the slave. Any device with a MIDI Out can, in theory, act as a master.

More than one slave can be controlled by a master device, which is where the MIDI Thru connection is useful. The MIDI Out from the master is routed to the MIDI In of the first device, and the MIDI Thru of each device is connected to the MIDI In of the subsequent device. (See Figure 10.11.) The practical limit of a MIDI Thru chain

Figure 10.11

The standardization of MIDI In, MIDI Out, and MIDI Thru jacks enable the interconnection of a series of MIDI devices.

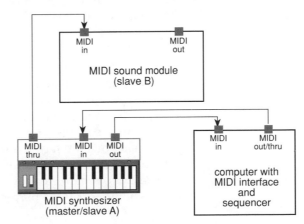

is approximately three devices. (Longer chains can be accommo-dated with the use of a MIDI Thru box that splits the MIDI signal into multiple MIDI Out connections.)

Most MIDI devices have all three types of connections. A device without a MIDI Thru jack must be placed at the end of a MIDI chain since it has no means of passing its signal on to another device. Some instruments combine the functions of the MIDI Out and Thru jacks into a single jack labeled MIDI Out/Thru or MIDI Echo. The data coming into the device's MIDI In jack is merged with internally generated data and the combined data is passed on through this single jack. The functionality can sometimes be switched internally.

❖ Channel Messages

MIDI information takes the form of messages sent from masters to slaves. *Channel messages* are used primarily to route information to specific devices via one or more of the 16 MIDI channels. This information typically describes the performance content, such as the notes and their nuances. Although most of this data is transpar-ent to the user during performance, it can often be enabled or dis-abled categorically on MIDI devices, and the individual data elements can be edited with great detail and accuracy in MIDI sequencers.

MIDI modes

Receiving devices can be set to one of four different MIDI modes provided for in the MIDI spec. In Mode 1, or *omni mode,* a slave re-sponds to information coming in on all channels. Mode 2 is mostly obsolete. In Mode 3, or *poly mode*, the instrument responds with one homogenous sound to information on a single channel. In Mode 4, or *mono mode*, an instrument capable of producing more than one timbre simultaneously assigns information on discrete chan-nels to discrete timbres.

Note-on, note-off

The most common form of MIDI data describes what note is being played, how fast/hard, and when it is released. The MIDI protocol provides for the sequential numbering of notes over a ten octave range, starting with 0 at the low end and ending with 127 at the high end. Since various instruments have differing quantities of keys or analogous pitch controls, Middle C has been standardized as MIDI note number 60 with few exceptions. (See Figure 10.1.)

A *note-on* command sent on a given channel dictates that a spe-cific note number is to be played by any devices receiving on that channel. Note-on commands also include a velocity parameter ranging from 0 to 127 in value. Velocity is equivalent to the force used in striking a key and is typically routed to control the volume of the associated note in a slave instrument. (Some inexpensive MIDI instruments do not offer velocity-sensitivity. Instead, they send a fixed velocity parameter assigned by the manufacturer.)

The note-on command remains in effect until a *note-off* command is sent on the same channel. Although the MIDI spec also provides for a note-on with a velocity of zero to be interpreted as a note-off, this is rarely implemented. Similarly, note-off commands have a provision for release velocity that is rarely implemented.

Mono pressure

Some instruments provide for *mono pressure*—also known as *aftertouch* or *channel pressure*—response to additional pressure that is applied after a note-on occurs. This is commonly routed to parameters such as volume, brilliance, or vibrato. Additional pressure on any key will result in the routed effect being applied to all engaged notes on that channel. Pressing harder on one key while holding down a chord, for example, will result in the entire chord being affected by vibrato or another specified effect. Most master devices that offer velocity sensitivity also offer mono pressure.

Poly pressure

Unlike mono pressure *poly pressure* provides for discrete amounts of pressure to be associated with individual notes on a given channel. Like mono pressure, this information can be routed to a variety of destinations. Poly pressure is rarely implemented.

Continuous controllers

Continuous controller data communicates channelized information about variable performance controls such as sliders, joysticks, and footpedals. This information is typically routed to parameters such as vibrato, master volume, and stereo pan. While the MIDI spec provides for a value range of 16,384, most manufacturers only use values ranging from 0 (minimum) to 127 (maximum).

Continuous controllers are also used to communicate on/off values such as a footswitch or sustain pedal: 0 signifies off, 127 signifies on, and all other values are typically ignored. The actual continuous controller destinations are numerically identified from 0 to 127, not to be confused with the data value being sent to those destinations. (See Table 10.1.)

Table 10.1. *Commonly used MIDI controller numbers.*

Controller #	Controller type	Controller #	Controller type
01	Modulation wheel	67	Soft on/off
02	Breath controller	80-83	General purpose controllers 5-8
04	Foot controller	92	Tremolo depth
05	Portamento time	93	Chorus depth
06	Data entry slider/knob	94	Detune depth
07	Main volume	95	Phaser depth (phase shifter)
08	Balance	96	Data increment
10	Pan	97	Data decrement
11	Expression controller	124	Omni off
16-19	General purpose controllers 1-4	125	Omni on
64	Sustain (damper pedal) on/off	126	Mono on
65	Portamento on/off	127	Poly on
66	Sostenuto on/off		

Pitch bend

Most electronic instruments have a joystick, wheel, or similar device dedicated to bending or sliding the instrument's pitch up and down. This is commonly used to add nuance similar to that of a guitar string being bent. Corresponding *pitch bend* data is sent as a dedicated data type on a given channel so that the pitch of a slave can track the same nuance. Since pitch can be bent both up and down, values range from 0 to 16,384, with 8,192 representing standard pitch.

Pitch bend performance controls can typically be restricted to bend a given internal as a maximum. This setting must be the same for master and slave(s) for the pitch bend data to have accurate effect.

Program change

The combinations of parameter settings in synthesizers and other electronic instruments are saved as programs or presets. These setting combinations are easily recalled by entering the program number via buttons on the front panel. This also sends a matching *program change* command on the current transmission channel. Devices receiving on that channel will change to that same program number. Program change commands carry a value between 0 and 127. While various manufacturers use different internal numbering systems for program locations on their products, all are ultimately mapped to the standard program change values for MIDI transmission and reception.

❖ System Messages

System messages are global data types received by all devices in a MIDI chain. System messages can be used to communicate at an intimate level with a given manufacturer's products. Beyond that, most system messages are used in synchronizing multiple time-based MIDI devices. System messages are invoked transparently to the user when using higher level functions, but a quick understanding of what's happening behind the scenes is important.

System exclusive

Each manufacturer of MIDI products is given a registered manufacturer ID number. *System exclusive* messages (*sys ex* for short) begin with a manufacturer ID. All connected devices made by that manufacturer will try to interpret the associated data; all others will ignore it. All subsequent data is assumed to be part of the system exclusive message until an *end of exclusive* message is sent. (Many system exclusive data transfers implement handshaking, requiring that the MIDI Out of both devices be connected to the MIDI In of the other.)

Unlike the rest of the MIDI spec, manufacturers can do whatever they please within system exclusive messages. The most common use for system exclusive is accessing the unique parameters of the device, both individually and globally. On the individual level, discrete parameters can be modified remotely as if you were making modifications directly on the device's front panel. On the global level, complete programs or sets of programs can be sent and received via MIDI. This allows MIDI-based computer systems to act as librarians and editors for electronic sounds, for example, as will be discussed in Chapter 11.

MIDI Clock

MIDI Clock provides a simple timing reference for synchronizing time-based devices such as a MIDI sequencer and drum machine. MIDI Clock provides a clock pulse at a rate of 24 pulses per quarter note (ppq). Slave devices must be set to respond to external synchronization mode in order to respond and synchronize to the master clock. Each time the master clock sends a clock pulse, the slave device advances its playback by one clock pulse. The timing reference is relative to the tempo of the master clock. MIDI Clock is a "dumb" clock, in that it doesn't know where it is in the composition.

Start, stop, and continue

The MIDI *start* command tells a device to begin playback at the beginning of the song. Playback continues until the end of the song or until a MIDI *stop* command is issued. The MIDI *continue* command begins playback from the point at which playback was stopped.

Song Position Pointer

Using MIDI Clock to synchronize the playback of two or more devices does not accommodate random access of any point in the song. Jumping, fast-forwarding, or rewinding to an arbitrary position on the master does not change the location of the slave. *Song Position Pointer* keeps track of the position relative to the beginning of the song in sixteenth notes. When the master is started from an arbitrary position, both machines begin playback at the closest sixteenth note. This approach is obviously more useful than simple MIDI Clock.

❖ MIDI Time Code

While Song Position Pointer adds more flexibility to synchronization, it is based on musical time rather than absolute time. SMPTE Time Code, the international standard for synchronizing various audio and visual elements for professional applications, deals with absolute time—hours, minutes, seconds, and frames. This is much more effective than relative timing such as that provided by MIDI when syncing non-musical elements. Even within the realm of synthesizers, samplers, and sequencers the exact timing of events—such as sound effects to visual events—is much more expedient and intuitive when referencing absolute time. (SMPTE is discussed in Chapter 13, as it is primarily used in video production. Conversion of SMPTE to MIDI timing is described in Chapter 11.)

This disparity in timing references was addressed with the addition of *MIDI Time Code* (MTC) to the MIDI spec. MTC embodies the hours:minutes:seconds:frames information of SMPTE within the MIDI data stream. Special SMPTE-to-MTC converter boxes read a SMPTE source and translate it to the MIDI data equivalent.

The two most important pieces of MTC information are the Full Message and the Quarter-Frame message. The *Full Message* is a total of 10 bytes that specify the SMPTE format (24, 25, 30, or drop frame) and the time in the same hours:minutes:seconds:frames format as SMPTE.

Since it is not feasible to send a 10-byte message over MIDI every 1/30th of a second due to bandwidth, the *Quarter-Frame Messages* are used in between. A total of eight 2-byte messages are sent in quarter-frame intervals and combined to provide a complete time ID every two frames. The Full Messages are then sent after each group of eight Quarter-Frame Messages.

If the Full Message seems redundant, consider that MTC can only lock up to SMPTE at a complete reference provided by a Full Message or eight Quarter-Frame Messages. For this reason, it takes two to four frames to lock up.

❖ General MIDI Mode

Although MIDI is commendable in its standardization, no standard originally defined what sounds are available in electronic instruments or where they are located. Lack of standards in this area has made it difficult to deliver arrangements to the mass market that will have predictable orchestration. For example, a piano performance can be placed on a sequencer track transmitting on a specific MIDI channel, but where will the piano sound be found in a given user's synthesizer or sound card?

The addition of *General MIDI Mode* to the MIDI spec addresses this problem. General MIDI Mode defines specific and predictable sounds for each of 128 program locations. This allows composers and producers to include program change commands in compositions that will configure the timbres appropriately for the tracks. Program #1 will always contain a piano, program #23 will always contain a harmonica, and so forth. (See Table 10.2.) General MIDI Mode also reserves Channel 10 for percussion and standardizes percussive sounds that respond to specific MIDI note numbers. (See Table 10.3.)

The quality of the sounds in a General MIDI device is still up to the individual manufacturer, but the generic sonic palette is always provided for categorically. While some instruments are designed specifically as General MIDI devices, many manufacturers will add General MIDI via *program mapping*. A piano sound might reside in any location, for example, but any program change commands calling program #1 in General MIDI Mode will be mapped to call the piano's actual program location.

Devices compatible with General MIDI must also be able to respond to each of the 16 MIDI channels with unique timbres simultaneously. A compatible device must have at least 24 voices available that can be dynamically allocated, or 16 dynamically allocated voices for pitched timbres and 8 dedicated voices for percussion sounds. (Voices and voice allocation are discussed in Chapter 11.)

While not yet supported by all instruments, general MIDI paves the way for mass delivery of MIDI soundtracks. This is a particularly powerful solution when integrating soundtracks and speech in an interactive environment. The difference in file size between

Table 10.2. *General MIDI Mode standardizes a palette of sounds and their program locations.*

Preset	Instrument	Preset	Instrument	Preset	Instrument
1	Acoustic piano	44	Contra bass	87	Synth lead 7
2	Bright piano	45	Tremolo strings	88	Synth lead 8
3	Electric piano	46	Pizzicato strings	89	Synth pad 1
4	Honky tonk piano	47	Orchestral harp	90	Synth pad 2
5	Rhodes piano	48	Tympani	91	Synth pad 3
6	Chorus piano	49	String ensemble 1	92	Synth pad 4
7	Harpsichord	50	String ensemble 2	93	Synth pad 5
8	Clavinet	51	Synth strings 1	94	Synth pad 6
9	Celesta	52	Synth strings 2	95	Synth pad 7
10	Glockenspiel	53	Choir aahs	96	Synth pad 8
11	Music box	54	Voice ooohs	97	Synth FX 1
12	Vibraphone	55	Synth voice	98	Synth FX 2
13	Marimba	56	Orchestra hit	99	Synth FX 3
14	Xylophone	57	Trumpet	100	Synth FX 4
15	Tubular bells	58	Trombone	101	Synth FX 5
16	Dulcimer	59	Tuba	102	Synth FX 6
17	Hammond organ	60	Muted trumpet	103	Synth FX 7
18	Percussive organ	61	French horn	104	Synth FX 8
19	Rock organ	62	Brass section	105	Sitar
20	Church organ	63	Synthbrass 1	106	Banjo
21	Reed organ	64	Synthbrass 2	107	Shamisen
22	Accordion	65	Soprano sax	108	Koto
23	Harmonica	66	Alto sax	109	Kalimba
24	Tango accordion	67	Tenor sax	110	Bag pipe
25	Nylon string guitar	68	Baritone sax	111	Fiddle
26	Steel string guitar	69	Oboe	112	Shanai
27	Electric guitar (jazz)	70	English horn	113	Tinkle bell
28	Electric guitar (clean)	71	Bassoon	114	Agogo bells
29	Electric guitar (mute)	72	Clarinet	115	Stool drum
30	Overdriven guitar	73	Piccolo	116	Woodblock
31	Distorted guitar	74	Flute	117	Taiko drum
32	Guitar harmonics	75	Recorder	118	Melodic drum
33	Acoustic bass	76	Pan flute	119	Synth drum
34	Electric bass (finger)	77	Blown bottle	120	Reverse cymbal
35	Electric bass (pick)	78	Shakuhachi	121	Guitar fret noise
36	Fretless bass	79	Whistle	122	Breath noise
37	Slap bass 1	80	Ocarina	123	Seashore
38	Slap bass 2	81	Synth lead 1	124	Bird tweet
39	Synth bass 1	82	Synth lead 2	125	Telephone ring
40	Synth bass 2	83	Synth lead 3	126	Helicopter
41	Violin	84	Synth lead 4	127	Applause
42	Viola	85	Synth lead 5	128	Gunshot
43	Cello	86	Synth lead 6		

Table 10.3. *General MIDI Mode maps percussive sounds to MIDI note numbers on Channel 10.*

Note #	Instrument	Note #	Instrument
35	Acoustic bass drum	59	Ride cymbal 2
36	Bass drum 1	60	Hi bongo
37	Side stick	61	Low Bbongo
38	Acoustic snare	62	Mute hi conga
39	Hand clap	63	Open hi conga
40	Electric snare	64	Low conga
41	Low floor tom	65	High timbale
42	Closed hi h	66	Low timbale
43	High floor tom	67	High agogo
44	Pedal hi hat	68	Low agogo
45	Low tom	69	Cabasa
46	Open hi hat	70	Maracas
47	Low mid tom	71	Short whistle
48	High mid tom	72	Long whistle
49	Crash cymbal 1	73	Short guiro
50	High tom	74	Long guiro
51	Ride cymbal 1	75	Claves
52	Chinese cymbal	76	Hi wood block
53	Ride bell	77	Low wood block
54	Tambourine	78	Mute cuica
55	Splash cymbal	79	Open cuica
56	Cowbell	80	Mute triangle
57	Crash cymbal 2	81	Open triangle
58	Vibraslap		

digital audio and corresponding MIDI performance data is also noteworthy. These topics are explored in greater depth in Chapter 18.

❖ ❖ ❖ ❖ ❖ ❖

The audio concepts presented in this chapter are common to many audio tools. The next chapter describes the tools themselves.

CHAPTER 11

Audio Tools

Audio production tools that were only available in professional recording studios ten years ago are now affordable to anyone who is serious about working with sound. The evolution of MIDI and digital audio technologies has changed the way compositions and recordings are realized. Although many of these tools are geared toward the working musician/composer, they are readily transferable and equally important to multimedia soundtrack production.

MICROPHONES

Microphones (*mikes* for short) transduce sound pressure waves into electrical waveforms. Proper microphone choice for quality audio is very important, considering the weakest link and GIGO principles. Microphones can be categorized according to the type of circuit and the type of transducer technology they use.

The circuit is either balanced or unbalanced as described in Chapter 3. In ideal circumstances, balanced microphones are preferable to unbalanced mikes, especially when long cables and/or mixers are involved. Many devices, such as cassette decks and sound cards for PCs, only accept unbalanced mikes, however. Microphone transformers can be used to convert between balanced and unbalanced signals.

Various microphone designs are currently in use, each one optimized for a specific application. The design parameters include directionality, transducer design, sensitivity, and frequency response. Suggestions for common miking situations can be found in Chapter 12.

❖ Directionality

All microphones are designed to pick up sound according to specific directional patterns. (See Figure 11.1) Some of the more expensive microphones can be switched to exhibit different response patterns.

Figure 11.1

Microphones are designed to pick up sound according to specific patterns.

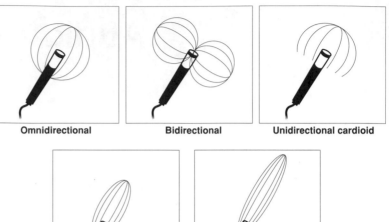

Omnidirectional   Bidirectional   Unidirectional cardioid

Unidirectional supercardioid   Ultradirectional hypercardioid

Omnidirectional

Omnidirectional microphones pick up sounds equally from all directions. They offer high overall sound quality and are relatively inexpensive due to simple construction. They are best suited for situations in which the sound source being recorded is isolated, since ambient sounds and background noise will be picked up through the rear and sides. Omnidirectional microphones are good choices when recording a live event in which all of the sounds of the surrounding environment are desirable.

Cardioid

Cardioid or *unidirectional microphones* are named for their heart-shaped pickup pattern. They reject sounds coming from the rear and accept sounds coming from the front. Sounds from the side are accepted to certain degrees according to the microphone's design or setting. Cardioids are good for situations where the sound source is not ideally isolated, such as a live ensemble or public speaking.

Cardioids have two basic drawbacks. First, some degradation in fidelity results from phase cancellation in the pickup pattern. Second, a low-frequency boom known as *proximity effect* results when a cardioid microphone is placed too close to the source.

Supercardioid

Supercardioid microphones have one main heart-shaped pattern pointing from the front and a smaller one pointing from the back. Their advantage is that sounds from the side are rejected more than with standard cardioids. Their disadvantage is that sounds from the rear are picked up. They are most effective at isolating individual adjacent sound sources, such as two vocalists side by side.

Hypercardioid

Hypercardioid microphones are an extension of the supercardioid design. The main pickup pattern is more focused and extends further from the front of the mike, while the rear pickup pattern is diminished. This makes hypercardioids ideal for situations where the microphone must be placed further from the sound source, such as in a staged performance or an electronic news gathering situation.

Bidirectional

Bidirectional microphones exhibit a figure-eight pattern that allows them to pick up sounds from opposite sides of the mike. Sounds coming from the other sides, as well as the traditional front and rear orientations, are largely rejected. Bidirectional microphones are designed for situations where two singers or spokespersons are facing each other in close proximity. Some new stereo mikes owe their abilities in part to bidirectional design, as well. Note, however, that the two pickup patterns are not highly focused and do not reject that much overall ambient noise.

❖ Transducer Types

Microphones perform the fundamental process of transducing sound to electricity by several different methods. Design differences have a great deal to do with the microphone's ability to handle transients and various sound pressure levels.

Condenser microphones

Condenser microphones utilize a charged diaphragm and adjacent back plate that form a capacitor. (Capacitors used to be called condensers.) Vibrations in the diaphragm alter the voltage output of the circuit in a mirror image of the sound pressure waves. This design accommodates delicate diaphragms and high sensitivity to subtleties in the sound. Condenser mikes are usually the design of choice when recording vocals, melodic instruments, and other featured sounds.

The weak signals generated by condenser circuits require that preamps be built into the microphone. Pads are usually included to ensure that the optimal level is sent to the console. The capacitive circuits and preamps in condenser mikes require a source of DC power. While batteries can be used, power is usually supplied externally in the form of *phantom power* from a dedicated box or from the microphone inputs of a console through balanced lines. The *electret* is a variation on the condenser mike in which the diaphragm and back plate are permanently charged, thereby requiring no phantom power for that function. (Batteries are still needed for the amplifying transistor.)

Dynamic microphones

Dynamic microphones have a diaphragm encircled by a coil of wire suspended in a magnetic field. Sound pressure waves hitting the diaphragm cause a fluctuation in the coil position that induces an electric current analogous to the sound waves. Dynamic microphones can handle higher sound pressure levels than condensers and are suited for applications such as close-miking drums or electric guitar amps. On the down side, they exhibit poorer transient response and frequency response than condensers.

Ribbon microphones

Ribbon microphones employ a diaphragm made of a ribbon of thin foil suspended between magnetic poles. The differences in pressure cause the ribbon to cut through the magnetic flux lines, inducing a voltage into the ribbon. This yields a very warm sound, but little tolerance for high sound pressure levels. Ribbon microphones are inherently bidirectional. However, opening and closing various ports on properly designed microphones allow the user to physically alter the directionality. Ribbon microphones are not in wide use today.

❖ Frequency Response

The overall frequency response specifications of a microphone are as important as those of other audio components. In particular, they should be matched to the frequencies emitted by the source being recorded or amplified. Generally speaking, mikes with smaller diaphragms are better suited for higher frequencies, while those with larger diaphragms are better for low frequencies. Moreover, the frequency response changes with the curvature of the polar patterns. The axis of a microphone is an imaginary line running through the front and back of the microphone. The further off axis the sound source is, the less flat the frequency response. Better microphones offer flatter frequency response further distances off axis.

ANALOG TAPE RECORDERS AND FORMATS

Analog tape recording works on the same basic principles of magnetic recording and media outlined in Chapter 2 and shared by disk drives and video decks. Analog tape is divided linearly into separate tracks, each capable of holding its own discrete audio information. You can envision tracks as the parallel lanes on a highway. The variety of tape formats in use today all share some common features.

❖ Common Attributes of Analog Tape

The quality of magnetic recording depends a great deal on tape formulation and bias. Equally important is the density of magnetic particles available during the recording process.

Bias and tape formulation

Magnetic recording is not practical without bias—an additional signal that compensates for the nonlinear frequency response of a magnetic formulation. Optimal recording depends on proper matching of the tape formulation and the bias setting on the deck.

The formulation of the tape has a great deal to do with the quality of any recording. The original ferric-oxide formulation is now referred to as *Type I*, or *normal bias*. The more uniform the oxide coating and tape thickness, the better sound you get from Type I tapes. *Type II* tapes use chromium-dioxide particles for improved performance over ferric oxide. *Type III* is rarely used today. *Type IV* employs metal particles, requiring the highest bias and offering the best performance and high-frequency response.

Effects of speed and width on fidelity

Along with the properties of the media, the amount of magnetic particles available determines the frequency response and dynamic range of the signal that can be recorded. In addition, greater numbers of magnetic particles are often less susceptible to *dropouts*— a degradation or loss of signal due to tape wear or to dirt in the tape path.

The width of the tape head determines the width of the track and with it the number of particles available in one spatial dimension. This is a major reason why cassette decks have lower fidelity than open reel decks: the open-reel decks have wider tracks. However, the width of a tape must account for more than the aggregate width of the tracks. A certain amount of *guard space* must be provided between tracks to avoid *crosstalk* or audio bleed between tracks.

The other spatial dimension in question runs along the length of the tape. The number of particles passing the head at a given moment is determined by the tape speed. Doubling the tape speed can double the frequency response and dynamic range. Tape speed is measured in *ips* (inches per second).

❖ Analog Tape Formats

Tape format refers to the combined attributes of the tape width, the number of tracks, and their usage. Tape formats fall into the basic categories of non-multitrack and multitrack.

Non-multitrack decks

The average decks the consumer is exposed to—the cassette and older stereo open-reel—are obviously stereo devices with two tracks. Two-track devices are used primarily for mastering, distribution, and acquisition. Tracks and channels are not necessarily the same, however.

Consider the standard audio cassette. The tape is said to have two sides, each of which has two tracks. Both sides of the tape actually share the same tape surface, though. Although the cassette has four tracks, only two are available at a time as playback channels. (See Figure 11.2.)

Some people still have the 1/4-inch open-reel decks that were popular before cassettes. These are called *quarter-track* since they exhibit a 4-track, 2-channel configuration functionally similar to the cassette. The open-reel decks still used in professional mastering are *half-track decks*. These offer greater fidelity because they are only 2-track, 2-channel in the same amount of tape. The reels are not flipped over. Half-track decks come in 1/4-inch and 1/2-inch formats, with the latter offering greater fidelity.

Most open-reel decks offer selectable tape speeds. Semi-pro decks operate at 7-1/2 ips and/or 15 ips. Professional 1/4-inch and

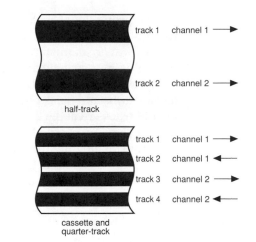

Figure 11.2

Common analog tape formats.

1/2-inch mastering decks run at 15 and/or 30 ips. By contrast, the cassette is a mere 1/8-inch wide and runs at a speed of 1-7/8 ips. The difference in fidelity can be attributed to the difference in magnetic surface area and tape speed.

Multitrack decks

Multitrack decks allow discrete performances to be recorded on parallel tracks. (See Figure 11.3.) The ability to engage the record function on each track separately makes it possible for the various tracks to be recorded either simultaneously or at different times. These tracks are then mixed under controlled circumstances to a non-multitrack format.

Figure 11.3

Multitrack decks allow more than two tracks to be recorded selectively.

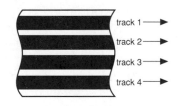

The individual tracks on multitrack formats must share valuable magnetic real estate with their neighbors as more tracks are squeezed into a given tape width. All else being equal, 8 tracks on 1/2-inch tape will have better fidelity than 8 tracks on 1/4-inch tape. Multitrack decks usually have multiples of four tracks: 4-, 8-, 12-, 16-, and 24-track machines are all in use. (Professional digital multitracks come in 32- and 48-track formats.)

The professional analog multitrack recording standard continues to be 2-inch, 24-track at 30 ips. This is decidedly not a desktop format, however. Manufacturers of semi-professional multitracks are becoming increasingly adept at squeezing higher performance out of tapes with lesser widths. Much of the credit goes to better tape formulations and noise reduction. Today's 1/4-inch 8-tracks and 1/2-inch 16-tracks rival the 2-inch 24-tracks of a decade ago at a fraction of the price. A variety of proprietary formats abounds. Akai offers a 12-track analog multitrack with good fidelity that utilizes videocassettes, for example. In addition, 8-track formats on cassette and 16-track formats on 1/4-inch tape perform remarkably well for the money.

❖ Noise Reduction

The other factor contributing to higher fidelity on smaller formats is noise reduction. All analog tape has an inherent tape hiss that is audible on a blank tape. While the hiss is less apparent in louder recorded passages, it is a constant frustration to musicians and engineers. Noise reduction circuitry aimed at reducing that hiss is licensed for use in various products by two primary manufacturers— dbx and Dolby.

The differences between dbx and Dolby are perhaps best described by saying that dbx offers greater noise reduction (around -30 dB), while Dolby offers less coloration to the sound. (dbx has a tendency to breathe, or pump, due to the companding process described later in this chapter.) Dolby C offers -20 dB of noise reduction, while the older Dolby B provides -10 dB. Dolby S and SR offer increased performance but carry significantly higher price tags at this writing.

❖ Tape Heads

An individual electromagnetic head is required for each track of tape. A *head stack* incorporates all the heads required to access all the tracks in a given format. Tape decks employ either two or three head stacks. An erase head is always first with regard to tape travel. The second head on a two-head machine combines the record and playback functions. These functions are separated on three-head decks. The amount of energy required to record and playback tape tracks is formidable enough that a single head stack cannot usually perform both functions simultaneously without incurring unacceptable amounts of crosstalk. Most cassette decks have two heads and can only record or play at a given time, for example.

Multitrack machines must, therefore, perform a synchronization function during overdubs that might not be initially apparent. Since the playback head must be a reasonable distance from the record head (usually about an inch), the machine must perform a *self-sync* function to synchronize the newly recorded track with the playback tracks. While this is transparent on many current models, some older machines require the user to select this mode to perform overdubs.

❖ Transport Mechanism

Considerations involving the basic transport mechanism are two-fold. First, the *direct-drive* mechanism in better decks offers more traction, accuracy, and control than those with *belt drives*. Second, the *transport controls*—such as play, stop, fast-forward, rewind, and pause—employ solenoids on better decks, rather than mechanical interfaces. Both direct-drive and solenoid controls are mandatory for decks that will be used synchronized as slaves in an environment such as video scoring. These features usually go hand in hand with a digital counter as well.

The more professional the deck, the more bells and whistles you get. (As with cars—you can live without the power windows and sunroof, but they make the experience smoother.) *RTZ* (return-to-zero) locates the transport to the zero point on the counter. Programmable memory locations make it easier to find points like a verse or chorus. *Automated rehearse* will play a defined passage over and over again to practice a take. Automation and footswitches offer two different approaches to punch-in and punch-out of over-dubs. Nicer decks come with remote panels offering full transport functions and counter, as well as full *autolocation* to programmable memory locations or an arbitrary counter or SMPTE number.

DIGITAL TAPE RECORDERS

Digital multitrack tape recorders are rapidly replacing their analog predecessors in professional recording studios. As with most every-thing, this technology is filtering down to the desktop. The advantages over analog are improved frequency response, dynamic range, and recording linearity. The signal-to-noise ratio is also vastly improved because tape hiss is not a concern: the digital information on the tape is either on or off. This also eliminates the need for noise reduction circuits.

The disadvantages of digital tape are price and the fact that it does not lend itself to the physical splicing possible with analog tape. Editing is often performed using the direct-to-disk recording systems discussed later in this chapter, with digital tape taking the role of acquisition, long-term storage, and some distribution.

❖ PCM Encoding

As with all digital audio, DACs, ADCs, bit resolution, and sampling rates all come into play with digital tape recorders. The additional twist is how the audio is actually placed on the tape. The most common encoding technique is *PCM* (pulse code modulation). PCM converts a stream of bits into a chain of narrow rectangular pulse waves that represent the bit value. This stream of pulses is written to the tape. On playback, the process is reversed, and the pulses are converted back to bit values.

While the information has all of the positive attributes of digital information, the medium of tape is still capable of flaws and drop-outs. Digital information is usually written redundantly to tape so that the information has an on-the-fly backup in case of error. To accommodate this process, data is sometimes interleaved onto the tape via the same rotating head technology that is used in video decks. This interleave process makes it impossible to edit digital tape by hand.

❖ Digital Tape Formats for the Desktop

Digital tape recording is becoming an integral part of audio production at all levels. On the desktop, however, affordable products are relegated primarily to 2-track formats with a few exceptions.

DAT

DAT (digital audio tape) is a 2-track format that utilizes specially-designed cassettes. The format is quite viable, but it got off to a slow start in the consumer market because of legal issues regarding protection of copyrighted materials. The recording quality is so good that the recording industry demanded that a copy protection scheme be incorporated into machines to prevent digital copies of recording artist's material. Copy protection in the form of *SCMS* (Serial Copy Management System) is applied to the analog I/O and to S/PDIF on some machines; AES/EBU I/O is unaffected.

The performance and price of DAT machines depends upon the quality of the ADCs and DACs and whether the deck offers digital I/O.

The transfer of material between DAT and another digital medium such as direct-to-disk recorders is far superior using digital protocols such as S/PIDF or AES/EBU that bypass an intermediate analog stage.

As with analog devices, higher price tags bring more advanced features. If your situation requires the synchronization of digital audio to SMPTE time code, only a few high-end decks currently support SMPTE. Higher price tags also bring more sophisticated transport controls. A few manufacturers also include serial control that allows computer control.

F1

Before the advent of DAT, PCM encoders and decoders were available in the form the *Sony F1*. The F1 comprised the electronics—standard video decks were employed as transports. Although this was great stuff at the time, the video transports and nonintegrated system left much to be desired. With the exception of existing archives, F1 has been largely made obsolete by DAT.

Sony 1630

The *Sony 1630* operates on the same basic principle as F1, but utilizes 3/4-inch video decks instead. SMPTE time code is also supported, and editing systems are also available. The Sony 1630 is not used for real-time recording, however, and is designed primarily to prepare digital audio files for CD mastering.

Digital multitracks

At this writing, the first digital multitrack tape deck under $5,000 has been released in the form of the Alesis A-DAT. It provides for eight digital tracks on an inexpensive VHS or S-VHS videotape. Several other manufacturers are also on the verge of releasing similar products using 8 mm videotape.

COMPUTER-BASED DIGITAL AUDIO TOOLS

Computer-based digital audio products utilize the technology of ADCs to digitize audio, and DACs to transform the numeric representations back into analog form. The hardware required for this and the treatment the digital representation during the process define the primary differences between simple audio digitizers and hard disk recording systems.

❖ Basic Audio Digitizers

Audio digitizers typically utilize inexpensive ADC hardware to transform the signal from an unbalanced line-level input (or an inexpensive microphone) into a sampled version of the audio waveform. The quality is usually 8-bit, with sampling rates of 22KHz down to 11KHz—sometimes even lower. The DAC and output circuitry exhibit the same basic specs and quality. This level of quality is acceptable for speech, and for music that doesn't need to sound better than an AM radio station. Stereo is available in some formats.

As an example, the Macintosh offers built-in digital audio playback with 8-bit quality and up to 22KHz playback rate. Products such as the popular MacRecorder and the built-in microphone on newer Macs serve as inexpensive input devices. Similarly, the Amiga's built-in 8-bit audio DACs can play samples digitized with one of several inexpensive input devices. While the PC offers no built-in digital audio abilities, the popular SoundBlaster adds both input and output with 8-bit quality.

Software accompanying audio digitizers provides basic control over input and output levels. A waveform display of a recorded file can be used to select areas of the sound file and perform rudimentary cut, copy, and paste editing functions. Some products also offer additional basic signal processing functions.

The original file formats or operating system extensions for most of these products were confined to RAM-based operations. (The Macintosh .SND file is an example of a RAM-based format.) The file size was limited to available memory, which not only confined content to short audio snips, but raised issues of load time and shared memory resources. As faster hard disks and processors have evolved, schemes similar to virtual memory have evolved that access the disk in real time during record and playback operations. RAM buffers are still used for immediate access, acting as a sort of middle-man between the hard disk and the ADC and DAC circuitry. Macintosh AIFF and Windows .WAV files are examples of digital audio file formats that can access the hard disk.

❖ Hard Disk Recorders

Hard disk recorders—such as Digidesign's AudioMedia and Turtle Beach's 56K—utilize specialized circuit boards to increase fidelity to CD-quality audio with 44.1KHz sampling rates at 16-bit resolution. Designed for more demanding applications, these systems also incorporate professional analog audio inputs and outputs. The better versions offer digital I/O, facilitating direct digital transfer between other digital audio devices such as DAT recorders.

CD-quality stereo sampling requires storage devices with access times faster than 28 milliseconds. This precludes some optical storage devices from being used with these systems. Hard disk recorders offer 2-track mastering and multitrack recording, a track architecture similar to tape decks. Current disk access times limit designers to two to four tracks per hard disk. Multitrack systems beyond four tracks employ multiple hard disks. Systems utilizing more than four tracks usually attach the drives directly to proprietary DSP cards to bypass speed issues associated with the system bus. These types of hard disk recorders are often referred to as *direct-to-disk recorders*.

The biggest advantage of hard disk recording over digital tape formats is random access and the editing it enables. As with software accompanying audio digitizers, recorded waveforms can be displayed and edited. (See Figure 11.4.) After recording, signals can be *normalized* (boosted to their maximum levels before clipping) with the click of the mouse—without adding noise! DSP techniques can apply equalization permanently to the sound file, again without adding noise. (This is typically not a real-time proposition, however.) Sample rates can be converted for different devices, similar to the way that image processors convert digital graphic formats and resolutions.

Figure 11.4

Hard disk recording systems provide visual display and editing of the recorded waveform.

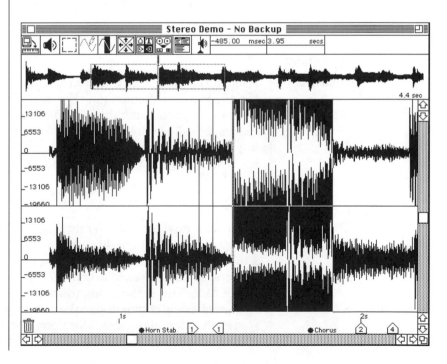

Recent advances include the ability to shift pitch without altering timbre, which is handy for tuning pre-recorded material to another reference (such as a piano). Conversely, *time compression* can be used to reduce or expand the overall length of a passage without altering the pitch. This is particularly useful when a piece of music or dialog must fit a visual segment of slightly different length.

The techniques described so far fall in the category of *destructive editing*, in that the sound file is altered permanently. *Non-destructive editing* doesn't alter the data, but how it is played back. Most systems provide for a playlist that identifies specific regions of the sound file, then calls them in a given order and/or at specific times. This technique is used in creating 12-minute dance mixes out of 3 minute songs, for example. You just record a chorus, audio logo, or sound effect once, and invoke it as often as you like via the list. Crossfades between regions are also typically provided for.

Most hard disk recording systems can also synchronize global or regional playback to SMPTE time code. This makes them valuable production tools for video soundtracks. (SMPTE is covered in Chapter 13.) Some systems also provide basic MIDI Start and MIDI Clock to slave playback of a MIDI sequence. A few manufacturers are offering more integrated systems that allow MIDI sequence tracks and digital audio tracks to be recorded, viewed, edited, and played back simultaneously.

MIXING CONSOLES

A *mixing console* (*mixer*, *console*, or *board* for short) is used to control the process of combining the outputs of two or more audio sources. Beyond that, mixers come in all shapes, sizes, and price ranges. Features differ between brands and models, but the following discussion describes the main attributes that you may encounter in selecting the right mixer for a given job.

❖ Architectural Overview

All mixers provide a way to mix multiple inputs into a single mono or stereo output for amplification and/or recording. The simplest situation requiring a mixer would be a live presentation where a microphone is to be used in conjunction with music from a computer, CD, or tape. This is the straightforward function of individual *input channels* feeding common signal paths called *buses* that are, in turn, routed to external devices. More complex live presentations and larger halls require the additional ability to provide a separate *monitor mix* allowing the performers to hear the sound clearly—a situation largely beyond the realm of desktop multimedia and this book.

Mixer requirements grow more complex in the multitrack recording environment where multiple tracks are built up in successive passes, then mixed. During the recording session, different combinations of signals from the input channels must be selectively routed to discrete tracks via buses. Simultaneously, previously recorded tracks must be monitored for reference via *tape returns*. (See Figure 11.5.)

After everything is recorded via physical and/or MIDI sequenced tracks, the results are then combined during the mixing session. This involves rerouting the track outputs to input channels, with the combination going to the *stereo output bus* or *master bus*. The output of the stereo bus is connected directly to a computer-based

---

Figure 11.5

The basic architecture of a recording console relies on various buses to route and combine audio signals.

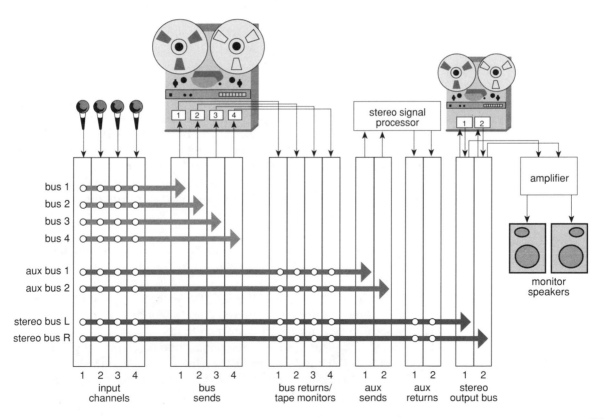

digital audio recording system or to the inputs of a mastering deck such as a DAT, cassette, or 2-track open reel.

The input requirements of the console therefore change from the recording session to the mixing session. During the recording session, the process involves combining many input channels and routing them to one or more tape tracks on each of several passes. At this stage, a high degree of control is needed over what is being recorded. Previously recorded tracks must be monitored, but don't require ultimate control. On mixdown, the emphasis on control shifts to the previously recorded tracks.

The expensive way to satisfy these requirements is to buy enough input channels to simultaneously accommodate all the original sources and the tape tracks. A less expensive and less elegant method involves changing input connections on a few channels so that the source signals and tape returns required at any given moment are available. A more practical solution is to use a mixer that supports a *tape monitor* section and switchable inputs. A dedicated no-frills monitor section provides basic volume pots over tape returns while leaving all the input channels free. Prior to mixdown, simple switches allow the tape returns to be rerouted to the input channels.

❖ Input Channels

The first thing to look for on input channels is the types of inputs that are supported. The least expensive mixers support only line level inputs. Mike level inputs are more expensive, and balanced XLR mike inputs cost even more. If you're working with all electronic inputs, you won't have a problem. Some manufacturers compromise by adding mike inputs to only the first few channels. If you need to connect more mikes, it's cheaper to buy a mixer that supports them on more channels than buy outboard mike preamps.

Effects sends

Effects sends enable each input channel to send a certain amount of signal to a common *effects bus* or *aux bus*. The bus output then goes to a shared effects device such as reverb during either recording or mixdown. The output of the effects device is typically returned to the stereo output bus. A stereo effects bus or two mono effects buses are necessary to drive stereo effects.

If an effects send is *prefader* (positioned electronically before the fader in the input channel), the effects send level will not be affected by fader movements. Conversely, postfader effects sends will be affected by the fader. Although the ability to switch between pre- and postfader is optimal, postfader is the more useful: during a mix, you'll want the volume of the effect to follow that of the main signal.

Channel insert

A channel insert is a simple in/out patch point within the channel electronics that allows effects devices to become part of the insert channel. This is sometimes preferable to tying up an effects bus for a dedicated effect.

EQ

EQ, or *equalization*, provides a mechanism for cutting and boosting specific frequencies or frequency ranges. (Dedicated equalizers are discussed in greater depth later in this chapter.)

Mixers come with varying levels of EQ on each input channel. The least expensive implementation takes the form of treble and bass controls that boost and cut at preset frequencies. Other methods of gaining more control involve adding controls for more frequency ranges or adding the ability to switch the affected frequency ranges or to dial them in exactly. The ultimate EQ section combines these two approaches, providing separate attenuation of three or four bands of selectable frequency ranges.

A few other features make EQ more flexible. The ability to switch the EQ section in and out provides a quick way to compare the input signal with the equalized version. If the EQ is positioned before the effects send, the EQ settings will alter the effects; positioning the EQ after the effects send will not. Both have their advantages, and the better mixers allow you to switch between the two.

Bus assign

Ideally, a mixer will be able to route the signal selectively from each input channel to any bus. The primary use for this function in multitrack recording is to route buses to track inputs on a multitrack recorder, providing an elegant assignment method.

Direct send

A *direct send* allows the output of an input channel to be routed directly to an external device, typically a track input on a multitrack recorder. Since bus electronics can add another level of noise before the signal gets to tape, direct sends are cleaner.

Pan

Pan controls determine the placement of the associate sound within the stereo field. This function relates to the stereo field of the master bus and to that of individual buses used for track assignment and submixes.

Mute and solo

Many mixers have mute and solo switches on each channel. The *mute* switch silences the channel without changing the position of the level control. The *solo* button routes the channel output to the *solo bus*. Anytime one or more solo buttons are engaged on the console, the overall mix is replaced in the control room monitors by the solo bus. This is quite useful in auditioning or making fine adjustments to individual audio elements during a session.

Faders

While the cheapest mixers have simple knobs for channel volume, *faders* (sliding potentiometers) are desirable for two reasons. First, they afford more smooth and exacting controls. Second, complex mixes often require multiple fingers on multiple faders. Faders with longer throws and less friction are generally better.

❖ Cue Mix

Anytime live talent is performing into a microphone, a *cue mix* must be supplied to headphones. Ideally, this is a separate mix providing the blend of aural components required by the talent. Although professional consoles provide for multiple cue mixes for multiple musicians, this feature is beyond the price tag of desktop-level mixers.

Cue mixes can be implemented in a variety of ways. Some consoles have dedicated cue sections. Others provide a cue send knob on each input channel. Cue mixes can also be created using generic aux sends. If cue mixes are required in your situation, consider how the console taps effects sends into cue mixes so that the talent hears the effects.

❖ Monitors

During both the recording and mixing processes, a *control room monitor* knob allows those at the console to adjust their listening level independently of the record levels. More advanced sessions take advantage of the ability to switch specific aspects of the mix into the control room monitors, such as effects buses or record buses. Similarly, a *studio monitor* knob allows those in a separate recording area to hear the playback at separately controllable volume. *Talkback* allows those at the console to use a microphone to speak to performers in the studio without using an input channel. The presence of these monitoring features largely distinguishes a recording console from one designed for live sound reinforcement.

❖ Buses

As previously described, the signals from any input channels can be routed selectively to buses. The number of buses varies from mixer to mixer, and buses cost more money. Ideally, the number of buses will match the number of tracks on your multitrack recorder since buses are often used to route inputs selectively to track inputs on the tape deck.

Buses are also used as *submixes* or *subgroups*. This allows global processing or fader control over mix elements that have something in common—such as all music or all voice-overs. Advanced bus designs exhibit more sends, receives, EQs, and other goodies common to input channels.

❖ Metering and Overload Indicators

The more metering a console has, the more control you have over your sound. Meters are indispensable when it comes to monitoring the output of each input channel, submix bus, and stereo master bus. Some mixers provide meters that can be switched to reflect the levels of the effects bus, cue mix, headphone jack, and more. While meters are not economically or physically practical at every stage, overload indicators in the form of LEDs compensate nicely. For example, a meter on an input channel will tell you the channel's signal level going into the mix, but will not indicate whether the channel input is overloading. An overload indicator on the input will. The more level indicators available, the more control you have over the weakest link principle.

❖ Automation

Full automation over all parameters of a console is very expensive. In general, two kinds of automation are available at moderate prices—mute automation and fader automation.

Mute automation provides on/off control over the mute functions on a console. Combinations of mute status are stored as presets that can be called up via MIDI program change commands. This allows a MIDI sequencer to trigger changes in the mix.

Fader automation reads and writes fader moves for volume automation. Moving fader automation involves rather expensive mechanisms that alter the fader positions on playback according to the movements you make during recording. Alternately, a few companies make more affordable external packages that place voltage-controlled amplifiers controlled by remote faders on the channel outputs. Fader moves are typically recorded with a MIDI sequencer as MIDI continuous controllers. On playback the recorded commands control the amplifiers for an automated mix.

PORTABLE MINISTUDIOS

Manufacturers of recording and mixing equipment recently lowered the entry point for personal recording by combining the two categories in the *ministudio*—a combination mixer/multitrack recorder. How much sophistication, quality, and flexibility you get in each category will be dictated by the model/manufacturer, the price point, and your needs. Most employ a standard audio cassette in a 4-track, 4-channel configuration—often using a higher speed to improve fidelity. Remember: one way in which costs are kept down is by cutting corners and having many functions do double duty. Consider carefully how you would actually use the product.

SIGNAL PROCESSING DEVICES

Signal processors or *effects* bring a diverse set of tools to the recording and live sound environments. They can be used to simulate various acoustic spaces, create effects that are impossible acoustically, and bring clarity, warmth, and other desirable attributes to the sound.

Although classic signal processors are external devices, they are found increasingly in electronic music instruments and mixing consoles. Many are able to call up preprogrammed setting combinations at the touch of a button or in response to MIDI program change commands. Some even allow remote alteration of individual parameters via MIDI system exclusive messages.

Most effects share some common functions such as input and output level controls. This helps to integrate the device into various parts of the audio chain at optimum levels. *Mix* controls provide a way to determine the blend of the original and processed signals at the processor's output. (The original signal is referred to as *dry*; the processed signal is *wet*.)

Every time you turn around, somebody invents a new type of signal processor. Moreover, many manufacturers incorporate multiple functions into a single device, although dedicated effects often offer great functionality and/or quality per effect. Many *multi-effects processors* can provide several effects simultaneously. The following discussion provides an overview of the mainstream effect categories. Tips for usage are provided in Chapter 12.

❖ Reverb

Reverb is used to simulate acoustic space. Less expensive units offer preset spaces. More advanced models offer control over the number of reflections, the delay between them, and the intensity of the reflections. Separate control over the initial reflection parameters provides the greatest flexibility.

❖ Digital Delays

Digital delays provide a number of effects based on time delay. Some of these effects require an LFO which subtly alters the pitch of the delayed signal to add an animated quality. Modulated time delays on the order of a few milliseconds alter the harmonic structure in an effect called *flanging*. (Flanging is a sort of tearing or pipe-like sound popularized on Jimi Hendrix recordings.) Modulated delays in the 10 to 35 millisecond range create a *chorusing* effect that thickens the sound. Delays ranging up to about 80 milliseconds create doubling—the effect of two instruments or voices performing almost in unison. Still longer unmodulated delays are perceived as echo with various intervals.

❖ Phase Shifters

Phase shifters do just what the name implies—alter the phase of the signal. Modulation is typically used to animate the effect. While this effect was popular in some musical circles in the 1970s, it is not used much today outside of science fiction soundtracks.

❖ Dynamic Effects

Compressors reduce the dynamic range of the sound according to a user-controlled ratio. A compression ratio of 3:1 indicates that for every 3 dB of signal input there will be only 1 dB of signal output.

Compression is useful when recording highly dynamic or transient material (such as rock drums), since it reduces the chance of tape saturation due to temporary signal overload and allows higher over-all levels to be recorded. This, in turn, yields a higher signal-to-noise ratio. Compression is also handy when ensuring that a signal with unwanted dynamic variations, such as narration, maintains a fairly steady level.

Limiters prevent a signal from exceeding a given output level regardless of the input level. Compressor/limiter combinations are popular because the limiter will provide an arbitrary level ceiling after the compressor does its best. (Too much compression results in a dull sound due to a lack of dynamics.)

Expanders perform the opposite function of compressors. A 1:3 expansion ratio would produce 3 dB of output for every 1 dB of input. The use of compression on recording and expansion on playback forms the basis of classic noise reduction. This combination is often called *companding*.

❖ **Noise Gates**

Noise gates allow the user to set a threshold below which output will be muted and above which the signal will be passed. This is useful in amplifying or recording signals in an environment where the ambient noise is undesirable, yet uncontrollable. Ideally, the threshold is set at the highest possible level that will still accept the desired source sound.

❖ **Equalizers**

Equalizers provide equalization or EQ—control over specific frequency ranges. The individual ranges are referred to as *bands*, and greater numbers of bands offer simultaneous control over more independent frequency ranges. The *graphic equalizer* usually has fixed frequency bands with sliders offering a cut or boost amount for each band. The attenuation affects surrounding frequencies according to a predictable slope. (See Figure 11.6.) Graphic equalizers are best suited for adjusting the overall sound output to compensate for deficiencies in the frequency response of speakers and/or the listening environment.

The *parametric equalizer* offers three basic controls for each band: the exact frequency at the center of the band, the width of the band, and the cut/boost attenuation. (See Figure 11.7.) Parametrics are useful in homing in on the exact frequencies that cause feedback in live sound or in clarifying mixes where the harmonic content of two or more elements are competing at the same frequencies.

Figure 11.6

Graphic equalizers cut and boost fixed ranges of frequencies.

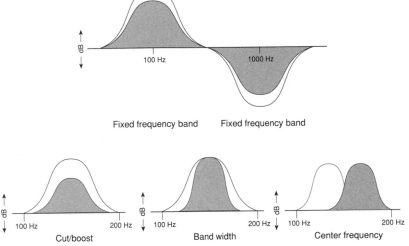

Figure 11.7

Parametric equalizers allow the ability to dial in the exact frequency and bandwidth to be cut or boosted.

SYNTHESIZERS

A *synthesizer* is an electronic musical instrument capable of generating sound by exercising real-time control over the key parameters of sound—frequency, timbre, amplitude, and duration. The first synthesizers consisted of modular panels of knobs and switches that had to be interconnected via *patch cords* and set manually. Moreover, they were largely *monophonic*—capable of responding only one note at a time—for the first decade or so.

Synthesis has come a long way since the days of Switched-On Bach. Circuitry that once resembled an old telephone switchboard now fits in a keyboard, in rack-mount *sound modules*, or on a card for a computer bus—usually with many times the power. The settings for a plethora of parameters can be stored as *programs* and called up with the press of a button. (Programs are also called *patches*, a carryover from the days of the patch cord.) Storage options include RAM and ROM cartridges, floppy disks, and system exclusive transfers.

Most synthesizers also have rather extensive MIDI send and receive capabilities. In fact, MIDI is the only way in which sound modules and many computer sound cards lacking keyboards can be controlled. The hottest trend for MIDI in multimedia is the incorporation of the synthesizer with General MIDI presets into an internal sound card or external box for use with the computer and its software sequencing abilities.

❖ **Architecture**

Virtually all modern synthesizers are *polyphonic*—capable of sounding many notes at a time. In the simplest terms, the degree of polyphony corresponds to the number of *voices*—essentially individual monophonic synthesizers—available in the device. Many synthesizers build more complex sounds by stacking more than one voice per note, thereby reducing the polyphony accordingly.

Polyphonic synthesizers can be further differentiated according to whether they are multitimbral or not. *Multitimbral* instruments can sound unique timbres with each voice; those that cannot do so are more like a traditional instrument in which all voices share the same sonic qualities. The ability to play unique timbres simultaneously in response to discrete multiple MIDI channels enables a single synthesizer to orchestrate a multitrack sequence. This capability is enhanced with *dynamic voice allocation*—the ability of the instrument to float individual voices and assign them as needed to MIDI note-on commands complete with the appropriate timbres.

Many synthesizers also sport built-in drum sounds, sequencers, and signal processors in various combinations and degrees of sophistication. Although this self-contained music workstation approach can be quite valuable for personal and semi-pro composition, most of these categories are more sophisticated in their dedicated forms discussed throughout this chapter.

❖ **The Classic Synthesizer**

Synthesizers utilize a wide variety of methods to generate sounds. The classic synthesizer architecture uses *subtractive synthesis*. This term comes from the fact that the timbres of notes are shaped by removing or filtering harmonics from rich waveforms. The voice architecture of many synthesizers today is patterned after perhaps the most classic of synthesizers—the Minimoog.

Oscillators, filters, and amplifiers

The basic sound is generated by one or more *oscillators*, typically offering a choice of simple waveforms—rectangular, sawtooth, and triangular. Coarse and fine tuning are provided for each oscillator. The more oscillators available per voice, the more complex the raw waveforms, octave combinations, and beat frequencies will be. *Noise generators* are also available to provide sound effects and breath effects.

Oscillator outputs are mixed and routed through one or more *filters*. A low-pass filter is most essential for subtractive synthesis. The arbitrary cutoff frequency influences the basic tone color by filtering out certain harmonics. The filter *resonance*, or *Q*, provides a variable degree of emphasis at the cutoff frequency. The filter output is then routed to an internal amplifier.

The real power of subtractive synthesis is the ability to modulate parameters such as oscillator pitch, filter cutoff, and amplifier level with external signals that vary with time. Components of the classic synthesizer, such as the keyboard, emit a control voltage that can be accepted by *voltage-controlled oscillators* (VCOs), *voltage-controlled filters* (VCFs), and *voltage-controlled amplifiers* (VCAs). (See Figure 11.8.) While voltage control is still used in some instruments, digital control is in greater use today, giving us the *DCO*, *DCF*, and *DCA*.

Figure 11.8

The basic signal chain used in subtractive synthesis.

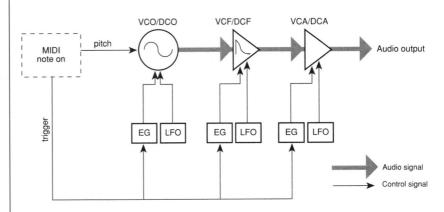

Modulation sources

The most basic modulation source is the keyboard and/or MIDI controller source. Routing to the oscillator provides basic control of musical pitch. Routing to the filter or oscillator controls the cutoff frequency and amplitude, respectively, according to the note being played. Routing MIDI parameters such as velocity, aftertouch, and continuous controllers to various components can expand the expressiveness of the electronic instrument

Real power to shape sounds comes with the *envelope generator* (EG). Envelopes dictate the way a control level changes over time, typically using parameters that are basic corollaries to acoustic parameters—attack, initial decay, sustain level, and release. Applying an envelope to the filter cutoff alters the harmonic content and, therefore, the timbre over time. Routing an envelope to the amplifier shapes the overall loudness of the sound over time. Most synthesizers have at least two envelope generators per voice to accommodate independent filter and amplifier modulation. The ability to

319

affect oscillator pitch with an envelope can also be useful for instrument inflections and sound effects.

The other common modulation source is the *low-frequency oscillator* (LFO). The influence of the LFO is determined both by the waveform and the routing. A triangle wave will modulate pitch to produce *vibrato*, modulate filter cutoff to produce a "wah-wah" effect, and modulate amplitude to produce *tremolo*. A rectangular wave will produce abrupt level changes in the destination, and so forth. The amount of modulation dictates the range of the level change in the destination. Instrument vibrato and sirens are closely related triangle wave modulations, for example. Vibrato has a higher modulation frequency in subtle amounts, while the siren has a lower modulation frequency in greater amount.

Modulation sources can affect one another. Since natural instruments exhibit shorter amplitudes with higher pitches, the keyboard or MIDI note-on information can be made to modulate the envelope that in turn is modulating the amplitude. Routing velocity to influence either the filter cutoff or the filter envelope will help to simulate the natural phenomenon of increased brightness with increased amplitude.

Performance controls

Performance controls can be used to manually affect the nuances of electronic instruments in real time. One left-hand control is typically dedicated to pitch bend. A second left-hand control can usually be programmed to control the amount of modulation to a given destination—typically vibrato. (These two common performance controls sometimes take the form of a single device, such as a joystick, that controls separate parameters via the x- and y-axes.) Velocity and pressure can be routed to control various modulation sources. Footpedals and footswitches round out the traditional complement of programmable performance controls.

Summary of synthesized sound

The range of sounds that can be produced by a classic synthesizer are limited only by the available sources and destinations and their individual parameters. The key to creating your own sounds is to experiment with individual parameters and build a knowledge of how they interact. While effective sound synthesis is an art form, all modern synthesizers come with an impressive selection of presets and/or programs that require little or no alteration. Subtle changes to a parameter or two are often all that is required to customize a sound to the needs of a given passage.

❖ Other Forms of Synthesis

Many other synthesis technologies are available in addition to classic subtractive synthesis. Many borrow some of the same concepts and components. Most also share similar performance controls.

Variations of subtractive synthesis

The most common variation on subtractive synthesis is the use of digitally-sampled waveforms in the oscillator stage. Combined with the classic filter, amplifier, and modulation structures, this dramatically increases the sonic palette available through subtractive synthesis. *Wavetable synthesis* adds to this potential by providing oscillators with a series of different sampled and synthesized waves in rapid succession.

FM synthesis

Originally developed at Stanford University, *FM synthesis* was popularized in the mid-1980s in the form of the Yamaha DX7 and related products. FM synthesis derives its name from the fact that sound is created almost entirely by modulating the frequencies of one or more oscillators with those of others. Low-frequency modulation influences the sound at discernible intervals. When the modulating frequency reaches a pitch above about 15Hz, it actually alters the perceived harmonic content of the destination.

In FM synthesis, the oscillators are called *operators*. Operators can usually be used as carriers or modulators. Each operator is influenced by an envelope generator. Envelopes related to carriers determine the amplitude of fundamental frequencies; envelopes related to modulators influence the harmonic content over time. (See Figure 11.9.)

Figure 11.9

FM synthesis creates timbres by modulating fundamental frequencies with other frequencies under envelope control.

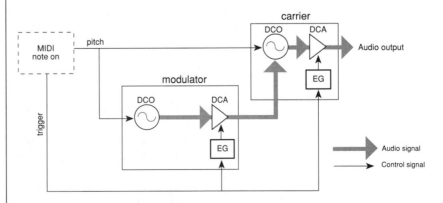

Greater numbers of operators increase the potential for musical complexity and usefulness. While the DX7 had six operators, the popular SoundBlaster card for the PC employs a Yamaha chip with two operators per voice. Yamaha has unveiled a four-operator chip that is being incorporated into several PC sound cards.

Achieving good results from FM synthesis is considered by most people to be less intuitive and, therefore, more difficult than with subtractive synthesis. However, libraries of preprogrammed sounds address this problem. In general, FM is more realistic in creating pitched percussive timbres and bell-like sounds than smooth sounds such as orchestral string sections.

Additive synthesis

Additive synthesis builds sounds from scratch by providing direct control over the individual sine wave harmonics. For additive synthesis to be effective, real-time control over the amplitude of each harmonic is required. This process is computation intensive, requiring control of 16 harmonics at least and 32 preferably. For this reason, early additive synthesizers were little more than computer-generated organs.

Although today's processors can handle additive synthesis, the requirements of polyphony still carry a relatively high price. While controlling sound in this way is a direct corollary to the way sounds work in nature, the other drawback is that an intimate knowledge of harmonic content is required in order to manipulate additive synthesis. At this writing, additive synthesis is not in use on the desktop.

DIGITAL SAMPLERS

In their simplest form, *digital samplers* are devices capable of digitizing sounds from other sources and playing them back on demand. Sampled sounds are RAM-based: they can be stored on disk, but must be in memory to be played back. Like synthesizers, samplers take forms such as keyboards, rack-mount modules, and computer cards.

Samplers share many of the attributes of subtractive synthesis voice architecture. Most are multitimbral, capable of responding to multiple MIDI channels discretely with unique samples. More often than not, today's samplers include filters, amplifiers, LFOs, and envelopes.

Digital sampling works on the same basic principles of resolution and sampling rates common to all digital audio devices. A-to-D converters are used in the sampling process and D-to-A converters are used for playback. While the goal of the average digital recorder is to play back sounds at the same rate at which they were recorded, the sampler intentionally alters the playback rate. Digital samples sound higher in pitch when the playback rate is higher than the sample rate, and lower in pitch when the playback rate is less than the sample rate.

Sampled sounds are only credible, however, when the pitch is altered by a few semitones. Pitch variations on the order of octaves result in sounds associated with monsters and chipmunks. On the other hand, individual samples for each musical pitch are too memory intensive for most budgets. As a compromise, most manufacturers provide for *multisampling*—the ability to assign a unique sample every third semitone or so and to alter the playback rate within that range. (See Figure 11.10.) The process of assigning samples to notes or ranges is known as *sample mapping*. This process also entails digitally tuning the sample so that it matches the pitch to which it is being assigned.

Figure 11.10

Multisampling technology provides the ability to assign unique samples to respond to specific note ranges.

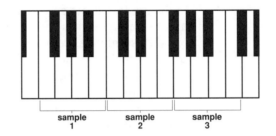

The sample sizes required to accommodate sounds with lengthy sustains can be formidable. To work around this, samplers can loop sections of the digital waveform during the sustain portion of the envelope. Some samplers also invoke loops during the release stage as well.

Attributes that distinguish samplers from one another include the control afforded by the voice architecture, the number of voices, sample memory, storage devices, available sound libraries, and the quality of the sampling circuitry. Better samplers record in stereo and play back via stereo voices. Output circuitry is another factor, regardless of mono or stereo design. On less expensive models, the output circuitry is multiplexed so that the multiple voices share a common D-to-A converter. All else being equal, individual converters for each voice provide better fidelity—not to mention individual mix outputs for each voice.

323

Sample playback devices

Aside from storage, two major parts of the digital sampler are the sampling circuitry and the voices to play back the samples. Due to the sound acquisition, keyboard mapping, and looping processes, more people are interested in playing back sampled sounds than in recording their own. Sample playback devices with synthesizer voice architecture and large sound libraries are therefore in high demand. At least one manufacturer, E-mu Systems, provides an OEM chipset that other manufacturers are using to integrate ROM- or RAM-based sample playback and subtractive voice architecture into computer-based sound cards for multimedia. The lines continue to blur between sample-playback devices and synthesizers.

MIDI SEQUENCERS

Combined with an inexpensive MIDI interface card, MIDI sequencer software provides the equivalent of multitrack recording for MIDI data. The software has on-screen controls that emulate a tape deck, including transport controls, mute, and solo. The sequencer can also be thought of as the conductor of the electronic orchestra.

MIDI sequences require significantly less storage and throughput than digital audio files. A four-minute composition of average complexity might require about 50K in MIDI form, instead of 40MB for CD-quality audio! MIDI sequences are, therefore, easy to modem and deliver. While many sequencers offer more complex proprietary file formats, most manufacturers also support the MIDI spec's standard file formats for sequences.

❖ Track Record and Playback

In its simplest form, the sequencer has independent tracks that can hold discrete passages of MIDI performances. These passages can be captured in real time by playing on any device whose MIDI Out is connected to the computer's MIDI In while recording. Alternately, *step-entry* allows people lacking musical dexterity to enter notes in nonreal time: duration is selected from on-screen icons, and pitch can be entered either from a MIDI device or an on-screen keyboard. Punch-in and punch-out functions for rerecording small portions of passages are typically automated as well.

Once recorded, tracks can be assigned to any of the 16 MIDI channels. Combined with MIDI sound sources, this paves the way for the orchestration process. (See Figure 11.11.) Let's say you record a piano performance on track 1, a bass performance on

Figure 11.11

*Entire electronic orchestra-
tions can be accomplished
by matching the MIDI
receive channels on instruments and MIDI transmit
channels on individual
sequencer tracks.*

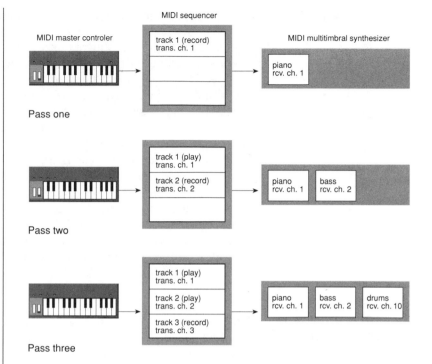

track 2, and a drum performance on track 3. To keep things simple, let's also channelize the outputs so that tracks 1 through 3 transmit on MIDI channels 1 through 3 on playback. Connect the MIDI Out of the computer to one or more MIDI instruments, then assign a piano sound to receive on channel 1, a bass sound to receive on channel 2, and a drum kit to receive on channel 3. Voila—instant jazz trio!

This channelization process can be applied to a single multitimbral instrument or to multiple devices whether they are multitimbral or not. Either way, this arranging process provides for a tremendous amount of experimentation. A myriad of sound combinations can be auditioned by calling up different instrument programs. The program parameters can be tweaked in real time as the passage is playing back, and sounds can be layered by assigning track outputs to more than one channel.

Sequencers can also record more than note data. Other MIDI performance parameters—program changes, continuous controllers, pitch bend, pressure, and velocity information—can be recorded, then edited later. This makes sequencers appropriate for controlling automated fader packages, mute automation consoles, MIDI-controlled effects devices, MIDI-controlled lighting systems, and more.

❖ Editing

As with most other digital data, MIDI sequence data can be cut, copied, and pasted. The pitch and duration of individual notes can also be altered after recording. Entire passages can be *transposed* to a different key without affecting timing. Quantization allows all notes to be moved to a specified value such as eighth notes. All velocity values can be altered globally by arbitrary amounts, percentages, or curves, providing some basic automated mixing. All of these functions would require rerecording entire passages or tedious punch-in and punch-out using traditional analog or digital recording methods.

Sequencers that support *song section architecture* offer an added bonus for pop-oriented composition. Composers can perfect individual song sections such as intro, verse, chorus, and bridge, then try different arrangements by calling them in various orders. (This is similar to the playlist in hard disk recording systems.) Can't decide whether to end with two or three iterations of the chorus? The difference is only a mouse click away!

❖ Tempo and Synchronization

Altering the tempo of a MIDI sequence or portion thereof has no effect on the MIDI note values that dictate pitch. This means that you're free to experiment with tempo after the composition is recorded or anytime during the composition/recording process.

Most current MIDI sequencers support Song Position Pointer and can synchronize to either internal or external clock. Support for MIDI Time Code is a little less common, but you'll typically only need this if you envision working with events in absolute time against SMPTE time code.

The more sophisticated sequencer software incorporates *tempo maps*. These are used in conjunction with SMPTE-to-MIDI converters to alter tempo during a composition when scoring extremely dynamic and complex soundtracks against pictures.

OTHER MIDI SOFTWARE AND HARDWARE

Many other MIDI software and hardware categories have evolved parallel to the sequencer. Here's a quick categorical look at some of the other things you may encounter in your MIDI travels.

❖ MIDI Interfaces

Computers require MIDI interfaces to communicate with external MIDI devices. Since MIDI is a part of the MPC standard, interfaces are often built into MPC sound cards. Virtually all personal computers have dedicated MIDI interfaces available from a variety of third-party sources.

The basic MIDI interface offers a MIDI In and a MIDI Out jack. MIDI Thru jacks are less common because sequencers usually offer a software thru that allows the musician to audition a remote sound module while recording. Interfaces with multiple MIDI Outs can be handy when driving many different MIDI devices. Two MIDI Ins with merge capabilities allow the signals from a MIDI input device to merge with those from an external sync converter. (Some interfaces incorporate a sync converter.)

Beyond that a MIDI patchbay allows users to route multiple MIDI masters to multiple MIDI slaves without having to change the physical connections. In a parallel concept, a few manufacturers offer sequencer/interface combinations supporting multiple 16-channel MIDI buses to address 32 to 512 channels in very large MIDI setups!

❖ MIDI Sync Converters

If you need to synchronize MIDI soundtracks to external devices, some form of *sync converter* is required. The most rudimentary is *FSK-to-MIDI conversion* that simply reads and writes a dumb clock onto tape. *SMPTE-to-MIDI converters* provide Song Position Pointer information to be correlated to SMPTE time code. More advanced versions provide for tempo maps in the converter hardware or as a software accessory. *SMPTE-to-MTC converters* derive MIDI Time Code from SMPTE sources. The majority of SMPTE-based converters will also write SMPTE time code to tape.

❖ Hybrid Sequencer/ Recorders

Several manufacturers offer packages that combine powerful MIDI sequencing in parallel with direct-to-disk recording. This product is aimed at those who compose and record primarily with MIDI, yet need a track or two for vocals or other acoustic elements. The two components are integrated seamlessly so that passages containing tracks of both MIDI and digital audio information can be edited as a whole.

❖ Music Notation

Although some sequencers offer rudimentary display and printout of music notation, dedicated notation software does this better. That's because some fancy artificial intelligence is required to bridge the gap between human expression and the literal nature of the computer. Conversely, notation software usually offers some basic sequencing but lacks the control of dedicated sequencer software. Standard MIDI files can usually be used to transport files between these two types of software.

❖ Patch Editors and Librarians

The number of parameters on electronic music products has increased while the number of buttons used to access them has decreased. Most devices use parameter lookup buttons to step through a sea of menus, cursor keys to move around the current menu in a small LCD display, and a data entry mechanism such as a keypad, slider, or buttons.

Patch editor software turns your monitor and mouse into a graphic interface for the parameters inside a MIDI device. Since this is accomplished via system exclusive codes, most patch editors are designed for a given instrument. Generic versions are available, but you should make sure your instrument is already supported unless you want to dive head first into the MIDI bit stream!

Some electronic music instruments are supported by libraries of hundreds and even thousands of alternate sound programs. Combined with any programs you create yourself, the task of organizing and archiving libraries of sounds becomes formidable. *Patch librarians* serve as a sort of database for individual patches, as well as groups of patches that you commonly use together. Although these applications employ system exclusive, the bulk transfer information is less involved than manipulating the individual parameters. A reasonable number of generic librarians are available, but the same caveat about instrument support applies. (Some companies also offer hybrid patch editor/librarians.)

POWER AMPLIFIERS

An audio power amplifier takes the preamplified sound from a console or other preamp and boosts it to levels required by the speakers. As such they are pretty straightforward. Examining the specifications regarding frequency response, distortion, and the like are all well and good, but you can usually let your ears be the judge.

More importantly, the output impedance should match the input impedance of the speakers you intend to drive. You should also use a wattage rating that will drive your speakers at their optimum level. About the closest thing to an average rating is 75 watts into 8 ohms. All things considered, you should have enough power so that the speakers are driven to the desired level without having to push the mixer output past its optimum output.

SPEAKERS

Speakers are the mechanisms by which electrical representations of sound are transduced into sound waves. The basic speaker consists of a diaphragm connected to a cone (usually paper) on one end and a plastic core surrounded by a coil of wire attached to the other. A permanent magnet is fixed behind the coil/core. Alternating current from an audio amplifier is applied to the coil which causes fluctuations in the magnetic field of the fixed magnet, thus forcing the entire diaphragm/cone assembly to move back and forth. The electrical energy is thus translated into sound pressure waves.

The gory details of speakers is a subject audiophiles can argue about forever. The following discussion points out some of the key concepts involved in speaker choices. Beyond these parameters, your ears are as good a reference as anything.

❖ Basic Concepts

The size of the speaker cone determines the frequency ranges that can be reproduced accurately. As with all other natural sound sources, the larger the speaker, the lower the frequencies it can produce. Similarly, the smaller the speaker, the higher the frequencies it can produce. Just as smaller speakers (*tweeters*) don't do a good job of handling low frequencies, larger speakers (*woofers*) aren't good at reproducing higher frequencies.

The solution is to place an array of different sized speakers in a common cabinet. A *crossover circuit* is placed between them to isolate the frequency ranges. A *passive crossover* is typically a high-pass filter that prevents the low frequencies from reaching the smaller speakers; the woofer still has to try to deal with the high frequencies. This is less optimal than an *active crossover* that actually isolates the frequency bands. Ideally, a passive crossover is inserted between each speaker size.

Speakers and their cabinets go hand in hand. Together they determine the frequency response and the optimal sound pressure levels. The ports, or holes, in the fronts of speaker cabinets *tune* the cabinet to help flatten the frequency response. One of the major specifications to consider in purchasing any speaker cabinets is the flatness of the frequency response.

Speakers can only handle certain power ratings. Be careful to match the power amplifier output with the speaker's wattage rating, taking impedance into consideration. Driving speakers with signals that exceed their handling abilities results in blown speakers and expensive repair bills. Conversely, some speakers simply sound better when driven at higher levels.

❖ The Right Speaker for the Job

Speakers are designed for specific purposes. Those used in live sound in large venues are engineered more for sound pressure level and dispersion than for fidelity. Speakers for studio monitoring are designed more for fidelity and accuracy than for power. Moreover, monitor speakers are built to be most efficient in a room of specific size, driven at a specific power level, and placed at a given proximity to the listener.

Near-field monitors have very narrow fields and are specifically designed to be used within a few feet of the listener at moderate volumes. As such, they are usually found perched atop or just behind the console. They are fairly small and don't require much power. More sizable studio monitors are designed to play the louder mixes and cover the entire room. Most professional studios have the ability to switch between these two types of speakers.

❖ ❖ ❖ ❖ ❖ ❖

This chapter has discussed the various tools available for recording, shaping, and playing back sound. The next chapter provides tips and techniques to help you get the most out of your audio productions.

CHAPTER 12

Audio Production

Typically, the efforts of many specialists go into the production of the audio that accompanies visuals in television and the movies. Many tools are now available that allow an individual to produce and manipulate high-quality sound on the desktop. Teaching musicianship, composition, and the myriad permutations of studio engineering is beyond the scope of this book. This chapter offers perspectives on effective use of desktop audio tools at a variety of levels.

SOUND IN MULTIMEDIA PRODUCTIONS

In some ways, sound is the multimedia orphan. Most productions emphasize visual content much more than audio. This is due to several reasons. Although multimedia's family is diverse, one of its ancestors is the slide presentation—a largely silent medium. Computer technology has also emphasized graphics, right down to the fact that every computer has a monitor while not all have speakers or audio circuits. The most popular desktop computer—the PC clone—can barely bleep and bloop without additional hardware. Indeed, the addition of audio can place a serious burden on multimedia platforms already pushed to the limit with animation and video.

The audio elements of a production can be as important in the communication process as the visual elements, however. Soundtracks can convey a sense of realism, time, place, and emotion. Moreover, today's audiences are accustomed to receiving information aurally. Multimedia without sound is as one-dimensional as the Silver Screen was before the talkies. Indeed, much can be learned—both technically and aesthetically—from Hollywood's use of sound.

You can verify the crucial role of audio simply by turning down the sound on your TV and experiencing only the visual elements. You'll soon see that pure action has little meaning without the emotional cues given by an accompanying soundtrack.

❖ Categorizing Sound

Sound can be broken down into the categories of music, speech, and sound effects. Another delineation is literal sound versus abstract sound. Literal sounds are those necessary to support reality: for example, the words spoken by an actor, the music performed by a group, or the sounds associated with environments or moving objects. Abstract sounds, although not essential to the content, help communicate the message emotionally. The musical scores of episodic television programs and movies fulfill this role.

A related categorization divides sounds into those that occur on-screen and off-screen. All abstract sounds are off-screen, but literal sounds can fall in either category. Dialog is typically on-screen, whereas narration is as often off-screen as on. The off-screen sounds of explosions, screeching tires, or a blood-curdling scream can convey a great deal without direct visual support. Indeed, much more can be communicated by showing something else on the screen at the same time—someone's reaction to the sound, for example.

Another distinction can be made between productions where audio supports the visuals, as opposed to music-video style productions where the music drives the imagery. These differences are not just aesthetic, but procedural as well. Most music for television and movies is created in parallel with or after the visuals; music videos are always based on completed music that dictates both the shooting and editing processes.

Regardless of categorization, the first step in realizing effective productions is the seamless and synergistic integration of audio, rather than the addition of sound to go with the imagery.

❖ Conveying Realism

Conveying realism extends beyond simply recording a real world event to communicating a sense of proximity and environment to the listener. In some cases reality must be enhanced or replaced to have the proper impact.

Proximity

Matching sound levels so that they communicate the proximity of the viewer to a literal sound source is important in conveying realism. If the camera is moving toward an actor from across a crowded room, the actor's voice will become louder as the camera nears. The level of ambient noise, on the other hand, will remain the same. (*Ambient noise* is the combination of any signals that are relatively constant throughout an environment.)

Distance diminishes brilliance as well as loudness. Obstacles such as walls and doors significantly affect both parameters due to absorption. The successive reflections in a reverberant environment are also less brilliant than their predecessors.

Environment

Sounds can seem unrealistic if the expected acoustic qualities of an environment are lost. Studio recordings are routinely made in dry environments for optimum control and flexibility. Signal processors like reverb units are used to add the expected ambiance artificially.

Expected acoustic qualities extend to the presence of certain extraneous sounds as well. Outdoor scenes might benefit from the ambient sounds of chirping birds or nearby traffic, just as restaurant scenes warrant background sounds of conversation and cutlery on china.

Enhanced sound effects

Obtaining optimum sound recordings during a visual shoot is sometimes difficult, since a microphone might become an unwanted element in the picture. Hollywood technicians spend a great deal of effort recreating sound effects. The *Foley artist* is the person in the recording studio who watches the picture and manually creates sound effects for everything from footfalls to door slams to breaking glass. Foley artists often employ tricks to fake sounds, such as simulating a crackling fire by crumbling cellophane near a microphone. Larger sounds—such as explosions and car crashes—have been pulled from tape libraries until recently, as have ambient tracks. Many of today's sound effects are performed using digital samplers, including some of the those traditionally done via Foley.

Sound effects can also be exaggerated to heighten the sense of reality. Sound designers routinely do things like compositing multiple explosions to make a single explosion and/or playing them at half speed to make them sound larger than life. Cartoon reality is created through sound effects, and visions of the future in science fiction are embellished not only with the improbable bleeps and bloops of equipment, but also with the impossible whooshes of spaceships and rocket engines in the soundless vacuum of space.

❖ Conveying Meaning

Although the task of conveying realism is fairly mechanical, that of conveying abstract meaning requires additional creativity. Devices such as melody, harmony, rhythm, instrumentation, musical genre, time signature, tempo, structure, and even silence can imply much more than what is being said and/or portrayed visually. Producers can guide composers or select music from existing libraries according to the message and style to be conveyed. The following look at the impact of the soundtrack provides guidelines for evaluating and implementing audio.

Emotion

Music is an extremely powerful vehicle for conveying emotion. Taken out of the context of literal performance, musical genres can be broadly associated with moods. Circus music might imply that a scenario is ludicrous or comical. A light jazz ensemble could suggest the stealth of a cat burglar or cool sophistication. A classical repertoire can imply elegance and class, and rock music often communicates fast-paced excitement. These are merely examples; many hybrids and variations on a theme abound.

The differences in soundtracks for several popular science fiction TV programs and movies can be used to illustrate the role of music in relation to imagery. The music from the *Star Trek: The Next Generation* television series opens with a soft ponderous theme that implies a sense of the wonder of "space...the final frontier." As the transition is made to the USS Enterprise warping through space, the music shifts to a bright, up-tempo, brassy theme that characterizes the mission of the crew to "boldly go where no one has gone before." In contrast, many of the space scenes from *2001: A Space Odyssey* are accompanied by Strauss waltzes, communicating a calm, stately mood. And the appearance of Darth Vader's flagship in the *Star Wars* series is accompanied by ominous "bad guy" music.

The selection of instruments and the way they are mixed is as important to a soundtrack as the hues of the artist's palette is to a painting. An acoustic guitar, a hollow-body jazz guitar, and a screaming Eddie Van Halen sound-alike convey different things to the ear even if they are playing exactly the same notes. One reason an orchestra has so many different kinds of instruments is that they each convey different personalities, qualities, and emotions.

Soundtracks from the old Warner Brothers cartoons illustrate this point in timeless fashion. As a generalization, tubas say big and sluggish, bassoons say quirky, clarinets and oboes say playful, piccolos say tiny, trumpets say bold and exciting, timpani say dramatic, and so forth.

Sound effects can also lend emotion to a scene. The sound of a ticking clock instantly brings the concepts of time, waiting, and anticipation to mind. The sound of a rifle being cocked leads the listener to anticipate a shot—possibly in association with fear for a hero's safety or pleasure in a villain's impending demise. Silence can also add tension to a scene if most other imagery is accompanied by sound.

Tempo also conveys emotion. A moderate to slow tempo invokes a romantic or laid-back aura. Faster tempos imply action and upbeat spirits. Exaggerated tempos in either direction can convey humor or distorted reality. Accelerating tempos, increasing volumes, and/or rising pitches communicate emotional build-up; opposite stimulus conveys that things are calming down.

Time

Soundtracks can also establish or reinforce a sense of time. Given properly dated repertoire, the marching band might convey the 1890s, the jazz band might take you to the 1950s, the orchestra might imply that the calendar has been set back to the Victorian Age, and screaming guitars might bring you back to more current times. The soundtracks for *Dueling Banjos*, *The Sting*, *Casablanca*, and *Saturday Night Fever* are exemplary in their use of musical genres that leave no question as to the era in which the story takes place.

Time of day can also be reinforced through sound effects. Alarm clocks and coffee grinders signal morning, while crickets and owls spell evening. The chimes of a clock can be used to establish any hour.

Geographic location

Since different cultures have styles and instruments with unique musical signatures, a sense of place can also be conveyed with these vehicles. A polyrythmic thundering of native drums spells tribal African, flamenco guitar and castanets are unmistakably Spanish, the sitar conjures images of India, and the koto takes the mind to Japan. Use of ethnic instruments in combination can imply the modern global community.

Association

Musical style can also communicate subconsciously to the hearts of a targeted audience. Demographics are very important in advertising and entertainment. The movie industry attempts to establish automatic integration of new releases into pop culture by incorporating songs by well-established music superstars in their soundtracks. The music and instrumentation for *Happy Days*, *The Wonder Years,* and *thirtysomething* pull at the subconsciousness of an aging Baby Boom generation. Brewing companies augment images of sexy women with the sounds of rock and roll to associate a fantasy lifestyle with their products in the minds of young men. Fast-food chains use rap music to sell hamburgers to a younger audience.

Musical genre is not the only tool for communicating to a target audience. When Richie Havens' voice is heard singing a modern jingle, the listener doesn't have to make a conscious identification in order for some part of the subconscious to travel back to the days of Woodstock—thereby making a positive association with viewers of a target age group. Similarly, another advertising trend resurrects pop songs from the '60s and '70s, changing the words slightly to suit the needs of a car company or other advertiser. This is a powerful communication tool: not only is a cultural association made, but the melody of the advertiser's jingle is already familiar to the audience.

The voice-over also offers another platform for association. Actors with distinctive voices, such as Patrick Stewart and James Earl Jones, are in high demand because their voices are familiar. In addition, the delivery style, accent, or use of slang can help target the message to a specific demographic group.

Signature and continuity

In the early days of soundtracks, characters, places, and events often had distinct themes. George Reeves' version of Superman would never dream of flying through the sky without his special theme music. The ominous two-note motif from *Jaws* is a telltale sign of impending danger. Each of the myriad characters on *Pee Wee's Playhouse* has a distinct theme that serves as a musical signature. And unique instruments were used to identify each character in *Peter and the Wolf*. Such signatures provide associative references for the audience and lend continuity to the entire experience. Indeed, musical elements should be chosen both for effectiveness and continuity with the rest of the soundtrack.

Musical signatures are less overt that they once were. Where Charlie Chan movies blatantly employed an overused Oriental motif to describe Chinatown, for example, contemporary movies like *Big Trouble in Little China* and *Black Rain* season contemporary Western styles more subtly with Oriental flavors.

One of the keys to establishing continuity without succumbing to clichés is flexibility. The classic theme from the James Bond movies has been orchestrated in many different ways within individual movies and throughout the series, for example.

Sound effects also serve to identify people, places, and things. Classic examples include the shrieking violins from the shower scene in *Psycho*, the electronic dialog of *Star Wars*' R2D2, and the sonic environment heard on the Enterprise bridge in the original *Star Trek* series. Each of these sounds is easily recognized and associated even when heard out of context.

Memorability

The best main themes are those that the audience retains long after the viewing experience is over. More people than not can remember the classic themes of *Pink Panther* or *Star Wars* movies. The more memorable the theme, the more memorable the entire presentation and its message. Similarly, Madison Avenue's ultimate goal in all those catchy radio and television jingles is to implant a combination of words and melodies so beguiling that the unsuspecting masses walk around subconsciously singing the product advertisements to themselves.

Although such strength in main themes is desirable, the music that underlies important action or dialog should be almost invisible. Supportive music should be felt on an emotional level more than heard at the conscious level. Major themes excluded, one of the best compliments that can be paid to a film composer is that you don't remember the music, but the viewing experience as a whole was incredible. This concept reinforces the need for synergy between audio and visual elements.

A recent experience ties these concepts of memorability and subtlety together in an interesting way. I recently heard a radio commercial for a product that employed the theme from *Miami Vice* behind the announcer's voice. I don't know what the product or the message was because I couldn't get past the mental images of Don Johnson, flamingos, and speedboats that I associate with that music.

CREATING AN AUDIO PRODUCTION ENVIRONMENT

One of the first steps in preparing to work with sound is optimizing the workspace for audio recording and production. This involves establishing a controlled sonic environment. Your own circumstances will dictate the degree to which you need to be concerned with issues like isolation and diffusion. The following suggestions may help you obtain better results from your audio productions. The more complex your recording efforts are, the more you may need to consult professional studio designers.

❖ Eliminating Sonic Reflection

While sonic reflections can contribute desirably to a listening environment like a concert hall, reflection is largely an unwanted characteristic in a production situation. Reflection can be attributed to surface materials and parallel surfaces.

As outlined in Chapter 10, harder and smoother surfaces generally reflect more sound. Tile and concrete are extremely reflective, for example. Glass is highly reflective as well, which is why most professional recording studios have no unnecessary outside windows. In more temporary or multipurpose situations, windows may be a fact of life. Drapes or blankets can be used to cover windows during production. Thicker material also helps counter the other window problem—sound exchange with the outside world.

Parallel surfaces can cause room resonance and standing waves. The somewhat exotic look of professional recording facilities owes much more to the acoustic mandate of unparallel walls than to visual design aesthetics. Not only are the walls at different angles, but the ceiling is angled uniquely from the floor. The glass separating the control room from the recording space is also set at an angle.

The use of unparallel walls diffuses sound waves on a large scale. Smaller *diffusers* in the form of movable baffles and irregularly shaped objects are also employed to disperse the angles of reflection at various wavelengths. Most diffusers are constructed from materials that also absorb some sound. Walls are often padded with material such as *Sonex* that exhibits three-dimensional surface patterns in foam that both absorbs and diffuses sound waves.

Acoustic tile found in many modern office ceilings is moderately good at diffusing and absorbing sound. Sonex, foam, carpeting, egg cartons, and other absorptive materials can be placed on portable baffles that can be positioned at various angles as needed. Decorative rugs can be hung on walls, and blankets can be suspended from the ceiling or a frame.

❖ Isolation

Isolation is also important to a controlled recording environment. After all, you don't need extraneous noise, like passing traffic or ringing telephones, reaching your microphones. Of course, other people should not be disturbed by the noise you generate either. Fortunately, studio isolation solutions usually address both issues at the same time.

External isolation

The methods outlined for using absorptive materials to eliminate reflections also go a long way in preventing sound from penetrating the recording environment. By extension, the more insulation in the walls, floors, and ceilings, the better the isolation will be.

All the padding in the world will not prevent low frequencies from coupling into the walls. In essence, a building acts somewhat like a speaker cabinet for long wavelengths at high enough levels. Professional studio designers often "float" rooms within rooms, using as little connecting surface area as possible. Many a band has converted an unassuming garage into a private recording studio using this method. Professional advice or more extensive reading is advisable when isolation from the outside world is that serious an issue.

Internal isolation

Isolation is also an issue within the studio. The goal here is control. Most engineers prefer to record each instrument or voice in complete isolation on a separate track, because this provides the greatest flexibility throughout the recording and mixing process. To this end, direct input of electronic instruments into the console is desirable. When microphones must be used, sonic isolation of acoustic and amplified sound sources is crucial.

Recording studios employ a *control room* for the engineer, producer, and other nonperformers that is isolated from the live performance area. Additionally, an *isolation booth* (*iso booth* for short) is used to separate a vocalist, drummer, or other talent sonically from the rest of the performers. In the recording of ensembles where performers must be in the same room, baffles are often used to help isolate and direct the sound of given performers into individual microphones.

In post-production facilities or smaller studios, the live room is usually unnecessary, but the iso booth is invaluable for voice-overs. With the advent of the MIDI studio and desktop multimedia tools, productions often involve only one or two people in a single room. This is only a problem when some live sound, like a voice-over, must be recorded. Speakers must be turned off and closed-cup headphones used so that existing program material doesn't bleed into the microphone. Equipment noise, such as that generated by computer fans and tape deck transports, creates an isolation problem. The most obvious solution is to put distance between the open microphone and the offending gear. Localized isolation can also be created by using small baffles or a padded voice-over tent.

❖ Equipment Setup

Ergonomics is a critical concern when a lot of equipment is involved in any kind of production. The centerpiece of any audio production environment should be the mixing console. The control room monitor speakers should be positioned so their axes of projection are focused to meet at the precise point at the console where the mixing will occur. The monitors should be far enough apart to establish a good stereo field, yet not so far apart or to the side as to be atypical of the average listening environment. Adhere to the monitor manufacturer's specifications regarding proper listening proximity.

A great deal of audio equipment comes in standard 19-inch rack-mount configurations. Go for it whenever possible—racks can help optimize the use of space. Similarly, keyboard stands are available in various versions that provide for stacking keyboards and other assorted gear. Equipment that you interact with infrequently—such as power supplies, amplifiers, and computer CPUs—can be placed in less accessible positions than the equipment that must be accessed constantly.

The more equipment you have and the more frequently you change it, the more important it is to have adequate room to move behind the gear. Crawling behind equipment with a flashlight every time you need to plug and unplug something gets old really fast. Patch bays can make your life easier; allowing enough space makes connecting the equipment to them easier also. The comments in Chapter 3 regarding cable routing, power, grounds, and interference should all be taken into consideration as well.

MICROPHONE TECHNIQUES

Chapter 10 discussed the different types of microphones in use today. Each recording situation has unique miking considerations, and no two engineers will use microphones in the same way. This section takes a quick look at general approaches to miking and a more specific look at the most common use of microphones in multimedia production—recording human speech. (Recording live audio during a video shoot is discussed in Chapter 15.)

❖ General Concepts

The main issues in all miking situations are frequency response, sensitivity, and isolation. Matching these considerations to the characteristic performance of microphone categories is the best way to choose a microphone. Microphones with larger diaphragms typically can handle higher sound pressure levels and lower frequencies. Those with smaller diaphragms usually are more responsive to subtle dynamics.

The pickup patterns of the various microphones discussed in Chapter 15 should be correlated to the recording environment. Omnidirectional mikes are the best choice when the intention is to capture ambiance. Unidirectional microphones are more popular for recording a single source well while rejecting other sound from the environment. The higher the need for rear and side rejection, the more a mike exhibiting cardioid and hypercardioid patterns is required. The use of bidirectional microphones is dictated by the need to use one mike to capture two opposing sound sources, or to record in stereo.

One effective way of visualizing proper microphone usage is to correlate the sonic pickup patterns to the visual projection of various lighting instruments. Sounds outside the pickup patterns are effectively in aural shadow. In this sense, an omnidirectional microphone is correlated to a plain light bulb, while unidirectional microphones can be equated to various spotlight settings.

Proximity

Often the greatest sonic presence can be obtain by *close-miking* a sound source—placing the microphone in close proximity. Many microphones tend to produce a booming sound when placed too close to a source of sound pressure waves of any magnitude. This is aptly referred to as the proximity effect. Many microphones have a switch that rolls off low frequencies to counter the proximity effect. Such a device should therefore be chosen for close miking.

Using multiple microphones

Multiple microphones are frequently used in recording situations to obtain several different sonic perspectives. A guitar might be close-miked for presence, with a second microphone placed further away to capture the instrument's ambiance in the room. Improper placement of multiple microphones can result in phase shift or even phase cancellation. One way to avoid phase problems is to employ the *three-to-one rule*—the distance between multiple microphones should be no less than three times the distance of the microphones to the sound source. If the microphones are positioned one foot from the sound source, for example, they should be no closer than three feet apart. This rule is actually more of a guideline. While closer ratios invite phase cancellation in some situations, they can provide more musically pleasing results in others.

Stereo miking

In a stereo recording, the output of two microphones is recorded to discrete channels in order to capture the placement of sound sources in their natural stereo field. One of the goals of stereo miking is good *localization*—perception of the placement of individual elements within the stereo field. The microphones should be a matched pair—the same make and model. Phase is critical in stereo miking. Two signals that are out of phase will cancel out one another just as in any other medium. If they are in phase, the composite level will be 3 to 6 dB higher than a mono recording. Signals that are partially out of phase can cause problems if stereo recordings are later reduced to mono. One way to ensure mono compatibility is to test the results of stereo placement by monitoring in mono.

In addition to acoustic phase, the two microphones must also be electrically in phase to obtain proper results. If each channel individually produces appropriate levels at the console but the level drops when the channels are combined, the wiring of one microphone cable may be the reverse of the other. One solution is to rewire one of the cables or replace it with a properly wired cable. Most better recording consoles also have a phase reverse switch on microphone input channels that flips the polarity; toggling this switch on one of the two channels in question will also bring the two mikes into phase.

There are many approaches to stereo miking, most of which trade off the effectiveness of the stereo imaging for overall sound quality. The most obvious method is to place the two mikes perpendicular to the sound source and spread them equal distances from the center. Omnidirectional condenser microphones are the primary choice in this situation, since the focus of unidirectional microphones tends to lend off-axis coloration and less accurate localization of individual elements within the stereo field. In general, this method yields a fuller sound but less distinct stereo imaging. Ideal spacing is usually about 75 percent of the width of the source while adhering to the three-to-one rule. (See Figure 12.1.)

X–Y miking or *coincident miking* uses two directional microphones that are placed in the center of the stereo field. They share a vertical axis, with the diaphragms aligned on top of each other so that their pickup patterns are crossed. This can be accomplished using two mike stands or a stereo adapter bar on a single stand.

With X–Y milking, acoustic phase cancellation is rarely a problem, since sounds arrive at both diaphragms at very nearly the same time. In general, wider angles yield wider stereo fields. Cardioids are most commonly used and can be placed at angles ranging from 90 degrees to 135 degrees. The tighter pickup patterns of hypercardioids dictate that they be placed on the narrower side of the this range, although they can be placed further away to compensate. X–Y miking offers better localization of elements within the stereo field than spaced miking and better compatibility with mono, but is less full in overall sound quality.

Near-coincident miking adds warmth to the sound of coincident miking by angling the two microphones out from the center side by side. Although localization is preserved in this configuration, this approach can result in some mono compatibility problems down the road since sounds may arrive at both diaphragms slightly out of phase.

Figure 12.1

Different microphones and placement techniques offer various trade-offs in stereo recording situations.

Spaced miking

X-Y miking

Near-coincident miking

One of the most advanced stereo miking systems is the M–S (middle–side) method. It employs two microphones, often in the same housing. An omnidirectional or cardioid microphone is positioned toward the sound source, while a bidirectional mike is positioned to pick up the sound from the sides. M–S systems include dedicated circuitry to merge the signals properly and can be a bit expensive as a result.

❖ Direct Recordings of Speech

The subject of recording live sound during a video shoot is addressed in Chapter 15. Narration, announcements, radio-style interviews, and voice-overs are all best recorded in a controlled environment such as an isolation booth. (A *voice-over* is essentially off-camera narration; the name comes from the fact that the voice is often superimposed over music and/or background sounds.) Not only is control important, but narration will often be mixed later with music or other sounds set in particular acoustic spaces. Adding narration with its own pronounced acoustic space would lend incongruity to the composite soundtrack.

In some cases, a narrator speaks on camera some of the time and off-camera at other times. If the off-camera work is recorded in a different environment, the difference in ambiance, microphones, and the like may be very noticeable to the listener. Although this can be overcome with good engineering and the right equipment, it's usually easier to record everything in the on-camera environment given this situation.

When ambiance cannot be avoided during the recording of narration, it is often advantageous to take some extra time and tape to record a long passage of the ambiance alone. This can be mixed into the final tracks in places where there is no narration, thereby avoiding any continuity problems as the voice comes and goes.

Miking a single voice

Directional microphones are optimal since they reject unwanted sounds and reflections that might come from other directions than the announcer's voice. The talent must direct their speech according to the polar pattern of the microphone, however. For this reason, extremely tight pickup patterns can be restricting.

In general, soft-spoken people should be closer to the mike than those who speak loudly. Although levels can be boosted electronically, speaking too far away from the microphone dilutes the sound power and distances the speaker perceptually from the listener. (Recall that sound waves follow the Law of Inverse Squares.) On the other hand, speaking too close to the mike can result in the proximity effect and/or overload. A bit of experimentation is often required to establish the proper proximity to the microphone— sometimes called the *sweet spot*.

Another common problem in miking voices is unwanted speech artifacts like sibilance (such as the hiss from the letter "s"), pops (such as from the force of the letter "p"), and mouth noises (such as smacking lips). One solution is to use a *pop filter* or a microphone that has one built in. Placing a sock over the mike will also work, as will cutting a foam sheath for the mic. Such make-shift solutions can reduce high frequencies, however.

The other way to eliminate unwanted speech artifacts is to place the microphone so that the speech is channeled across the mike rather than directly into it. The trick here is to make certain that the speech still falls within the microphone's pickup pattern. A commonly used angle is 45 degrees.

A table, copy stand, or music stand should be used to avoid rustling papers. Computers or other electronic prompting devices are best for long scripts. Even in the controlled environment of an iso booth, reflection problems can be caused by such seemingly innocent objects as tables, copy stands, and CRTs, however. Where possible, microphones should be angled so that reflections off of the these hard surfaces do not enter into the pickup pattern. Alternately, such surfaces can be covered with softer materials.

Achieving even levels

Today's listeners are accustomed to the smooth voices of professional announcers. Several techniques (in addition to rehearsing) can be used to enhance everyday recorded speech. Most people speak from the throat. Disc jockeys and professional announcers speak from the diaphragm to produce a deeper effect. The diaphragm is the area just above the stomach that actually causes air to move in and out of the lungs. Try making your voice emanate from there. With a little practice, your speech will sound deeper and fuller. Similarly, most people are lazy speakers. Awareness of the need to enunciate on the part of the speaker can make a great deal of difference in recorded results.

Most people's speech patterns fluctuate in sound level. This results in a dynamic range that can make some words hard to distinguish. When a voice must dominate over music or sound effects in a mix, fluctuating dynamics can be even more problematic. The first place to start in addressing this problem is at the source: people should be encouraged to speak at more uniform levels.

To even out the dynamic range, you can use a compressor usually in conjunction with a limiter to place a ceiling on the signal level. Although compression can be applied to prerecorded speech, it is usually more convenient to employ the compressor/limiter during the recording process. This not only helps ensure that the recording is not distorted, but makes for one less thing to worry about while mixing. Care should be exercised in setting the compression ratio. Too little compression won't accomplish the desired effect, but too much will literally squeeze the life out of a spoken passage.

Miking more than one voice

An interview situation can be handled several ways. Ideally, the two speakers should face one another with the microphone(s) in the center. Separate unidirectional mikes can be used for each person if the mikes are positioned back-to-back so that each rejects the signals accepted by the other. A bidirectional microphone can be placed so that the two pickup patterns are aligned with the speakers. If the people speak at uniformly different volumes, the microphone can be placed closer to the softer-spoken person. Radical differences should be handled with separate microphones since the difference in tonal qualities and perceived proximity will be noticeable to the listener.

Panel situations with more than two speakers are handled most easily by employing separate mikes. Microphones with narrower pickup patterns, such as hypercardioids, can help in avoiding isolation and phase cancellation problems.

It's one thing for the person doing the recording to understand proper microphone placement and characteristics; the talent is a whole separate issue. Those unused to microphones invariably ignore them or nearly swallow them! Where possible, explain the ideal speaking position and proximity to the speakers before you begin and conduct a few recording tests.

RECORDING BASICS

The nature of the recording process and the engineering procedures involved vary widely depending upon the project and genre. The circumstances of live concert sound are vastly different from those of studio recordings. Even in the studio, the processes of recording classical, jazz, and pop are unique, as is the experience of producing audio for CDs, film, television, and radio. This section focuses on the lowest common denominators—the basic ways to approach the recording and mixing processes.

❖ **Phases of Soundtrack Production**

The process of creating a soundtrack can be divided into four phases—preproduction, recording, mixing, and postproduction. The lines blur a bit on the desktop, but the basic ideas are still the same.

Preproduction is everything that happens before the actual recording process begins. This phase typically includes determining overall goals and timing needs, writing, choosing, or acquiring the music, auditioning and choosing talent, budgeting, picking the right equipment, and establishing logistics. In situations where out-of-house facilities are to be booked at a charge, anything that can economize on expensive time later should be done in advance. In this case, preproduction can also include picking the right facility.

The *recording session* is used to acquire any previously unrecorded sonic elements that will become part of the soundtrack. In the case of in-house desktop audio tools, musicians can shift some or all of the composition and arranging processes from the preproduction phase to the recording phase.

Mixing is the process of combining some or all of the previously recorded elements into a final sonic entity. A music mix, for example, would distill all of the melodic and rhythmic components into a finished song or composition, although it may or may not include the narration or sound effects.

In *postproduction* all of the elements are combined and processed for final distribution on media. In the recording industry, the process is referred to as *mastering*—preparing the mixed recording for the final process of conversion to masters and the plethora of distribution copies they stamp out in the form of albums, tapes, and CDs. In video production, the term *sweetening* is used to describe the process of transferring the audio elements to their final form on videotape. The term postproduction is mostly used to describe the process of integrating all of the audio and visual elements.

The remainder of this section focuses on the recording and mixing processes. Preproduction and postproduction of multimedia as a whole are explored in greater depth in Chapter 18. The use of audio in video postproduction is covered in Chapter 15.

❖ **Multitrack Recording**

Until the perfection of multitrack recording in the mid-1960s, most of the elements had to be recorded concurrently. Although we take multitrack recording technology for granted today, it revolutionized the recording industry only a few decades ago. The ability to *overdub*, or record different performance elements separately, made for significantly better miking isolation and, therefore, better sound quality and creative flexibility. Multitrack's inherent ability to relegate different instruments or performances to separate tracks also made it possible to correct small errors selectively and experiment with changes without forcing the entire ensemble to "take it from the top again."

Multitrack paved the way for much more complex sonic combinations. The Beatles' *Sgt. Pepper's Lonely Hearts Club Band* LP is one of the first, and still foremost, examples of this potential. Today several other developments in personal recording equipment and MIDI sequencing allow even a lone musician to aspire to similar heights in a desktop environment.

Preparation

The recording process starts with proper preparation. For starters, make certain that the tape bias/type matches that which the deck is set for, or vice versa. Buy the best tape your deck will handle—a few dollars isn't worth a single dB less in quality. Clean the heads and transport of the deck regularly for optimal performance. The heads and metal components of the transport should be cleaned with isopropyl alcohol or special head cleaner; rubber pinch rollers must be cleaned with special rubber cleaner. (The alcohol that saves the heads can destroy rubber.)

Reset the tape counter to zero at the head of the tape. Create a track sheet to document the content of the tracks, as well as any comments. Even if you don't need any reminders now, it can save time a month or a year from now if you ever need to remix the tape. Similarly, place a strip of removable white tape across the mixer channels on which you can write each channel's current function.

The recording process sometimes involves taping things several times in hopes of obtaining a better take or version. Returning to the beginning for such a take is simplified by resetting the tape counter, entering the counter position as a transport memory location, or at least documenting the location number. Each take should also be *slated* before it is recorded. Slating is the process of using a microphone to identify each take verbally. In conjunction with the counter, slating makes it a lot easier to distinguish between takes.

All instruments should be tuned to A-440 using an electronic tuner or similar device. Adherence to the A-440 standard ensures that the recording will be in tune with production music from other sources, as well as instruments with relatively fixed tuning such as acoustic pianos.

Professional studios place *test tones* at the beginning of each tape that allow other production facilities to calibrate their equipment to your tape. Although test tones are not as necessary in more self-contained productions, consult an engineer if your tapes need to go elsewhere.

Providing for synchronization and tempo guides

When building a composition track-by-track in a multitrack recording environment, a tempo track is one of the first things recorded. Even recording a simple metronome provides a common tempo reference that can be used until the actual rhythm is strong enough.

If there is any chance that your tape will have to be synchronized with other recording decks, MIDI sequencers, or video, record a sync track first. Sync and tempo are closely related; with MIDI sequencers, the guide tempo can be derived directly from the sync track. MIDI synchronization is discussed later in this chapter.

Tracking logistics

When recording compositions from scratch, you must decide early on how the tracks will be built up. In general, rhythm tracks such as drums, bass, and basic chords are recorded first. This provides a framework over which to record vocals, leads, and subtle embellishments. In the case of the one-man band, for example, a drum beat is usually established first, then bass, then chords, and so forth.

When recording a band or other ensemble that is accustomed to performing together, trying to build each track with overdubs can be disastrous. One way to get the best of both worlds is to record the basic tracks in ensemble performance with good enough isolation that individual performers can rerecord their parts later with the recorded ensemble.

Bouncing tracks

Multitrack recorders inherently have the capacity of *bouncing* tracks. Used in conjunction with a recording console, two or more tracks can be mixed to another track (or stereo pair of tracks). The original tracks can then be erased, freeing to record new overdubs. (See Figure 12.2.) On the downside, the combined elements on the destination track can no longer be manipulated individually: volume, EQ, processing, and stereo positioning are later adjusted as one or not at all.

There is no physical limit to the number of times you can bounce tracks, but each bounce on analog tape adds a considerable amount of noise. This restricts the practical limit to only a few such passes before the signal is completely degraded with noise. In addition, some high frequencies are usually lost with each generation, lead-

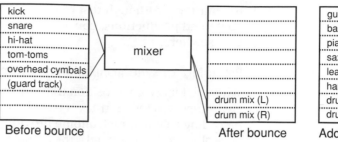

Figure 12.2

Bouncing tracks allows existing tracks to be freed by submixing them to other locations.

ing to the practice of boosting the high end of the source tracks during the bounce. Generation loss is not an issue with digital recording, as long as the transfer is entirely digital. The use of DACs and ADCs will cause some degradation.

Many multitrack tape decks cannot bounce to adjacent tracks. On a 4-track deck, for example, you can typically bounce tracks 1 and 2 to track 4, but not to track 3. Even when physically possible, the use of a blank guard track is recommended to avoid crosstalk. Therefore, careful track planning is in order if bouncing is to be employed.

Establishing optimum levels

One of the engineering goals during the recording process is to establish optimum signal levels within the console and on tape. These levels are largely independent of those that each element will have in the final mix. As a general rule, the signal level at each electronic stage should exhibit the highest possible signal-to-noise ratio without clipping. Where feasible, establish levels in the same order of signal flow in deference to the GIGO principle.

As the signal chain becomes more complex, however, it becomes harder to implement these processes since each stage has its own input, output, signal-to-noise, and distortion characteristics. In the end, a balance must sometimes be struck that yields the cleanest signal at the end of the chain that the combined components will allow.

Analog recorders offer one of the greatest challenges in optimizing signal levels. The tape itself has a noise floor that is higher than that of the electronic components alone. Ideally, recording levels should be established that keep the meter as close to 0 VU as possible. The more dynamic the content is, the more difficult this becomes. Noise reduction provides for lower recording levels, but can sometimes add unwanted coloration to the sound.

Outboard compressors can be used to tighten up the dynamic range of the signal being recorded. The overall output of the compressor can be boosted, making it possible to record with higher levels. As with all compression, however, you can have too much of a good thing. After all, the element of dynamics is integral to a lot of popular music. Transients such as the crack of a rock snare drum can cause temporary level jumps that saturate the tape and trigger the peak indicators, even though the rest of the music maintains a steady level around 0 VU. While compression can help, too much compression can make the sound lifeless. Simply reducing the overall level to the point where the transients don't peak might jeopardize the overall signal-to-noise level in analog tape.

These issues emphasize two aspects of analog tape. First, program material such as pop music is often so continuous that it masks the noise floor. Second, some distortion—especially on an aperiodic sound like a snare—is not only acceptable, but sometimes desirable. Many engineers prefer the warmth of analog's overall subtle distortion to the pristine nature of digital recording media. The meters on most analog recorders can be pushed upwards of +3 VU before crossing the fine line between acceptable warmth and unacceptable distortion.

Crosstalk can also influence level settings on analog tape. At points where signals approach saturation, the magnetic field associated with a track can be so strong as to affect neighboring tracks. On decks with less favorable crosstalk specs, a particularly hot snare might be heard faintly on an adjacent track, for example. To avoid this, allocate tracks so that those adjacent to high-level tracks are either empty or have strong, continuous content.

Each situation is different, and all of these factors taken together dictate record levels. If all else fails, do some record tests at various levels before committing to one for each track.

The guidelines for setting levels in digital recording differ significantly from analog. On the signal-to-noise side, no noise floor or tape hiss exists in the medium itself. On the other hand, clipping occurs arbitrarily at the level corresponding to the highest digital value. When combined, these factors typically dictate lower recording levels than would be used with analog tape. The lack of noise floor, however, should not be taken as an invitation to record with significantly low levels, since the levels of the tape returns on the console might have to be set higher than optimum and the dynamic range of the recording would be reduced. Given these factors, compression and limiting have their place in digital recording.

Achieving the cleanest signals

The greatest levels in the world are meaningless if the signals are fraught with noise. As a rule, the more circuitry there is in the sound chain, the more the signal will be degraded. Remove any unnecessary equipment from the recording chain.

The mixing console contains various electronic stages that each add noise. If no adjustments are necessary, routing the sound source directly to the deck input is the cleanest signal path. When a one-to-one relationship between sound sources, mixer channels, and tape tracks exists, the direct outputs on each mixer channel can be routed to the deck inputs to avoid the bus electronics. Unless the mixer does not feature direct outs, record buses should only be used when mixing more than one channel to an individual tape track. To audition what's going on the tape, switch the console settings so that you are listening to the tape returns while recording.

Signal processing while recording

You will have to decide whether to apply signal processing during the tracking or mixing phase. Compression and limiting for purposes of optimizing recording levels obviously need to be applied while tracking. Effects that are crucial to a performance or characteristic sound—such as the array of effects pedals used by most guitarists—should be recorded with the performance.

Once an effect is part of a track, there's no getting rid of it. For this reason other effects are usually applied during the mixing stage. This assumes, however, that there are enough effects devices to provide all of the simultaneous processing desired during the mix—and enough hands to make any changes that are necessary. When these issues are problematic, effects that are certain to go unchanged can be recorded during tracking.

This same logic applies to equalization. Although necessary gross EQ changes can be made while tracking, leaving the raw signal intact during recording provides for greatest flexibility during the mix.

Obtaining the best performances

When performances of talent are being recorded, the concept of quality extends to the performance. The producer must strike a balance between time constraints and the creative space of the performer(s). Few people will deliver their best performances if somebody is breathing down their necks while watching the clock. On the other hand, time is money. One of the most effective ways to reconcile these issues is through proper planning in the preproduction stage.

One of the oldest tricks in the book is to record a dry run without the knowledge of the talent. Many performers—especially less experienced ones—tighten up under the pressure of rolling tape. Even stars like Janet Jackson have wound up with rehearsal tracks on the final recording. In the words of Jeff Baxter, a former Doobie Brother and a producer in his own right, "always roll tape."

Often a great performance will be marred by a blooper or two. The good parts may never be recoupable by wiping the track and starting over. Where possible, use a punch-in/punch-out technique to replace the error and leave the rest intact. (A *punch-in* is usually accomplished by placing the transport in record, but engaging the track record function only at the beginning of the passage to be replaced. *Punch-out* refers to disengaging the track record function at the end of a corrected passage.) Punches should be done where a little gap of silence occurs so that there are no glitches. In many cases punches are made without the performer monitoring the track in order to record the passage as if it were the first take.

Another way to take the pressure off and achieve better performances is to keep going after a good take. If the extra tracks are available, keep the first as a safety, turn off the tape monitor on that track, and record another with a different goal. Go for a performance with a completely different quality—silly, sad, wild—and repeat this process. Although any of these tracks alone may be surprisingly better, pieces of various performances can be mixed down to a single track that sounds like one very emotional one.

❖ The Mixing Session

Once all of the elements have been recorded or acquired, they must be mixed into a single sonic entity. Many of the considerations that apply to the recording process apply to mixing as well, such as attaining optimum levels and signal quality. The mixing process also addresses issues of level balances, tonal enhancement, stereo imaging, perceived environment, and special effects.

Balancing levels

The levels of all of the audio elements must be set in such a way that everything is clearly audible, yet the more dominant elements such as melody and voice stand out. This is not as easy as it sounds. It is not unusual for novices to continue boosting individual track volumes selectively, only to find themselves with all the faders up, overloading levels, and a continued imbalance. Volume is not the only factor that affects clarity. Since every sound is comprised of many frequencies, boosting the level of one track may increase frequencies that mask the distinguishing frequencies of other tracks.

For this reason the EQ controls on individual mixer channels are invaluable during the mixing process.

Adding distinction between a kick drum and bass guitar in a mix provides a classic example of the selective application of EQ. Since both are low-frequency instruments, it's not uncommon for them to share certain frequencies. Boosting the overall level of either instrument could partially mask the other. The solution is to cut and boost different frequencies on one or both tracks. Basic EQ may only be able to make one brighter and the other more boomy. More sophisticated EQ devices can dial in exact frequencies to be cut and boosted. Experimenting with EQ will help determine the resonant and component frequencies that serve as a sonic signature for each instrument. These are among the most important frequencies to clarify.

Stereo placement

In stereo recordings, consideration must be given to the placement of the individual sounds within the stereo field. After all, stereo is a wasted effort if everything is perceived to be in the center! The primary factor in dealing with stereo is that a stereo field is just that—not simply left or right, but a panorama. Few sounds are panned completely to one side or the other, and certain sounds are best left in the center. (See Figure 12.3.) One of the keys to proper use of the stereo field is that stereo adds perspective that, in turn, heightens the reality of the listening experience. Improper positioning of elements therefore stands out as unnatural and distracting.

Figure 12.3

The stereo field should be treated as a panorama to separate and place sounds.

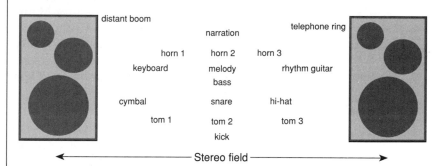

Single-source speech such as narration is distracting if not placed in the center, because we typically turn to face someone who is speaking. Most melodic instruments and lead vocal lines are placed in the center for the same reason. Dialog, on the other hand, can enjoy a certain degree of separation since no two people can be at exactly the same position.

In the case of a music mix, proper use of the stereo field can help in the process of distinguishing sounds from one another. The kick drum, snare drum, and bass are usually centered with the lead. The remaining components of the drum kit are usually dispersed through the stereo field in relationships mimicking those in the real world. Instruments that share similar frequencies can be panned in opposite directions for distinction.

Sound effects are candidates for the most severe positioning, since in reality many come from distinct positions relative to the listener. In the case of sounds whose orientation changes relative to the ear over time—such as a passing car or plane—the sense of reality can be dramatically heightened by accommodating the motion in the stereo field. With effects recorded in mono, the illusion of stereo can be created by manually rotating the pan pot. Ambient tracks recorded in stereo can add a surprising degree of realism. To retain the original placement of elements in the stereo field, these should be mixed in with the right track panned hard right and the left track panned hard left.

Even with sound effects, it is inadvisable to pan individual elements complete hard left or hard right unless you are certain of the controlled listening environment. In a presentation to a large group of people, for example, some people sitting on one side of the room may hear little, if anything, from the speaker cabinet on the other side.

Perceived environment and proximity

While the goal of the recording process is often to record dry, flexible sounds, the goal of the mixing session is to bring them to life in the desired way. Signal processing such as reverb and digital delay can be instrumental in placing some or all of the sonic elements in a perceived environment and proximity to the viewer. As with many aspects of audio, establishing the right amount of reverb is partly scientific and partly subjective. Too little reverb gives an abrupt, unnatural feel; too much destroys clarity.

The easiest reverb choices to make are those that are purposeful, such as placing an orator in a virtual environment like a room of specific size—an auditorium or gymnasium, for example. Many modern reverb devices have presets that simulate standard environments and are named accordingly.

In more subtle situations, envision the optimal listening environment for the given type of sound. Normal conversation requires as little as 0.5 second to 1.0 second delay times. A small ensemble might play in a room of moderate size—up to 1.5 seconds. An orchestra requires the larger venue of a concert hall—up to 2.5 seconds.

Not all sonic components of a mix should get the same treatment. Low-frequency components are usually kept dry to avoid boominess. More than a little reverb can make narration sound hoaky. Elements with various intended proximities to the listener require different settings as well. In a hypothetical scene in front of a church, for example, the organ inside could bear a great deal of reverb, but a passing car horn would warrant very little.

Special effects

Signal processors and EQ can also be used to create special effects. The possibilities are endless. Here are a few examples to start your creative juices flowing: A single instrument or voice can be made to seem like more than one source using a chorus setting on a digital delay. A normal voice can be made to sound like it is coming through a telephone or radio by significantly boosting the mid-range frequencies and completely cutting the low frequencies. Intense echo along with heavy phasing, flanging, and/or pitch shift is a cheap and dirty way to lend a futuristic quality to a sound. Phil Collins' trademark drum sound is attained by applying a noise gate with a high threshold setting so that the sound is choked off almost immediately. Rock recordings from *Sgt. Pepper's* on offer a tremendous education in signal processing for the enlightened listener.

Submasters

Submaster buses can be used during mastering to group input channels for common control. Assigning all the tracks that comprise music, dialog, and sound effects, respectively, to three separate buses allows easy common control over each conceptual group. Submasters can also be used to route a group of tracks to a single signal processor in order to apply a common effect. As with the recording process, however, buses add another stage of potential noise and should be bypassed when they serve no function.

Listening environment

Although sonic accuracy is the paradigm for audiophiles, the average playback system is far from flat or accurate. Radio stations, for example, often boost the low frequency content of everything they broadcast to compensate for the poor bass response of the average portable radio or car stereo. If possible, it is to your advantage to determine the circumstances in which a mix ultimately will be played back. Considerations include the frequency response of the medium and monitors, listening level, and the size and contents of the room.

If you mix at loud levels using monitors the size of Montana in a studio, that mix will sound shallow when played back on small speakers because the larger speakers give a false impression of bass. On the other hand, mixes that sound good on small monitors at low volumes usually sound acceptable when played through larger ones. Most studios have at least one pair of small, average monitors that can be used for a reality check during the mix. If you're doing a presentation or installation for specific monitors, try to mix using those same monitors. If the presentation will ultimately be on videotape or played back using the speakers built into a video monitor, use the same setup to judge the mix. Due to the equal loudness curves of the human ear, monitor levels during the mix should be similar to those anticipated for playback.

Ear fatigue

The mixing process often requires playing the same passage over and over again. No amount of equipment or forethought during a mix can overcome *ear fatigue*. Quite simply, the brain loses its objectivity after listening to the same thing over and over again. Therefore, take regular breaks to give your ears a rest.

Audio card performance

The less expensive digital audio cards available for desktop multimedia sometimes have ADCs of lesser quality than their DACs. This represents yet another incarnation of the GIGO principle. Better results can be obtained by mastering to more professional systems with high resolution and high sampling rates, then converting the files digitally to a format that can be used by the consumer-level playback cards. If the sound files are to be ported to different digital audio formats, it is usually advisable to convert the files from the high-quality master for each individual format.

DACs can introduce noise into the system on playback, making it desirable to have the highest possible levels to optimize signal-to-noise ratio. One way to do this is to use compression while recording in order to restrict the dynamic range and realize higher record levels without clipping. (This will often yield better quality in the ADC stage also.) Another approach is to optimize the levels after recording either by increasing the gain uniformly or applying a normalize function.

MIDI SEQUENCING TIPS

As with everything else in audio production, mastering the MIDI sequencing process can be a topic of great depth. This section examines some of the most common factors involved in composing with MIDI.

❖ Humanization

One of the challenges of sequencing is to maintain a human feel to the music. Quantization, found on virtually every MIDI sequencer, is a great tool for correcting performances that exhibit poor timing. Of course, arbitrary quantization that rounds all notes to values such as eighth notes can produce a mechanical feel—great for high-tech music and electronic passages. However, human performers are not automatons. Quantization can take the human expression right out of music that should show some feeling.

To avoid dehumanization, record with quantization turned off, so the natural performance is captured. Quantization can then be applied selectively. Advanced sequencers enable you to specify that only notes whose timing is off past a certain amount be quantized or that notes be brought closer to absolute timing values by a specified percentage. Mastering these quantizing parameters can greatly affect the feel of the music. When all else fails, the timing of individual notes can be edited by hand for final touches.

Just as human performances do not exhibit perfect timing, nor do they exhibit uniform volume either. Use of a velocity-sensitive keyboard goes a long way in humanizing sequences. (Velocity-sensitivity can be likened to drawing with a pressure-sensitive tablet rather than a mouse in the graphics world.)

The cut-and-paste and song section capabilities of sequencers provide arrangement shortcuts that are often welcome, but overuse of these features can dehumanize a composition. A drummer, for example, often adds subtle variations to a basic beat, as well as unique turnarounds between song sections. Multitrack recording techniques such as punch-in/punch-out can be used for variety, as well as to fix Bloopers. On another level, two of the finest musicians playing in unison will have subtle timing differences that cannot be accurately reproduced with cut-and-paste or digital delays. As with traditional multitrack recording, performing and recording a second identical track provides much more character.

❖ Automatic Playback Setup

When a MIDI sound source is to be used to play back a prerecorded sequence during delivery, the MIDI device must be set up with the appropriate programs assigned on the proper channels. This can be accomplished by manually inserting program change commands into the tracks at the beginning of the sequence—often after inserting a blank first measure specifically for this purpose. If, for example, track 1 contains a piano performance and you're relying on General MIDI mode, assign track 1 to channel 1 and place a program change command dictating program 1 at the beginning of the track.

Interruption of a previous sequence could have left the device with a controller or pitch bend value, or with hanging notes that were not properly turned off. Eliminate any variables pertaining to the state of the MIDI device in general by setting all continuous controllers to zero. Use a MIDI *all notes off* command to ensure against hanging notes. Create these setup parameters once, then paste them into other sequences later.

Ambitious musical productions may employ more than 16 distinct instruments during a sequence, even though there are only 16 MIDI channels. Although a MIDI device can respond to only 16 channels of information simultaneously, program change commands can be embedded in sequence tracks so that one channel can be used for different instruments at different points in a composition.

❖ Maximizing MIDI Voices

The number of voices available to play back a MIDI sequence depends on the individual MIDI sound source(s) and whether the selected sound programs stack multiple voices for each note to realize complex sounds. Since most MIDI sound sources employ dynamic voice allocation, careful planning can help to access more voices. The key is to avoid simultaneous events. Drums are the strongest rhythmic element, and drum sounds therefore need to take priority with regard to exact timing. Usually percussive sounds are relatively short. In some cases, short elements with less crucial timing can be offset just enough so that they use a voice immediately after it is deallocated from a percussive instrument. (If the drum track was not entered with a percussion controller, use the visual editor to make certain that the note durations are no longer than the sounds require.) While this allocation technique requires some experimentation and will not work in all circumstances, it can be a lifesaver.

A doubling effect and a strange lack of voices during the creation of a MIDI sequence may indicate that you have an unwanted MIDI loop. This usually results when an instrument is being used as both a controller and a sound source and when software thru is being used on the sequencer to channelize the performance. If the *local on* function of the instrument is engaged, voices are used twice—once directly when the key is depressed and again when the note-on it generates goes through the sequencer and back into the same instrument's MIDI In jack. The solution is to switch to *local off* so that the instrument only responds to the version sent through the sequencer.

❖ Creating Special Effects with MIDI

Most sequencers have editing provisions for cutting, copying, pasting, transposing tracks, altering velocities, and shifting entire tracks forward or backward in relation to one another. These features can be used to create special effects by copying a track and then manipulating the copy. Digital delay, for example, can be simulated by delaying the duplicate track by a timing interval such as an eighth note, then reducing the velocity by a factor of, say, 50 percent. Treating a series of duplicates in this fashion creates more intricate delays. Altering the transposition of the delayed tracks can produce even more complex effects.

Similar techniques can help you avoid synthesizer patch editing. Octaves or other intervals can be added by simply transposing a duplicate track. If the attack of a violin sound is too long, you can shift the violin track ahead a bit to compensate instead of reprogramming the attack.

❖ Synchronizing MIDI to Tape

Two situations call for synchronizing MIDI sequencers to tape: integration of virtual MIDI tracks with multitrack and scoring to video. In both cases, SMPTE time code is the preferred universal synchronization method. (SMPTE is discussed in Chapter 13.)

Recording time code onto audio tape

The first step is to use some type of SMPTE generator to record a time code track. (Simply copying SMPTE from one tape to another can degrade the signal.) Since the strength and continuous nature of the signal can cause crosstalk, a blank guard track is usually needed between the time code track and the track containing program material. This ensures that the SMPTE signal won't be audible and that the SMPTE track will not be made unreadable by adjacent audio. If you cannot avoid using an adjacent track, be sure to use it for something with no more than moderate record levels along with a minimum of transients and frequencies in SMPTE's 2400 to

4800Hz ranges. To conserve tracks, time code is placed on an out-side track of the multitrack—track 1 or 8 on an 8-track, for example. Generally the highest track number is used. On a 2-track machine, SMPTE is usually placed on track 2.

Record levels on the deck are typically set at around -3 to -5 VU. The exact level will vary slightly according to the tape deck as well as devices being used to read and write the time code. Establish the optimum level by conducting a few experiments. Levels that are too low won't be tracked by the SMPTE reader; those that are too high can be too distorted for accurate reading and may cause additional crosstalk problems. Time code should be recorded with no compression or noise reduction. Record more time code than you anticipate the need for in the event that a composition runs long or more takes are required. It is common practice to record time code on the entire tape before proceeding.

Correlating SMPTE and MIDI

SMPTE is an absolute timing reference. MIDI song pointer position information is a relative timing reference that tracks position from the beginning of the composition. A start point and a tempo must be established to reconcile the two references. The start point or SMPTE offset simply identifies the SMPTE frame MIDI is to treat as the beginning of the song. The tempo provides a reference for converting absolute time to relative time. (More cinematic scores might employ tempo and meter map capabilities, although implementing these is beyond the scope of this book.) Stand-alone SMPTE-to-MIDI converters allow both of these parameters to be set in hardware. Converters designed to connect directly to computers use an accompanying software utility or the sequencer itself to set the start point and tempo.

Once these parameters are set and the sequence is placed in external sync mode, the sequencer transport should follow the tape transport. When the two transports first synchronize after the tape is relocated, a small delay is normal as the two positions are reconciled. A metronome on the sequencer can be engaged to generate an audible click track.

Synchronizing virtual tracks

The term *virtual tracks* is used to describe MIDI sequencer tracks that do not actually exist in audio form. The flexibility of virtual tracks allows the composition—and sound effects triggered via MIDI—to be completely malleable right up to the mix. In multimedia delivery systems with MIDI capability, tracks can remain in virtual form and never be recorded as audio. Ideally, virtual tracks can be employed for any electronically-generated tracks, using tape only for non-MIDI performances. This opens up more tape tracks and avoids unnecessary signal degradation with analog tape.

It is not uncommon to desire orchestrations that require more voices than a given MIDI instrument or complement of instruments can reproduce simultaneously. One solution is to sequence part of the orchestration, record the instruments' performance of the sequence to tape tracks, then mute those virtual tracks and continue building new ones while synchronized to tape playback. In a variation on that theme, the composition stage might involve sequencing using simple sounds that each require a minimal number of voices. When the arrangement is polished, individual virtual tracks can be soloed, assigned to more complex voicings, and their performance recorded to individual tracks on the multitrack deck. Given a limited number of voices, this approach simultaneously provides for the greatest flexibility during composition and arrangement and the best sound quality in the final production.

If some timbres associated with certain virtual tracks exceed the dynamic or frequency capabilities of the multitrack, these tracks should remain in virtual form right through the mix. Highly transient drum tracks, for example, often lose some dynamics when transferred to tape. Similarly, instruments with high frequency content, such as a piccolo, might lose some frequency response on less expensive multitracks or ministudios. Both are candidates to remain in virtual form.

❖ Music Libraries

Just as electronic clip art has been invaluable in the graphics side of desktop production, *music libraries*, or *clip music*, also make it possible to take advantage of prerecorded music when time or musical skills are lacking. Music libraries have long serviced the industrial and broadcast video markets and literally thousands of audio CDs and tapes are available, offering quick and easy digitization of selected pieces onto hard disk. Several companies have also begun packaging music libraries in both digital audio and MIDI form on CD-ROMs, which is ideal for the desktop multimedia production environment.

Music libraries are typically sold with the license to reuse the material as often as needed in everyday productions, although many require additional fees for broadcast rights. Material by recognized musicians must invariably be negotiated on a per-use basis. The legal issues of incorporating the work of other people into your productions are discussed in greater detail in Chapter 19.

❖ ❖ ❖ ❖ ❖ ❖

This chapter concludes the discussion of sound by examining various ways to achieve better results with audio—from both an aesthetic and engineering standpoint. Chapter 13 shifts the focus to video and its underlying technology.

PART V

Video

In the strictest sense of the word, video in itself is multimedia since it combines visual and aural information. The seamless integration of video and computers represents the most difficult aspect of multimedia from a technology standpoint, and the most rewarding from a communication standpoint.

No degree of integration obviates the technology, tools, or techniques that have changed the way we communicate over the past half century. Chapter 13 discusses the fundamental technology behind all video. Chapter 14 covers the various tools that are used in the production of video. Chapter 15 offers perspectives on the actual process of creating video productions. ❖

Video Technology

Most experts feel that digital video holds the real key to multimedia's ultimate success. However, digital video has a long way to go before it will completely replace analog video. Therefore, this chapter begins with a discussion of analog video technology.

Attempting to distinguish between the terms *television* and *video* is as much an exercise in futility as attempting to sum up their impact on the way we communicate. Television is associated with the concept of broadcast or cable delivery of someone else's programming on someone else's timetable. Video is associated with the power to record, edit, or view programming according to one's own needs and schedules. Until interactive television becomes a reality, multimedia offers a great short-term promise of expanding the video paradigm. Video technology is so closely tied to that of television that a bit of perspective on the latter is appropriate. The concepts in this chapter are key to understanding the video tools and their use presented in the next two chapters.

My apologies to readers in countries that use other broadcast standards than NTSC for the bias shown toward NTSC. Although the technical issues involved in reconciling the various video standards in the world are formidable, the basic concepts of video are fairly universal and transferable.

ANALOG VIDEO

The CRTs in television sets and video monitors are extremely similar to those used with computers. (Chapter 7 offers an overview of CRT technology.) Although the CRTs used with television and video accept and display RGB signals, the signals used to convey video information through cables and in broadcasts are very different. Television receivers include circuitry that translates the video signal to RGB. The best way to understand the video signal is to take a brief look at history.

❖ NTSC Video Standards

One reason television became so pervasive so quickly in the United States was that it was standardized early on. The FCC (Federal Communications Commission) allocated 13 basic VHF television channels in 1945, thus standardizing frequencies. (The frequency band usurped by Channel 1 was given back to mobile radio in 1948.) The *NTSC* (National Television Systems Committee) was formed in 1948 to define a national standard for the broadcast signal itself. After five years of reconciling the wishes of manufacturers, broadcasters, and the FCC, the standard for black-and-white television was cast in stone in 1953 and ratified by the *EIA* (Electronics Industries Association) as the *RS-170 specification*.

The NTSC standard defines all of the parameters that allow any television set in North America to receive any broadcast television signal transmitted in North America. NTSC dictates a display rate of 30 frames per second in interlaced fashion—odd lines in one pass, even lines in the next. This divides each frame into two fields and, therefore, each second into 60 fields. NTSC also specifies other parameters for equipment compatibility that are explored throughout this chapter.

Video resolution

The easiest way to understand NTSC is to start with the black-and-white television system. Black-and-white TV is, of course, actually monochrome with many levels of gray. A black-and-white video camera creates an electronic representation of an image by scanning its photosensitive surface and transmitting the corresponding voltage at each point. This voltage level represents the luminance.

Vertical resolution is determined by the number of rasters, or scanlines, a system standard dictates. While NTSC consists of 525 scanlines, some are usurped by the vertical blanking interval, leaving NTSC equipment with a visible resolution of 484 lines.

Horizontal resolution is determined by how fine or small the scanning point in a given camera is. The benchmark for measuring horizontal resolution is a series of fine vertical lines that alternate between black and white. When the size of the scanning point is smaller than the line width, the lines will be reproduced; when the scanning point is larger than the line width, the lines will not be reproduced accurately. Horizontal resolution is described by the number of vertical lines—black and white—that can be accurately represented in an area as wide as the overall image is tall. Thus, a system that can reproduce 200 white lines and 200 black lines in an area the same width as the 484 lines are tall (in NTSC) is said to have a 400-line resolution.

From black-and-white to color

Color television did not replace black-and-white television, it evolved out of it. By the time color video technology matured, black-and-white TV sets were firmly ensconced in millions of homes. For this reason, the NTSC developed a way to add color to the existing standard so that millions of television receivers would not become obsolete overnight. In some ways the solution is ingenious and admirable. On the other hand, we are still using a standard that is 50 years old and very long in the tooth by today's standards.

The NTSC solution to color broadcast wasn't entirely altruistic. A broadcast bandwidth of 4.5MHz had already been established in the rapidly crowding airwaves of the electromagnetic spectrum to accommodate monochrome images. Broadcasting separate signals for red, green, and blue signals theoretically would have required three times the bandwidth and would have added synchronization problems.

The solution to all of these problems was to add a separate *chrominance* or *chroma signal* to the existing luminance signal. The luminance signal represents the brightness at a given point in the image, while the chrominance signal represents the color. The chrominance signal is a sine wave that is modulated onto the luminance signal as a *subcarrier*. The combined use of luminance and chrominance to represent images in any system is referred to as *composite video*.

The concept of various trichromatic color systems described in Chapter 7 applies to video as well. Through the use of luminance, the color space used by video is closest to HSV-type color spaces. Color information must then represent both the exact color (hue), as well as how much (saturation). The phase of the sine wave determines the hue, while its amplitude determines saturation. For example, 0 degrees is yellow-green, 90 degrees is red, 180 degrees is a purplish-blue, 270 degrees is green, and so forth.

For technical reasons, chrominance information is amplitude-modulated onto the steady frequency of the color subcarrier at two different phases: the *I* or *in-phase value* at 0 degrees, and the *Q* or *quadrature value* at 90 degrees. The luminance signal in color video is called the *Y signal*. Taken together, NTSC composite video is then represented as a *YIQ signal*. This method of adding color to the NTSC monochrome signal became the *RS-170A specification*.

Fortunately, the details of YIQ, modulation, and color phase are transparent to the end user. The closest consumers usually get are the tint and color controls that govern the hue and saturation, respectively, on the average television set. Professional video equipment such as the waveform monitors and vectorscopes discussed in the next chapter provide additional tools to ensure the accuracy of the video signal.

The addition of color to NTSC had two other effects on the video signal. First, all the math involved in adding color to the existing frequencies used by monochrome broadcasts dictated a rate of 29.97 frames per second rather than 30. This also resulted in a field rate of 59.94Hz. Second, the way in which the color information is modulated results in the chrominance being 180 degrees out of phase at the end of a single frame. It therefore takes two frames to bring the color back into phase again. As such, some video equipment requires two consecutive frames of information—a color frame—to perform operations such as still-frame capture.

Broadcast versus direct video

In order to be viewed on standard television receivers in North America, all video must not only be in the form of an NTSC composite signal, but also be modulated onto the RF carrier waves that correspond to assigned broadcast channels. This conversion adds another level of degradation to the video signal, including opening it up to the world of RF interference. On the standard television, RF signals go from the antenna into a tuner or receiver where they are converted back into regular composite video. These signals are then decoded into RGB signals for the CRT. (See Figure 13.1.)

Figure 13.1

RF conversion further degrades the composite video signal.

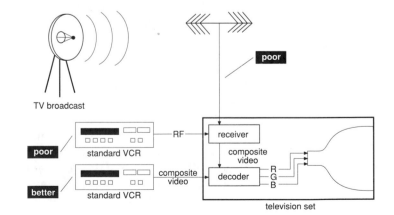

Consumer video decks also have RF outputs that can be assigned to output on a specific broadcast channel, thereby providing for connection to any television. The issues of signal conversion and degradation with RF are still just as valid across a few feet of cable as they are across ten miles of airwaves.

Broadcast NTSC also has another problem. Approximately 1MHz of bandwidth is required for every 80 lines of horizontal resolution. The 4.5MHz bandwidth set aside for broadcasting NTSC therefore yields a theoretic maximum of approximately 360 lines—not the greatest.

For these reasons the RF stage should be bypassed wherever possible. Connecting the direct video output of a VCR to the direct video input of a monitor combination will result in a much better picture than connecting the RF out of the same VCR to the antenna input of a receiver stage driving that same monitor. The RF stage is always bypassed in production work to eliminate this incarnation of the weakest link principle.

Even excluding the RF stage, composite video is still several steps removed from the RGB form a video signal ultimately takes in the CRT. The process of modulating the chrominance onto the luminance still results in some interference between the two—especially when luminance information occupies frequencies close to that of the subcarrier.

In recent years *component video* in several forms has gained increasing acceptance for production work. Component video is not a standard, but a concept where components of the video signal are kept separate to yield greater control and image quality. The most popular incarnations maintain separate luminance and chrominance signals. The chrominance channel retains the hue and saturation information in a single component (C). (See Figure 13.2.) This type of component video signal is therefore known as *Y/C*. The luminance in component video is also recorded at a higher frequency, making it possible to exceed 400 lines of resolution. (S-VHS and Hi8 employ component Y/C video.)

Figure 13.2

Component video maintains distinctions between the components of the video signal such as luminance and chrominance.

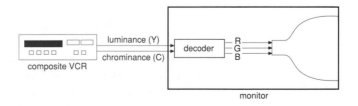

❖ Other Video Formats

Video standards vary with geography. In addition to North America, NTSC is used in Central America, Japan, parts of the South Pacific, and parts of South America. The other main standards are PAL and SECAM.

PAL (Phase Alternation Line) offers 25 interlaced frames per second with 625 scanlines. Developed after NTSC, PAL provides greater bandwidth for chrominance modulation, yielding better color resolution. The chrominance signals here are referred to as U and V; taken with luminance, composite PAL signals are said to operate in a YUV color space. PAL was adopted by the United Kingdom, West Germany, and The Netherlands in 1967, and extends to some other parts of the world as well. Brazil alone uses a version of PAL called *PAL–M* that combines improved chrominance bandwidth with 30 frames per second and 525 lines.

SECAM (Séquential Couleur Avec Memoire) provides the same interlaced frame rate and resolution as PAL, except that FM is used to encode the chrominance signal. This system also provides color superior to NTSC. SECAM is used in France and its former colonies, the former Eastern bloc, and parts of the Middle East. To complicate things, two versions of SECAM exist—SECAM vertical and SECAM horizontal.

The point of this discussion is not to prepare you for working directly with PAL and SECAM. Instead, it is to emphasize that productions intended for other parts of the world or footage coming from other parts of the world must undergo *standards conversion*. The equipment required to convert between video standards is too dedicated and expensive for the average production facility to purchase. Facilities that specialize in standards conversion can be found in most metropolitan areas, however.

HDTV (High Definition Television) is being developed to improve the audio and video quality of broadcast television—and possibly to replace the film cameras used in movie production. Toward that end, the aspect ratio of HDTV is 3 x 5 rather than the 3 x 4 ratio of traditional video. Japan has a working system in place with a 60Hz field rate, a vertical resolution of 1125 lines, and a horizontal resolution in the 600- to 700-line region. Several variations have been prototyped in other parts of the world. One of the main differences is analog versus digital implementation. The optimal goal will be one HDTV standard for the entire world.

HDTV presents several problems, not the least of which is incompatibility with existing standards. Another is price. Finally, the extra resolution and image space places significantly higher burdens on bandwidth, storage, and throughput for broadcast as well as on computer integration capacities. Compression technology is very much a part of putting HDTV to practical and universal use.

❖ Video Waveform

The video waveform actually represents three signals at once—luminance, chrominance, and sync.

Video levels

As mentioned earlier, the video camera produces a voltage for each point in its image scan. A voltage range describes the luminance range from black (minimum) to white (maximum). Levels exceeding the maximum voltage cause distortion; images using less than the full electrical range to represent a full brightness range will have less clarity and be more susceptible to noise. Voltage levels below those used to represent luminance are used for synchronization. All voltages within a system are therefore calibrated to the same standards for optimal results.

To accommodate different systems, the *IRE* (Institute of Radio Engineers) developed a calibration method that is system independent—appropriately called *IRE levels*. (The IRE later evolved into the modern-day *IEEE*—Institute of Electrical and Electronics Engineers.) In NTSC video, 1-volt peak-to-peak corresponds to a range of 140 IRE.

IRE levels in the NTSC waveform

Ideally, in the NTSC system the minimum luminance or *black level* is 7.5 IRE, and maximum luminance or *white level* is 100 IRE. (The 7.5 reference is also called the *pedestal* or *setup level*.) All of the levels in between 7.5 and 100 IRE represent luminance values in the image.

Two additional facts from Chapter 7 come into play here—the electron guns are turned off during horizontal and vertical blanking, and the rasterizing process as a whole operates with precision timing. Blanking is controlled directly from the video waveform; the guns are turned off anytime the level drops below 7.5 IRE. The precise timing required by all video equipment takes the form of sync pulses corresponding directly to a -40 IRE level. (See Figure 13.3.)

One other signal is represented in the video waveform is *color burst*. Color burst takes the form of nine consecutive cycles with absolute peaks of 20 IRE and -20 IRE. It serves as a color sync signal and communicates proper hue to a video monitor. The lack of a color burst signal indicates black-and-white video.

Figure 13.3

_A video waveform
describes luminance,
blanking, synchronization,
and color._

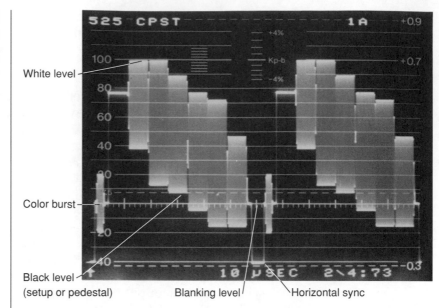

White level

Color burst

Black level
(setup or pedestal)   Blanking level   Horizontal sync

Although video can certainly be produced without paying any attention to the parameters of the video waveform, the ability to monitor and control these parameters is one of the distinguishing features of professional video productions. Chapter 14 describes the tools available for this purpose.

Synchronization

Maintaining synchronization within a video waveform is critical to the integrity of the image. Vertical sync keeps the picture from flipping. Horizontal sync keeps the image from being skewed. Color sync ensures that the proper colors are displayed. The timing of all of these signals is interrelated within the video waveform.

Unlike audio, synchronization must also be maintained for video signals to work together. Simply mixing two or more video signals results in a waveform that is no longer distinguishable as video. Similarly, editing video segments together without regard for synchronization results in discontinuity in the sync and a temporarily garbled picture. Various devices and methods described in Chapters 14 and 15 are used to ensure that video waveforms are in phase when they must work together.

Distortion

White noise in the video signal manifests as snow. (The image on a TV receiver when there's no incoming signal is 100 percent random noise or snow.) As with other media, higher signal-to-noise ratios are optimal. In the video world 46 dB represents about a 200:1 signal-to-noise ratio and is considered good; 50 dB is great. Snow becomes noticeable when the signal-to-noise ratio falls below about 40 dB.

DIGITAL VIDEO

Analog video experiences all of the problems associated with any analog medium—signal path degradation, generation loss, and influence by the medium itself. Digital video promises to eliminate those problems while integrating moving images and sound more seamlessly into a computerized world.

On the whole, digital video technology is nothing unusual compared to digital audio or computer graphics. Analog signals from a video source like a camera are converted to digital information via an ADC. (The video signal is typically converted to YUV or similar color space before being digitized.) The images can then be manipulated, stored, or transmitted in digital form. The digital information must be transformed back into analog form via a DAC in order to be viewed on a monitor or used in conjunction with other analog devices. The concepts of sampling rates, resolution, Nyquist theorem, aliasing, and quantizing described in Chapter 2 all apply to digital video.

❖ Dealing with Data

One storage medium for digital video is videotape. This works like DAT, where the digital information is transformed into a recordable analog representation using PCM or similar method. At this writing, digital video decks, such as D1 and D2, are only affordable for high-end postproduction facilities. In addition, tape is still a linear medium external from the computer environment.

The ultimate goal of digital video is to integrate it into the computer. This paradigm provides random-access editing, interactivity, image processing, seamless integration with computer graphics, integration into various types of computer documents, storage on hard drives and CDs, and transmission across networks and phone lines.

As with digital audio, the biggest challenge posed by digital video is the volume of data involved and how it bears on storage, transmission, throughput, and display. A video image the size of the average 640 x 480 computer display with a resolution of 24 bits per pixel and a standard NTSC frame rate of 30 fps represents a little over 26MB of data per second of video—not counting audio! At that rate, a 1GB hard disk could store only about 38 seconds of video.

Even if storage space were not an issue, throughput is an impasse. At this writing, the fastest drives can transfer approximately 7MB per second without considering access time and system overhead; transfer time with most storage devices is significantly lower. System bus speeds average from 8MB per second to 2MB per second. As for networks, Ethernet's 10MBits per second can hardly handle this bulk of video information either.

Integrating video completely into the computer is obviously a tall order. As with other electronic media, the solution entails compromises, compression technology, and dedicated hardware.

❖ Compromises in Digital Video

At this writing, you cannot have full-frame (image that fills the screen), full-fidelity (millions of colors at screen resolution), full-motion (30 fps) video pumping through a computer. Rather, compromises must be made in one or more of these areas.

Image size is typically the first parameter sacrificed. After all, we are accustomed to seeing video on screens of all different sizes. In addition, many multimedia applications that involve digital video require some screen space for menus and other graphic elements.

Solutions for reducing the amount of data associated with image fidelity are similar to those for computer graphics. Fewer bits can be used to represent colors: 12-bit or 16-bit color yields fairly acceptable image quality. CLUTs are another possibility in conjunction with smaller palettes.

The frame rate can be reduced to about 16 fps before the illusion of motion is replaced by the perception of a series of frames. Even above that threshold, some flicker may be noticeable at less than full frame rates.

❖ Video Compression

The most promising solutions for integrating video and computers center on various compression technologies, which are still in their formative stages at this writing. Due to the massive amount of data involved and the need for a high compression ratio, most approaches are lossy in nature and take advantage of the quirks of the human visual system. Most are also adaptive—they can be implemented so that the compression algorithm can be optimized for a given image or series of images.

One prominent approach averages color areas to take advantage of the brain's lack of sensitivity to slight color changes. Subtle variations in a basic color area can be quantized so that redundancy compression is more useful.

The other area of interest is motion compression, similar to that used by animation programs. In scenes that involve little action, significant data reduction can be achieved by saving only the pixels that change from frame to frame. Motion compression is of little help when the camera or zoom changes, however. Motion compression also poses a problem with regard to the random access that is desired for interactivity and video editing, in that many frames are described over time rather than as absolute images. Moreover, either the compression process must be a nonreal-time proposition or the algorithm must be *predictive*—able to guess what the next change will be. Predictive algorithms are not trivial to implement.

Another solution being explored takes advantage of the fact that the brain doesn't perceive much detail in a moving image. This makes it possible to blur the frames in a fast motion sequence to a degree where image compression can make a significant difference, then revert to clearer frames when the motion stops. Transforming this concept from theory into practice is also a major undertaking.

Most video compression solutions combine various approaches such as these to yield optimum results. Such is the case with one of the first video compression standards—Intel's DVI technology. JPEG is being used in conjunction with at least the initial release of Apple's QuickTime. (See Chapter 7 for an introduction to JPEG.) A plethora of solutions are being explored—some proprietary, some not. MPEG (Motion Picture Expert Group) is one group involved in pursuing an open standard.

❖ **Dedicated Hardware**

Compression and decompression do not come without processing overhead of their own. Until video compression chips become part of the computer motherboard, dedicated hardware must always be used for the initial compression. A *balanced system* or *symmetrical system* employs the same level of hardware to compress (record) and decompress (play back) video. Both functions provide similar speed. An *unbalanced system* or *asymmetrical system* utilizes different levels of hardware for the compression and decompression stages. In some cases, such as QuickTime, decompression can be accomplished using nothing more than standard computer hardware.

Some technologies can straddle the gap between unbalanced and balanced approaches. While QuickTime Movies can be played back on most Macs, for example, the results leave much to be desired. The advent of QuickTime accelerator cards with hardware decompression chips allows more impressive results. To satisfy the quest for common multimedia delivery platforms video decompression chips are more likely to become part of the motherboard than compression chips. One current view is that the chip sets that are targeted to bring HDTV to the masses will also bring affordable and effective hardware video compression and decompression to the desktop.

SMPTE TIME CODE

In the early days of video, editing was a difficult, laborious process. Standards began to emerge to identify frames uniquely in order to provide for a more accurate and automated editing process. The industry's penchant for standards came to the rescue—this time in the form of SMPTE (Society of Motion Picture and Television Engineers). SMPTE (pronounced "simp-tee") time code was quickly adopted by the EBU (European Broadcasters Union). Today, SMPTE is the universal reference for synchronizing video and audio equipment.

SMPTE readouts are displayed in the format of hours:minutes:seconds:frames. A SMPTE display of 01:13:56:04 indicates one hour, 13 minutes, 56 seconds, and four frames. Using this identification method, each frame can be identified, addressed, and relocated accurately time and time again. Moreover, each frame can be identified universally by any machine capable of reading SMPTE time code.

❖ Frame Rates

SMPTE also defines references for the various frame rates in use around the world—24 fps for international film, 25 fps for non-NTSC video, 30 fps for black-and-white NTSC, and 30 fps drop frame for color NTSC. *Drop frame* is used to compensate for the 29.97 actual frame rate that accommodates the addition of chrominance mentioned earlier in this chapter. With a timing reference of 30 fps, you wind up being off by 108 frames for each hour—3.6 seconds. Although this may not seem like much, it is critical in broadcasts and other professional situations that are timed right down to the split-second. Drop frame compensates for this by omitting references to two frames each minute except for every tenth minute. The frames themselves are not skipped—the reference simply jumps ahead. The next frame after 00:08:59:29 in drop frame, for example, would be labeled 00:09:00:02. In practice, the 30 fps non-drop frame format is used in most non-broadcast industrial productions.

❖ SMPTE Bits

SMPTE takes the form of a linear stream of pulse waves that represents the references to sequential frames of SMPTE time code. These pulses can be recorded directly onto videotape and audiotape using a *time code generator* in a process known as *striping* a tape. The pulse waves fluctuate between 2400Hz and 4800Hz. If you were to audition this track, it would sound like electronic chatter. To SMPTE gear, however, a 2400Hz pulse corresponds to a digital 0; a 4800Hz fluctuation represents a digital 1. A *SMPTE reader* translates and assembles the stream of bits into meaningful information.

Dividing 2400Hz by 30 frames/second yields 80 bits of data correlating to each NTSC frame. The 80-bit word that parallels each frame identifies the frame uniquely and in sequence compared to its neighbors. Different groups of bits represent different aspects of the identification: 20 bits represent the hours (0–23), minutes (0–59), and seconds (0–59); 6 bits express the frame (0–29); and a single bit signifies drop frame status. A color frame bit provides a means for distinguishing between even and odd interlace fields. A 16-bit sync word is used to identify frame boundaries and indicates in which direction the tape is moving. Five bits go unused.

The remaining 32 bits are used optionally for user information—such as recording date, reel number, etc.—in the form of four letters, eight numbers, or a combination of the two. This information must be recorded at the same time as the rest of the code. Not all equipment can read and write this user information, however.

❖ LTC versus VITC

Two completely different methods of recording SMPTE time code on tape are used—LTC and VITC. Both are capable of representing the same information.

LTC

LTC (Linear Time Code) resides on a linear track, such as the audio track of a multitrack tape deck or the audio track of a video deck. LTC cannot be read at transport speeds significantly higher or lower than normal playback rate. When the transport is in fast forward, the LTC audio signal may be distorted to the point where it is difficult or impossible to read. The machine must therefore be equipped with wideband amplifiers and broadband reproduce heads—expensive stuff.

Conversely, at slower transport speeds the machine must have good low frequency response and higher-gain amplifiers as the frequency and amplitude of the time code decreases. At slow shuttle speeds or freeze-frame, the voltage being seen by the heads is so low that the time code cannot be read. To make up for this, most SMPTE readers switch over to reading tach pulses or address tracks from the transport to maintain an approximate location. However, this is not nearly as accurate as SMPTE.

VITC

VITC (Vertical Interval Time Code) is stored in the vertical blanking interval of the video signal itself. The advantage to VITC (pronounced "vitsy") is that the SMPTE time code is available and readable whenever the picture is visible—even in freeze-frame when the transport is stationary. This is very important with respect to the frame accuracy required when editing video. In helical-scan VTRs, the heads are always in contact with the tape, and VITC allows time code to be read at literally any transport speed. This negates the need for special signal processing and amplification and frees up an audio track on the VTR.

VITC also provides additional information that provides for greater accuracy. VITC contains an extra 10 bits of data for a total of 90 bits per frame. One of these extra bits is a field bit that allows VITC readers to index each field of interlaced color video. This provides a resolution of half a frame (or 1/60th of a second) that can be useful in ensuring that edits occur on the first field of a frame. The additional bits also provide a method for comparing SMPTE information to verify accuracy. The possibility of error is virtually eliminated because VITC is printed twice in each vertical blanking interval on nonadjacent scan lines. Given two fields per frame, the code is actually printed four times for each frame!

By nature VITC can only be used with VTRs. Audio decks and electronic equipment like computers require the use of LTC. A *VITC-to-LTC converter* is required for an audio deck or other non-VTR equipment to track VITC. VITC-compatible products are typically more expensive than their LTC counterparts. Finally, VITC cannot be striped onto a tape in advance—it must be recorded when the video is recorded.

CONTROL STANDARDS

Any method of automated editing requires some form of control that allows the edit controller to operate the transport controls of the video decks remotely. Most pro and semi-pro decks have an RS-232 serial port that provides the most direct method for communicating with computers. (Since serial protocols are bidirectional in nature, they allow a complete dialog between the computer/controller and decks.) Serial implementations are less common as you approach the consumer end of the VCR spectrum. The NEC PC–VCR and Panasonic Selectra AG-1960 are two examples of S–VHS machines offering serial communications.

A few years ago the average home VCR had no provision for external control of the transport, short of the handheld remote. All the people generating endless vacation footage created a demand for inexpensive video editing and accurate transport control. This brought some consumer electronics equipment one step closer to their professional counterparts.

Low-end transport control takes several forms. The *Control-S protocol* essentially provides a means whereby any transport function that can be controlled by an infrared remote can also be controlled via a hard-wired connection. Control-S is a one-way street: there is no provision for the deck to provide information to the outside world.

The *Control-L* or *LANC* (*Local Area Network Control*) format is much more useful than Control-S because communication is bidirectional. Not only can you tell a deck to shuttle to a given frame, but it can send a message back when it gets there. Moreover, you can identify where the transport is at any time. Coupled with an accurate transport, you can establish the kind of dialog that takes place between an editing deck and an edit controller.

No computer has provisions for a Control-S or Control-L connection, however. For a computer to control the transport of one or more video decks using Control-S or Control-L, a method of converting between these formats and serial protocols is required. That's exactly what the Sony Vbox does. The Vbox offers connections for Control-S, Control-L, and Sony's *ViSCA* (*Video System Control Architecture*). ViSCA combines a serial connection with a command protocol that includes Control-L, along with transport control, tape addressing, polling, and other commands that enhance the functionality of decks in an editing environment. ViSCA's addressing is frame accurate, but it cannot bring frame accuracy to a transport that is inherently not frame accurate in the first place! ViSCA can also handle Sony's *RC* (*Rewritable Code*) time code—a proprietary longitudinal reference found on some of their high-end decks and camcorders.

ViSCA also provides for daisy-chaining, allowing up to seven compatible devices to be addressed and controlled simultaneously. (Audio and video connections must still be routed by hand or through some form of switching device.) An interesting aspect of ViSCA and Vbox is that a low-end computer-based editing environment can utilize Control-L compatible camcorders as editing decks. Sony has made ViSCA an open protocol so that other manufacturers can incorporate it into their equipment.

Video control standards are being developed at a staggering pace. Video Media's V-LAN is an example of the new trend toward bringing the concept of local area networks to multiple video machine control.

CONNECTIONS

The connections on a traditional TV antenna and the input to a television set are 300-ohm. The cable coming into your home and the connectors on the back of cable-ready televisions are 75-ohm *F-connectors*. Both types of connections are used in conjunction with RF-modulated signals associated with broadcast and/or cable channels. The little box that allows conversion between these signals is a form of simple impedance-matching transformer.

With the exception of the 300-ohm antenna, all cables used to carry video signals are coaxial to shield against RF. On consumer gear, RCA plugs are often used for both audio and composite video connections. More professional equipment employs twist-locking *BNC* connectors for composite video and balanced XLRs for audio. (See Figure 13.4.)

Figure 13.4

Standard video connectors include BNC, RCA, and F-connectors.

F-connector   **BNC connector**   **RCA connector**

The discussion of video levels earlier in this chapter indicated that NTSC composite signals are approximately 1 volt peak-to-peak. Video gear actually generates a 2-volt signal internally. When combined with a built-in 75-ohm output resistor and a 75-ohm load on the attached cable, a 1-volt signal is actually available on the output connector. If the load deviates from 75 ohms, the voltage will deviate from the 1-volt standard. To ensure a stable load, 75-ohm termination is implemented on the output of the final piece of equipment in any video chain—even if it's just a VCR connected to a monitor.

Termination is accomplished with a switch labeled "75Ω" or "Hi-Z," or by inserting a *75-ohm terminator* plug on the final output. If no termination is implemented, the receiving equipment receives all 2-volt signals—resulting in a very bright, washed out picture. If the output of more than one device in a chain is terminated, the multiple loads result in each device receiving less than 1-volt signals—yielding a very dim picture.

❖ ❖ ❖ ❖ ❖ ❖

This chapter has provided the foundation upon which all video technology is predicated. Chapter 14 explores the various categories of video equipment that employ this technology.

Video Production Tools

As with many other media, video equipment has made a gradual transition from professional use to industrial use to consumer use. The lines between these categories continue to blur at an ever-quickening pace.

In the world of video equipment, the term *professional* is typically associated with the quality, durability, and accurate synchronization required for world-class broadcast. Professional equipment is quite expensive and requires a great deal of expertise to use and maintain. *Industrial* implies rugged design and quality high enough for use in markets such as business and education. *ENG* (electronic news gathering)—field acquisition for broadcast—has been partially responsible for bringing better quality to more portable and affordable equipment. The upper end of today's consumer or "prosumer" equipment offers quality that rivals the industrial standard of only a few years ago.

Just as the price:performance ratio of video equipment has improved, so has that of computers. The union of these two technologies has led to the phenomenon of *desktop video*. Many traditional video tools are still used both on the desktop and in bringing production elements to and from the desktop. This chapter focuses on the equipment available to desktop producers in the prosumer and industrial markets.

VIDEO RECORDERS AND FORMATS

Video recorders, or decks, work on principles similar to their audio counterparts. As with audio, the density of information that can be recorded onto the tape with reference to time dictates a great deal about fidelity. Due to the comparatively high amount of information contained in the video signal, video transports employ a *helical scan* system in which the record/playback heads are mounted on a spinning *head drum*—allowing information to be recorded in greater density without creating impractically high tape speeds. Further, the drum is mounted at such an angle that the information for each frame is recorded at a diagonal across the tape—effectively providing greater magnetic surface area for each frame. (See Figure 14.1.) All decks have at least two heads, one on each side of the head drum. *Four head decks* allow stable pictures while the transport is paused.

Figure 14.1

The helical scanning system places video signals on tape at a diagonal to increase the effective surface area of the tape.

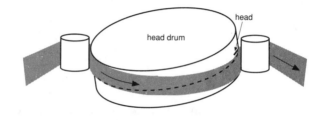

Anytime the video must be viewed, the transport opens the protective case on the videocassette and uses mechanical arms to pull a section of tape out and wrap it around the head drum. If one section of tape is constantly exposed to the rotating head, the friction can have an abrasive effect on the tape—both degrading the signal and clogging the heads. For this reason the tape is disengaged from the heads when it is stopped, rewound, or fast-forwarded. Most decks will kick out of pause mode after approximately eight minutes in order to prevent damage to the tape and heads. While video transports allow shuttling the tape forward and backward while watching the picture, fast-forward and rewind create less wear and tear since the tape is removed from the heads during the latter operations.

❖ Tracks

Video decks actually record and play back three or four different kinds of information. (See Figure 14.2.) All tracks except the video track are linear and use stationary record and playback heads.

Figure 14.2

Videotape contains various tracks for video, audio, control, and address information.

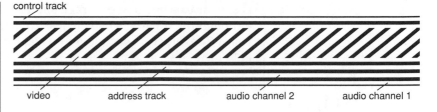

control track

video   address track   audio channel 2   audio channel 1

Audio tracks

All video formats provide at least one dedicated track for analog audio, and many provide for stereo. Many decks offer an *audio dub* that allows audio to be recorded without disturbing existing video—a desirable feature for video production and editing. More professional decks extend this feature to independent recording of video as well as each audio track. In addition, better decks provide manual gain controls and accompanying meters for the audio track(s) rather than the *automatic gain control* (AGC). AGCs attempt to maintain a uniform level—even between silence and program material. The result is often a pumping effect that boosts noise noticeably in quiet passages.

Some formats offer the ability to encode audio as digital information, typically using PCM or FM technology. Once encoded, the information is embedded in the video tracks. This usually means that the encoded audio will be lost if the video is rerecorded. For this reason, audio is also recorded onto standard longitudinal audio tracks in parallel.

Control track

The combination of moving tape and moving heads poses a potential threat to the critical timing required to preserve the integrity of the video signal. All formats therefore include a longitudinal *control track* consisting of a series of pulses that serve to establish a timing reference. During recording, every other vertical sync pulse from the incoming signal—the one associated with the beginning of each frame—causes a corresponding pulse to be placed on the control track. On playback, the control track regulates the movement of the capstan and the head drum to maintain proper synchronization.

Address or cue track

Since the control track consists of a series of identical pulses, it is incapable of providing information about the relative position of the tape. More advanced decks provide an *address track*, or *cue track*, that is used to record time code—typically SMPTE time code. This is similar to a linear audio track and can indeed be used as such, although the quality is usually less than that of a dedicated audio track. Conversely, a second audio track can be used for longitudinal time code.

❖ Flying Erase Heads

Most video decks have a *stationary erase head* that erases information on all tracks simultaneously as the tape goes by. This erase head is positioned in the tape path before the head drum containing the record/playback heads. When record is pressed on the transport, all information is erased—including the control track—before new information is recorded. The loss of control track results in visible glitches when recording a new segment where an old one used to be.

Better decks have a pair of *flying erase heads* mounted on the head drum. This allows only the video and/or audio tracks to be erased a split second before new information is recorded. Since the control track is left intact, glitches are obviated or greatly reduced when performing insert edits. (Insert editing is described later in this chapter.) Freeze-frame pauses with four-head decks are also much cleaner.

❖ Formats

As with their audio counterparts, video formats are referenced primarily by their tape widths. All tapes recorded on a given format can be played back on other machines of that same format. All *VTRs* (video tape recorders) originally used reel-to-reel formats that required threading and were susceptible to dust. All that remains of open-reel VTRs today are the 1" and 2" formats used in broadcast television. All modern industrial and consumer VTRs employ cassettes in which the tape and reels are permanently mounted and protected—hence the alternate term *VCR* (video cassette recorder). These formats range from 3/4" to 8mm.

Many factors besides tape width influence the performance afforded by different formats. As with audio recording, higher tape speeds and better tape formulations offer higher quality. Some formats record composite video, others higher-quality component video. Some broadcast formats such as D-2 offer digital recording, but all "prosumer"-level tape formats at this writing are analog.

Designers of nonbroadcast video gear reduce the bandwidth requirements by encoding the color information at a lower frequency than luminance. This *color under* process reduces picture detail and color resolution and increases chroma noise. These by-products are particularly noticeable in copied generations. The color under process is found in 3/4", 3/4" SP, VHS, Betamax, S-VHS, 8mm, and Hi8.

3/4" U-Matic

The *3/4" U-Matic* format was introduced in 1971 and remained the undisputed standard format for industrial production for almost two decades. This format is still in fairly wide use today by virtue of existing equipment investment and existing tape libraries. It offers two longitudinal analog audio tracks, an address track, and a control track, in addition to composite video. Tape speed is relatively slow, and the luminance resolution of 3/4" is 260 lines.

3/4" SP

The recent *3/4" SP* format improves on the original U-Matic design, recording composite video at a higher resolution (340 lines) and audio with Dolby C. U-Matic tapes can be played on 3/4" SP, but not the other way around.

VHS

In the early to mid-1980s, the consumer market experienced a format war between the 1/2" *VHS* and *Betamax* formats. Although Betamax yielded better audio-visual quality, VHS won out—partially because Sony tightly controlled the licensing of the Betamax standard, and partially because VHS was the first to offer movie-length recordings on a single cassette with acceptable quality. (As a result, Betamax is virtually obsolete today.)

VHS includes tracks for composite video and stereo hi-fi audio. With a resolution of 240 lines, VHS is a final mass distribution format and not a recommended production format.

S-VHS

JVC introduced the *S-VHS* format in 1987. It uses the same sized cassettes as VHS but with better tape formulation. More importantly, luminance and chrominance are processed as separate Y/C signals for improved resolution (400 lines). S-VHS also yields better signal-to-noise ratio in both luminance and chrominance than either VHS or 3/4". The standard also provides the ability to record high-fidelity audio onto the video tracks as well as the longitudinal tracks. S-VHS machines can play VHS tapes, but not the other way around.

8mm

Introduced in 1985 as a joint standard by several manufacturers, *8mm* uses the smallest tape width and cassette size to date, making it popular for lightweight camcorders. (8mm is approximately 1/4".) The relatively small surface area of the tape is offset by the use of metal particle tape capable of retaining much higher signal levels— approximately the visual fidelity of 3/4". The tape also wraps around about 30° more of the head, providing enough room for the video heads to record PCM audio tracks rivaling the quality of audio CDs. In addition, 8mm decks include *ATF* (automatic track finding) that obviates the need for manual tracking adjustments.

Hi8

Sony introduced the *Hi8* format in 1989 as an improvement to 8mm. The luminance carrier frequency range is boosted to 5.7–7.7MHz from the 8mm range of 4.2–5.4MHz. As a result, resolution is increased to more than 400 lines, and color is improved as well. Hi8 can also record time code discretely. Hi8 decks can play 8mm tapes, but not the other way around.

Betacam SP

Betacam SP is the second generation version of Sony's Betacam format. It has become quite popular in the high-end industrial and low-end broadcast markets since it employs a form of component video on 1/2" tape and does not downgrade bandwidth and color quality via the color under method. Betacam SP can use standard oxide tape formulations, and performance can be improved with metal particle tape. Two longitudinal audio tracks supplement FM encoding of hi-fi audio into the video tracks.

M-II

The *M-II* format is the second generation version of the M-format originally introduced by Matsushita and RCA and is a direct competitor of Betacam SP. M-II does not use color under and employs special metal particle tape exclusively to record its component video signal. It also features full-range FM audio encoding in parallel with the two longitudinal audio tracks.

❖ External Control

The more control external devices can provide over a VCR, the more useful it is in an editing environment. The simplest form of remote control is one-way, such as that afforded by Control-S or standard

VHS camera control. One-way remote makes it possible to control transport operations from an edit controller or camera, but data such as location information cannot be received from the decks. Some decks also have proprietary edit connectors that allow play and pause operations on a master to engage and disengage the record function of another deck—provided that both decks are made by the same manufacturer.

Control-L's two-way communication is more popular for consumer editing gear, and some computer-based edit controllers include cables that provide these connections. More advanced decks such as NEC's PC-VCR have RS-232C serial ports that allow even more information to be communicated between deck and computer. Sony's ViSCA protocol also provides for similar control.

External sync connectors allow the VCR to be synchronized to other video sources such as a camera. (Synchronization of multiple video sources is discussed later in this chapter.)

❖ Other Features and Functions

Manufacturers are cramming more and more features into smaller and smaller boxes. Here are some of the more common features and controls found on today's video decks. (While many consumer VCRs include tuners and timers for recording television broadcasts, these features are beyond the scope of this discussion.)

Skew

Skew adjusts tape tension during playback which, in turn, controls how snugly the tape wraps around the head drum. Skew adjustments become necessary as older machines go out of alignment or as worn tapes begin to stretch. The need for skew adjustment is manifested by wavering of vertical lines toward the top of the screen—a phenomenon known as *flagging*. Extreme cases cause the image to lose sync altogether.

Tracking

Tracking adjusts the position of the moving tape in relation to the head drum to ensure that the heads are tracking the recorded information accurately during playback. Poor tracking is manifested in different ways on different formats, including snow localized at the top or bottom of the image, or dispersed throughout. Some decks include tracking meters that provide a more scientific reference for optimal tracking. Many newer decks feature automatic digital tracking.

Jog wheel

A *jog wheel* is a knob that supplements the transport controls in finding particular footage or edit points. When playback is engaged, turning the jog wheel left or right from the center détente shuttles the tape backward or forward, respectively. The further the knob is turned from the détente, the faster the tape is shuttled.

Index search

Many decks have the ability to log *indexes* with the push of a button during the recording and playback processes. Indexes are "dumb" electronic markers placed on the control track. When an *index search* button is pressed, the transport will shuttle to the next logged index point. Most decks with this feature can search either forward or backward for the next index on demand.

Input selector

The input selector selects which signal is coming into the VCR. Input choices might be made between tuner and line input or between multiple line inputs, depending on the deck. The *dub* position on some input selectors disables input processing and is used while transferring footage from one VCR to another.

Fade control

Some newer decks have the ability to fade to or from black on playback. This feature is often accompanied by simultaneous audio fades. The fade feature can be useful in a presentation and can smooth transitions in low-budget cuts-only editing situations.

VIDEO CAMERAS

Video cameras, whether in stand-alone form or integrated into camcorders, represent the beginning of the traditional video chain. The visual equivalent to the microphone, the primary function of the video camera is to transform light waves into electronic signals representing images. In the simplest terms, the optics system of the camera focuses the image on the transducer, which performs the conversion. The quality of the imagery produced by a video camera is largely attributed to these two components.

❖ Camera Transducers

The camera transducer, or image sensor, is the element that transforms light into electricity. Two basic types of transducers are currently in use—the vacuum tube and the CCD.

Tubes

The first video cameras employed special vacuum tubes, called *vidicon* tubes, as transducers. Improved vidicons are still in use today in some low-end cameras. Further embellishments have resulted in the midrange *saticon* and high-end *plumbicon* tubes used in industrial and broadcast work, respectively. (Several other "-cons" are in less widespread use.) Tube transducers range between approximately three and six inches in length and one-half to one inch in diameter. All else being equal, the bigger the tube, the better the image quality.

In the simple monochrome camera, the lens system focuses the light onto the glass face of the tube. Light passes through the glass onto a photosensitive layer. Behind that layer lies the *target*—a thin element bearing a slight positive charge. As light strikes each point on the photosensitive layer, the charge at the corresponding point on the target varies according to the intensity of the light. The rest of the process is essentially the reverse of the CRT. An electron beam is directed by deflection coils in such a way that it scans the face of the target. The different charges the beam encounters at each point in the target are translated to different voltages and then assembled into a video signal and sent on.

Color tube systems modify this process in one of several ways. The original color cameras employed *dichroic* mirrors to separate the light into red, green, and blue components and direct them to separate tubes. The critical alignment required by this system relegates them to high-end studio use. The *prism block* system uses a prism and color filters to separate the additive primary colors and direct them to three separate tubes. This system simultaneously requires less alignment and offers improved image quality. Both of these systems result in a *three-tube camera*. The use of multiple tubes requires the cameras to be registered regularly, especially if they are transported. (Poor registration is exhibited by fringe colors around the edges of objects.)

The *single-tube* color camera employs a *stripe filter* on the face of the tube—a series of fine red, green, and blue filters that separate the light and send the components sequentially to a single tube. The stripe filter system has the advantage of being smaller, lighter, simpler, and less expensive, but has the disadvantage of reduced sharpness and color control. As such, this technique is relegated to low-end applications.

Regardless of the system, designers of tube transducers face common problems. Targets are often slow to respond to abrupt changes in brightness—a phenomenon known as *lag*. One visible manifestation of lag is when a moving object leaves a trail behind it. A similar form of artifacting called *comet-tailing* gets its name from the fiery red tails that occur when the camera is unable to process reflective highlights in a scene. Larger areas of the target can also be overloaded easily. This results in *blooming*, typified by a dark halo around a bright object. When pointed at a stationary and/or bright image for extended periods, a ghost of the image can be permanently embedded in the photosensitive surface—a phenomenon referred to as *burn in*. Tubes are not very sensitive to low light, either. Finally, all vacuum tubes wear out with age, causing color imbalances and poor contrast.

CCDs

The *CCD* (charge-coupled device) is a solid-state chip about the size of a postage stamp designed to replace the tube and its problems. (Cameras that use CCDs are referred to as *chip cameras*.) The chips incorporate thousands of photosensitive semiconductors that store electrical charges corresponding to the light intensity. Each of these semiconductors corresponds directly to a pixel; more advanced models can have as many as 300,000 pixels. The charges are transferred to a second layer that acts as a frame buffer, from which the pixels are read in the appropriate sequence and transformed into a video signal.

Lower-priced chip cameras employ a single CCD in conjunction with a stripe filter. Better color chip cameras employ three CCDs, mounted directly on the prism block. A new generation of two-chip cameras uses one chip for luminance and one for chrominance— the latter with a stripe filter. These designs offer image quality that is near that of RGB. All chip cameras eliminate registration problems. Unlike tubes, CCDs don't lag, comet-tail, bloom, burn in, or wear out. They are also more sensitive to light than tubes. Although they work better than tubes in low-light conditions, CCDs are overloaded more easily in extremely bright conditions, sometimes resulting in white columns or rows when associated pixels are overloaded. While under constant improvement, CCDs still offer lower resolution than tubes. The size and weight make CCDs ideal for camcorders— in fact, they dominate the consumer market. CCDs are also used in more industrial cameras that need to stand up to rugged use.

❖ Camera Optics

The camera *optics* are responsible for focusing imagery on the transducer. The optics system consists of a series of lenses that operate in much the same way as the optics found in cameras used for still photography.

Focal length

Focal length describes the distance between the center of the lens and the focus point on the transducer. Median focal lengths are associated with standard lenses and approximate human vision. Short focal lengths form the basis of the *wide-angle* lens—the view is wider, close objects are magnified, and objects at median to longer distances appear small. Long focal lengths form the basis of the *telephoto* lens—the view is much narrower, but distant objects are greatly magnified. (Many cameras also have a switch that converts to a *macro* lens capable of extreme close-up work.)

Better video cameras are equipped with a *zoom* lens capable of variable focal lengths ranging from wide-angle to telephoto in a continuous motion. (See Figure 14.3.) To *zoom in* is to extend the focal length to maximum; to *zoom out* is to retract the lens to the shortest focal length. The zoom lens consists of a complex system of internal lenses in groupings that move in relationship to one another. Fortunately, the internal operation is transparent to the user.

Figure 14.3

The zoom lens can vary continuously from wide-angle to telephoto.

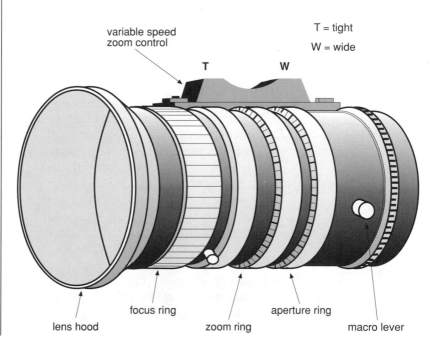

The focal characteristic of a zoom lens is specified by the zoom range or ratio. A lens specified as 10:1 or 10X, for example, has a maximum focal length that is ten times that of the shortest focal length. This figure is often accompanied by the shortest focal length. A lens specified as being 12.5 x 10, for example, has a zoom factor of 12.5, a minimum wide-angle focal length of 10mm, and a maximum telephoto focal length of 125mm.

Different ranges of focal lengths are optimal for different types of work. Lenses optimized for outdoor shoots such as sporting events typically offer higher zoom ratios—from 10:1 to 30:1—since the action is often far away. On the other hand, the short distances associated with indoor work rarely require more than a 6:1 ratio. Decent all-purpose consumer-grade lenses average between 6:1 and 8:1. Systems offering higher zoom ratios without a physical increase in size require more light—a consideration if a camera optimized for outdoor work is used inside.

Lens controls

Three main lens controls affect the image the transducer receives—zoom, focus, and aperture. All three take the form of circular rings around various portions of the lens barrel.

The *zoom ring* (often found in the middle of the barrel) controls the focal length manually. Most cameras supplement this with an automatic zoom control that motorizes the process through a switch mounted in or close to the handle. Automatic zoom provides for smooth zoom operations at a preset speed. More advanced models provide pressure-sensitive switches that allow the user to control the zoom speed with finger pressure.

The *aperture ring* controls the *iris*. Like the iris in the human eye, the camera's iris determines the size of the lens opening, or *aperture*, and the amount of light reaching the transducer. Darker environments require proportionally more light and larger apertures; brightly lit scenes require proportionally less light and smaller apertures. In camera optics, the aperture is calibrated according to a standard scale of *f-stops*. The numbering system works inversely to aperture size in that smaller f-stops such as f-1.4 are the largest openings, and the larger f-stops such as f-22 are the smallest openings. Aperture settings also contribute significantly to the depth of field, as discussed in Chapter 15.

The *focus ring* determines how sharply the image of an object at a given distance will be focused on the transducer. *Auto-focus* systems employing various technologies abound, especially on consumer gear, but they are not intelligent—they have no way of knowing which element in a visual composition you wish to be in focus. The most popular implementations assume that the center of the image is the focus point, although this is not always the case. Most professional videographers disengage the auto-focus.

❖ Additional Camera Features and Controls

So many cameras, so little time. While video manufacturers are always coming up with something new, here are a few more common functions found on midrange cameras.

Gain controls

Many cameras now have an *automatic gain control* (AGC) that automatically boosts the video signal level being recorded when the picture becomes too dark. One problem with AGCs is that they calculate the required gain by averaging the levels in the overall image. The other is that transient elements in the picture, such as passersby wearing bright clothes, can temporarily upset the levels and contrasts in an established shot. When AGC is disengaged, the gain is determined by the aperture.

A separate *gain control* can be used to manually boost the video signal level and improve color reproduction in low-light situations. This control can only be used with moderation, since boosted signals include boosted noise.

White balance

Various lighting conditions and instruments produce different color components. The light from a fluorescent bulb has a cold blue-green tint, for example, while the color of sunlight is perceived differently according to the time of day and cloud conditions. This can cause a simple color imbalance from a video standpoint, but the issue escalates when various scenes for a single video are shot in multiple locations or at different times of day. *White balance* controls address these problems by adjusting the balance of the red, green, and blue additive components that yield white in the video signal to the environment. Manual versions are used in conjunction with built-in meters. *Automatic white balance* buttons make calibration as simple as pointing the camera at a white card or surface and pressing a button.

Automatic setup

Automatic white balance is a form of automatic camera setup. *Black balance*, or *auto black*, is used to establish the black level of the video signal. This is typically performed by capping the lens and pressing the black balance button for a few seconds. A *registration*, or *auto-centering*, button is used to align the three color components in the camera. Most modern cameras with these features also have a memory feature that retains these automatic settings after power is turned off.

External sync

In simple shooting situations, the camera generates the video sync that becomes part of the signal. In situations where several pieces of video equipment need to work in sync—such as in a multicamera production—the camera will require an external sync input and switch.

❖ Camera Accessories

Various accessories make working with cameras easier and produce better results. Most fall into the categories of physically stabilizing the camera or altering the image coming into the lens.

Stabilizers

Hand-held shooting requires a great deal of proficiency in steadying the camera. Professional videographers rely on a variety of stabilizing devices when circumstances permit. The most common is the *tripod*, similar to those used in still photography. The combination of three telescopic legs and pivots at the head where the camera is mounted allows the camera to be stabilized at a wide range of heights and angles. Simple tripods employ *friction heads*—straightforward mechanics at the point where the head rotates and tilts. Better tripods have *fluid heads* for smoother operation. Tripod accessories include *spreaders* to spread and hold the legs for additional stability, and *dollies* that provide a wheeled base designed to roll the position of the entire camera/tripod assembly smoothly.

A *monopod* is a simpler device that mounts the camera on a single telescopic pole. Monopods are typically used in conjunction with a sling worn by the operator in such a way that the user's legs form the other two points of a living tripod. Monopods are less stable than tripods, but provide for greater agility.

The *Steadicam* was designed to allow professional camera operators to walk and run while maintaining a smooth image. The device is essentially a system of weights and balances to which the camera is mounted; the entire assembly sort of floats on the shoulder of the operator. While Steadicams are pricey and designed for heavy motion picture cameras, prosumer versions are available for videography work.

Filters

Various filters can be used in conjunction with better cameras. Some simply screw onto the end of the lens assembly, and some cameras actually have a wheel of different filters mounted between the lens assembly and the transducer. Filters perform two basic functions—correction and special effects. Corrective lenses compensate for things like color imbalances associated with different lighting environments or remove glare caused by light reflecting off surfaces or the outer lens itself. Special effects lenses can be used to create effects such as starbursts, diffusion, or simulated fog.

CAMERA/ RECORDER COMBINATIONS

Cameras and video recorders are often used in conjunction or in integrated packages for remote work. Regardless of the method of integration, the functions of the two components are basically the same as their stand-alone versions. The three basic forms are portable systems, dockable components, and camcorders.

❖ Portable Systems

Portable systems consist of a separate camera and VCR connected by an umbilical. Camera and tape formats can be mixed and matched as required. The VCR is either carried via a shoulder strap or mounted in a two-wheeled cart that often includes a small monitor and heavy-duty battery pack.

❖ Dockable Components

Dockable components are designed in such a way that a camera and VCR can be used separately or attached to operate as one unit. This approach has several advantages. First, cameras with different fortes can be combined with decks of various formats as needed. While the same is true of portable systems, the dockable solution yields a single compact unit that has a great deal of flexibility. Second, each component can be upgraded as needed. Finally, the deck can be detached and used separately in the editing process without the awkward camera portion.

❖ Camcorders

Camcorders permanently integrate camera, recorder, and microphone components. The dedicated components can be miniaturized without concern for connectivity. Since the main goal of consumer camcorder design is minimal size, weight, and price, low-end camcorders do not have many of the features required for more demanding production work. High-end camcorders, on the other hand, offer much of the quality and many of the features previously reserved for industrial video gear. Some can also be controlled externally via Control-L, ViSCA, or similar protocol, allowing them to double as source decks in the editing process. Regardless of the level of sophistication, the permanent integration of camera and format provide no mix-and-match or upgrade path.

EDIT CONTROLLERS

Cameras and VCRs are used to gather raw or *source footage*. Small *segments* of this source material are typically edited in a sequence to create the final production. Unlike audiotape, splicing videotape is next to impossible, because of sync issues and the diagonal nature of the video tracks. The video editing process therefore entails transferring segments electronically from a *source deck* to a *record deck* (also called a *master deck* or *edit deck*). The first frame in the transferred segment represents the *edit-in point*; the last frame in the segment is the *edit-out point*.

Consider the following scenario: Video footage is transferred from the source deck to the record deck, and the record deck is then stopped at the point where the next segment is to begin. Along with the video and audio tracks, the control track is transferred as well. New source material is then located and played and the record deck is put into record mode. The new material is accompanied by its control track. If the control tracks from the two passes are not in sync (as they won't be most of the time), a visible glitch will occur at the transition point.

To complicate matters, many edits require extreme accuracy at the beginning and ending frames of the segments. With 30 frames per second flying by, it's often hard to engage the decks at exactly the right frame.

These problems are overcome through the use of an *edit controller*. (Edit controllers are also referred to as *video editors*, but this term is easily confused with persons bearing the same title.) Software-hardware combinations are now available that turn most desktop computers into edit controllers. Either form deals with synchronization of the source and record decks and accuracy in the edited segments.

❖ Classifications of Video Editing

Video editing ranges from simple to complex. Several different methods of classifying the editing process bring issues to bear regarding the equipment and time required to yield finished production of a given quality. These classifications include on-line versus off-line, assemble versus insert, single-source versus multiple source, and control-track versus address code editing.

On-line versus off-line

On-line editing uses actual source tapes to create the finished production. Most low-budget and/or small-format productions take this form by default. In high-end and/or large-format production, on-line editing poses several problems. First, the equipment required for this type of editing work in professional situations is typically so expensive that time is billed in the hundreds of dollars per hour—not exactly an environment that encourages creative freedom and trial-and-error. (Many high-quality facilities keep their equipment so heavily booked that scheduling can also be an issue.) Second, the constant shuttling and previewing of tape associated with the editing process can cause wear and tear on the source tape.

The solution to these issues is *off-line editing*, where less expensive equipment is used to make a low-quality mock-up of the production. *Workprints*, or dubs, of the source material are typically used to preserve the source tapes for the on-line process. In addition to providing a test tape before committing to the final production, the off-line edit generates an *edit decision list* (EDL) that is used to guide the subsequent on-line edit. At its simplest, the EDL can take the form of a *paper edit*—a simple written log of the addresses associated with the edit points. The more advanced form is an electronic list of the edit points that can be transferred via disk to the on-line system, thus automating the final session to a great degree. The *CMX* standard is the most widely used form of EDL.

Assemble versus insert editing

The most straightforward type of editing involves assembling the desired takes one after another onto a new master tape—a process appropriately known as *assemble editing*. Assemble editing uses a stationary erase head to erase all tracks including the video, audio, and control tracks before the tape reaches the head drum. Fresh signals for all of those tracks are then recorded simultaneously by the head drum.

The problem with assemble edits is that a blank spot always occurs on the tape at the end of a segment. Placing another segment at this point causes the picture to break up, since there is a momentary loss of control track and the associated sync. Therefore, extra footage must be placed on the master tape beyond the desired edit-out point. (Technically speaking, assemble editing has no edit-out point.) The subsequent segments must then be recorded over the extra frames, thereby taping over the potential glitch. (See Figure 14.4.) Unfortunately, synchronization can still be problematic.

Figure 14.4

Assemble editing erases the control track and can only be used for sequential edits.

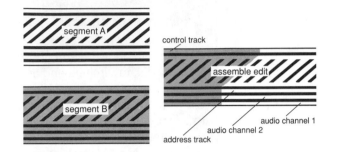

Insert editing is the preferred editing method because it does not erase the control track. The flying erase heads erase only the video and/or audio tracks specified by the user. (The stationary erase head is not used.) Since the control track is not erased, continuity and synchronization are maintained at the edit points. The result is a smooth, glitch-free edit. (See Figure 14.5.) Insert editing therefore dictates that a control track already exists on the tape for the duration of the intended production. Segments can still be conceptually assembled in sequence using the insert edit process. Additionally, segments can be dropped into the middle of existing material, since insert editing employs true edit-in and edit-out points.

Figure 14.5

Insert editing does not erase the control track and can be used for more selective and flexible editing.

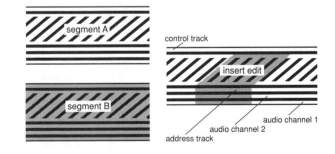

Single-source versus multiple-source editing

As the name implies, *single-source editing* employs only one source deck. Since this involves transferring one segment, locating the next, transferring it, and so on, only one video source can be on the screen at any given time. This means that single-source productions cannot show a second video source in a window or via a split-screen effect. Although few productions require those effects, the less obvious and more salient issues have to do with transitions. A single-source editing environment only provides for *cuts-only editing* (also known as *butt edits*)—an abrupt pop from one segment to another. (See Figure 14.6.) Any type of transition that goes directly from one video source into another requires portions of both segments to be on the screen simultaneously regardless of their relationship—wipe, crossfade, spin flip, etc. The best you can get with cuts-only editing is fade to black, cut, and fade up from black—certainly adequate for many industrial projects, but limiting nonetheless.

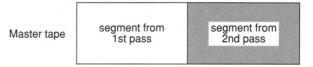

Multiple-source editing employs more than one source deck under simultaneous and independent control of the edit controller. This addresses all of the shortcomings of single-source editing. Multiple video sources can be made to play in separate windows or via split screens, and transitions can move smoothly between one video source and another. (All of these effects require the use of video switchers discussed later in this chapter.) The source decks in multiple-source editing are referred to alphabetically. The most common form employs two source decks and is therefore called *A/B roll editing*. (See Figure 14.7.)

Figure 14.7

A/B rolls employ two source decks, providing for transitions in which two video sources can be seen simultaneously on the master.

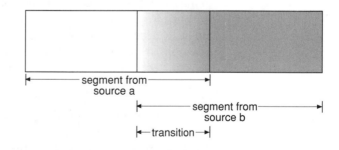

An extension of the multiple-source, *multi-format editors* are capable of controlling different machine formats simultaneously. For example, source deck A might be S-VHS, source deck B might be Hi8, and the record master might be 3/4".

Control track versus address code editing

The video editing process assumes a knowledge of the relative locations of segments within the tapes. Low-end edit controllers use the control track not only to maintain synchronization, but to establish location. Since all control track pulses are identical, they carry no absolute reference information. Whatever counter number happens to be showing in the display when a new tape is inserted will be the reference for the current location (unless the counter is reset to zero). The edit controller counts control track pulses as the tape is played and shuttled forward or backward at various speeds. This makes for an inherent amount of inaccuracy, ranging from a few frames within a short segment to seconds when locating scenes over longer lengths of tape.

In addition to inaccuracy, *control track editing* has another problem in that it does not provide for repeatability. Counter readings become invalid when swapping source tapes. In addition, all information pertaining to the edit points is lost when power is shut off. Since there are no absolutes, the use of control track editing for off-line work provides for only rough timing and aesthetic evaluations.

Address code editing employs some form of time code—typically SMPTE—to identify each frame uniquely. The edit controller reads the exact frame location from the address track or VITC of each deck at any given moment, thus providing complete frame-accuracy in the editing process. Since the time code is married to the video, edit decision lists can be memorized, stored, retrieved, and transferred to other systems.

❖ **Edit Controller Functions**

The previous discussion goes a long way in describing the differences in functionality between edit controllers. Virtually all models provide for both insert and assemble editing. Simple edit controllers are single-source and use only the control track as a timing reference. The next step up typically incorporates time code and provides for an edit decision list. The most advanced versions control multiple source decks. Owing to the nature of their complexity, these units offer greater programmability—often with the ability to automate the on-line process according to an EDL generated off-line.

Regardless of its class, an edit controller's primary functions center on remote transport control of the various decks and setting their edit-in and edit-out points. (Some models employ a single set of controls for these functions, along with a toggle that switches them to affect either the source or record deck.) In addition to the standard transport controls, a search control in the form of a jog wheel, joystick, and/or buttons allows the operator to quickly locate a desired point in either the source or master footage. Counters also display the current position according to pulse-count or time code, depending upon the system.

The edit-in and edit-out buttons for the source deck set the current counter location as the beginning and end points (respectively) on the source footage that will be transferred to the master. The analogous buttons for the record deck determine the segment of the master footage to which the source segment will be transferred. Associated *trim buttons* will increment or decrement any of the edit points one or a few frames at a time, depending upon the accuracy of the system.

Video decks typically require at least five seconds to play footage and stabilize the video signal after the transport is engaged. *Pre-roll controls* are used to specify how far in advance of the edit-in points the decks begin playing the footage. *Post-roll controls* determine how long playback continues after passing the edit-out points. The minimum amount of pre-roll time is dictated by how long the decks need in order to stabilize. A small amount of post-roll should be used to accommodate for slight inaccuracies in the transfer process. Longer pre- and post-roll times are used to achieve a better feel for the continuity of the edited scene.

The controller is also used to select between assemble and insert edit modes. Insert edits can be performed on the video and/or audio tracks. Inserting video is useful only for changing the imagery while maintaining a continuous soundtrack. Inserting audio is handy for creating or replacing a soundtrack after the video has been edited.

Once everything is set up properly, the edit controller performs all of the calculations to engage the transports of the decks at the right time and control their functions on the fly for the actual edit. A *preview* button allows the edit to be auditioned without altering the record master; both decks start playing back at the appropriate points, and the controller switches the record deck's input mode to show the source signal during the segment where the footage would be transferred during the actual edit. The *perform edit*, or *auto-assemble*, button actually executes the edit; the *review* button plays the edited segment for verification purposes.

VIDEO SWITCHERS

Video edit controllers are indispensable for controlling the timing of video segments and compiling them into a cohesive order. When used alone, however, they offer little or no aesthetic control over the actual video signal. Switching, real-time transitions between multiple video sources, and basic special effects all require the addition of a *video production switcher*. As such, the production switcher is the visual equivalent of the audio mixing console. (Unlike audio, however, the input signals must be synchronized by devices such as genlocks and TBCs described later in this chapter.) The functions of better switchers can be automated if they are connected to or integrated into a computer, allowing many complex operations to be *cascaded* (combined in sequence) and performed predictably.

Production switchers accept video inputs for various devices, such as multiple VCRs, cameras, a character generator, and computer graphics. The front panel has several buses, each one of which contains switches corresponding to the various input jacks. (See Figure 14.8.) Pressing one of the switches selects the corresponding input to be sent to the bus output. Each bus has a unique function.

Figure 14.8

The video production switcher routes and mixes multiple video sources for specific bus outputs.

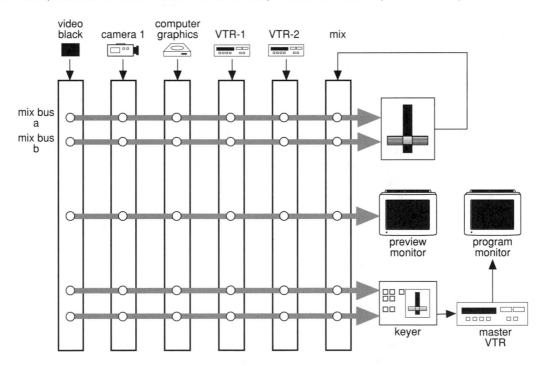

❖ Program Bus

The *program bus* (also called the *direct bus*) determines what is sent to the record deck. The results can be viewed on a monitor connected between the switcher and the record deck, or connected to the output of the record deck. (Such a monitor is called a *line monitor* or *program monitor*.)

❖ Preview Bus

The *preview bus* allows any video source to be shown on a separate monitor—aptly called the *preview monitor*—allowing the user to audition another video source without affecting what's being recorded from the program bus.

❖ Mix/Effects Buses

Most switchers have a built-in *special effects generator* (SEG) that is typically associated with at least one pair of *mix/effects buses*. (A pair of mix/effects buses is sometimes called a *bank*.) Separate video sources can be assigned to each mix/effects bus, and a manual *fader bar* and/or programmable control determines the ratio of the two mix/effects bus signals at the bank output. The input source choices on the program and preview buses each include a button that allows routing of the mix/effects to either destination.

Fades and dissolves

Various transitions can be associated with a bank. A *fade* is a transition from a video source to black or vice versa. (Black is usually a dedicated video source button on the various buses.) A *dissolve* is the same as a fade, except that it is a transition between two non-blank video sources. A partial dissolve superimposes two images—an effect called a *super* in the video world.

Wipes

A *wipe* replaces one source with another according to the *wipe pattern* provided on a given switcher. (See Figure 14.9.) A horizontal wipe, for example, has the effect of sliding a vertical line across the screen with one side of the line showing the one video source and the other side showing a second. (Note that new source only replaces the original, rather than pushing it off the screen.) Fixing the transition half-way through provides for a *split-screen* showing parts of two images side-by-side. The center of the wipe pattern can sometimes be positioned on the screen via a joystick; combined with

Figure 14.9

Various transitions enhance
edits between two scenes.

Dissolve (switcher)

Horizontal wipe to center (switcher)

Push on (DVE)

Perspective distortion (DVE)

Spin-zoom (DVE)

various patterns, this provides for small windows containing a portion of another image. The edges of the wipe pattern can often be
adjusted to appear hard or soft.

❖ **Keying**

While fades, dissolves, and wipes can provide some special effects,
they are primarily designed for transitions between two video
sources. *Keying* allows portions of video sources to be merged

selectively by replacing areas of one video image with the corresponding area of another.

Luminance keying

Luminance keying (also called *luma keying*) uses luminance levels to determine which areas will be transparent. (See Figure 14.10.) The *key level*, or *clip,* control determines the luminance threshold. Everything brighter than the threshold level will be solid; everything below it will be transparent to the other video source. A common technique in video production is to place white title letters on a black background, then use luminance keying to eliminate the black background and "key" the white letters over a video segment.

Figure 14.10

Luminance keying is often used to superimpose the bright areas of a title over a video image.

Video source

Key source

External key source

Luminance Key

External key

Matte keying

Matte keying applies a third video source to a luminance key. The most common third source is a built-in colorizer that creates a background in any solid color selected using hue, saturation, and lightness controls. Using such a background as a matte will effectively colorize the white text. Alternately, some switchers allow the keyed area to be filled with any available video source.

Chroma keying

Chroma keying replaces areas of a given color in one image with corresponding areas of another. The selected color is typically blue because there is no pure blue in human skin tones. (The term *blue screen* is often used in association with chroma keys in this default color.) The most common example of this technique is the classic TV meteorologist standing in front of what appears to be a large animated weather map. In actuality, the talent is standing in front of a large blue screen, and the camera image is chroma keyed over a separate video signal carrying the graphic. The biggest trick is ensuring that nothing in the foreground is blue—otherwise the background would show through in its place! Uniform background paint saturation and even lighting (as well as proper adjustment of the chroma key level) influences how clean the edges of the transition areas are.

Downstream keyers

On less expensive switchers, keying is implemented between mix buses in a bank. This restricts the creative process to either one transition or one special effect at a time. More advanced models employ *downstream keyers*—key and matte components that operate on the output of the program bus. This allows the mix buses to be used for transitions and other effects, while providing keying and matting via the downstream keyer.

DIGITAL VIDEO EFFECTS

All of the special effects described so far have a common limitation—all manipulations are performed without altering the size of any of the video images. A wipe, for example, does not change the size relationships of the two images involved, but merely alters the relationship of the windows through which they are viewed. Altering size, position, orientation, and other aspects of images is the domain of a *DVE* (digital video effects) device.

DVEs are so named because the analog video signal is converted into a digital format that can be easily manipulated. Once in digital form, images can be altered in an almost endless number of ways similar to those associated with image processing software in Chapter 8. Images can be scaled, stretched, squashed, rotated, flipped, given perspective, posterized, solarized, turned into mosaics, mapped onto surfaces, and so forth. In addition, these effects are dynamic—they can be applied in real time. This capability provides for everything from zooms to spin-flips to a trail of visual echoes on demand.

DVEs also provide for positioning and combining images in a variety of relationships. One image can push another off the screen in a desired direction, for example, or an image might slide apart like a curtain to reveal another one behind it. DVEs can also provide for multiple moving images in various areas of the screen.

News broadcasts will often use a more complex effect like zooming out of a full-screen action shot to a position that appears to be behind and to the side of a spokesperson's head. In situations where an anchorperson is interviewing several people from remote locations, the DVE is often used to position multiple apparent viewing screens side by side (complete with perspective); the interviewer is actually shot on a blue screen and a chroma key is used to place him "in front" of the remote "monitors."

Given their digital nature, DVEs are inherently programmable. This allows complex effects to be perfected, then recalled at the touch of a button or automated in sequence. Although traditional DVEs are not cheap, DVE technology and effects are becoming more affordable as digital video becomes more integrated into the desktop.

CHARACTER GENERATORS AND TITLING SOFTWARE

Titling and other text is created in traditional video production through the use of a *character generator*. On the desktop this function is replaced by *titling software*. (Highly stylized type can also be created and integrated into a sophisticated title screen using the text capabilities of graphics and animation software.) The obvious requisite of such tools is a wide choice of fonts, sizes, colors, and the ability to easily add stylistic effects such as drop shadows. Ideally, control over justification, kerning, and leading is included.

Character generators and titling software offer several other features not found in an all-purpose graphics program, however. First is the ability to animate a long list of text vertically or horizontally. Vertical text animation—called a *scroll*—is used for things like the moving credits at the end of a production. Horizontal text animation—called a *crawl*—is used for moving banners such as a stock market ticker tape. The other unique attribute of character generators and titling software is the ability to store and recall pages of titles representing the various text required through a production and accommodating fast sequences of titles on the fly.

Character generators are typically brought into a switcher on a dedicated input and are often used in conjunction with a luminance key in order to superimpose the titling over a video image. The same can be accomplished with computer graphics and titling packages, provided the computer signal is converted to NTSC video format using an RGB-to-NTSC encoder described later in this chapter. Like many other video components, both stand-alone and computer-based character generators require synchronization in order to be used in an editing environment—the next subject of discussion.

SYNCHRONIZATION DEVICES

As described in Chapter 13, video signals are literally defined by precision timing. Unlike audio, mixing two video signals together results in a chaotic waveform that simply isn't a video signal anymore—unless the source signals are synchronized. Similarly, editing two nonsynchronous video signals back-to-back will cause a visible glitch in the picture. Simply put, any time two or more video signals are combined—either simultaneously or in series—seamless synchronization must be maintained.

Turning this concept into practice, all inputs to a video switcher must be "marching to the same drummer." (See Figure 14.11.) One device capable of sending a video sync signal must be designated as a sync master, and all others must be slaved to it. The master device is often a dedicated sync generator whose sole purpose is to generate master, or *house sync*—especially in larger facilities. Cameras and other production devices have external sync connectors and switches as well. The same house sync must be routed to all devices connected to the switcher.

Figure 14.11

All video signals that are to be mixed in a production must be synchronized.

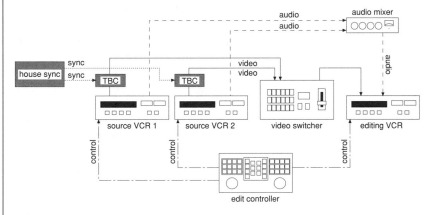

❖ Genlocks

The process of synchronizing one video device to a source of external timing is known as *genlocking*. Devices that aid in this process are aptly named *genlocks*. The most prevalent use of genlocks in desktop production work is in synchronizing the timing of the computer with other video sources in order to record computer graphics onto video. Genlocks for computer graphics are described later in this chapter.

❖ **Time-Base Correctors**

VCRs must also be synchronized to house sync in order to be used in a switcher. (Cuts-only editing with a single-source deck doesn't pose a problem because the video isn't being mixed with anything, and the editor only performs edit-ins and -outs during the vertical blanking interval.) Unfortunately, synchronizing video decks presents an additional problem due to the physical nature of the transport and tape. VCRs (and the analogous components of camcorders) don't produce a pristine video signal due to factors such as stretched tape, inconsistent tape wrap around the head drum, dropouts, and other anomalies. While monitors are fairly forgiving when viewing a single source, these timing anomalies throw the perfect sync of the editing/switching environment out of whack.

The solution is to place a *time-base corrector* (TBC) between the output of every video deck and the corresponding switcher input. TBCs come in various forms that correct for the problems on different scales. Professional video decks that have external sync jacks often need compensation just for a few jitters and color anomalies. TBCs designed to work with specific models of these decks have only a small window of correction—they correct for only a few dozen scanlines at a time.

TBCs designed to work with a wide range of VCRs (including those without external sync provisions) have frame buffers capable of holding an entire frame of video. (Due to the cost of the memory required, some take in only one field of each frame and duplicate it to create a frame with lower vertical resolution.) In advanced devices, one frame buffer is taking in a new frame, another is correcting the lines of the previously accepted frame, and a third is outputting the previously corrected frame. TBCs also include genlocks so that the frames are output in sync with the rest of the system. TBCs with the capability of holding entire frames are also called *frame store synchronizers* and can often be used to freeze and hold a frame of still video for production purposes.

Many TBCs are now available as boards designed to reside in computer card slots. TBCs also commonly include some of the other video features—such as proc amps and drop-out compensators—discussed later in this chapter.

VIDEO PRODUCTION ACCESSORIES

Various video hardware devices are available to monitor and modify a video signal. The latter are best at tweaking minor problems and are no substitute for good source video.

❖ Proc Amps

Proc amps (short for *processing amplifiers*) provide controls to modify various parameters of the video signal. Proc amps allow adjustment of the overall gain of the video signal, the pedestal or setup level, sync pulse, color burst, as well as the luminance, hue, and saturation factors that can provide color correction.

❖ Dropout Compensators

Dirt in the tape path of the VCR or physical damage to the magnetic particles on the videotape result in *dropout*—anomalies in the video signal that appear as colored specs on the video monitor. A *dropout compensator* (DOC) corrects for these problems by detecting dropout areas and replacing them with pixels from the previous scanline.

❖ Image Enhancers

Image enhancers are especially helpful in retaining image quality when copying video cassettes. Controls are typically provided for sharpening, noise (graininess) reduction, color intensity, brightness, and contrast. Some consumer-level devices include other goodies like fade to and from black.

❖ Waveform Monitors

Waveform monitors are essentially specialized oscilloscopes that display the waveform of an incoming video signal. While they don't actually adjust the signal, waveform monitors are useful for identifying adjustments that other video devices affect, such as peak white and pedestal, to ensure the best signal.

❖ Vectorscopes

Waveform monitors can only show that color is present in the video signal. *Vectorscopes* are used to display the chrominance information.

❖ Time Code Generators

Time code generators create fresh SMPTE time codes that can be recorded onto a track of audiotape or videotape. Standard controls are provided to set the SMPTE frame-rate format and the starting time reference. Many time code generators can also regenerate fresh time code that mirrors an incoming stream of SMPTE time code—handy since copying time code directly is not recommended. Some models also include the combination of a dedicated character generator and keying circuit that provides a *window dub*—a small window containing the time code numbers superimposed over the video footage for off-line editing reference.

COMPUTER-BASED VIDEO TOOLS

A plethora of products are now available that marry computer and video technologies in one way or another. These tools involve various permutations of transferring computer graphics onto video, getting video into the computer, controlling the transports of video equipment, and processing the video signal.

❖ NTSC Meets RGB

Any situation in which NTSC video and RGB computer graphics signals meet must take into account the inherent differences in the two technologies. Different manufacturers implement solutions to address these differences; a brief discussion of the problems and common solutions follows.

Spatial differences

Video images are *overscanned*—the image area extends beyond the physical viewing area bounded by the plastic cowl on the front of the monitor. RGB monitors are *underscanned*, having a black border around the edges of the image area. Conversion between NTSC and RGB must take this difference into account.

Another factor that must be considered is the *aspect ratio*—the ratio of the horizontal and vertical dimensions. The viewing areas of standard RGB and NTSC monitors have a physical ratio of 3:4— three units high by four units wide. A video image is comprised of approximately 720 x 484 pixels, while the average RGB display is 640 x 480. The ratios of these two sets of numbers reveal a difference in aspect ratios at the pixel level. The pixels on computer monitors are square with a 1:1 aspect ratio; those on video monitors are taller than they are wide with an aspect ratio of about 1:1.17. Without compensation, converting NTSC to RGB results in an image that appears to be vertically squashed; converting RGB to NTSC results in an image that appears to be vertically stretched. Scaling must be performed in order to maintain a perceived 1:1 aspect ratio when converting between these two formats.

Color and luminance differences

The *color gamut*—the range of displayable colors—differs between RGB and NTSC. RGB can handle more highly saturated colors than video can. Oversaturation of color in a video signal can result in bleeding colors. (Video is particularly unforgiving with saturated reds.)

Color definition also differs between the two technologies. Digital RGB images are capable of immediate transition between any valid colors on a pixel-by-pixel basis. The way in which color is encoded in analog video often requires several color cycles—and therefore several pixels on a scanline—in order for a color to change.

On the other hand, video is capable of a greater range of luminance than RGB. Bright white in the best computer graphics systems is only about 85 IRE by video measurements rather than 100 IRE.

Interlace

While all video displays are interlaced, most computer displays are not. When a noninterlaced frame is converted to an interlaced frame, horizontal lines that are one scanline tall appear to flicker because they are present on only one field of the frame and begin to fade before being refreshed. (The same problem applies to single pixels to a lesser degree.) Graphics to be displayed on video should therefore be designed with horizontal lines at least two pixels high.

Conversely, when the two sequential fields of an interlaced frame are merged into a single noninterlaced field when doing a frame capture, fast motion can result in a blurred image. Significant differences between fields can have a sort of "comb" effect with every other line. One solution is to find a frame that exhibits less difference between the fields. Another is to duplicate the lines from one field and substitute them for the other field, although this effectively halves the vertical resolution. A far more advanced technical solution involves electronically averaging the differences between fields.

❖ NTSC Encoders

Recording computer images onto videotape or displaying them on video monitors requires an *NTSC encoder*. (Some computers such as the Amiga actually incorporate this circuitry to provide video output without additional hardware.) When designing NTSC encoders, manufacturers must address the issues of overscan, aspect ratio, and other previously described problems. They must also decide whether to incorporate outputs for component video formats in addition to composite video.

Better NTSC encoders incorporate genlocks so that the resulting video signal can be integrated with other video signals. Products that go this far typically include the ability to key, or *overlay*, part of the computer image on top of the incoming video image and output the composite image—ideal for titling. The keying process is implemented in different ways depending upon the graphics display technology. In the case of a color lookup table of eight bits or less, one color register or more is designated as being transparent—any pixels painted with that register will be replaced with corresponding pixels of the video image. This is often referred to as *color keying*. In the case of 32-bit graphics, 24 bits are used for the full-color image and the additional 8 bits are used as an *alpha channel* to determine 256 transparency levels for the video image. However, 16-bit high-color technology on the PC employs 5 bits for each of the RGB values (a total of 15 bits) and reserves 1 bit for each pixel to determine keying.

❖ Frame Grabbers

Frame grabbers (sometimes called *video capture boards*) sample a single-frame of video on the fly, converting it to a computer graphic file. One of the aspects that dictate image quality is the conversion process. Most products convert from YUV to RGB formats at four times the color subcarrier frequency. Each sample contains luminance information; the way that the U and V color components are converted makes the real difference in performance as well as price. In the most professional implementation, the U and V components are sampled each time as well. This is known as *4:4:4* (four times oversampling of each component). The next most effective approach alternates sampling the U component every other time—known as *4:2:2*. The least effective approach—*4:1:1*—uses fewer bits for each sample. Only half of either the U or V information is encoded with each sample, resulting in the poorest translation of color.

Some frame grabbers actually have two buffers and digitize two consecutive frames, since a complete cycle of color information requires a color frame. In some cases the captured results can exhibit a temporary jitter as the display flickers between the two frames. The image is then distilled to a single video frame using the color information from the complete color frame. These systems sometimes require trial-and-error in order to capture a pair of frames that share the same complete color cycle.

A non-real time approach to capturing still video images involves digitizing the red, green, and blue components from the video image in separate passes—typically over the course of 20 seconds or so. This obviously works best with the perfectly frozen frames that are no problem for laserdiscs, but are hard to come by with low-end VCRs. In a variation on a theme, systems like NewTek's DigiView provides a color filter wheel consisting of red, green, and blue gels for three different passes with any black-and-white camera (such as an inexpensive security camera). This provides a color scanning option when used in conjunction with a copy stand.

❖ **Video-in-a-window Adapters**

The simplest way of integrating motion video into a computer-based presentation is with separate monitors for the computer and video images—obviously not the most elegant solution. *Video-in-a-window* display adapters allow both types of images to be displayed on the computer monitor. They work on a principle similar to frame grabbers; however, full-motion video from an external source is accommodated by integrating the information into an RGB window on the computer monitor rather than storing the data. (Single frames can usually be stored, but typically not motion video.) The same conversion technology considerations apply to video-in-a-window products as to frame grabbers. Some models also incorporate TV tuners—handy for watching TV or cable stock quotes while working, but little more.

The video-in-a-window approach has several advantages and disadvantages over true digital video as a data type. The most practical form of external video for applications like education, training, and kiosks is the laserdisc because of the longevity of the medium and its random-access capability. Unfortunately, producing, mastering, and updating the content of a laserdisc can be prohibitively expensive—and laserdisc players aren't cheap either. On the other hand, the problems associated with recording, storing, manipulating, and displaying video as computer data are obviated since video is produced and stored externally. In addition, fidelity is not compromised by video compression considerations.

❖ **Frame Controllers**

As described in Chapter 8, the process of rendering a single frame of 3-D animation can take a considerable amount of time. Recording each frame of an animated sequence to tape by hand would be tedious at best. *Frame controllers* provide remote control functions for video decks, and the software that accompanies them allows the computer to automate the process of compiling 3-D animations. Of course, a frame-accurate video deck is a requisite. A frame of animation is rendered, the frame controller locates the exact next video frame in the sequence being recorded, engages record, disengages, the next frame is rendered, and the process continues.

Used in conjunction with video capture and NTSC encoders, frame controllers can also be used to automate the process of applying computer-based effects to a video sequence. A frame is captured, an effect such as an image processor filter is applied, the modified image is recorded back out to the same frame, the transport is advanced to the next frame, and the process continues end-on-end.

❖ Integrated Components and the Video Toaster

Computer technology has blurred the lines between product categories, and many add-on devices now perform more than one function. At this writing, the one that has changed desktop video production most fundamentally has been NewTek's *Video Toaster* for the Amiga. The Toaster combines a four-input video switcher complete with transitions and keying, two frame buffers, DVE effects, 3-D rendering software, and a character generator—all at a reasonable price. This combination is so compelling that many Mac and PC users dedicate a Toaster/Amiga combination to video production. While the Toaster offers video editing, several third-party packages are also available to add that functionality. (Note: while the price of the Toaster seems amazingly low, the cost of TBCs for each source VCR, memory, and hard disk can add to the equipment budget considerably.)

❖ Computer-based Digital Video Systems

As described in Chapter 13, integrating motion video completely into the computer is one of the fastest developing areas of multimedia. Whether Apple's QuickTime, Intel's DVI, Microsoft's AVI, or another technology, a motion video digitizer board is required to get video into the computer, compress it, and store it—all in real time. Like single-frame digitizers, the conversion technology dictates much of the quality; in addition, the type of the compression used makes a difference as well.

With the help of system-level software drivers, some formats like QuickTime and AVI can play back without additional hardware. (In some cases, accelerator boards will help to improve one or more of the parameters that affect compressed video playback—image size, frame rate, and color quality.) More ambitious systems such as DVI require special hardware to play back motion video from hard disks and CD-ROM.

Nonlinear editing

Tape-based video editing is *linear editing*—the source material must be searched, auditioned, and transferred to the master according to the constraints of the linear medium of videotape. The ability to transfer motion video source material onto a hard disk paved the way for a new era in video production—*nonlinear editing*. Various video clips can be random-accessed almost instantly, providing for auditions of source clips and test edits that don't require tape shuttling (and don't incur the associated tape wear). (See Figure 14.12.) Editing is nondestructive: edit-in and -out points are simply pointers that dictate how the video footage is to be played back. Modifying an edit simply moves the pointer, making edit decisions a what-if process. Titling, traditional graphics, transitions, and special effects can usually be incorporated into the production, although the latter two usually require some calculations before previewing the edit.

Figure 14.12

Typical user interface for a nonlinear editing system.

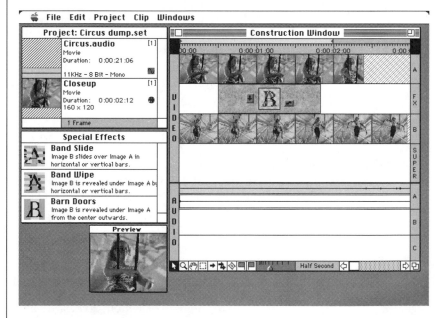

The basic off-line and on-line scenarios apply to nonlinear editing. In terms of off-line, the nonlinear edit using footage on the hard drive can generate an edit decision list that can be transferred to an on-line system. Some more advanced disk-based systems also incorporate traditional tape-based editing and switching: the EDL from the low-resolution disk-based edit can immediately be used to edit the original tape footage. Nonlinear on-line editing with quality high enough to replace tape editing is just now emerging with fairly large price tags—not to mention a heavy requirement for storage media and overall system speed. In cases such as QuickTime and AVI where lower-quality compressed video is the final form, off-line and on-line can be thought of as being one and the same.

❖ ❖ ❖ ❖ ❖ ❖

This chapter has provided an overview of the basic types of video equipment used in desktop productions. As with any other medium, tools alone do not a great production make. Chapter 15 provides some perspective on how to use these tools to produce good video that people actually want to watch.

Video Production

Regardless of the subject matter or equipment used, the process of creating a video can be broken down into three main phases. Plans are made during preproduction, elements are gathered during production proper, and everything comes together during postproduction. Whether traditional or desktop video production tools (or a combination of the two) are used, getting a handle on the techniques employed for decades by television and movie production professionals can make a big difference in creating videos that are compelling, entertaining, and informative. This chapter focuses on the various phases of the video production process and examines effective techniques for using the tools discussed in Chapter 14.

PREPRODUCTION

As with most processes, a little planning goes a long way. In video, preproduction is the stage where decisions are made about the message, the way it is to be communicated, design and style, script, storyboards, budgets, personnel, equipment, facilities, and many other aspects. Most of these traditional video preproduction processes are a subset of those used in creating integrated media in general. As such, they are covered in Chapter 18.

❖ Orchestrating the Shoot

One of the most important aspects of preproduction is translating the script into a shot list. This need will become more clear, both with experience and over the course of this chapter. The audiovisual elements acquired during the production process can make or break the postproduction editing process—which can make or break the overall results. Effective preproduction includes a full visualization of the edited final product in order to ensure that the required elements are acquired during the production process. While storyboards are often employed to help visualize the flow of a production, an actual list of shots provides the best guide during the shoot.

Several types of camera shots are so common in video production that they have formal names. (See Figure 15.1.) The *extreme long shot* (ELS or XLS) and long shot (LS) are used primarily as *establishing shots*—those that give the viewer a frame of reference for locale or mood. The *medium shot* (MS) is typically used as a transition to the *close-up* (CU), which is used to establish intimacy or detail. The *extreme close-up* (ECU or XCU) is used primarily to register intense emotion.

The *bust shot* and *knee shot* show approximately the upper one-third and two-thirds of the body, respectively. The *2-shot* and *3-shot* are used to frame two and three people, respectively, who are relatively side-by-side. The *over-the-shoulder shot* is one in which the person speaking is seen over the shoulder of the person to whom he or she is talking. *Cutaways* are shots of surrounding scenery that can be used later in editing as transitions between main shots.

❖ Preparing for a Location Shoot

Full-blown dramatic production involves personnel and equipment that is beyond the scope of this book. Some of the related issues include casting, wardrobe, catering, production crews, equipment rentals, toilet facilities, critical scheduling, and location scouting. The latter may be the most common consideration in smaller productions. Permission should be obtained before shooting in a private facility. While shooting in public is generally not a problem unless you are obstructing pedestrian or vehicular traffic, contacting the public relations authorities not only is prudent, but can sometimes result in unexpected help and cooperation.

❖ Television versus Film-style Production

Most feature films are shot using a single camera. The task of providing various angles of the same action that can later be edited together is accomplished through a series of sequential takes. Where actors are involved, they reenact their performances for each take. If your desktop productions become ambitious, this film-style single-camera production technique will likely be the method of choice.

Figure 15.1

*Several types of video shots
are so commonly used
that they have industry-
standard names.*

Extreme long-shot

Extreme close-up

Long shot

Over-the-shoulder-shot

Medium shot

Two-shot

Close-up

Three-shot

The other alternative is the multicamera shoot used in live television production. There are two basic variations on a theme. In
one, multiple cameras and various video sources such as VTRs are
externally synchronized to a common house sync and routed to a

production switcher. The director determines how the cameras are positioned and how the signals are mixed in real time. In this style of television production, very little editing is done in postproduction, since the lion's share of the creative decisions are made live. (The teamwork, pressure, and split-second accuracy involved in producing something like live television newscasts is nothing short of incredible.)

The second variation also involves live direction on multiple cameras. The output of each camera is recorded on a separate VTR, all with common time code. This allows the edit decision process to be reserved for postproduction.

Either form of multicamera production involves a lot more equipment and people than single-camera film-style work. Combined with the fact that most multimedia and desktop video content lends itself more to film-style production aesthetics, further discussion of multicamera shoots is beyond the scope of this book. (Multideck editing is certainly more prevalent and is discussed later in this chapter.)

PRODUCTION LIGHTING

Until the advent of the low-light CCD camera, shooting video in most lighting conditions other than direct sunlight required additional lighting equipment. Even though many of today's consumer and industrial cameras can operate with relatively little illumination, considerations of both available light and artificial light can make the difference between a flat-looking production and one with visual depth. (A review of the basic properties of light can be found in Chapter 7.)

Certainly the most basic function of lighting is to make sure that everything that must be visible to the viewer is illuminated adequately. Good lighting goes beyond illumination, adding not only a sense of dimension, but conveying mood and character, and playing on the fact that the human eye is attracted to light. Lighting can be evaluated and used according to several basic criteria—intensity, color temperature, and quality.

❖ Intensity

The basic unit for measuring light intensity is the *foot-candle* (fc)—the amount of illumination a candle produces on a target that is one foot away. Light is also measured in *lux*, which is approximately 10 foot-candles. The light in our daily experiences ranges from about

.01 fc on a moonlit night to around 10,000 fc on very bright days, as the following list shows.

Moonlit night	.01 fc
Average indoor room	20 to 40 fc
Video studio	200 fc
Sunlight	3,000 to 10,000 fc

Video cameras can often create perceptible images with as little as one-half foot-candle; however, 20 fc is usually necessary for a decent color image; 75 to 90 fc yields an image with richer color.

Contrast ratio

Contrast ratio is the difference between the darkest and brightest light levels in a given scene. Contrast ratio is a relative measurement, irrespective of absolute intensity. While the human eye can perceive contrast ratios on the order of 1,000:1, the average video camera only differentiates contrast ratios of about 30:1 in a given shot. The challenge is to restrict the image coming into the camera at any point in time to these illumination constraints.

❖ Color Temperature

What the human eye perceives as white is relative to the overall field of vision at any moment. In actuality, "white" exhibits more red at lower intensities and more blue at higher intensities. A candle gives off a warm red-yellow glow, while a fluorescent light emits a harsher bluish-green tone. The balance of colors that make up white is known as *color temperature*—measured on the *Kelvin* (K) scale. Simply put, various sources of white light emit a mixture of spectral frequencies that center on a particular frequency. As that frequency increases through the spectrum, the color temperature also increases.

Color temperatures can vary from as little as 1,800°K for a candle flame to about 25,000°K for the brightest, clearest skylight. This presents one of the challenges of shooting different video scenes under various lighting conditions: differences in color temperature between scenes can result in noticeable color tints from scene to scene as they are edited together. In professional television production, color temperatures for white are standardized at 3,200°K for indoor scenes and 5,600°K for outdoor scenes. Most video cameras are balanced for 3,200°K, and a slightly reddish filter wheel is rotated into the lens path to compensate for outdoor shoots. The white balance should also be set to fine-tune the color balance electronically each time the lighting conditions change.

❖ **Hard Light versus Soft Light**

The focus of the light source determines much of the definition in an image. *Hard light* is directly transmitted from a small focused source such as a spotlight or midday sun. When hard light strikes a textured surface at an angle, there is a rapid transition or *falloff* from the light areas to the dark ones. (See Figure 15.2.) The result is high contrast between very crisp highlights and well-defined shadows. The associated subconscious effect is one of depth and dimension.

Figure 15.2

Hard light from focused sources exhibits fast falloff and high contrast; soft light from diffused sources exhibits slow falloff and low contrast.

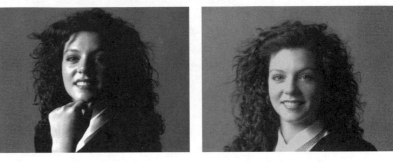

Fast falloff   Slow falloff

Soft light, on the other hand, is unfocused or diffused and comes from a comparatively large source or many points. The falloff between light and dark areas is much smoother with soft light than with hard light. The result is overall illumination, but with little contrast or detail. Soft light is often very appropriate for softening the appearance of the human face, for example. The exclusive use of soft light can result in a flat-looking image that lacks dimension. In most cases, ideal lighting results from a combination of both hard and soft lighting.

❖ **Lighting Instruments**

Many different types of lights are used for specific purposes in professional video production, the most basic categories being spots for harder focused light and floods for softer diffused light. The details of professional lighting instruments are quite involved and are beyond the scope of this book. The most common artificial light source used for low-budget production work is the portable tungsten-halogen light.

Tungsten-halogen lights

An incandescent bulb similar to that used in the home has several problems when boosted to the required color temperature for video lighting. The biggest is that it burns out very quickly. During the short lifespan, color temperatures also decrease rapidly.

Rather than the nitrogen in the traditional incandescent bulb, the *tungsten-halogen light* uses gases that help the boiled-off tungsten atoms to recombine with the tungsten filament. This eliminates the problems of varying intensity and color temperatures associated with incandescent lamps. In order for this process to work, the bulb of the tungsten-halogen lamp must maintain a temperature above 250°C. This makes the use of glass impractical and has led to the use of quartz instead. (Tungsten-halogen lights, therefore, are often called *quartz lamps*.) The color temperature conforms to the 3,200°K standard for indoor video shoots. This type of light has become the most popular for consumer and many industrial-level video productions.

However, reducing the voltage to tungsten-halogen lights via a traditional dimmer reduces the color temperature. Therefore, physical methods of controlling the intensity of these lights are required.

Two main caveats are associated with tungsten-halogen lights. First, plenty of ventilation is required since the high temperatures can melt mounts, gels, and even the lamp itself. Second, never touch the lamp. Not only is it very hot when operating, but the oil from fingerprints can cause the lamp to heat unevenly and fail quickly. Gloves or a clean cloth should be used when touching the actual lamp, even when it is turned off.

HMI lights

The biggest problem with incandescent lights (including tungsten-halogen lights) is that they require a great deal of power, most of which is simply converted to heat. The *HMI light* (hydrogen medium-arc-length iodine) requires less power and generates less heat. This not only is less demanding on available power, but also leads to a more comfortable shooting environment. Like the tungsten-halogen lights, HMI lights have good stability in the areas of intensity and color temperature. As an added bonus, the color temperature conforms to the 5,600°K standard for outdoor shooting.

HMI has several problems also. First, the lights can be quite expensive and bulky. Second, they require about a minute to warm up. Finally, the starter ballasts themselves can be large, hot, and noisy. These factors combined make them practical only for important, carefully staged productions.

❖ **Lighting Techniques**

One basic lighting approach is to establish the *baselight*—the proper overall illumination the camera requires to function properly. The baselight for indoor shooting is ideally in the range of 75 to 300 foot-candles, depending upon the camera and desired mood. Once the baselight requirements are satisfied, additional lights can be placed to handle problem areas. This method is often the only practical way to go when time constraints prevent more elaborate lighting setups.

The more desirable approach is to light the main elements in the image with spotlights, then fill in the shadows with softer lights. While it provides greater control and visual character, this method takes more time to experiment with and perfect.

Measuring light

A *light meter* can be very helpful in evaluating the technical effectiveness of lighting. There are really two types of evaluations—incident light and reflected light. *Incident light* is a direct measurement of the light falling on an area. The light meter is pointed at the camera lens and provides a good indication of baselight. *Reflected light* is measured by pointing a light meter at the objects in close proximity. Taking various readings throughout the area viewed by the camera provides information about contrast ratios. Ratios exceeding that of the camera indicate that attention must be given to dimming highlights or illuminating shadows. Meters alone do not good lighting make, however: they should be used ultimately to verify the results of lighting created according to the naked eye and a video monitor.

Controlling light

The most basic method of controlling light is by changing the distance between the light and the subject. Recall from Chapter 1 that light from a diffuse source falls off according to the law of inverse squares. Moving a light twice as far away, for example, will result in one-quarter of the illumination. Another basic method is choosing lighting fixtures with wattage and foot-candle ratings that are appropriate for a given proximity.

Some lights have mechanisms that allow the beam to be defocused and focused by moving the bulb forward or backward in relationship to the fixture's aperture. Others are specifically designed to provide hard light or soft light. The quartz lamps most commonly used as all-purpose light sources in desktop-level productions are fairly focused and thus provide relatively hard light. Transforming them into soft lights involves diffusing their effect. One such method is bouncing them off a ceiling or an umbrella—a technique similar to that used with flash photography. Another is placing a diffusing *scrim* made from cloth, spun glass, or frosted glass between the light and subject. In cases where reflections are extremely problematic, a *light tent* can be helpful. A "tent" is constructed from white cloth like a sheet with an opening only large enough for the camera lens; bright light is projected onto the cloth from the outside, illuminating the inside with diffuse light.

Some lights have two or four *barn doors* on the front that can be positioned to direct and shape the beam. Many lights also have provisions for attaching color gels to colorize lights for effects and/or mount *cookies*—cutouts in various shapes that can be used to add patterns.

❖ Single-Source Lighting

Sometimes a single light, often in the form of a camera attachment, is the only lamp available. While this is the most mobile approach, the results can appear flat since the light is on the same plane as the lens. In addition, the light is both imposing and annoying to anyone who happens to be the subject. Better results can be attained by placing the light somewhere off axis from the camera. Placing the light off to the side of the camera creates some depth.

A low ceiling can often be used as a built-in reflector to diffuse light as it falls on the subject. Establishing the proper angle is important, since too sharp an angle can result in shadows around the eyes and similar unwanted phenomena. In small rooms, light can be reflected off the back wall, then off the ceiling. (See Figure 15.3.)

Figure 15.3

Reflective surfaces are useful in directing and amplifying light.

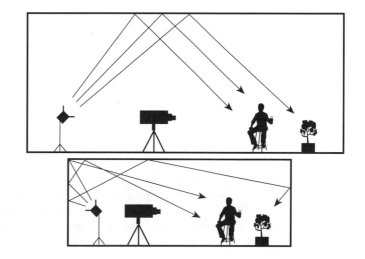

Hand-held or mounted *reflectors* are also handy for bouncing light. They can be used either in the path between light and subject or to fill in shadows on the opposite side of the subject from the light source. A home-made reflector can be made from a piece of white posterboard, covering one side with crinkled aluminum foil and leaving the other plain. The foil side provides a brighter reflection while the plain side is softer.

A single focused light source can also be used to create special effects, depending upon its position. Light from the front and above is natural and communicates normalcy; light from below is abnormal and intimates danger or mystery. Light from the side communicates drama through contrast. Illuminating a figure or object from the rear creates a somewhat surrealistic effect.

❖ Three-point Lighting

It is almost impossible to satisfy the requirements of baselight, contrast ratio, depth, and mood with a single light source. The classic problem is communicating the three-dimensional depth of the real world on the two-dimensional medium of the video monitor. The classic solution is the use of three separate lights—a technique known as *three-point lighting* or *triangle lighting*.

Key light

The *key light* is the major light source perceived by the viewer. As such it is responsible for the illumination that establishes the basic shape of the object, as well as establishing the direction of the light source via highlights and shadows. Key lights are typically more focused light sources such as spots. Since most natural light comes from above, they are positioned above and in front of the subject pointing down at an angle of approximately 45 degrees. They are also placed on one side of the camera or the other to add depth. (See Figure 15.4.)

When placed too high, key lights can create shadows under protruding objects, such as the eyebrows, nose, and glasses of the human face. Lowering the position of the key lights or diffusing the light more will help overcome this problem. Placing key lights too low can result in longer overall shadows cast by the subject.

Back light

While the key light produces shadows, it is often difficult to distinguish the dark areas of the subject from the actual shadows the subject casts. The *back light* is used to add definition to these areas.

Figure 15.4

The classic three-point lighting system employs a key light, back light, and fill light to illuminate the subject.

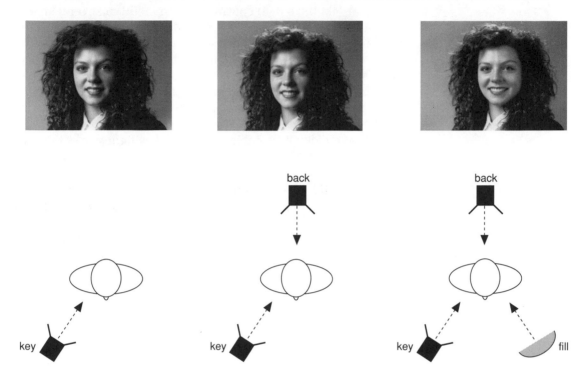

Typically a spotlight is placed directly behind the subject, with careful attention to angle. When placed too low, the back light can create a halo effect—fine for special effects, but undesirable for everyday shots. When placed too high, the back light can illuminate too much of the shadow effect created by the key light. An angle of 45 degrees is typically the most effective at adding proper contour. This sometimes requires adjustments in the shooting environment so that the subject is far enough in front of a back wall to permit such an angle.

The back light is typically about the same intensity as the key light; light-colored subjects, such as people with light hair and clothes, require less backlight than do their darker counterparts. Boosting the intensity of the back light to as much as one-and-one-half times that of the key light can serve to add a slight aura or sparkle outlining the subject.

433

Fill light

The combined effect of key light and back light may still exhibit fast falloff that results in high contrast, not to mention several shadows opposite the key light. The *fill light* adds some illumination to the problem areas. It is a more diffuse fixture such as a flood, typically placed at about 30 degrees in relation to the subject and on the opposite side of the camera from the key light. The fill light is typically about 50 percent the intensity of the key. Less definition in the scene results as the ratio of intensity between fill light and key light becomes more even. In many situations, a reflector placed on the opposite side of the subject from the key light works fine as a fill light.

Additional lighting considerations

In situations where the subject and/or camera moves, the fill light often takes the form of a second key light. Where motion is expected, the fields of the various lights should be made to overlap so that the subject does not have the opportunity to move in and out of shadow.

In more elaborate productions, the three-point lighting solution is applied primarily to the subject. A *background light* or *set light* is used to illuminate the backdrop. This light may be diffused if uniform illumination is desired; alternately, focused lights with gels and/or cookies can be used to "paint" the backdrop with light. Background lights can also be helpful in establishing things like location, mood, and time of day. *Cameo lighting* illuminates the subject and leaves the background in shadow. *Silhouettes* are created by removing illumination entirely from the foreground subjects and using background lights exclusively.

A *kicker* is a focused light that is placed behind and to the side of the subject. Like the back light, it serves to add contour and delineation between the subject and the background. The additional effect created by the kicker's unique positioning is to create the effect that light is being cast from another source such as a neon sign or moonlight.

❖ Available Lighting

Lighting and proper use of the video camera go hand in hand. This is especially true when using some form of *available light* (light that's already part of the environment), such as existing lighting fixtures, sunlight, or windows.

Cloudy days

Outdoor lighting presents its own unique circumstances. While it would seem that one can exercise little control over the sun, a variety of things can make daylight shots more effective. Cloudy days present the smallest lighting challenge, since the light is uniform and amazingly bright. The overall effect is diffused and flat, however. To make up for this, a reflector is sometimes used to focus some light on the subject. In some circumstances, artificial lights can also help.

In most cases, the iris can be left on the auto-iris setting since the light is fairly uniform. Care should be taken not to place the subject in front of a bright background, as the circuit would favor the background and risk underexposing the subject. If you are given no choice in such a shooting situation, use the manual iris setting and zoom in as much as possible to eliminate the bright background.

Bright sunlight

Sunny days can pose many lighting and contrast problems. The first thing is to have the sun work for you rather than against you. The sun can definitely work against you since the bright background will make iris settings and proper contrast ratios almost impossible. (Shooting directly into the sun can also ruin the tubes in tube cameras.) The sun to your back will create much better results, although the flat appearance and/or having the sun directly in a person's eyes can be problematic. Ideally, the sun can be used as a natural key light. Like a key light, the sun can cast very hard shadows. To compensate, a reflector can be carefully positioned to direct light into the shadows, serving the same purpose as a fill light.

Almost all circumstances involving outdoor shoots dictate manual iris control. There's simply too much opportunity for the camera's auto-iris circuitry to adjust to a bright light or reflection. When shooting into the sun is inevitable, try zooming in on the subject to eliminate the bright background. In addition, use any available lights and reflectors to light the subject artificially.

Shooting outdoors often has the additional problem of extremely bright reflections. *Blooming* occurs when a bright spot, such as the glint off a shiny chrome car bumper, overloads the camera circuitry. Other than changing camera angles, the most common solution is to dull the reflection with tape or a special spray such as Krylon.

Tube cameras overload when more light comes in than can be processed by the electronics, resulting in a persistence of the bright portions of the image. *Lag* or *comet tailing* occurs when the camera is moved quickly while overloaded, leaving a bright trail across the screen. The solutions to this include avoiding the bright spot, dulling it as just described, or avoiding fast camera motion. In the case of something like the headlights of a moving car, it is best to avoid them.

Lens flare occurs when the sun is reflected directly on the camera lens. While this can be a very artsy effect, it is usually unwanted and can be eliminated by placing a shade (called a *flag* in the video world) directly in the path between the sun and lens.

Windows

Shooting indoors has similar challenges where sunlight is involved. Shooting in a sunlit window can present the same problem in iris setting—the difference between the bright window and foreground subject is way outside the contrast ratio of the camera. The subject will either appear silhouetted, or the background will be over-exposed. The obvious solution is to avoid shooting into a window. One approach is to shoot from the side to avoid the window, have the talent turn, and use the light from the window as a key light. An artificial light or reflector can serve as a fill to round things out. (If a light is used, an HMI light or appropriate filter for the tungsten-halogen light should be used to compensate for color temperature differences.)

Tracing paper or lighting gels can also be placed over the window, if necessary, to cut down the intensity of the incoming light. If a particular angle must be maintained, draw blinds or curtains. If that's not possible, waiting for a cloudy day or until late in the day can make a significant difference.

Fluorescent lights

Many public buildings rely on fluorescent lights for illumination. Fluorescents have a more imbalanced set of spectral frequencies than regular incandescents and tungsten-halogen. One solution is to turn off the fluorescents, but this is not always possible and can eliminate the baselight. Another is to rely on the available light of the fluorescents and set the camera's color temperature controls accordingly before doing the white balance. Situations that require both types of light can be dealt with by placing a dichroic filter over the camera lens to shift the color temperature of the fluorescents to a standard color temperature. Using both types of lights and no filter, the best you can do is to set the white balance color temperature for 3,200°K.

SHOOTING VIDEO

Whether using a consumer camcorder or a broadcast-quality camera, the guidelines for acquiring good video footage apply across the board. Aside from lighting, the most important concepts are proper use of the lens, proper framing and image composition, and recording sound.

❖ Using the Lens

The concepts of focal length, viewing angle, iris opening, and focus explored in Chapter 14 are all intertwined.

Lens angles and field of view

A bit of simple physics shows that a given distance between the lens and image target dictates the available viewing angle. (See Figure 15.5.) Since the image target is of fixed size, the angle dictates the *field of view*—how much of the scene fills the video frame. The ratio is inversely proportionate: doubling the focal length fills the image target with half the field of view, and vice versa. A wide-angle lens has a short focal length that includes more of the scene compared to a normal lens; a narrow-angle lens has a long focal length that includes less.

Figure 15.5

Varying the focal length of the lens determines the field of view.

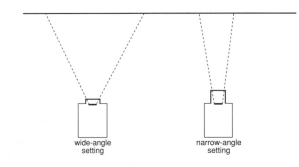

wide-angle setting   narrow-angle setting

While the lenses of some inexpensive video cameras have only a fixed lens, most offer a zoom lens that can serve the functions of many types of lenses. When the zoom lens is retracted all the way, it becomes a wide-angle lens and the image appears to move away; when extended all the way, it becomes a narrow-angle lens and the image appears to move closer.

Depth of field

When the focus ring on the camera is turned, the position of the lens is adjusted slightly to make certain objects appear more sharply and clearly. *Depth of field* describes the range of distances from the camera in which other objects around the focal point will be in focus—one-third in front of the focused point and two-thirds behind. (See Figure 15.6.) Depth of field is simultaneously influenced by focal length, aperture, and the distance of the camera to the object. At the widest lens angle the depth of field is infinite, so objects at all distances will be in focus; this range compresses as the angle of the lens gets sharper. Small apertures (large f-stops) provide great depth of field; large apertures (small f-stops) yield shallow depth of field. Longer distances between camera and object provide greater depth of field; shorter distances result in shallower depth of field. The best way to master how these factors interact is through experimentation.

Figure 15.6

Depth of field describes the range of distances from the camera in which objects will be in focus.

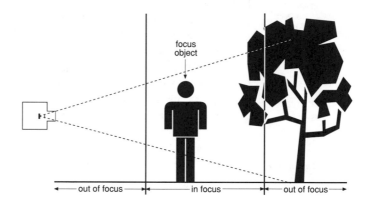

Different depths of field have advantages and disadvantages. Great depth of field puts just about everything in focus, even when the distance between the camera and subject change. This, combined with the greater field of view associated with wide-angle shots, makes it difficult to draw the viewer's eye to any particular element, however.

Shallow depth of field makes it easy to focus the viewer's attention on objects that are at a given distance from the camera—although the rest of the image can be so out of focus that it is distracting. The focus is so critical that small changes in the distance between camera and object require refocusing. This can be turned to artistic advantage since quickly changing the focus can shift the emphasis from a foreground element to a background element or vice versa—a technique called *rack focus*.

A median depth of field obviously splits the difference between these two extremes. Focus is more forgiving, and the viewing angle accommodates the average framing needs.

Spatial relationships

The focal length of the lens has another effect on the image—the perceived size of objects and their spatial relationships. A zoom lens set at a median focal length offers spatial relationships close to those perceived with the naked eye. These relationships are altered by wide-angle and narrow-angle settings. (See Figure 15.7.)

Figure 15.7

Extreme depth of field settings alter the spatial relationships of objects in the frame.

Normal setting

Wide-angle setting

The most obvious effect of the wide-angle lens position is that more of the scene fits into the frame. The side effect is that the perceived depth in the image is exaggerated. Elements going into the distance appear stretched and elongated. Elements closer to the camera seem larger than life, while those at even a moderate distance can seem very far away. In a way this exaggeration of depth actually backfires, since the normal object size relationships by which we judge depth are distorted. Since we usually judge speed by object size, linear motion along the depth axis seems to accelerate when closer to the lens and decelerate when further away.

The narrow-angle lens position basically has the opposite consideration from its wide-angle counterpart. Less of the scene fits into the image than in the normal position. As a result, apparent depth is compressed and objects at various distances from the camera appear closer together than they really are. The side effect is that very little motion along the depth axis is perceived.

Use of zoom

Zooming in or out on a subject during a take is considered to be the signature of the amateur videographer. It should never be used to imply movement, since the spatial relationships change as the focal point changes. Movement is communicated much more effectively by physically moving the camera forward or backward in relation to the subject. (Doing this smoothly requires a dolly—a camera stand mounted on wheels.)

If you must zoom during a take, zoom in on the subject first and focus before shooting. Even if you then zoom out to begin shooting, the scene will still be in focus when zooming in makes the depth of field shallower. Then, don't just zoom out: Be sure to adjust the framing properly for the best image composition at all times.

Auto-focus

Most video cameras have an auto-focus switch that tries to keep everything in focus. The problem is that the camera has no idea which element you wish to focus on. While using auto-focus can occasionally have its advantages when there is no setup time or the subject is in motion, manual focus is much better in most situations.

Auto-iris

Auto-iris switches allow the camera to control the size of the iris opening automatically. Auto-iris only evaluates the amount of light coming into the lens, not where it's coming from. If someone is wearing a white shirt in a medium shot, the iris may adjust to that light level rather than the more important one of the person's face. Much better results can be obtained by zooming in on the person's face, manually adjusting the iris, and then zooming back out for the take. Like auto-focus, use of the auto-iris setting should be reserved for fast shots that don't allow proper setup time.

❖ Good Composition

Shooting good video footage entails a lot more than simply pointing the camera at the subject and starting to record. In fact, the term "shooting video" actually implies the first mistake the amateur videographer typically makes—using the viewfinder like a gunsight. Instead, one of the jobs of the videographer is to compose images just as a good photographer does. Here's a look at some creative considerations in the composition process.

Keep it simple

If the mission of the video is to tell a story, unnecessary elements that appear in the frame dilute the story, and with it the audience's attention. While photographs can be cropped and sized to fit on a page, the video equivalent is much more of a technical and time-consuming challenge. In essence, good videographers "crop" the video image while shooting through proper composition, manipulation of the lens, and camera position.

On the other hand, viewers only see what you let them see through the lens. The important thing is finding the right balance so that you give the viewers exactly the information they need—no more and no less. A common approach to this concern is to use different shots for different purposes. A wide-angle shot can be used to establish a location or scenario. Once that's accomplished, cutting to a close up that focuses exclusively on the action works just fine.

Provide a size reference

Objects whose size is unknown to the viewer and/or important to the message should be given a frame of reference. People (or parts thereof) are the most commonly used size reference, but any object of known size that fits in context will work. Without a frame of reference, the viewer psychologically evaluates object size by the amount of space it takes up on the screen.

Avoid conflicts in the frame

Backgrounds can sometimes conflict with the subject. One way this happens is through clashing colors or patterns. Another is through colors that are too similar or brightness levels that lack contrast. Perhaps the most embarrassing is when background objects such as telephone poles appear to be sticking out of a person's head. The solution is proper evaluation of the scene's composition before shooting. Problems like these are solved by simply moving the subject or the camera.

Use asymmetry

Objects placed in the center of the screen imply stability. A lone TV news anchorperson is indeed anchored in the middle of the screen unless room is being made for an over-the-shoulder graphic. Artists and philosophers as far back as the ancient Greeks decided that centering an object in the field of vision is much less interesting than an off-center placement, however. Moving an object away from the center tends to destabilize the image, adding character and visual interest. (See Figure 15.8.) By extension, placing objects or lines of force on opposite sides of the center creates a compelling tension.

There are two classic approaches to describing and applying asymmetry—the Rule of Thirds and the Golden Area. The *Rule of Thirds* conceptually divides an image into three rows and three

Figure 15.8

Images are often more interesting with the destabilizing effect of asymmetric composition.

Symmetry

Asymmetry

columns and, at its simplest, suggests that items should be placed at the one-third or two-thirds point in either direction. More complex implementations involve placing important items in, say, the upper left and lower right. The *Golden Area* principle is similar, dividing the image area into three units high by five units wide. Objects are ideally placed in the middle of the three horizontal rows and approximately three-fifths of the distance from left to right.

These are merely guidelines, however: putting them to use involves individual style, subject matter, and circumstances. Creating an interesting asymmetric effect often means adjusting the set by adding, removing, or rearranging elements.

Lead the eye with vectors

Various vectors in an image can lead the eye. *Motion vectors* are the most obvious and powerful vector force. *Index vectors* are created when a person or object literally points at something, leading the eye to focus on an object on-screen or creating the anticipation of seeing something next. *Graphic vectors* result from the lines of objects in the frame. They are less obvious, less directional, and less powerful than motion and index vectors.

Vectors can work for and against the videographer. The graphic vector of a road going off into the horizon will naturally lead the viewer's eye down the road, for example. If that's the point in the video when you're about to take the viewer on a journey, great— that's where you want their eyes to go! If the message is instead about something happening along the side of the road, this vector will be distracting. Maintaining the same graphic vector in the horizon is also important when doing several shots of the same distance.

Unlike simple people shots, strong index vectors dictate continuity in angles between two sequential shots. If, for example, someone is pointing to something off the screen to the right, the subsequent shot of whatever they were pointing to should be from the same angle. (See Figure 15.9.)

Figure 15.9

Index vectors should be used to dictate the camera angle of a subsequent shot.

Shot 1

Shot 2

As described in Chapter 9, the Western eye is more comfortable being led from left to right—even when not reading text. This applies to static lines like the hypothetical road, as well as to passing action. Elements on the right side of the screen receive greater viewer attention.

Speaking of leading the eye, remember that the eye is attracted to bright areas. Light sources can be used to focus the viewer's attention on the desired subject and to downplay the background and incidental elements.

Consider vertical relationships

The camera's vertical position relative to the subject can communicate equality or lack thereof. (See Figure 15.10.) Pointing the camera down on the subject gives the viewer the sense of psychologically looking down on it from a position of superiority. Parallel vertical positions provide a sense of equality. As you might expect, pointing the camera up on a subject gives the viewer a psychological sense of inferiority.

Figure 15.10

The vertical relationship of the camera to the subject communicates equality or lack thereof.

Use interesting angles

Shots that have nothing but vertical and horizontal lines in them often seem boring. Strive to include objects that have various angles. Actually tilting the camera can exaggerate this effect to create the impression of motion, interest, or abnormality. Tilting the camera is an all or nothing proposition, however: either ensure that the horizon is perfectly level (as it would be in normal vision) or use an angle significant enough to have a dramatic effect.

Provide for closure

Imagination is closely linked with getting an audience emotionally involved. *Closure* is the ability of the viewer subconsciously to fill in missing parts of an image—much as a good novel provides just enough information to fuel the imagination. Closure manifests when enough of the object is showing that we can easily envision the rest, yet enough is missing that the imagination is still engaged. Consideration of closure is extremely important at times when it is impossible to get an entire object into the frame. Framing a head perfectly is an example of bad closure because the mind will not try to imagine the rest of the body; including the neck (and optionally the shoulders) provides more fuel for the imagination. (See Figure 15.11.)

In the extreme, closure reinforces the KISS principle. A shot that shows only fingers drumming on a table, for example, could easily communicate greater tension than if the entire person was shown—the imagination runs wild, possibly conjuring up even more severe scenarios.

Figure 15.11

Proper framing engages the viewer by allowing the mind's eye to fill in the missing part of the scene.

Poor closure

Better closure

Frame people properly

Shots involving people require a bit of extra attention from a psychological standpoint. From the audience's standpoint, a person on the screen is a real person and the monitor is their world. If possible, try to avoid cutting off the top of people's heads. (The exception to this is the extreme close-up, which should employ the Rule of Thirds to place the eyes in the top third and the mouth in the bottom third.) Moreover, some *headroom* should be left between the top of the head and the top of the screen. Similarly, when a person is facing right or left, some *leadroom* or *noseroom* should be left to buffer the face from the edge of the screen. (See Figure 15.12.)

Figure 15.12

The human head requires special attention to proper framing to ensure enough headroom and noseroom.

No headroom

Better headroom

445

When parts of the body must be cut off by the edge of the screen, enable closure by framing the shot in such a way that the break doesn't occur right at a key point such as a joint. In a similar vein, framing a shot so that the boundary between the person and the background coincides with the boundary of the screen can leave a disorienting effect that should be avoided.

Employ variety

Applying a little psychology again, the viewer will feel more intimate with the subject at close range. This leads to the logical conclusion that tight shots are much more desirable than long shots. Strict application, however, leaves the audience with one of the biggest faux pas in video production—the dreaded "talking head." Shooting footage from several positions provides for some variety during editing. When changing distance, the angle should be varied at least 30 degrees if cuts-only edits are to be used. (Not only does the audience expect a significant change at a cut, but the person appears to pop back and forth if there is no angle change between edited segments. Editing any two segments together that lack the necessary spatial transition results in an unwanted *jump cut*.)

Varying the angle with distance comes with a caveat, however. Consider a line or axis extending straight out from the subject to the normal viewing angle. Care should be taken to keep the shots on the same side of the axis to prevent the viewer from becoming disoriented. (See Figure 15.13.) Alternately, shots in which the camera angle jumps to the other side of the axis should include deliberate movement on the part of the talent to face or move toward the camera. The combined effect communicates redirection or motion.

Figure 15.13

Various shots of a subject designed to add interest should be taken from the same side of the axis and with at least a 30 degree difference in angle.

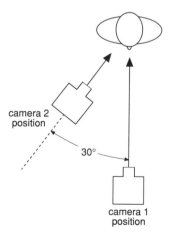

camera 2 position

30°

camera 1 position

Consider frame magnetism

The edges of the screen act as magnets for visual elements—an effect that can work for and against the videographer. Placing objects at the top of the screen can help suspend them. The sides of the screen can emphasize width, but tend to pull two subjects apart. Overall positioning of an object close to all edges communicates large size.

Use a tripod or dolly

The shaky picture that typically results from hand-held shots is another mark of amateur video. With the exception of ENG work, almost all professional TV and film imagery is shot with the use of a tripod or dolly. This not only keeps the image steady, but provides for smooth moves such as a *pan*—a smooth turn of the camera to accommodate its namesake panorama. If the scene is to be panned, first make sure the camera can turn as smoothly as possible on the tripod (which hopefully is outfitted with a fluid head). Record at least 15 seconds at the initial position, then turn the camera uniformly to the end position at a speed appropriate to the subject, and record at least another 15 seconds. The extra time at the beginning and end may come in quite handy later during editing. The same concepts apply to *tilts*—smoothly angling the camera vertically, such as sweeping the view up the side of a tall building.

Trucking is the process of physically moving the camera position parallel to the ground during a take. (An example of trucking might be keeping up with someone as they are walking.) While dollies are designed specifically for this purpose, necessity can certainly be the mother of invention. A smooth-gliding cart, wheelchair with soft tires, or slow-moving car are examples of makeshift dollies that make smooth trucks possible. If forced to resort to hand-held operation, practice shuffling with knees bent. It may look a bit silly, but it can get you out of a pinch.

Craning entails moving the camera along the vertical axis. While Hollywood can afford specially-designed cranes, this type of effect is a bit trickier on low budgets. Short of slow stoops and rises, options include glass elevators, escalators, sliding boards, and cherry pickers.

When considering camera motion, remember that use of compressed digital video—such as QuickTime—as the ultimate delivery vehicle causes more frame-to-frame image change, larger files, and slower performance. Use a stationary camera where possible.

Move the camera for a reason

The audience should never be aware of the videographer. One way this translates is that camera moves should have a reason. The camera should follow the action of the scene, fulfilling the viewers' expectations or satisfying their curiosity. If someone makes a face on camera, for example, we obviously want to see the object of their frustration in the next shot. If a camera move is desired for logistical reasons, try to find a subject to carry or justify the motion. Panning down a street or road, for example, is often accomplished by following a person or vehicle to the desired location.

Shoot along the axis of motion

Excessive camera motion quickly manifests when trying to follow action such as a tennis game from the side. If possible, shoot along the axis of motion—in this example, down the court rather than across it. Put another way, position the shot so that action takes place at different depths. This not only makes for less camera movement, but enhances basic frame composition by adding dimension.

Video Composition Tips

- White balance the camera in each new lighting situation.
- Use tripods, manual focus, and manual iris settings whenever possible.
- Focus attention by keeping the composition simple.
- Establish size using a known reference and/or frame magnetism.
- Use asymmetric composition, angles, and various positions to add interest.
- Lead the eye with vectors.
- Frame people properly and facilitate closure.
- Move the camera for a reason; shoot along the axis of motion.
- Shoot more than you need and document each take.

❖ Additional Shooting Tips

Here are a few more things that will help make life in the fast lane a bit easier.

Always use the best tape

The weakest link and GIGO principles apply to video as well as any other media. If the results of a shoot are for serious use, always spend the extra buck to get the highest recommended grade of tape for your camera.

Shoot more than you need

Always shoot more video footage than you need—it's better to have too much than not enough later during editing. This is true in every aspect. Hold on shots before and after the action takes place in case extra time must be filled. Shoot several takes of the same scene if necessary, varying action, speed, lighting, and lens settings as needed to compensate for any suspected problems. If possible, shoot a scene repeatedly from several different positions to provide variety and choice during editing. Also, shoot incidental shots, long shots, and cutaways that might come in handy later as editing transitions.

Document the shoot

When shooting multiple takes, it is often hard to distinguish them later. Identifying the takes is a two-step process. First, identify each take on tape if possible. Professionals use a slate to visually record the scene and take number. In lieu of a visual indicator, simply describing the take verbally into the microphone will help later. Second, when a good take is recorded, document it in some way. Write down the take number and either the counter number or time code number. These steps will save a lot of time later during editing.

❖ Recording Location Sound

Elements such as soundtrack music, sound effects, and voice-overs are best integrated during the postproduction phase of a video project. Obviously, video shoots such as interviews and drama in which the sound is an integral part of the content require simultaneous audio recording. Most productions at the desktop level will use the audio tracks of the videotape as the audio recording medium. The alternative is a dedicated high-quality audio recorder synchronized to the video recorder via time code.

The biggest decision in recording audio usually will be the choice of microphone and its location. (Basic microphone technology and usage are covered in Chapters 11 and 12, respectively.) The microphone built into your video camera will be acceptable under certain conditions; other times connecting an external microphone into the camera will be required for better results. In general, dedicated microphones will provide better flexibility and sonic quality. If the relationship between the subject and camera will fluctuate, an external microphone will definitely be needed to ensure continuity in the sound. Beyond that, the type of microphone should match the situation regardless of whether it is built in or external.

Three basic approaches will be most effective for recording the average on-camera spokesperson. The small clip-on *lavaliere* microphone is widely used because it is unobtrusively attached to the speaker's lapel and maintains a fixed distance to the mouth. (Lavalieres are usually omni-directional with a relatively short range.) Roving reporters use unidirectional microphones because they eliminate a great deal of ambient noise. Care must be taken to ensure that the mike is positioned so that people speak into it. The mikes built into some cameras are unidirectional and will work if the camera is close enough to the subject. In situations where the subject cannot be close-miked and the camera's mike is too far away, a hypercardioid shotgun mike is used to span the distance.

POSTPRODUCTION AND EDITING

Postproduction is where all the elements of a video production come together. In general, everything you need to integrate into the final edited product should be on hand—much as a cook lines up all the ingredients before starting to tackle a recipe. This not only translates to greater productivity at the desktop level, but lots of dollars saved if your final work is being done at a professional video post facility.

❖ The Pre-post Process

Chapter 14 described the difference between off-line and on-line editing. Certainly in many desktop productions there is no distinction—the video footage is simply edited with decisions made on the fly. Time and/or equipment permitting, there are several good reasons for adding the off-line step. If, for example, the final edits will be performed at a high-priced facility or even on in-house equipment that is in heavy use, what-if situations should definitely take place in an environment where the clock is not ticking. Even if the editing system is your own, repeated use of your source tapes during trial-and-error situations can cause wear that degrades the tape.

Making a workprint

Ideally, the source tapes are played twice after they are shot—once to make a *workprint* or working copy, and once for the final edit. (If the editing environment is entirely digital, degradation is not generally a factor.) Being expendable, the workprint is used in the process of viewing, logging, and performing off-line test edits.

The workprint can take several forms. If the off-line system is a traditional tape-based one, the workprint is a tape copy in whatever format is appropriate. The ability to digitize motion video into digital data equivalents such as DVI, QuickTime, and AVI files provides the alternative of using the computer for off-line editing. This brings the added advantage of random-access to the editing process.

The availability of time code makes a great deal of difference in the effectiveness and accuracy of the off-line process. Without time code, the off-line process serves only as a rough guideline—the process of fine-tuning must be performed again during the on-line session. If the same time code is shared by the workprint and the source tapes, the edit points can be exacted during the off-line process and transferred directly to the on-line system.

Workprints are often created with the time code displayed in window dubs. Since this creates a small window in the video displaying the time code, this provides for exact in and out points to be established in non-editing environments. The simple home VCR, for example, can be used to establish the desired edit points for segments. A written log of the desired segments and edit points then becomes a paper edit—a list of numbers that can be transferred manually to the on-line editing system to save time and money.

Window dubs are optional during actual off-line editing. Here it is more important for the time code to be in machine-readable LTC or VITC form. More advanced off-line editing systems can then translate the sequence of edit points to an electronic edit decision list that can be transferred to the on-line system either manually or via floppy disk.

Some cameras can generate or record time code while shooting. In this case, making a workprint entails using a time code generator to regenerate the same stream of numbers for recording onto the workprint while the video is being copied. (In most cases, time code cannot simply be copied.) When the source tape lacks time code, there are two approaches to adding it. Equipment permitting, the time code generator can lay fresh LTC on both the source and workprint simultaneously—the source deck in audio dub or time code dub mode and the workprint deck in full record mode. This approach still only plays the source tape once. Alternately, LTC can be dubbed to the source tape first, then the source tape is used to make the workprint with time code.

Logging the footage

After a workprint is made, the next step is usually to review the footage in order to document the specific segments and takes that are likely candidates. This not only provides a map that makes finding the desired footage easy, but also provides a feel for how much material there is and how it correlates to the desired length of the final program. (If a workprint is not made, this same process can be applied to the original footage.)

This procedure often extends directly into the paper edit process. The paper edit is essentially a list defining the sequence in which segments are to be edited. Each includes the tape number, sequential scene number, take number, the edit-in point and -out point, length, sound description, and a space for comments. The numbers from the paper edit can then be used to drive the actual editing process.

Transferring audio

Some audio elements, such as ambient tracks or a simple continuous music track, can be added loosely to the production without regard for perfect synchronization. Using this *wild sound* technique, an audio device can simply be started manually at the appropriate time. Since the original audio source is used, there is no generation loss that would be associated with an intermediate tape.

In many situations, however, it is desirable to be able to control music and sound effects with the same accuracy as the video elements. Newer DAT machines with SMPTE capabilities, as well as some hard disk recording systems and direct-drive tape decks, provide the necessary control to be used both off- and on-line. In lieu of these tools, music and other sound effects are traditionally transferred to videotape. This allows the music to be triggered and edited predictably according to the same time code that governs the visual elements.

❖ The Editing Process

As described in Chapter 14, there are many different types of editing procedures and equipment. The most common for desktop video involving VCRs are cuts-only edits using a single source deck. A/B editing using two source decks is becoming more popular as the price/performance ratio of consumer and industrial gear improves. The concepts of A/B roll also apply to computer-based digital video technologies such as QuickTime: the digital images from two or more virtual video clips can be mixed on a frame-by-frame basis to result in an edited video within the computer.

Common preparatory procedures

Several preparatory steps are important regardless of the type of editing you plan to do or the equipment you plan to use.

- As with the process of acquiring the footage, use the best tape available for the edit master.

- If you will be insert editing, record control track on the entire edit master—a process known as *blacking* or *blanking* the tape. This can be accomplished either by recording video black from a switcher or by using no video input. (Some people prefer to use color bars as the video source.) If time code is to be used, record LTC simultaneously with video black. Since control track and time code can only be recorded in real time, this process is typically done during down time.

- If you will be assemble editing, record video black and control track for at least the first 30 seconds of the tape so that the machines have something to cue up to.

- Set up the sync. If house sync or a TBC is driving the decks, set them for external sync. If not, set them for internal sync.

- Set up the video. Switch the record deck's input to the "line" or "dub" position as specified by the manufacturer. If the master record deck has a control for video record level, adjust it so that it reads 0 VU while the source tape is playing. If necessary, adjust tracking and skew on the source deck to stabilize the image.

- Play a portion of the video black signal recorded on the record deck and adjust the tracking of that deck if necessary.

- Set up the audio. The audio output switch on the source deck should be set according to the audio content of the source material. Then play the loudest portion of the source material and adjust the record deck's audio record level so that they read 0 VU. If an audio mixer is inserted between the source and record decks, ensure that the levels are set optimally there as well. Use the volume control on the actual sound system only to adjust listening level.

- Set the editor's preroll time for both decks to five seconds to give the video signal enough time to stabilize before the edit-in points. Some better decks require less time to stabilize, and the preroll can be adjusted accordingly.

- Rewind both tapes to the beginning, then reset the counters on the decks and edit controller to zero.

- Cue the tape in about 20 seconds from the beginning of the edit master before recording anything but black. The beginning of the tape quickly becomes worn and stretched after repeated use and should therefore not be used for content.

- If your equipment provides for it, record 30 seconds or more of color bars and a test tone at 0 VU. This will be helpful in calibrating equipment when the tape is played back and/or duplicated.

- Optionally, record or slate a title on the record tape that identifies the programs on the tape and their locations. This will make it easier to find things down the road.

- You may want to record a visual countdown from ten seconds down to two seconds. This is a professional practice that is helpful in situations where the tape will be used in other production or duplication environments.

- Cue the record tape ahead so that there are two seconds of video black after the color bars and/or slate before the actual program material starts.

Cuts-only editing

While most low-budget editing procedures employ a single source deck and a master record deck, there are many variations on a theme and equipment. As a rule, insert editing is recommended in order to eliminate potential glitches at edit points. A rundown of the basic steps in a cuts-only insert edit process follows:

- Select the type of insert edit you wish to make—in this case both audio and video.

- Enter the edit-in point for the source deck—the first frame of the desired scene. This can be accomplished by locating the approximate position and using the jog controls to locate the exact frame. Then use the appropriate button on the edit controller to set or mark the edit-in point for the source deck. Some systems will also allow the edit-in point to be marked "on the fly" while watching the picture.

- Use the same process to enter the edit-out point for the source deck—the last frame of the desired scene.

- Enter the edit-in point for the record deck. When simply cutting segments together, this will usually be the same as the edit-out point for the previously recorded segment.

- Select Preview on the edit controller. The editor will perform a test edit allowing you to preview the edit before committing to it.

- Use the editor's trim controls to adjust any of the edit points, if needed, then preview the edit again. Repeat this step as necessary until the edit looks the way you want.

- Commit to the edit. The appropriate button will be labeled something like Start Edit, Auto-Edit, or Perform.

- If your controller has a Review button, press it to verify the results of the edit that was just made. Otherwise, manually rewind the tape to review the edit.

- Repeat the last eight steps until the desired sequence has been assembled.

There are certainly variations on a theme with the single-source editing process. One is whether the source or master deck is assigned an edit-out point. (An edit-out point need only be specified on one deck.) Consider a situation in which a long segment of someone being interviewed has been laid down. To break things up in the middle of the segment, you wish to cut to a visual example of what the person is talking about while the dialog continues. This can be accomplished with a video-only insert edit over the existing material on the record deck; setting the edit-out point on the record deck rather than the source deck will probably be more intuitive and exacting for this process.

Another variation is the addition of fades as transitions. Fades can be performed during editing by switchers, some inexpensive video enhancers, and even some VCRs. In general, the fade-out begins before the edit-out point and reaches full black at the edit-out point; the fade-in starts from black at the edit-in point of the next segment and makes a transition to full intensity. The exact timing is up to you and your equipment and may require a few trials while previewing the edit. If your equipment does not facilitate fades, many cameras today allow the user to fade in at the beginning of a shot and fade out at the end. Although this is not as flexible as fading during the editing process, fades while shooting source footage are an alternative when carefully planned.

Audio and video can also be inserted separately. Let's say that several video sequences are to be cut together along with a narration that spans all of them. The video segments can be cut together first, then the narration added via an audio insert; alternately, the audio track can be laid down first and the video segments inserted. The order in which you lay audio and video may vary from scene to scene; the element that is most time-critical should be the one that is recorded first.

A simple audio patchbay and/or mixer will help also. The patchbay allows the signals from either channel of the source deck (and other audio sources) to be directed to either channel of the record deck. The mixer will allow the audio from the source deck to be mixed with other sound sources while editing.

A/B roll editing

As described in Chapter 14, A/B roll editing employs two source decks so that two video signals can appear on the screen simultaneously for transition effects such as dissolves. Most A/B roll systems use some form of time code to ensure accuracy. The subject of A/B roll quickly reaches beyond the desktop and into the professional video studio. The following provides an initial frame of reference for using two source decks on the desktop and a perspective on how projects will be fulfilled when taken to a professional post-production facility for on-line work.

There are two basic methods of performing A/B rolls. The *checkerboard editing* approach requires that odd numbered shots and even numbered shots be placed on two different source tapes, respectively. Although this provides for automation in high-end facilities, it incurs a generation loss as the source material is transferred to the intermediate tapes.

Matched frame editing permits the original source tapes to be used. The following listing is an example of how a sequence of dissolves between three shots would be implemented. For sake of example, we'll assume that scenes 1 and 3 are on source deck A and scene 2 is on source deck B. The transition between scene 1 and 2 will be transition 1; the transition between scene 2 and 3 will be transition 2. (See Figure 15.14.)

Figure 15.14

Matched frame editing uses an exact point in a previously edited pass to begin the next edit.

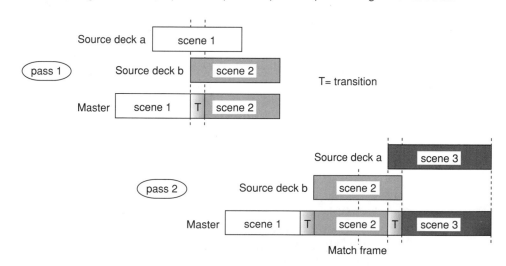

- Enter the edit-in point for the first segment on source deck A.
- Enter the edit-out point for source deck A after the point where transition 1 will be completed.
- Enter the edit-in point for the second segment on source deck B before the intended transition point.
- Enter the edit-out point for source deck B after the point where transition 2 will be completed.
- Enter the edit-in point for the record deck.
- Preview the edit and practice the transition from source deck A to source deck B.
- Perform the edit and transition.
- Review the edit to verify its integrity.
- Locate a frame on the edit master that is after the edit/transition just performed and before the next desired transition point. Enter that frame number as the edit-point for both the record deck and source deck B.
- Enter an edit-out point for source deck B after the next transition.
- Enter an edit-in point for scene 3 on source deck A before the point where transition 2 will begin.
- Enter an edit-out point for source deck A after the point where the next transition will be completed.
- Preview the edit and practice the transition from source deck B to source deck A.
- Perform the edit and transition.
- Review the edit to verify its integrity.

As with cuts-only editing, matched frame editing has many variations. One deck can be used to add a second audio component to the audio coming from the main source tape. (Both signals would be fed to a mixer in order to adjust their relationship.) Alternately, the two source tapes might be playing simultaneously in different areas of the screen. The possibilities are endless.

❖ **Advanced Audio for Video**

As the emphasis on creative aesthetics in productions increases, audio requirements become more sophisticated. Audio sweetening, laybacks, intimate synchronization, and music-video style productions are some of the primary ways in which sound plays a greater role in video production.

Audio and video synchronization

Many of the more advanced uses of audio in video production require that the audio source be synchronized perfectly to the video via time code. (Video is always the master since constant transport speed is integral in preserving the video signal.) If the audio device is a direct-to-disk recorder, it will need to be able to accept time code either directly or via a SMPTE-to-MTC converter. Synchronizing is a fairly straightforward process since the digital audio is random-accessed and playback rates are easily changed on the fly by varying the rate at which data is fed to the DAC.

If the audio source is a tape deck, it will need to have a direct-drive transport and a free track for SMPTE. Most ATRs don't have the onboard electronics to make the decisions about slowing down and speeding up to stay in perfect sync. This is the job of the synchronizer. This little wonder reads and compares SMPTE time code from both master and slave machines to determine if they are maintaining their alignment. If the slave gets ahead of the master, the synchronizer slows the slave down ever so slightly; if the slave is behind, the synchronizer speeds up the slave a bit to compensate. This process, while imperceptible to the operator, is constantly going on behind the scenes.

So far we're talking about syncing via time code alone. Reading SMPTE requires that the heads be in contact with the tape, which is not the case during normal rewind, fast-forward, and auto-location operations. In a code-only sync environment, rewinding or fast-forwarding the master has no analogous effect on the slave. When you play the master, the slave will have to relocate to the proper point before it can lock up—an undesirable trait. For this reason, some synchronizers also read *tach pulses*—sort of a high-speed electronic click track—from both capstans. This allows the slave to roughly follow the master during these transport operations; when normal play resumes, SMPTE once again takes over the synchronization. The term *chase-lock* refers to this highly desirable combination of tach pulses and SMPTE for complete transport synchronization.

Synchronizers come in various flavors. Virtually all perform the functions just described. More advanced units can control the basic transport functions of the master VCR in order to act as central controllers. These units often include auto-location, SMPTE generators, SMPTE-to-MIDI/MTC converters, support for multiple slaves, and programmable switch closures to trigger non-SMPTE devices such as CD players and cart machines. Some synchronizers are modular in design, allowing you to plug in additional circuit cards for these added functions.

Synchronizer-to-deck connections are fairly straightforward since they usually employ multipin connectors. The biggest thing to understand is the concept of programming a SMPTE *offset*. Simply put, the SMPTE numbers in matching sections of your audio and video tape will typically not match up. You must tell the synchronizer what the difference between those numbers is; it will calculate this difference when comparing the SMPTE locations of the two machines during synchronization. For example, let's say you've striped your audio tape starting at 00:00:00, you want to start 10 seconds into the stripe, and the scene you have to score is at 1:05:24 on the video-tape. That means you'll need to program an offset of 00:55:24.

Audio sweetening

Audio sweetening is the process of enhancing the audio during or after the on-line editing process. At it simplest, sweetening involves attenuating the audio of various passages as they are edited in order to ensure level continuity and proper balance. If narration and music are both fairly continuous, levels must be established that allow the narration to be heard clearly above the music. In some upbeat productions, it is sometimes desirable to have the music loud when there is no narration, yet pulled back during narration—a process known as *ducking*.

Other examples of audio sweetening include applying EQ to various audio passages to smooth out tonal differences and ensure tonal continuity. Spatial enhancement such as reverb is often added at this stage as well. In more advanced situations, a multitrack audio deck containing various music, speech, and sound effect tracks can be synchronized so that it follows the same time code as the editor. This allows complex audio elements to be mixed right to one or more audio tracks on the edit master during the editing process.

Audio laybacks

Some complex soundtracks warrant an additional step in assembling the audio components. Let's say that the production needs to include the spoken dialog of people on screen, a well-timed soundtrack, and perfectly timed sound effects. The video segments would be edited together first, with the only audio being the accompanying dialog. When completed, the entire audio track can be transferred to a track of a multitrack audio deck while synchronized to the video via time code. Additional tracks on the multitrack can then be used to compose a soundtrack or transfer one from an existing source. Still other tracks can be used to record specific sound effects and ambient tracks. If the multitrack is synchronized to the time code from the video deck, the additional tracks can be created while viewing their relationship to the picture.

When all elements are intact, they can be mixed to and recorded over the original audio tracks on the edit master, using the same time code for synchronization. (Alternately, they can be mixed to an audio master in the form of a two-track deck, hard disk recorder, or DAT while regenerating time code. The audio master can then be synchronized to the video while being transferred.) The key to either of these audio *layback* processes is perfect synchronization of the audio and video equipment via time code.

Music video considerations

Music video production brings special considerations because any video cut showing performers in action has to be perfectly synchronized with a continuous music track. This dictates that at least a rough mix of the music be produced in advance of the shoot in order for the on-camera talent to have something to perform to. Music-video production also impacts the editing flow: the music track (or a working version) must first be placed on the master videotape, and all of the desired video takes must be edited in perfect sync to that music. While this obviously requires the use of time code, each video take normally will be recorded with time code that is distinct from that of every other take and with no relation to the music. Later in editing, if there's no relationship between the time code associated with each source cut and the time code from the music, the only solution is to get the offset close and tweak it until it looks right.

While some editors have no problem working this way, others prefer more exacting approaches that hinge on establishing a well-defined reference between audio and video elements. The first step is to ensure not only that the music is recorded first, but that the working master has continuous time code. The audio deck being used as a reference during the video shoot must play back at exactly the same rate every time in order to prevent sync problems. On top of that, it must be able to lock onto a video sync signal to ensure proper sync with the video. (Video sync is used as a common "pacemaker" to ensure that all equipment in the shoot is "marching in step" with everything else.) The garden-variety cassette or two-track won't cut it.

The film industry uses Nagras—special crystal-clocked, sync-ready, open-reel decks—due to their conformity to video requirements. A tape recorded on one Nagra will play back at exactly the same speed on all Nagras at all times. Although their purchase price can be prohibitive, Nagras can be rented for shoots in most metropolitan areas.

The other type of machine that will work is the more common servo-controlled open-reel audio deck driven by an external synchronizer that accepts video sync. Although these machines guarantee that a tape will play back at exactly the same rate every time, there's no guarantee that a tape recorded on one servo-controlled deck will play at exactly the same overall speed on another. (While this might not be a problem in some industrial productions, it drives musicians and producers crazy in more musically-oriented projects.)

Several solutions get around the potential speed discrepancy. One is to record the musical passage from the machine on which it was mastered directly to the servo-controlled deck to be used for playback in the video shoot. Another is to use an R-DAT machine as a stable transfer vehicle between machines in different physical locations. (At this writing, R-DATs don't support the combination of external sync and dedicated SMPTE track, so they can't be used as an audio reference during the shoot itself.) Perhaps the simplest solution is to transfer the master audio and its time code to a video deck to be used as a master sync source during the shoot.

So what we wind up with is two SMPTE references—the master time code originating with the audio master that later winds up on the editing master, and the unique field time codes associated with each video take. This means that offsets have to be calculated in order to edit in each cut. The solution is to establish a common reference between the two so that offset calculations are no-brainers. This can be accomplished during the shoot by recording the time code from the music master onto the videotapes in parallel to the time code being originated by the video gear.

The professional way to do this is to route the master code into the user bits of the field code, with the composite signal going to both an LTC address track and/or VITC. This can be accomplished with the time code circuitry of many modern professional video decks; alternately, a SMPTE generator/reader capable of addressing user bits will do the trick. Later in editing, editing gear capable of reading user bits can access the master code from the user bits while syncing via the field code. Establishing an offset is a matter of pushing a button.

A simpler twist that demands less sophisticated equipment is to put the master time code onto an audio track of the VCR during the shoot while the field code goes to an LTC address track and/or VITC. In postproduction, a second SMPTE reader can be used to display the master code from the address track. While this number will have to be entered into the editor by hand, an offset can still be established without trial and error.

Finally, all audio and video gear must be driven by a common video sync generator during the shoot. For each video take, locate the audio deck to a point at least five seconds before the shot you want, start audio playback, then begin video recording.

❖ Editing Aesthetics

Like everything else in video, directing and editing is an ongoing learning experience even for professionals. In fact, the creative aesthetics of video editing can vary dramatically with genre, content, and purpose. Nonetheless, the most important thing that all video productions share is consideration of overall audience impact. Does the story flow? Does the overall effect engage the audience on an emotional level? Does the pacing hold the viewers' interest? Is there continuity in style? Is the production process invisible?

Many of the following video editing checkpoints directly reinforce the concept of getting the best footage in the field in the first place. Careful attention to the proposed editing process and desired production results will drive the type of footage that is acquired. This is a much better solution than letting the footage dictate what is possible and what is not in the editing phase!

Edit for continuity

Editing for continuity might be described as the process of making the audience feel comfortable and normal. The surroundings, directional orientation, subject, and mood are not only known, but carried through so that attention is focused on the message rather than distracted with questions. Establishing shots (typically medium or long shots) are traditionally used at the beginning of a new scene to show the audience where you are taking them. Then, when editing from an establishing shot to a close-up, for example, the inclusion of a medium shot will smooth the change in distance and ensure that the subject's identity is maintained across it.

This style of editing is aptly named *continuity editing*. There is a case for breaking these rules of continuity called *dynamic editing*. Dynamic editing is intended to shake the audience up through spatial distortions (such as the use of unusual camera positions and angles) and temporal distortion (such as parallel occurrences, flashbacks, and premonitions). Dynamic editing is primarily used in artistic and dramatic productions.

Ensure vector continuity

Continuity in angles and vectors is also important. If two people are facing one another in a two-shot, for example, the individuals should appear at the same angles during close-ups. As mentioned in the section on good composition, a shot of someone looking or pointing off screen should be followed by a shot of the object in question—a shot from the viewing angle of the person in the previous shot.

Edit with a reason

Just as the camera should only be moved for a reason, the scene should only be edited for a reason. Good reasons include focusing on the various people speaking in a conversation, breaking up a boring scene, and following a vector off scene to its target. Cutting to another shot just because you haven't done so for some arbitrary period of time is not.

Include only the necessary footage

One of the reasons why home movies are so stigmatized is that—due to lack of editing—the viewer is usually subjected to everything that happened. Although this is an extreme example, even edited video can often seem long and drawn out. Today's audience has a very short attention span. Always ask yourself if the message can be communicated with less—less overall footage, and less of any given scene.

Avoid jump cuts and matched cuts

As mentioned earlier, jump cuts occur when two segments of videotape are edited together in such a way that the camera position changes too radically without a transitory position. If you must edit between two scenes that are only slightly different, the dreaded jump cut can be avoided by editing to a cutaway shot as a buffer.

Similarly, unwanted *matched cuts* occur when the camera remains stationary between edited segments, yet the subject moves. This occurs most often when editing together only the salient portions of a single-camera interview. The best solution here is to employ some form of artsy transition that masks the jump.

Avoid talking heads

Excessive and unfocused dialog combined with heads-only speaker shots is commonly reffered to as *talking heads*. Footage of this kind is boring and should be avoided as much as possible. Plan to capture a variety of interesting footage during the shooting process, such as different positions and angles, audience reactions, and so forth. If this isn't possible, search for other devices to cut to, such as video graphics or stock footage that reinforce and illustrate the points being made.

Edit motion carefully

Footage containing motion has special considerations. When editing footage containing a moving subject from two positions, edit during the motion rather than before or after. This provides for greater interest and better flow. When doing so, make certain that the camera remains on the same side of the perceived subject/audience axis to ensure that the motion is perceived as having the same direction. If the only available shots break this rule, use a cutaway as a buffer.

Avoid editing between scenes with different color temperatures

If various scenes have been shot under different lighting circumstances and therefore have different color temperatures, try to cut regularly only between scenes with the same temperature. These differences are natural when moving from indoors to outdoors, for example, but can be distracting otherwise.

Use sound effects to establish locale and continuity

A wide variety of sounds form part of our daily experience. Extending them to the video soundtrack can heighten reality. Ambient tracks can help not only to establish realism, but to lend continuity. Let's say that you've got a long shot on the edge of a woods, a close-up of an animal that is your subject—and no medium shot. Although cutting away to a shot of the sky will help, the addition of a constant ambient track of chirping crickets and birds will help smooth everything together with continuity.

Use music that reinforces the mood

Choosing the right music can make or break a video production. Criteria for choosing music are discussed in Chapter 12.

Edit rhythmically

If upbeat music is the unifying factor in a production or segment, record the music first and cut on the beat. This extends the musical rhythm to the entire experience. When slower musical passages are a driving force, slow dissolves often complement the effect.

Edit for pacing

Good editors are always aware of pacing. On a localized level, certain types of subjects dictate the duration of associated shots. The fast action of a car chase dictates faster cuts than the tranquility of a babbling brook, for example. On the broader scale of the entire production, the pacing should change so that there are peaks and valleys in the action. This provides contrast, emotion, and greater interest. Also, be careful not to provide the big peak too soon: boredom quickly sets in if everything else is downhill. Conversely, a carrot must often be dangled that piques and maintains the viewers' interest as you are building to the most important part of the message.

Employ continuity in transitions

While an A/B roll environment provides a wide variety of transition effects, haphazard use of them becomes disorienting and intrusive. In most cases, a single type of transition with its variations on a theme lend the proper continuity.

❖ Designing and Integrating Video Graphics

Graphics and titles are also added at the postproduction stage. In some situations, especially static computer-based images, the output of the computer's NTSC encoder can be fed directly into the line input of the source deck and passed on to the record deck without the generation loss associated from transferring the graphics to tape. In situations where timing is more critical, such as a real-time animation, the graphics will usually have to be transferred to a videotape so that they can be integrated more effectively into the editing environment.

Many of the concepts that apply to creating computer-based graphics and titling have already been discussed in previous chapters. A review of Chapter 9 will provide insight on innovative design and typography. Chapter 14 addresses some of the technical issues in converting noninterlaced RGB signals to interlaced NTSC signals. A few of those concepts are worth reiterating in conjunction with a few new ones.

Avoid single-pixel lines

Due to the interlaced nature of video, a single pixel in a scanline of one field will flicker if not matched by a corresponding pixel on the next scanline in the opposite field. Lines with a height of two pixels or greater should therefore always be used.

Video Editing Tips

- Establish and stick with a style of continuity editing or dynamic editing.
- Ensure continuity through establishing shots, vectors, transitions, sound, and color temperature.
- Edit with a reason and include only necessary footage.
- Avoid jump cuts, matched cuts, and talking heads.
- Edit with pace and rhythm in mind.
- Edit during motion rather than before or after.
- Use sound effects to establish locale, and music to communicate mood.

Restrict text to the safe titling area

The overscanned video image not only extends past the visible portion of the picture tube, but the degree to which it does so varies from television to television. As a result, portions of the image, such as titles that have a comfortable margin in relation to the edge of the screen on a production monitor, may seem tighter or even extend off of the screen when viewed on another monitor. This has led video professionals to restrict titling and other important graphic elements to the *safe titling area*—the central 80 percent of the screen. In other words, leave at least 10 percent on all sides as a margin—preferably a little more.

Use large font sizes

NTSC is considerably muddier than RGB. Use font sizes that are at least 18 points, preferably 24 points. Smaller fonts are difficult to read on video monitors and often are illegible on standard televisions driven by standard VCRs. If serifed fonts are used, pick ones with slab or similarly thick serifs that do not result in single pixels on a horizontal line.

Restrict the palette to NTSC-legal colors

Since the color gamuts of NTSC and 24-bit RGB do not completely overlap, the color palette for video work should be restricted to those that NTSC can display accurately. In general, NTSC oversaturates very easily, causing colors to bleed into adjacent areas of the image. Bright red is the worst offender, with bright blue a close second. (Other colors, notably purple, are difficult to translate to exactly the same hue.) Use the HSV or similar color space to restrict the saturation values of all colors in the image to a maximum of 85 percent to 90 percent. High-contrast colors in adjacent areas of an image should also be avoided where possible, since these quick changes are difficult for video electronics to represent accurately. Some graphics and media integration programs come with optional palettes specifically designed for video, and some image processors can filter the colors of any image to be NTSC-legal.

Don't rely on exact colors for user interaction

The colors in an NTSC video cannot be guaranteed to reproduce identically on every monitor. It is therefore recommended that the user interface not rely on things like "push the red button" since it may appear as orange or pink! Instead, user interface choices should be primarily distinguished by text or graphic content.

Conduct NTSC tests during design

When creating computer graphics and titles that will be used with video, use an NTSC encoder to test how the colors and safe titling area appear on the video monitor. This is obviously a much better time to uncover any problems than when you are actually in the editing process.

❖ Stock Footage

Just as clip art, stock photography, and music libraries help save time and money in other media, *stock footage* of existing film and video are also available for licensing. Most firms specialize in certain types of imagery—everything from vintage newsreels to underwater scenes to feature films. Some offer a one-time buyout with unlimited rights, while others have per-use charges. Most TV networks and film studios have offices that handle licensing of their productions. You can even license scenes from *Top Gun* to promote a product or service if you have enough money!

❖ ❖ ❖ ❖ ❖ ❖

This chapter concludes our discussion of video. Producing compelling moving imagery that tells a story or communicates a message is an art form as old as the first motion picture and as new as tomorrow. The best way to learn is to take the guidelines presented here as a starting point for your own explorations and to use them to see the work of masters from Hitchcock to Spielberg—and from CNN to MTV—through new eyes. The next section examines one of the most important driving forces in multimedia communication—media integration.

Media Integration

While graphics, animation, sound, and video have all come to the desktop in their own right, their true power lies in their integration and interactive user control. These two factors have largely defined the term *desktop multimedia*. The ability to distribute the massive amounts of data associated with these technologies is closely related to proliferation of the genre.

Chapter 16 examines the optical technologies associated with interactive media such as CD-ROM and laserdiscs. Chapter 17 discusses the hardware tools that use these technologies and the software applications that are used to integrate the various media into cohesive productions. Chapter 18 covers some of the production processes involved in integrating media. ❖

Optical Technologies

Magnetic media such as hard drives and floppy disks are certainly interactive. Optical media are gaining more and more importance since they can store massive amounts of data in a form that is durable, inexpensive to duplicate, and easily distributable. This chapter focuses on the CD-ROM and laserdisc technologies that are helping to spearhead the multimedia market. The information provided here is by no means complete in its technical detail—such documents are several feet thick! Instead, the information provides a synopsis designed to help take some of the mystery out of the various optical formats and their practical differences.

CAV AND CLV

Rotating media operate in two basic methods—CLV and CAV. Both methods operate on the principle that, given a fixed disk rotation speed, concentric or spiral tracks go by the record and/or play head faster toward the center of a disk and slower toward the outside. Both are used in computer media and have their advantages and disadvantages.

❖ CAV

CAV (constant angular velocity) is the standard method by which the medium rotates at a constant speed. A record player is an example of CAV technology. CAV is also used in most floppy disks and hard disks. One advantage is less technology is required to keep a motor running at a constant speed than continuously regulating the speed to compensate for head position. Another is that any data can be accessed almost instantly by simply repositioning the head over the associated track and waiting for the desired sector to rotate under the head. The disadvantage to CAV is that the much greater physical area of the outside tracks can hold only the same amount of data as the smallest inner track—it's just spread out to compensate for the constant rotation speed.

❖ **CLV**

CLV (constant linear velocity) directly addresses the storage deficiency of CAV technology by adjusting the motor speed to compensate for the head position. By rotating more slowly toward the outer tracks and writing at the same speed, each track can hold the maximum amount of data. In the bigger picture, a great deal more data can be stored with CLV than with CAV. Part of this scheme involves recording the data in a stream on a continuous spiral track, with addressing in minutes, seconds, and sectors. This system is great for continuous audio or video tracks. Unfortunately, it's bad news for random-access applications that call for locating specific computer data or images. The best a CLV system can do is position the head approximately, change motor speed accordingly, then read an address and make positioning adjustments until the exact address is found. The trade-off for greatly enhanced storage capability, then, is painfully slow access time.

COMPACT DISC TECHNOLOGY AND FORMATS

The amount of digital data required to represent significant content—such as audio, photorealistic images, and graphics—quickly pushes the limitations of any storage media. The additional requirements of random-access and mass distribution have spawned rapid advancements in optical media. One popular result has been the *compact disc* (CD). It weighs next to nothing, is relatively impervious to physical abuse, can be mass-produced at prices around one or two dollars, and delivers up to 74 minutes of high-quality audio, or more than 500MB of digital data.

As a result, CD technology in its various forms is one of the driving forces behind multimedia production and consumer acceptance. One of the reasons for this success is the joint definition of standards by Philips and Sony. Although the most familiar incarnation is the audio CD that has taken the consumer electronics market by storm, CD-ROM is gaining rapid acceptance with computer users, and CD-I represents the move toward stand-alone interactive products for home, education, and business. The various implementations of CD technology are referenced by the colors of the documentation binders defining them and will be discussed shortly. First, let's review the many facets these standards have in common with one another.

❖ Common Technology

All CD-based media work on the basic optical media principles described in Chapter 2 and on the CLV technology described at the beginning of this chapter. CDs share a common physical format—a 120 mm disc with a 15 mm center hole and 1.2 mm thickness—that allows any CD to physically fit into any CD drive. (It also allows all CDs to be stored and shipped in the standard plastic *jewel case* like those your audio CDs come in.) The information takes the form of pits in a transparent medium that adheres to a strict index of refraction—typically polycarbonate plastic in mass-produced versions and glass in the master. The pitted surface is covered with an extremely thin layer of aluminum to add reflectivity, then a protective plastic film onto which the label is printed. The laser in the player reads the reflective pits on the non-label side of the spinning disc.

The area from the outer circumference to the center of the disc is subdivided for specific purposes. The innermost 6 mm around the center hole is the *clamping area* the drive mechanism uses to keep a firm hold on the disc and does not contain data. Next comes a *lead-in* area approximately 4 mm wide that contains the *VTOC* (volume table of contents) for the disc. The next 33 mm contains the program data on one long spiral of approximately 20,000 iterations. (The tracks evolve from the inner portion of the disc out toward the edge.) A 1 mm *lead-out* area signifies the end of the disc. A 3 mm area around the edge is reserved for handling and contains no data. (See Figure 16.1.)

Data encoding

The surface of a CD consists of *pits* (which actually look like bumps to the laser) and *lands*—the normal surface level between pits. The laser beam striking a land area is reflected into a photosensor, representing a form of "on" state. When the laser strikes a pit, the light is scattered in such a way that it does not reflect in the photosensor; this essentially turns the photosensor off to represent a form of "off" state.

Figure 16.1

The physical structure of a compact disc.

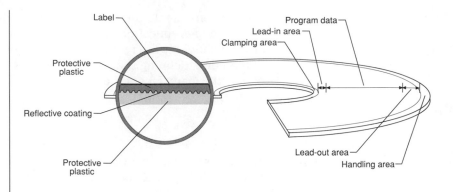

The pits and lands themselves do not represent actual on/off bit data as one might expect. The transitions between pits and lands and the associated timing represent *channel bits*. Fourteen channel bits make up a data symbol that translates to a traditional 8-bit data value. This system incorporates data redundancy that provides for greater accuracy. The process of encoding 8-bit data values to 14-bit channel values to create the pits and lands during the mastering process is called *eight-to-fourteen modulation* (EFM). The ROM in each CD player contains a lookup table that reverses the process to decode the modulated data.

Frames and blocks

Data on a CD is organized in groups of channel bits called *frames*. Each frame can contain either 24 bytes of computer data or twelve 16-bit audio samples (six stereo samples). In addition to the 14 channel bits for each of these bytes, a frame also contains 24 channel bits for synchronization, 14 channel bits for each of eight 8-bit error correction parity words, 14 channel bits of an 8-bit control and display word, and the three *merge bits* separating each data symbol—a total of 588 channel bits.

Groups of 98 frames are called blocks in CD audio and sectors in CD-ROM and CD-I. The block or sector is the smallest addressable unit in CD technology. There are 75 blocks or sectors for every second of CD rotation, yielding a total of 7,350 frames per second.

Error correction

Although optical media is one the most reliable and impervious methods of storing data, errors can occur during the manufacturing process and from severe damage to the disc surface. CDs therefore employ a form of error correction called *CIRC* (Cross Interleaved Reed-Solomon Code). CIRC combines three types of error correction methods. Although you don't need to know the gory details, here's a brief overview. *Cross-coding* rearranges the bits out of sequence according to a key during encoding, then uses the key on playback to arrange the bits back in the original order. This scatters the effects of longer errors throughout the data, leaving the gist of the information largely intelligible when decoded. Another attempt at minimizing large errors—*interleaving*—delays data for a fixed period of time during encoding before intermixing it with the data stream and reverses the process during decoding on playback. Finally, *Reed-Solomon coding* is optimized to correct small anomalies that commonly result from a scratched disc.

Subcode channels

The *control and display word* for each channel consists of 14 channel bits that translate to 8 data bits. Each of the eight data bits corresponds to a *subcode channel* described with the letters P through W. The information in a given subcode channel is encoded as a stream of single bits, each control and display word throughout the frame carrying a set of single bits for each channel. A block of subcode data for each channel is 98 bits long, thereby spanning 98 frames. The first two bits of the data stream for each subcode channel are always used as synchronization bits; the remaining 96 can be used in various ways for data.

Channels R through W can be defined by various permutations of the CD specification. The *P channel* represents a *music channel separator flag*. (Don't worry about this one!) The 98-bit stream of a *Q channel* block has its own well-defined architecture: The first two bits are the standard sync bits. Another four control bits specify the number of audio channels, type of data on the track, copy protection (allowing or disallowing a consumer DAT recorder to make a digital copy, for example), and audio pre-emphasis setting. The 4-bit *ADR flag* describes which mode the subsequent 72 data bits use. Finally, the last 16 bits are used for CRC error detection for the channel data. (See Figure 16.2.)

The ADR flag signals one of three basic methods of using the 72 data bits in the Q channel. Q-channel Mode 1 (the most common) is used to hold the absolute time, playing time, and selection number that appears on the front-panel display of an audio CD player, as well as the data address in the form of minutes, seconds, and data block or sector. Q-channel Mode 2 uses the Q channel to represent the catalog number in the UPC/EAN standard format used internationally for bar-coding products. Similarly, Q-channel Mode 3 identifies the product uniquely in the format of the *ISRC* (International Standard Recording Code).

Figure 16.2

Each block of the Q subcode channel has a standard format.

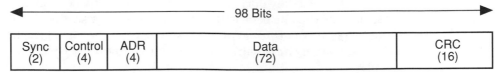

Tracks

Although the program area of a CD actually contains one long physical track, it is logically organized into anywhere from 1 to 99 tracks. A given track can only contain one type of information, such as digital audio or computer data, but different tracks can contain different types of data.

❖ CD-DA (Red Book)

CD technology as a whole was initially developed for audio. The standard CD audio player found in the home relies on the *Red Book* standard. These CDs are formally known as *CD-DA* (as in digital audio). The features common to all CD technologies outlined so far in this chapter were developed as part of the Red Book specification. The only missing ingredient is that the data take the form of stereo 16-bit audio using PCM encoding at a 44.1KHz sampling rate.

The Nyquist theorem dictates that 20KHz frequency response requires a sampling rate of at least 40KHz, but the reason for the exact specification of 44.1KHz may seem a bit elusive. An intimate understanding of CD technology solves the mystery. Twenty-four 8-bit symbols per frame yield twelve 16-bit stereo samples—six for the left channel and six for the right. Six samples per frame multiplied by 98 frames per block times 75 blocks per second yield 44,100 samples per second per channel—44.1KHz!

The CD+Graphics addendum

The original Red Book specification did not utilize subcode channels R through W and set the values of their data streams to zero. This translated to more than 24MB of wasted space on an audio CD. Several addenda were made to the specification that define their use for *CD+Graphics*. The intended application of CD Graphics was to display still images while the music played. A separate subcode output on the CD player is required to access the CD Graphics.

Suggested uses ranged from multilingual text, electronic sheet music, and album graphics on separate channels. Unfortunately, the maximum image resolution of 288 x 192 in 16 colors (combined with the seven seconds required to assemble an image) left audiences flat—with the exception of words for the karaoke sing-along phenomenon in Japan. Manufacturers dropped the added expense of subcode jacks for models intended for distribution in the West, effectively sealing the fate of CD+Graphics.

❖ CD-ROM (Yellow Book)

CD technology was quickly seen as a storage medium for large amounts of any type of digital data, not just sound. Sony and Philips were quick to introduce the *Yellow Book* specification for *CD-ROM* (Compact Disc-Read Only Memory) that is essentially a superset of the Red Book standard. The significant differences are use of the data areas for information other than digital audio and more stringent error correction routines. The overall Yellow Book specification is also much more open-ended than its audio-only relative. It specifies the method by which bits are encoded, as well as their organization into frames and sectors. Methods of organizing sectors into logical blocks of information, as well as how those logical blocks are accessed by the filing system, are left open to interpretation.

Data encoding

Just as in Red Book, EFM is used to encode information into frames—here strictly twenty-four 8-bit data bytes. The data streams of subcode channels R through W are not used and are set to zero. Although the grouping of 98 frames into blocks is only important with regard to subcode channels in CD-DA, CD-ROM technology uses the 98-frame block or sector implicitly to record and access data. A little arithmetic shows that 24 bytes per frame multiplied by 98 frames yield 2,352 bytes per sector. A sector always begins with a 12-byte sync field and a 4-byte header field containing the sector address in minutes:seconds:sector. Sectors are addressed sequentially, typically on a single track that runs the length of the CD-ROM. (The first sector is 00:00:00, the next sector is 00:00:01, and so forth. The next sector after 00:00:74 would be 00:01:00.) The first three seconds of each sector are reserved and may not be used for user data.

Modes 1 and 2

The header also contains a *mode byte* describing how the remaining 2,336-byte data portion of the sector is to be used. *Mode 1* provides 2,048 user bytes along with 288 bytes employed for additional error correction. A method called *EDC/ECC* (Error Detection Coding/Error Correction Coding) is used on top of the standard CIRC method. (The CIRC error-correction used in CD-DA is fine for audio where a few bits won't be missed, but additional measures are required to ensure the integrity of most computer data.)

Mode 2 adds no error correction, thus providing the full 2,336 user bytes per sector. As a rule, Mode 1 is used in most regular CD-ROMs. Mode 2 was quickly expanded into the CD-I Green Book specification discussed later in this chapter.

The two modes also differ in effective storage capacity and data retrieval speed. While a CD-DA is capable of holding 74 minutes of audio, manufacturers often have problems recording more than 60 minutes of data accurately. Sixty minutes multiplied by 60 seconds per minute times 75 sectors per second therefore yields a total practical limit of 270,000 sectors. At 2,048 user bytes per sector, Mode 1 can store 552,960,000 bytes (527MB) and read data at a rate of 153,600 bytes (150K) per second. Mode 2 calculates to 630,720,000 bytes (601MB) of storage with a fixed data rate of 175,200 bytes (171K) per second.

Mixed mode CDs

The term *mixed mode* is used in two different ways with regard to CDs. One usage refers to a disc that contains both audio and data tracks. Since the Yellow Book spec is built on that of Red Book, this is certainly possible. Track 1 is typically the data track, and the audio tracks start at Track 2. A CD-ROM track begins with a dead space called a *pregap* if it is preceded by a CD-DA track and ends with a *postgap* if succeeded by a CD-DA track.

The other reference to mixed mode (generally considered the more proper one) describes a disc that has both Mode 1 and Mode 2 formats on it. There can only be one mode for any given track.

High Sierra

As indicated earlier, the Yellow Book standard ensures uniformity at the levels of data encoding/decoding and frame and sector architecture—however, the higher level methods by which computer operating systems access this information is left open. Once again the issue of platform cross-compatibility (or lack thereof) rears its ugly head. The path of least resistance would be to extend an operating system from a platform such as Macintosh HFS, DOS, or AmigaDOS to the CD. Indeed, that is often the case with the aid of software drivers in the host machine that know how to deal with the differences between traditional track/sector architecture and the minutes:seconds:sector system of CD-ROM. Unfortunately, this makes a CD-ROM accessible only to that one system.

Shortly after the announcement of the Yellow Book standard, representatives from a handful of key manufacturers gathered at a resort in the Sierra Nevada mountains for the purpose of developing a common method of organizing files and indexes so that they can be accessed universally. This successful effort was named *High Sierra* for obvious reasons. High Sierra standardizes the organization and positioning of a universal VTOC. Moreover, the VTOC holds information representing the direct path to each file to avoid having to search and navigate through layers of directories—an especially painstaking task at CD-ROM speeds. High Sierra also provides for multiple CD-ROMs to act as multiple volumes within a set, enabling even more massive amounts of information to be accessed.

The result is that if a host computer has a driver that can translate between the native disk operating system and the High Sierra standard, any file on a High Sierra CD-ROM can be located and accessed. The data within a file itself must still be in a form that is compatible with a given application in order for the contents to mean anything. In other words, a text file in the universal ASCII format poses no problem to multiple platforms; a PC graphics application still won't know what to make of an image in Macintosh PICT format, however. For this reason, many CD-ROMs in High Sierra format that contain things like image libraries actually contain duplicate images in a variety of popular formats.

ISO 9660

High Sierra's success led to its submission to the *ISO* (International Standards Organization)—a body that does just what its name implies. A few minor changes were made and the resulting *ISO 9660* specification was released as a worldwide standard. As with High Sierra, the inclusion of a simple ISO 9660 software driver in the host operating system allows that system to access files in any ISO 9660 CD-ROM. The same caveats apply to compatibility between data files and applications.

❖ CD-I
(Green Book)

The problems of disparate operating systems and file formats, not to mention proper hardware like display adapters and audio cards, led Philips and Sony to release the *Green Book* specification for *CD-I*

479

(Compact Disc-Interactive). The specification for CD-I media is directly tied to the specification for a standard CD-I player. According to this specification, a CD-I player must have the following:

- a 16-bit 68000-based microprocessor
- RTOS operating system
- a CD-ROM drive with PCM decoder and DAC capable of handling CD-DA audio
- 1MB RAM minimum with expansion capabilities
- a video processor for decoding and displaying graphics in various formats
- an audio processor for decoding various audio formats
- a user input device

RTOS operating system

RTOS (Real-Time Operating System) is a derivative of the OS9/68000 operating system. The use of a standard operating system ensures that all CD-I discs can be accessed by all CD-I players. (All files to be used with CD-I must be created in or converted to files that are accessible by RTOS.) The real-time aspect handles the special needs of synchronizing and prioritizing the graphics, text, audio, video, and data associated with multimedia.

CD-I sound

Like all CD devices, CD-I players can play standard audio CD-DAs without ceremony. The CD-I system itself, however, supports six types of digital audio formats—three quality levels in either mono or stereo. All employ *ADPCM* (Adaptive Delta Pulse Code Modulation)—a technique that encodes audio according to changes between amplitude values rather than the absolute values. As such, fewer bits are required to convey a given quality of audio. *Level A audio* offers approximately the quality of an LP and requires about half the data as Red Book audio. *Level B audio* is equivalent to the best FM broadcasts. *Level C audio* offers quality similar to the average portable cassette deck.

The trade-off of sound quality versus data storage and throughput requirements is helpful when balancing the other media needs in an audiovisual production. A total of 16 channels of 72 minutes each is available for use by the various formats, although using the full capacity leaves no storage for other data. These can be used for anything from 2 hours of stereo Level A audio to 19 hours of relatively continuous Level C audio to 16 discrete narration tracks

Table 16.1. *CD-I provides for various trade-offs in audio quality and storage.*

Audio level	Resolution	Sampling rate	Bandwidth	Concurrent channels	Storage for 1 minute of stereo
CD-DA	16-bit	44.1KHz	20KHz	2 stereo	10.09MB
CD-I Level A	8-bit	37.8KHz	17KHz	2 stereo, 4 mono	4.33MB
CD-I Level B	4-bit	37.8KHz	17KHz	4 stereo, 8 mono	2.16MB
CD-I Level C	4-bit	18.9KHz	8.5KHz	8 stereo, 16 mono	1.08MB

in different languages. Higher levels employ several channels simultaneously. (See Table 16.1.)

CD-I video

CD-I players include composite video outputs. Three video formats are provided for graphic display—NTSC, PAL, and a *compatible* format that is designed to be interpreted by either of the other two formats. Unfortunately, images in the compatible format will appear slightly stretched along the vertical axis when displayed on NTSC, while appearing slightly squashed on PAL systems. Thus, the compatible format is best reserved for only those productions that demand international content.

Several forms and resolutions of imagery are available. (See Table 16.2.) Although full-screen, full-motion video is not possible at this writing, several workarounds permit reduced-quality motion video and run-length encoded animation at respectable frame rates. Photorealistic images can be encoded using *DYUV* (Delta-YUV—a version of YUV that tracks changes between adjacent pixels rather than absolute values). Direct RGB format with five bits per channel (32,768 colors) and color look-up tables of up to eight bits (any 256 colors) are also available for images. Transitions such as wipes, fades, scrolls, and partial screen updates are also available.

The Green Book also provides for a backdrop plane that can be used for an unspecified video source, a background graphics plane, a foreground graphics plane, and a cursor plane. The ability to use distinct graphics planes for specific purposes opens many possibilities for creative expression in developing content. Character set bitmaps and support of standard 7-bit ASCII and 8-bit international character sets are also included.

Table 16.2. *CD-I offers a choice of several video resolutions.*

Video	Normal resolution	High resolution
NTSC	360 X 240	720 X 480
PAL	384 X 280	768 X 460
Compatible	384 X 280	768 X 460

Forms and tracks

Recall that the Yellow Book specification provides Mode 1 for extra error-checking of computer data and Mode 2 without error-checking for audiovisual data that can survive the occasional loss of bits. CD-I is, in effect, an extension of CD-ROM Mode 2. (In fact, pure ASCII text files in Mode 2 High Sierra CD-ROMs can often be accessed by CD-I players.) The same error-correction issues come into play. CD-I, however, has a heavy emphasis on integrated media that makes it desirable to interleave data such as error-sensitive text and less-sensitive audio on the same track—and the spec dictates only one mode per track. Hence, the development of CD-I Mode 2 Forms 1 and 2. *Form 1* provides the same 2,048 bytes of user data per sector as CD-ROM Mode 1, complete with the same EDC/ECC error correction. *Form 2* offers no error correction and is similar to CD-ROM Mode 2 except that eight fewer bytes are sacrificed to a header—a total of 2,328 bytes of user data per sector.

CD-I discs have only one track of Mode 2 data—Track 0. (This track could span the whole disc if necessary.) Different sectors can have various types of data, some of which can be designated as normal (sent to RAM) and some of which can be designated as real-time (prioritized and interleaved). A CD-I disc can also incorporate CD-DA tracks beginning with Track 0.

❖ CD-ROM XA

One of the banes of developing multimedia CD-ROMs for computers is that while the content often demands sound and visual imagery simultaneously, the computer's microprocessor can only access one type of data at a time. Consequently, the graphics are loaded into RAM first, then the audio is located, and finally the graphics are displayed while the audio plays back. The processor is extremely busy during all of this and glitches between the audio and visuals often result. Extensive use of audio can bring up storage issues, even on a CD-ROM.

CD-ROM XA (Extended Architecture) was developed in part to overcome these problems. It is essentially an extension of the Yellow Book CD-ROM standard with ISO 9660 compatibility that incorporates elements from CD-I such as Mode 2 Forms 1 and 2 for interleaving data and Level B and Level C ADPCM audio. CD-ROM XA drives contain dedicated chips that can decompress the ADPCM audio as well as access and synchronize audio and visual data that is written to the disk in interleaved form. This removes the task of synchronization from the microprocessor and the burden of pre-loaded graphics from system RAM, while providing smoother integration of audio and visuals. As an added advantage, the use of compressed audio requires less space on the CD. It also provides developers with a partial bridge between the CD-ROM and CD-I markets.

❖ CD-R (Orange Book)

For the most part, CDs have been mastered at service bureaus and then mass-duplicated for distribution. Machines capable of writing to CD-ROMs are plummeting in price, however. The *Orange Book* specification for *CD-R* (Compact Disc-Recordable) was recently introduced as a guideline for standardizing the process of creating discs that don't require the mastering process. (CD-R is also known as CD-Writable.) CD-R discs can be written so that they are compatible with CD-DA, CD-ROM, and/or CD-ROM XA players.

One of the major challenges addressed by the Orange Book spec is the fact that the files and VTOCs of previous CDs were cast in stone. Even if additional data could be written to another area of the disk, the master directory could not be updated to provide access to it. Orange Book offers *multisession* abilities—the option of writing data to different parts of the disc at different times. (See Figure 16.3.) You might think of it as a bridge from the original VTOC that looks to another area of the disk to see if a second VTOC exists as a result of more information having been written in a later session.

Figure 16.3

The relationship of the various CD specifications..

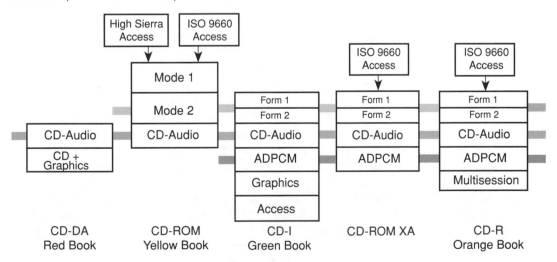

❖ Kodak Photo CD

Although CD-I has been around for several years, consumers have not been stampeding to buy it. Eastman Kodak hopes to change this lack of interest with their introduction of *Photo CD*. The main purpose of Photo CD is to place photographs on a compact disc and allow consumers to view them on home television screens with a special Photo CD player. (Philips CD-I players can also play Photo CDs.) Mode 2 CD-ROM drives and drivers that can access Photo CDs via desktop computers also allow these images to be used for tasks such as desktop publishing, multimedia development, and presentations.

Photo CDs are mastered at Kodak service bureaus around the country from negatives or 35mm slides via CD-R technology. The CDs are delivered in a jewel case along with a sheet of printed thumbnails that serves as an index for the images. (You get the developed slides or photos back as well.) Color thermal prints can also be ordered from these facilities. Each image is provided in an *Image Pac* that actually contains versions in the following resolutions:

- a thumbnail for preview purposes (128 lines x 192 pixels)
- a low-resolution snapshot for purposes such as experimental manipulation and FPO (for placement only) in desktop publishing (256 lines x 384 pixels)
- a medium-resolution version designed for display on televisions (512 lines x 768 pixels)
- an HDTV version (1024 lines x 1536 pixels)
- a high-resolution version for image manipulation and printing (2048 x 3072 pixels)

Photo CD utilizes CD-Writable technology and stores images in Kodak's proprietary *Photo YCC* format. Since this process employs compression based (in part) on eliminating redundancy, the amount of disc space required for an Image Pac depends upon the image content. The average Image Pac takes between 3MB and 6MB, so the average Photo CD will hold about 100 Image Pacs. The cost is approximately one dollar per image—a significant improvement over traditional drum scans for publishing work. Photo CDs are multisession, so images can be added until the media is full. Kodak records the first session in ISO 9660 format so that most Mode 2 CD-ROM drives can access the images; drives must support multisession formats in order to be able to access images from subsequent sessions. Kodak supplies drivers to facilitate access by Mac and PC, and many major hardware and software manufacturers are embracing the Photo CD technology.

At this writing, Kodak is still developing the ability to scan existing print images and accept digital data. Also announced but not delivered is the ability for multimedia producers to add sound, graphics, and interactivity to the medium. When these plans are fulfilled, Photo CD promises to be a powerful multimedia development and presentation tool at the least. If accepted by the consumer market, it could also open a whole new market for multimedia titles. The only caveat is that Photo CD players at this writing do not have the computing power of CD-I and other products vying for the consumer market such as CDTV.

LASERDISC TECHNOLOGY

The 12-inch laserdisc paralleled videotape in the race for acceptance as the household video media standard. VCRs won, primarily because they offered the user the ability to record television programming and camera input. Laserdiscs have been kept alive by the interactive training needs of corporations, government, and the military, and perseverance has led to greater acceptance in today's consumer market.

Indeed, laserdiscs have several advantages over videotape. For openers, the image quality is superior. NTSC still has its shortcomings, but the optical media offers none of the degradation associated with magnetic tape. Equally important, the media does not wear noticeably with repeated use. Still-frame images are crystal-clear and rock-solid during pause operations. Perhaps most importantly, the random-access technology involved allows for almost instantaneous access to properly indexed image or segment.

The combination of these factors makes laserdisc technology a very useful component of multimedia systems such as kiosks and training stations. The video output can be integrated with computer images in several ways: viewed on a dedicated monitor, on the computer screen via a video-in-a-window adapter, or by overlaying computer graphics on an NTSC monitor. The serial control ports on most industrial laserdisc players provide a method by which computers can access the appropriate information.

Laserdiscs operate on the same basic optical technology ascribed to CD technology earlier in this chapter, although rotation speed is significantly higher. Both sides of a laserdisc can be encoded with data. The pits and lands instead translate to FM signals that represent the video signal. Beyond that, laserdiscs fall into two basic categories—CAV and CLV.

❖ CAV Laserdiscs

CAV laserdiscs employ the constant angular velocity technology described at the beginning of this chapter. There are 54,000 tracks in a continuous spiral on a laserdisc, each taking one complete rotation and containing the two fields of a single video frame. The disc rotates at 1800 rpm to achieve the NTSC standard of 30 frames per second. One side of a 12-inch CAV laserdisc therefore contains at total of 54,000 frames—30 minutes of video.

Control functions

CAV offers *frame search* (the ability to locate any single frame immediately) and *stop motion* (the ability to freeze any frame indefinitely by simply repeating the track). This alone is very powerful, but *step motion* adds the ability to move forward or backward a single frame at a time—very useful for showing a sequence of conceptual or how-to steps, for example. Playback speed for *slow motion* can be set anywhere from step motion to *normal play. Fast motion*—double or triple the speed of normal play—is attained by skipping tracks. *Scan mode* provides fast previews at approximately 20 times normal speed via the same method.

Chapters

The unique address of each of the 54,000 frames is stored in the vertical blanking interval. Up to 80 *chapters* or segments of frames can be defined on each side. These chapters can be used to locate segments logically rather than having to keep track of the associated start frame. Two caveats about using chapters: they can be no shorter than 30 frames, and all frames on a side must be associated with one chapter or another. Chapter stop codes can also be encoded so that a segment freezes automatically on the last frame—although not all laserdisc players support this feature.

❖ CLV Laserdiscs

CLV laserdiscs use the constant linear velocity technique of altering the disc rotation speed to pack more information onto the longer tracks—1800 rpm nearest the hub and 600 rpm at the outermost track. There is no fixed correlation of frames to tracks on CLV laserdiscs, making it difficult to identify and access individual frames. Frame search, stop motion, step motion, and slow motion are sacrificed on most players. Chapters can still be implemented and accessed quickly.

The advantage of CLV is that storage is effectively doubled, yielding up to an hour per side. CLV is therefore useful when the emphasis must be placed on program length rather than extensive interactivity. (A laserdisc can be pressed with CLV on one side and CAV on the other.)

WRITABLE OPTICAL MEDIA

One of the problems with CD and laserdisc technologies is that they must be mastered. Aside from the issue of cost, this means that they can't be used in everyday activities that demand instant recording. (Mastering devices are coming down in price but are still unusual on the desktop.) Several technologies integrate some of the benefits of optical technology with the ability to record data to the drives incrementally on demand. Any such technology is often categorically referred to as *DRAW* (direct read after write). Although not considered distribution media, DRAW devices can be helpful in the production process.

❖ WORM Drives

WORM (write-once, read-many) drives allow data to be written to any used portion of the disk at any time. Once data has been recorded over a given area, however, it cannot be altered. This makes WORM drives most practical for archiving data that will not need to change. Manufacturers use many variations on a theme, but the general idea is that a thin layer of magnetic film is permanently altered by the laser when the data is recorded.

❖ Magneto-optical Drives

The *magneto-optical* (M-O) drive combines optical and magnetic recording technologies. An M-O disk contains a spinning platter inside a removable cartridge just like removable magnetic media. The platter, however, is made of three layers—a layer of special crystalline alloy pressed between a top layer of clear plastic coating, and a backing layer of aluminum. This alloy is not normally susceptible to magnetic fields, but becomes so when heated to its Curie point. When a bit is to be written, a laser instantly heats the desired pinpoint on the disk to the Curie point and an electromagnetic field polarizes the magnetic patterns in one direction or the other. When the laser is turned off, the alloy cools back down. Since it can no longer be influenced by magnetism, the magnetic pattern is cast in stone. (The data can be rewritten at a later date, however, using the same method.)

To read the data back, the laser is directed at the surface at a power level that does not cause the media to reach the Curie point. The beam shines through the crystal alloy and reflects off the aluminum backing into an optical sensor. The angle of reflection signifies the polarity of the magnetic field to the sensor so that the bit can be evaluated as a binary 0 or 1.

M-O technology has several big advantages over straight magnetic recording. First, data cannot be accidentally erased by stray magnetic fields; the laser has to be used again at high power in conjunction with the electromagnetic head in order to alter the magnetic patterns. Second, the pinpoint accuracy of the laser allows large amounts of data to be stored on small, light, and relatively inexpensive cartridges. The M-O cartridges used in the NeXT computer store 256MB; Sony and others make M-O drives that store 600MB per side on double-sided removable cartridges (1.2GB total). Finally, since M-O drives lack heads that float over the platter, the possibility of head crashes is eliminated.

The down side to M-O technology is slower speed. This is due in part to an average access time of 90 ms at this writing, as well as to the fact that each write operation takes three passes: erase, write, and verify.

❖ ❖ ❖ ❖ ❖ ❖

This concludes the discussion of optical technology. The next chapter describes how it is utilized by hardware, as well as the software used to create productions.

CHAPTER 17

Media Integration Tools

The tools presented so far throughout this book play a role in creating various pieces of the multimedia puzzle. This chapter focuses on some of the specialized tools that pull those pieces of the puzzle together.

MEDIA INTEGRATION HARDWARE

The first CD hardware success story was the consumer CD audio revolution. A second success is building as CD-ROMs take their place in more and more computer setups. A classic chicken-and-egg story, mass acceptance of multimedia is in many ways dependent on a larger installed base of CD-ROM players; conversely, the impetus to buy the hardware is tied to the availability of software. Although compressed video is positioning itself to take over, the laserdisc player still plays an important role in industrial installations where video quality is important.

❖ CD-ROM Drives

All CD-ROM drives are not created equal. Based on the discussion of the various CD specifications presented in Chapter 16, here's a quick look at some of the things to consider when evaluating CD-ROM drives.

Speed

As with magnetic media, there are two aspects of speed in which optimal performance is desirable—access time and transfer rate. Where earlier CD-ROM drives took as long as 1500 ms to find something, the state of the art at this writing offers access times of 350 ms or better. Since even this is about 20 times slower than the average hard drive, the fastest possible access time is obviously important in a CD-ROM drive.

As for transfer rate, CD-ROM Mode 1 would seem to dictate a constant flow of data at 150K per second. Normally, the drive waits for the operating system to send a request for the next sector in line—a process that can seriously impede throughput. *Continuous-read* drives constantly grab the next few sectors and place them in a buffer so that they are instantly transferable on request. The result is a steady flow close to or equal to 150K per second. Many drives have buffers that are at least 32K, but 64K is recommended.

Given all the numbers from the Red Book and Yellow Book specs, 150K per second would appear to be the fastest transfer time possible for CD-ROM. Since this is another thorn in the side of ambitious content developers, drive manufacturers are moving to double-speed and even quad-speed CD drives that rotate at two and four times the regular speeds, respectively. When a CD-DA audio track is encountered, the drive resumes normal speed. Obviously, these drives represent a welcome improvement.

Audio outputs

All CD-ROM drives can read CD-DA digital audio tracks. The audio data is not transferred to the host computer, however, but is played back entirely by the drive. That means that in order to play CD-DAs or CD-DA tracks embedded in a CD-ROM, the drive must have the necessary electronics to decode PCM, as well as the 16-bit DACS to transform the digital data into analog audio. Translation: If you want CD-audio capabilities in your CD-ROM drive, make sure that it has audio outputs. If you plan to do multimedia work, pass by models that only offer headphone outputs and go for one with line-level jacks. (Most drives that offer audio outputs in some form also will come with either a remote control and/or a software utility that simulates the controls of the consumer CD player.)

Compatibility

Most drives today come with software drivers for the various operating systems, as well as High Sierra and ISO 9660. The remaining compatibility questions concern the CD-ROM XA extension and

Kodak Photo CD. The XA extension typically costs several hundred dollars more due to the extra circuitry required. Although XA has not really taken off at this writing, increasing demands on media synchronization and IBM's integration of the format into their Ultimedia series may indicate an increasing need for compatibility. As for Photo CD, the main issue is whether a drive supports the Mode 2 multisession format or will only access the first ISO 9660 session.

Physical attributes

The most obvious physical attribute to consider is internal drives versus external drives—as much a matter of personal taste as anything. Internal drives are harder to install and place another burden on the PC's power supply; external drives are easier to install and transport, but cost more and require some desk space.

Dust is one of the biggest enemies of the CD drive. Models in which the enclosure seals after the disc is inserted are less prone to accumulating dust. Some newer models have self-cleaning photosensor lenses that eliminate most of the remaining contamination problems.

Multiple disc access

Several external drives are available that allow up to six CDs to be placed in a magazine caddy for automatic access. Although rare, even larger numbers of CDs can be accessed via CD *jukeboxes*— similar in operation to the familiar musical jukebox.

Integrated extras

The inclusion of CD-ROM in the MPC specification has led to a proliferation of MPC upgrade kits. These products often include other components required by MPC, such as a MIDI synthesizer, digital audio circuitry, and a rudimentary audio mixer.

Connections

Finally, consider how the CD-ROM drive connects to the computer. SCSI is the only choice on Macs. PC users choose between special IDE- and SCSI-controlled models. SCSI models are generally a bit faster and can be used with other platforms, but they can be more expensive. Also be careful to avoid some SCSI implementations on the PC that are nonstandard. You want "true SCSI"—and SCSI II isn't a bad idea while you're at it.

❖ CD Recorders

The increasingly lower price tags on CD-R recorders are threatening to bring the desktop publishing phenomenon to optical media. (At this writing, the first machine under $6,000 has just been introduced.) The discs used are already formatted with *pregrooves* that the laser uses for tracking purposes during the recording process. The reflective surface is made from a material that is dissolved when subjected to the beam of the recording laser, thereby creating deformations that act as pits. The resulting disc is then immediately playable on a standard CD-ROM player.

The advent of the affordable desktop CD mastering does not signal the end of large mastering and duplication facilities. CD recorders are good for tests, masters, archives, and short runs, but the technology is currently prohibitive for mass production. As for their use as everyday storage devices, CD access times are still significantly slower than magnetic media. Moreover, some CD recorders have most of the intelligence built in to convert native system data to CD format, while others require the CD mastering software described at the end of this chapter. Recordable CD is a new technology at this writing and may be a very interesting tool for multimedia production as the technology becomes more entrenched and understood.

❖ CD-I Players

Although the CD-I standard has been published for years, the consumer market has only recently been deemed by Philips to be ready for interactive technology. Indeed, Philips is the only manufacturer at this writing to market CD-I players. The basic requirements for CD-I players are described in Chapter 16 along with the CD-I Green Book specification to which they are integral.

❖ CDTV

CDTV is a CD-based interactive multimedia player aimed at the consumer market. Although similar to CD-I in its target audience and use, it is a proprietary system. CDTV is essentially a black box with the guts of an Amiga 500, a CD-ROM reader, NTSC video output, stereo audio outs, and a full-function infrared remote. In fact, the CDTV can be upgraded to an Amiga with the addition of a keyboard, mouse, and floppy drive. The multimedia capabilities of the Amiga are discussed in Chapter 5.

❖ Laserdisc Players

Feature choices in laserdisc players are fairly straightforward. Most laserdisc players manufactured in recent years will play both CAV and CLV discs. From there prices and features increase proportionately. (The laserdisc players specifically designed for karaoke have additional features that are beyond the scope of this book.)

Computer control

All laserdisc players can be controlled via infrared remotes. Probably the most important criteria for multimedia use is the ability to accept computer control for the transport commands and frame addressing, as well to receive verification from the laserdisc player. This communication is accomplished via an RS-232 port—a feature that is typically found only on industrial-quality decks.

Frame buffer

Chapter 16 revealed that CLV discs do not facilitate stop motion. A few new machines are breaking down this barrier by including a built-in frame buffer that stores the last frame. By displaying the contents of the frame buffer, freeze-frame and slow motion functions become possible.

Playing more than one side

Perhaps the biggest drawback with laserdiscs is the limited playing time on each side of the disc, especially with CAV. New players are reaching the market that can move the laser and photosensor in order to access either side of a disc. This process causes a delay of approximately 10 to 15 seconds. A few models even accept two laserdiscs, making it possible to access up to four sides without human intervention.

❖ Touchscreens

Touchscreens allow the user simply to touch a portion of a screen in order to interact with it and make a selection. They offer one solution to developers in addressing issues of durability in public displays such as kiosks. Although available for years, touchscreens have not met with incredible success for several reasons—not the least of which is expense. People are not used to interacting with CRTs in this fashion, and such interaction can often smudge the viewing screen. Finally, the fingertip simply has lower resolution than a mouse-driven cursor for all-around computer tasks. Nonetheless, they fill a definite need in some interactive projects.

The two most popular underlying technologies are resistive membranes and piezo-electric. *Resistive membrane* technology places a conductive membrane of thin material such as polyester over a glass or plastic panel. When a finger touches the membrane, it closes a conductive path that allows the associated circuitry to determine the location of the touch. In a variation on this theme, the conductive material is sandwiched between two layers of transparent material for protection and is constructed in such a way that it expands to make its own contact when pressure is applied.

Piezo-electric technology sets up a series of high-frequency waves in the glass panel. When a finger touches the panel, the wave pattern changes. The way in which the waves are altered is sensed by the associated circuitry and is used to derive the position.

Both of these systems have their advantages and disadvantages. Although resistive membranes have greater resolution, they form a thin mesh that absorbs some of the screen brightness. The mesh is also susceptible to environmental damage unless embedded between a layer of glass and a layer of plastic. In this case, the plastic can also cut down on clarity. On the other hand, piezo-electric technology is less accurate, uses nothing but clear glass, and is more expensive.

Regardless of the sensing technology, touchscreens come with controller circuitry that is fed into the host computer via a serial port or card slot. They also come with drivers that emulate the mouse, thereby making them easy to integrate into the working environment.

MEDIA INTEGRATION SOFTWARE

All multimedia productions require software to glue all the pieces of the puzzle together and control the flow of the presentation. This category has been one of the hottest areas of software development in recent years. The additional process of distributing such productions via CD-ROM raises its own issues that until recently have been a black art. New mastering and premastering software is beginning to pave the way for less expensive factory masters and to utilize the potential of the new desktop CD recorders. These two areas of production software are the focus of the rest of this chapter.

❖ Software for Presentation and Media Integration

Various names are used to categorize software packages that pull disparate media elements together into a cohesive production. *Presentation software* is generally entry-level software for creating productions that mimic the traditional slide show. *Multimedia production software* is more ambitious in the forms of internal and external media it combines and in its ability to synchronize them. *Authoring systems* tend to emphasize interactive navigation, database access, and preparation of productions for mastering and/or distribution.

The lines between these categories are rapidly blurring. Half the paint and draw programs today seem to come with a presentation utility. An increasing number of everyday applications are including support for dynamic media types such as QuickTime. Production tools include everything from animation routines to interactive scripting. The following discussion focuses, then, not on inefficient category names, but on the kinds of features that are available in this entire genre of *media integration packages*, and how they bear on various types of productions.

Supported media

The types of media that are supported by a media integration package will dictate what types of productions are possible. The more extensive and ambitious the media needs of a production, the narrower the choice of software tools becomes. Just about every package supports text and graphics, but animation, sound, and video are another matter. If sound is required, the options include MIDI sequence playback, 8-bit digital audio, and 16-bit digital audio. If video is to be included, the options include compressed digital video, such as QuickTime or AVI, more advanced DVI, or external control capabilities for laserdiscs or video decks.

Timing and synchronization

The timing for most presentation packages is sequential—after this image, display the next one. Additional control over timing usually takes the form of delays measured in nebulous units of time like "wait 20." Absolute time references like minutes and seconds aren't always used because some programs run at different speeds on different processors. Twenty units of time might be 20 seconds on a 486 and 40 seconds on a 286, for example. Implementation of these forms of relative time does not allow the user to ensure that an event starts at an exact time or that two or more events, such as video and a soundtrack, will end at the same time.

Synchronizing simultaneous playback of two or more media types is made difficult by this same scenario if the only provision is wild sync—simply starting playback of two types of dynamic media files simultaneously. Let's say that animation and 8-bit 22KHz digital audio—both of which are processor-intensive—are playing back at the same time. The frame rate of the animation can be adjusted on the production computer so that it is reasonably synchronized to the audio. When played back on a computer with a processor running at a different speed, however, the digital audio must be prioritized to maintain a playback rate of 22KHz. In doing so, the animation speed will usually be retarded on slower machines and accelerated on faster machines.

Establishing an absolute timing reference resolves these problems. The issue of intimate control over when events start and stop is typically handled by placing elements along a time line or on a grid of cells representing frames. (See Figure 17.1.)

Figure 17.1

Macromedia Director associates events with one or more frames in an audiovisual score.

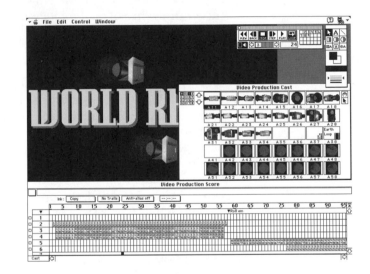

Implementation of the time line alone doesn't address the problem of maintaining synchronized relationships between computers running at different speeds. To do so the package must have the ability to translate the clock speed of various processors to an absolute timing reference such as minutes:seconds:frames and to synchronize playback of media elements accordingly. This is one of the basic elements of Apple's QuickTime (which, at this writing, is being adopted by other platforms as well). QuickTime Movies, for example, will drop frames of compressed video as necessary to keep the basic content flow of visual information in sync with the accompanying audio. Passport Producer is an example of a program that uses QuickTime as a timing foundation, then translates it to a time line that can be displayed in real time or SMPTE for compatibility with the rest of the audiovisual world. (See Figure 17.2.)

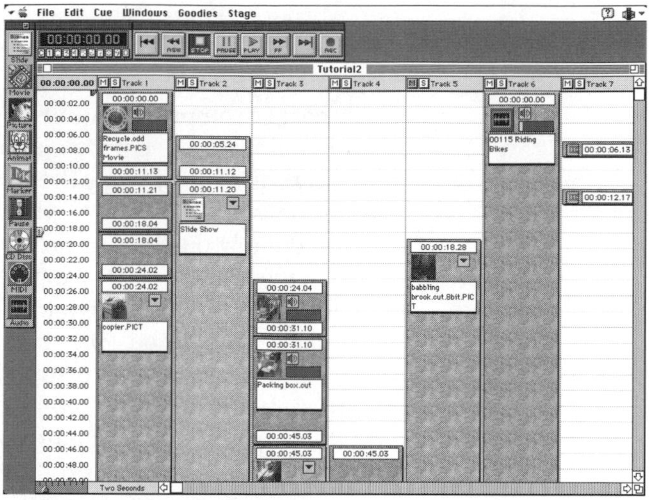

Figure 17.2

Passport Producer provides an absolute time line that can be set to measurements corresponding to SMPTE time code.

Viewing metaphor

In a related concept, different applications use various metaphors for the viewing area. Claris HyperCard, Asymetrix ToolBook, and related programs rely primarily on the metaphor of a stack of screens that contain similar architecture and information. These systems are primarily oriented toward the interactive navigation of information. Applications billed as presentation packages (such as Aldus Persuasion and Microsoft PowerPoint) typically use the metaphor of sequentially presented slides. Production-oriented applications such as Macromedia Director and Passport Producer employ the metaphor of a stage upon which actors, media files, and other types of cues are performed.

Transitions

Segues between graphic elements are much more interesting given transitions such as fades, wipes, and so forth. Most visually-oriented software will offer some transitions between graphic screens. The issue then becomes their quality, speed, and control. Although quantity is also a factor, having transitions that are the most visually effective (and the least distracting) is more important than the sheer number of available effects.

Palette handling

Many applications can handle RGB images in up to 24-bit color, but the time required to access and display such images is often prohibitive. Most presentation graphics therefore employ CLUTs for indexed color. The question is how they handle the CLUTs associated with different images. Some will map colors from the image palette to the closest color registers in a common palette used throughout all or part of the presentation. (The common palette might be the system palette or one provided by the package.) Those that do no mapping will typically use the palette associated with each image. Part of the issue is color integrity, and part of it has to do with transitions that show portions of two images on the screen simultaneously.

Packages that map image palettes to a common presentation palette have the advantage that the palettes of source images do not necessarily have to be optimized or conformed to those of other images. All colors will be mapped to the closest available values— and therein lies the rub. If you've got emerald green in an image and the closest thing in the presentation palette is lime green, the color differences may be problematic.

Packages that use the palette of each image typically provide greater color fidelity. However, the computer can only handle one CLUT at a time. During a transition such as a wipe where portions of both images share the screen for any period of time, the palette from the first image will typically be used until the second image has completely replaced it—then the palette from the second image takes effect. Unless the palettes are identical, the color register values from the first image will cause the colors of the second to be wrong during the transition. Simple fades to and from black in the style of cuts-only video are typically the best solution here.

Built-in animation

Presentation packages often have the ability to animate the appearance of elements such as text bullets. The simplest form of text animation is a *build*—each bullet pops on in sequence after a delay. More ambitious versions add motion to the build. This feature is implemented in a variety of ways, ranging from "slide from right" to drawing a path that the text will follow. (Even in packages that support externally-created animations, rudimentary built-in routines for animating text provide a more painless way of spicing up slide-show style images.)

Text handling

Products for the Macintosh and Windows will typically support any font installed in the system at any desired size. DOS presentation packages, however, are limited to the fonts that are compatible and available. Chapter 9 examined the importance of choosing the right typeface to communicate a message. Moreover, the choice of font sizes under DOS applications is typically very restricted. Font availability and accessibility is therefore a serious consideration under DOS.

Regardless of the platform or environment, typographic control is also a consideration. Control over leading, kerning, word space, letter space, tabs, and the like determines the level of visual refinement that can be exercised.

Charting

Some presentation packages are oriented toward communicating business information that incorporates facts and figures—information that is often contained in spreadsheets. Many packages include the ability to convert spreadsheet data automatically into bar charts, pie charts, graphs, and other forms of visualization. In addition to availability, use of this feature depends upon how much control the user has over style, color, size, dimensionality, labels, and the like.

Outlines and speaker notes

Business presentation packages often incorporate text tools for outlining the speaker's message. Graphic elements can be associated directly with each level or item, and the outlined text can even be part of the slide. The presentation flow is adjusted automatically as the outline is changed or rearranged. Speaker notes often can be associated with each level: the text won't become part of the onscreen image, but can be printed out to provide notes or an entire written script for the presenter.

Style sheets

Style sheets are electronic templates that allow easy development of a presentation. A template can be created for a "major points" screen, for example, that always displays the title in the upper-left corner of a special background in 48-point red Garamond type followed by a sequence of text bullets in 18-point blue Futura type. Each time a major point is to be made, the template is summoned and the words are inserted. This not only speeds up the production process, but ensures visual continuity in the presentation as well.

Internal media creation and editing

The quantity and level of tools for creating and editing media that are included in the integration package vary widely. As a general rule, an internal tool set will rarely be as comprehensive as a standalone application designed specifically for that task. On the other hand, it's very nice to be able to create simple elements and perform rudimentary edits without having to leave the media integration package to access other software. If budget and available resources are a problem, more extensive implementation of these features is obviously desirable.

Media libraries

As competition heats up between manufacturers of media integration packages, the inclusion of clip media is becoming a significant marketing strategy. Let's face it—if the task is to get a quick-and-dirty presentation done yesterday, then clip art, backgrounds, stock photos, music libraries, animations, and so on are a welcome asset even if you have creative talents in all of the those areas. Of course, the inclusion of such libraries is more critical if you don't have those skills and/or the time and budget to commission someone who does.

Object overlays

As productions become more ambitious, it is desirable to be able to control individual graphic elements separately. Various small graphic elements can be displayed and removed selectively over a static background. These objects may have their own transitions or motion paths. Some systems allow a given color (such as register 0 in a CLUT) to be transparent so that a solid background in the object will be replaced with the overall screen background.

File preloading

Pacing is important in keeping the audience interested, and a pause while the next graphic element loads is an easy way to lose the viewers' attention. Some media integration packages allow selected files to be preloaded into RAM so that they can be accessed instantly. Some do this at the beginning of the production, others during the presentation. More advanced packages also have the ability to purge a file from memory after it is used in order to free up space for more preloads during playback.

Interactivity

Interactivity—the ability of the user to determine the flow of information—adds a whole new level to evaluating media integration packages. Virtually every computer-based presentation package has the ability to insert time-out delays to hold an image on the screen for a given period of time or until a key or mouse button is pressed. The next level of interactivity is assigning markers associated with points in the production to keystrokes (such as the numeric keys), allowing the speaker or user to return to or jump to a given point on demand.

True interactivity provides the user with (1) onscreen choices that encourage a response, (2) a way for the user to make a choice, and (3) a method for the program to respond with an appropriate action. Interactive programming has come a long way in recent years. A decade ago little more existed than pressing a letter or number on the keyboard that corresponded to a list of text items on the screen. Today, productions are few and far between that do not allow the user to make choices from much more visually intuitive screens via mouse, trackball, or touchscreen.

One way to implement onscreen selections is to poll the program as to whether the mouse has been depressed and, if so, evaluate the cursor coordinates to determine whether they correspond with an area depicting an onscreen choice. If they do, the appropriate action is taken; if not, the mouse click is ignored and the program continues. More complex productions—such as some interactive adventures or educational programs—use this approach when allowing the user to select various items or areas of an image that don't necessarily look like buttons.

More intuitive products allow for elements that are known to the program as objects or buttons. The program can automatically distinguish whether such a button is being pressed or not. Various attributes can be ascribed to these buttons, such as a graphic or text display to enhance the user interface, an alternate graphic depicting the button's engaged or depressed state, and an action to be taken when the button is depressed. This action can be as simple as a link or jump to another area of the production, or an entire series of actions. Such buttons can also be transparent, allowing this function to be imparted to any area and element on the screen.

Hypertext

Hypertext is essentially the ability to link specific text to related text or, in some cases, visual elements. While there are many variations on this theme, HyperCard provides the most common example. Invisible buttons can be positioned around words or phrases with links to such things as other usage of the word, a glossary definition, or even a graphic example. As such, hypertext represents one of the underlying concepts of the new media paradigm for education, training, and interactive books.

Programming environment

How all of this happens and how easy it is to implement largely depends upon the programming environment offered by a given application. There are three basic approaches—icon-oriented, scripting, and a hybrid of the two.

Icon-oriented applications typically let you drag icons representing a media type onto a flowchart or time line. (See Figure 17.3.) A specific disk file—as well as other attributes such as duration, transition, and screen coordinates—can then be associated with the icon. The flow of the production can be altered by moving, adding, copying, and deleting icons. Some systems also offer a hierarchical approach in which icons or groups of icons can become "children" of "parent" icons: when the parent is moved, the children move with it. Icon-oriented applications are generally the most intuitive and simplest to use.

Figure 17.3

Commodore's AmigaVision provides an example of an icon-oriented production environment.

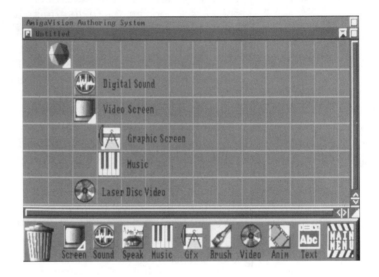

Scripting resembles the process most people think of when they think of programming computers. In most cases, the scripting language resembles relatively plain English and consists of commands that are optimized for multimedia production. Scripting languages require learning, remembering, and (usually) typing the proper commands in their proper syntax, or acceptable order. Scripting languages are generally the hardest to use, but usually offer control not available in an icon-oriented environment.

Hybrid systems offer the best of both worlds. The main environment is icon-oriented, allowing the majority of the work to be done with relative ease. Scripting is available at a lower level when you really need to get silicon under your fingernails. A button might be created and positioned in the everyday icon-oriented level, for example, yet a detailed script might be attached to the button and invoked when the button is activated. Hybrid systems are typically the choice of professionals when interactivity is involved.

Database support

Advanced interactive productions sometimes require access to a database. (A *database* is essentially a series of similar records that can be accessed and searched according to common types of information *fields*. A Rolodex is essentially a real-world database with fields for name, address, phone number, and so forth.) As a simple example, let's say that you are going to put a kiosk containing an interactive catalog in a store. A database will be devised in which each record contains the product type, manufacturer, model, feature list, and product photo. The user can browse through a list of product types and select one. The database is then searched for all records in which the product field matches that criteria, and a list of the valid products is displayed. The user then chooses a specific product, and the system retrieves and displays the feature list and photo.

That's an example of searching a database in a multimedia environment. Being able to input information into a database in such a situation is also useful. The kiosk can ask if the person wants more information on the product sent to their homes. A separate database containing a mailing list can be accessed and a new record created. Users can then enter their name and address into the database.

Databases usually add to the price tag of an authoring environment, and not every application needs one. A decisive factor in setting up a database is whether you will ever have to access enough similarly structured, interrelated information that adding to a database and maintaining a common access method is more efficient than dealing with integrating and defining circumstances for each element individually.

Run-time distribution

One-time productions can be played back using the production application. Mass-distribution or installation on multiple machines raises the issue of licensing. Most software manufacturers stipulate that one copy of their application may be installed on only one machine at a time. Moreover, distributing the entire production package can be bulky and confusing. The solution is a *run-time player* module that many manufacturers of presentation software include and encourage users to distribute freely with their productions. Some applications will compile the production, related files, and run-time player into a single file that can be viewed by double-clicking. Others simply have you include the player module on the same disk as the production files.

Cross-platform compatibility

One of the banes of multimedia producers is that productions created on one platform generally don't play on another. (While there are many platforms, the reality is that Macs and PCs account for 90 percent of the presentation and desktop multimedia markets.) Some manufacturers do address this challenge, however. Programs such as Aldus IntelliDraw that are available on both the Mac and PC offer the ability to transport productions between two platforms. Other programs allow files to be compiled into a form that can be read by a player module on the other platform. Although cross-platform conversion isn't always seamless, cleaning up a few anomalies is usually preferable to creating two separate versions of a project using two completely different tool sets.

System requirements

Like all types of software, various authoring programs impose different requirements on the system in terms of processor speed, memory, disk space, and the like. Certainly the first consideration is whether your production system meets those requirements. Mass-distribution raises a secondary consideration about the system requirements for the run-time player module.

❖ CD Premastering and Mastering Tools

CDs can be mastered or premastered using software tools from manufacturers such as OMI and Meridian Data. These systems handle all the gory details of EFM coding, organizing tracks, creating all the header, sync, and control and display bytes, subcode channels, VTOC—in general, everything that is required to format data before actually committing it physically to a CD. Virtually anything on your hard disk can be converted into the necessary format.

The output of these systems can be used in several ways. First, a virtual image of the CD can be accessed from the hard disk for testing purposes. The output can be transferred to a medium that can be shipped to a facility that specializes in mastering and duplication. Alternately, the software can be used to drive a desktop CD recorder to write a CD.

❖ ❖ ❖ ❖ ❖ ❖

This chapter has focused on the tools that bring media together. The next chapter concludes the discussion of media integration with a look at the processes involved.

CHAPTER 18

Producing Multimedia

The exact procedures used to integrate media into a cohesive production vary with each project, combination of media, and complement of tools. All productions nonetheless share common goals and processes. The role of the multimedia producer also shares many commonalties across projects. This chapter examines what it takes to pull together successful and rewarding multimedia production experiences.

THE ROLE OF THE MULTIMEDIA PRODUCER

In the entertainment community, the *producer* is typically the person that pulls all the pieces of the puzzle together, including selling the project to a studio, acquiring funding, managing the budget, and hiring the director. The *director*, in turn, hires the right talent to realize the production from a creative and procedural standpoint. In the world of multimedia, these roles are often one and the same. Moreover, the tendency is to be scriptwriter, artist, animator, engineer, composer, videographer, programmer, and more. The roles that you take on personally in producing multimedia will be governed by your talents, desires, schedule, and resources.

❖ Interfacing with the Client

If you are doing a production for your own purposes, you've obviated one of the hardest tasks of being a producer—interfacing with the client. Don't get me wrong: clients make the world go around. The challenge is effective communication with someone who is on a different wavelength. Clients typically don't care about the gory details of CD-ROM transfer rates, bit planes, audio resolution, and video compression. They only care about their message, timetable, and budget—and rightfully so. The producer's job is to worry about the rest. In this light, the producer must also take on the role of communicator, acting as a buffer between client and production staff—as well as between message and medium. (Effective communication is important even if your boss is commissioning an in-house project.)

The three big tradeoffs

Many clients have no concept of the time, money, and equipment required to produce multimedia. Many service industries have adopted the axiom that among the three main aspects of production—quality, price, and speed—you can have any two. This axiom applies equally to multimedia production. If the client wants the project produced yesterday, either the quality must suffer or the price must reflect a rush charge (often to compensate for the contracting of additional resources). Conversely, if the client is willing to wait for high quality, the price can remain reasonable.

One of the most difficult things about multimedia production is the pace at which technology is evolving and the lack of standardized tools. The multimedia industry does not yet have the equivalent of the seamless audio-video production suite or standardized VHS tape as a delivery vehicle. One of the factors that must be built into any production more ambitious than a computerized slide show is the extra time to make it all work with a given set of tools. The more ambitious the production, the more you should be doubling and tripling the amount of time you schedule into and compensate for in the budget.

Talking money

It is very common for a prospective client to describe a half-baked concept and ask how much the production will cost. An instant reply framed in hard dollars is a sure path to failure. The best thing to do is put the issue of money aside temporarily and invest some time establishing what the client wants to accomplish. Equally important, try to get the client to open up enough to let you into their "mind's eye." One goal of this process is to make sure you are both on the right wavelength from the start. Another is to ensure you are comparing apples with apples when the conversation returns to pricing. (If the client is envisioning a slide presentation and you're thinking Hollywood, your bid will seem out to lunch. Conversely, you'll live to regret bidding on a slide presentation if the client expects Hollywood.)

While most prospective clients are loath to divulge their budget, it is necessary, at least to establish a ballpark figure. After all, there is a tremendous amount of esthetic difference and production resources involved in the productions associated with budgets of $1,000, $10,000, and $50,000. People can often relate to the variance of cost per finished minute associated with video. You can have talking heads shot on a camcorder for $100 per finished minute, or Madison Avenue for $100,000 plus per finished minute. Another corollary is the difference between an ad in the *Yellow Pages* and one in *The New Yorker*. These more common frames of reference can help get prospective multimedia clients to loosen up a bit in divulging budget restraints.

Production costs versus delivery costs

Cost will also be determined by the technology requirements of the project. It is important to separate the cost of production from the cost of delivery and distribution. If the discussion hinges on a series of 100 kiosks for a retail chain, for example, it is usually best to distinguish the cost of your production services from the cost of delivery system. (The term *delivery system* refers to the equipment required to play or deliver the completed production in the final setting.) There are lots of variations on the theme and alternate (competitive) sources for delivery hardware. Unless you are specifically in the business of being a VAR (value-added reseller), establish what your production services are worth separately. There's plenty of legitimate value in providing the client with the additional service of researching, reselling, and installing the delivery hardware if you desire. The distinction between service and product often makes things easier to deal with for both parties.

❖ **Moving Forward**

It quickly becomes obvious that the first step in a project is to establish what clients really want and reconcile that with what they're willing to pay. Going through an exercise with the client will help both parties to visualize the production needs, goals, scope, style, and purpose. This phase typically turns prospects into clients, and ideas into game plans. A series of questions I find extremely valuable at this critical stage will follow shortly.

Some form of written agreement is advisable to solidify commitments. The scope of the project and your potential liability will determine whether a legal contract and the associated costs are

Production Visualization Questions

- What is the purpose of the production?
- How will the success of the production be measured?
- Who is the audience—professionally, demographically, and psychograpically?
- What is the proposed length of the production?
- How will the production be delivered?
- What are the circumstances under which the production will be viewed?
- What is the balance of information detail versus excitement level?
- What is the desired action on the part of the audience?
- What is the audience's current attitude toward the subject?
- What problems does the production or its subject solve for the viewer?
- What are the main five points of the message in order of importance?
- What is the subliminal message or benefit?
- What should the product or subject feel, look, and sound like stylistically to the viewer?
- What should be the pace?
- How much motion will be effective? Will the product need to move? Will the viewer's perspective need to move?
- Do any other overall stylistic treatments come to mind such as drama, nostalgia, science fiction, mystery, or parody?
- What image is to be portrayed about the company, product, or subject?
- Do any existing materials, styles, and themes (such as logos, slogans, artwork, ads, photos, videos, and brochures) need to be carried over for continuity and synergy?
- Do any usable source materials exist, especially in electronic form?
- Do elements of this production need to be carried over into other projects?
- What production elements—video, animation, 3D, music, and so forth—are envisioned?
- Is the use of any particular platform, hardware, or software mandated?

(continued...)

Production Visualization Questions
(continued)

- What is the production and delivery timetable—including performance and payment milestones?
- Assuming one gets what one pays for, what are the minimum and maximum amounts of money that can be budgeted for the project?
- Who has the authority to sign off on ideas, budgets, and schedules?

appropriate. Most circumstances dictate a letter of agreement accompanied by a purchase order. The letter of agreement should describe the production, establish milestones, payment schedules, liabilities, recourse for unsatisfactory performance, and a framework for modification. (More than one client has been known to dictate massive changes at the eleventh hour that should be considered above and beyond the original agreement.) Even if the production is in-house, a variation on the letter of agreement can be very helpful in verifying responsibilities, budgets, expectations, and timetables.

PREPRODUCTION

As with all media, the preproduction phase in multimedia is the invaluable planning stage. When implemented effectively, it provides a map that guarantees the production process to be as smooth and effective as possible—both procedurally and monetarily.

❖ Concept Treatments

Most productions start with a written *treatment* of the concept, largely designed to get all the basic ideas out on the table. This can be anything that provides a concise overview, from a paragraph or two to several pages of prose. The treatment ensures that the goal is clear to both you and the client before any significant time is invested in creative work. Even if you are your own client, the treatment serves to clarify the vision of what you intend to communicate to the audience.

❖ **Scripts and Storyboards**

The script is the traditional method of establishing content at an exacting level in film and video production. You will probably find that traditional scripts are only important for the video portion of your production, as well as any area where narration is required.

The more useful tool for most multimedia productions is the *storyboard*—a sequence of rough images that represent key frames of the content at different stages. (See Figure 18.1.) Ad agencies and video producers use storyboards to help clients visualize specific creative treatments of the content. The key frames are traditionally hand-drawn sketches laid out on posterboard in such a way that the sequence can be viewed as a whole. With the proliferation of computers, storyboard software is making the job easier and the results more polished. (Initial storyboards shouldn't to be too polished, however, since they are still part of the idea stage.)

Figure 18.1

The storyboard is used as a visualization tool in the preproduction phase of the project.

❖ Content Flowcharts

Interactive productions bring the extra challenge of non-linearity. Since the order in which the material will be presented on playback will be determined by the user, it is prudent to extend the storyboard concept to a flowchart that enables you to visualize the various paths, what elements lie along them, and how they are navigated. (See Figure 18.2.) The flowchart can also help ensure against dead ends in the interactive navigation process.

Figure 18.2

The flowchart helps envision the overall architecture and flow of the content.

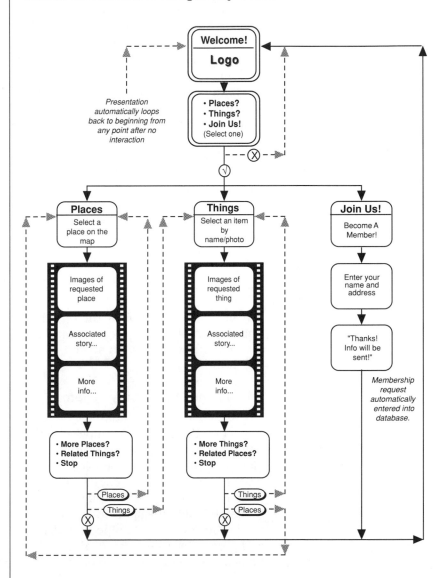

❖ Project Timelines

Part of the producer's job is to manage schedules. As with any project, milestones must be established—both to stay on schedule and to provide some sanity and sense of accomplishment for those involved during the production. The project timeline also provides a reality check. It's easy to fantasize that various things can be accomplished in a given period of time; mapping it all out together against the reality of the calendar reveals problem areas and timing intricacies that are best dealt with in advance.

There's plenty of generic project planning software available that can easily be applied to multimedia productions. Many people also rely on low-tech erasable wall-mount production calendars that focus on short periods of time. While different people employ different management styles, you will probably find it beneficial for all parties involved in the production to visualize the scheduling milestones and consequences in the scope of the overall project.

❖ Budgets

No preproduction phase is complete without a budget. The budget is more than just the sum total the client is willing to spend. It provides a breakdown that allocates costs to specific production phases, tasks, people, equipment, supplies, overhead, and the like. Spreadsheet software is invaluable in the budgeting process.

❖ The Right Tools for the Job

The old adage of choosing the right tool for the job most assuredly applies to multimedia production. Hardware and software can be divided into two conceptual entities—production tools and delivery systems.

Establishing the delivery system

Obviously, the specifications of the delivery system can have an impact on the budget. A simple VHS deck or garden-variety 286 computer is one thing—interactive control of full fidelity audio and video is another. Even the choice of a mainstream desktop computer model is an important cost consideration if the project will require numerous delivery points, such as multiple kiosks.

Establishing the specifications of the delivery system is also important from the standpoint of driving the production values and processes. The most ideal situation is that of a production to be delivered with your own hardware. Situations such as one-time productions or permanent installations can withstand custom hardware and software requirements that are under your control.

Productions intended for remote delivery or mass distribution add other issues. Establishing that all delivery systems, such as kiosks, will have VGA graphics and no more, for example, dictates the graphic format to be produced. Establishing that all systems will use 33MHz 80386 processors results in predictable speed for things like animations.

On the other hand, the content needs can also dictate the hardware. If a certain type of technology required to produce or deliver a certain type of technology or effect is only available on a certain platform, price becomes less of a deciding factor.

Productions intended for mass distribution, such as on a floppy disk, cannot rely on any standards with regard to entrenched hardware or software and must therefore be created using the lowest common denominator. Unless you are targeting an audience using a single platform such as a Macintosh or PC, versions for multiple platforms will also have to be developed. Given the requirements of multimedia content, mass-distributed productions are often shipped with a disclaimer about minimum system requirements for effective playback. (While it is not interactive, the least common denominator for mass distribution today is still the VHS tape.)

Choosing the right production tools

The production process can take advantage of many different types of tools that do not have to be available on the delivery system. Given cross-platform compatibility of various file formats, there's nothing dictating that all pieces of the puzzle be produced on the same platform. The focus turns to productivity, available resources, and cost-effectiveness.

Sheer processor speed is a factor when considering resources. 3-D rendering provides a classic example, in that rendering can usurp tremendous amounts of time, especially when it comes to animation. Faster machines obviously reduce this time but cost more money. The question often becomes whether an investment in the faster machine will pay for itself, either during this project or over future projects. More than dollars alone must be considered, such as whether the purchase frees up another machine that could be used elsewhere in your business.

Resourceful producers also turn to other solutions when caught between small budgets and less than optimal resources. Many types of equipment can be rented on a short-term basis—often a viable option when you need a workhorse around a given project. Other options for short-term equipment include leasing, borrowing, trading services, and so forth. In many cases, the best solution is to contract the services of others who own the necessary tools and are experienced in using them.

Choosing the right people for the job

One of the challenges of desktop multimedia is that, in theory, anyone can produce anything given enough time, talent, and money. Most producers quickly realize that there is rarely enough of any one of these resources, let alone all three. Moreover, few people truly possess equal creative and technical skill across multiple media. Movies, television broadcasts, magazines, and other world-class projects invariably rely on the talents of many skilled professionals.

One way to look at using other talent is reluctantly admitting that there's not enough time to do it all yourself. The more positive realization is that it opens up the opportunity not only to work with and learn from other creative individuals, but to have the luxury of choosing from the stylistic fortes of each artist, musician, videographer, animation, writer, and so on. Assembling a good team can be an extremely rewarding experience for both the producer and the client.

The role of the producer then becomes equated to that of a ship's captain: the captain is qualified to supervise and coordinate the talents of others because he has worked in the engine room, the communications shack, and the galley (and has probably swabbed the decks as well). In the role of producer/captain, effective communication and production processes become as important as steering the ship.

There are plenty of ways to find freelance talent. One is to look within organizations whose members specialize in a given field. Another is to frequent places and events where talented people congregate and/or patronize. A music store is a good place to find a certain type of musician or at least a recommendation on one, for example. Similarily, art exhibits showcase the talents of local artists. If a magazine or video has contained art that appeals to you, call the publisher and get a referral. Another source is in gainfully employed professionals who moonlight on the side.

Colleges, high schools, and vocational schools can often recommend talented students and some schools even have an "earn while you learn partnership" with community businesses. (While students work for less money than experienced professionals, they are often unaccustomed to the pace and responsibility required for serious production schedules.)

PRODUCTION

The production process is often one of the easiest parts of the job—especially if preproduction has been done properly. Ideally, one enters the production phase with road maps for content, schedules, budgets, equipment, and personnel.

❖ Using a Master List

As one of the first steps, the storyboard, script, and flowchart should lead to a master list itemizing all the pieces of the content puzzle. This includes all still images, animations, video segments, music passages, narration, text, and so on. Each should include their source, intended final form, who is to do the associated work, and when. Each item should also have a checklist for status—raw materials in, edited, converted to proper format, file format, and so forth. The larger the project is in scope, the more important the master list becomes in keeping track of what has been and what yet needs to be accomplished. It also provides coworkers with a task assignment that allows them to work more autonomously. The master list is, in a word, organization.

❖ Choosing the Right Production Processes

Choosing the right production processes is just as important as choosing the right tools and talent. In many cases, there are multiple ways to accomplish a task. Some are more efficient; some produce better results. The ideal process accomplishes both of these goals. Investing a little time to test theories on the front end can save tremendous amounts of time and money during the production process.

On a related note, desktop multimedia seems to continually place producers on the "bleeding edge" of technology. Just because Product A works with Product B and Product A works with Product C doesn't guarantee that Products B and C will work together! Always test a production theory and the end results before committing to a given technology, tool set, file format, and process.

It's easy to forget all of the variations on a theme that you've tested. When testing various permutations of a production process, write down the steps and the associated results. This provides a clear review at any point of what has been tested along with the associated results.

Making lemonade

Multimedia production and technology is filled with caveats. The adage mentioned earlier about choosing any two among the factors of time, money, and quality, has a corollary with regard to

515

compressed video technology, for example. Given full frame, full motion, and full fidelity you can have any two—if you're lucky! And the more multimedia elements you combine such as audio, video, and animation, the more demands are placed on the hardware.

Ambitious productions all come down to delivery, hardware, storage, and throughput. The smaller the amount of data, the better. Many methods of reducing data overhead and throughput demands have been examined throughout this book. They include reduced color palettes, JPEG image compression, color cycle animation, real-time object animation, MIDI soundtracks, compressed video, RAM disks, file preloading, and more.

Even on the most powerful desktop machines there often seems to be a losing battle against processor speed, hard disk storage and access, and memory limitations. You've undoubtedly heard the phase "when life gives you lemons, make lemonade." This adage is often the saving grace of multimedia producers. Establish what the limits of the technology are and use them creatively. Let's say that the fastest we can get video of acceptable quality off of a given storage medium is 10 frames per second, thus making the video appear extremely choppy. One solution would be to add motion blur to each frame in order to enhance the effect to one of deliberate stop action. This effect can be heightened by timing one frame per beat along with a soundtrack. Additional effects, such as posterization or painting on each frame, can serve to engage the viewer enough to disguise the motion deficiencies even further.

❖ Work Smart

Working smart usually means working less. Templates, for example, ensure uniformity and often make the work flow easier. Even if a given software package doesn't support templates per se, written notes about positions, color values, settings, timing, and so on provide a manual equivalent.

Electronic media invite the process of writing over the original files with modified versions. Unless storage media is at a critical level, keeping track of the source material and the evolutionary steps eliminates the need to start completely from scratch if the end result is unsatisfactory. Also establish conventions by which files are to be named. This allows anyone involved with the production to identify a file's contents and status at a glance. This is especially important when a file evolves through several steps during the course of the production.

In the computer world, the need to save your work and back up your files on a regular basis can never be overemphasized. Doing work is one thing, doing it twice is quite another! In a work for hire situation, failure to save and back up your files adequately can turn from inconvenience to law suit should your data befall some mishap.

❖ Legal Issues

These days it is almost impossible to create multimedia without considering the legal issue of *copyrights* in one way or another. The following is a brief look at the overall concepts and implications of copyrights. Copyright law is not only complex, but subject to interpretation. Moreover, the basic foundation was created long before the advent of multimedia and the associated complexities. It is highly recommended that you engage the services of a copyright lawyer or entertainment lawyer if any copyright issues arise.

Basic copyright concepts

Title 17 of the U.S. Code embodies the United States Copyright Act and contains many subsections. In general, the Copyright Act provides for the copyright owner to reproduce the copyrighted work, prepare derivatives, distribute copies, perform the work, and display the work. It also empowers the owner to authorize others to do the same. By extension, those unauthorized to do the same are in violation of copyright law. (There are several *fair use* exemptions to the copyright law for educational and archival purposes.)

One of the fundamentals of the copyright is that an idea cannot be copyrighted, only its implementation. In other words, Disney can't copyright the idea of a talking bipedal mouse, but they can very definitely copyright the embodiment of that idea in the form of Mickey Mouse.

Copyrights generally extend fifty years past the death of the holder. Material for which the copyright has expired falls into the *public domain* and is free for use. Material created by the U.S. Government is automatically in the public domain.

As a result of recent litigation, the copyright comes into being when the work is created and requires no registration or copyright notice. It is highly recommended that a finished work be registered with the Copyright Office, since it carries a great deal of evidence should litigation ever be required. (Contact: Register of Copyrights, Copyright Office, Library of Congress, Washington, DC 20559.) Similarly, the display of the copyright notice (©) on the package and at the beginning of your production is also recommended.

In general, the subject of copyrights can be broken down into two areas: the use of outside material in your productions, and the protection of your original work.

Using outside material

The key question in using outside material in your productions is whether any of it is owned by other parties. It is illegal, for example, to use a Michael Jackson recording or the likeness of Bart Simpson in a public display such as a trade show unless the rights to use them have been obtained in writing through the proper legal channels. Even if you only show the production in a boardroom to a dozen people with no chance of the copyright holder ever knowing about it, the legal implications are the same.

A great deal of clip media is available to multimedia producers in the form of clip art, library music, stock photography, and stock video footage. In most cases, you are not buying the material, only a limited license to use it. Some of this media is *buy-out* material, meaning that you purchase the right to unlimited usage as long as you don't repackage it as clip media. Others sell one-time usage rights—further usage requires an additional fee. Many forms of clip media stipulate that embodiment in a mass-distributed or broadcast production require an additional license.

The copyright for work for hire and work done for employers by employees generally falls to the employer unless otherwise stipulated in the contract. (Allowing a creative party to retain a copyright on their contribution does not preclude you from copyrighting the overall production.) The importance of retaining the copyright to all materials will depend upon the production, the intended distribution, and the professional level of the creative talent.

One of the keys to using copyrighted material is whether it is recognizable. If you image process an Andy Warhol painting or signal process a Beatles song beyond recognition, there's little issue. Video footage or photography depicting recognizable people or works of art, on the other hand, generally requires signed releases even if they are not the main subject.

The first rule when using outside material, then, is to establish who owns it and what it takes to license usage in your situation. The second rule is to determine if the rights of others are infringed incidentally. The third rule is to obtain any appropriate licensing before public performance and distribution. (Many trade show promoters have even taken to prohibiting music in exhibitors' displays unless proof of license is available.) The fourth rule is to spell out all issues of copyright ownership and licensing when contracting the services of others to create original work.

Protecting your work

Just as it is in the interest of others to protect their work, it is in your interest to protect yours. Your entire production should be copyrighted before public display if there is a longevity and value attached to it. Certainly, this does not apply significantly to a one-time business presentation in an environment such as a trade show. An interactive entertainment CD designed for public distribution represents a much more serious concern that warrants the services of a lawyer specializing in copyrights and entertainment law.

POST-PRODUCTION

The lines between production and post-production blur easily on the desktop. In general, I like to create all of the pieces of the puzzle in the production phase, then "glue them together" in the post-production process. On larger interactive projects, programming can be done in parallel to element production using place holder files for the different media files that will eventually be plugged in.

❖ Programming Basics

In projects that involve authoring, some semblance of programming is usually involved. Many of the same considerations from the production process apply to post-production programming as well.

Document the process

Variable names should be logical and intuitive enough that their use will be apparent if the program/script is reviewed months or years later or by someone else. Similarly, documenting the procedures with embedded remarks will help keep everything easy to understand both during and after the programming process.

Use modular programming and variables

Modular programming can save an incredible amount of time, as well as keep things simple. Ideally, the main body of the script does little more than call subroutine modules—which themselves may call other subroutines. This approach allows global changes to be implemented by editing a single entry. As described in Chapter 3, the use of variables provides another shortcut that can drastically simplify the programming process.

While not a complete program nor written in a formal language, the following plain-English programming example shows the power of both subroutines and variables in presenting and testing a simple set of lessons. Let's say that we have digitized speech saying "Right!"

in one file, and "Wrong!" in another bearing that same file name. Let's also assume that the image, text, and correct answer for each of 10 lessons is stored in a series of files. Those for lesson 1 are named "Image1," "Text1," and "Answer1," those for lesson 2 are named "Image 2," "Text2," and "Answer2," and so on.

```
[main  routine]
   execute  setup
   execute  welcome  routine
   execute  display  information  routine
   execute  response  routine
   execute  more  routine
   Goto  execute  welcome  routine

[setup  routine]
   set  variable:  rightsound  =  "Right!"
   set  variable:  wrongsound  =  "Wrong!"
   set  variable:  lessons  =  10
   return  to  calling  routine

[welcome  routine]
   set  variable:  filenumber  =  1  (reset  to  first  file)
   set  variable:  correct  =  0     (reset  for  next  user)
   set  variable:  rightanswer  =  0
   display  welcome  image
   play  welcome  audio
   return  to  calling  routine

[display  information  routine]
   display  file  "Image"filenumber
   display  text  "Text"filenumber
   load  file  "Answer"filenumber
   rightanswer  =  first  field  of  answer  file
   filenumber  =  filenumber  +1  (increment  to  point  to  next  files)
   return  to  calling  routine

[response  routine]
   prompt  "What  is  the  correct  answer?"
   get  user  input
   if  user  input  =  rightanswer
     play  rightsound
     correct  =  correct  +  1
   else
     play  wrongsound
   return  to  calling  routine

[more  routine]
   if  filenumber  =  lessons  +  1
     execute  end  lessons  routine
   else
     prompt  "Would  you  like  to  continue?"
     get  user  input
     if  user  input  =  yes
```

```
          forget  calling  routine
          goto  execute  display  information  (loop  to  next  lesson)
    if  user  input  =  no
       forget  calling  routine
       execute  end  lessons  routine

[end  lessons  routine]
    display  "Your  score  was  "  correct  "right  out  of  "  filenumber
    pause  20  seconds
    forget  calling  routine
    goto  execute  welcome  (loop  to  top  of  main  routine  for  next  user)
```

The primary benefit of using subroutines is that the basic flow of the main routine is uncluttered and very easy to understand. The other is that any changes need only be made once. The prompts, for example, can be altered globally by making changes to a single line of the script. In addition, a routine could easily be developed to handle all of the circumstances surrounding user input, then called at each point where "get user input" appears. The use of specialized routines provides the additional advantage of creating libraries of small modules that can be reused in other productions.

Variables also played a strong role in this example. The variable "correct" simplifies the scorekeeping process. The use of files numbered to match each lesson also allowed variables to be used to retrieve the associated files for each lesson. Given this design, the same script could just as easily accommodate the presentation and testing of 100 lessons as 10 files: After creating the additional lesson files with the appropriate number suffixes, the variable "lessons" would simply be changed from 10 to 100. In addition, different audio files could be associated with right and wrong answers by simply changing the variable for "rightsound" and "wrongsound."

❖ Interactive Aesthetics

A great deal of research has been conducted on the subject of effective user interaction with computers. Here's a quick look at some of the major considerations.

Keep the interface simple

One of the greatest faux pas of interactive media production is providing the viewer with an interface that is anything less than intuitive. For starters, that means limiting the number of choices. (Nine choices on any one screen is generally acknowledged to be the comfortable maximum for the user.) If more choices are necessary, break them down into nested categories from which the user can choose.

Let's say that you're doing an interactive program on the animal kingdom. Listing every animal at the onset is obviously prohibitive. The logical solution would be to break them down into initial categories of mammals, reptiles, fish, and birds. Each of these would lead to a list of subcategories. Mammals, for example, would lead to choices such as felines, canines, rodents, marsupials, and so forth. Each of these would lead, in turn, to the actual species. Felines would lead to lions, tigers, jaguars, bobcats, and the like. Finally, selecting one of these would lead to the presentation on that animal. This provides a reasonable and logical hierarchy.

Too many nested levels can be just as frustrating, however. The addition of another few levels to our interactive exploration of the vast subject of the animal kingdom would make the process tedious. One solution is to present useful information at the various levels along the way. The level describing felines could provide information about that branch of the animal kingdom that makes them unique. Navigating further to a specific species then becomes more of a matter of curiosity than a chore.

Make the interaction compelling

Certainly the proper choice of style and aesthetics for both visual and aural elements discussed in previous chapters is important when designing a production for a given client or audience. Interactive multimedia should not only draw the user in with sights and sounds, however, but make the interactive experience exciting. Capitalize on the fact that people love to explore: provide a framework for interaction that fires the imagination and the desire to learn. An educational program might be framed as a treasure hunt, or a corporate training program can be framed as a mystery to be explored. The possibilities are endless when a little creative vision is applied.

Delays should be avoided whenever possible. Preloading files at the beginning of the production or during natural pauses is one way to cut down on the delays associated with loading large files. Programs that do not accommodate preloads can often be worked around by loading the necessary files into a RAM disk—provided you have enough memory. Another common delay—directory access to CD-ROMs—can be avoided by using a utility that loads the directory into RAM to allow fast access to files. When delays are inevitable, the first rule is to let the user know that something is happening. If at all possible, provide some diversion in the interim such as music or an interesting graphic.

Make the user comfortable

There are still plenty of people who are afraid of computers or, at least, are uncomfortable with them. The controls themselves should be intuitive, uniform in operation, and simple to use. Don't rely on hand-to-eye coordination unless you're making video games for kids. Always make it obvious to the user what action is expected of him and clarify what the choices are. Equally important, provide clear choices for moving forward, backward, laterally, and exiting. Add printed or verbal instructions if necessary. People will linger to explore much longer if they know where they are and that they can move on intelligently at any time.

Another way to make the user comfortable is to supply positive feedback. Whether the feedback is aural, visual, or both, let the user know that her action was accepted and is being acted on in some way. If an erroneous choice is made, point the way to the correct one.

Don't make people read

Multimedia provides an opportunity to use almost every form of communication in combination for the most effective results. If a picture is worth a thousand words, a video or animation is certainly worth many more.

Even when still images are used, one of the first rules is to avoid making people read. Society in general is accustomed to being spoon-fed information on television. Even viewers who enjoy books often find detailed reading on a CRT or video monitor to be tedious. Ideally, a video segment will both show and tell the viewer about the subject. Even when motion video is not possible, digital audio can be used to provide narration tracks that communicate the information in a much more palatable form than streams of text thrown on the screen.

Consider audience deficiencies

Another reason why it's a bad idea to make people read is that many people require reading glasses in order to read much more than titles. In general, deficiencies in human sensory perception are a valid concern. As Chapter 7 revealed, a surprising percentage of the population experiences color anomalies in their vision. On-screen choices should therefore be clearly identified through the use of icons and/or words in addition to any distinction made through color. Similar consideration should be given to those who are hard of hearing. Ideally, the equivalent of closed captioning should be provided in interactive productions designed for the masses.

In truth, most multimedia productions have not evolved to the level where potential handicaps and deficiencies on the part of the audience are accommodated. Nonetheless, it will become a more important consideration as the interactive technologies become more accepted. In actuality, interactive media provides the perfect means by which individuals with sensory deficiencies can customize the way information is accessed.

Provide for non-linear content

One of the greatest challenges of interactive media is non-linearity. In other words, scripts, videos, and soundtracks have simply played from start to finish—until recently. When the user is empowered to change the flow of the content, the producer must accommodate this in the production design.

Traditional soundtracks, for example, are the result of music, sound effects, and speech mixed together into a single entity. If a user decides to navigate elsewhere while such a soundtrack is playing, there is little choice but to interrupt it and start up at another point. A more effective way to accommodate interactivity in a soundtrack is the parallel use of MIDI or CD for the musical score and computer-based digital audio for short snips of narration. This approach allows the user's actions to guide the choice of narration, while the MIDI or CD soundtrack plays seamlessly in the background. The separation of speech and music also allows the narration to be recorded and played in several different languages without having to remaster the soundtrack.

Ideally, the production software will provide for both aural and visual transitions that can be called on the fly in response to user navigation requests. This would allow the digital audio narration in the previous example to fade out elegantly when the user wishes to navigate elsewhere. Similarly, computer control of audio levels allows the music to be lowered in volume during narration, then returned to a normal level—a process known as *ducking* in the audio world. In a parallel concept, a video clip should ideally make a more graceful transition than simply popping off if the user exits in the middle of a video segment.

Test, then test again!

In general, all producers are wise to test their productions on non-crucial audiences. Hollywood studios screen films and TV shows before their final release. Ad agencies conduct market surveys to ensure that the message hits the desired mark. Game designers subject their products to the torture only kids can inflict. Multimedia production should be no different. If the production will play back on one or more different machines than the production machine, test all the feasible hardware combinations.

Interactivity is an added impetus for testing. The test is not only for content and aesthetic impact, but for intuitivity and ease of use. Every navigation possibility should be explored to ensure against dead ends and improper routing. Then subject it to the "gorilla test," where all the keys and actions are tested: it may never occur to you to press F1 while holding the shift and control keys simultaneously—but if that combination will cause the program to crash, somebody will try it somewhere, sometime!

Interactive Guidelines

- Keep the interface simple, intuitive, and uniform. Use a moderate number of nested levels with interesting information along the way.
- Make the content interesting and compelling.
- Don't make people read much more than titles.
- Don't base choices on color or sound alone if you wish to compensate for human deficiencies.
- Make it obvious where the user is and what actions are expected of them.
- Accommodate non-linear content as elegantly as possible through multiple media and transitions on demand.
- Test everything repeatedly.

DELIVERY

Many multimedia productions are created with great expenditures of time and money without a thought to the ultimate environment in which they will be viewed. If your production will be viewed in an environment over which you have any control, exercise it!

Amplify the media if necessary

Make sure your audience can see and hear the presentation. Various overhead and video projection systems are available for rent or purchase that ensure everyone can see the presentation comfortably. Similarly, the use of sound systems ensures the aural portion of the production can be heard without straining.

Eliminate distractions

One way to help focus the audience's attention on the presentation is to eliminate distractions. Where possible, isolate the production in an area free from conversation, noise, motion, and other media devices. Take steps to eliminate other light sources that cause glare on a CRT or wash out the images from projectors. Dimming the lights in general will heighten the focus on the presentation. Place the speakers at ear level. Make certain that the audio level is not too loud to be offensive or distorted, and that any tone controls are adjusted for the best balance of clarity and warmth.

Put your best foot forward

Finally, consider anything else you can do to lend class, character, and credibility to the presentation environment. The physical attributes of a kiosk, for example, will play an important role in how people perceive the system. In a boardroom presentation, hide the computer and cables if possible. In a larger presentation, treat the front of the room as a stage to be dressed. Incorporate the drama of lights and other theatrical devices if possible and appropriate. In short, treat your production as Hollywood—and treat the delivery as theater.

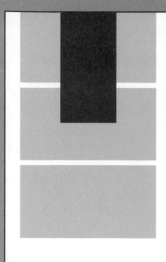

Appendices

Appendix A

Additional Reading

PERIODICALS

❖ Multimedia

CD-ROM Professional
Pemberton Press, Inc.
CD-ROM Professional
462 Danbury Road
Wilton, CT 06897
(800) 248-8466

Desktop Communications
International Desktop Communications, Ltd
P.O. Box 941745
Altanta, GA 30341
(404) 493-4786

New Media
Hypermedia Communications Inc.
901 Mariner's Island Blvd., Suite 365
San Mateo, CA 94404
(415) 573-5170

Publish
Integrated Media, Inc.
P.O. Box 55400
Boulder, CO 80322
(800) 274-5116

QuickTime Forum
Multi-Facet Communications
110 West Iowa Ave.
Sunnyvale, CA 94086
(408) 749-0549

Verbum
The Gosney Company, Inc.
670 Seventh Ave. 2nd Floor
San Diego, CA 92101
(619) 233-9977

❖ **Video**

AV Video
Montage Publishing, Inc.
701 Westchester Ave.
White Plains, NY 10604
(914) 328-9157

Post
Testa Communications
25 Willowdale Ave.
Port Washington, NY 11050
(516) 767-2500

Video Systems
Intertec Publishing Corporation
9221 Quivira Road
P.O. Box 12901
Overland Park, KS 66212
(913) 541-6628

Videography
P.S.N. Publications
2 Park Avenue, Suite 1820
New York, NY 10016
(212) 779-1919

Videomaker
Videomaker Inc.
P.O. Box 558
Mt. Morris, IL 61054
(815) 734-1112

❖ **Music and Audio**

Electronic Musician
Act III
P.O. Box 41094
Nashville, TN 37204
(800) 888-5139

Keyboard
Miller Freeman, Inc.
Box 58528
Boulder, CO 80322-8528
(800) 289-9919

Mix
Act III
P.O. Box 41094
Nashville, TN 37204
(800) 888-5139

Recording Engineer/Producer
Intertec Publishing Corporation
9221 Quivira Road
P.O. Box 12901
Overland Park, KS 66212
(913) 541-6628

❖ **Graphics**

Computer Artist
PennWell Publishing Company
Subscription Services
P.O. Box 3188
Tulsa, OK 74101
(918) 831-9423

Computer Graphics World
PennWell Publishing Company
One Technology Park Drive
Westford, MA 01886
(508) 692-0700

Computer Pictures
Montage Publishing, Inc.
701 Westchester Ave
White Plains, NY 10604
(914) 328-9157

MacArtist
MacArtist, Inc.
901 E. Santa Ana Blvd. Suite 103
Santa Ana, CA 92701
(714-973-1529)

Step-By-Step Design
Step-By-Step Publishing
6000 North Forest Park Drive
Peoria, IL 61614
(309) 688-2300

Step-By-Step Electronic Design
Step-By-Step Publishing
6000 North Forest Park Drive
Peoria, IL 61614
(309) 688-2300.

❖ ## Computer

AMIGA WORLD
TechMedia Publishing, Inc.
80 Elm Street
Peterborough, NH 03458
(603) 924-0100

Byte
McGraw-Hill
One Phoenix Mill Lane
Peterborough, NH 03458
(603) 924-9281

MacUser
Ziff-Davis Publishing Company
P.O. Box 56986
Boulder, CO 80322-6986
(800) 627-2247

MacWEEK
Coastal Associates Publishing
P.O. Box 1766
Riverton, NJ 08077-7366
(609) 461-2100

MACWORLD
Macworld Communications, Inc.
501 Second Street, 5th Floor
San Francisco, CA 94107
(415) 243-0505

PC Magazine
Ziff-Davis Publishing Company
P.O. Box 54093
Boulder, CO 80322-4093
(800) 289-0429

PC WORLD
PC World Communications, Inc.
501 Second Street, #600
San Francisco, CA 94107
(415) 243-0500

BOOKS

❖ Graphics

Ashford, Janet, Linnea Dayton, and Michael Gosney
The Verbum Book of Postscript Illustration
Redwood City, CA
M&T Books, 1990

Ball, Jennifer, Linnea Dayton, and Michael Gosney
The Verbum Book of Digital Typograpy
San Diego, CA
M & T Publishing and Michael Gosney, 1991

Beaumont, Michael
Type: Design, Color, Character & Use
Cincinnati, OH
Quarto Publishing, 1987

Brady, Philip
Using Type Right
Cincinnati, OH
North Light Books, 1988

Burke, Clifford
Type from the Desktop
Chapel Hill, NC
Ventana Press, 1990

Chang, Phil Inje, Linnea Dayton, and Michael Gosney
The Verbum Book of Scanned Imagery
Redwood City, CA
M&T Books, 1991

Cook, Alton, and Robert Fleury
Type & Color
Cincinnati, OH
Rockport Publishers, 1990

Dayton, Linnea, Paul Goethel, and Michael Gosney
The Verbum Book of Digital Painting
Redwood City, CA
M&T Books, 1990

Fenton, Erfert
The Macintosh Font Book
Berkeley, CA
Peachpit Press, 1989

Finberg, Howard, and Bruce D. Itule
Visual Editing: A Graphic Guide for Journalists
Belmont, CA
Wadsworth Publishing Company, 1990

Garchik, Morton
Creative Visual Thinking
New York
Art Direction Book Company, 1989

Glassner, Andrew
3D Computer Graphics
New York
Design Press, 1989

Gosney, Michael
Making Art on the Macintosh II
Glenview, IL
Scott, Foresman and Company, 1989

Irwin, Richard
Drawing on the Macintosh
Homewood, IL
Deke McClelland Publishing Resources, 1991

Irwin, Richard
Drawing on the PC
Homewood, IL
Deke McClelland Publishing Resources, 1991

Koren, Leonard, and Wippo Meckler
Graphic Design Cookbook
San Francisco
Chronicle Books, 1989

McNeill, Dan
Mastering Graphics on the Macintosh
Greensboro, NNC
Compute Publications, 1989

Newcomb, John
The Book of Graphic Problem-Solving
New York
R. R. Bowker Company, 1984

Pettersson, Rune
Visuals for Information: Research and Practice
Englewood Cliffs, NJ
Educational Technology Productions Inc., 1989

Powell, William F.
Color: And How To Use It
Tustin, CA
Walter Foster Publishing, 1984

Rogondino, Michael
Computer Type
San Francisco
Chronicle Books, 1991

Swann, Alan
How to Understand and Use Design and Layout
Cincinnati, OH
Quarto Publishing, 1990

White, Jan
Editing by design
New York
R. R. Bowker Company, 1982

White, Jan
Using Charts and Graphs
New York
R. R. Bowker Company, 1984

Zelanzny, Gene
Say It With Charts
Homewood, IL
Business One Irwin, 1991

❖ **Video**

Anzovin, Steven
Amiga Desktop Video
Randor, PA
Compute Books, 1989

Compesi, Ronald, and Ronald Sherriffs
Small Format Television Production
Needham Heights, MA
Allyn and Bacon, 1990

Edmonds, Robert
The Sights and Sounds of Cinema and Television
New York
Teachers College Press, 1982

Handbook of Recommended Standards & Procedures
New York
International Teleproduction Society, 1987

Hausman, Carl
Institutional Video
Belmont, CA
Wadsworth Publishing Company, 1991

Luther, Arch C.
Digital Video in the PC Environment
New York
Intertext Publications/Multiscience Press, Inc., 1991

Mortier, Shamms
Amiga Desktop Videography
Newark, DE
MichTron, 1991

Singleton, Ralph
Film Scheduling/Film Budgeting Workbook
Beverly Hills, CA
Lone Eagle Publishing Company, 1989

Whittaker, Ron
Video Field Production
Mountain View, CA
Mayfield Publishing Company, 1989

Wright, Guy
Amiga Desktop Video Guide
Grand Rapids, MI, 1990

Zettl, Herbert
Television Production Handbook
Belmont, CA
Wadsworth Publishing Company, 1984

❖ Multimedia Production

Anzovin, Steven
Macintosh Desktop Presentations
Radnor, PA
Compute Publications, Inc., 1990

Apple Computer
Inside Macintosh QuickTime
Reading, MA
Addison-Wesley Publishing Company, 1992

Bergman, Robert, and Thomas Moore
Managing Interactive Video/Multimedia Projects
Englewood Cliffs, NJ
Educational Technology Publications, 1991

Cole, Margaret, and Sylvia Odenwald
Desktop Presentations
New York
AMACOM, 1990

Crawford, Tad
Legal Guide for the Visual Artist
New York
Allworth Press, 1990

Franklin, Carl, and Susan Kinnell
Hypertext/Hypermedia in Schools
Santa Barbara, CA
ABC-CLIO, 1990

Imke, Steven
Interactive Video Management and Production
Englewood Cliffs, NJ
Educational Technology Publications, 1991

Jacobsen, Linda
CyberArts
San Francisco
Miller Freeman Publishing, 1992

Ken Pohlman
The Compact Disc Handbook
Madison, WI
A&R Editions, 1992

Laurel, Brenda
The Art of Human-Computer Interface Design
Reading, MA
Addison-Wesley Publishing Company, 1990

Montgomery, Paula, and H. Thomas Walker
Media Production & Computer Activities
Santa Barbara, CA
ABC-CLIO, Inc., 1990

Perlmutter, Martin
Producer's Guide to Interactive Videodiscs
White Plains
Knowledge Industry Publications, 1991

Philips International, Inc.
Compact Disc-Interactive: A Designer's Overview
Berkeley, CA
McGraw-Hill, 1988

Powell, James
Designing User Interfaces
San Marcos, CA
Microtrend Books, 1990

Rabb, Margaret
The Presentation Design Book
Chapel Hill, NC
Ventana Press, 1990

Tay Vaughn
Multimedia: Making it Work
Berkeley, CA
Osborn/McGraw-Hill, 1992

Wilson, Linda Lee
Make it Legal
New York
Douglas Design Associates, 1990

Zettl, Herbert
Sight, Sound, Motion: Applied Media Aesthetics
Belmont, CA
Wadsworth Publishing Company, 1990

❖ | **Audio**

Alten, Stanley
Audio in Media
Belmont, CA
Wadsworth Publishing Company, 1990

Anderton, Craig
MIDI for Musicians
New York
Amsco Publications, 1986

Anderton, Craig
The Electronic Musician's Dictionary
New York
Amsco Publications, 1986

Bartlett, Bruce
Recording Demo Tapes at Home
Indianapolis, IN
Howard W. Sams & Company, 1989

Campbell, Murray, and Clive Greated
The Musician's Guide to Acoustics
New York
Schirmer Books, 1988

Casabona, Helen, and David Frederick
Using MIDI
Sherman Oaks, CA
Alfred Publishing Company, 1987

Chamberlin, Hal
Musical Applications of Microprocessors
Rochelle Park, NJ
Hayden Book Company, 1980

Dictionary of Creative Audio Terms
Framingham, MA
Creative Audio & Music Electronics Organization, 1979

Eargle, John
The Microphone Handbook
Plainview, NY
Elar Publishing

Goldberg, Michael
The Ultimate Home Studio
Menlo Park, CA
Digidesign, 1991

Huber, David, and Robert Runstein
Modern Recording Techniques
Indianapolis, IN
Howard W. Sams & Company, 1986

Multi-Track Recording
Milwaukee, WI
Hal Leonard Books, 1988

Rachlin, Harvey
The Songwriter's and Musician's Guide to Making Great Demos
Cincinnati, OH
Writer's Digest Books, 1988

Wadhams, Wayne
Dictionary of Music Production and Engineering Terminology
New York
Schirmer Books, 1988

Woram, John
The Recording Studio Handbook
Plainview, NY
Sagamore Publishing Company, 1979

Yavelow, Christopher
Macworld Music & Sound Guide
San Mateo, CA
IDG, 1992

❖ | ## Computers/General Media

Aaron, Alex, and Bud Aaron
Upgrading PCs
Berkeley, CA
McGraw-Hill, 1991

Aker, Sharon, and Arthur Naiman
The Macintosh Bible
Berkeley, CA
Goldstein & Blair, 1991

Albrecht, Bob
Simply PCs
Berkeley, CA
McGraw-Hill, 1992

Anis, Nick, and John Dvorak
Dvorak's Guide To Dos & PC Performance
Berkeley, CA
McGraw-Hill, 1991

Anis, Nick, and Craig Menefee
The PC User's Guide
Berkeley, CA
McGraw-Hill, 1991

Buddine, Laura and Elizabeth Young
The Brady Guide to CD-ROM
New York
Brady, 1987

Dunuloff, Craig
The System 7 Book
Chapel Hill, NC
Ventana Press, 1991

Freedman, Alan
The Computer Glossary
New York
AMACOM, 1991

Goodman, Danny
The Complete Hypercard Handbook
New York
Bantam Books, 1987

Johnson, Laura, and Ed Teja
IBM PC and PS/2 Graphics Handbook
San Marcos, CA
Microtrend Books, 1990

Kussmann, Ralf
PC File Formats & Conversions
Grand Rapids, MI
Abacus, 1990

Lorenz, Lori, and Michael O'Mara
Windows 3 Companion
Louisville, KY
Microsoft Press,1990

Norton, Peter
Inside The IBM PC and PS/2
New York
Brady, 1990

Roberts, Russell
Understanding Hard Disk Management on the Macintosh
San Francisco
SYBEX, 1989

Rubin, Charles
The Macintosh Bible Guide to System 7
Berkeley, CA
Goldstein & Blair, 1991

The Macintosh Memory Guide
San Mateo, CA
Connectix, 1992

Woram, John
The PC Configuration Handbook
New York
Bantam Computer Books, 1987

Professional Organizations

ACM (Association for Computing Machinery)
11 West 42nd St.
New York, NY 10026
(212) 869-7440

Electronic Artists Group
P.O. Box 580783
Memphis, MN 55458
(612) 331-4289

IICS (International Interactive Communications Society)
P.O. Box 1862
Lake Oswego, OR 97035
(503) 649-2065

IMA (Interactive Multimedia Association)
3 Church Circle, Suite 800
Annapolis, MD 20401
(410) 626-1380

IMA (International MIDI Association)
5316 West 57th St.
Los Angeles, CA 90056
(213) 649-6434

ITVA (International Television Association)
6311 North O'Connor Rd. DB51
Irving, TX 75039
(214) 869-1112

NCGA (National Computer Graphics Association)
2722 Merrilee Drive, Suite 200
Fairfax, VA 22031
(800) 225-6242

Optical Publishing Association
7001 Discovery Blvd. #205
Dublin, OH 43017
(614) 793-9660

SMPTE (Society of Motion Picture and Television Engineers)
595 West Hartsdale Ave.
White Plains, NY 10607
(914) 761-1100

Software Publishers Association
1730 M St. NW Suite 700
Washington, DC 20036
(202) 452-1600

Appendix C

Product Listing

SOFTWARE LISTINGS BY PRODUCT

❖ ### 3D rendering/modeling software

3D Workshop
Brown Wagh Publishing
130-D Knowles Drive
Los Gatos, CA 95030
(408) 378-3838

Alias Upfront
PC, Mac
Alias Research, Inc.
Style! Division
P.O. Box 202347
Austin, TX 78720
(800) 447-2542

Alias Sketch
Mac
Alias Research, Inc.
Style! Division
P.O. Box 202347
Austin, TX 78720
(800) 447-2542

Autodesk 3D Studio
PC
2320 Marinship Way
Sausalito, CA 94965
(800) 525-2763

Caligari
Amiga
Octree Software Inc.
311 W. 43rd Street, Suite 901
New York, NY 10036
(212) 262-3116

DesignCAD 3-D
PC
DesignCAD, Inc.
One American Way
Pryor, OK 74361
(918) 825-4848

ElectricImage Animation System
ElectricImage Inc.
117 E. Colorado Blvd., Suite 300
Pasadena, CA 91105
(818) 577-1627

Envision
Mac
ModaCAD Inc.
1954 Cotner Ave.
Los Angeles, CA 90025
(310) 312-6632

Infini-D
Specular International
233 N. Pleasant St.
P.O. Box 888
Amherst, MA 01004
(413) 549-7600

Life Forms
Mac
MacroMedia, Inc.
600 Townsend
San Francisco, CA 94103
(415) 442-0200

MacroMind Three-D
Mac
MacroMedia, Inc.
600 Townsend St.
San Franciso, CA 94103
(415) 442-0200

MacroModel
Mac
MacroMedia, Inc.
600 Townsend St.
San Franciso, CA 94103
(415) 442-0200

ModelShop ll
Mac
MacroMedia, Inc.
600 Townsend
San Francisco, CA 94103

NetRenderMan
Mac, Unix
Pixar
1001 W. Cutting Blvd.
Richmond, CA 94804
(510) 236-4000

Ray Dream Designer
Mac
Ray Dream, Inc.
1804 N. Shoreline Blvd.
Mountain View, CA 94043
(415) 960-0768

RenderMan Developer's Kit
PC
Pixar
1001 W. Cutting Blvd.
Richmond, CA 94804
(510) 236-4000

Sculpt-Animate 4D
Mac, Amiga
Byte by Byte Corporation
9442-A Capital of Texas Highway N., Suite 650
Austin, TX 78759
(512) 795-0150

Showplace/MacRenderMan
Mac
Pixar
1001 W. Cutting Blvd.
Richmond, CA 94804
(510) 236-4000

StrataVision
Mac
Strata Inc.
2 West, St. George Blvd., Suite 2100
Saint George, UT 84770
(800) 869-6855

Super 3D
Mac
Aldus Corporation
411 First Avenue, S.
Seattle, WA 98104
(800) 333-2538

Swivel 3D Professional
Mac
MacroMedia, Inc.
600 Townsend St.
San Franciso, CA 94103
(415) 442-0200

Topas and MacTopas
PC, Mac
AT&T Graphics Software Labs
3520 Commerce Crossing, Suite 300
Indianapolis, IN 46240
(317) 844-4364

Typestry
Mac
Pixar
1001 W. Cutting Blvd.
Richmond, CA 94804
(510) 236-4000

Virtus Walkthrough
Mac
Virtus Corporation
117 Edinburgh South, Suite 204
Cary, NC 27511
(919) 467-9700

❖ ## 3-D clip objects

Swivel Art series
MacroMedia, Inc.
600 Townsend St.
San Franciso, CA 94103
(415) 442-0200

TV Objects
Amiga
Slide City
6474 Highway 11
Delon Springs, FL 32130
(904) 985-1103

❖ | ## Animation clips

Animation clip art collections
Mac
Visual Magic
620 C. Street, #201
San Diego, CA 92101
(800) 367-6240

Clip Animation Vol 1 & 2
Mac
Illusion Art
P.O. Box 21398
Oakland, CA 94611

Video Visions
Amiga
CV Designs
61 Clewleyroad
Medford, MA 02155
(617) 391-9224

❖ | ## Animation software

ADDmotion
Mac
Motion Works Inc.
1020 Mainland St., Suite 130
Vancouver, British Columbia, Canada V6B2T4
(604) 685-9975

Animation Stand
Mac
Linker Systems
13612 Onkayha Circle
Irvine, CA 92720
(714) 552-1904

Animation Works
PC, Mac
Gold Disk, Inc.
385 Van Ness, Suite 110
Torrance, CA 90501
(310) 320-5080

Animation Works Interactive
PC
Gold Disk, Inc.
385 Van Ness, Suite 110
Torrance, CA 90501
(310) 320-5080

Animation Studio
Walt Disney Computer Software Co. Inc.
500 S. Buena Vista St.
Burbank, CA 91521
(818) 567-5340

Autodesk Animator and Animator Pro
PC
Autodesk Multimedia Business Unit
2320 Marinship Way
Sausalito, CA 94965
(800) 525-2763

Cinemation
Mac
Vividus Corp.
651 Kendall Avenue
Palo Alto, CA 94306
(415) 494-2111

Deluxe Animation
PC
Electronic Arts
1820 Gateway Drive
San Mateo, CA 94404
(415) 571-7171

Deluxe Paint
PC, Amiga
Electronic Arts
1820 Gateway Drive
San Mateo, CA 94404
(415) 571-7171

Director
Mac
MacroMedia, Inc.
600 Townsend
San Francisco, CA 94103
(415) 442-0200

Grasp
PC
Paul Mace Software
400 Williamson Way
Ashland, OR 97520
(800) 523-0258

Magic
Mac
MacroMedia, Inc.
600 Townsend
San Francisco, CA 94103
(415) 442-0200

On the Air
Mac
Meyer Software
616 Continental Road
Hatboro, PA 19040
(800) 643-2286

PC Animate Plus
Brown Wagh Publishing
130-D Knowles Drive
Los Gatos, CA 95030
(408) 378-3838

PROmotion
Mac
Motion Works Inc.
1020 Mainland St., Suite 130
Vancouver, British Columbia, Canada V6B2T4
(604) 685-9975

Sculpt-Animate 4D
Amiga
Byte by Byte Corporation
9442-A Capital of Texas Highway N., Suite 650
Austin, TX 78759
(512) 795-0150

❖ ## Authoring software

Ask•Me 2000
Innovative Communications Systems (ICS)
7100 Northland Circle, Suite 401
Minneapolis, MN 55428
(612) 531-0603

Audio Visual Connection
IBM
IBM Corp.
Multimedia Information Center
P.O. Box 2150
Atlanta, GA 30301
(800) 426-9402

Authorware
Mac, PC
MacroMedia, Inc.
600 Townsend St.
San Franciso, CA 94103
(415) 442-0200

CanDo
Amiga
INOVAtronics
8499 Greenville Ave., Suite 209B
Dallas, TX 74231
(214) 340-4992

Course Builder
Mac
TeleRobotics International
7325 Oak Ridge Highway, Suite 104
Knoxville, TN 37921
(615) 690-5600

Director
Mac
MacroMedia, Inc.
600 Townsend
San Francisco, CA 94103
(415) 442-0200

Grasp
PC
Paul Mace Software
400 Williamson Way
Ashland, OR 97520
(800) 523-0258

Guide
PC
OWL International
2800 156th Avenue, S.E.
Bellevue, WA 98007
(206) 747-3203

HSC InterActive
Harvard Systems Corp.
1661 Lincoln Blvd., Suite 101
Santa Monica, CA 90404
(310) 392-8441

HyperCard
Mac
Claris Corporation
5201 Patrick Henry Drive
Box 58168
Santa Clara, CA 95052
(408) 987-7000

HyperWriter
PC
NTERGAID
2490 Black Rock Turnpike, Suite 337
Fairfield, CT 06430
(203) 368-0632

IconAuthor
PC
AimTech Corporation
20 Trafalagar Square
Nashua, NH 03063
(603) 883-0220

Image Q
PC
Image North Technologies
180 King Street South, Suite 360
Waterloo, Ontario, Canada, N2J1P8
(519) 570-9111

Linkway Live!
IBM
IBM Corp.
Multimedia Information Center
P.O. Box 2150
Atlanta, GA 30301
(800) 426-9402

MacPresents
Mac
Educational Multimedia Concepts, Inc.
1313 Fifth SE, Suite 202E
Minneapolis, MN 44414
(612) 379-3842

Magic
Mac
MacroMedia, Inc.
600 Townsend
San Francisco, CA 94103
(415) 442-0200

MediaBlitz
Asymetrix Corp.
110 110th Ave. N.E., Suite 717
Bellevue, WA 98004
(206) 462-0501

MediaMaker
Mac
MacroMedia, Inc.
600 Townsend
San Francisco, CA 94103
(415) 442-0200, (415) 442-0200

Multimedia Make Your Point
Asymetrix Corp.
110 110th Ave. N.E., Suite 717
Bellevue, WA 98004
206) 462-0501

Spinnaker PLUS
PC, Mac
Spinnaker Software Corp.
201 Broadway
Cambridge, MA 02139
(800) 826-0706

Storyboard Live!
IBM
IBM Corp.
Multimedia Information Center
P.O. Box 2150
Atlanta, GA 30301
(800) 426-9402

SuperCard
Mac
Aldus Corporation
411 First Avenue, S.
Seattle, WA 98104
(800) 333-2538

TourGuide
American Training International
12638 Beatrice St.
Los Angeles, CA 90066
(310) 823-1129

ToolBook
Asymetrix Corp.
110 110th Ave. N.E., Suite 717
Bellevue, WA 98004
(206) 462-0501

Quest Multimedia Authoring System
Allen Communication Inc.
5225 Wiley Post Way, Suite 140
Salt Lake City, UT 84116
(801) 537-7800

❖ **Clip art/backgrounds**

Adobe Collector's Edition: Textures and Patterns
Mac, PC
Adobe Systems, Inc.
1585 Charleston Road
Mountain View, CA 94039
(415) 961-4400

ArtRoom CD
PC, Mac
Image Club Graphics
Suite 5, 1902 11th Street
SE Calgary, Alberta, Canada, T2G3G2
(800) 661-9410

Backgrounds, textures, and images on CD ROM
Texture City
3215 Overland Avenue, Suite 6167
Los Angeles, CA 90034
(310) 836-9224

Background and clip art collections
Mac
Educorp
7434 Trade Street
San Diego, CA 92121
(619) 536-9999

Background and clip art collections
Mac
Wayzata Technology
P.O. Box 807
Grand Rapids, MN 55744
(800) 735-7321

Backgrounds for Multimedia
Mac
ArtBeats
P.O. Box 1287
Myrtle Creek, OR 97457
(800) 444-9392

Chinese Clip Art
Mac
Pacific Rim Connections
3030 Atwater Drive
Burlingame, CA 94010
(415) 697-9439

Design Clips
PC
LetterSpace
338 E. 53rd Street, #2C
New York, NY 10022
(212) 935-8130

Designer's Club Collection
PC, Mac
Dynamic Graphics, Inc.
6000 N. Forest Park Drive
Peoria, IL 61614
(800) 255-8800

Dover Clip Art Collection-CD
PC, Mac
Alde Publishing Inc.
6520 Edenvale Blvd., Suite 118
Eden Prairie, MN 55346
(612) 934-2024

DrawArt Professional Clip Art
PC
Migraph Inc.
32700 Pacific Hwy. S. Suite 12
Federal Way, WA 98003

EduClip Images
Mac
Teach Yourself By Computer Software, Inc.
3400 Monroe Avenue
Rochester, NY 14618
(716) 381-5450

EPS Clip Art collections
PC, Mac
3G Graphics, Inc.
114 Second Avenue South, Suite 104
Edmonds, WA 90202
(206) 774-3518

EPS Clip Art collections
PC, Mac
T/Maker Company
1390 Villa Street
Mountain View, CA 94041
(415) 962-0195

EPS Clip Art collections
PC, Mac
Dream Maker Software
7217 Foothill Blvd.
Tujunga, CA 91042
(800) 876-5665

EPS Clip Art collections
PC, Mac
Online Arts
700 E. Redlands Blvd., Suite 309
Redlands, CA 92373
(714) 794-0013

EPS Clip Art collections
PC, Mac
Pixel Perfect
P.O. Box 2470
Escondido, CA 92033

EPS Map Art collections
PC, Mac
MicroMaps Software
9 Church Street
Lambertville, NJ 08530
(800) 334-4291

Japanese Clip Art
Mac
Qualitas Trading Co.
6907 Norfolk Road
Berkeley, CA 94705
(415) 848-8080

MacKids Kolor Klips
Mac
Nordic Software, Inc.
917 Carlos Drive
Lincoln, NE 68505
(402) 488-5086

Media Line
Amiga
Free Spirit Software, Inc.
58 Noble Street
Kutztown, PA 19530
(215) 683-5609

Medical Clip Art
PC, Mac
TechPool Studios
1463 Warrenville Center
Cleveland, OH 44121
(800) 777-8930

MultiWare CD ROM
PC, Mac
BeachWare
5234 Via Valarta
San Diego, CA 92124
(619) 492-9529

Native American Art Collection
Mac
Grafx Associates
P.O. Box 12811
Tucson, AZ 85732
(800) 628-2149

Poem for Windows
PC
Iterated Systems, Inc.
5550 Peachtree Parkway
Norcross, GA 30092
(404) 840-0310

Power Backgrounds
Mac
California Clip Art
17951 Sky Park Circle, Suite E
Irvine, CA 92714
(714) 250-0495

ProArt
Mac
Multi-Ad Services, Inc.
1720 W. Detweiller Drive
Peoria, IL 61615
(800) 447-1950

SoftClips
Amiga
SoftWood Inc.
P.O. Box 50178
Phoenix, AZ 85076
(800) 247-8330

TV Graphics
Amiga
Slide City
6474 Highway 11
Delon Springs, FL 32130
(904) 985-1103

Visual Delights CD-ROM
Mac
SunShine
P.O. Box 4351
Austin, TX 78765
(512) 453-2334

Vivid Impressions
PC, Mac
Cassady & Green, Inc.
P.O. Box 223779
Carmel, CA 93922
(800) 359-4920

Wraptures Vol. 1 & 2
Mac
Form and Function
1595 17th Avenue
San Francisco, CA 94122

❖ ## Communication/network software

MicroPhone II
PC, Mac
Software Ventures, Inc.
2907 Claremont Avenue, Suite 220
Berkeley, CA 94705
(510) 644-3232

Send Express
Mac
Gizmo Technologies
P.O. Box 14177
Fremont, CA 94539
(510) 623-7899

❖ **Compression software**

DiskDoubler
Mac
Salient Solutions, Inc.
124 University Avenue
Palo Alto, CA 94301
(415) 321-5375

PicturePress Plus
Mac
Storm Technology Inc.
1861 Landings Drive
Mountain View, CA 94043
(415) 691-1111

StuffIt Deluxe
Mac
Aladdin Systems, Inc.
Deer Park Center, Suite 23A-171
Aptos, CA 95003
(408) 685-9175

SuperStar
PC
AddStar, Inc.
3905 Bohannon Drive
Menlo Park, CA 94025
(415) 688-0465

❖ **Cross-platform conversion software**

AccessPC
Mac
Insignia Solutions
526 Clyde Avenue
Mountain View, CA 94043
(415) 694-7600

DOS Mounter
Mac
Dyna Communications
50 S. Main Street, 5th Floor
Salt Lake City, UT 84144
(801) 531-0600

GraphPorter
Mac
GSC Associates
2304 Artesia Blvd., Suite 201
Redondo Beach, CA 90278
(213) 379-2113

MacLink Plus PC
PC, Mac
DataViz, Inc.
55 Corporate Drive
Trumbull, CT 06611
(203) 268-0030

MetaPICT
Mac
GSC Associates
2304 Artesia Blvd., Suite 201
Redondo Beach, CA 90278
(213) 379-2113

RunPC
Mac
Argosy Software, Inc.
113 Spring Street, 5th Floor
New York, NY 10012
(212) 274-1199

SoftPC
Mac
Insignia Solutions
526 Clyde Avenue
Mountain View, CA 94043
(415) 694-7600

Software Bridge
Mac
Argosy Software, Inc.
113 Spring Street, 5th Floor
New York, NY 10012
(212) 274-1199

❖ **Drawing software**

Adobe Illustrator
PC, Mac
Adobe Systems, Inc.
1585 Charleston Road
Mountain View, CA 94039
(415) 961-4400

Arts & Letters Graphics Editor
PC
Computer Support Corporation
15925 Midway Road
Dallas, TX 75244
(214) 661-8960

Canvas
Mac
Deneba Software
3305 N.W. 74th Avenue
Miami, FL 33122
(800) 622-6827

CorelDraw!
PC
Corel Bldg.
1600 Carling Avenue
Ottawa, Ontario, Canada K1Z8R7
(613) 728-8200

Designer
PC
Micrografx, Inc.
1303 Arapaho
Richardson, TX 75081
(800) 272-3728

Designworks
Amiga
New Horizons Software
206 Wold Basin Road, Suite 109
Austin, TX 78746
(512) 328-6650

Freehand
PC, Mac
Aldus Corporation
411 First Avenue, S.
Seattle, WA 98104
(800) 333-2538

IntelliDraw
PC, Mac
Aldus Corporation
411 First Avenue, S.
Seattle, WA 98104
(800) 333-2538

Logo Design Software
PC, Mac
Decathlon Corporation
4100 Executive Park Drive, Suite 16
Cincinnati, OH 45241
(513) 421-1938

MacDraw Pro
Mac
Claris Corporation
5201 Patrick Henry Drive
Box 58168
Santa Clara, CA 95052
(408) 987-7000

Professional Draw
PC, Amiga
Gold Disk, Inc.
20675 S. Western Avenue, Suite 120
Torrance, CA 90501
(310) 320-5080

Relational Objex
Mac
Softstream International, Inc.
10 White Chapel Drive
Mount Laurel, NJ 08054
(800) 252-6610

Satellite 3D
Calliscope
801 Church Street, Suite 1112
Mountain View, CA 94041
(415) 964-8550

SuperPaint
Mac
Aldus Corporation
411 First Avenue, S.
Seattle, WA 98104
(800) 333-2538

Windows Draw
PC
Micrografx, Inc.
1303 Arapaho
Richardson, TX 75081
(800) 272-3728

❖ ## Fonts

Adobe Postscript Fonts
PC, Mac
Adobe Systems, Inc.
1585 Charleston Road
Mountain View, CA 94039
(415) 961-4400

Bullets & Boxes
Mac
Casey's Page Mill
6528 S. Oneida Court
Englewood, CO 80111
(303) 220-1463

Fluent Laser Fonts
PC, Mac
Casady & Greene, Inc.
P.O. Box 223779
Carmel, CA 93922
(800) 359-4920

Initial Caps
Mac
Berkana International
216 Downing Avenue N.
North Bend, WA 98045
(206) 361-1633

KARA FONTS
Amiga
Kara Computer Graphics
2554 Lincoln Blvd., Suite 1010
Marina Del Rey, CA 90291
(213) 578-9177

LetterPerfect Fonts
Mac
LetterPerfect Corporation
6606 Soundview Drive
Gig Harbor, WA 98335
(206) 851-5158

MoreFonts
PC
MicroLogic Software
1351 Ocean Avenue
Emeryville, CA 94608
(510) 652-5464

Ornate Typefaces
Mac
Ingrimayne Software
P.O. Box 404
Rensselaer, IN 47978
(219) 866-6241

SoftType
PC
ZSoft Corporation
450 Franklin Road, Suite 100
Marietta, GA 30067
(404) 428-0008

❖ **Font manipulation software**

Effects Specialist
Mac
Postcraft International Inc.
27811 Hopkins Avenue, Suite 6
Valencia, CA 91355
(805) 257-1797

Metamorphosis Pro
Mac
Altsys Corporation
269 W. Renner Road
Richardson, TX 75080
(214) 680-2060

MoreFonts
PC
MicroLogic Software
1351 Ocean Avenue
Emeryville, CA 94608
(510) 652-5464

TypeStyler
Mac
Broderbund Software
17 Paul Drive
San Rafael, CA 94903
(415) 492-3200

Typestry
Mac
Pixar
1001 W. Cutting Blvd.
Richmond, CA 94804
(510) 236-4000

❖ | ## Graphics utilities software

CanOpener
Mac
Abbott Systems
62 Mountain Road
Pleasantville, NY 10570
(800) 552-9157

Capture
Mac
Mainstay Software
5311-B Derry Avenue
Agoura Hills, CA 91301
(818) 991-6540

ClickPaste
Mac
Mainstay Software
5311-B Derry Avenue
Agoura Hills, CA 91301
(818) 991-6540

DiskFit Pro
Mac
Dantz Development Corporation
1400 Shattuck Avenue, Suite 1
Berkeley, CA 94709
(510) 849-0295

DoDot
PC
Halcyon Software
10297 Cold Harbor Avenue
Cupertino, CA 95014
(408) 378-9898

Envision It
PC
Envisions Solutions Technology, Inc.
822 Mahler Road
Burlingame, CA 94010
(800) 321-3689

EPS Exchange
Mac
Altsys Corporation
269 W. Renner Road
Richardson, TX 75080
(214) 680-2060

Image Grabber
Mac
Sabastian Software
P.O. Box 70278
Bellevue, WA 98007
(206) 861-0602

FullShot
PC
INBIT
P.O. Box 391674
Mountain View, CA 94039
(415) 967-1788

JAG
Mac
Ray Dream, Inc.
1804 Shoreline Blvd.
Mountain View, CA 94043
(415) 960-0768

Pizazz Plus
PC
Application Techniques
10 Lomar Park Drive
Pepperell, MA 01463
(508) 433-5201

PictureEze
PC
Application Techniques
10 Lomar Park Drive
Pepperell, MA 01463
(508) 433-5201

Poem for Windows
PC
Iterated Systems, Inc.
5550 Peachtree Parkway
Norcross, GA 30092
(404) 840-0310

Postility
Mac
Postcraft International Inc.
27811 Hopkins Avenue, Suite 6
Valencia, CA 91355
(805) 257-1797

ScanMatch
Mac
Savitar Communications
139 Townsend Street
San Francisco, CA 94107
(415) 243-3030

SmartScrap
Mac
Solutions, Inc.
30 Commerce Street
Williston, VT 05495
(802) 865-9220

SnapIt
PC
Window Painters, Ltd.
P.O. Box 39424
Minneapolis, MN 55439
(612) 897-1305

SnapJot
Mac
Wildflower Software
21 W. 171 Coronet Road
Lombard, IL 60148
(708) 916-9350

Streamline
PC, Mac
Adobe Systems, Inc.
1585 Charleston Road
Mountain View, CA 94039
(415) 961-4400

TextureSynth
Mac
Pantechnicon
P.O. Box 738
Santa Cruz, CA 95061
(408) 427-1687

Vistapro
Amiga
Virtual Reality Landscapes, Inc.
2341 Ganador Court
San Luis Obispo, CA 93401
(805) 545-8515

❖ ## Image processing software

Adobe PhotoShop
Mac
Adobe Systems, Inc.
1585 Charleston Road
Mountain View, CA 94039
(415) 961-4400

Aldus PhotoStyler
PC
Aldus Corporation
411 First Avenue, S.
Seattle, WA 98104
(800) 333-2538

Color It!
Mac
MicroFrontier, Inc.
3401 101st Street, Suite E
Des Moines, IA 50322
(800) 388-8109

Color Studio
Mac
Fractal Design Corporation
335 Spreckels Drive, Suite F
Aptos, CA 95003
(408) 688-8800

Halo Desktop Imager 1.1
PC
Media Cybernetics
5201 Great America Parkway, Suite 3102
Santa Clara, CA 95054
(408) 562-6076

PhotoFinish
PC
ZSoft Corporation
450 Franklin Road, Suite 100
Marietta, GA 30067
(404) 428-0008

Picture Publisher
PC
Micrografx, Inc.
1303 Arapaho
Richardson, TX 75081
(800) 272-3728

PixoFoto
PC
PixoArts Corp.
4600 Bohannon Drive, Suite 220
Menlo Park, CA 94025
(415) 323-6592

Publisher's Paintbrush
PC
ZSoft Corporation
450 Franklin Road, Suite 100
Marietta, GA 30067
(404) 428-0008

Gallery Effects
PC, Mac
Aldus Corporation
411 First Avenue, S.
Seattle, WA 98104
(800) 333-2538

Image-In Pro
PC
Image-In Incorporated
406 79th Street
Minneapolis, MN 55420
(800) 345-3540

RazzaMa Tazz Filters
Mac
Performance Resources
220 Hickory Street
Stranton, PA 18505
(800) 944-4151

Speciality Plug-in Filters
Mac
Andromeda Software
849 Old Farm Road
Thousand Oaks, CA 91360
(800) 547-0055

WinRIX
PC
RIX SoftWorks Inc.
18552 MacArthur Blvd., Suite 200
Irvine, CA 92715
(714) 476-8266

❖ ## Media database software

Mariah
Mac
Symmetry
8603 E. Royal Road, Suite 110
Scottsdale, AZ 85285
(602) 998-9106

MediaTree
Mac
Tulip Software
P.O. Box 3046
Andover, MA 01810
(508) 475-8711

Multi-Ad Search
Mac
Multi-Ad Services, Inc.
1720 W. Detweiller Drive
Peoria, IL 61615
(800) 447-1950

Portfolio
Mac
SoftShell International
715 Horizon Drive, Suite 390
Grand Junction, CO 81506
(303) 242-7502

❖ **Music libraries**

MultiWare CD-ROM
PC, Mac
BeachWare
5234 Via Valarta
San Diego, CA 92124
(619) 492-9529

MusicBytes
PC, Mac
Prosonus
11126 Weddington
North Hollywood, CA 91601
(818) 766-5221

QuickTunes
Mac, PC
Passport Designs Inc.
100 Stone Pine Road
Half Moon Bay, CA 94019
(415) 726-0280

❖ | ## Music Software

Alchemy
Mac
Passport Designs Inc.
100 Stone Pine Road
Half Moon Bay, CA 94019
(415) 726-0280

AudioShop
Mac
Opcode Systems Inc.
3950 Fabian Way, Suite 100
Palo Alto, CA 94303
(415) 856-3333

Audio Trax
Mac
Passport Designs Inc.
100 Stone Pine Road
Half Moon Bay, CA 94019
(415) 726-0280

AudioView
V-22, V22m, V-24s, V-24sm
Voyetra Technologies
333 Fifth Ave.
Pelham, NY 10803
(800) 233-9377

Beyond
Mac
Dr. T's Music Software Inc.
100 Crescent Road
Needham, MA 02194
(617) 455-1454

Cakewalk, Cakewalk Pro
PC
Twelve Tone Systems
44 Pleasant St.
Watertown, MA 02172
(617) 926-2480

Cubase, Cubase Audio
Mac
Steinberg Jones
17700 Raymer St., Suite 1001
Northridge, CA 91325
(818) 993-4091

Digital Performer
Mac
Mark of the Unicorn
222 Third St.
Cambridge, MA 02142
(617) 576-2760

Master Tracks Pro-5
Mac, PC
Passport Designs Inc.
100 Stone Pine Road
Half Moon Bay, CA 94019
(415) 726-0280

Monologue
PC, Mac
First Byte
19840 Pioneer Avenue
Torrance, CA 90503

Performer
Mac
Mark of the Unicorn
280 Mass Ave.
Cambridge, MA 02138
(617) 576-2760

SampleVision
PC
Turtle Beach Systems Inc.
Cyber Center, Unit 33
1600 Pennsylvania Ave.
York, PA 17404
(717) 843-6916

SoundEdit Pro
Mac
MacroMedia, Inc.
600 Townsend St.
San Franciso, CA 94103
(415) 442-0200

Studio 3.04
PC
Midisoft Corp.
263 N.E. 90th St.
Redmond, WA 98502
(206) 8817176

StudioVision
Mac
Opcode Systems Inc.
3950 Fabian Way, Suite 100
Palo Alto, CA 94303
(415) 856-3333

Trax
Mac, PC
Passport Designs Inc.
100 Stone Pine Road
Half Moon Bay, CA 94019
(415) 726-0280

TurboSynth
PC
Digidesign Inc.
1360 Willow Road, Suite 101
Menlo Park, CA 94025
(415) 688-0600

Vision, EZ Vision
Mac
Opcode Systems Inc.
3950 Fabian Way, Suite 100
Palo Alto, CA 94303
(415) 856-3333

Wave for Windows
PC
Turtle Beach Systems Inc.
Cyber Center, Unit 33
1600 Pennsylvania Ave.
York, PA 17404
(717) 843-6916

❖ **Paint software**

ColoRIX VGA Paint
PC
RIX SoftWorks Inc.
18552 MacArthur Blvd., Suite 200
Irvine, CA 92715
(714) 476-8266

Deluxe Paint
PC, Amiga
Electronic Arts
1820 Gateway Drive
San Mateo, CA 94404
(415) 571-7171

Lumena
PC
Time Arts Inc.
1425 Corporate Center Parkway
Santa Rosa, CA 95407
(707) 576-7722

Oasis
Mac
Time Arts Inc.
1425 Corporate Center Parkway
Santa Rosa, CA 95407
(707) 576-7722

Painter
Mac, PC
Fractal Design Corporation
335 Spreckels Drive, Suite F
Aptos, CA 95003
(408) 688-8800

Photon Paint
Mac, Amiga
MicroIllusions
P.O. Box 3475
Granada Hills, CA 91394
(818) 785-7345

Studio/32
Mac
Electronic Arts
1820 Gateway Drive
San Mateo, CA 94404
(415) 571-7171

Tempra Pro
PC
Mathematica Inc.
402 S. Kentucky Ave., Suite 210
Lakeland, FL 33801
(813) 682-1128

WaterColor
Mac, PC
AXA Corp.
17752 Mitchell, Suite C
Irvine, CA 92714
(714) 757-1500

❖ ## Photography, stock

Digital photography collections
Mac
Educorp
7434 Trade Street
San Diego, CA 92121
(619) 536-9999

Digital photography collections
PC
Starware Publishing Corp.
P.O. Box 4188
Deerfield Beach, FL 33442
(305) 426-4552

Digital photography collections
Mac
Wayzata Technology
412 Pokegama Ave North
Grand Rapids, MN 55744
(800) 735-7321

Digital Photographics CD ROM
Mac
Husom & Rose Photographics
1988 Stanford Avenue
St. Paul, MN 55105
(612) 699-1858

MultiWare CD ROM
PC, Mac
BeachWare
5234 Via Valarta
San Diego, CA 92124
(619) 492-9529

❖ | **Presentation/Production software**

Action
Mac, PC
MacroMedia, Inc.
600 Townsend St.
San Franciso, CA 94103
(415) 442-0200

ANIMaxx
PC
North Coast Software
P.O. Box 343
Barrington, N.H. 03825
(603) 332-9363

Applause II
PC
Borland International, Inc.
1800 Green Hills Road
Scotts Valley, CA 95067
(800) 437-4329

Arts & Letters Graphics Composer
PC
Computer Support Corporation
15925 Midway Road
Dallas, TX 75244
(214) 661-8960

Astound
Mac
Gold Disk, Inc.
20675 S. Western Avenue, Suite 120
Torrance, CA 90501
(310) 320-5080

Canvas
Mac
Deneba Software
3305 N.W. 74th Avenue
Miami, FL 33122
(800) 622-6827

Charisma
PC
Micrografx, Inc.
1303 Arapaho
Richardson, TX 75081
(800) 272-3728

Cinemation
Mac
Vividus Corp.
651 Kendall Avenue
Palo Alto, CA 94306
(415) 494-2111

Comic Strip Factory
Mac
Foundation Publishing, Inc.
14228 Shore Lane
Prior Lake, MN 55372
(612) 445-8860

CorelDraw!
PC
Corel Corp.
1600 Carling Avenue
Ottawa, Ontario, Canada K1Z8R7
(613) 728-8200

Curtain Call
PC
Brown Wagh Publishing
130-D Knowles Drive
Los Gatos, CA 95030
(408) 378-3838

DeltaGraph Pro
Mac
Deltapoint, Inc.
2 Harris Court, Suite B-1
Monterey, CA 93940
(800) 367-4334

EasyFlow
PC
Haven Tree Software Limited
P.O. Box 1093-N
Thousand Island Park, NY 13962
(800) 267-0668

Elan Performer
Amiga
Elan Design
P.O. Box 31725
San Francisco, CA 94131
(415) 621-8673

Executive Graph-in-the-Box
PC
New England Software Inc.
Greenwich Office Park, #3
Greenwich, CT 06831
(203) 625-0062

Filevision
Mac
TSP Software
4790 Irvine Blvd., Suite 105-294
Irvine, CA 92720
(714) 731-1368

FracTools
PC
Bourbaki Inc.
615 W. Hays Street
Boise, ID 83702
(208) 342-5849

FracZooms
PC
Bourbaki Inc.
615 W. Hays Street
Boise, ID 83702
(208) 342-5849

GeoQuery
Mac
GeoQuery Corp.
475 Alexis R. Shuman Blvd., Suite 380E
Naperville, IL 60563
(800) 541-0181

GraphMaster
Mac
Visual Business Systems
380 Interstate N. Parkway, Suite 190
Atlanta, GA 30339
(404) 956-0325

GraphShow
PC
Chartersoft Corp.
80 Fennel Street
Winnipet, Manitoba, Canada R3T3M4
(204) 453-4444

Hollywood
PC
Claris Corporation
5201 Patrick Henry Drive
Santa Clara, CA 95054
(408) 987-7000

Innovision
Amiga
Elan Design
P.O. Box 31725
San Francisco, CA 94131
(415) 621-8673

interFACE
Mac
Bright Star Technologies, Inc.
1450 114th Avenue SE, Suite 200
Bellevue, WA 98004
(206) 451-3697

KaleidaGraph
Mac
Synergy
2457 Perkiomen Avenue
Reading, PA 19606

LinksWare
Mac
LinksWare Corp.
812 19th Street
Pacific Grove, CA 93950
(408) 372-4155

MacDraw Pro
Mac
Claris Corporation
5201 Patrick Henry Drive
Santa Clara, CA 95054
(408) 987-7000

MacSpin
Mac
Abacus Concepts
1984 Bonita Avenue
Berkeley, CA 94704
(415) 540-1949

MapViewer
PC
Golden Software, Inc.
809 14th Street
Golden, CO 80401
(303) 279-1021

Mathematica
PC, Mac
Wolfram Research, Inc.
100 Trade Center Drive
Champaign, IL 61820
(217) 398-0700

MetaDesign
PC, Mac
Meta Software Corporation
125 Cambridge Park Drive
Cambridge, MA 02140
(617) 576-6920

More
Mac
Symantec Corporation
10201 Torre Avenue
Cupertino, CA 95014
(408) 243-9560

Mum's the Word
Mac
Terrace Software
P.O. Box 271
Medford, MA 02155
(617) 396-0382

On the Air
Mac
Meyer Software
616 Continental Road
Hatboro, PA 19040
(215) 675-3890

Passport Producer
Passport Designs Inc.
100 Stone Pine Road
Half Moon Bay, CA 94019
(415) 726-0280

Persuasion
PC, Mac
Aldus Corporation
411 First Avenue, S.
Seattle, WA 98104
(800) 333-2538

PowerPoint
Mac, PC
Microsoft Corp.
1 Microsoft Way
Redmond, WA 98052
(800) 227-4679

Presenting Now...
Mac
ISM, Inc.
2103 Harmony Woods Road
Owings Mills, MD 21117
(410) 560-0973

StatView
Mac
Abacus Concepts
1984 Bonita Avenue
Berkeley, CA 94704
(415) 540-1949

Stanford Graphics
PC
3-D Visions Corporation
2780 Skypark Drive
Torrance, CA 90505
(301) 325-1339

Super Nova
Mac
Abacus Concepts
1984 Bonita Avenue
Berkeley, CA 94704
(510) 540-1949

Tempra Show, Tempra Showmaster
Mathematica Inc.
402 S. Kentucky Ave.
Lakeland, FL 33801
(813) 682-1128

TopDown
Mac
Kaetron Software Corp.
12777 Jones Road, Suite 445
Houston, TX 77070
(713) 890-3434

❖ **QuickTime movie tools**

Adobe Premier
Mac
Adobe Systems, Inc.
1585 Charleston Road
Mountain View, CA 94039
(415) 961-4400

CameraMan
Mac
Vision Software
3160 De La Cruz Blvd., Suite 1104
Santa Clara, CA 95054
(408) 748-8411

DiVA VideoShop
Mac
DiVA Corporation
222 Third Street, Suite 3332
Cambridge, MA 02142
(617) 491-4147

MovieWorks
Mac
Interactive Solutions
1720 Sol Amphlett Blvd., Suite 219
San Mateo, CA 94402
(415) 377-0136

MultiWare CD ROM
PC, Mac
BeachWare
5234 Via Valarta
San Diego, CA 92124
(619) 492-9529

PACo Producer
Mac
COSa
14 Imperial Place, Suite 203
Providence, RI 02903
(401) 831-2672

QuickTime Starter Kit
Mac
Apple Computer Inc.
20525 Mariani Ave.
Cupertino, CA 95014
(408) 996-1010

VideoFusion
Mac
VideoLake, Ltd.
1722 Indian Wood Circle, Suite H
Maumee, OH 43537
(419) 891-1090

❖ ### Storyboarding/project management software

Active Memory
Mac
ASD Software
4650 Arrow Highway, Suite E-6
Montclair, CA 91763
(714) 624-2594

CalenDar
Mac
Psybron Systems, Inc.
P.O. Box 431
Charleston, WV 25322
(304) 340-4260

Contact!
Mac
Psybron Systems, Inc.
P.O. Box 431
Charleston, WV 25322
(304) 340-4260

Fair Witness
Mac
Chena Software
905 Harrison Street
Allentown, PA 18103
(215) 770-1210

First Things First
Mac
Visionary Software
6600 Silacci Way
Gilroy, CA 95020
(800) 522-5939

IdeaFisher
PC, Mac
Fisher Idea Systems
2222 Martin Street, Suite 110
Irvine, CA 92715
(800) 289-4332

Idea Generator Plus
PC
Experience In Software
2000 Hearst Avenue, Suite 202
Berkeley, CA 94709
(510) 644-0694

In Control
Mac
Attain Corporation
48 Grove Street
Somerville, MA 02144
(614) 776-1626

Info Select
PC
Micro Logic
P.O. Box 70
Hackensack, NJ 07602
(201) 342-6518

Inspiration
Mac
Ceres Software, Inc.
2920 S.W. Dolph Court, Suite #3
Portland, OR 97219
(503) 245-9011

MindLInk Pro
PC, Mac
MindLink Inc.
P.O. Box 247
North Pomfret, VT 05053
(802) 457-2025

MacSchedule
Mac
Mainstay Software
5311-B Derry Avenue
Agoura Hills, CA 91301
(818) 991-6540

PLANMaker
Mac
POWERSolutions for Business
1920 S. Broadway
St. Louis, MO 63104
(314) 421-0670

Project KICKStart
PC
Experience In Software
2000 Hearst Avenue, Suite 202
Berkeley, CA 94709
(510) 644-0694

Synchronicity
Mac
Visionary Software
2641 S.W. Huber Street
Portland, OR 97219
(800) 522-5939

WindowWatch
Mac
ASD Software
4650 Arrow Highway, Suite E-6
Montclair, CA 91763
(714) 624-2594

❖ **System utilities software**

911
Mac
Microcom, Inc.
P.O. Box 51489
Durham, NC 27727
(919) 490-1277

DiskQuick
Mac
Ideaform Inc.
P.O. Box 1540
Fairfield, IA 52556
(515) 472-7256

Frontier
Mac
Userland Software, Inc.
490 California Avenue
Palo Alto, CA 94305
(415) 325-5700

HandOFF
Mac
Connectix Corporation
2655 Campus Drive
San Mateo, CA 94403
(415) 571-5100

Help!
Mac
Teknosys
3923 Coconut Palm Drive, Suite 111
Tampa, FL 33619
(800) 873-3494

Icon Creator
PC
Software Workshop, Inc.
75 S. Mountain Way
Orem, UT 84058
(801) 224-6865

INITPicker
Mac
Microseeds Publishing, Inc.
5801 Benjamin Center, Suite 103
Tampa, FL 33634

Kiwi Power Windows
Mac
Kiwi Software, Inc.
6546 Pardall Road
Santa Barbara, CA 93117
(805) 685-4031

MacDisk Manager
Mac
Weber & Sons, Inc.
P.O. Box 104-PR
Adelphia, NJ 07710
(908) 431-1128

MacEKG
Mac
MicroMat Computer Systems
7075 Redwood Blvd.
Novato, CA 94950
(415) 898-6227

Mac Tools Deluxe
Mac
Central Point Software
15220 N.W. Greenbrier Parkway, #200
Beaverton, OR 97006
(503) 690-8088

Maxima
Mac
Connectix Corporation
2655 Campus Drive
San Mateo, CA 94403
(415) 571-5100

Microsoft Windows
PC
Microsoft Corp.
1 Microsoft Way
Redmond, WA 98052
(800) 227-4679

Norton Desktop
PC
Symantec Corporation
10201 Torre Avenue
Cupertino, CA 95014
(408) 243-95600

Now Utilities
Mac
Now Software, Inc.
520 S.W. Harrison Street, Suite 435
Portland, OR 97201
(503) 274-2800

OnCue
Mac
ICOM Simulations, Inc.
648 S. Wheeling Road
Wheeling, IL 60090
(708) 520-4440

PC-Kwik PowerPak
PC
Multisoft Corporation
15100 S.W. Koll Parkway
Beaverton, OR 97006
(503) 646-8267

PC Tools
PC
Central Point Software
15220 N.W. Greenbrier Parkway, #200
Beaverton, OR 97006
(503) 690-8088

ProKey
PC
Rosesoft Inc.
P.O. Box 70337
Bellevue, WA 98007
(206) 562-0225

Quick Tools
Mac
Advanced Software, Inc.
1095 E. Duane Avenue, Suite 103
Sunnyvale, CA 94086
(408) 733-0745

Redux
Mac
Microseeds Publishing, Inc.
5801 Benjamin Center, Suite 103
Tampa, FL 33634

Snooper
Mac
Maxa
116 Maryland Avenue
Glendale, CA 91206
(800) 788-6292

Soft-ICE/W
PC
Nu-Mega Technologies Inc.
P.O. Box 7780
Nashua, NH 03060
(603) 889-2386

SpeedyCD
Mac
ShirtPocket Software, Inc.
P.O. Box 40666
Mesa, AZ 85274
(602) 966-7667

Tiles
Mac
CE Software
P.O. Box 65580
West Des Moines, IA 50625
(515) 224-1995

Virex
Mac
Microcom, Inc.
P.O. Box 51489
Durham, NC 27727
(919) 490-1277

❖ **Video stock footage**

ClipVideo
VHS
The Publishing Factory
310 Dover Road
Charlottesville, VA 22901
(804) 973-8254

❖ **Video editing and production software**

Deluxe Video III
Amiga
Electronic Arts
1820 Gateway Drive
San Mateo, CA 94404
(415) 571-7171

D/Vision-Pro
TouchVision Systems Inc.
1800 W. Winnemac
Chicago, IL 60640
(312) 989-2160

Photon Video Edit Decision
Amiga
MicroIllusions
P.O. Box 3475
Granada Hills, CA 91394
(818) 785-7345

Photon Video Transport Controller
Amiga
MicroIllusions
P.O. Box 3475
Granada Hills, CA 91394
(818) 785-7345

Sundance 2.0
Mac
Sundance Technology Group
6309 N. O'Connor Road, Suite 111
Irving, TX 75039
(214) 869-1002

Video Director
PC
Gold Disk, Inc.
20675 S. Western Avenue, Suite 120
Torrance, CA 90501
(310) 320-5080

VideoToolkit
Mac
Abbate Video
83 Main Street
Norfolk, MA 02056
(508) 520-0197

VideoWare
HSC Software
1661 Lincoln Blvd., Suite 101
Santa Monica, CA 90404
(310) 392-8441

Virtual/Video Producer
PC
V_Graph Inc.
1275 Westtown Thornton Road
Westtown, PA 19396
(215) 399-1521

HARDWARE LISTINGS BY MANFACTURER

❖ **Graphics and digital video hardware**

Avid Technology Inc.
Media Composers
Avid Series 200 and Avid Series 2000
3 Burlington Woods
Burlington, MA 01803
(617) 221-6789

Digital F/X Inc.
Video F/X Plus *Mac*
755 Ravendale Drive
Mountain View, CA 94042
(415) 961-2800

Digital Vision Inc.
ComputerEyes/RT
270 Bridge St.
Dedham, MA 02026
(617) 329-5400

E-Machines
QuickView Studio *Mac*
QuickView Studio QT *Mac*
9305 S.W. Gemini Drive
Beaverton, OR 97005
(503) 646-6699

Editing Machines Corp.
Emc2
Emc-PC *PC*
1825 Q St. N.W.
Washington, DC 20009
(202) 232-4597

Fast Electronics U.S. Inc.
Video Machine Mac, Video Machine PC
5 Commonwealth Road
Natick, MA 01760
(508) 655-3278

FutureVideo Products Inc.
EditLink V-Station
28 Argonaut
Aliso Viejo, CA 92656
(714) 770-4416

IBM Corp.
ActionMedia II *IBM*
ActionMedia Capture Module *IBM*
Multimedia Information Center
P.O. Box 2150
Atlanta, GA 30301
(800) 426-9402

IEV International Inc.
ProMotion Multimedia Engine *PC*
3030 S. Main St., Suite 300
Salt Lake City, UT 84115
(801) 466-9093

Lazerus
ExpressWay *PC*
P.O. Box 13249
Oakland, CA 94661
(510) 339-6263

Mass Microsystems Inc.
QuickImage 24 *PC*
410 W. Maude Ave.
Sunnyvale, CA 94086
(408) 522-1200

Matrox Electronic Systems Ltd.
Matrox Studio *PC*
Personal Producer
1055 St. Regis Blvd.
Dorval, Quebec, Canada H9P 2T4
(514) 685-2630

New Media Graphics Corp.
Super Motion Compression
780 Boston Road
Billerica, MA 01821
(508) 663-0666

New Video Corp.
EyeQ 750/8 AS *Mac*
1526 Cloverfield Blvd.
Santa Monica, CA 90404
(310) 449-7000

NewTek, Inc.
Video Toaster
Amiga
215 SE 8th St.
Topeka, KS 66603
(913) 354-1146

Panasonic Communications & System Co.
Extensive line of video products
2 Panasonic Way
Secaucus, NJ 07094
(800) 742-8086

Radius Inc.
VideoVision *Mac*
Assorted monitors and display cards
1710 Fortune Drive
San Jose, CA 95131
(408) 434-1010

RasterOps Corp. *Mac*
24MxTV
24STV
24XLTV
MediaTime
MoviePak
Assorted monitors
2500 Walsh Ave.
Santa Clara, CA 95051
(408) 562-4200

RGB Computer & Video Inc.
AmiLink/PM
4152 Blue Heron Blvd. W., Suite 118
Riviera Beach, FL 33404
(407) 844-3348

Sony Corporation of America
Assorted video and computer peripherals
655 River Oaks Parkway
San Jose, CA 95134
(800) 352-7669

SuperMac Technology
Digital Film *Mac*
VideoSpigot *Mac*
Assorted monitors and display cards
485 Potrero Ave.
Sunnyvale, CA 94086
(408) 245-2202

Truevision Inc.
Bravado-16 *PC*
NuVista+ *Mac*
7340 Shadeland Station
Indianapolis, IN 46256
(317) 841-0332

VideoLogic Inc.
MediaStation
245 First St.
Cambridge, MA 02142
(617) 494-0530

Videomedia Inc.
Video control hardware *PC*
175 Lewis Road
San Jose, CA 95111
(408) 227-9977

❖ ## Digital audio hardware

Ad Lib Inc.
Ad Lib Gold *PC*
50 Stanford St., Suite 800
Boston, MA 02114
(800) 463-2686

Antex Electronics Corp.
AudioPort
Z-1
16100 S. Figueroa St.
Gardena, CA 90246
(310) 458-1214

Creative Labs Inc. *PC*
Sound Blaster
Sound Blaster 16
Sound Blaster Pro
1901 McCarthy Blvd.
Milpitas, CA 94035
(408) 428-6600

MacroMedia Inc.
MacRecorder *Mac*
600 Townsend St.
San Franciso, CA 94103
(415) 442-0200

Media Vision Inc. *PC*
Audioport
Pro AudioSpectrum 16
Pro AudioSpectrum Plus
3185 Laurelview Court
Fremont, CA 94538
(510) 770-8600

Mark of the Unicorn
Digital Waveboard *Mac*
1280 Mass Ave.
Cambridge, MA 02138
(617) 576-2760

ProMedia Technologies
Audio Canvas XA-16 *PC*
1540 Market St., Suite 425
San Francisco, CA 94102
(415) 621-1399

Steinberg Jones
Cubase Audio
17700 Raymer St., Suite 1001
Northridge, CA 91325
(818) 993-4091

Turtle Beach Systems Inc.
MultiSound *PC*
54k *PC*
Cyber Center, Unit 33
1600 Pennsylvania Ave.
York, PA 17404
(717) 843-6916

❖ ## MIDI hardware

Advanced Gravis Computer Technology Ltd.
Ultrasound
7400 MacPherson Ave., Suite 111
Burnaby, British Columbia, Canada V5J5B6
(604) 431-5020

Altech Systems
Altech Dual Interface
122 Faries Industrial Park Drive
Shreveport, LA 71106
(318) 868-8036

Apple Computer Inc.
Apple MIDI Interface *Mac*
20525 Mariani Ave.
Cupertino, CA 95014
(408) 996-1010

Computer Music Supply
CMS MIDI interface boards
382 N. Lemon
Walnut, CA 91789
(800) 322-6434

IBM Corp.
Music Feature *IBM*
Multimedia Information Center
P.O. Box 2150
Atlanta, GA 30301
(800) 426-9402

JL Cooper
MacNexus *Mac*
Sync•Link *Mac*
13478 Beach Ave.
Marina Del Rey, CA 90292
(213) 306-4131

Kee Electronics Inc.
MIDIator MS-101, MS-103, MS-114
MIDIator MS–123, MS–124, MP–128
7515 Chapel Ave.
Fort Worth, TX 76116
(800) 533-6434

Mark of the Unicorn
MIDI Time Piece Mac *Mac*
MIDI Time Piece Windows *PC*
MIDI Time Piece II Mac *Mac*
MIDI Time Piece II Windows *PC*
1280 Mass Ave.
Cambridge, MA 02138
(617) 576-2760

MIDIman
Macman *Mac*
Mac Syncman *Mac*
MM–401
236 W. Mountain St., Suite 108
Pasadena, CA. 91103
(800) 969-6434

Opcode Systems Inc.
Studio 3 *Mac*
Studio 4 *Mac*
Studio 5 *Mac*
Studio Plus II *Mac*
3950 Fabian Way, Suite 100
Palo Alto, CA 94303
(415) 856-3333

Roland Corp. U.S.
LAPC-1
MPU-IMC, MPU-IPC, Super MPU/AT
SCC-1
7200 Dominion Circle
Los Angeles, CA 90040
(213) 685-5141

❖ ## Monitors/projection systems

3M Corp.
5300 Panel
5800 Panel
5900 Panel
3M Austin Center
P.O. Box 2963
Austin, TX 78769
(512) 984-1800

Barco Inc.
OCM 2846
OCM 3346
SCM 2846
SCM 3346
1000 Cobb Place Blvd., Suite 100
Kennesaw, GA 30144
(404) 590-7900

Boxlight Corp.
Boxlight 1320
Boxlight 2040V
17771 Fjord Drive N.E.
Poulsbo, WA 98370
(800) 762-5757

Dukane Corp.
Magniview 494
Magniview 492
2900 Dukane Drive
St. Charles, IL 60174
(708) 584-2300

In Focus Systems Inc.
TVT-3000
7770 S.W. Mohawk St.
Tualatin, OR 97062
(800) 327-7231

Mitsubishi Electronics America Inc.
AM-2752A monitor
AM-3151A monitor
AM-3501R monitor
Professional Electronics Division
800 Cottontail Lane
Somerset, NJ 08873
(800) 733-8439

Mitsubishi Electronics America Inc.
Diamond Pro 37 monitor
Diamond Scan 33 monitor
Diamond Scan 37 monitor
Information Systems Division
6665 Plaza Drive
P.O. Box 6007
Cypress, CA 90630
(714) 220-2500

NEC Technologies Inc.
MultiSync 3PG Data Monitor
1255 Micheal Drive
Wood Dale, IL 60191
(708) 860-9500

nView Corp.
MediaPro
ViewFrame Spectra
ViewFrame Spectra Plus
11835 Canon Blvd.
Newport News, VA 23606
(800) 736-8439

Panelight Display Systems Inc.
Panelight 185
1040 Ferry Bldg., Box 263
San Francisco, CA 94111
(800) 726-3599

Proxima Corp.
Ovation
Ovation sx
6610 Nancy Ridge Drive
San Diego, CA 92121
(619) 457-5500

Sayett Technology Inc.
Datashow 256C
17 Tobey Village Office Park
Pittsford, NY 14534
(716) 264-9250

Sharp Electronics Corp.
QA-1150 *Mac*
Sharp Plaza
Mahwah, NJ 07430
(201) 529-8200

Telex Communications Inc. *Mac, PC*
MagnaByte 1000
MagnaByte SC
MagnaByte 6001
9600 Aldrich Ave. S.
Minneapolis, MN 55420
(612) 884-4051

❖ ## MPC kits (PC)

CompuAdd Corp.
325S Low Profile
433 DLC
12303 Technology Blvd.
Austin, TX 78727
(800) 627-1967

Creative Labs Inc.
Sound Blaster Multimedia Upgrade Kit
1901 McCarthy Blvd.
Milpitas, CA 94035
(408) 428-6600

Media Vision Inc.
MPC Upgrade Kit Plus
3185 Laurelview Court
Fremont, CA 94538
(510) 770-8600

Turtle Beach Systems Inc.
MultiSound MPC Ugrade Kit
Cyber Center, Unit 33
1600 Pennsylvania Ave.
York, PA 17404
(717) 843-6916

Tandy Corp.
Tandy MPC Upgrade Kit
700 One Tandy Center
Fort Worth, TX 76102
(817) 878-4969

❖ | ## Platforms

Apple Computer Inc.
Macintosh line of computers
20525 Mariani Ave.
Cupertino, CA 95014
(408) 996-1010

Commodore Business Machines
Amiga line of computers
1200 Wilson Drive
West Chester, PA 19380
(215) 431-9100

IBM
PS-2 and Ultimedia lines of computers
Multimedia Information Center
P.O. Box 2150
Atlanta, GA 30301
(800) 426-9402

Philips
CD-I Players
1 Philips Drive
Knoxville, TN 37914
(800) 722-6224

NeXT
NeXT line of computers
900 Chesapeake Drive
Redwood City, CA 94063
(415) 366-0900

Silicon Graphics
Iris Indigo
2011 N. Shoreline Blvd.
Mountain View, CA 94039
(415) 960-1980

❖ **CD-ROM hardware**

Apple Computer Inc.
AppleCD 150 *Mac*
20525 Mariani Ave.
Cupertino, CA 95014
(408) 996-1010

CD Technology Inc.
CD Porta Drive-T3301
766 San Aleso Ave.
Sunnyvale, CA 94086
(408) 752-8500

Chinon America Inc.
435 series
535 series
615 Hawaii Ave.
Torrance, CA 90503
(800) 441-0222

Hitachi Home Electronics Inc.
CDR-1700S, CDR-1750S
CDR-3700, CDR-3750
Multimedia Systems Division
401 W. Artesia Blvd.
Compton, CA 90220
(310) 537-8383

MicroNet Technology Inc.
Micro/CD-ROM
20 Mason
Irvine, CA 92718
(714) 837-6033

NEC Technologies Inc.
CDR-74, CDR-84
MPC-84, MPC-74, MPC-37
1255 Michael Drive
Wood Dale, IL 60191
(708) 860-9500

Peripheral Land Inc.
PLI CD-ROM
47421 Bayside Parkway
Fremont, CA 94538
(800) 288-8754

Philips Consumer Electronics
Philips CM205XRS CD-ROM
1 Philips Drive
Knoxville, TN 37914
(800) 722-6224

Relax Technology Inc.
Vista CD-ROM
3101 Whipple Road
Union City, CA 94587
(510) 471-6112

Storage Devices Inc.
CD-ROM Subsystem
6800 Orangethorpe Ave., Ste. J
Buena Park, CA 90620
(714) 562-5500

Texel
DM-3024, DM-5024
1605 Wyatt Ave.
Santa Clara, CA 95054
(800) 886-3935

Todd Enterprises Inc.
TCDR-7000M
TCDR-75050U
224-49 67th Ave.
Bayside, NY 11364
(800) 445-8633

Toshiba America Information Systems Inc.
TXM-3401E series
TXM-3401E series
9740 Irvine Blvd.
P.O. Box 19724
Irvine, CA 92713
(714) 583-3000

Index

Left margin: SND • CGM • GIF • IFF • RIB • RIF • DWG • EPS • CUT • RLE • X11 • GEM • HPGL • DXF •

Free Offer!!!

Special offer for readers of *The Desktop Multimedia Bible*.

The Desktop Multimedia File Format Guide

Get Jeff Burger's guide to the various file formats used in multimedia—free! Covers Mac, PC, and Amiga formats. You'll find information on AIFF, WAV, BMP, PCX, TIFF, TIF, PICT, PICS, FLI, TGA, SND, CGM, GIF, IFF, RIB, RIF, MIDI and much more—all in one handy reference booklet.

..Yes! Rush me Jeff Burger's free *Desktop Multimedia File Format Guide*. Here's $3.00* to cover shipping and handling.

Name: _____ Company: _____

Street Address: _____

City: _____ State: _____ Zip: _____ Country: _____

Daytime phone: _____

Help us decide what to do next! Would you be interested in:
- ❑ Knowing about future revisions to the book.
- ❑ A companion videotape to *The Desktop Multimedia Bible*.
- ❑ Product demos by mail. ❑ Mac ❑ PC ❑ Amiga ❑ Other _____
- ❑ A newsletter containing late breaking multimedia updates.
- ❑ An interactive CD-ROM version of *The Desktop Multimedia Bible*.
- ❑ A dictionary of electronic media terms.
- ❑ A local seminar on multimedia production with Jeff Burger.
- ❑ What else? _____

Mail $3.00* shipping and handling to:

Creative Technologies
2995 Woodside Rd., Suite 400
Woodside, CA 94062

(*Readers outside the U.S. please send an international money order for $5.00 US.)